America
in the
Twentieth
Century

THIRD EDITION

George Donelson Moss
City College of San Francisco

Prentice Hall, Upper Saddle River, New Jersey   07458

Library of Congress Cataloging-in-Publication Data

Moss, GEORGE,
    America in the twentieth century / George Donelson Moss. — 3rd
ed.
        p.   cm.
    Includes bibliographical references and index.
    ISBN 0–13–569336–5
    1. United States—History—20th century. 2. United States—
Politics and government—20th century. I. Title.
E741.M67 1997
973.9—dc20   96–26166
                                                   CIP

To Linda, who knows why, and to Morris, who doesn't.

Editorial director: *Charlyce Jones Owen*
Acquisitions editor: *Sally Constable*
Editorial/production supervision: *Kim Gueterman*
Cover designer: *Wendy Alling-Judy*
Photo research: *Sherry Lee Cohen*
Buyer: *Lynn Pearlman*

This book was set in 10/12 Palatino by BookMasters, Inc.
and was printed and bound by R. R. Donnelley & Sons Company.
The cover was printed by Phoenix Color Corp.

 © 1997, 1993, 1989 by Prentice-Hall, Inc.
Simon & Schuster/A Viacom Company
Upper Saddle River, New Jersey   07458

Printed in the United States of America
10 9 8 7 6 5 4

ISBN   0-13-569336-5

Prentice-Hall International (UK) Limited, *London*
Prentice-Hall of Australia Pty. Limited, *Sydney*
Prentice-Hall of Canada Inc., *Toronto*
Prentice-Hall Hispanoamericana, S.A., *Mexico*
Prentice-Hall of India Private Limited, *New Delhi*
Prentice-Hall of Japan, Inc., *Tokyo*
Simon & Schuster Asia Pte. Ltd., *Singapore*
Editora Prentice-Hall do Brasil, Ltda., *Rio de Janeiro*

Contents

Preface

For the better part of three decades, I have been trying to explain the mysteries of modern American history to my students and to anyone else who showed an interest in the subject. This textbook derives naturally and inevitably from my vocation as a tribal historian, one of the professional keepers of the nation's collective memory of itself. It represents my best efforts over many years to write a comprehensive narrative synthesis spanning the years of the twentieth century.

The book focuses on the public life of the American people. Historically Americans have come together in the public sphere to compete and to cooperate with one other; it is where the action has been. It is within the public sphere that the great decisions for war and peace, for reform and reaction, that shaped the democratic life of the American people, have been determined. It is within the public arena that powerful contending ideologies and interests have sought allegiance, and economic and cultural forces have shaped the destiny of the nation and forged the character of its people.

The narrative also incorporates much demographic, economic, social, and cultural history to bring the experiences of all Americans into the mainstreams of history. It is an inclusive account that records the historical experience of those groups who used to be ignored or neglected in conventional histories. Special attention has been given to the history of women, African Americans, Hispanics, Asians, Native Americans, and to other Americans who have come together to create the most successful multicultural society in the history of the planet.

I have also devoted a lot of space to describing and defining the major role that the United States has played in world affairs in the twentieth century. Such a focus is particularly appropriate for the half century following World War II when the United States has been the preeminent national power in the world and has forged a network of global interests.

I am delighted to have an opportunity to offer this third edition of *America in the Twentieth Century.* During the years that the book has been available to students and teachers, I have received many letters, phone calls, and faxes from readers. Most have written to tell me that they found the book informative, enjoyable reading. They have also included constructive criticisms and suggestions for improving the book. My correspondents will discover that I have incorporated many of their suggestions into this new edition: suggestions that have tightened the organization of the book, strengthened its analyses, and clarified some of the writing.

The book has been thoroughly revised. Each chapter has been carefully reworked; and in some cases restructured and revamped. In some chapters new material has been added, in others material has been abbreviated or deleted.

In my view, confirmed by the testimony of readers, the strengths of the book are: it is well-written. I employ a clear, concise style that avoids social scientific jargon, psychobabble, and esoteric intellectual constructs. The book is accessible to anyone who wants to understand the major contours of modern U.S. history. It is a good place to begin your study of modern and post-modern America.

The book is also well-organized. The story of America in the twentieth century unfolds chapter-by-chapter in carefully structured and coherent categories. Each chapter carves out a chronological segment. Within each time frame, the particular topics that define an era and give it its historical significance are developed. The master themes of modern American historical development undergird the events and personalities treated in individual chapters. These themes provide the story of America with its underlying coherence and continuity. They include: the growth in the size, cost, power, and scope of authority of the national government; the expanding role the United States plays in world affairs that often involves fighting in wars; the development and application of new systems of technology; the development of the consumer economy; the continued growth of a vital popular culture and systems of mass communication; the increasing plurality and diversity of American social life; and the continuing commitment to democratic values and practices.

The book was written for use in survey courses in twentieth-century U.S. history taught in high schools, community colleges, and the lower divisions of four-year colleges. It can also be used in upper division courses at four-year colleges and universities in classes for students who are not history majors or do not have extensive backgrounds in U.S. history.

My stance toward my subject is serious, detached, and objective, if slightly ironic. I have no interest in imposing my political affiliations or ideological allegiances disguised as historical interpretation on my readers. In fact, I strive mightily to resist such unprofessional tendencies. I have no axes to grind and no hidden agenda. My only goal is *to help you learn how to think about twentieth century U.S. history, not what to think.*

ACKNOWLEDGEMENTS

Mark Twain once said that he could remember anything, whether it happened or not. Alas, professional historians are not permitted the luxury of mythic invention, nor even of inadvertent error. Fortunately, I have had a tremendous amount of help in creating this book and revising it twice. That help has eliminated errors and brought forth a far better book than I could have created on my own.

One of the great pleasures of historical scholarship is that it is so much a collective enterprise. Scores of friends, students, colleagues, and other scholars have shared in the challenging task of producing a comprehensive narrative history of twentieth century America. I want them all to know that I am exceedingly grateful and beholden to them. I also cherish their encouragement and support while doing the book and revising it.

I also want to acknowledge my deep gratitude to many outstanding people affiliated with my publisher, Prentice Hall, who managed the quasi-magical task of transforming an ungainly manuscript into a beautiful book. Sally Constable, acquisitions editor, a person of many talents, made the decision to revise the book for a third edition. Kim Gueterman took charge of the production process, kept on schedule, and kept me informed of its progress with unusual efficiency and tact. I want to especially express my profound appreciation to Rodney P. Carlisle, Rutgers University, and James A. Jolly, Millersville State College of Pennsylvania for their thorough reading of the entire manuscript and excellent critiques.

Lastly, special thanks to two special people: To Mary Chatelier, who used her skills as historian/detective to retrieve dozens of original photographs from the confines of the not entirely user-friendly National Archives photo collections. They have enriched the book. And to the lovely Linda, who steadfastly refuses to accept anything less than the best work I can do. I know that I have odd ways of showing my gratitude, but I am grateful.

CHAPTER 1

Prologue: A Society in Transition

The face of America was transformed during the last three decades of the nineteenth century. A predominantly rural nation whose people inhabited small towns and villages had become an urban industrial giant. As late as the 1870s, most Americans had earned their livings as farmers, shopkeepers, and small businessmen, or else as employees of farmers, merchants, and small manufacturers. By the end of the nineteenth century, large corporations increasingly dominated the economic landscape, and America was fast becoming a nation of employees. Three historical forces transformed America as the nineteenth century ran its course: industrialization, urbanization, and massive immigration. Behind these powerful forces lay the application of new technologies. Rapid technological change was the powerful engine driving the transformation of America at the dawn of the twentieth century.

A DEMOGRAPHIC PORTRAIT

The population of the United States grew from 60 million in 1890 to more than 76 million by 1900. As the twentieth century began, America was the fourth most populous nation in the world (after China, India, and Russia) and contained the most rapidly growing population of any large nation in the world. The rapid rate of population growth was a function of both a high birthrate among the native-born population and the unprecedented massive inflow of immigrants. During the decade of the 1890s, over 6 million immigrants traveled to America, 75 percent of whom comprised the "new" immigration, people coming from the countries of southern and eastern Europe, principally Poland, Italy, and Russia. According to the census of 1900, 26 million of the nation's 76 million inhabitants were either immigrants or the sons and daughters of immigrants. In addition to the inflow of new immigrants, two other major population movements characterized *fin de*

1

siècle America: People, especially farmers, continued to trek westward to farm new lands in Texas, the high plains, and California. Millions more moved from rural areas to the large towns and cities, especially in the northeastern regions of the nation. As the twentieth century began, three-fourths of the American population inhabited the eastern third of the nation; they resided east of the mighty Mississippi River.

Even though the census of 1900 showed that nearly two-thirds of American families still resided in towns of fewer than 2,500 people, the nation had undergone a rapid growth in urban population during the 1890s. The rapid urbanization of American society during the last decades of the nineteenth century was its most salient demographic trend. Population growth within the surging metropolises of America had been nothing short of spectacular. New York City, the commercial and cultural capital of the nation, had grown from 1.5 million people in the 1870s to 3.5 million by 1900! Chicago, which had only become a city during the Civil War, was approaching 2 million people by 1900. Other large cities showed similar dramatic increases. It was in the growing large cities of America during the 1890s where one could see the population diversity and cultural pluralism that was creating the world's first genuinely multicultural society. While the countryside contained relatively homogeneous enclaves of families whose forbears had emigrated from northern and western Europe, the great cities of America were increasingly populated by the world's most diverse populations.

As the twentieth century began, Americans were living longer than ever before and family size was declining. Divorce rates were increasing, but they remained quite small compared to modern figures. Of the approximately 30 million people in the workforce, two-thirds were employed in nonagricultural pursuits. Of these nonagricultural workers, perhaps 12 million held "blue-collar" jobs in industries of various kinds. The median annual wage for a blue-collar worker in 1900 was about $500, barely enough to support a family. The industrial workforce also included 6 million women and perhaps 2 million children (age fifteen and below). The typical work week included sixty hours. As the twentieth century began, millions of working class families endured a life of poverty with scant opportunities for themselves or their children to rise up to middle-class status.

ECONOMIC GROWTH

Economic growth characterized all regions of America during the late nineteenth century, although it was most extensive in the northeastern and Great Lakes regions. Within a generation, America had developed the world's largest industrial economy. Economic growth influenced the lives of nearly all Americans. Geographic and social mobility were enhanced. American manufacturing flourished during the decades of the late nineteenth century for many reasons. New natural resources were being discovered and exploited. The nation also expanded geographically as the West was wrested from the Plains Indians. Western expansion added to the size of national markets, which were also protected from foreign competitors by tariff walls erected by congressional legislation. Additional ingredients composed the recipe for economic growth. America raised a class of bold, skillful entrepreneurs, many from poor backgrounds, who organized and built large industrial corporations. And, the dominant values of the age promoted and celebrated economic growth and material acquisition. Manufacturing also flourished because it was a time of rapid advance in basic science and technology. New machines that increased productivity appeared, and engineers harnessed new power sources.

Constructing the nation's industrial infrastructure, particularly the transportation revolution wrought by the building of the railroads, made an essential contribution to the industrial revolution. Railroads formed the most important element in American economic development for several reasons. They constituted an important industry in themselves, the nation's first big business. During the 1880s, 7,000 miles of track were laid annually. By 1890, feeder lines, regional roads branching off the main east-west trunk lines, linked together most cities and towns in the country. As the century ended, the nation's railroads owned 193,000 miles of tracks, more than half of the world's total trackage. As the nation's railroad industry expanded, it also became concentrated. By 1900, seven giant interregional railroad combines (including the New York Central, the Baltimore and Ohio, the Pennsylvania, and the Southern Pacific) controlled 90 percent of the nation's railroad mileage.

Railroads also stimulated the growth of a large-scale manufacturing economy. Before the national system of railroads was in place, manufacturing was largely confined to small businesses that sold to local markets. The railroads created national markets. Industrialists borrowed money, bought new machines, purchased raw materials in large quantities, hired more workers, and employed sales people. Branch offices and new factories were opened. Those manufacturers who most successfully tapped the national markets created by the railroads became the nation's largest businesses. Railroads made big business possible. By 1900, the national system of railroads had created a unified continental-size national economy, the largest and most productive economy in the world.

Rapid, large-scale expansion of manufacturing enterprises formed an integral part of the American industrial revolution. In 1900, the American gross domestic product (GDP) reached $40 billion, a sixfold increase in twenty years. The most impressive advances in manufacturing during the late nineteenth century occurred in the steel industry. Inventors discovered a means of mass-producing steel cheaply that transformed iron manufacturing during the 1860s. The United States, which had no steel industry at the time of the Civil War, became the world's largest steel manufacturer in 1880. The steel industry was centered at Pittsburgh because of its nearness to iron and coal deposits and its easy access to both railroad and maritime transportation. Andrew Carnegie, who came to America as a penniless immigrant boy, became the steel master of America. When he retired from business in 1901, his

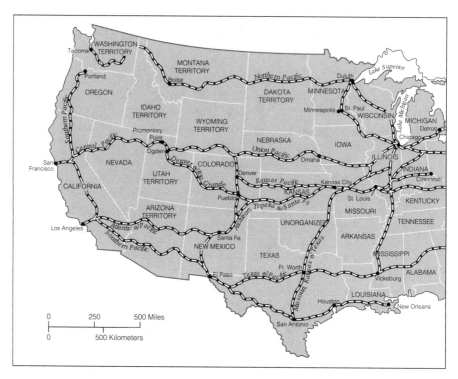

Railroad network, 1885.   *Source:* Moss, *The Rise of Modern America* (Englewood Cliffs, NJ: Prentice Hall, 1995) p. 3.

Carnegie Steel Company was the world's largest. His personal fortune was estimated at $500 million. He devoted the rest of his life to giving away most of his vast fortune to support various philanthropic enterprises, including more than twenty-five hundred projects such as libraries, public buildings, and foundations.

The American petroleum industry also grew rapidly during the late nineteenth century. The first producing oil well was drilled in western Pennsylvania in 1859. As the oil industry mushroomed during the 1860s, its most important product was kerosene, used mainly to light people's homes at night. One giant firm emerged to monopolize the oil refining industry in America; this was the Standard Oil Company, headed by John D. Rockefeller. Rockefeller had entered the oil business in 1863 when it was competitive and chaotic. Within a few years, Standard Oil's efficient operation made it the largest refiner. Standard Oil forced railroads to grant it rebates, giving it a tremendous competitive advantage over rival refineries. It then proceeded to buy up its competition. Competitors who initially refused to sell were driven to the verge of bankruptcy and forced to sell. The Standard Oil Trust, formed in 1882, controlled 85 percent of America's oil refining capacity, and Rockefeller had become the nation's first billionaire. He, too, retired from business and gave away huge sums of his money to various philanthropic enterprises.

Two other important industries evolved during the late nineteenth century, the telephone industry and the electric utility industry. Alexander Graham Bell invented the telephone in 1876. Two years later, the first commercial telephone exchange was installed in New Haven, Connecticut. During the last two decades of the nineteenth century, telephone use spread rapidly. By 1900, Americans were using over 800,000 telephones, mostly for commercial purposes. In that same year, the American Telephone and Telegraph Company acquired its monopoly. Thomas Edison, the most famous inventor in American history, played a key role in the emergence of both the telephone and electric utility industries. He vastly improved telephonic transmission, but his most significant achievement was his perfection, in 1879, of the incandescent lamp (what we now call the electric light bulb) at his Menlo Park, New Jersey, laboratory. At Christmastime, he decorated his lab with a few dozen of the new lights. People came long distances to see this miraculous invention of the "Wizard of Menlo Park." Here was an invention that promised to obliterate the dark, to transform the way people lived and worked.

In 1882, Edison's company built the first power station in New York, which supplied the city with electric current for lighting for eighty-five customers. By 1898, there were three thousand operating power stations in the country. The Edison system employed direct current at low voltage; this limited the distance electric power could be transmitted to about 2 miles. George Westinghouse, another versatile inventor of the era, understood that alternating current, stepped up to high voltages by transformers, could be transmitted cheaply over long distances and then reduced to lower voltages for safe use by consumers. He formed the Westinghouse Electric Company in 1886 to compete with Edison's company. Westinghouse soon surpassed Edison as a supplier of electricity.

While entrepreneurs and inventors developed the new corporate forms of organization and the new technological systems that created the American industrial infrastructure, other business leaders built extensive marketing organizations of their own. The first advertising agencies appeared during the 1870s. Ad writers created copy and devised images to promote national sales of brand names such as Quaker Oats and Kellogg. Large department stores such as Macy's in New York and Wanamaker's in Philadelphia made their appearance. "Chain stores" such as the Atlantic and Pacific Tea Company (the A & P grocery) and F. W. Woolworth's "five and dimes" proliferated. As the major department and chain stores plied their urban customers with a cornucopia of goods, Sears, Roebuck and Montgomery Wards sold to rural customers through mail-order catalogues. Sears's and Ward's mail-order businesses could only flourish within a literate and affluent society that had evolved efficient and reliable transportation and communication systems.

As industries physically expanded, they also tended to become concentrated: fewer and fewer firms of a larger and larger size were controlling production in most of the important sectors of the economy. One major reason for the concentration of so many industries during the late nineteenth century was because only through concentration could the new technological systems be fully utilized. Another important reason for the concentration that accompanied expansion was

J.P. Morgan was one of the richest and most powerful men in America during the late nineteenth century. He reorganized railroad companies, created the world's largest steel company, and once used his vast financial resources to save the U.S. Treasury from bankruptcy. *Source:* Edward Steichen.J. Pierpont Morgan (1906). Photogravur from Camera Work, 8 1/8 x 6 1/4". The Museum of Modern Art, New York. Gift of A. Conger Goodyear.

falling prices. As prices fell, profit margins decreased and competition intensified. Rival concerns lowered their prices to retain or to increase market shares; successful firms either destroyed or absorbed their beaten rivals.

According to classical economic theory, competition kept prices low and ensured that only the most efficient producers survived and prospered. But, in practice, competition often led to ruinous consequences for both business and its customers. For example, railroads were forced to cut their freight rates to keep up with their competition. Rate reductions cut deeply into their profits. So they tried to compensate by increasing volume. They also often resorted to granting secret rebates (rates lower than their published rates) to selected large shippers such as Standard Oil. Small shippers continued to pay regular rates, which were much higher. Railroads often charged high prices where they had monopolies to make up for the low rates they had to offer in major competitive markets. Many railroads went bankrupt, especially during recessions and depressions. The public would not tolerate bankrupt railroads' going out of business because they were the only means of transportation available, and the courts placed bankrupt lines in the hands of receivers, who, reluctantly, had to keep them running, but usually inefficiently.

Railroads responded to price competition and its adverse consequences by reorganizing via mergers and takeovers; they combined lines into giant interregional systems during the 1880s. During the severe depression of the early 1890s, some of these combines went bankrupt. Bankers, led by J. P. Morgan, intervened to refinance and restructure the railroad systems. The financiers saved the railroads from bankruptcy and stabilized the nation's primary transportation system. The price paid for an orderly operating environment for the industry included higher rates for freight and passengers, banker control of many of the nation's largest railroads, and interregional monopolies.

At this time, most Americans were committed to economic individualism and the philosophy of free enterprise. In theory, they opposed government regulation of the economy. In practice, they accepted considerable governmental activity in the economic sphere—protective tariffs, internal improvements, and land grant subsidies to the railroads—because these governmental actions promoted geographical expansion and economic growth. They also generated jobs.

By the 1880s, many Americans had been frightened by the emergence of large industrial corporations such as the giant railroad systems and the Standard Oil Trust. Farmers, craftsmen, and small businessmen feared that these large corporate enterprises had become too big, too powerful. Big businesses were seen as posing threats to society. Lacking competition, unrestrained by government, they could charge their customers whatever they wanted. Even worse, monopolists were destroying economic opportunity and threatening democratic institutions. Thoughtful citizens worried about the survivability of democracy in a society increasingly characterized by a widening gap between rich and poor. Celebrations of industrialization were undercut by fears of its consequences, and reformers called for government action to tame the trusts.

The first to act were midwestern farmers and merchants who pressured state legislatures to regulate railroad rates. These state efforts were generally ineffective because railroads were large regional businesses whose operations spanned several states. The Supreme Court, after initially approving such state efforts, declared state regulatory efforts unconstitutional in 1886. In 1887, Congress enacted the Interstate Commerce Act to provide a measure of railroad regulation. It called for rates to be "reasonable and just," outlawed rebates, required railroads to publish and to stick to their rate schedules, and outlawed some monopolistic practices. Most important, it created the Interstate Commerce Commission (ICC), the first federal regulatory agency, to supervise railroads, investigate complaints, and enforce the law.

In practice, the ICC proved no more successful than the state regulatory commissions. The ICC's chief weakness was its lack of power to set rates; it could only take the railroads to court and try to persuade the courts to order the railroads to reduce their rates. The ICC's small staff could handle only a few complaints. These cases were often tied up in courts by lengthy litigation. When cases were resolved, they usually ended in victories for the railroads.

At the same time that some states and the federal government were trying unsuccessfully to regulate the railroads, attempts were also made to tame the trusts. As with railroad legislation, the first antitrust laws originated in the states. They were usually vague and unenforceable. Federal action came in 1890 when Congress enacted the Sherman Antitrust Act. The act declared any trust or other combination found to be "in restraint of trade" illegal. Persons forming such trusts could be fined and jailed. Individuals and businesses found to have suffered losses caused by illegal actions could sue in federal court for triple damages. The Supreme Court quickly emasculated the Sherman Act. In *United States* v. *E. C. Knight Company* (1895), it found that a sugar trust that controlled 98 percent of all domestically refined sugar was not in restraint of trade. The Court held that the E. C. Knight Co. had been formed to manufacture sugar, not to trade sugar, and was therefore a commercial activity, exempting it from prosecution under the Sherman Antitrust Act. Business continued to centralize as the nineteenth century ended. Big business got bigger.

LABOR

Wage earners were affected in many ways by industrialization and the rise of big business. Some effects were beneficial, others damaging. More efficient production methods enabled industrial workers to increase their output. Real wages rose 25 percent between 1870 and 1890. Work became physically less arduous, and the average work day was shortened from eleven to ten hours.

But as machines replaced human skills in shops and mills, jobs required less skill and became repetitive and monotonous. As manufacturing units grew larger, employee-employer relations became impersonal. The bargaining leverage of workers declined, and opportunities for workers to rise from the ranks of laborers and become manufacturers themselves decreased. Industrial work often proved dangerous. Nearly a million workers were injured annually in work-related accidents. In an age when laissez-faire attitudes dominated, there were no safety regulations or compulsory worker compensation programs. Workers and their families received no compensation, even for crippling or fatal accidents that occurred on the job. Industrialization also caused more frequent and larger swings in the business cycle. Workers and their families were often victimized by the increasing instability of the industrial economy. Periods of expansion would be followed by periods of depression and high unemployment.

During the 1880s and 1890s, only a small percentage of industrial workers joined trade unions, and most who did were skilled artisans, such as printers and carpenters, who joined craft unions. Most of the immigrants, who made up the bulk of the industrial workforce, were either unwilling or unable to join unions. Unions also excluded most African Americans and women from their ranks. The Knights of Labor, organized in 1869 by a group of garment workers in Philadelphia, managed to survive for a time. During the 1880s, it led successful strikes against railroads, and its membership reached 700,000. It declined after that. It failed to survive the end of the nineteenth century.

The only labor organization to establish itself during the Gilded Age was the American Federation of Labor, organized in 1886. It took a pragmatic, businesslike approach to unionism. It eschewed radicalism and politics. It concentrated on organizing skilled workers and fighting for "bread and butter" issues such as better wages and shorter hours. Its chief weapon was the strike. It grew steadily and had 1 million members by 1900.

Striking steel workers at the Carnegie mills in Homestead, Pennsylvania, prepare for a clash with armed Pinkerton detectives hired by Andrew Carnegie to break the strike. *Source:* Library of Congress.

Worker frustration and discontent mounted in the late nineteenth century. Workers felt threatened by the huge size of large corporate employers, by technology, and by periodic recessions and depressions, which meant unemployment in a laissez-faire economy. Most of all, they were frightened and angered by the stubborn arrogance of corporate employers, nearly all of whom opposed trade unions, fired workers for joining unions, and refused to bargain with union representatives. Strikes, which became frequent during the 1880s and 1890s, often became bitter, violent confrontations.

A savage railroad strike in 1877 convulsed the nation. For a time, about two-thirds of the nation's railways were shut down. Violence erupted in several locations in Maryland and Pennsylvania. Workers were shot; railroad properties were sabotaged. Federal troops were called out to keep order. In 1892, a strike occurred against Carnegie's steel factory in Homestead, Pennsylvania. During the strike, a fierce battle erupted between armed strikers and company guards, claiming seven lives. The strike lasted for months before the company won, fired many of the strikers, and crushed their union.

The most important strike occurred in 1894 when workers at the Pullman Company near Chicago went on strike to protest wage cuts during a severe depression. Some Pullman employees belonged to the American Railway Union, led by Eugene V. Debs. They refused to work on trains with Pullman cars. The resulting strike tied up rail traffic in and out of Chicago. The railroad companies appealed to President Cleveland to send troops, and he did, on the pretext that they were required to ensure the movement of mail. When Debs defied a federal injunction, he was jailed for contempt of court and the strike was broken. The crushing of the Pullman strike demonstrated the power of the courts to break strikes. In 1897, Debs converted to socialism and later ran for president five times on the American Socialist Party (SDP) ticket.

IMMIGRANTS

The industrial revolution stimulated a huge increase in immigration to America and tapped new population sources. Most of the immigrants who had come to America before 1890 had emigrated from the British Isles or the countries of western and northern Europe. After 1890, large numbers continued to emigrate from these traditional sources, but the majority of immigrants arrived from countries of southern and eastern Europe (Italy, Poland, Russia, and the Balkan countries), countries that had previously furnished few, if any, immigrants. These southern and eastern Europeans made up the new immigration. They were a predominantly peasant population pushed out of their homelands by decaying feudal economies and political and religious persecution. They flooded into America, pulled by the promise of economic opportunity and personal freedom.

Their first experiences were often harsh. They braved an uncomfortable, sometimes dangerous sea voyage and worried through inspections at Ellis Island and other immigration depots, often arriving in America with few possessions, little money, no education, and no job skills. They crowded into immigrant neighborhoods in large cities. There they found living quarters and the company of their ethnic brethren. These immigrant communities centered around old-country institutions such as the church and synagogue.

Although most of these new immigrants had come from peasant backgrounds, few went into agriculture in America. They lacked the capital and knowledge required to farm in America, which was a specialized business. Also, the economic possibilities and cultural attractions of the cities were more inviting than those of rural areas. The new immigrants were fed into the urban, industrial workforce. They lived in tenements near the factories that employed them. Many went into construction work, digging sewers, installing utilities, and paving the streets of expanding metropolises, in which the only constant appeared to be ceaseless growth. They worked hard, often for long hours, six days a week. At night, they returned to their crowded apartments in slum neighborhoods.

Even so, these harsh living and working conditions were better than what most of them had left behind. They worked no harder and earned no less than the native-born workers who were doing the same kind of work. Many immigrants acquired the income and knowledge to leave the ghettos. If they could not, their children, benefiting from educational opportunities, often achieved middle-class occupations, income, and status. There were many victors as well as victims among the immigrant groups that poured into the United States during the 1890s.

However, the oppressive living conditions prevailing in the immigrant slums and the failure of many of the newcomers to assimilate into the mainstream of American life angered and alarmed reformers. One of them, Jacob Riis, called attention to the immigrants' plight in an influential book, *How the Other Half Lives*, published in 1890. The book consisted of sketches of life in New York's immigrant ghettos drawn from Riis's years as a reporter. He illustrated the articles in his book with photographs. He piled one pathetic case upon another, his prose full of anger and shock. He declared the slums to be the children of "public neglect and private greed." A reformer, he advocated decent, low-cost housing as the chief means of solving these savage social problems.

A year before Riis published his spirited book, Jane Addams opened a settlement house in a slum neighborhood of south Chicago, where she and her fellow social workers provided services to the residents, who were mainly new immigrants. She called it Hull House, and it became the largest and most famous of the hundreds of settlement houses opened in American cities during the last fifteen years of the nineteenth century. Hull House offered its clients a day-care center, arts and crafts, counseling, playgrounds and baths for children, cooking classes, schools, an employment referral service, and access to medical and dental care. It also brought middle-class social workers into contact with immigrants, giving those professionals an opportunity for firsthand observation of immigrant problems.

The tremendous influx of new immigrants also provoked a nativist backlash on the part of some old-stock native-born Americans. Nativists resented what they perceived to be flood of poor, illiterate, and unskilled people who could never become productive citizens. A body of pseudoscientific studies attempted to prove that immigrants from southern and eastern European countries belonged to races that were "inferior" to northern and western Europeans and their American descendants. During the 1880s and 1890s, nativists organized for action and became a potent political force. The most influential nativist organization was the American Protective Association (APA); the APA was founded in 1887 primarily to promote Americanism and Protestant religions, which members equated with American national culture. Their chief targets were Roman Catholics, the Catholic Church, and Catholicism itself.

Other less prejudiced and extremist voices joined the call for excluding new immigrants or at least severely reducing the size of the inflow. During the 1890s, the leaders of organized labor called for the adoption of literacy tests to screen out immigrants. Congress moved to bar "undesirable" immigrants from entering the country; at various times it excluded convicts, insane people, contract laborers, paupers, anarchists, and people with serious illnesses.

CITIES

The enormous expansion of industry was the chief cause of urban growth during the late nineteenth century when modern American metropolises appeared. A steadily increasing proportion of the American urban population was made up of immigrants. By 1900, immigrant populations composed the majority of the population in several of the largest American cities. According to the 1900 census, first- or second-generation immigrants made up over 80 percent of New York City's nearly 3.5 million inhabitants.

These immigrants often got blamed for all the problems that afflicted American cities of the late nineteenth century; this accusation was both exaggerated and unfair. The main cause of urban problems was the rapid expansion of cities. Cities suffered from acute growing pains; city services could not begin to keep pace with the rate of urban growth. Severe problems with water supplies, sewage, garbage disposal, and police and fire protection arose. Crowded, substandard housing was the worst problem, with its attendant physical discomfort, psychological stress, juvenile delinquency, vice, and crime. Slums spawned street gangs, epidemic diseases, and high infant-mortality rates.

Gradually the basic facilities of urban living improved. Streets were paved; electric lights pushed back the dark after nightfall. Major improvements were made in urban transportation. The major innovation was the electric trolley. These "streetcars" changed the character of urban life. They extended the range of the traditional "walking city" from 2.5 miles to more than 6 miles, which meant that the geographic areas of cities expanded enormously. Population shifts occurred as the affluent classes fled from inner cities to the outer neighborhoods, the suburbs. They left the immigrant working classes clustered in the downtown areas. Segregated residential patterns emerged in every city, separating people by income and economic class, which correlated with ethnic and racial divisions.

WOMEN, CHILDREN, AND WORK

During the last decades of the nineteenth century, 6 million American women entered the workforce. Many entered manufacturing industries such as shoemaking, food processing, and textiles, and became factory workers. By 1890, over 300,000 women worked in textile factories, constituting over half of the labor force. They also took clerical jobs in business as typists, bookkeepers, and salespersons. Employers were willing to hire millions of women because they could pay them less, substantially less, in most cases, than men. Women worked for about one-third to one-half of what men received for comparable work. In 1900, about 90 percent of working women were young and single. Prevailing attitudes barred married women from the workplaces of America. When a young working girl married, she usually had to quit her job. Female workers sometimes organized their own unions, carrying out successful strikes and achieving higher wages. Working women forged the first broad-based women's union in this country, the Women's Trade Union League (WTUL), founded in 1903. Women also entered most of the professions, albeit in small numbers. Women became doctors, lawyers, engineers, and university professors. By 1900, most public school teachers and librarians were women.

Women workers in one of the nation's "sweatshops" during the Gilded Age. *Source:* Library of Congress.

Most working children labored on their parents' farms, but they also flooded into industrial occupations in the late nineteenth century. Children under age fifteen worked in coal mining, textiles, and other industries. Other children worked in the streets selling newspapers and shining shoes.

NATIVE AMERICANS

During the 1870s and 1880s, as the American economy expanded and the building of the railroads opened the West for economic development, the Plains Indians became victims of the westward expansion. They were conquered, their culture fragmented, and they were deprived of much of their lands. The survivors were tucked away on arid reservations to endure a life of poverty and isolation.

Indian resistance was heroic; they held off the encroaching whites for years, but they inevitably succumbed to overwhelming firepower and vastly superior numbers. It was the destruction of the buffalo herds that fatally undermined the ability of the Plains Indians to resist the U.S. Army. Two vast herds had roamed the prairies, furnishing the Indians with food, clothing, shelter, and tools. By the 1880s, these herds had been hunted to the verge of extinction. With the destruction of the buffalo herds, the Plains Indians' way of life was undermined. General Philip

Sheridan, the Civil War hero who commanded U.S. Army forces conquering the Plains Indians, understood why the Indians fought and expressed sympathy for the people his soldiers were destroying. He wrote that

> We took away their country and their means of support, broke up their mode of living, their habits of life, introduced disease and decay among them and it was for this and against this they made war. Could anyone expect less?[1]

Plains Indians also suffered at the hands of civilian agencies entrusted with administering Indian affairs. Government agents were political appointees. They were often incompetent, corrupt, and indifferent to Indian welfare; they exploited the people they supposedly served. There were cases of crooked agents selling food supplies intended for reservation Indians to miners and pocketing the money, leaving the helpless Indians to starve.

In 1887, Congress passed the Dawes Act, which was designed to eliminate tribal life and to convert the surviving Plains Indians to the white man's way of life. Reservation lands were divided into small units, with each head of an Indian household allotted 160 acres. Indians who accepted the allotments and "adopted the habits of civilized life" were granted U.S. citizenship. A clause in the Dawes Act prevented Indians from selling their allotted lands for twenty-five years. Funds were also appropriated to provide education for Indian children. Intended as a reform to help Indians, in practice the Dawes Act proved disastrous. It shattered the remnants of Indian culture without enabling them to adopt the white man's ways. Most of the land allotments ended up in white hands, and the Indians remained dependent on government aid. The Dawes Act was the final destructive act in a long chronicle of white atrocities committed against Native Americans.

The last Indians to abandon the unequal struggle against the whites were the Chiricahua Apaches, who inhabited the desert of the Southwest. Relentless warriors, they waged a bitter, savage guerrilla struggle against the U.S. Army in Arizona Territory. In 1886, the Army succeeded in capturing their chieftain, a resourceful warrior named Geronimo. The Apaches finally yielded, and the nearly 300-year cycle of genocidal warfare waged by the European invaders of North America against Native Americans came to an end.

There was a tragic final footnote to the Euro-American conquest of the Native American people written in the snow at Wounded Knee, South Dakota, in December 1890. A Paiute shaman named Wovoka had developed a religion based on a ceremonial rite known to whites as the Ghost Dance. Wovoka promised his people that there would come a time when the dead would reappear and the land would be returned to Native Americans. He converted the Lakota Sioux to his new faith. U.S. soldiers attacked a Sioux religious observance. Heavily armed cavalrymen massacred the Indians as they tried to flee, butchering scores of people, including women and children.

---

[1]Thomas C. Leonard, "The Reluctant Conquerors," *American Heritage,* XXVII:5 (August 1976), 34–40.

Indian land cessions 1850—1890

Ceded prior to 1850

Ceded 1850—1870

Ceded 1870—1890

Indian reservations in 1890
(principal tribes labeled)

Indian land cessions, 1850–1890. *Source:* Moss, *The Rise of Modern America,* p. 16.

As the nineteenth century ended, a Native American population that had numbered in the millions and consisted of hundreds of intact cultures at the time Europeans established their first permanent settlements on the Atlantic seaboard had been reduced by centuries of warfare and oppression to perhaps 50,000 individuals. Social scientists predicted that these degraded remnants would soon die out; that the early twentieth century would bear witness to the extinction of the Amerindians.

AFRICAN AMERICANS

While Native Americans fell victim to western expansion, the status of black people in the South deteriorated in the aftermath of Reconstruction. The Republican party abandoned southern blacks in exchange for the presidency in 1877. Throughout the decade of the 1880s, the status of African Americans in the South was ambiguous. They retained legal and political rights. They still voted, but they were deprived of effective political power because the Republic party organization had been destroyed.

During the 1890s, with Mississippi leading the way, southern states rewrote their constitutions to include provisions that disfranchised most African Americans. Various subterfuges were used to circumvent the Fifteenth Amendment, the most common of which was the "understanding clause." This clause required potential voters to read and understand any section of their state constitution before registering and left enforcement of this rule to voter registrars. Registrars used it as a vehicle to disfranchise African Americans by imposing stringent standards on them, meanwhile allowing illiterate whites to register by taking their word that they "understood" the state constitution. Other exclusionary devices included literacy tests and poll taxes. Black disfranchisement ensured Democratic control of southern politics. Disfranchisement also excluded large numbers of white voters, particularly those who had formerly voted Republican.

By 1900, only 5 percent of eligible African Americans voted in the South. Disfranchisement also opened the door for the enforcement of legal segregation in all important areas of southern life. Elaborate segregation ordinances evolved everywhere in the South, depriving black people of equal access to public accommodations. By 1900, southern blacks were disfranchised, segregated, and deprived of equal educational and economic opportunities. There was a tremendous increase in the amount of violence directed against black people during the 1890s. Lynch mobs roamed the South murdering hundreds of African Americans. By the end of the nineteenth century, rights acquired during Reconstruction became a faded memory for black people.

The application of "Jim Crow" (the systemic segregation and suppression of black people) had been possible because the Supreme Court had retreated from its commitment to racial democracy in the aftermath of Reconstruction. In 1883, the Court nullified the Civil Rights Act of 1875, which had outlawed segregation of public accommodations. In 1896, the Supreme Court put the seal of constitutional

Booker T. Washington, born a slave, rose to become a prominent leader in education and the foremost spokesman for African Americans during the 1890s.   *Source:* Hampton Institute.

approval upon segregation. In a notorious case, *Plessy* v. *Ferguson,* the Court sustained a Louisiana statute that segregated the races on railroads. The Court found segregation to be constitutional if "separate-but-equal" facilities were provided. Separate-but-equal facilities did not violate the equal protection clause of Section One of the Fourteenth Amendment. One Supreme Court justice vigorously dissented from the majority decision: John Marshall Harlan, a southerner and conservative, wrote that the Court "had inflicted a terrible blow to the principle of equal protection before the law."

Plessy v. *Ferguson* resolved a conflict between American professions of equality and institutionalized racism when the Court also held that segregation did not imply that black people were inferior. The timing of *Plessy* v. *Ferguson* was also important. It removed the last barrier to the general drive to deprive African Americans of rights, and, in the words of historian C. Vann Woodward, the decision "unleashed the floodgates of racial aggression." Segregation would be constitutional for the next fifty-eight years.

Out of this era of decline and danger for African Americans emerged Booker T. Washington, who became the foremost spokesman for black people. Deeply concerned about the ability of African Americans to survive in racist America, he developed a strategy he hoped would lead to racial harmony and common progress. In a speech delivered at an Atlanta exposition in 1895, he preached self-help, economic progress, thrift, and racial solidarity. He told black people that if they learned to advance themselves by getting agricultural or vocational training, saving their money, and acquiring property, they would earn the respect and acceptance of whites. Washington assured white leaders that African Americans accepted disfranchisement and segregation in order to concentrate on economic gains. In return, he asked southern white business leaders and politicians to support black education and hire black workers. Washington's proposed accommodationist strategy made him popular among whites. It enabled him to raise millions of dollars from northern philanthropists for black technical and vocational training.

Other African American leaders, rejecting Washington's accommodationist strategies, proposed that blacks challenge racism and legal segregation, that African Americans demand full equality now. The most prominent African American scholar in 1900, William E. B. Dubois, told blacks that they should demand the best university educations available, that they should demand the right to vote in order to battle the segregation system through the political process.

During the 1890s, over 90 percent of African Americans resided in the South, most living outside the boundaries of industrial society. Most were forced to live within the confines of an oppressive environment without political power and with inferior legal rights. African Americans were bound by a rigid and stringent caste system that deprived blacks of equal opportunities; indeed, that forbade any expression of equality. In many regions of the South, African Americans were entrapped in a kind of economic bondage. They worked as sharecroppers or tenants, perpetually in debt, caught up in a credit system that enabled landowners, merchants, and bankers, to hold them in virtual peonage.

Despite their difficult lives within an oppressive and unjust social system, many capable and hardworking African Americans achieved considerable successes. They enjoyed strong, stable family lives. They established strong communities built around black churches and schools, and black-owned businesses. Thousands of black farmers were able to acquire their own farms. According to the census of 1900, African Americans owned about 12 million acres of land in the South.

ASIAN AMERICANS

Chinese people first emigrated to the United States during the 1840s, when they came to California to mine gold. Initially, they were welcomed. These immigrants were mostly young men who came as sojourners to make their fortunes in the region they called "Gold Mountain" and then planned to return to their villages and families in China. Many came from the Toison district of Canton Province in southern China. During the 1860s, perhaps 25,000 Chinese were working in California's gold fields. As the gold ore played out, former miners went to work building railroads.

During the 1860s, about 12,000 Chinese worked for the Southern Pacific railroad, constructing the western half of the first transcontinental railroad, which was completed in 1869. During the 1870s, Chinese immigrants in California worked in agriculture, in the fishing industry, and in service businesses such as restaurants and laundries. They were ineligible for American citizenship under a 1790 law that limited that privilege to white people. Many prospered despite encountering considerable, often violent, anti-Chinese prejudice. In 1882, about 30,000 Chinese immigrants entered the country, bringing the national total to 150,000, mostly concentrated on the West Coast.

Many white Americans had resented the Chinese for years. Anti-Chinese prejudice was especially strong among working-class whites. They viewed the Chinese as economic competitors who took their jobs, worked for lower wages, and could be used as strikebreakers. Unions held "anti-coolie" meetings and demonstrations protesting the Chinese presence and calling for a ban on further Chinese immigration. There were violent attacks on Chinese, including lynchings, burnings, and the destroying of their homes and businesses. Pressure from West Coast politicians prompted Washington to conclude an agreement with China that restricted immigration. Congress implemented the ban by enacting the Chinese Exclusion Act in 1882 that barred most Chinese immigration to the United States for ten years. The Chinese were the first national group to be formally barred from emigrating to America.

Japanese emigration to America began during the late 1880s on a small scale. By 1900, about three thousand Japanese immigrants had reached America, most settling in California. They also encountered anti-Asian prejudice, which hindered their opportunities. White Californians began a drive to exclude Japanese immigrants that would continue intermittently until World War II.

FARMERS

The economic position of many farmers declined during the late nineteenth century, for several reasons. Ironically, one of the major reasons for agricultural decline lay in the fact that the American industrial revolution had enabled American farmers to mechanize, to farm larger acreages, and above all, to increase productivity. Both American and world agricultural production increased, and the European market, the American farmers' major overseas outlet, shrank. Farm commodity prices tumbled. Corn, which sold at 78¢ per bushel in 1869, brought 28¢ in 1889. Wheat brought $2 per bushel in 1867, 70¢ in 1889. As farm commodity prices fell and farm income dropped, individual farmers responded by increasing production. Increased production further depressed prices and farm income continued to spiral downward.

Farmers also had to pay more for equipment and other supplies because manufacturers, protected from foreign competition by tariff barriers, had raised their prices. Good land was increasingly expensive in many areas either because it was growing scarce or because the railroads and large land companies controlled it. Flour-milling and meat-packing industries forced farmers and stock owners to sell them grain and beef at lower prices. Railroads, especially in regions in which they enjoyed a transportation monopoly, often charged farmers exorbitant rates to haul their crops.

Harvesting wheat on one of the "bonanza farms" in western America ca. 1890.   *Source:* Library of Congress.

Midwestern farmers organized to try to improve their economic situation. During the 1860s and 1870s, they formed Granges. These groups organized purchasing cooperatives, and they lobbied state governments to regulate railroads, particularly to limit the shipping rates that railroads charged farmers. These efforts were generally futile. By the late 1870s, many farmers were in serious economic difficulty. Farm income continued to fall, and many farmers were deeply in debt for equipment and land that they had purchased previously. Unable to make mortgage and tax payments, they faced the loss of their farms.

In their distress, some farmers turned to currency inflation to rescue them from economic disaster. During the Civil War, the government had issued "greenbacks"—hundreds of millions of dollars of paper money that was not redeemable in silver or gold. Farmers, joined by small merchants and other hard-pressed groups, called for the government to issue more greenbacks. They reasoned that currency inflation would cause price levels to rise, their income would increase, and they could pay their debts. In 1880, they formed the Greenback-Labor party, a single-issue alternative party, which attracted 300,000 votes. It faded thereafter, but the idea of easing farmers' debt burdens via currency inflation did not.

POLITICS

Politics during this era were characterized by passive presidents and strong senators. The Senate dominated the federal government. Many of its members were either political bosses preoccupied with forging alliances, winning elections, and controlling patronage; or, they were pawns of corporate interests. In either case, they tended to neglect the real issues of the day. The House of Representatives was more responsive to the public interest, but it was too unstable to play an effective legislative role. Frequent, close elections meant a constant turnover in House membership, and neither party was able to control the House long enough to enact a legislative agenda. At local and state levels, corrupt political machines frequently controlled government.

Political machines stayed in power by turning out the vote on election day to support the organization's candidates. Control of elections meant power—power to distribute city jobs to supporters, to award franchises to companies for providing city services in exchange for bribes, and to award building contracts to construction companies willing to pay for them. Corrupt contractors often profited excessively from these contracts by overcharging the taxpayers and using cheap, substandard materials. Even though these machines were corrupt and inefficient, they got urban utility and transport systems installed rapidly.

Immigrant neighborhoods formed the popular base of big-city political machines. It was common for individuals to register illegally in several precincts and vote many times on election day. And, in exchange for his votes, a voter often benefited from machine favors—a job, a cheap rental, help if there were trouble with the police, and assistance in acquiring citizenship. Frequently, a member of the political machine appeared at baptisms, weddings, and funerals. The political boss and many of his henchmen were often immigrants themselves, and newcomers could identify with their success and power. The machine also ran ethnically balanced tickets to appeal to a broad range of immigrant nationalities and to give members of immigrant groups an opportunity to achieve political office and to participate in politics. Political machines often sponsored dinners, fairs, and picnic outings for their immigrant constituents. These events not only entertained the voters but also ensured their continuing political support.

Presidential elections were invariably corrupt, and close. The two major political parties were evenly matched. There were few significant issue differences between them, and no ideological differences. Usually Republican presidential candidates won narrowly. Grover Cleveland was the only Democratic president to hold office during the 1880s and 1890s. Elections were not decided by the issues. Voters generally voted a straight party ticket; occasionally, they were attracted by the personal qualities of a candidate.

THE PEOPLE'S PARTY

By the late 1880s, continuing hard times meant that farmers continued to organize in efforts to solve their economic problems. Farmers' Alliances appeared in the Midwest and South. During the late 1880s, the Alliances claimed a membership of white and black farmers that approached 2 million. They formed cooperatives and entered politics at the local level. Alliance members, encouraged by local political successes and angered by both major parties, which had continued to be unresponsive to their concerns, met in St. Louis in February 1892 to form a new national third party, the People's Party, also called the Populist Party, or the Populists. They gathered again in Omaha, Nebraska, on July 4, 1892, to choose their candidate for president and to adopt a platform. In a noisy, emotional gathering, which resembled a religious revival, they denounced bankers and business leaders who exploited the farmers and workers of the country.

The major plank in their platform called for currency inflation. But it was no longer a call for more greenbacks, which the farmers had abandoned as an unrealistic goal. They wanted the free and unlimited coinage of silver to gold at a ratio of sixteen to one. They wanted to inflate the currency, expanding the money supply by requiring the U.S. Treasury to buy and to coin, free of charge, all silver brought to it. They wanted silver dollars to contain sixteen times as much silver, by weight, as gold dollars would contain gold. That sixteen-to-one ratio would ensure that silver would be more valuable as money than it would be as a precious metal, given the prevailing prices for gold and silver. Therefore, silver would remain in circulation as money, and the currency would become inflated. This money plank appealed to western silver miners as well as farmers, and it appealed to some small business owners who saw inflation as a cure for their economic woes. Free silver also had symbolic uses: It represented the liberation of the toiling masses from economic bondage to banks and railroads. Free silver would redeem their Jeffersonian birthright and restore their claim to a fair share of society's benefits.

Other Populist planks called for government ownership of railroads and telephone lines, an income tax, a single term for the president, and the direct election of senators. Populists tried to attract the support of labor by calling for an eight-hour day, by denouncing contract labor (importing aliens as workers who took jobs from American workers and could be used as strikebreakers), and by demanding an end to the use of Pinkerton detectives to break up strikes.

At the time of the Populist movement, there was a great deal of discontent among the urban working classes. Strikes and unemployment marches were symptomatic of the unrest seething in the land at the time of the Populist revolt. Some of these angry workers made common cause with the embattled farmers from the Midwest and South. In 1894, Jacob Coxey led an "army" of about 600 unemployed workers in a march from his home in Ohio to the nation's capital. Middle-class Americans were alarmed by the growing signs of social instability in their increasingly frayed society.

The Populists nominated James B. Weaver, a former Civil War general and Greenback-Labor leader, for president. Running as a third party in 1892, the Populists waged an energetic campaign. They had able leaders such as Mary E. Lease, an attorney and powerful orator, who exhorted Kansas farmers to "raise less corn and more hell." On election day, the Populists gathered over a million votes, 8.5 percent of the total. They showed strength in two regions: the South and the newer states of the Midwest. They won many local elections, elected some representatives and a few senators, and won control of the Kansas legislature. They also picked up twenty-two electoral votes. It was a good showing, good enough to alarm the established parties in the South and Midwest.

During 1893 and 1894, the nation was mired in the worst depression in its history. Banks and businesses failed by the thousands. Railroads controlling about one-third of the trackage in the country went bankrupt. Farmers, unable to meet mortgage payments, lost their farms. Millions of industrial workers were unemployed. Late in 1894, the U.S. Treasury faced a desperate financial crisis. Its gold reserves dwindled to $41 million, not enough to pay debt obligations that would soon come due. Only an emergency bond issue that was floated by a banking syndicate headed by J. P. Morgan, which raised $62 million, saved the American government from bankruptcy.

The Populist vote increased in the 1894 elections as they continued to demand the unlimited coinage of silver to gold at a ratio of sixteen to one. The depression and his failure to solve it discredited President Cleveland's administration. The Democrats in the South and Republicans in the Midwest feared they would lose large numbers of their followers to the Populists in 1896.

The Republicans met to nominate a candidate in St. Louis in 1896 and chose an Ohio congressman with a good record, William McKinley. The Republicans adopted a platform maintaining the gold standard and a protective tariff.

At the Democratic convention held in Chicago in July 1896, President Cleveland lost control of the delegates, and they rallied to the candidacy of a thirty-six-year-old Nebraskan named William Jennings Bryan. Bryan won the nomination with a dramatic appeal for silver, ending his speech, "You shall not press down upon the brow of labor this crown of thorns; you shall not crucify mankind upon a cross of gold." The convention promptly adopted a platform calling for the "free and unlimited coinage of both gold and silver at the present legal ratio of sixteen to one" and nominated Bryan for president.

The Democrats' actions confronted the Populists with a Hobson's choice. If they supported Bryan and free silver, they risked losing their identity as a political party. If they ran their own candidate, they ensured McKinley's election and the defeat of the silver issue. Most Populists ended up supporting Bryan and the Democrats. After 1896, Populist support declined rapidly. The Democrats had co-opted the Populists' major issue and most of their followers.

In the contest between Bryan and McKinley, issues did matter. The Republicans had many advantages they could exploit during the campaign. The Democrats were saddled with Cleveland's discredited depression presidency and were on

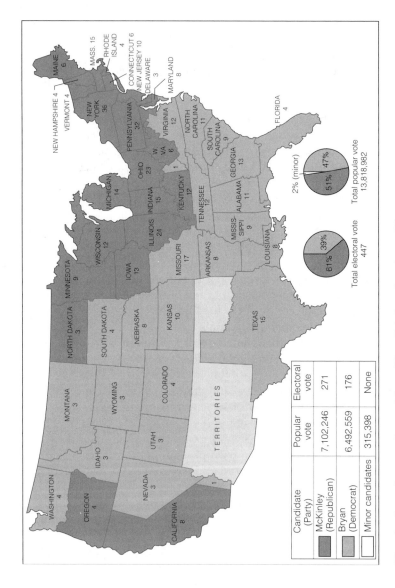

The election of 1896. *Source:* Moss, *Rise of Modern America,* p. 25.

Candidate (Party)	Popular vote	Electoral vote
McKinley (Republican)	7,102,246	271
Bryan (Democrat)	6,492,559	176
Minor candidates	315,398	None

Total electoral vote 447

61% 39%

Total popular vote 13,818,982

51% 47%

2% (minor)

the defensive. McKinley ran a well-organized, well-financed campaign orchestrated by an Ohio businessman, Marcus A. Hanna. Hanna raised $3.5 million. His campaign organization flooded the nation with millions of pieces of campaign literature and fifteen hundred speakers. Theodore Roosevelt said that Hanna "advertised McKinley as if he were a patent medicine." Hanna's electoral strategy called for McKinley to stay home, conducting a dignified "front porch" campaign. Selected delegates representing various national constituencies would be brought to his home. McKinley would greet them and make a speech calculated to appeal to their interests. Hanna saw to it that McKinley's "front porch" speeches got national attention.

The Democrats had little money, a weak organization, and few prominent supporters. But they had William Jennings Bryan, who waged an energetic one-man campaign. He traveled over 18,000 miles and made over 600 stump speeches. He had a powerful voice—loud, clear, and eloquent. He spoke, without amplification, to crowds as large as 10,000. All could hear and most cheered. Bryan's campaign speeches were dominated by a single theme—silver. His was mainly a single-issue campaign, in contrast to McKinley's pluralistic and nationalistic approach.

In November, McKinley won decisively. He got over 7 million votes to Bryan's 6.5 million. He received 271 electoral votes to Bryan's 176. The Republicans also rolled up large majorities in both houses of Congress. Organization and money had beaten eloquence. Pluralism had defeated silver. Nationalism had bested sectionalism. The silver issue carried the South and Midwest, but it did not travel well outside these regions. Bryan also failed to reach industrial workers. The Republicans got the support of most urban voters, most business voters, and most middle-class voters, and they carried the farm vote in several midwestern states such as Illinois and Ohio, which ensured their victory.

IMPERIALISM

For much of the Gilded Age, Americans were preoccupied with internal events such as industrialization, the building of the railroads, the settlement of the West, and urban affairs. But toward the end of the nineteenth century, the United States turned outward. It became involved in world affairs, built a modern navy, expanded its overseas trade, fought a war with Spain, and acquired a colonial empire. By 1900, the United States had emerged as a world power.

Many forces converged to revive American expansionism and to direct American attention overseas. Powerful economic forces stemming from industrialization played a major role. Industrialization diversified and increased American exports, creating a search for new overseas markets and a drive to expand existing ones. Andrew Carnegie discovered he could sell a ton of steel to an English railway cheaper than English steel manufacturers could. John D. Rockefeller's Standard Oil monopoly soon dominated the European market for kerosene. Other American business leaders looked to Latin America, long a market for British manufacturers, for increased sales. American imports also increased, and many came from American-owned enterprises in foreign lands. American investment capital poured into Canada, Mexico, and Cuba during the 1890s.

Other forces promoted expansion. Captain Alfred T. Mahan, an avowed expansionist, urged Congress to modernize and expand the U.S. Navy. In books and essays, he used the example of Great Britain, the world's preeminent power, to prove his contention that sea power undergirded all great powers. He linked together expanding sea power with expanding commercial ties and overseas colonial possessions. His arguments influenced many members of congress and two future presidents, Theodore Roosevelt and Woodrow Wilson.

The missionary movements of many churches also promoted overseas activity. In their earnest desire to save souls and do good works for the greater glory of God, they were servants of expansion, particularly in Asia. By the 1890s, hundreds of American missionaries lived and worked in China. Reverend Josiah Strong, a Congregational minister from Ohio, actively promoted American missionary expansionism. Blending a concept of religious mission with nationalism and racial ideologies, he prophesied that

> This race of unequaled energy, with all the majesty of numbers, and the might of wealth behind it—the representative, let us hope, of the largest liberty, the purest Christianity, the highest civilization . . . will move down upon Mexico, down upon Central and South America, out upon the islands of the sea.[2]

Social Darwinists also advocated American expansionism. They applied the Darwinian concept of "struggle for survival" to international power politics. They were confident that what they called the mighty American "Anglo-Saxon race" was destined to acquire colonies and to expand its influence until it dominated the world. Social Darwinist foreign policy ideas also influenced men such as Theodore Roosevelt and Henry Cabot Lodge, who helped forge America's expansionist foreign policies from 1898 to World War I.

An amalgam of powerful economic, strategic, and ideological forces provided an expansionist dynamic. Together they turned a hitherto inward-looking and parochial continental power into an expansionist and international power during the last decade of the nineteenth century.

American expansion initially focused on the South Pacific. As the century came to a close, the United States gained ownership of two island chains, Samoa and Hawaii. Samoa, which lay some 4,000 miles southwest of San Francisco, commanded important shipping lanes in the South Pacific. Its splendid natural harbors of Apia and Pago Pago were desired as way stations for America's growing trade with New Zealand and Australia.

In 1878, the United States concluded a treaty with the Samoans that gave the United States rights to a coaling station at Pago Pago. The Germans and British also negotiated treaties with Samoa, and the three nations disputed each other's interests in the archipelago. All three nations sent warships, and for a time war threat-

2Josiah Strong, *Our Country*, ed. Joseph Herbst (Cambridge, MA: Belknap Press, 1963), reprint of the 1891 revised edition. See chap. 14, "The Anglo Saxon and the World's Future," pp. 213–18.

ened among them. The three imperialistic powers resolved their conflicts diplomatically at a conference held in Berlin in 1889. They created a three-power protectorate that proved inherently unworkable as conflicts over economic and strategic interests continued. In 1899, the Samoan archipelago was divided between Germany and the United States, with Britain gaining territory elsewhere. Germany got the two largest islands, America the remaining islands, including Tutuila, with its harbor at Pago Pago.

American involvement with the Hawaiian islands dated from the 1820s, when New England missionaries settled there to convert the population. During the 1840s, American whaling ships made Hawaii a major port of call. American cultural influence had become dominant in the islands by mid-century, and some expansionists were calling for annexation. A reciprocity treaty was signed between Hawaii and the United States in 1875, which lowered tariffs on both sides. These arrangements permitted Hawaii to ship sugar duty-free to the United States, causing the islands' sugar industry to boom. It also tied the Hawaiian economy to mainland markets. Economic dependency became a strong force for political union with the United States. The reciprocity treaty was amended in 1887 to grant American ships exclusive right to use the magnificent Pearl River Harbor as a naval station.

By 1890, planters of American descent controlled the sugar industry and owned about two-thirds of the land. In that year, changes in American tariff laws favoring domestic sugar growers caused mainland demand for Hawaiian sugar to drop sharply, plunging the Hawaiian economy into depression. Hawaiian sugar planters favored annexation with the United States to regain their lost markets. There were additional motives for annexation. In 1891, Queen Liliuokalani became the Hawaiian monarch. Resenting the growing influence of Americans, she abolished the existing constitution that had granted Americans control of the islands' political life. She tried to reassert the absolute prerogatives of the traditional Hawaiian monarchy. Her actions provoked an American-led coup that overthrew her government. The planter revolutionaries turned to the American minister to Hawaii, John Stevens, for help.

On January 16, 1893, Stevens, a strong advocate of annexation, arranged for 150 marines from the USS *Boston,* then in Pearl Harbor, to take up stations near Queen Liliuokalani's palace. The next day, Stevens officially recognized the new revolutionary regime. Grudgingly, the haughty Queen yielded her authority. Two weeks later, Stevens declared Hawaii an American protectorate and advised Washington to proceed with annexation: "The Hawaiian pear is now fully ripe, and this is the golden hour for the United States to pluck it." A delegation from the new Hawaiian government came to Washington to negotiate an annexation treaty. In mid-February, less than a month following the coup, President Harrison submitted an annexation treaty to the Senate for approval.

The Senate had not yet voted on the proposed treaty when a new president, Grover Cleveland, took office. Cleveland, who opposed annexation, withdrew the treaty from Senate consideration. He sent a special commissioner, former

Congressman James Blount, to Hawaii to find out if the native Hawaiians favored annexation. Blount reported to Cleveland that the coup against the Queen could not have succeeded without U.S. complicity, and that the Hawaiians both opposed annexation and wanted their monarch restored. The president blocked annexation and tried to restore the Queen to her throne, but the American planters now controlling the Hawaiian government refused to step down.

In 1897, President William McKinley came to office favoring annexation. Another treaty was negotiated and sent to the Senate, which failed to approve it. It took the outbreak of the Spanish-American War to provide the necessary votes for the annexation of Hawaii. Advocates argued that Hawaii was needed to send supplies and reinforcements to American soldiers in the Philippines. Captain Mahan argued that the United States required Hawaii to protect the American mainland from future attacks. He also argued the United States should take Hawaii lest it fall into the hands of a hostile power such as Japan. War fever and imperialism carried the day. The annexation treaty passed. On July 7, 1898, Hawaii became an American territory.

Another major area of American interest was the Caribbean. In 1895, U.S. attention focused on Cuba, when the Cubans rose in rebellion against Spanish rule. The fighting between the rebels and the Spanish troops was vicious. The Spanish commander, General Valeriano Weyler, in an effort to deny the guerrillas popular support, herded the Cuban people into concentration camps. Thousands of Cubans perished from disease, starvation, and mistreatment. Americans, who mostly sympathized with the rebels, were appalled by General Weyler's notorious *reconcentrado* policy and its ghastly results. American newspapers also carried exaggerated and distorted accounts of Spanish activity in Cuba, further inflaming public opinion against the Spanish. Two large New York City dailies, Joseph Pulitzer's *New York World* and young William Randolph Hearst's *New York Morning Journal*, competing fiercely for readers, ran many sensational, inaccurate accounts of the war.

Irresponsible journalism may have stirred the people, but it did not cause the United States to go to war in Cuba. Other forces were at work. Anti-Spanish sentiment was intensified in early February 1898 when Cuban rebels released a private letter that had been written by the Spanish Ambassador to the United States, Enrique Dupuy de Lome. In the letter, de Lome had criticized President McKinley, calling him "weak and a bidder for the admiration of the crowd."

A week after the publication of the letter, there occurred the event that probably made war inevitable. On the evening of February 15, the American battleship *Maine* was blown up in Havana Harbor. The ship was demolished, killing 260 sailors. The cause of the blast has never been determined, but at the time Americans held the Spanish responsible. Political pressure built for America to go to war against Spain. People marched through the streets chanting "Remember the *Maine*! To hell with Spain!" The most fervent pro-war advocates in Washington were Democratic and Populist members of Congress who invoked the "spirit of 1776," calling for a war to liberate the Cuban people from Spanish colonialism. They also identified the rebel struggle with their own efforts to escape from economic bondage.

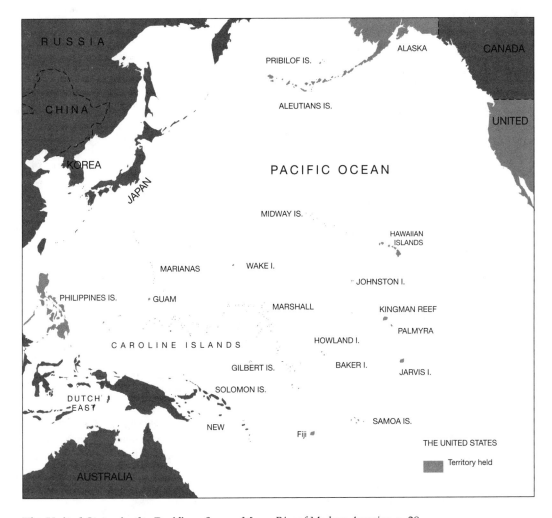

The United States in the Pacific.　*Source:* Moss, *Rise of Modern America*, p. 29.

President McKinley, wishing to solve the Cuban crisis by diplomacy, tried to avoid a war that he did not believe served the national interest. He tried to moderate the press and public responses to avoid being forced to war. He was particularly concerned about the popular "rush to judgment" after the sinking of the *Maine.* Backed by Wall Street bankers and business leaders who saw war as disrupting trade with Cuba, McKinley demanded that Spain revoke the *reconcentrado* policy and grant an armistice to the rebels. In early April 1898, Spain, desperately wishing to avoid a war it could never win, agreed to these terms.

But Spain's concessions were too little too late. McKinley had decided to grant Congress the war it and the American people demanded. Internal political pressures had forced McKinley's hand. On April 11, he sent a war message to Congress in which he also noted the Spanish concessions that really made war unnecessary. But, on April 18, Congress, in a jingoistic frenzy, issued an ultimatum directing the Spanish to vacate Cuba and ordering a naval blockade of the island. Four days later, Congress followed these acts of war against Spain with a formal declaration of hostilities. The United States, surrendering to belligerent emotions, stumbled into a war it could have avoided.

Although all eyes were on Cuba where the crisis in relations between Spain and the United States had brought war, the opening battle of the Spanish-American War occurred on the other side of the world in Manila Bay in the Philippines. On May 1, Commodore George Dewey's squadron destroyed a Spanish fleet trapped in the bay. In August, U.S. Army forces occupied Manila, the capital of the Spanish colony. An American expedition later occupied the Spanish colony of Guam, which lay 1,500 miles east of Manila.

In May, the Spanish sent a fleet of seven ships to Cuba. They anchored in Santiago Bay at the southeastern tip of the island. An American fleet, discovering their presence, hovered outside the bay, waiting until the U.S. Army arrived to attack the city of Santiago and force the Spanish ships out of the bay. On June 22, about seventeen thousand American troops landed. This expeditionary force included the "Rough Riders," a cavalry unit whose second-in-command was Lieutenant Colonel Theodore Roosevelt. The Army encountered stiff resistance from the Spanish defenders but succeeded in capturing the heights above the city and bay. Roosevelt led one of the assaults. The Spanish fleet then tried to run past the American ships, but the much more powerful American squadron destroyed it. Two weeks later, the city surrendered. Spanish power in Cuba was broken.

The Spaniards sued for peace in August and the war ended. The Spanish-American War was one of the most popular wars in national history. It lasted only four months, and the United States won every battle at slight cost in lives and dollars. There was no draft, the economy boomed, and the civilian population suffered no shortages or deprivations of any kind. The war also signaled the arrival of a new imperial great power on the world scene.

At a peace conference that met in Paris from October to December 1898, the victorious American forced Spain to cede Guam, the Philippines, and Puerto Rico to the United States, for which the Americans paid the Spanish $20 million. The Spanish also ceded Cuba to the United States, but Cuba soon became an independent republic. The Platt Amendment, forced on the Cubans in 1901, made Cuba an American protectorate and curtailed Cuban sovereignty in numerous ways. What had begun as a war to liberate Cuba from Spanish colonialism turned into a war for American empire.

Ironically, before it could impose its colonial rule, the United States had to fight a war in the Philippines from 1899 to 1902 to crush a Philippine nationalist insurgency. Filipino insurgents, led by Emilio Aguinaldo, already in rebellion against their Spanish overlords before the arrival of Dewey's fleet, had helped the Americans defeat the Spaniards. Aguinaldo, who believed that American leaders,

The Spanish-American War: Caribbean Theater. *Source:* Moss, *Rise of Modern America,* p. 31.

including Dewey, had promised his country independence if he joined American forces in defeating the Spanish, felt betrayed by the Paris treaty. He and a group of prominent Filipinos organized a government at Malalos, wrote a constitution, and proclaimed a new independent Philippine republic in January 1899. One month later, fighting erupted between his and American forces.

The war Americans called the "Philippine insurrection" lasted nearly three years and claimed the lives of over 4,000 U.S. troops and perhaps 220,000 Filipinos, most of them civilian casualties of American counter-insurgency war-fare. The conflict was one of the ugliest in American history; both sides committed atrocities. When McKinley sought reelection in 1900, while war was raging, his young vice-presidential candidate, Theodore Roosevelt, himself a hero of the

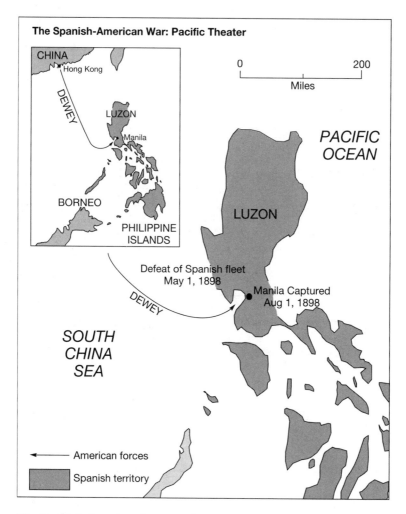

The Spanish-American War: Pacific Theater   *Source:* Moss, *Rise of Modern America,* p. 33.

Spanish-American War, defended the U.S. war in the Philippines. He called it a necessary part of the American mission to create a democratic Filipino government and to teach the Filipino people the blessings of civilization and individual liberty.

Following the suppression of the insurrection, the United States established a colonial administration in the Philippines. American teachers, engineers, nurses, and doctors flocked to the islands to modernize Filipino society. English was made the official language. In 1908, the University of the Philippines opened to train a pro-American governing elite that would gradually implement political democracy and prepare for the independence promised for the future. Linkages between American business interests and Filipino planters and merchants provided the

U.S. troops fighting Filipino nationalists.   *Source:* Library of Congress.

foundation for forty years of U.S. colonial rule in the islands as well as a growing commerce between the two countries.

In 1898 and 1899, there was much opposition to colonial imperialism within the United States. Senate opponents of imperialism nearly blocked ratification of the Treaty of Paris, which transferred Spanish colonies to the United States. Many prominent Americans joined the anti-imperialist cause, including Mark Twain, Grover Cleveland, and Samuel Gompers. The Democratic presidential candidate in 1900, William Jennings Bryan, made anti-imperialism a major issue, although President McKinley easily won reelection. If the 1900 election is taken to be a referendum on imperialism, a large majority of Americans enthusiastically embraced it.

A major reason the United States acquired the Philippines was to enhance its strategic and trading interests in the Far East, particularly in China. American traders had long dreamed of a vast China market and U.S. missionaries had talked excitedly about winning millions of Chinese souls for Christ. During the 1890s, Americans had to watch from afar as powerful European nations and Japan carved China into spheres of influence following its disastrous defeat in the Sino-Japanese War, 1894–1895.

With the annexation of the Philippines, and with growing trading and missionary interests in China, the United States became more actively engaged in Chinese affairs. In September 1899, Secretary of State John Hay issued a note that announced a new American policy toward China, which he named the "Open Door." The Open Door policy called for equal trade in China's ports. Hay's approach endeavored to secure American commercial opportunities in the various spheres of influence without having to use military force. The Open Door fixed itself in the American mind as the guiding principle of American foreign policy in regard to China.

At the time that Hay was promulgating the Open Door, the decadent Chinese government under the Manchus could not resist the foreign invaders dominating and exploiting China. In 1900, nationalistic Chinese, resentful of the sad state that had befallen their once mighty kingdom, led by a secret society called the *I-ho ch'uan* (the "Boxers"), rose up to try to throw out their imperialist oppressors. The Boxers murdered thousands of Christian missionaries and their Chinese converts. They also laid siege to the foreign legations in Beijing. Responding to the Boxer Rebellion, the United States sent twenty-five hundred troops to join an international expeditionary force of fifteen thousand soldiers that lifted the siege of the Beijing legations within a few weeks.

Following the suppression of the Boxers, Secretary of State Hay issued another note dated July 3, 1900. It reaffirmed the Open Door and called for the preservation of Chinese territorial integrity. Hay hoped to preserve American trade opportunities in China by keeping the country intact. The Open Door policy was not completely successful because Japan and the European powers with spheres of influence in China did not always respond to American concerns. U.S. trade and investment in China remained small; comparatively few Americans lived and worked in China. But Hay's two Open Door notes reinforced the growing notion in American minds that the United States had become a world power with vital interests in Far Eastern affairs.

As the twentieth century began, the United States had become an imperial democracy and one of the great powers of the globe. It held colonies in the vast Pacific basin, the Far East, and the Caribbean. It had become the overlord of the Caribbean region and had pledged itself to preserve the Open Door in China. Its overseas investments were expanding, and it had developed an export trade amounting to $1.5 billion annually. Its economy had become the largest in the world. Its yearly steel production, which equaled that of France, Germany, and Britain combined, symbolized America's new industrial might. It had built a navy that annihilated the Spanish fleet and ranked sixth in the world.

Many Americans were proud of the new role the United States played in world affairs. Some were distressed by the contradictions between America's democratic professions and its imperial conquests. But most Americans believed the United States had an imperial destiny and arrogantly assumed American imperialism would benefit its victims.

SOCIAL DARWINISM

The American industrial revolution had a profound effect on the ways Americans felt and thought during the Gilded Age. Technological innovations revolutionized the communication of ideas. Materialistic values impinged upon literature, art, and public education. Darwin's evolutionary theories influenced American philosophers, social scientists, lawyers, and most educated people. Simultaneously, Americans clung to older ideas of romantic individualism and Jeffersonian democracy. American thinking during this era remained diffuse, a mixed bag of old and new forms.

While American enterprise was expanding and consolidating, fashionable intellectual currents encouraged the exploitative drives of the people. Charles Darwin's *Origins of Species,* first published in England in 1859, had begun to influence public opinion in this country during the late nineteenth century. The idea that nature had ordained inevitable progress governed by the natural selection of individuals best adapted to survive in a competitive environment appealed to most Americans. "Let the buyer beware," intoned sugar magnate Henry O. Havemeyer. "You cannot wet-nurse people from the time they are born until the time they die. They have to wade in and get stuck, and that is the way men are educated." Havemeyer's views represented efforts to apply evolutionary theory to the marketplace.

The key tenets of Social Darwinism were derived from classical economics and were as old as Adam Smith. Individuals would compete fiercely within a laissez-faire economy. A few would succeed and grow rich. Most would fail and remain poor. Social Darwinists wanted a minimalist state, a "night watchman" that only prevented crime and enforced contracts. Government had no regulatory or welfare functions. The poor were responsible for their fate and by definition unfit. Government interference in economic affairs would be futile and impede progress, which was inevitable, but incremental. Trade unions had no social or economic roles to play according to the logic of Social Darwinism. Andrew Carnegie counseled all who would heed him: "Leave things as they now are." The foremost American Social Darwinist, Yale sociologist William Graham Sumner, told his students "it's root, hog, or die." It was each against all, struggling to survive in an economic jungle. Money and power were the measures of success; increasing productivity the clearest sign of progress.

RELIGION

The transformations in American social life and culture accompanying the industrial revolution had a major impact on organized religion in the late nineteenth century. The most obvious effect was a rapid secularization of American life. Churches found themselves playing less important social roles and saw their influence decline. Even so, religious institutions continued to thrive in urban industrial America. Most churches increased their memberships, especially the Catholic Church. The "new" immigration brought millions of Catholics to America during the 1890s.

Darwin's theory of evolution challenged the traditional religious conception of human origins. If humans evolved from apes by natural processes, then the Biblical account of creation was false, and the idea of humans being formed in God's image was also untrue. A bitter controversy pitted biological science against revealed religion. But evolutionary theory did not undermine the religious faith of most Americans. They either did not learn of evolutionary theory or they dismissed it. But most American intellectuals were converted to the evolutionary theory. Some theologians reconciled the two views: They argued that evolution was merely God's way of ordering the universe.

Traditional Protestant churches in the late nineteenth century were made up primarily of middle-class congregations. Ministers preached the Protestant ethic and personal responsibility for sin. Even though many of their communicants were slum dwellers, leaders of the Catholic Church also echoed the social conservatism of the Protestant ministry. Even evangelists such as Dwight Moody, the foremost preacher of the time, who endeavored to reach the urban masses by establishing mission schools in slum neighborhoods, concentrated on convincing individuals to give up their sinful ways and come to Christ. All of these religious institutions and individuals focused on the Christian drama of sin and redemption at the personal level. They were unconcerned about the causes of urban poverty, vice, and crime.

But within religious ranks, some ministers tried a different approach. These "social gospelers" tried to improve living conditions instead of saving souls. They advocated economic and social reform. The most influential social gospel minister was Washington Gladden. He supported trade unions, the regulation of industry, and other reforms. Some of these Christians also called for slum clearance, public housing, and the nationalization of industry.

EDUCATION

The modern American system of public education was forged during the era of the industrial revolution. Americans had long held a commitment to public education, but it was only during the decades following the Civil War that the growth of large cities provided the population concentrations necessary for economical mass education. Only then did industrialization generate the increase in wealth required to finance such a vast undertaking as providing education for everyone.

Steady progress occurred in public education during the Gilded Age. School attendance increased from 6.8 million children in 1870 to 15.5 million in 1900. Public spending on education rose from $63 million in 1870 to over $214 million in 1902. During these years, the number of secondary schools increased from perhaps one hundred to more than six thousand. By 1900, it was possible for youngsters living in cities to attend high school if their economic circumstances permitted. National illiteracy declined from 20 percent to 10 percent between 1870 and 1900. The goal of universal education, however, was only partially achieved during the late nineteenth century. About two-thirds of school age children received a few years of formal education by the 1890s. School sessions were often short and many students dropped out after a few years of spotty attendance. Most states did not have compulsory attendance laws, which meant school attendance was voluntary. The census of 1900 showed the median national educational attainment to be 5.5 years of schooling.

Institutions of higher learning also multiplied during the Gilded Age. Between 1870 and 1900, the number of colleges and universities in America doubled, from about five hundred to almost a thousand. Curricula expanded and diversified. Harvard's president, Charles W. Eliot, introduced the elective system, added many science and engineering courses, and experimented in new teaching techniques. Much of the expansion in college enrollments occurred as a consequence of the Morrill Land Grant Act of 1862 that created state universities in the Midwest and South.

Women attended college in growing numbers. By the end of the nineteenth century, women accounted for about one-third of the 300,000 students enrolled in the nation's institutions of higher learning, with one-third of these female students attending women's colleges. In the South, college life was segregated, and African Americans, both young men and women, continued to suffer from inferior opportunities to achieve a higher education. During the Gilded Age, on many college campuses in all parts of the nation, intercollegiate athletics had become a central feature of student social life.

There was a tremendous demand for popular education outside the schools and colleges in the late nineteenth century. The Chautauqua movement developed to fill an important cultural gap. Started in upstate New York in 1874 as a summer course for Sunday School teachers, it grew into a massive popular education system. It offered traveling lecturers on hundreds of topics, correspondence courses, and a monthly magazine. Chautauqua had hundreds of imitators. Standards on its popular lecture circuits varied and could be low. Speakers were often chosen for their celebrity status or their skill as entertainers. Teachers could vary from distinguished experts to assorted phonies and incompetents. To quote historian John Garraty: "Chautauqua reflected the prevailing tastes of the American people—diverse, enthusiastic, uncritical, and shallow."

MASS MEDIA

Newspapers and magazines proliferated during the Gilded Age. Technological innovations in printing made possible the mass production of attractive, cheap periodicals. Increasing population and rising levels of literacy created a larger demand for printed matter. Joseph Pulitzer created the modern style of journalism and the mass-circulation daily newspaper. He built up the *New York World* until its circulation during the 1890s reached more than 1 million, the largest in the world. He increased circulation with a variety of innovations and techniques. He hired talented journalists and paid them well. He went in for sensational headlines. He often sent his investigators nosing around city hall looking for scandals; he launched crusades and he held banquets and carnivals to raise funds for the poor. His paper was the first to have comics. For educated readers, there was plenty of hard and serious political, economic, and international news. He also kept the price low. The *New York World* was good value at $.02 an issue. Pulitzer was later imitated by an ambitious young journalist, William Randolph Hearst, who soon outdid Pulitzer when it came to sensationalism in his *New York Morning Journal*. Because of innovations in printing technology, publishers also produced high-quality weekly and monthly magazines. By the end of the nineteenth century, magazines such as *Cosmopolitan, The Saturday Evening Post,* and *McClure's* enjoyed mass circulations.

LITERATURE AND PHILOSOPHY

In literature, a new age of realism developed during the 1870s and 1880s, influenced by the same forces that were transforming all other aspects of American life—industrialization, the rise of cities, and evolutionary science. Novelists wrote about social problems, depicted realistic settings, and created more complex characters. They took their characters from a wide range of classes and regions. One expression of the new realism was the local color school. Regional writers looked to the areas they knew best for their stories and novels. During the 1880s, Joel Chandler Harris published his *Uncle Remus: His Songs and His Sayings*, which accurately reproduced the speech dialects of blacks in rural Georgia.

Mark Twain (Samuel Langhorne Clemens) was the first great American realist and writer from the West. The story that brought Twain his first national recognition was "The Celebrated Jumping Frog of Calaveras County," and the book that made him famous was *Innocents Abroad*, published in 1869. The latter was a travelogue that made fun of Gilded Age Americans traveling abroad. Twain was both participant and chronicler of the Gilded Age. The 1873 novel that he coauthored with Charles Dudley Warner, *The Gilded Age,* gave the era its enduring name. *The Adventures of Tom Sawyer* came out in 1876, and his masterpiece, considered by many critics to be the finest American novel, *The Adventures of Huckleberry Finn,* was published in 1884. No one surpassed Twain in creating characters, in writing dialogue, and in depicting a scene. He possessed a comic genius. Inside Mark Twain, the funnyman who made Americans laugh uproariously at themselves and their culture, beat the heart of a serious moralist. Twain was outraged, disgusted, and anguished by his age's untrammeled greed, prevalent political corruption, and heartless exploitation of the poor. His laughter at times turned bitter and mocking.

One of Twain's finest short stories is called "The Man That Corrupted Hadleyburg." It opens with a portrayal of a quiet, peaceful town. The people are not rich but they are happy, contented, and good. They care for each other. One day a stranger rides into town, deposits a sack of money in front of the post office, then dashes off. He is never seen again. The rest of the story describes what happens to the townspeople as they discover the money, try to decide what to do with it, and fall to quarreling over it. As the tale ends, Hadleyburg has become a hellish place. Its inhabitants are filled with rage and hate. They are all quarreling and fighting over the money. Twain's story served as a parable for the age.

By the end of the nineteenth century, some writers had moved beyond realism to naturalism. Naturalists concentrated on industrialization and the social dis-

Mark Twain, the most famous writer in American history. Photo by Matthew Brady. *Source:* National Archives.

integration and destruction of individuals that it caused. Naturalists served up stark and pessimistic portrayals of the human condition—individuals trapped in deterministic environments that degraded and often destroyed them. Naturalistic writers depicted human beings as animals governed by instincts and base passions. One of the finest naturalistic novels was Theodore Dreiser's classic *Sister Carrie* (1900). Many readers were shocked and outraged by naturalism, by its pessimism and moral nihilism, and by its portrayals of individuals as passive victims of powerful natural and social forces.

There also developed in this era a new kind of American philosophy called *pragmatism*. Pragmatists asserted that ideas were true only if they worked in the world; if they were useful and achieved practical results. Experience, not logic, proved the truth of an idea. The main creators of philosophical pragmatism were Charles Peirce, William James, and John Dewey. Pragmatism inspired much of the reform spirit of the early twentieth century. James subverted Social Darwinism and laissez-faire capitalism by proving that social changes came about because of the willed actions of reformers, not from impersonal environmental forces. Educational reformer John Dewey and social worker Jane Addams embraced pragmatic approaches to social change.

CIVILIZATION AND ITS DISCONTENTS

As the Gilded Age ended, the majority of Americans, especially comfortable middle-class Americans, residents of small towns, shopkeepers, many farmers, and skilled workers, remained confirmed optimists, uncritically admiring of their civilization and proud to be citizens of America, no doubt the best country in all the world. However, African Americans, Asians, Native Americans, immigrants, hard-pressed western and southern farmers, and all the other people who failed to achieve the good life found little to celebrate and much to protest in their increasingly industrialized and urbanized society. Giant monopolies flourished; the gap between rich and poor was widening; and poisonous slums infected every city. Shallow industrialists worshiped the almighty dollar and made getting it their religion. America's greatest poet, Walt Whitman, famed for his poetic celebration of democracy, called his fellow Americans the "most materialistic and money-making people ever known."

Many thoughtful and well-informed middle-class people, whose own lives were comfortable and prosperous, recoiled in horror at the social consequences of industrialization, urbanization, and massive immigration. They were alarmed by social instability and outraged at both the greed of businessmen and the degraded lives of the struggling masses. Many indulged a romantic nostalgia for a vanished America of small, homogeneous communities and tranquil, orderly lives. As the nineteenth century ended, the voices of discontent with the new industrial way of life formed a rising chorus. Calls for reform resounded across the land.

IMPORTANT EVENTS

1874	The Chautauqua movement is founded
1876	Alexander Graham Bell invents the telephone
1877	The Great Railroad Strike occurs
1879	Thomas Edison perfects the incandescent lamp (electric light)
1882	Congress enacts the Chinese Exclusion Act
1883	Joseph Pulitzer takes over the *New York World*
1884	Mark Twain's *The Adventures of Huckleberry Finn* is published
1886	The American Federation of Labor is organized
1887	Congress enacts the Interstate Commerce Act
1887	Congress enacts the Dawes Act
1889	Jane Addams opens Hull House in Chicago
1890	Congress enacts the Sherman Antitrust Act
1892	The People's Party (the Populists) is founded
1894	The Pullman strike occurs
1895	Booker T. Washington delivers his "Atlanta Compromise" speech
1898	The Spanish-American War is fought
1898	Hawaii is annexed
1899	War breaks out in the Philippines
1899	John Hay announces the Open Door policy

BIBLIOGRAPHY

Note to the reader: Carefully chosen bibliographic entries follow each chapter. They are chosen for their scholarship, readability, and accessibility. They are books and articles that students will understand and enjoy reading, and are sources from which they will learn much.

There are many fine books available that cover various aspects of late nineteenth-century U.S. history. They have been written by scholars whose learning is vast and who possess genuine literary talent. Many have achieved the stature of classics in their fields. Most libraries will have these books, and they are available in paperback editions. Robert H. Wiebe, in *The Search for Order,* has written a brilliant account of the transformation of American life in the late nineteenth and early twentieth centuries and how middle-class intellectuals understood and reacted to this transformation. See also Samuel P. Hays's *The Response to Industrialism, 1885–1914.* A well-written account of the Gilded Age is Ray Ginger's *The Age of Excess.* Sam Bass Warner, Jr., in *A History of the American City,* offers the best account of the rise of American cities in the late nineteenth century. The best-written book about the politicians and business leaders who dominated the Gilded Age remains the classic work of Matthew Josephson, *The Robber Barons.* The best social history of the American industrial revolution is *The Age of Enterprise,* by Thomas C. Cochran and William Miller. Herbert Gutman's *Work, Culture, and Society in Industrializing America* is a collection of essays reflecting the new labor history that focuses on the culture of work. Nick Salvatore's *Eugene V. Debs: Citizen and Socialist* is the finest biography yet rendered of the greatest figure in American socialism. Oscar Handlin's *The Uprooted* is a famed account of the new immigrants who flooded into America between 1890 to 1914. A fine recent study is that of Alan Kraut, *The Huddled Masses: The Immigrant in American Society, 1830–1921.* In Jane Addam's *Twenty Years at Hull House,* the pioneer social worker and humanitarian tells the story of the first and most famous settlement house in the United States. C. Vann Woodward, in *The Strange Career of Jim Crow,* gives a brilliant history of the rise of legal segregation in the South. Louis R. Harlan has written a splendid two-volume biography of Booker T. Washington. A fine book on the conflict between Europeans and Native Americans is S. L. A. Marshall's *The Crimsoned Prairie.* Justin Kaplan, in *Mr. Clemens and Mark Twain,* offers a good biography of America's most famous writer. Two histories of reform in broad perspective are Eric Goldman's *Rendezvous with Destiny* and Richard Hofstadter's *Age of Reform.* In *Imperial Democracy,* Ernest R. May gives a brief account of the emergence of the American empire at the turn of the century.

CHAPTER 2

The Progressive Era

Americans have been infatuated by quantitative measures as indicators of progress. At the turn of the century, publicists boasted about growing American industrial might as measured by statistics of production: tons of steel produced, miles of railroad trackage lain, and barrels of oil refined. Other boosters bragged about the huge geographic size of the country, its large cities, and its ranking as the fourth most populous nation on the planet. More thoughtful Americans concerned themselves with issues pertaining to the quality of American life. They worried about some of the negative consequences of industrialization such as corporate domination of the economy, pervasive political corruption, and the presence in all large cities of masses of impoverished immigrants. For these "Progressives," as they called themselves, progress would be better measured by their success as reformers, as problem solvers who restored the promise of American life to all people during the years between the Spanish-American War and the American entry into World War I, when an urgent desire for change swept the nation. The combined efforts of many reformers shaped the age that historians label the Progressive Era.

MODERN SOCIETY

Progressive Era America was a time of rapid social development. Prosperity had returned after the depression and disorders of the 1890s. Farms and factories were once again prospering. In 1901, the economy approached full employment and economic growth spurted. Farm prices rose almost 50 percent between 1900 and 1910 as farmers entered a "golden age." In 1900, the median industrial wage was $418 per year. By 1915, it was about $800 per year and rising. A Boston newspaper in 1904 enthused, "The resort to force, the wild talk of the nineties are over. Everyone is busily, happily getting ahead."

Americans were excited by the prospects abounding in the new century. Wild celebrations everywhere had marked the beginning of the twentieth century. Americans had faith in the capacities of business enterprises and new technologies to shape a more abundant future. *New* became a favorite buzzword of the times. Everywhere there was talk of the new city, the new art, the new democracy, and the new morality.

Another favorite theme was *mass.* Americans celebrated the quantitative aspects of their national experience. They were proud of the size and scale of America—its massive economy and large population. They flocked to mass entertainment, read mass-circulation magazines and newspapers, and took mass transit from the suburbs to central cities. They even boasted of the large crowds that turned out to watch major league baseball and college football games, as if they believed national virtue resided in population statistics.

Cities grew rapidly and on a colossal scale compared to earlier eras. Downtowns became clusters of tall buildings, large department stores, warehouses, and hotels. Strips of factories radiated out from the center. As streetcar transit lines spread, American cities assumed their modern patterns of ethnic, social, and economic segregation, usually in the form of concentric rings. Racial minorities and immigrants were packed into the innermost ring, circled by a belt of crowded tenements. The remaining rings represented increasing status and affluence, radiating outward toward posh suburbs where the rich and elite classes lived. The largest cities were New York, Chicago, and Philadelphia. They had become huge industrial, urban centers whose factories and shops churned out every kind of product used by American farmers, merchants, and the growing legions of consumers.

Los Angeles, a city of 300,000, passed a series of ordinances in 1915 that created modern urban zoning. For the first time, legal codes divided an American city into three districts of specified use: a residential area, an industrial area, and an area open to both residences and light industry. Other cities quickly followed suit. Zoning gave order to urban development, ending the chaotic, unplanned growth of cities that was characteristic of the Gilded Age.

Zoning not only kept skyscrapers out of factory districts, and factories out of suburbs, it also had important sociological and political consequences. In southern cities, zoning became another tool to extend segregation. In northern cities, it was a weapon that could be used along with others against blacks and ethnic minorities—against Jews in New York City, against Italians in Boston, and Poles in Detroit. In Chicago, New York, Detroit, and Cleveland, zoning laws helped confine rapidly growing black populations to particular districts, creating ghettos.

The consumer economy of the 1920s originated in the prewar era. As factories produced more consumer goods, they also spent more money for advertising. Ads and billboards promoted sales of cigarettes, perfumes, and cosmetics. Advertising agencies grew and market research began. The first public opinion polls began as efforts to sample consumer preferences in the marketplace.

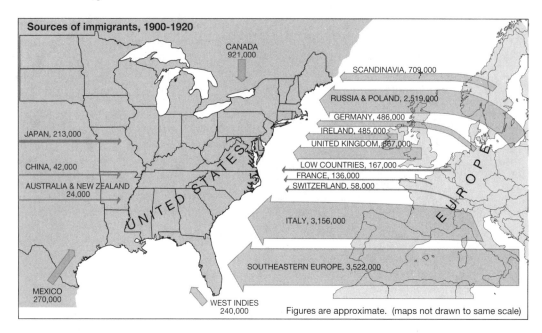

Sources of Immigrants, 1900–1920.   *Source:* Moss, *Rise of Modern America*, p. 43.

Between 1900 and 1910, almost 10 million immigrants entered the country, more came than in any other decade in American history. These newcomers continued the trend established during the late nineteenth century. Most of them were "new" immigrants from southern and eastern European countries. The largest number emigrated from Italy, Poland, Russia, and Austria-Hungary. About 1.5 million were eastern European Jews, mainly from Poland and Russia. Most new immigrants were Catholic or Jewish; about 40 percent were illiterate; and most, coming from peasant backgrounds, arrived without money or job skills. About two-thirds of these immigrants were males.

These new immigrants were a diverse lot who had little in common with one another except their poverty and desire to come to America. Traffic moved both ways across the Atlantic. A large number of immigrants returned to their native lands after a stay in America, either because they were disillusioned or because they had never intended to stay permanently. Those who returned to Europe were known as "birds of passage." The percentage of returnees varied with different nationalities. Those who came with their families, such as the Jews, rarely returned. Many Serbs and Poles, who tended to come as single young men, worked to earn money to buy a farm or business back home. The most numerous "birds of passage" were Italian men, thousands of whom became trans-Atlantic commuters. They worked in American industry for a year, returned to Italy, and were back in America the next year.

Mulberry Street, New York City—the heart of the immigrant area of the Lower East Side in the early 1900s.   *Source:* Library of Congress.

Despite the newcomers' tremendous cultural diversity and varying aspirations, old-stock Americans and business owners who employed the new immigrants tended to lump them all into simplistic stereotypes. They were "foreigners" who had to be "Americanized," and the quicker the better. Henry Ford, the man whose technological wizardry would put the nation on wheels during the 1920s, employed thousands of immigrants in his River Rouge assembly plant near Detroit. Ford also ran an "Americanization" school, which his immigrant employees were required to attend. They were first taught to say: "I am a good American." There was a graduation ceremony for the employees who completed Ford's program. At the ceremony, the workers acted out a giant pantomime skit, in which, clad in their native dress, they filed into a large "melting pot." When they emerged from the pot, they were each wearing identical American-made suits and carrying a small American flag. Ford's forced-draft process of Americanization cleansed ethnics of any lingering old-country cultural baggage.

Nativist sentiment, which had accompanied earlier waves of immigration, intensified in the wake of the massive influx of new immigrants. Old-stock Americans looked down their noses at the newcomers' appearance, behavior, and language. Racial theorists stressed the superiority of northern European "races" over those from the south and east of Europe. Some hostility toward the new immigrants reflected anti-Catholic and anti-Semitic prejudices. Nativism crystallized into anti-immigration movements of growing strength. These movements aimed to restrict the new immigration, but they failed to do so before World War I brought almost all immigration to a halt. Nativists would achieve their goal of restriction during the mid-1920s.

POPULAR CULTURE

Major signs of progress in early twentieth-century American life included rising wage levels and growing leisure for American workers. The average workweek for manufacturing workers had shrunk to fifty hours by 1914. By the first decade of the new century, white-collar workers worked nine-hour days Monday through Friday and a half-day on Saturday. People had more money to spend and more time to enjoy spending it on play and recreation. Increasing income and leisure promoted a flourishing mass culture in the cities.

Spectator sports were attracting large crowds. Baseball entrenched itself as the national pastime. In 1903, the pennant winners of the two major leagues met in the first World Series to determine the national champion. The Boston Red Sox, winners of the American League title, beat the National League champions, the Pittsburgh Pirates, five games to three. College football was another popular spectator sport. Crowds of fifty thousand or more often gathered to watch powerhouse Ivy League and midwestern teams play. On New Year's Day, 1902, the first Rose Bowl game was held in Pasadena, California. The University of Michigan overwhelmed an upstart team from Stanford 49 to 0.

Progressive reformers attacked college football for its violence and for its use of "tramp athletes," nonstudents whom colleges paid to play for them. In 1905, 18 players were killed and 150 suffered serious injury. President Roosevelt called a White House conference to clean up college football and other sports. The conference founded the Intercollegiate Athletic Association, which became the National Collegiate Athletic Association (NCAA) in 1910. True to its progressive origins, the NCAA has functioned as a regulatory agency for collegiate athletics ever since.

Attendance at "movies" rose even faster than for spectator sports. Thomas Edison and a young assistant, William Dickson, had invented a process for making motion pictures in 1889. Commercial movies made their appearance during the 1890s. These early films were crudely made, their audiences recruited mainly from the ranks of immigrant populations, who were crowded into the large eastern cities. Early movie houses were store fronts and parlors called "nickelodeons," a name derived from combining the price of admission with the Greek word for theater. After 1900, the new industry expanded rapidly.

By 1910, there were ten thousand theaters in the country showing motion pictures, attracting a weekly audience of 10 million. The most popular films were about fifteen to twenty minutes in length and featured comedy, adventure, or pathos. The early center of American filmmaking was New York. In 1909, the largest companies formed a trust to control the production and distribution of films. In 1910, a group of independent filmmakers discovered Hollywood, a sleepy farming community near Los Angeles. In Hollywood, they could escape the movie trust and take advantage of the sunshine and mild weather abounding in southern California. Also, within a few miles of the studios, could be found outdoor scenes that would substitute for almost any locale a plot might call for, whether it was Arabia, Sherwood Forest, or the Old South. In 1915, D. W. Griffith, the best of the new Hollywood moviemakers, produced the first movie spectacular, *Birth of a Nation.*

Before 1910, band concerts were the country's most popular mass entertainment. Thousands of amateur bands offered free concerts in parks on Sunday afternoons. The most popular American band, led by John Philip Sousa, the "March King," toured the nation, attracting large crowds everywhere. Sousa was also a composer and wrote the famed "The Stars and Stripes Forever" in 1896. This robust, patriotic march became wildly popular during the Spanish-American War, making its author rich and famous.

By the end of the first decade of the new century, recorded music was taking much of the audience away from public band concerts. Phonograph and recording companies were selling millions of "records." Record players became fixtures in homes that could afford them. Early recordings usually featured vaudeville skits. The first orchestral recording was made in 1906. As record sales increased, families sang less and listened more.

Ragtime, a musical idiom featuring fast syncopated rhythms, became popular, especially after 1911 when Irving Berlin wrote "Alexander's Ragtime Band." Ragtime set young people to dancing fast, replacing traditional waltzes and polkas. The new dances often had animal names—Fox Trot, Bunny Hop, Turkey Trot, and the Snake. The "fast set," enjoying some of these new dances, ran afoul of the moralists who worried about partners' getting too close and becoming sexually excited (nine inches between dance partners was the approved distance).

Vaudeville, increasingly popular after the turn of the century, flowered in the decade preceding World War I. Drawing from the immigrant experience, it featured skits, songs, dances, comedy, magicians, and acrobats, all expressing the color and variety of polyglot American urban life. Vaudeville performers also expanded the limits of what was permissible in public entertainment. Vaudeville dancers bared their legs and later their midriffs. Vaudeville comics told "dirty" jokes and got away with it. The leading impresario of vaudeville, Florenz Ziegfeld, produced his famed "Follies," featuring elaborate dance numbers by beautifully costumed "Ziegfeld girls."

Popular fiction flourished along with vaudeville. Genteel novels centering around family life, often set in rural New England, were popular. Westerns also sold well. The most popular western story was Owen Wister's *The Virginian,* whose gunman hero became a prototype for later "Westerns," both novelistic and cinematic. Wister was a friend of Theodore Roosevelt, who was an avid fan of Westerns and a writer of western history. Readers also enjoyed detective thrillers and science fiction, which featured tales set in the future about spaceships, ray guns, and gravity neutralizers.

Fiction for young people sold widely. Edward L. Stratemeyer applied mass-production techniques to the business of publishing popular fiction for young people. He formed a syndicate that employed a stable of writers who turned out hundreds of books in series featuring Tom Swift and the Rover Boys for boys, and the Bobbsey Twins for girls. Gilbert Patten created the character of Frank Merriwell, a wholesome college athlete attending Yale. The name of his athletic hero expressed the character qualities that Patten stressed: He was frank and merry by nature, and well in mind and body. Patten's books sold by the millions.

Horatio Alger's books continued to sell well during the Progressive Era, although Alger had died in 1899. Alger, like Patten, wrote fiction for adolescent boys. In more than 130 novels, Alger stressed the same theme: how poor boys rise from the streets of cities to become successful businessmen. The secret of success in Alger books is always the same—moral character. Alger heroes succeed because they are good, because they have self-discipline, and because they work hard. A little luck often aids the hero as he makes his way up in the world. Alger's novels sold by the millions during the years preceding World War I, and his name was added to the culture. Today's media frequently call attention to "Horatio Alger heroes" who rise from "rags to riches."

LITERATURE AND ART

Along with the simplistic sentimentalities of popular culture, serious art also fared well in Progressive Era America. Isadora Duncan and Ruth St. Denis transformed modern dance. Abandoning traditional ballet, both dancers stressed emotion, the human body, and individual improvisation. Duncan danced "the way she felt," giving expression to inner emotion and communicating ideas. Her ideas and innovative techniques swept the country. Duncan, a flamboyant personality with a zest for life, became a reigning celebrity of the age.

Greenwich Village, a seedy district of New York City, became a haven for young artists, writers, and poets committed to experimenting with new forms of expression. A group of painters, including Robert Henri, John Sloan, and George Bellows, was named by its critics the "Ashcan School" because of its interest in social realism. These artists preferred to paint the subjects they found in the Village and other parts of the city—street scenes, colorful crowds, slum children swimming in the East River, the tenements, and portraits of ordinary people. Their paintings honestly expressed the inherent beauty and vitality found in the lives of the urban masses.

In 1913, a show at the New York Armory introduced American viewers to European modernist paintings, sculptures, and prints. Americans got their first exposure to the works of Picasso, Van Gogh, Gaughin, and Cézanne, among many others. The Greenwich Village crowd was dazzled and excited by the show. Traditionalists attacked the exhibits as worthless and wicked. But the artists featured in the exhibit would have a profound effect on the direction American art would take in the twentieth century, and many future American painters' works would reflect their influence.

Chicago was the center of a flourishing new poetry. Harriet Monroe started *Poetry* magazine in Chicago in 1912. Many of America's most promising young poets published some of their poems in her magazine, including Ezra Pound and T. S. Eliot. Other poets experimenting with new techniques were Robert Frost, Edgar Lee Masters, and Carl Sandburg. Sandburg's most famous poem, "Chicago" (1916) celebrated the vitality of America's second city.

The culture of the early twentieth century, both in its popular and highbrow forms, foreshadowed developments in the 1920s. Changes were underway before World War I. Evidence of ferment and change could be found everywhere—in the movie houses, in popular music, in art galleries, and in the new literary magazines. The Progressive Era was the seedtime of the modernist spirit in American culture.

THE ROOTS OF REFORM

Progressivism's immediate origins lay in the 1890s, when many people responded to the transformation of American life and the social problems that it generated, particularly the many undesirable consequences of industrialization. Large industrial corporations dominated their industries, controlled prices, and exploited their workers and customers. Corruption corroded government at all levels; from two-bit ward heelers on the streets to the upper echelons of the federal government. The cities, filling with a rising tide of immigrants, threatened to become home to a permanently dispossessed and alienated underclass. The great urban centers of America spawned slums, crime, and poverty. Monopoly, corrupt politics, and mass poverty challenged the central promise of American life; they suggested that equality of opportunity for all was a myth. The American dream increasingly appeared beyond the reach of millions of American families. Progressive reformers, as they sat out to solve these massive and often interrelated problems, did not form a unified national crusade. Rather, progressivism constituted a remarkably diverse aggregation of many, often unrelated, even mutually antagonistic, efforts to achieve economic, social, and political reforms.

Progressives sought to solve these problems by ending abuses of power and eliminating unfair privilege. They intended to replace the wasteful, competitive, anarchic industrial society with one that was efficient, orderly, and based on cooperation between business and government. They wanted to restore the orderly American community that they believed had prevailed in preindustrial times, and they wanted to use modern methods and scientific techniques to bring it back. They would restrain the powerful and protect the powerless in order to bring about the restoration of an orderly and just American commonwealth.

Progressivism's roots lay buried deep within American political traditions, but its proximate origins could be found in a series of unrelated reform movements that erupted in this country during the 1890s. One of these comprised the agrarian insurgents of the Midwest and South. These embattled farmers called for state intervention to curb the power of the railroads, banks, and other big businesses. Within the cities, the social strains caused by rapid, large-scale industrialization activated the Social Gospelers and other pioneer advocates of social justice. During the 1890s, a literature of protest and exposure foreshadowed the Muckrakers. Henry Demarest Lloyd wrote *Wealth Against Commonwealth* (1894), a scathing indictment of the Standard Oil Company. Describing the wholesale corruption of state governments carried out by Standard Oil's henchmen, Lloyd wrote, "Standard Oil did everything to the Pennsylvania legislature but refine it." A new generation of social scientists joined the assault on privileged wealth and irresponsible power. A new generation of intellectuals challenged the assumptions and precepts of Social Darwinism. The growth of a large urban middle class, many of whose members were well-educated young businessmen and professionals, got involved in urban reform movements during the 1890s. These concerned individuals were outraged by the existence of widespread monopoly, political corruption, and social distress. As the twentieth century began, they were increasingly involved in the proliferating reform movements that constituted the Progressive Era.

SOCIAL JUSTICE

Among the most important strands of Progressive reformers were the diverse movements that have been collectively labeled the social justice movement. Many well-educated, young, middle-class women were in the front ranks of many social justice reform activities. Florence Kelly worked to bring about safer working conditions for factory workers, and she was a pioneer advocate of consumer protection legislation. Jane Addams, the social worker who founded Hull House, was the most prominent woman active in social justice causes. In addition to her settlement house work, Addams worked to strengthen trade unions, abolish child labor, and achieve women's suffrage. When the United States entered World War I in 1917, Addams joined other Progressive reformers opposed to American participation in the war. Between 1900 and 1915, social justice reformers could count many victories. During this period, most states enacted laws that provided for workers' compensation, limited the hours of work for women, and restricted child labor. Sometimes the courts curtailed or nullified these Progressive social reforms.

Not all social justice reformers came from middle-class or business ranks. Industrial workers supported progressivism in some urbanized industrial states such as California and New York. They formed coalitions with middle-class reformers to press for improvements in housing and in health care, for safer factories, for shorter hours, for workers' compensation, and for disability insurance. More militant members of the social justice movement moved beyond coalition politics to direct action. In 1909, the Women's Trade Union League (WTUL) and the local chapter of the International Ladies Garment Workers Union (ILGWU) waged

A young mill worker in a textile factory ca. 1910. Child labor was a scandalous aspect of American industrial society during the Progressive Era.   *Source:* Library of Congress.

a long, bitter strike against New York City's garment district sweatshops. After three months, they gained a partial victory that resulted in the unionization of some of the sweatshops. A year later, in Chicago, Sidney Hillman led the Amalgamated Clothing Workers Union in a strike that achieved similar gains, including organizing the workers at Hart, Shaffner, and Marx, one of the largest clothing manufacturers in America.

Immigrant and working-class neighborhoods occasionally elected progressive reformers who had backgrounds in machine politics but were neither corrupt nor conservative. Alfred E. (Al) Smith, a Catholic and the son of immigrants, rose through the ranks of Tammany Hall to become a progressive governor of New York. Smith worked with middle-class reformers and progressive legislators to enact labor and social welfare legislation.

Some advocates of radical change during the Progressive Era wanted more than reform; they wanted to create a fundamentally different society. They rejected progressivism for socialism. Their ranks included some immigrant Jewish intellectuals, factory workers, former Populists, western miners, and lumberjacks. A radical trade union, the Industrial Workers of the World, led by William (Big Bill) Haywood, tried to unite the nation's unskilled workers into one big union that would control their factories. It led a series of strikes in textile factories in Lawrence, Massachusetts, and in the West. It never had more than 150,000 members and never established a stable organizational structure, and its radical ideology kept it alienated from other trade unions. It faded into obscurity during World War I when federal prosecutors sent most of its leaders to jail for obstructing the war effort.

Most socialists of the Progressive Era supported the American Socialist Party (SDP) and its dynamic leader, Eugene Debs. American socialism grew rapidly during the Progressive Era. By 1912, hundreds of socialist candidates had been elected to city councils and county boards of supervisors. Over fifty socialists served as mayors, and Wisconsin sent a socialist, Victor Berger, to Congress. American socialists published over three hundred newspapers, one of which, *The Appeal to Reason,* claimed 700,000 weekly subscribers. Popular writers and journalists such as Jack London and Upton Sinclair were avowed socialists. Debs ran for president five times. He and his party made their best showing during the 1912 election when he polled 900,000 votes and hundreds of socialists got elected to local and state offices.

But American socialism and the SDP declined after 1912. Socialists opposed American entry into World War I and incurred the wrath of most patriots. Socialists suffered severe repression at the hands of the federal government. Many of its members, including Debs, were imprisoned. The party was further weakened by internal factionalism during the 1920s and lost membership to the American Communist Party. It managed to survive on the political fringes until the 1960s when its aged leaders disbanded the remnants of a once-vital movement.

MUCKRAKERS

Progressive reformers were aided by socially conscious journalists, writers, and artists, whom Theodore Roosevelt dubbed "muckrakers." A small army of these investigative reporters fed their middle-class readers sensational reports covering a wide range of economic, social, and political evils afflicting American life in the early twentieth century. Their articles appeared in *McClure's* and other slick, mass-circulation magazines. Millions of middle-class people became aware of the many ways the American social reality contradicted the ideal image of America. Readers were alarmed, outraged, and anguished by muckraker revelations, and they were often motivated to support reform efforts to combat wrongdoing. Muckrakers contributed significantly to progressive reform movements. They also established a category of reportage that became an integral part of American journalism. Consumer advocate Ralph Nader used the muckraker approach to call attention to lax safety standards in the auto industry during the 1960s. Today, the popular television show *60 Minutes* allows electronic journalists to perpetuate the muckraking style of reportage.

Important muckrakers included Ida Tarbell, who wrote a two-volume history of the Standard Oil Company describing the ruthless, illegal methods it had employed to forge its refining monopoly. Lincoln Steffens wrote a series of articles for *McClure's*, later published as a book, *The Shame of the Cities* (1904), which exposed political corruption in several large eastern and midwestern cities. David Graham Phillip's *Treason of the Senate* (1906) depicted many senators as rich corporate servitors. John Spargo's *Bitter Cry of the Children* (1903) was a fact-filled, excruciating account of child labor in factories and mines. Burton J. Hendrick's *Story of Life Insurance* (1907) exposed scams that cheated widows out of their benefits.

The most famous muckraker was a young radical novelist, Upton Sinclair, whose realistic novel *The Jungle* (1906) highlighted the brutal exploitation of workers in the meat-packing industry. His book also conveyed vividly the filthy conditions prevailing in the packinghouses as they processed tainted and sometimes spoiled meat for public consumption. In the following passage Sinclair describes how sausage was prepared:

> There was never the least attention paid to what was cut up for sausage; there would come all the way back from Europe old sausage that had been rejected and that was moldy and white—it would be doused with borax and glycerine, and dumped into the hoppers and made over again for home consumption. There would be meat that tumbled out onto the floor, in the dirt and sawdust, where the workers had tramped and spit uncounted billions of germs. There would be meat sorted in great piles in rooms; and the water from leaky roofs would drip over it. It was too dark in these storage places to see well, but a man could run his hands over these piles of meat and sweep handfuls off of the dried dung of rats. These rats were nuisances, and the packers would put out poisoned bread for them; they would die, and then rats, bread and meat would go into the hoppers.[1]

Sinclair's novel had an immediate effect. When it was published, President Roosevelt read it and promptly sent for Sinclair. He asked Sinclair if the conditions that he described in his novel truly existed. When Sinclair assured him that they did, Roosevelt ordered an investigation of the meat-packing industry. Federal investigators confirmed most of Sinclair's charges. *The Jungle* also helped move out of Congress a Meat Inspection Act and the Pure Food and Drug Act, two pioneer consumer protection laws enacted in 1906.

The Jungle is a classic example of muckraking. Ironically, Sinclair intended to expose the horrors of working in a meat-packing plant to show corruption in Chicago politics and to promote socialism as the only solution to what he termed "wage slavery" under capitalism. Most of his middle-class readership, however, reacted most strongly to his lurid descriptions of the unsanitary conditions under which the public's breakfast, lunch, and dinner meats were prepared. As Sinclair noted, ruefully, "I aimed at their hearts and hit their stomachs."

---

[1]Upton Sinclair, *The Jungle* (New York: New American Library of World Literature, 1905, 1906), p. 136.

WOMEN REFORMERS

When the Progressive Era began, feminists sought liberation from domestic confines and male domination. Many women joined a women's club movement. By 1900, the General Confederation of Women's Clubs claimed a million members. Feminist reformers brought a particularly female dimension to progressivism. Because women were excluded from politics before 1920, they tended to move into social reform. They sought social goals such as the regulation of labor conditions for women and children, housing reform, and consumer protection. Many college-trained women became active in settlement houses and worked for educational reform.

Some women joined a birth control movement led by Margaret Sanger. Sanger began her career as a nurse visiting Manhattan's immigrant neighborhoods. She distributed birth control information among poor immigrant women to help them prevent unwanted pregnancies. Her cause attracted the interest of middle-class women who wanted to limit the size of their families as well as control the growth of the immigrant masses. In 1921, she founded the American Birth Control League. Birth control entered the realm of public discussion for the first time. Because of Sanger's efforts, many middle-class families were using contraception by the 1920s. But most states prohibited the sale of contraceptives, and most women during the Progressive Era opposed birth control because they believed it threatened their status as women.

The number of working women expanded rapidly during the Progressive Era. Perhaps as many as 7 to 8 million women were working by 1912. Charlotte Perkins Gilman became an advocate for working women. An early economic feminist, Gilman challenged the traditional satisfactions attributed to domesticity. She insisted that women, like men, could find full freedom and satisfaction only through meaningful work. At the time, Gilman's ideas applied mostly to the relatively small number of middle-class professional women. Most working-class women came from the ranks of immigrants, African Americans, and the rural poor, who worked mostly at low-paying, low-skill, and low-status jobs. These women had no economic power or political clout, and scant opportunity for meaningful or creative work.

The major feminist issue of the Progressive Era was suffrage. The crusade for the vote had begun in the mid-nineteenth century as a spin-off from the Abolitionists' insistence that all Americans, regardless of sex or race, were equal and deserved the same rights. But male resistance made the struggle for women to get the vote long and hard: The Supreme Court, in *Minor* v. *Happersett* (1875), ruled that women could not vote even though they were citizens. Suffragists achieved their first victories at the local level. Wyoming was the first territory to grant women the right to vote. By 1912, nine states, all of them in the West, had granted women the vote. The National American Women's Suffrage Association (NAWSA), the most important suffragist organization, claimed eighty-five thousand members in 1912.

In 1915, a talented organizer, Carrie Chapman Catt, took over the leadership of NAWSA, and the women's suffrage movement quickly gathered momentum.

She refocused suffragist energies away from state-by-state campaigns and toward achieving a constitutional amendment in order to place all women's right to vote beyond the reach of restrictive Supreme Court decisions. Many different groups worked for the cause. Some moderates relied on propaganda campaigns. Militants such as Alice Paul, influenced by radical English suffragists, used direct action tactics. The decisive factor was women's participation on the home front during World War I. Women worked in factories and as medical volunteers. Their efforts convinced legislators to propose what became the Nineteenth Amendment, ratified in 1920. The 1920 presidential election was the first in which all women could vote.

Because so many women had fought so hard so long for the vote, they had come to believe that achieving women's suffrage would bring the dawn of a golden era in American political life. Voting women would put a quick end to boss and business domination of politics. The moral tone of the nation's civic life would be uplifted. Those women, and some men, who expected a rapid transformation of the public life of the nation were quickly disillusioned. Women did not vote as a unified movement. No women's agenda emerged. Only about 25 percent of eligible women voters availed themselves of the opportunity during the election of 1920. Most of these newly enfranchised women apparently voted the ways that their fathers, brothers, and husbands did. Feminists, to their dismay, found that the vote did not bring empowerment for women; they did not attain the influence required to enact the programs they favored or to change the way politics and government worked.

Nevertheless, attaining the suffrage for women was a great victory, an overcoming of powerful and stubborn obstacles. The Nineteenth Amendment represented a great democratic advance, one of the crowning political achievements of the Progressive Era. Very quickly, women's voting came to be accepted as a given, as a normal part of the political life of the nation. Very quickly, it was forgotten that women's suffrage took seventy years of hard struggle to achieve, and that virtually to the day that it carried, powerful men denounced women's suffrage and rhetorically prophesied the end of the republic.

AFRICAN AMERICANS

The Progressive reform impulse rarely extended to the 10 million African Americans, over 85 percent of whom still lived in the South in 1910. Southern blacks were victimized by a repressive system that disfranchised, segregated, and frequently brutalized them. In 1910, fewer than 1 percent of high-school-age blacks attended high schools. Southern white political leaders, many of them Progressives, perfected a demagogic politics based on the rhetorical denunciation of blacks and keeping them at the bottom of the socioeconomic pyramid. During the first decade of the twentieth century, white southerners extended and refined the systematic legal segregation of blacks and whites. Between 1910 and 1914, white mobs lynched

Alice Paul, leader of the National Woman's Party, sews a ratification star on the party's flag to celebrate the ratification of the Nineteenth Amendment in 1920, which granted women aged twenty-one and older the right to vote.   *Source:* Schlisinger Library, Radcliffe College.

scores of African Americans. White progressives shared the prevailing racist view that African Americans were inherently inferior and incapable of full citizenship. Few protested the "color line" that everywhere separated black America from white America. Most southern blacks resided in rural areas. They worked as share croppers and tenants, earning a median annual income of approximately $100. Many were tied to the land by labor contracts and perpetual indebtedness to local merchants and planters. Many African Africans appeared to have traded the legal slavery endured by their parents and grandparents for a form of economic bondage in the Progressive Era. Institutionalized racism and segregation also afflicted African Americans residing in northern cities. Oppression of blacks was a national not merely a regional problem in Progressive America.

Booker T. Washington remained the most prominent spokesman for black people, and he continued to advocate accommodation as a policy during the Progressive Era. Most white reformers welcomed Washington's accommodationist strategy because it urged African Americans not to protest and to remain in their places. But to a few black Progressives, Washington appeared to be favoring second-class citizenship for African Americans. In 1905, a group of black leaders met near Niagara Falls to endorse a more militant strategy. They called for equality before the law, voting rights, integration, and equal educational and economic opportunities for African Americans. The chief Niagara spokesman was William E. B. Dubois, who could not accept Washington's submission to white dominance. Dubois insisted: "The way for a people to gain their reasonable rights is not by voluntarily throwing them away."

Dubois demonstrated that accommodation was a flawed strategy, but his militant protest strategy was ineffective. He believed that a highly educated African American elite, whom he called the Talented Tenth, would lead the way by impressing whites and setting an example for blacks. Such a strategy appealed to some white middle-class Progressives, but his elitist strategy held little meaning for the African American masses who were mainly sharecroppers and unskilled workers. When Dubois and his allies formed the National Association for the Advancement of Colored People (NAACP) in 1909, with its objective of attacking racial discrimination through the courts, its leadership consisted mainly of white Progressives.

Whichever strategy they pursued, accommodation or protest, African Americans during the Progressive Era faced continued oppression. During the presidency of Woodrow Wilson, a southern progressive Democrat, the federal civil service was resegregated. African Americans struggled against long odds to achieve their portion of the American dream. And, their pride made it difficult for blacks to celebrate their American identity in a country dominated by racist whites who oppressed African Americans.

ASIAN AMERICANS

Progressive reformers were generally no more concerned about the welfare of other nonwhite minorities than they were about African Americans. Chinese Americans and Japanese Americans, mostly clustered on the West Coast, continued to experience discrimination and hostility. In 1902, Congress made the Chinese Exclusion Act permanent. In October 1906, the San Francisco school board ordered all Asian children to attend a segregated Oriental school. The Japanese government, concerned about the treatment of Japanese in foreign lands, protested this action in Washington. President Roosevelt, concerned about maintaining good relations with a rising power in Asia, intervened to persuade the school board to repeal its offensive order. An informal agreement was worked out, the Gentlemen's Agreement of 1908. According to its terms, the school board rescinded its order against the children of Japanese subjects, and the Japanese government, for its part, agreed to restrict the emigration of Japanese peasant laborers to the United States.

Other acts against Japanese in California occurred. In 1913, Progressives in the state legislature enacted an alien land law that forbade aliens to lease land for periods greater than three years. Later laws further restricted alien leases of farmland. Such laws were ineffective in practice because Japanese farmers leased lands in the names of their American-born children, and the state supreme court nullified some of these laws. In 1924, Congress, responding to political pressure from California representatives, prohibited further Japanese emigration to the United States. This irrational act profoundly insulted and angered the Japanese government, and it was, in the long run, a contributing cause of World War II in Asia.

NATIVE AMERICANS

Native Americans were ignored by progressive reformers. American Indian policy during the Progressive Era was officially guided by Dawes Act principles. Officials in the Bureau of Indian Affairs continued to pay lip service to assimilation; but under the cover of the Dawes Act, they expropriated allotment lands, neglected schooling for Indian children, and tried to keep Indians confined to working as cheap farm laborers and domestic servants at the margins of society.

One remarkable Indian spokesman, Carlos Montezuma, became an advocate of Native American rights during the Progressive Era. A full-blooded Apache, he had been reared by an itinerant Italian musician, who treated him as a son. He went to the University of Illinois and became a prominent physician. Wealthy, learned, and articulate, Montezuma criticized Bureau of Indian Affairs policies. He formed organizations and raised funds for Indian causes. He urged Indians to help themselves, to leave the reservations, and to stop being "papooses," dependent on the white man for survival. Proud of his Indian heritage, Montezuma also urged Native Americans to honor and retain their traditional culture and Indian identity.

MORAL REFORM

Many Progressive reformers were determined not only to improve institutions, but also to improve human behavior. They set out to purge society of drinking, prostitution, and gambling. Their campaign to outlaw alcohol was their most important moral crusade. The formation of the Anti-Saloon League in 1893 marked the beginning of the prohibitionist drive that eventually forced abstinence upon the entire nation. The League joined forces with the Women's Christian Temperance Union to portray alcoholism as a social menace which ruined lives, destroyed families, caused diseases, created poverty, and robbed the economy of productive work. Between 1893 and 1900, many states, counties, and cities outlawed or restricted the sale and consumption of alcoholic beverages. As the twentieth century began, about one-fourth of the people lived in "dry" communities. After 1900, prohibitionists concentrated their formidable energies on achieving a national law forbidding the manufacture, sale, and use of alcoholic beverages.

The enemies of drink got their chance during World War I. The government forbade using grain to manufacture whiskey in wartime in order to conserve food. Prohibitionists pressured the government into forbidding sales of alcoholic beverages near military bases and training camps. Citizens were encouraged to abstain from drinking as a patriotic sacrifice in support of America's soldiers fighting in

France. Because Germany was the enemy and many American breweries were owned by German American families, prohibitionists urged Americans to boycott beer. Prominent industrialists called for prohibition. Henry Ford enthused, "A sober worker is an efficient worker." Prominent national political leaders became converts to the cause in wartime, and Congress proposed a constitutional amendment outlawing booze. The Eighteenth Amendment was ratified in 1919 and implemented by the Volstead Act in 1920, which strictly defined the term *alcoholic beverage*. Prohibition would be the law of the land for nearly fourteen years. Not all prohibitionists were Progressives and not all Progressives were prohibitionists, but the Eighteenth Amendment symbolized the progressive urge to use governmental power to improve the nation's morals.

Progressives also attacked prostitution. Muckrakers exposed the operations of "white slavery" rings that kidnapped young women and forced them into prostitution. Jane Addams wrote about the pressures of poverty that forced immigrant and black women into prostitution. In 1910, Congress enacted the Mann Act, which prohibited transporting women across state lines for "immoral purposes." By 1915, every state had outlawed brothels and the public solicitation of sex. Most states also outlawed gambling and closed casinos. California Progressives also banned professional boxing and barred betting at race tracks, forcing horse owners to close all their tracks because outlawing betting deprived them of their source of revenue for financing the sport.

EDUCATIONAL REFORM

Progressive reformers envisioned education as an important means for improving society. Before it could, however, progressive educators demanded that schools abandon traditional nineteenth-century curricula that stressed moralistic pieties and rote memorization. John Dewey, the foremost progressive educational reformer, stated that the chief role of public schools in a democratic society was to prepare children for productive citizenship and fulfilling personal lives. In two influential books, *The School and Society* (1899) and *Democracy and Education* (1916), Dewey expounded his theories of progressive education: Children, not subject matter, should be a school's focus. Schools must cultivate creativity and intelligence. From kindergarten through high school, children learned from experience, and curricula must be tailored to those experiences. The school should be a laboratory of democracy.

During the Progressive Era, the percentage of school-age children enrolled in public and private schools expanded rapidly. By 1920, 78 percent of all five- to seventeen-year-olds attended school, a huge increase over the attendance rate during the Gilded Age. School construction expanded significantly. Administration and teaching were professionalized, and salaries were raised. These gains reflected the progressive commitment to education as well as taxpayer willingness to fund the costs of an expanding public school system.

Prohibition brought many changes to the American scene. Here the former bar of a New York hotel has been converted to a library after the advent of the Eighteenth Amendment.   *Source:* Library of Congress.

College curricula and enrollments also expanded rapidly during the Progressive Era. By 1910, there were over one thousand colleges and universities in America, more than in the rest of the world. Much of the growth in college enrollments occurred at public colleges and universities. The first community colleges appeared during the era, products of progressive educational theories. The enrollment of women at colleges and universities expanded greatly; most of them attended coeducational institutions. By 1920, women accounted for almost half of those enrolled in college.

POLITICAL REFORM

Traditional Jeffersonian notions of limited government eroded during the late nineteenth century because of industrialization. Corporate executives, paying lip service to laissez-faire slogans, aggressively sought government aid and protection. Angry farmers called for government takeover of railroads and monopolies. Urban representatives demanded government action to correct social

The public school system expanded rapidly during the early twentieth century, providing clerical training to meet the demand for growing numbers of office workers.
Source: Metropolitan Life Insurance Company.

problems. By the dawn of the Progressive Era, middle-class reformers believed that the use of government power was necessary to counter corruption and exploitation. But before reformers could use political power, they would have to reclaim government from the political machines and corporate interests that controlled it. So Progressives turned first to politics to root out corruption and favoritism from government. They sought to gain control of the political process to reform society.

Progressive reformers had a strong aversion to party politics. They wanted to scrap political machines and bosses. To improve the political process, Progressives wanted to nominate candidates by direct primaries instead of party caucuses. They called for nonpartisan elections to bypass the corruption that party politics bred. To get people involved directly in the democratic process, Progressives advocated three reform devices: the initiative, which enabled voters to propose new laws; the referendum, which allowed voters to accept or reject laws; and the recall, which permitted voters to remove incompetent or corrupt officials from office before their terms expired. All these reform mechanisms aimed to make politics more rational, efficient, and accountable to the electorate. Progressive reformers also achieved a major political victory in 1913 when the states ratified the Seventeenth Amendment providing for direct election of senators. Senators had been elected by state legislators since the Constitution was adopted. Legislative selection of senators had often been corrupted by corporate interests and manipulated by political bosses.

Some business executives became Progressive reformers. They supported federal regulation of industries as a means of protecting themselves from more radical proposals, such as trust busting or nationalization, and a bewildering variety of state regulations. Corporate leaders also saw advantages to federal regulation that created a stable operating environment for business by eliminating cutthroat competition and boom-and-bust cycles. The U.S. Chamber of Commerce and the National Civic Federation, both business and trade associations, favored limited government political and economic reform.

Progressive reformers started in the cities. They created the city manager and city commission forms of urban government, which employed trained administrators instead of political cronies to staff municipal agencies. They bought up public utilities so that gas, water, streetcar, and electrical companies could not corrupt city governments and exploit customers. Soon Progressive reformers expanded their horizons; they moved from local to statewide reform efforts. They formed political coalitions to elect state legislators and governors. Reform aims varied regionally. In the urban-industrial East, Progressives concentrated on breaking corrupt political machines and enacting labor reforms. In the Midwest and West, they focused on railroad regulation and direct democracy.

The most successful state Progressive reform leader was Wisconsin's governor, Robert La Follette. A small-town lawyer, he rose through the political ranks to become governor in 1900. He and his supporters implemented a broad reform program including direct democracy, a fair tax system, railroad regulation, labor reform, and social welfare. Wisconsin Progressives also generously supported the University of Wisconsin, making it a leading public university. In turn, the university furnished many experts to staff state agencies and to study problems, enabling the government to use the resources of modern science and technology. After serving three terms as governor, La Follette was elected senator and took his progressive crusade to Washington.

California also featured vigorous progressive reform. Hiram Johnson, a San Francisco attorney, led the California Progressives. He won the 1910 gubernatorial election on a promise to curb the power of the Southern Pacific railroad that dominated the state politically and economically. In office, Johnson and his supporters regulated the railroad. They also created a Public Utilities Commission empowered to set rates for utilities companies operating in the state.

State Progressive reformers also enacted a range of labor protection and social welfare laws that affected industrial workers more directly than did political reforms. Many states enacted factory inspection laws, and most implemented compulsory disability insurance to compensate victims of industrial accidents. They also enacted employer liability laws. They passed laws establishing minimum ages of employment, varying from ages twelve to sixteen. They also prohibited employers from working youngsters more than eight to ten hours per day. Most states enacted legislation limiting the workday for women to ten hours. In 1914, Arizona became the first state to create pensions for the elderly. But all these laws proved difficult to enforce: Many employers refused to comply with them, and the courts often weakened or nullified them.

THE ADVENT OF THEODORE ROOSEVELT

Progressive reformers looked to the federal government as the main engine of change. But the federal government was incapable of positive action during the 1890s. It was controlled by two political parties that were mainly responsive to special interests if they acted at all. Suddenly, in September 1901, a deranged anarchist murdered President McKinley, vaulting young Theodore Roosevelt into the White House. As governor of New York, Roosevelt had angered Republican party bosses by supporting regulatory legislation. They got rid of him by pushing him into the vice presidency in 1900. They never dreamed that they were giving the nation its most forceful president since Abraham Lincoln, a man who would revitalize the office, give it much of its twentieth-century character, and make it the most powerful branch of the national government.

Roosevelt did not appear presidential. He was short and near-sighted. He had big teeth and talked with a high-pitched voice. He had been a sickly child, undersized and suffering chronic asthma attacks, but he worked hard to develop his body and participated in vigorous sports. At Harvard, his small size kept him off the football team, but he did compete on the boxing and wrestling teams. In the 1880s, he lived on a cattle ranch in the Dakota territory, working cattle and sharing the rugged life of his cowboys. A bright man, he had a wide range of intellectual interests. He was a serious naturalist, specializing in ornithology. He was also a successful historian, writing *The Naval War of 1812* (1882) and *Winning of the West* (1889). A descendant of a distinguished New York family, he lived on inherited wealth. He also inherited a sense of civic responsibility and became a professional politician. A Republican party partisan, he held various New York state offices during the 1880s and 1890s. In 1897 President McKinley appointed him Assistant Secretary of the Navy. He resigned his office to fight in Cuba during the Spanish-American War. He returned from that war a hero and got elected governor of New York, then vice president in 1900.

President Roosevelt became a reform leader. He shared the Progressive view that the Jeffersonian ideal of small government was obsolete in an age of giant industries and large cities. He was a Hamiltonian, calling for a powerful central government to regulate big business and other sectors of the massive American economy. His presidency began the federal regulation of economic affairs that has characterized twentieth-century American history. He moved against monopoly at a time when giant trusts controlled every important economic sector. Though Roosevelt acquired a reputation as a trust buster, he believed that consolidation was the most efficient means to achieve economic and technological progress. He had no quarrel with bigness or monopoly as such. He distinguished between "good" trusts and "bad" trusts. Good trusts did not abuse their power and contributed to economic growth. Bad trusts were those few combines that used their

Theodore Roosevelt. *Source:* Library of Congress.

market leverage to raise prices and exploit consumers. Roosevelt made it his goal to stop the bad trusts from resorting to market manipulations. If necessary, he would use antitrust prosecutions to dissolve bad trusts.

Roosevelt's first successful antitrust action came in 1904 when the Supreme Court agreed with his contention that a railroad holding company, the Northern Securities Company, had been formed mainly to exploit customers, thus violating the Sherman Antitrust Act. The court ordered it dissolved. But Roosevelt preferred a cooperative relationship between big government and big business. He directed the newly formed Bureau of Corporations to work with companies when they proposed mergers. He hoped through monitoring and investigation to exert pressures on business to regulate itself. He cultivated friendly relations with prominent business and financial leaders.

Roosevelt pushed for regulatory legislation, especially after he won election in his own right by a landslide margin in 1904. He displayed impressive political skill in steering the Hepburn Act through a reluctant Congress in 1906. The Hepburn Act strengthened the Interstate Commerce Commission and imposed stricter controls on the nation's railroads. The energetic leader also supported consumer protection legislation. The outcry against fraud and adulteration in the patent-medicine and processed-meat industries intensified after the publication of Sinclair's muckraking novelistic exposé in 1906. Roosevelt supported the Pure Food and Drug Act and the Meat Inspection Act, both enacted by Congress in 1906.

Roosevelt also took a progressive stance toward labor-management relations during his presidency. In 1902, the United Mine Workers struck against coal companies in the anthracite fields of Pennsylvania. The Mine Workers wanted a 20 percent pay raise, an eight-hour day (a reduction from the then ten-hour day) and a recognition of their union as the miners' bargaining agent. Company officials refused to negotiate with union leaders and the strike dragged on. Roosevelt intervened, offering the progressive services of investigation and arbitration. Company officials rejected his offer, refusing to meet with union representatives. George Baer, spokesman for the mine owners, asserted that

> The rights and interests of the laboring man will be protected and cared for—not by the labor agitator, but by the Christian men to whom God in his infinite wisdom has given the control of the property interests of this country.[2]

With winter approaching and city dwellers facing the prospect of acute fuel shortages, Roosevelt rallied public opinion in support of government arbitration of the coal strike. He appointed a commission to arbitrate a settlement and pressured both sides into accepting its recommendations. The commission granted the miners a 10 percent pay increase and a nine-hour day. It did not force the companies to recognize the United Mine Workers, and it permitted them to raise their prices to cover their increased labor costs. The strike ended. Roosevelt, pleased with the outcome, observed that everyone got a "square deal." Roosevelt's enlightened role in the coal strike contrasts powerfully with Democratic President Cleveland's performance during the Pullman Strike of 1894. Cleveland used the powers of the federal government to break the strike and destroy the American Railway Union. Roosevelt also extended the progressive concept of federal regulation to labor-management relations to protect the public interest. The chief beneficiary of the square deal turned out to be Roosevelt himself because the strike settlement enhanced significantly the stature of the young chief executive early in his presidency.

---

[2]George Baer, quoted in Henry F. Pringle, *Theodore Roosevelt* (New York: Harcourt, Brace, 1931, 1956), p. 186.

Roosevelt's most enduring contribution to Progressive reform came on the issue of conservation. An avid outdoorsman, Roosevelt was a determined conservationist. He used his executive authority to add 150 million acres of western virgin forest lands to the national forests and to preserve vast areas of water and coal from private development. He also strongly backed his friend, the Interior Department's chief forester Gifford Pinchot, who shared Roosevelt's conservationist goals. In 1908, Roosevelt hosted a Washington gathering of governors and resource managers called the National Conservation Congress. Roosevelt favored national planning for resource management and ordered growth. He was not a strict preservationist, but he sought to balance the needs of economic development with the desire to preserve the nation's wilderness heritage of forests, open land, lakes, and rivers.

In 1907, a financial panic forced some large New York banks to close in order to prevent depositors from withdrawing money. Financial titan J. P. Morgan stopped the panic by providing funds to rescue some imperiled banks and by persuading financiers to stop selling securities. Roosevelt, grateful to Morgan for preventing a possible recession, allowed Morgan's U.S. Steel Corporation to buy its main competitor, the Tennessee Iron and Coal Company, giving the gigantic company monopolistic control of the steel industry.

During his last year in office, Roosevelt became more progressive, straining his relations with conservative business interests within the right wing of the Republican party. He attacked corporate leaders whom he called "malefactors of great wealth," calling for stricter government regulation of business and increased taxation of the rich. Having promised in 1904 not to seek reelection, Roosevelt decided to back his good friend and political ally, Secretary of War William Howard Taft, as his successor. Roosevelt was confident that Taft would continue his reform efforts. The Democrats nominated William Jennings Bryan for the third time. Taft, aided by Roosevelt, won easily. The still-popular Roosevelt, who could have had another presidential term had he sought it, left the country to hunt lions in Africa.

TAFT VERSUS PROGRESSIVISM

Taft was an intelligent, experienced politician, and he was committed to Progressive causes. He also retained good relations with conservative and moderate Republicans. He appeared to be the ideal successor to the energetic Roosevelt. But he lacked Roosevelt's stamina and love of politics. He was an obese man, weighing well over three hundred pounds, and he did not work hard. He was easygoing and passive; he disliked conflict and hated to impose his views on people. He intended to carry the mantle of progressivism, but he lacked the energy and political resources to do so.

At the outset of his presidency, Taft aggressively pursued a Progressive agenda: He enforced the Sherman Antitrust Act vigorously and added millions of acres of land to national forests. He signed the Mann-Elkins Railroad Act in 1910, increasing the regulatory authority of the Interstate Commerce Commission over

Roosevelt's greatest achievements and most enduring legacies were his conservation efforts, represented here by the magnificent trees preserved in Roosevelt National Forest, located on the eastern slope of the Rocky Mountains in northeastern Colorado.
Source: National Archives.

the railroad industry. He supported labor legislation. He also called Congress into special session in 1909 to lower tariff rates, an issue that Roosevelt had avoided.

Taft favored lowering tariff rates, and the House passed a bill reducing tariffs on most imports. The Senate, dominated by protectionists, eliminated the cuts in the House bill. A group of Progressive senators, led by Wisconsin's Robert La Follette, denounced the protectionist changes, using statistical data to show how many proposed tariff rates were unreasonably high. But Taft signed the new tariff, named the Payne-Aldrich Tariff, calling it "the best tariff the Republican Party ever passed," even though it raised tariffs on many important imports. Taft's actions outraged La Follette and other Senate Progressives, who accused him of betraying the cause of tariff reform.

The Republican party was splitting into progressive and conservative factions. Following the tariff battle, House Progressives challenged the autocratic power of Speaker Joseph "Uncle Joe" Cannon, a conservative Republican whose control of committee assignments and debate schedules allowed him to determine the fate of most House legislation. Taft initially backed the insurgents then changed his mind and supported Cannon. His reversal angered House Progressives and they joined their Senate colleagues in denouncing the president as an apostate reformer.

Taft also alienated Progressive conservationists when he permitted Secretary of the Interior Richard A. Ballinger to open 1 million acres of forest and mineral lands for development. He also fired Gifford Pinchot for protesting Ballinger's sale of some public waterpower sites in Alaska to private interests. Taft was not opposed to conservation, he was mainly backing Ballinger in a political feud with Pinchot, but Progressives viewed Pinchot's dismissal as an ominous sign that Taft was betraying the conservationist cause. The Ballinger-Pinchot controversy got more complicated when Pinchot traveled abroad to seek out his old friend Roosevelt. Without consulting Taft, Roosevelt sided with Pinchot, angering the rotund president, who resented his former friend's lack of confidence in his presidency.

As the split within Republican ranks widened, Taft cast his lot with the conservatives with whom he was personally more comfortable, and Roosevelt sided with the Progressives. After returning from his world travels, Roosevelt denied any presidential ambitions, but he did speak out on the issues. He was easily the most famous living American, and his speeches made headlines. Speaking at Osawatomie, Kansas, in August 1910, Roosevelt came out in favor of a comprehensive progressive program he called the New Nationalism. He attacked "lawbreakers of great wealth" and called for a broad expansion of federal power. He asserted that progress must come through the national government.

THE ELECTION OF 1912

On January 11, 1911, Progressive Republican leaders met in the nation's capital to form the National Republican Progressive League. They elected Senator Bob La Follette of Wisconsin to head their new organization. At a conference held in Chicago later in the year, the new Progressive League chose La Follette as their favored candidate for the Republican presidential nomination in 1912.

Paralleling the growing Republican Party split between progressives and conservatives, there occurred a break between Taft and Roosevelt in October 1911, when the president ordered an antitrust suit against U.S. Steel, forcing the giant company to sell off its Tennessee Iron and Coal Company. Roosevelt reacted angrily because he thought the suit unwarranted. Also, he had approved U.S. Steel's acquisition of the Tennessee Iron and Coal Company during the financial panic of 1907. Taft's actions made Roosevelt appear either a supporter of monopoly or, worse, a dupe of big business. He attacked Taft's action publicly, and early in 1912, he announced that he would be a candidate for the Republican presidential nomination. He denounced Taft for betraying the reform cause. Progressive leaders rallied to Roosevelt's banner.

Roosevelt threw himself into the campaign. He was clearly the choice of the Republican Party rank and file. He was victorious in all states that held presidential primaries. He even beat President Taft in his home state of Ohio. But Roosevelt could not win the nomination through the primaries because not enough states held primaries in those days. President Taft's forces controlled the party machinery and came to the Republican party convention in Chicago with a small majority of the delegates. Roosevelt's forces challenged the credentials of 254 of Taft's delegates, some of whom had been chosen under dubious circumstances. The fate of Roosevelt's candidacy, the fate of the Republican Party, and the outcome of the 1912 presidential election depended on the selection of those 254 contested delegates. The Taft-controlled credentials committee awarded 235 of the disputed delegates to Taft and only 19 to Roosevelt. Having won control of the convention, Taft's forces beat back all efforts to seat more of Roosevelt's delegates and secured Taft's renomination, narrowly, on the first ballot.

Roosevelt, outraged, was convinced that the nomination that was rightfully his, had been stolen from him by the political bosses. He decided to run for president as the head of a third party organization. In August, delegates gathered in Chicago in the same convention hall where Taft had emerged victorious six weeks earlier to create the Progressive Party. In an emotional atmosphere that resembled a revivalist camp meeting, on the evening of August 6, delegates, who were mostly Republican Progressives, nominated Theodore Roosevelt as their presidential candidate and adopted his New Nationalism as the party platform. The delegates also chose California governor Hiram Johnson as Teddy's vice-presidential running mate. Roosevelt, in a rousing acceptance speech, told the delegates that we "stand at Armageddon and battle for the Lord." Teddy, proclaiming himself "as strong as a bull moose in the rutting season," urged adoption of the New Nationalist program that included regulation of corporations, a national presidential primary, the elimination of child labor, a minimum wage, women's suffrage, and many other Progressive reforms. Roosevelt's candidacy made it official: The Republican Party had split. Conservative Republicans supported President Taft's bid for reelection. Progressive Republicans, now formed into the Progressive third party, supported Roosevelt's candidacy.

The Democrats, meanwhile, had held their convention in Baltimore. The leading candidate for the Democratic presidential nomination in 1912 was Champ Clark of Missouri, a veteran Democratic leader and currently Speaker of the House. Clark was a disciple of William Jennings Bryan and also had the backing of media magnate William Randolph Hearts, who was also a power within the Democratic Party. Clark won most of the delegates during the primaries and came to the convention heavily favored to win the Democratic nomination. But Clark was challenged by a political newcomer, Woodrow Wilson, the Progressive reform governor of New Jersey, who for most of his adult life had been a college professor and administrator. A third candidate, Congressman Oscar Underwood of Alabama, had also entered the presidential lists. Underwood ran as a favorite son candidate and showed strength in other southern states.

When the Baltimore convention began June 25, 1912, Underwood and Wilson appeared to have no chance against Clark. On the initial ballot, Clark won a large majority of delegates, but he failed to get the required two-thirds vote needed for nomination. (The Democratic Party retained the two-thirds rule adopted in 1836 to give southern delegates extra clout in choosing the party's presidential nominees.) For many ballots, the Underwood and Wilson delegates held firm to deny Clark the nomination. On the fourteenth ballot, Clark made a deal with Tammany Hall to win the votes of the New York delegation. Outraged, the idealistic Bryan, still the most popular leader in the Democratic party, switched his support to Wilson. For three more days, the candidates continued to battle fiercely for delegates. Finally, on the forty-sixth ballot, Underwood's supporters switched to fellow southerner Woodrow Wilson and the nomination was his. Wilson chose Governor Thomas R. Marshall of Indiana for his vice-presidential candidate.

The Socialist Party nominated its perennial candidate, Eugene Debs. The stage was set for one of the most important elections of the twentieth century, one in which the American system was subjected to a thorough evaluation, and an election in which alternative public policy options were rigorously debated and offered to the voters.

There were four significant candidates in the race: on the Right, the Republican candidate was the incumbent President Taft; on the Left, Eugene Debs ran on a socialist slate calling for the nationalization of monopolies; in the Center stood two candidates—the Democratic nominee Woodrow Wilson, and the Progressive Party leader, former President Theodore Roosevelt, both of whom claimed the mantle of Progressive reform. Neither Taft nor Debs had a chance to win; the outcome turned on the battle between Wilson and Roosevelt.

Roosevelt ran on his New Nationalism program. Wilson countered with a Progressive program he called the New Freedom. Both candidates embraced Progressive principles, and there were similarities in their appeals; however, there were significant differences between them because they represented different varieties of progressivism. The candidacies of Roosevelt and Wilson revealed a deep ideological cleavage that had evolved within national progressivism. Their most important difference expressed a philosophical division within Progressive ranks over the fundamentals of progressive government. Roosevelt would not destroy the trusts, which he saw as efficient means to organize production. He favored establishing regulatory commissions staffed by experts who would protect consumer rights and ensure that concentrations of economic power performed in the public interest.

Wilson, whose New Freedom drew heavily upon the ideas of Progressive legal reformer Louis Brandeis, believed that concentrations of economic power threatened liberty and foreclosed economic opportunity. He wanted to break up trusts to restore competition, but he did not want to restore laissez-faire, which he believed to be obsolete. He favored what Brandeis called "regulated free enterprise." And, Wilson did not favor the cooperation between big government and big business inherent in Roosevelt's New Nationalism. He spoke passionately, sometimes in evangelical tones, of the need to emancipate the American economy from the power of the trusts, that government should provide for the man on the make, not for the man who has it made. The Democratic platform, which had been largely drafted by Bryan, also called for structural reforms to make the political system more democratic and for a downward revision of tariff schedules.

But on the central issue of the 1912 campaign, the role of the federal government in promoting the economic security and social welfare of the American people, Wilson and the Democrats were mostly silent or took refuge in vague generalities. The absence of social justice planks in the Democratic platform derived mainly from the party's ancient Jeffersonian allegiances. Democrats still adherred to states' rights doctrines and a general policy of modified laissez-faire at the federal level. Wilson was suspicious of both big business and big government, regarding them both as potential threats to liberty. If regulation were necessary, Wilson would have the states do it. In 1912, the Democratic Party position was that if laws were needed to protect working people they would come from state governments, not from Washington.

As he traveled the campaign trail in search of votes, Wilson highlighted the major themes of his New Freedom program. He would unleash the entrepreneurial energies of the American people by abolishing special privileges and restoring competition to the American system of free enterprise capitalism. He would achieve these goals by lowering tariffs, reforming the banking and currency systems, and strengthening the Sherman Antitrust Act.

Roosevelt dismissed Wilson's prescription for economic renewal as hopelessly reactionary and infeasible. Roosevelt reminded his audiences that big business was here to stay and that was a good thing. Large corporations were more efficient and more productive than small enterprises. They contributed greatly to national wealth and gave America a competitive edge in world markets. Roosevelt insisted that efforts to destroy large corporations were probably impossible and would undermine national prosperity. Roosevelt accepted a corporate-dominated economy, but one strictly monitored and regulated by a powerful central government in order to prevent trusts from abusing their power. Teddy called for the creation of a federal trade commission to regulate the nation's large corporations. Roosevelt hedged on the tariff by calling for the creation of a nonpartisan tariff commission to make "scientific adjustments in rates," which could be either up or down. Roosevelt, in keeping with the spirit of his New Nationalism, called for a host of social justice measures protecting farmers, women, children, and workers.

Election results showed Wilson the winner with only 42 percent of the popular vote—he was a minority president, but he carried forty states and captured 435 of 531 electoral votes. The Democrats also won control over both houses of the new Congress that would convene in 1913. Two-thirds of the gubernatorial elections held in 1912 also went to Democratic candidates. Roosevelt got about 27 percent of the popular vote, carrying six states with 88 electoral votes. Taft, who stayed at the White House and refused to make even one campaign speech, finished a distant third with 23 percent of the vote and 9 electoral votes. Debs, campaigning nationally, pulled down 902,000 votes, about 6 percent, the best ever by a socialist. Debs received the votes of many citizens who were not socialists but who knew Debs to be an honest man and a champion of the dispossessed.

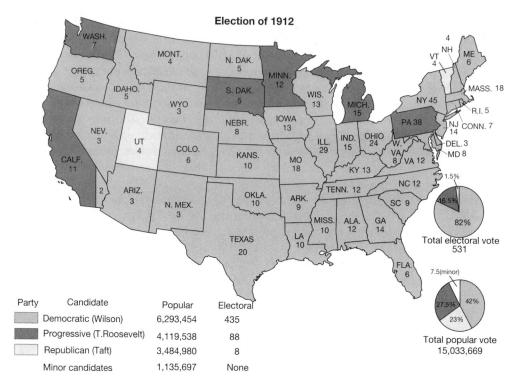

Election of 1912

Party	Candidate	Popular	Electoral
░	Democratic (Wilson)	6,293,454	435
▓	Progressive (T.Roosevelt)	4,119,538	88
▫	Republican (Taft)	3,484,980	8
	Minor candidates	1,135,697	None

Election of 1912.   *Source:* Moss, *Rise of Modern America,* p. 85.

The Republican Party split, as well as the failure of Theodore Roosevelt to win over the Democratic Progressives and thus forge a majority coalition of reform forces, made Wilson's electoral victory possible. Had the Republican Party been united behind a Roosevelt candidacy, he would have won handily. Even a Taft candidacy, running on a Progressive slate with Roosevelt's support, would probably have prevailed. Wilson, however, was able to maintain traditional Democratic constituencies and his New Freedom platform also kept Democratic Progressives within the party fold. Partisan political alignments more than the issues determined the outcome of the 1912 election.

WILSONIAN PROGRESSIVISM

Wilson made an unlikely president. He had been born in Staunton, Virginia, on December 29, 1856, the son of a stern Presbyterian minister. He grew up in South Carolina and Georgia during the era of the Civil War and Reconstruction. After getting a law degree and becoming an attorney, he opted for an academic career. He received a Ph.D. from Johns Hopkins University and became a professor of history and political science. (Wilson is the only U.S. president ever to have earned a Ph.D. degree.)

During a lengthy and distinguished academic career, Wilson taught at several different colleges and universities. From 1885 until 1902, he was a professor of history and government at Princeton University. He became an authority on the U.S. Constitution and one of the most eminent American scholars of his generation. He wrote several scholarly books, of which his most renowned was *Congressional Government* (1885). In this work, Wilson stated that the separation of powers within the U.S. Constitution made responsible leadership impossible. He advocated revising the Constitution to create a national government modeled along the lines of the British cabinet system. After observing Theodore Roosevelt transform the presidency from a passive office to a dynamic and powerful office from which he led the nation and promoted reform causes, Wilson changed his mind. He realized that a strong president could provide responsible leadership and could bend the Congress to his will, which corresponded to the will of the people.

Wilson entered politics in middle age. In 1902, he became president of Princeton University where he upset traditionalists with curriculum reforms. He resigned his presidency in 1910 during a dispute over university policy, intending to return to the classroom. But in 1910, the New Jersey Democratic Party needed a candidate for governor, and Wilson consented to run. The party bosses who secured his nomination needed his respectability, and they assumed he could be managed if he won. After winning the governorship, Wilson repudiated the bosses and embraced progressivism enthusiastically. He directed the passage of a host of legislative reforms that significantly improved politics in a state notorious for boss rule and corporate domination. His accomplishments in New Jersey made it possible for him to win the Democratic Party presidential nomination in 1912.

Wilson's manner reflected his religious and academic backgrounds. Tall, lean, and stiff, he looked sternly through his glasses at the world and its inhabitants. He could be aloof and often spoke self-righteously. Yet he proved to be an effective, even charismatic political leader. He took control of his party in Congress. He was a brilliant speaker; he could inspire support and intense loyalty with vivid religious imagery and ringing evocations of American principles in which he devoutly believed. Because he was steeped in the democratic and Judeo-Christian ideologies that undergirded progressivism, he could espouse reforms in moving, compelling, and irresistible phrases.

In a brilliant inaugural address, the new president spelled out his Progressive reform agenda to the American people. His top priority was tariff reform, long a Democratic Party staple and long a failed promise. Wilson called the new Congress into special session to revise the tariff. Breaking with tradition, the new president then went in person to deliver a forceful message to a joint session of Congress urging quick passage of the tariff bill. Wilson was the first president to address a joint session of Congress; the first to focus public attention directly on the lawmakers.

Tariff rates had been rising for years and had appreciably increased living costs for millions of Americans. Farmers had complained for years that protective tariffs raised their operating costs and lowered their commodity prices. All previous efforts at tariff reform had been blocked by Senate protectionist forces; for

Woodrow Wilson, the "schoolmaster in politics," was an eloquent champion of progressive reform causes. He is shown here making a campaign speech during the election of 1912.   *Source:* National Archives.

example, Taft's ill-fated effort at tariff reform in 1909. Oscar Underwood, Chairman of the House Ways and Means Committee, steered the administration's tariff bill through the House. It reduced substantially duties on hundreds of items and placed many more on the free list. The measure passed easily by a vote of 281–139, with a lot of Progressive Republican support.

In the Senate, like so many Furies, once again the lobbyists for special interests descended on the senators to press their amendments to maintain the protectionist rates. But unlike the lethargic Taft, President Wilson was prepared to battle the lobbyists. He made a dramatic appeal to the American people. He told them that, "The public ought to know the extraordinary exertions being made by the lobby in Washington. Only public opinion can check it and destroy it." Voters strongly responded to his appeal, and the Senate passed the measure with the reductions intact. The new president played a major role in bringing about the first reduction in tariff rates since the Civil War.

Wilson signed the new law, the Underwood-Simmons Tariff Act, on October 3, 1913. It reduced average import tax rates from about 40 to 29 percent, an 11 percent reduction across the board. Costs of living and of doing business for millions of Americans declined immediately. Imports to America increased dramatically. Reduced rates also meant that tax revenues declined sharply. Because tariff fees were the federal government's principal source of revenue, the new tariff bill levied a graduated income tax to replace its lost income, an option made possible by the recent ratification of the Sixteenth Amendment. The tax was small by today's standards. Incomes under $4,000 per year were excluded, which exempted over 90 percent of American families in 1914, the first year the tax was in effect. The income tax was originally intended to be a tax only on the affluent and wealthy. People in the $4,000 to $20,000 income brackets had to pay 1 percent income tax. The rate rose gradually to a top rate of 7 percent on incomes exceeding $500,000 per year. Such rates did not take much wealth from rich people and most Americans never noticed it, but the income tax had made its debut. Passage of the tariff reform was a major political victory for the rookie president. It gave him great leverage over Democratic leaders in Congress and won him the trust and respect of most Americans, who sensed that an effective leader was in power who could keep the Progressive faith and fulfill his campaign promises.

Wilson next turned his attention to another salient Democratic campaign promise—reform of the nation's banking and currency systems. Again, the new president intervened directly in the legislative process; he worked closely with key Democratic leaders in the House and Senate to ensure passage of the kind of measure that he wanted. Carter Glass of Virginia, Chairman of the House Banking Committee, introduced the federal reserve bill in early September. The House approved it quickly, but there was a long and tough battle to get the administration's bill through the Senate relatively unscathed. Wilson persisted, and the Senate approved the measure the day before Christmas.

The Federal Reserve Act constituted the most important progressive reform measure of Wilson's presidency. The law created the nation's first centralized banking system since Andrew Jackson had destroyed the Second Bank of the United States. It created twelve regional banks to hold the reserves of member banks throughout the nation. These district banks had authority to lend money to member banks at low rates of interest called the *discount rate.* By adjusting this rate, the regional banks could adjust the amount of money a bank could borrow and thereby increase or decrease the amount of money in circulation. In response to national need, the banks could either loosen or tighten credit by lowering or raising the discount rate. More elasticity was structured into the money supply, and interest rates for farmers and small business owners would be lower. A Federal Reserve Board made up of five members appointed by the president with the approval of the Senate ensured that the banking industry would be regulated in the public interest. The nation still uses the Federal Reserve system, although its powers have been significantly changed by subsequent legislation. The head of the Federal Reserve Board has the power to determine interest rates and the rate of monetary growth and is the most powerful nonelected official in Washington.

Following his victories on the tariff and banking bills, Wilson went after Congress to achieve his third major reform commitment, strengthening the Sherman Antitrust Act. Three measures, including one introduced by Henry Clayton of Alabama, cleared the House. The Clayton Act amended the Sherman Antitrust Act by outlawing monopolistic practices such as *discriminatory pricing* (the practice of a company's trying to destroy a smaller firm by lowering its prices in that company's market meanwhile keeping higher prices elsewhere) and *interlocking directorates* (the management of two or more competing companies by the same executives). Officers of corporations convicted of antitrust violations could be held individually responsible. The Clayton Act also contained provisions that exempted trade unions and agricultural organizations from antitrust laws, and it curtailed the use of court injunctions during strikes.

These acts, especially the Clayton Act, encountered serious opposition from the business community, including many small businessmen who had supported Wilson and the Democrats. They thought that these antitrust measures went too far; besides, it was proving impractical to try to prohibit by law every conceivable method of restraining trade. Facing both a practical and political problem, the Wilson administration executed a major ideological shift. Wilson dropped his support for antitrust legislation and supported instead a measure introduced by Congressman Raymond Stevens of New Hampshire that created a federal trade commission. Wilson signed the Federal Trade Commission Act on September 26, 1914. The Federal Trade Commission Act created the Federal Trade Commission (FTC), which replaced the Bureau of Corporations. The FTC was empowered to study corporate practices and issue cease-and-desist orders against unfair trade practices. The chief purpose of the new agency was to monitor business practices and proscribe unfair practices *before* they had put their competition out of business and ripped off their customers.

Ironically, Wilson had been forced to abandon a key plank in the New Freedom program, antitrust, in favor of a New Nationalist plank, a federal trade commission, that had been pushed by his arch political rival, Theodore Roosevelt. By 1914, corporate mergers were so extensive that restoration of free enterprise was impossible short of drastic antitrust actions that were unthinkable to Wilson and his key domestic adviser Brandeis, who favored the trade commission concept. Wilson and Brandeis accepted economic concentration and embraced Rooseveltian concepts of expanding the government's regulatory powers to prevent harm to the public interest.

During the first two years of his presidency, Wilson had been unconcerned about social justice legislation designed to provide federal protections for the exploited and disadvantaged classes of industrial America. Wilsonian progressivism was not responsive to the concerns of poor and powerless Americans. The president had no interest in helping African Americans; in fact, Wilson supported the resegregation of the federal civil service. Gradually, his interests turned toward social legislation. His shift towards the New Nationalism and embracing of the Federal Trade Commission Act signaled a change of direction. He realized that the national government had a positive role to play in promoting social welfare and enhancing economic security. Wilson also understood that he faced defeat in the 1916 election unless he supported a vigorous slate of New Nationalist reforms. The Democratic Party was still the minority party; unless Wilson could attract a large number of Roosevelt Progressive Republican voters, he would lose to the Republican Party candidate who would be backed by a reunified party.

In 1916, Wilson supported a whole range of social justice measures. Wilson supported passage of the Federal Farm Loan Act, which created banks to lend money at low interest rates to farmers. He also supported the Adamson Act, which gave all railroad workers an eight-hour day and time-and-a-half for overtime. Soon after signing the Adamson Act, Wilson signed a progressive tax measure that raised income tax rates, created a federal estate tax, and imposed excess profits taxes on large corporations. The tax measure represented the first effort in American history to use the tax powers of the federal government to effect a redistribution of wealth from the "haves" in the direction of the "have nots." Wilson further courted Progressive social reformers by backing laws outlawing child labor and granting federal employees workers' compensation. He also appointed Louis Brandeis to the Supreme Court. It was a controversial appointment because Brandeis was an outspoken critic of big business and also the first Jew ever appointed to the Court.

As Wilson approached the election of 1916, his presidency had been one of the most successful in American political history. His reform ideas set the direction of federal economic policy for much of the twentieth century. All major Progressive reform initiatives were enacted. Ironically, a major reason for the decline of progressivism that occurred after 1916 was that it was a victim of its own success. Its agenda was implemented—and exhausted. The "schoolmaster in politics," with scant prior political experience, in the judgment of many historians, turned out to be the greatest president since Abraham Lincoln.

PROGRESSIVISM IN PERSPECTIVE

The Progressive Era effectively ended with World War I, but a generation of reform had brought major changes. Late-nineteenth-century political, economic, and social institutions had been transformed. Laissez-faire had vanished. Public concern for poverty and injustice had reached intense levels, yet for every underprivileged American by 1920, at least three enjoyed material comforts and freedoms unprecedented in human history.

Progressivism was characterized by a jumble of reform movements that lacked unifying characteristics. There was no such thing as a progressive movement, only movements. Often, progressives worked oblivious to one another, even at cross-purposes to one another. Reform occurred at all levels, from neighborhood cleanup committees to national programs such as the New Freedom. Progressivism's diversity of aims, means, and achievements was its most salient characteristic. Its diversity reflected the pluralism of contemporary American society and political culture.

Many Progressive initiatives failed or only partially succeeded. Sometimes failure came from strong opposition, sometimes from inherent flaws in the reform movement. The courts struck down key Progressive reforms, most notably laws abolishing child labor. Political reforms such as the initiative and referendum failed to encourage greater citizen participation in politics and were exploited by special interest groups. Federal regulatory agencies lacked the resources to perform their investigative and monitoring functions thoroughly. They often obtained their data from the companies they were supposed to police, and they were staffed by people recruited from the industries they were supposed to monitor. Some political machines survived progressive assaults, and business influence at all levels of politics remained powerful.

Even so, Progressives compiled a solid record of achievement. Progressivism refashioned the nation's future. Big business became more sensitive to public opinion. The power of political autocrats was diluted. Progressive reforms protected consumers against price fixing and dangerous products. Social reforms alleviated injustice and human misery. Expanded school opportunities enabled the children of immigrants to achieve successful careers and fulfilling lives. Progressives challenged conventional ways of thinking. They raised urgent questions about the goals and qualities of American life. They provided both a new mode of public discourse and a method for solving public problems. They proved that concerned citizens could bring the promise of American life closer to fulfillment for millions of their fellow citizens.

IMPORTANT EVENTS

1901   President McKinley is assassinated; Vice President Theodore Roosevelt assumes presidency

1902   The government sues the Northern Security Company for antitrust violations and wins

1903	The first power-driven airplane flies at Kitty Hawk, North Carolina
1903	The first World Series takes place
1904	Ida Tarbell publishes her expose of Standard Oil
1905	The National Education Association is founded
1906	Upton Sinclair's novel, *The Jungle,* is published
1907	William James publishes *Pragmatism*
1908	Henry Ford manufactures the first Model T
1909	U.S. Marines go to Nicaragua
1910	The NAACP is founded
1911	Irving Berlin writes "Alexander's Ragtime Band"
1912	New Mexico and Arizona are added to the Union
1913	Henry Ford installs the first moving assembly line
1913	The Sixteenth Amendment establishes the income tax; the Seventeenth Amendment provides for direct election of senators
1914	World War I begins
1914	The Panama Canal is completed
1915	D. W. Griffith produces the first movie spectacular, *Birth of a Nation*
1916	Margaret Sanger founds the New York Birth Control League
1917	Congress enacts a literacy test for new immigrants
1918	World War I ends
1919	The Eighteenth Amendment, establishing prohibition, is ratified
1920	The Nineteenth Amendment, enfranchising women, is ratified

BIBLIOGRAPHY

The Progressive Era has a rich bibliography. Some of the most readable and accessible books include the previously mentioned studies of reform by Eric Goldman and Richard Hofstadter. David M. Chalmers's *The Social and Political Ideas of the Muckrakers* is the best study of the reform writers of the era. The role of women in the Progressive Era has been documented by William L. O'Neill in *Everyone Was Brave.* A first-rate biography of Margaret Sanger is David Kennedy's *Birth Control in America: The Career of Margaret Sanger.* Aileen Kraditor, in *Ideas of the Woman Suffrage Movement,* offers an original study of the drive to win the vote for women. Ruth Rosen's *The Lost Sisterhood: Prostitutes in America 1900–1918* is a fascinating study of this group of women. Elliot M. Rudwick's *W. E. B. Dubois: A Study in Group Leadership* is the best book about the most important black progressive. A classic study of national progressivism is found in *The Era of Theodore Roosevelt,* by George Mowry. The best intellectual history of progressivism remains Morton White's *Social Thought in America: The Revolt Against Formalism.* Lawrence Cremin's *The Transformation of the School: Progressivism in American Education* is the best study of an important era in education by the foremost American historian of education. An imaginative comparative study of the two greatest progressive reform leaders, Theodore Roosevelt and Woodrow Wilson, is *The Warrior and the Priest,* by John M. Cooper, Jr. Anyone who wants to know how Prohibition came to be the law of the land should read J. H. Timberlake's *Prohibition and the Progressive Movement.*

CHAPTER 3

America and the World

In the aftermath of its war with Spain, the United States pursued an interventionist foreign policy. It fought a war to crush a nationalist rebellion in the Philippines and joined other imperial powers to suppress the Boxer uprising in China. It sent its troops into many Latin American nations: Cuba, Panama, the Dominican Republic, Nicaragua, Haiti, and Mexico. Progressive foreign policy aimed to promote overseas trade and investment, to maintain regional order, and to fulfill the imperatives of the American missionary impulse to redeem the world. The foreign policy elite who formulated Progressive foreign policy believed that northern Europeans and their American descendants belonged to a superior race destined to dominate and to "civilize" the darker-skinned people of Latin America, Asia, Africa, and the Pacific islands. In 1917, the United States reached beyond the Caribbean and Pacific regions to intervene in Europe to ensure an Allied victory over Germany. World War I was a transforming experience for the United States and it opened a historic opportunity for America to assume primacy among the world's nations.

MANAGING THE AMERICAN EMPIRE

U.S. foreign policy during the Progressive Era was determined mainly by American expansionism during the 1890s and the acquisition of an overseas empire. Progressive diplomatists were concerned with the opportunities and problems encountered in managing, protecting, and expanding the American empire which reached from the Caribbean to the Far East. The American empire during the period between the Spanish-American War and World War I faced threats from restless nationalists, commercial rivals, and other expansionist nations.

Although Cuba did not become an American colony after the war with Spain, the United States dominated the new nation. American troops remained in Cuba until 1902, and Cuba was governed by General Leonard Wood, formerly the commander of the Rough Riders. To get rid of the American forces, Cubans were forced to accept the Platt Amendment, which was incorporated into the new Cuban constitution and later ratified as a treaty. The amendment conceded American hegemony over Cuba and impaired Cuban sovereignty. Cuba could make no treaties with another nation without U.S. approval. Cuba granted the United States the right to intervene "to maintain order and preserve Cuban independence." Cuba also had to lease a naval base at Guantanamo to the United States. The Platt Amendment governed United States–Cuba relations until 1934. Cubans protested the Platt Amendment to no avail. When a rebellion occurred in 1906, President Roosevelt intervened to reestablish a U.S.–controlled provisional government, supported by 5,000 American troops, that ruled for twenty-eight months. Over the next fifteen years, whenever political instability occurred in Cuba, the United States sent the Marines ashore to maintain order and to protect American lives and property.

The thirty-year-long American protectorate left its mark on Cuba. Americans helped Cubans improve transportation, develop a public school system, create a national army, increase sugar production, and raise public health levels. An American physician, Dr. Walter Reed, working with Cuban physicians, proved that mosquitoes carried yellow fever germs. American sanitary engineers eradicated the disease from the island. American investments in Cuba reached $220 million by 1913, and American exports to the island reached $200 million by 1917. The Platt Amendment, U.S. Marines, and U.S. investments made a mockery of Cuban sovereignty for decades. The Cuban nation developed with a colonial mentality. Cuban patriots nurtured a resentment towards the United States that in time became anti-Americanism.

Expanding American interests in the Caribbean and Asia made building an interoceanic canal across Central America an urgent American priority. Two obstacles had to be overcome before it could be constructed. First, the Clayton-Bulwer Treaty (1850) with the British, requiring Anglo-American control of any Central American canal, had to be canceled. In 1901, Secretary of State John Hay and Lord Pauncefote, the British ambassador to the United States, signed the second Hay-Pauncefote treaty, which gave America the right to build and fortify a transisthmian waterway. Second, a route for the canal had to be acquired. A possible route lay across the Colombian province of Panama, where a French company, the New Panama Canal Company, owned the right-of-way, having inherited it from the failed De Lesseps company, which had tried to build a canal during the 1880s. Only 50 miles separated the two oceans along this route, but the terrain was rugged and posed serious health hazards. Another possible route traversed Nicaragua. It was 200 miles long, but it would be an easier challenge because much of it included Lake Nicaragua and other natural waterways.

President Roosevelt considered both sites and chose the Panama route. His decision was influenced by the lobbying of Philippe Bunau-Varilla, a French engineer

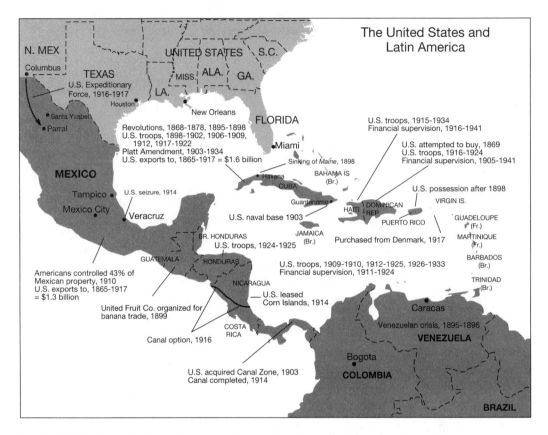

The United States and Latin America.   *Source:* Moss, *Rise of Modern America,* p. 95.

living in Panama who formerly had directed the defunct French canal project. On January 18, 1903, a commission agreed to pay the New Panama Canal Company $40 million for its right-of-way and equipment. Congress subsequently approved the Panama route. On January 22, 1903, Secretary of State John Hay negotiated a treaty with Tomas Herran, the Colombian chargé d'affaires. By its terms, the United States received a ninety-nine-year lease on a 6-mile-wide zone across the isthmus of Panama; in return, the United States granted an initial payment of $10 million to Colombia and $250,000 annual rental. But on August 12, 1903, the Colombian senate unanimously rejected the Hay-Herran treaty because the senators wanted more money and because the agreement, which severely infringed upon Colombian sovereignty, was unpopular with the Colombian people. The Colombian senators wanted an initial payment of $15 million from the United States and they also tried to extract $10 million from the New Panama Canal Company.

President Roosevelt could have negotiated an agreement with the Colombians who were eager to have the United States build the canal, but the imperious Roosevelt angrily denounced the Colombians, broke off negotiations and sought to get the canal right-of-way by other means. Panamanians, also eager for the Americans to build the canal, learning of the Colombian rejection and urged on by New Panama Canal officials, rose in rebellion on November 2, 1903. Roosevelt had previously given Bunau-Varilla indications that the United States would accept a Panamanian revolt.

That same day, an American fleet, led by the cruiser USS *Nashville*, arrived in Colon, Panama's Caribbean port. When Colombia landed 400 troops at Colon on November 3 to suppress the rebellion, the American Navy did not interfere. The failure of the U.S. Navy to intervene disappointed the Panamanian rebels, who had hoped for American help. Forced to rely on their own resources, the Panamanians outmaneuvered the Colombians. They bribed their leader into taking his troops back to Colombia. With the soldiers gone, the revolution succeeded. Joyous Panamanians declared their independence on the evening of November 3. At noon the next day, Secretary of State John Hay recognized the sovereign Republic of Panama. On November 18, Hay and the new Panamanian minister plenipotentiary, the resourceful Philippe Bunau-Varilla, negotiated a treaty, the Hay–Bunau-Varilla Treaty, granting the United States a zone 10 miles wide "in perpetuity" across the isthmus for the same money that Colombia had previously rejected. The New Panama Canal Company then received its $40 million for its right of way and properties. On February 24, 1904, the U.S. Senate overwhelmingly approved the new treaty. American public opinion also overwhelmingly approved the new treaty and the means required to achieve it.

Construction of the canal began in 1904 and the 50-mile-long canal opened to seafaring traffic on August 15, 1914. From opening day, the merchant ships of many nations and vessels of the U.S. Atlantic and Pacific fleets traversed the big ditch. Americans celebrated the opening of the canal by staging a world's fair honoring it, the Panama-Pacific Exposition held in San Francisco in 1915. Building the canal was a tremendous engineering feat that served the national interest economically and strategically. The United States fortified the Canal Zone, and guarding the canal and its approaches became a vital U.S. strategic interest. The terms of the treaty negotiated by United States and Panamanian officials made the Canal Zone an American colony. Panama was a sovereign nation in name only because of American control of the canal and a strip of Panamanian soil stretching across the heart of that small country.

Roosevelt's arrogant intervention in the internal affairs of Colombia, while popular with most citizens of the United States, frightened and angered Latin American nationalists who viewed the Panama canal as a symbol of "Yanqui" imperialism. In 1922, the United States paid Colombia $25 million in return for Colombia's recognition of Panamanian independence, a payment humorously dubbed "canalimony." In 1978, the United States and Panama concluded treaties that provide for turning over the Canal Zone to Panama in the year 2000.

Following his acquisition of the Canal Zone, Roosevelt turned the rest of the Caribbean into an "American lake," He was aided in these actions by the British, who were concerned to improve relations with the United States and tacitly accepted the American sphere of influence. London, perceiving the shifting power balance in the Western Hemisphere, acceded to American hegemony in Latin America. British acceptance of American dominance in the Caribbean area signaled a growing Anglo-American accord that cleared the way for U.S. regional expansionism without fear of British opposition and that blossomed into a full-fledged Anglo-American alliance during World War I. Both world powers benefited from their "great rapprochement."

Roosevelt said, "Speak softly and carry a big stick." He used the stick, but he seldom curbed his noisy rhetoric. In 1904, he announced his Roosevelt Corollary to the Monroe Doctrine, a warning to Latin American countries to put their governments and finances in order to forestall European intervention in their affairs. Roosevelt warned that

> Chronic wrongdoing . . . may in America, as elsewhere, ultimately require intervention by some civilized nation, and in the Western Hemisphere the adherence of the United States to the Monroe Doctrine may force the United States, however reluctantly, in flagrant cases of such wrongdoing or impotence, to the exercise of an international police power.[1]

The Roosevelt Corollary to the Monroe Doctrine transformed that hallowed prohibition upon European intervention in the Western Hemisphere into a firm assertion that the United States henceforth would arrogate to itself the role of regional policeman.

Roosevelt and his Progressive successors, Taft and Wilson, frequently implemented Roosevelt's corollary. Between 1900 and the entry of the U.S. into World War I, American troops intervened in Cuba, Panama, Nicaragua, the Dominican Republic, Haiti, and Mexico. American officials took over customs houses to control tariff revenues and government budgets, renegotiated foreign debts with American banks, and trained national armies; and they conducted elections. Frequent U.S. interventions into Nicaraguan affairs between 1907 and 1933 made that small and poor Central American country a U.S. protectorate.

Mexico appeared especially threatening to the Progressive managers of U.S. foreign policy. In 1910, revolutionaries overthrew Porfirio Díaz, an aged dictator who had maintained a favorable environment for U.S. and other foreign investments for forty years. During the next decade, the Mexicans changed governments several times as revolutionary factions struggled for power. At various stages of the Mexican revolution, American lives and property appeared to be imperiled.

But President Wilson appeared less concerned about protecting the U.S. Mexican investment of $1 billion than he was in guiding the Mexicans to establish an American-style political democracy. In the summer of 1913, Wilson attempted to remove General Victoriano Huerta from power and to replace him with a government led by Venustiano Carranza, the leader of the "Constitutionalists." When an arms embargo failed to work, Wilson sent American naval vessels to the Mexican gulf ports of Vera Cruz and Tampico.

---

[1]Theodore Roosevelt, quoted in Henry F. Pringle, *Theodore Roosevelt* (New York: Harcourt, Brace, 1931, 1945), p. 207.

On April 21, 1914, Wilson, learning that a merchant ship carrying arms for Huerta's forces was arriving at Vera Cruz, ordered a force of eight hundred U.S. sailors and Marines to enter the city and seize the customs house to interdict the arms shipment. Local Mexican forces fought the American invaders in the streets of Vera Cruz. Nineteen Americans and hundreds of Mexicans died in the battle. Although the U.S. invasion was intended to overthrow General Huerta, the American actions offended Mexicans of all political persuasions who viewed the U.S. actions as an affront to their nationalism and a threat to their independence. Appalled at the bloodshed that he had provoked, a chastened Wilson permitted mediation of the U.S.–Mexican dispute by Argentina, Brazil, and Chile. Mediation failed, but Huerta's rivals defeated him in battle and forced his abdication in July 1914. Carranza took power. Wilson withdrew American forces from Vera Cruz and extended diplomatic recognition to the new leader.

The Mexican revolution soon turned violent again when Carranza tried to crush one of the leading generals who had helped him achieve power, the former bandit, Francisco "Pancho" Villa. Sporadic fighting occurred between Carranza's and Villa's forces during 1915. On March 9, 1916, General Villa, who perceived Wilson to be an ally of Carranza, led his forces across the border and attacked the American town of Columbus, New Mexico, killing seventeen Americans before U.S. soldiers drove his forces back into Mexico.

Wilson reacted to Villa's daring raid by ordering the U.S. Army under the Command of General John J. "Black Jack" Pershing to invade Mexico and capture Pancho Villa. A force of some ten thousand U.S. soldiers eventually found themselves 350 miles into Mexico without ever spotting Villa's elusive forces. Instead, Pershing's soldiers found themselves fighting two pitched battles with Carranza's federal troops in April and June. Again, Wilson's military intervention had managed to anger and frighten all Mexicans.

On February 5, 1917, only when it became evident that the United States would soon enter World War I, did Wilson withdraw the U.S. Army from Mexico. Impending war in Europe forced Wilson to abandon his self-righteous and futile efforts to direct the political destiny of Mexico. Even so, U.S. cavalry units continued to patrol the U.S.–Mexican border regions until 1920 when Alvaro Obregon overthrew Carranza's government and the Mexican revolution finally ran its course. During the decade that revolution tore Mexico apart, U.S. efforts to influence the course of the upheaval served merely to increase Mexican animosity towards the United States. The chief legacy of Wilson's meddling has been Mexican resentment and mistrust of the United States.

The United States policed the Caribbean region during the Progressive Era for several reasons. American security and prosperity required order in these small, poor nations. Washington would not tolerate disorders that might threaten its new canal across Panama. Order also protected America's growing commerce and investments in Latin America. Between 1900 and 1917, American exports to Latin American increased from $132 million to $309 million. Imports from Latin America increased even more. American investments in Caribbean countries in sugar, tobacco, bananas, coffee, transportation, and banking expanded rapidly. Progressive diplomats also projected their reform urges outwardly. They wanted to remake Latin American societies in the image of the United States. Progressive idealists assumed all people, if given the chance, wanted to be like Americans; and, if they could be like Americans, they would be greatly improved. President Woodrow Wilson asserted "every nation needs to be drawn into the tutelage of America."

A salient characteristic of American foreign policy between the Spanish-American War and U.S. entry into World War I was insensitivity to the nationalism of other people. Americans did not understand or take seriously the Filipino resistance to American colonial domination, Cuban anger over the restrictions of the Platt Amendment, Colombian outrage over U.S. support of the Panamanian insurrection, or Mexican resentment over Wilsonian interventionism. The American empire that evolved comprised few colonies; it was an informal empire characterized by economic and political control instead of formal annexation and governance. The informal American empire, administered by paternalistic military officers, bankers, and reformers, many of whom displayed a contempt for the native people's culture, politics, and economies, wounded their national pride and infringed upon the sovereignty of their governments—all in the name of national security, profits, democracy, efficiency, progress, public health, and saving souls.

American foreign policy toward Europe during the Progressive Era was governed by three principles: (1) Europeans should not intervene in Western Hemispheric affairs now that American military force backed the Monroe Doctrine. (2) America should stay out of European affairs. When Roosevelt intervened to mediate a conflict between France and Germany over Morocco in 1906, he was criticized for entangling the United States in a European problem. (3) American interests were best served by cooperating internationally with the British, the world's preeminent power.

Possession of the Philippines and implementation of the Open Door policy had thrust the United States into Asian affairs. In the Progressive Era, American policy toward Asia was dominated by relations with Japan, a rising Asian power. When imperial conflicts over Manchuria and Korea provoked Japan and Russia to war in 1904, Japan scored quick victories. President Roosevelt mediated an end to the war at a conference in Portsmouth, New Hampshire, in 1905, trying to preserve the balance of power in the Far East. He failed. Later that year, the Taft-Katsura Agreement conceded Japanese control of Korea in exchange for a Japanese promise not to attack the American colony in the Philippine Islands. Roosevelt sent the American "Great White Fleet" on a world tour in 1907 and 1908 to impress the Japanese with American naval might. The Japanese were duly impressed, gave the Americans a lavish welcome, and began building bigger ships as soon as the Americans left. In 1908, the Root-Takahira Agreement recognized Japanese interests in Manchuria in exchange for another Japanese pledge to respect American colonial possessions in Asia.

Despite these arguments, United States–Japanese relations were not harmonious. The Japanese were offended by the racist mistreatment of Japanese in California during the Progressive Era. American economic activities in China also alarmed the Japanese, who worked to increase their economic concessions in that country. In the long run, Japanese–American relations would founder on conflicts over China, and the result would be World War II in Asia.

EUROPE GOES TO WAR

War erupted in Europe in August 1914, to the surprise and horror of most Americans. It had many causes, including decades of imperialistic rivalries over trade and colonies. By the first decade of the twentieth century, the great powers of Europe had joined two rival coalitions, each armed to the teeth. The Triple Alliance joined together Germany, Austria-Hungary, and Italy. The Triple Entente combined Britain, France, and Russia. All members had economic and territorial ambitions that involved them in the affairs of unstable countries and provinces in the Balkan peninsula. A series of crises in the Balkans caught the great powers of Europe in a chain of events that propelled them to war. Within the Balkans, Slavic nationalists sought to build a major power by prying territories from the Austro-Hungarian Empire and adding them to Serbia. One of these territories was Bosnia, which contained a large Serbian population. On June 28, 1914, at Sarajevo, in Bosnia, the heir to the Austrian throne, Archduke Franz Ferdinand, was assassinated by a Serbian terrorist, Gavrilo Princips.

Austria, backed by Germany, delivered an ultimatum to Serbia. Serbia appealed for help from its major ally, Russia. When Austria declared war on Serbia in late July, Russia began mobilizing her vast armies. Germany asked Russia to stop her mobilization. The Russians refused, and the Germans, convinced war was coming, declared war on Russia August 1 and on Russia's ally, France, two days later. Germany quickly followed these declarations of war with an invasion of neutral Belgium that was part of a preconceived plan to attack the French in order to defeat them quickly and avoid fighting a two-front war against France in the west and her ally Russia to the east. Germany's attack on Belgium brought the British into the war on August 4. Later, Turkey and Bulgaria joined Germany and Austria-Hungary. Japan joined the Entente powers, as did Italy after being freed from the Triple Alliance in 1915. (Germany and the nations allied with it were called the Central Powers. The nations allied in the Entente were called the Allies.) Six weeks after the assassination at Sarajevo, Europe was at war.

UNNEUTRAL NEUTRALITY

When the war began, nearly all Americans assumed that the United States would never become involved. There appeared to be no vital American interests at stake; it was a European war over European issues. As one American put it, the war was "none of our business." No one expected the war to last more than four to six months; "it should be over by Christmas," said the pundits.

World War I, 1914–1918.   *Source:* Moss, *Rise of Modern America*, p. 101.

President Wilson's response to the outbreak of war was an effort to isolate America from its effects; he declared America to be neutral. In a speech delivered before the Senate, he urged his countrymen to be neutral in their thoughts as well as acts. The United States, he asserted, would stand as an inspiring example of peace and prosperity in a deranged world. He also believed that the United States had to remain neutral; otherwise, he feared that its "mixed populations would wage war on each other." The war, he said, was one "with which we have nothing to do, whose causes cannot reach us."

Wilson's appeal for neutrality and unity at home proved impossible to attain. Ethnic groups took sides. Many German Americans and Irish Americans sided with the Central Powers. Americans of British, French, and Russian ancestry cheered the Allies. A large majority of Americans were drawn to the Allied side. They viewed the war as a struggle between democracy and autocracy. Germany's invasion of neutral Belgium at the outset of the war convinced many Americans that Germans were international outlaws, barbarian defilers of helpless innocents. Clever British propaganda reinforced this view of Germans as enemies of civilization.

America's economic ties to the Allies also made genuine neutrality impossible. War orders from France and Britain flowed into American farms and businesses, promoting a roaring wartime prosperity. In 1914, U.S. exports to the Allies totaled $753 million; in 1916, that figured soared to nearly $3 billion. During that same period, trade with Germany tumbled from $345 million to a paltry $29 million. Much of the war trade with the Allies was financed with credit extended by U.S. banks. They loaned the Allies $2.3 billion during the neutrality period. The Germans received only $27 million. President Wilson had initially banned bank loans to all belligerents in the hopes of shortening the war. He reversed himself when he saw that the war was going to be a protracted struggle. And, he understood that the Allied war trade had become important to the American economy. If credits were not made available to the Allies, their purchases of American goods would fall sharply, hurting manufacturers, farmers, and workers in this country.

Germany viewed the commercial and financial ties between the United States and the Allies as giving its enemies access to supposedly neutral American arsenals and credits. Wilson responded to German complaints by insisting that if America cut its ties with the Allies that would be an unneutral act favoring the Germans since under international law, the British, who controlled the seas, could, at their own risk, trade with neutrals. He maintained that it was Germany's responsibility to stop the trade with an effective blockade of the Allies. Wilson's view that American neutrality policy accorded with international law was true; British control of the seas turned this policy in favor of the Allies.

Wilson and nearly all his leading advisers were pro-Ally in the general sense that they preferred an Allied to a Central Powers victory. They believed that American interests and ideals would fare better in a postwar world that was dominated by the British rather than one that was dominated by Germany. Wilson envisioned a postwar world made safe for Progressive foreign policy principles of free-market capitalism and political democracy. He believed that only a free and prosperous world could ensure perpetual peace.

Although it is accurate to say that popular pro-Ally sentiments, economic and financial ties to the Allies, and Wilson's pro-Ally preference made genuine neutrality impossible, it is important to stress that Wilson did not seek to bring the United States into the war. He wanted desperately to avoid war, and he crafted a foreign policy that avoided war for nearly three years at the same time that it protected vital American interests and national honor. Repeatedly, Wilson sent his personal representative, Colonel Edward House, to Europe to try to mediate an end to the conflict. In early 1917, Wilson cried: "It would be a crime against civilization if we went in." No modern president has felt a greater horror of war and none tried harder to avoid engulfing his people in war than this profoundly religious and idealistic leader.

But Americans got caught in an Allies-Central Powers conflict. The British were determined to use their sea power to cripple the German economy and to undermine its war machine. An integral part of the British naval war against Germany was to sever its trade with neutrals like the United States. Britannia, ruling the waves, declared a loose, illegal blockade of Central Powers ports. The British defined contraband broadly to include foodstuffs and strategic raw materials. (*Contraband* was trade with belligerents forbidden to neutrals, traditionally arms and munitions.) The British also harassed neutral shipping. American ships hauling goods to Germany seldom reached their destinations. To neutralize German submarines, the British violated international law by arming their merchant ships, hauling armaments in passenger ships, and flying the flags of neutrals, including the U.S. flag.

President Wilson frequently protested British violations of American neutral rights. He told English leaders that neutrals had the right to ship noncontraband goods to all belligerents and pointed out, correctly, that the British definition of contraband was contrary to an international agreement that the British themselves had signed. The British defused American protests by easing their blockade periodically and by paying American companies for confiscated cargoes. Two other factors prevented American-British relations from deteriorating seriously because of British violations of American neutral rights. First, expanding Allied purchases of American goods more than made up for the lost Central Powers markets; the American war economy continued to expand. Second, the Germans violated American neutral rights by sinking ships and killing people, which made British offenses appear mild by comparison. British violations of international law were annoying, sometimes outrageous, but the English never sank any American ships nor killed any American citizens.

Germany, for its part, was determined to sever Allied-American trade. The German navy had conceded control of the seas to the British navy at the outset of the war. To try to cut the commercial links between the United States and the Allies, Germany resorted to submarine warfare. In February 1915, the German government announced that it was creating a war zone around the British Isles, a submarine counterblockade: All enemy ships entering the war zone would be sunk. They also warned all neutrals to avoid the war zone lest they be attacked by mistake, and told passengers from neutral nations to stay off enemy passenger ships. President Wilson reacted to this edict quickly and firmly. He told the German leaders that if any American property or lives were lost in the war zone, Germany would be held to "strict accountability." His message amounted to an ultimatum, a threat of war if the German attacks killed Americans.

International law in force at the time required commerce destroyers to warn merchant or passenger ships before attacking them in order to allow passengers and crew to disembark safely. Such rules assumed passengers and merchant crews were civilians, innocent noncombatants, and therefore exempt from attack. These rules predated the development of the submarine. Wilson refused to acknowledge the limitations of submarines that made it impossible for them to warn their intended targets and still function effectively. If submarines surfaced to warn ships, they would lose their chief advantage, surprise. Any merchant or passenger ship could easily outrun a surfaced submarine, and avoid its torpedoes. A surfaced submarine was an easy target for deck gunfire and was vulnerable to ramming, and the time it took for crew and passengers to debark usually gave a ship's radioman opportunity to call in nearby destroyers to attack the waiting U-boat. To Germans, it appeared that Wilson's strict accountability policy denied them effective use of the one weapon they possessed that could disrupt the Allies' ties with American producers and bankers, and enable Germany to win the war. Engaged in a brutal struggle for national survival, the Germans deeply resented Wilson's strict accountability policy with its dated, legalistic views of submarine warfare. Here lay a conflict between Germany and the United States that had ominous potential.

AMERICA GOES TO WAR

Since the Germans promised not to attack American ships in the war zone, an agreement they honored until the spring of 1917, the issue became the right of Americans to sail and work on belligerent ships. Germany's sinking of the British luxury liner *Lusitania* forced the issue. The 785-foot-long ship had left New York on May 1, 1915, with 1,257 passengers and a crew of 702 on board. It was also hauling much dubious cargo. The ship's manifest for its last voyage reads like a contraband shopping list. The *Lusitania* was hauling 4,200 cases of rifle ammunition, 1,250 cases of shrapnel, and 18 boxes of percussion caps. Other contraband cargo included motorcycle parts, metals, and cotton goods. Before the liner set sail, New York newspapers carried announcements from the German embassy warning passengers that Allied ships were "liable to destruction" in the war zone. Passengers ignored the warning, confident that the giant luxury liner could outrun any German submarines or torpedoes. At 2:10 P.M. local time on May 7, and 12 miles off the southern Irish coast, a German submarine, U-20, torpedoed the

Lusitania. The ship sank quickly in the dark Celtic Sea, carrying 1,195 people to their deaths, including 123 Americans.

Most Americans were horrified and outraged by the attack. Wilson angrily dismissed the idea that because the ship was hauling contraband, the Germans were justified in killing nearly 1,200 innocent people. But neither the American people nor Wilson wanted war over the incident. Wilson steered a middle path between Secretary of State William Jennings Bryan, who wanted to forbid Americans from traveling on belligerent ships and to prevent Allied passenger ships from hauling ammunition, and Theodore Roosevelt who was ready for war with Germany over the incident. Wilson sent a note to the German government insisting on the right of Americans to travel on belligerent ships. He also demanded that German submarines protect passenger ships and pay for U.S. losses. When Wilson refused to consider banning American travelers on Allied passenger ships, Bryan resigned. His replacement, Robert Lansing, supported Wilson's position.

At first, the Germans refused to apologize for the sinking of the *Lusitania* or to curb their submarines. Further notes were exchanged. To avoid war with America, the Germans eventually expressed regret for the loss of life and agreed to never again attack a passenger ship without warning. To charges from his critics that he was pursuing a double standard that favored the Allies, Wilson replied that the British were only violating property rights, whereas the Germans were violating human rights and murdering civilians.

On August 30, 1915, a German submarine torpedoed another British liner, the *Arabic;* two Americans were killed. The Germans hastened to apologize and pledged never again to attack passenger liners without warning. The *Arabic* incident fueled a debate in this country over the propriety of American passengers riding on belligerent ships. Critics of Wilson's "strict accountability" policy wanted the president to require American passengers to travel on American ships in the war zone. They believed such an order would avoid further incidents and the risks of war. They sponsored a congressional resolution prohibiting Americans from traveling on armed merchant ships or passenger ships hauling contraband, but the resolution failed to pass either house.

In March 1916, a German submarine attacked a French channel steamer, the *Sussex,* mistaking it for a minesweeper. Four Americans were injured. An angry Wilson ordered the Germans to restrict their submarines or he would sever diplomatic relations. The Germans, embarrassed by the incident and not wishing war with the United States, pledged not to attack merchant ships without warning. They observed the "*Sussex* pledge" for the rest of the year. Relations with Germany stabilized during 1916. "Strict accountability" was working. Meanwhile, the British stepped up their blockade activities, and their violations of U.S. neutral rights escalated. Relations between the United States and the British deteriorated as relations with Germany improved. A nearly genuine neutrality prevailed for much of 1916.

Wilson had to seek reelection in November 1916. He faced a formidable challenge from the Republicans. The party was reunited, its Progressive Party insurgents having returned to the fold. Republicans nominated an able candidate, Supreme Court Associate Justice Charles Evans Hughes, formerly a reform governor of New York. The 1916 presidential campaign was bitter, revealing deep divisions within America. Hughes attacked Wilson's social policies and accused him of not defending American neutral rights adequately against German assaults. The Democrats accused Hughes of being pro-German and Wilson implied that anyone who thought he was pro-British was disloyal. The key issue in the campaign was American foreign policy toward the warring powers. The Democratic Party campaigned on the slogan "He kept us out of war," referring to Wilson's policy, which had extracted the "*Sussex* pledge" from the Germans. And, Wilson's admirable record of achievement as a domestic reformer appealed to Progressive voters in both parties.

Hughes was favored to win when the campaign began, but he proved a poor campaigner. He was not a good speaker, and he inadvertently offended California Progressive Republican leaders and lost the presidency. In a close election, California, normally Republican, went for Wilson, giving him a narrow victory. A difference of fewer than 4,000 votes in California would have removed Wilson from the White House. His party fared no better. The Democrats retained a narrow majority in the Senate, but in the new House there would be 216 Democrats, 210 Republicans, and 6 Independents. It was not clear at election time which party would control the new Congress.

Despite the campaign slogan, Wilson knew that American neutrality was precarious as long as the war continued. A German submarine skipper could provoke a crisis any time he was tempted to ignore the "*Sussex* pledge." Wilson sent Colonel House on another mission to European capitals to find a formula that could serve as a basis for a cease-fire. He also appealed directly to the heads of the warring governments for "a peace without victory." His peace efforts failed because of events beyond his control.

The German government made a fateful decision to resume unrestricted submarine warfare on February 1, 1917. Henceforth, all ships, belligerent or neutral, warship or merchant, would be attacked on sight in the war zone. The Germans had decided to take a calculated risk, what they called their "gambler's throw," because their situation had grown desperate. The British blockade was severely pinching the German and Austro-Hungarian economies. Inflation was rampant and starvation widespread in both countries. The Germans gambled that an all-out submarine war would enable them to cut off shipments of vital foodstuffs and ammunition to the Allies, permitting Germany to win the war before American troops could be mobilized and ferried across the Atlantic in enough strength to affect the outcome. They knew their decision would provoke American entry into the war, but they assumed that they would win the race against time. They also believed that they were fated to lose a long-running war of attrition, for the Allies had superior resources—more population, more manufacturing capacity, and Allied sea power gave them access to their overseas colonies and the American arsenal. So they chose their "gambler's throw."

Wilson, as expected, promptly severed diplomatic relations in response to Germany's direct challenge to American neutrality, but he did not seek a declaration of war immediately. British Prime Minister Lloyd George and Senate Republican leader Henry Cabot Lodge accused Wilson of cowardice. The Germans began sinking American ships. During February and March 1917, German submarines sank scores of Allied merchant ships. On April 1, the British had only a six weeks' supply of grain on hand. Coal, sugar, and potatoes were scarce. The British people were feeling the privations of war. Once mighty lords of international banking, the British by the spring of 1917 had mortgaged themselves heavily to American creditors because of their purchases of huge quantities of ammunition. The British treasury was approaching bankruptcy. Lloyd George feared a combination of hunger, bankruptcy, and submarine warfare might force the British to accept Germany's peace terms, enabling them to win their "gambler's throw."

The French were also suffering that spring of 1917. General Robert Nivelle had tried to break the stalemated slaughter in the trenches with a spring offensive against the Germans at Champagne. The French fell into a trap set for them by the German commander, General Ludendorff, and were slaughtered. After sustaining two weeks' of massive losses under hellish conditions, the French soldiers mutinied. Nivelle was dismissed in disgrace. The French, exhausted and demoralized, were incapable of continuing the war much longer without help.

The spring of 1917 was also a fateful season for the other major Allied power, Russia. After nearly three years of war, the Russians had lost millions of men; czarist generals had herded unarmed peasants into fierce battles only to have them slaughtered like sheep. The civilian population had also been subjected to severe privation and suffering. The czar's government, aloof from the Russian people, could neither provide moral leadership nor organize the war effort efficiently. Having lost control of his army, the czar abdicated on March 15. Two days later, Russia became a republic for the first time in its history; a provisional government led by Alexander Kerensky came to power. Kerensky pledged to honor Russian treaty and commercial obligations and to continue the war.

The German chancellor, Theobald von Bethmann-Hollweg, watched Russian political developments closely. Aware that Russia was riven with factionalism, he decided that Germany ought to support the most extreme groups within Russia to promote chaos and cripple the Russian war effort. He arranged for a small group of radical Russian exiles living in Switzerland to return to Russia. The radicals, led by a man calling himself V. I. Lenin (his real name was Vladimir Ilich Ulyanov), traveled across Germany on a sealed train, and they were forbidden to get off the train while it was in Germany. Bethmann-Hollweg wanted to make sure that the radical political virus would infect only Russia. In mid-April, Lenin and his small band of "Bolsheviks" got off the train at Petrograd's Finland Station. In November 1917, he led a rebellion that toppled Kerensky's fragile government and took Russia out of the war. Lenin's goal was to establish a Communist state in Russia and to promote a socialist revolution, which would sweep across Europe in the wake of war. Germany was one of the first countries to experience a Communist uprising.

In late February, the British gave President Wilson a secret telegram they had intercepted and decoded, which was addressed to the German minister in Mexico from the German Foreign Secretary Arthur Zimmermann. The telegram instructed the minister to tell the Mexican government that if Mexico joined a military alliance against the United States, Germany would help the Mexicans recover their territory lost to the United States in 1848 in the Mexican-American war. Wilson took the Zimmermann note seriously. At the time, United States-Mexican relations were severely strained because Wilson had twice ordered American troops into Mexico during the Mexican revolution, and the two countries had verged on war. Soon after learning of the note, Wilson went before Congress seeking what he called an "armed neutrality." He hoped by arming American merchant ships to forestall war. As Congress debated his request, he released the Zimmermann note to the media. A wave of anti-German sentiment swept the country. Public opinion moved closer to war.

But a group of antiwar senators including Robert La Follette filibustered Wilson's armed neutrality proposal to death. Furious, Wilson excoriated them as a "little group of willful men, representing no opinion but their own, who have rendered this great nation helpless and contemptible." He then armed the ships on his own executive authority. But his action could not prevent German submarines from sinking American merchant ships. Cries for war resounded across the land.

Since the German decision to resume submarine warfare in mid-January, Wilson had hesitated to take the country to war for many reasons. He confided to a friend: "It was necessary for me, by very slow stages indeed and with the most genuine purpose to avoid war to lead the country on to a single way of thinking." Since the war began, Americans had disagreed about America's relationship to it and what course of action the nation should take. Also, in the spring of 1917, America stood at the end of nearly two decades of divisive political and social upheaval. The concentration of economic wealth and power, the many Progressive efforts to tame the trusts, the serious strikes, and the arrival of over 12 million immigrants since 1900 had opened deep social fissures. Wilson did not want to burden American society further with the strains of a major war effort. He knew what the war was doing to the political and social structures of the European belligerents. He asserted that "Every reform we have won will be lost if we get into this war." The President also feared the problems posed by the presence of millions of foreign-born residents in the country. He was particularly worried about the loyalty of those who had recently emigrated from Germany and the other Central Powers nations. If America went to war against Germany, could it count on the loyalty of its citizens who had come from the Fatherland?

But the time for decision had come. On March 20, Wilson met with his cabinet; its members unanimously favored war with Germany. The next day, Wilson called the newly elected Sixty-fifth Congress to special session beginning on April 2 to receive his war message. The President then secluded himself to prepare his speech.

He went before a hushed Congress the evening of April 2, 1917, to deliver a solemn, subdued speech. Missing were Wilson's usual rhetorical flights and resounding cadences. He recounted the many German violations of international law and American rights. He condemned German sabotage and spying within the United States and denounced the proposed German alliance with Mexico. He urged Congress to "formally accept the status of belligerent which has thus been thrust upon it."

Wilson then informed the assembled legislators what war would mean and what he intended to do. He planned to lend billions of dollars to the Allied nations already at war with Germany, to increases taxes to finance the costly American war effort, and to implement conscription. He also made it clear that he would insist more than ever on the preeminence of a strong executive. Although he acknowledged the loyalty of most Americans of German birth, he warned "if there should be disloyalty, it will be dealt with a firm hand of repression." An explosion of applause from the audience greeted that remark. As he neared the end of his speech, Wilson, with matchless eloquence, explained American war aims:

> The world must be made safe for democracy. Its peace must be planted upon the tested foundations of political liberty. We have no selfish ends to serve. We desire no conquest, no dominion. We seek no indemnities for ourselves, no material compensation for the sacrifices we shall freely make. We are but one of the champions of the rights of mankind . . . .
>
> It is a fearful thing to lead this great peaceful people into war, into the most terrible and disastrous of all wars, civilization itself seeming to be in the balance. But the right is more precious than peace, and we shall fight for the things which we have always carried nearest our hearts,—for democracy, . . . for a universal dominion of the right, . . . and make the world itself at last free. To such a task we can dedicate our lives and our fortunes, everything that we are and everything that we have, with the pride of those who know that the day has come when America is privileged to spend her blood and her might for the principles that gave her birth and happiness and the peace that she has treasured. God helping her, she can do no other.[2]

Wilson asked the Congress to commit the country to a distant war that had already butchered 7 million men and promised to add millions more names to the ledger of death before it ended. He had called for high taxes and the drafting of millions of young Americans who would be sent into that war. He had asked Congress to accept the expansion of presidential power, and he had called for the enforced loyalty of all Americans in a cause to which millions of his fellow citizens were hostile or indifferent.

Wilson's request for a war resolution provoked an extended debate among members of Congress that lasted four days. The outcome was a foregone conclusion. The proponents of war knew they had an overwhelming majority of the votes. But that reality did not inhibit the enemies of war who spoke against the resolution. The supporters of the resolution shared Wilson's view of the war as a struggle between the forces of democracy and the forces of autocratic tyranny, with America aligning itself on the side of virtue in a profound ideological conflict to

---

[2]Taken from a copy of Wilson's War Message found in Armin Rappaport, *Sources in American Diplomacy* (New York: Macmillan, 1966), pp. 211–12.

make the world a safe place for democratic nations. Some members of the Senate, like Warren G. Harding of Ohio, voted for war to uphold American rights that had been violated by German submarines.

Opponents of the resolution considered it hypocritical to demand war in the name of democracy. They considered the European conflict a contest between rival imperialisms. As they saw it, only territory and markets were at stake, not democratic principles. They also pointed out that many ardent supporters of the war were among the most determined opponents of Progressive reform efforts to make American institutions more democratic. Some midwestern Progressive opponents of war viewed the conflict as benefiting the rich at the expense of ordinary citizens. Republican Senator George Norris of Nebraska passionately declared that

> War brings no prosperity to the great mass of common patriotic citizens. . . . We are going into war upon the command of gold.[3]

Norris's Progressive colleague, Senator Robert La Follette, echoed his views. La Follette also charged the Wilson administration with having forced the war upon America by pursuing a pro-British neutrality policy. Other foes of war adhered to traditional isolationist views; they believed intervening in a European war was contrary to American interests and values. Jeannette Rankin, the first woman ever to sit in Congress, spoke with tears coursing down her cheeks: "I want to stand by my country, but I cannot vote for war."

Six senators and fifty representatives finally voted against American entry into the war, more than opposed any other war resolution in American history. There were others who opposed the war, but voted for it anyway. But all opponents of the war resolution made it clear that their opposition would cease once war was officially declared.

Wilson took the United States to war in the spring of 1917 for many reasons: to defend democracy, international law, morality, and the nation's honor. Wilson stressed these idealistic war aims in his stirring peroration. The United States also went to war to protect its commerce and national security. Further, Wilson and his advisers feared that the Allies could lose the war if the United States did not enter on their side. Another reason for entering the war was to ensure an American role at the peace conference. Wilson hoped to be a major influence in shaping the postwar world along Progressive lines; he perceived that unless America participated in the war, it would be excluded from the peace conference. Wilson took the United States to war not only to win the conflict, but also to shape the future.

The decisive event that brought the United States into World War I was the German decision to resume unrestricted submarine warfare in early 1917. This decision nullified Wilson's neutrality policy based upon "strict accountability" and

---

[3]Quoted in David Kennedy, *Over Here: The First World War and American Society* (New York: Oxford University, 1980), p. 19.

forced Wilson to choose between war and appeasement. Wilson's critics have cited his rigid conception of international law, which did not fit the reality of submarine tactics. They have also faulted his unyielding defense of the right of Americans to travel on belligerent ships, even those hauling contraband. But most Americans supported his neutrality policy, and when he told the people on April 2, 1917, that "neutrality was no longer feasible nor desirable," most supported his request for war.

OVER THERE

The United States had been preparing for possible combat during the years of neutrality. As early as 1915, President Wilson began planning a large military buildup. His proposals triggered a great debate within the nation over preparedness. Many congressmen and senators opposed the buildup. Pacifist Progressives led by Jane Addams formed an antiwar coalition, the American Union Against Militarism. Businessmen like Andrew Carnegie, who in 1910 had established the Carnegie Endowment for International Peace, helped finance peace groups. Henry Ford spent $500,000 in 1915 to send a "peace ark" to Europe to urge the European powers to accept a negotiated settlement.

Despite opposition from pacifists both in and out of government, Congress enacted the National Defense Act of 1916. It increased the size of the National Guard and established summer training camps for soldiers. The Navy Act established a three-year naval expansion program. To finance these expensive preparedness measures, Congress enacted the Revenue Act of 1916. It was a progressive tax increase, calling for a surtax on high incomes and corporate profits, a tax on large estates, and increased taxes on munitions makers. Despite these preparedness activities, the United States was not ready for war in the spring of 1917. The Army was small and equipped with obsolete weapons. Its most recent military action had been trying, and failing, to catch the elusive Pancho Villa in the wilds of northern Mexico. Its war planning was out of date, concerned with fending off a Japanese attack on the West Coast and a German invasion of the Caribbean.

Soon after the United States entered the war, Congress enacted a Selective Service Act implementing conscription. Antidraft forces challenged the constitutionality of the draft, but the Supreme Court quickly upheld it as a proper exercise of the "implied powers" principle. It required that all males between the ages of twenty and thirty register for the draft. In 1918, the ages for draftees changed to between eighteen and forty-five years of age. By war's end, 24 million men had registered for the draft, nearly 5 million had been conscripted, and 2 million had been sent to fight in France. Millions of draft-age men got deferments because they worked in war industries or had dependents. Over 300,000 evaded the draft by refusing to register or not responding when called. About 300,000 men volunteered for duty. The typical "doughboy" was a draftee, twenty-two years old, white, single, and with a seventh-grade education. Eighteen percent of American troops

Black troops fought in all-black, segregated units during World War I. This photo shows troopers from the 369th Infantry Regiment, who saw heavy combat on the Western Front in 1918. *Source:* National Archives.

who served in World War I were foreign-born, mostly from the European countries at war.

About 400,000 black men were drafted or volunteered. The American military, reflecting the society from which it was recruited, was segregated during World War I. African American soldiers were kept in all-black units and not allowed to enter many programs. They were not allowed to become aviators or to join the Marines. A separate officers' training program provided African American Army officers, who were never allowed to command white soldiers.

Even though the United States entered the war belatedly, and on a smaller scale than the other major combatants, its armed forces played major roles in the war. The Navy performed crucial service. In April 1917, when America entered the war, German submarines were sinking Allied merchant ships at a rate of 870,000 tons per month. American destroyers, teamed with their British counterparts, reduced, and eventually stopped, the submarine threat. American naval planners helped to develop the convoy system, in which destroyers and other warships escorted merchants ships across the Atlantic, effectively screening out German submarines. American troop ships were convoyed to France, and all 2 million men arrived safely. As Germany's plan for winning the war crucially depended on submarines, the U.S. Navy made a major contribution to the Allied victory.

As American troops arrived in France, General John J. Pershing, the commander of the American Expeditionary Force (AEF) refused to allow them to join Allied units. He refused to let American soldiers be fed into the mincing machine. Allied commanders had locked themselves into suicidal trench warfare, producing years of stalemate and ghastly casualty rates. Zig-zag trenches fronted by barbed wires and mines stretched across the 200-mile-long Western Front, which ran from the French channel coast, curving across northeastern France, to the Swiss border. In front of the trenches lay a region called "no man's land," cratered by heavy artillery bombardments. Allied soldiers, upon order, would charge the German lines on the other side of this deadly frontier. Rapid-fire machine guns mowed them down and chlorine gas poisoned them. Little territory would be gained yet the human cost was great. Then it would be the German's turn to be ordered to die in a futile charge. The stalemated slaughter went on for over three years. Before the advent of the Americans, the blood of millions of German, French, and British soldiers had spilled over the killing fields of northeastern France.

At the Battle of the Somme in 1916, the British and the French launched their greatest offensive of the war, losing 600,000 men, killed or wounded, to gain 125 square miles of territory. The Germans lost 500,000 men defending that small piece of blood-stained ground. The Germans also tried to break the impasse in 1916 by laying siege to a crucial French fortress at Verdun. The German strategy at Verdun was simple and horrible: Besiege the fort indefinitely, bleed France dry, relying on the numerical superiority of German manpower to guarantee eventual victory. The siege ended six months later with 350,000 French and 330,000 German soldiers dead. The front had not moved.

The entry of American men and material into World War I determined its outcome. With both sides on the verge of exhaustion, the arrival of fresh American forces tipped the balance decisively toward the Allies. Had America not entered the war, a German victory was possible. American forces began combat in March 1918 when the Germans launched a great spring offensive, their armies now strengthened by the arrival of thousands of battle-hardened veterans from the Eastern Front. In late May, advance units reached the Marne River, near the village of Château-Thierry, 50 miles from Paris. Early in June, 27,500 American soldiers fought their first important battle, driving the Germans out of Château-Thierry and nearby Belleau Wood. The size of the American forces expanded rapidly. In early July, near the Marne, 270,000 Americans joined the fighting, helping to flatten a German bulge between Reims and Soissons. On July 15, the German Army threw everything into one final effort to smash through to Paris, but in three days they were finished. Chancellor Bethman-Hollweg said, "On the Eighteenth, even the most optimistic among us knew that all was lost. The history of the world was played out in three days." The war had turned in favor of the Allies.

The Western Front.   *Source: Moss, Rise of Modern America, p. 115.*

The most important campaign in which American doughboys fought was the Meuse-Argonne Offensive in the fall of 1918. In forty days and nights of continuous fighting, U.S. troops sustained heavy casualties on their way to victory. *Source:* National Archives.

Between September 12 and 16, the American First Army, now 500,000 strong and fighting with French forces, wiped out a German thrust at Saint-Mihiel. Two weeks later, the Americans began their most important battle of the war: 1.2 million "doughboys" launched the Meuse-Argonne Offensive. In forty days and nights of heavy slugging in the region of the Argonne forest, the Americans eventually fought their way through the formidable defense of the Hindenburg Line. To the West, French and British forces staged similar drives. On November 1, the Allies broke through the German center and raced forward. On November 11, with German armies in full retreat and the German submarine threat neutralized by the Anglo-American convoy system, Germany signed an armistice. They were also lured toward an armistice by offers of a generous peace from President Wilson. After four years of killing, the war had ended. The Allies were victorious. The Americans had lost 48,909 men killed, with another 230,000 wounded. Losses to disease, mainly influenza, eventually ran the death total to over 112,000.

Ten months before the Armistice, Wilson had outlined a peace plan called the Fourteen Points in a speech to Congress. The first five points incorporated liberal principles upon which the peace must be based: open negotiations, freedom of the seas, free trade, disarmament, and a colonial system designed to serve the needs of subject peoples. The next eight points called for territorial transfers within Europe to implement the principle of "self-determination," which would permit all people possessing a distinct history, language, and ethnic identity to live under governments of their own choosing. The fourteenth point created an international agency to oversee the new order:

a general association of nations ... formed ... for the purpose of affording mutual guarantees of political independence and territorial integrity to great and small states alike.[4]

In the final weeks of the war, Wilson lured the Germans into overthrowing the Kaiser and surrendering by promising them a peace based on the Fourteen Points. He then pressured the Allies into accepting the Fourteen Points, somewhat modified, as the basis for conducting the impending peace conference. It was brilliant diplomacy by Wilson. His efforts made him immensely popular among Europeans. He was the savior who had delivered them from a murderous war and promised a just and lasting peace.

THE HOME FRONT

The war experience had a profound effect on American lives and institutions. Government had to quickly mobilize a vast military force, gear the economy for war, and prepare the American people to meet the rigorous demands of belligerency. The state had intervened in American life in unprecedented ways, and tremendous power had been concentrated in Washington. The size, cost, and power of the central government increased drastically during the two years of American involvement in World War I. Business and government became partners for the duration of the war. Hundreds of new government agencies, staffed mostly by businessmen, came into being to manage the war effort. Many of these agencies clamped controls on the economy. The Railroad Administration took over operation of the nation's railroads when they had broken down under the strains of wartime usage. The federal government also took over operation of the telephone and telegraph companies to avert strikes. The largest and most powerful wartime agency was the War Industries Board (WIB), created in July 1917. Headed by a friend of Wilson's, financier Bernard Baruch, the WIB coordinated the war economy. As the main instrument for mobilizing U.S. industrial capacity, the WIB imposed on American industry a system of production and price schedules keyed to military requirements.

Inexperience and inefficiency caused waste and delays in mobilizing the American economy for war. But Wilson proved to be a strong war leader, and America eventually delivered enough men and material to win the war. About 25 percent of American production went into the war effort. Farmers enjoyed boom years; they put more acreage into production, bought new farm machinery, and watched farm commodity prices soar. Farm income rose from $7.6 billion in 1914 to nearly $18 billion at war's end. Steel production doubled in wartime. The gross domestic product more than doubled between 1914 and 1920.

The most serious wartime economic problem was rampant inflation. One cause was increased demand for goods created by Allied and U.S. government purchases. But the major cause was governmental refusal to set price controls or ration

[4]Taken from a copy of The Covenant of the League of Nations found in Rappaport, *Sources in American Diplomacy,* p. 218.

scarce commodities. The cost of living doubled between 1914 and 1920. The war cost about $34 billion. The government financed one-third of its cost through taxes. The remaining two-thirds came from borrowing, including the issuing of Liberty Bonds sold to the people.

The War Revenue Act enacted in October 1917 established a graduated personal income tax, a corporate income tax, an excess profits tax, and an increased excise taxes on several items. It drastically elevated taxes in the highest brackets, from a top of 13 percent to 77 percent during the war. The number of income tax returns filed increased from fewer than 500,000 when the war began to nearly 7 million at war's end! Despite the higher war taxes, corporate profits in wartime reached historic highs. Net corporate income rose from $4 billion in 1913 to over $7 billion in 1917.

The Revenue Act of 1917 effected a fiscal revolution in federal taxation. It greatly increased the importance of income taxes and made the principle of progression a permanent fixture of the national tax system. When the war began, about 25 percent of federal revenues derived from income taxes; at war's end, that figure had risen to 75 percent. Income taxes had become, and would remain, the mainstay of federal financing.

Organized labor prospered in wartime also. The president of the American Federation of Labor, Samuel Gompers, gave a no-strike pledge to the Wilson administration during wartime. He and other labor leaders also served on wartime government agencies. The National War Labor Board protected the right of workers to organize unions and to bargain collectively. Union membership rose from 2.7 million in 1916 to over 4 million in 1919. Wages rose and many workers won an eight-hour day, but sharp inflation canceled most of the economic gains made by workers.

Disadvantaged groups also benefited in wartime. With 16 percent of the workforce off fighting the war and with immigration curtailed, war industries turned to women, African Americans, and Hispanic Americans to fill job vacancies. Women entered many industrial trades hitherto closed to them. The movement of women into previously all-male job categories generated controversy. Women were often paid less than men for the same work and excluded from unions. When the war ended, most of the wartime gains women had made were lost.

War-generated economic opportunities opened up for African Americans also. About 500,000 blacks fled poverty and oppression in the South, heading north for Detroit, Chicago, and New York City where the war industries were located. Most African American migrants were young, unmarried men in search of work.

New jobs and improved living opportunities for blacks in wartime provoked a white backlash. The Ku Klux Klan revived. There were savage race riots in several cities. During the summer of 1919, race riots rocked over twenty northern cities. The worst violence occurred in Chicago. On a hot July day, an incident at a beach started the rioting. Stabbings, burnings, and shootings went on for days. Thirty-eight people died and over five hundred were injured before National Guardsmen restored order.

During the war, thousands of women, hitherto excluded from many industrial occupations, found work in war industries. The wartime economic performance of women was a major factor in their getting the vote in 1920.   *Source:* National Archives.

CIVIL LIBERTIES IN WARTIME

Civil liberties were also a casualty of war. The targets of abuse were German Americans whose loyalty was suspect and other Americans who refused to support the war effort. These dissenters included pacifists, conscientious objectors, socialists, tenant farmers in Oklahoma who rebelled against the draft, and Progressive reformers like Robert La Follette and Jane Addams.

Soon after the United States entered the war, President Wilson appointed George Creel, a Progressive journalist, to head a Committee on Public Information (CPI). The CPI was a government propaganda agency created at Wilson's request to promote the war effort. It hired writers, scholars, filmmakers, and artists to mobilize public opinion in support of Allied war aims, and to arouse anti-German sentiments. Creel enlisted seventy-five thousand "four-minute men" who gave short patriotic speeches at public gatherings explaining war aims and celebrating American national virtues. CPI urged people to spy on their neighbors and report "suspicious" behavior to the authorities.

For a time, there was vigorous debate between the supporters of the war and antiwar critics. Creel Committee speakers were the most prominent defenders of the American effort. Wilson himself provided the most potent ideological defense of the war when he called it a struggle to preserve democracy. Linking the war to democracy made it a crusade, tying it to the ancient doctrine of American mission. World War I became a war to save democracy, to save Europe from itself, and to redeem mankind. America would send its young manhood to rescue the Old World from itself. The child of Western Civilization would save its parents. Wilson, an eloquent student of American history, tapped deep ideological wellsprings of emotion, giving the war transcendent meaning. Most Americans embraced the notion of a great war to make the world a safe place for democratic governments. Against Wilson's and the Creel Committee's defenses of the war, the arguments of critics, however plausible, were ineffective. Isolationist, populist, and humanitarian arguments collapsed. The champions of war won easily the battle to define the symbolic meaning of the war and to win the allegiance of most citizens.

But their propaganda victory had its costs. Congress passed repressive legislation to curb dissent in wartime, which President Wilson strongly endorsed. The Espionage Act, enacted into law on June 5, 1917, gave the government powerful tools for suppressing opponents of war. It levied fines up to $10,000 and prison terms as long as twenty years for persons who obstructed military operations in wartime, and up to $5,000 fines and five-year sentences for use of the mails to violate the law. It also prohibited any statement intended to impede the draft or to promote military insubordination, and it gave the Postmaster General power to ban from the mails any publication he considered to be treasonous. Armed with the powers of the Espionage Act, Postmaster General Albert Burleson barred many German American and socialist publications from the mails.

The Sedition Act, enacted in 1918, was more severe than the Espionage Act. It made it a crime to obstruct the sale of war bonds or to use "disloyal, profane, scurrilous, or abusive" language against the government, the constitution, the flag, and the military uniforms. It made almost any publicly voiced criticism of government policy or the war effort a crime punishable by fines, imprisonment, or both. The Justice Department prosecuted over 2,000 people under the two acts and many more people were bullied into silence. Jane Addams came under Justice Department surveillance. The most famous victim of wartime repression was Eugene Debs, the Socialist Party leader. Debs, who opposed the war, delivered a speech to a Socialist convention gathered in Canton, Ohio, on June 16, 1918. He spoke for over two hours. His speech was a general indictment of the American economic system and a call for socialism. He only mentioned the war in one passage that follows:

> The master class has always declared the wars; the subject class has always fought the battles. The master class has had all to gain and nothing to lose, while the subject class has had nothing to gain and all to lose—especially their lives.[5]

Justice Department agents in the audience wrote down his words. Within two weeks, he was indicted by a federal grand jury for violating the Sedition Act on ten different counts. He was tried in September. During his trial, Debs acknowl-

---

[5]Quoted in Ray Ginger, *Eugene V. Debs: The Making of an American Radical* (New York: Collier Books, 1949), pp. 376–7.

edged the offending remarks. His defense consisted solely of having his attorneys argue that the Sedition Act violated the First Amendment and was therefore unconstitutional. His remarks were therefore within the boundaries of constitutionally protected free speech. His defense failed because the Supreme Court had previously upheld the constitutionality of both the Espionage and Sedition Acts on the grounds that in time of war the government can legitimately curb free speech.

A jury convicted Debs on three counts of obstructing the draft, and he was sentenced to ten years in federal prison. His attorneys appealed the conviction. On March 10, 1919, the Supreme Court sustained his conviction. Debs began serving his sentence in April at a federal penitentiary near Atlanta, Georgia. Debs remained in jail until December 1921, when he was pardoned by President Harding. While in prison, Debs ran for president on the Socialist Party ticket during the 1920 election, campaigning from his Atlanta jail cell. He got 920,000 votes, the most votes he ever received in his many presidential campaigns.

State and local governments also joined the war against dissent. Officials removed what they considered pro-German books from school and libraries. Iowa refused to allow any foreign languages to be taught in its public schools. Teachers who questioned or challenged the war were dismissed.

Encouraged by government actions, vigilante groups and superpatriots went after alleged enemies and traitors. They became proficient at bookburning, spying on their fellow citizens, harassing school teachers, vandalizing German-owned stores, and attacking socialists. Radical antiwar figures were frequent vigilante targets. In April 1918, a Missouri mob seized Robert Prager, a young man whose only crime was that he had been born in Germany. He was bound in an American flag, paraded through town, and then lynched. A jury acquitted his killers on the grounds they had acted in self-defense.

The federal government, which encouraged and supported the campaign to crush dissent, concentrated its fire on the American Socialist Party and the Industrial Workers of the World, both of which openly opposed the war. By the end of the war, many leaders of both radical organizations were in jail and their organizations were is disarray. Neither organization ever regained the following it had enjoyed before the war.

President Wilson's own crusading zeal was partly to blame for the repression of the war years: persecution of minorities and aliens, attacks on socialist and radical labor organizations, arbitrary arrests and imprisonments, and censorship of the mails, the media, and personal speech. Victims totaled eight thousand to ten thousand individuals who suffered repression, imprisonment, mob violence, or deportation. Wartime repression reached its apogee in the formation of numerous private or quasi-official organizations to supplement official authority. These included the American Defense Society, and Knights of Liberty, and the largest of these groups, the American Protective League (APL). The APL claimed a membership in excess of 250,000. With the sanction of the Justice Department, the APL conducted private inquests into the loyalty of their fellow citizens that often veered toward vigilantism.

RED SCARE

Wartime suppression of dissent spilled into the postwar era during the Red Scare of 1919 and 1920. During this turbulent period, the targets of government prosecutors and vigilantes were Communists or Communist sympathizers, many of them aliens, suspected of plotting to overthrow the government. The Bolsheviks had come to power in Russia in November 1917. After the war, Communism did appear to be spreading westward. Communist uprisings occurred in Hungary and Germany. Americans fearfully looked at a Europe in chaos—shattered economies, weakened governments, and hungry millions struggling to survive in a world in which democracy appeared more imperiled than ever. In 1919, the Soviets established the Comintern to promote world revolution, and in that year two Communist parties were formed in the United States. War had also disrupted American race relations and family life. Inflation and unemployment were high. Nervous Americans, aware that a small, disciplined band of revolutionaries had come to power in Russia, worried that revolution might come to the United States.

Dramatic events occurring in 1919 intensified fears of revolution, provoking the Red Scare. Thousands of strikes, idling over 4 million workers, broke out. A general strike in Seattle was particularly alarming. In May, dozens of letter bombs were mailed to prominent business and political leaders, although none of the intended targets were killed or injured. Anarchist terrorists, plotting to undermine the government, were suspected of sending the bombs, but police never caught the conspirators. In September, the Boston police, who belonged to an American Federation of Labor (AFL) local, went on strike. For a few days, the streets of Boston belonged to rioters and looters. The governor of Massachusetts, an obscure Republican politician named Calvin Coolidge, became famous when he sent a terse telegram to Samuel Gompers, the president of the AFL, which read, "There is no right to strike against the public safety by anyone, anytime, anywhere." He also called out the Massachusetts National Guard which restored order and broke the strike.

The largest strike occurred in the steel industry when 350,000 workers walked off their jobs. The strikers wanted union recognition, a reduction in their seven-days-a-week, twelve-hours-a-day work schedule, and pay increases to offset inflation. Management refused to negotiate any of the workers' grievances and moved to break the strike. The companies hired strikebreakers, "goon squads" to assault workers, and launched a propaganda campaign to convince the public that the strike was a Bolshevik conspiracy. One strike leader, William Z. Foster, joined the Communist Party and his presence gave plausibility to the steel companies' charges that the strike was a revolutionary conspiracy.

In mid-1919, Attorney General A. Mitchell Palmer stepped forward to save America from Red revolution. A Progressive Democrat and ambitious to get the 1920 Democratic presidential nomination, Palmer claimed America was in imminent peril of revolution, as in the following passage:

The blaze of revolution was eating its way into the homes of the American workmen, its sharp tongues of revolutionary heat . . . licking the altars of churches, leaping into the belfry of the school bell, crawling into the sacred corners of American homes, burning up the foundations of society.[6]

To combat the Red menace, Palmer hired a young lawyer named J. Edgar Hoover to direct a new Bureau of Investigation. Hoover placed thousands of people and many organizations under surveillance. State and local governments took various repressive measures. Vigilantes, many of them war veterans, swung into action.

In January 1920, using information collected by Hoover, Palmer ordered raids in thirty-three cities across the land. Federal agents, assisted by local police, broke into homes and meeting halls. About six thousand people were arrested in the raids. The Palmer raids were preemptive. Palmer and Hoover intended to catch the conspirators plotting their revolutionary actions, to seize their maps, weapons, and the conspirators themselves before they could carry out their plans. There were wholesale violations of civil liberties. Many arrested were not radicals, not Communists, nor had they committed any crime. Eventually, most of those arrested were released. About 550 aliens were eventually deported for having violated immigration laws.

Investigations have never uncovered a revolutionary plot; it apparently existed only in Palmer and Hoover's imaginations. When Palmer's prediction that there would be a revolutionary uprising on May Day, 1920, proved mistaken, he lost credibility. Some Progressives also criticized his disregard of constitutional rights and due process. The Red Scare died out as the strikes ended, the Communist threat in Europe receded, and the nation returned to normal peacetime activities. Palmer's presidential bid collapsed.

One episode from the Red Scare has endured. On April 15, 1920, a paymaster and his guard were shot dead during the robbery of a shoe factory in South Braintree, Massachusetts. Three weeks later, Nicola Sacco, a shoe worker, and Bartolomeo Vanzetti, a fish peddler, both Italian immigrants and committed anarchists, were charged with murder. Both men were armed at the time of their arrest. The evidence against them was contradictory. During their trial, witnesses for the prosecution perjured themselves, and there were indications that the police had tampered with some of the evidence used against them. The judge in the case, Webster Thayer, was biased against the defendants. At one point in the proceedings, he called them "anarchist bastards."

When a jury convicted them of murder and Judge Thayer sentenced them to death, many believed Sacco and Vanzetti were innocent; they felt the two men had been convicted because they were radical immigrants. They had been convicted for what they were, not for what they had done. The case became a significant political controversy. The Massachusetts governor appointed a special commission to review the case. After a careful examination of the trial, the commissioners concluded

---

[6]Quoted in Mary Beth Norton and others, *A People and a Nation: A History of the United States,* 2nd ed., vol. II: Since 1865 (Boston: Houghton Mifflin, 1986), p. 669.

that justice had been done, although they reprimanded Judge Thayer for his derogatory remarks about the defendants.

The case of Sacco and Vanzetti assumed international proportions, engaging the passions of men and women around the globe. Anatole France, a Nobel Prize winning author, entered an eleventh-hour plea for their lives. All efforts were in vain. Despite the worldwide protests, both men were electrocuted August 23, 1927. By then millions of people in this country and around the world were convinced of their innocence. To this day, scholars of the case continue to debate its merits. Some believe Sacco and Vanzetti were innocent victims of political vengeance. Others cite evidence establishing their guilt. It is impossible to resolve the issue so the debate goes on.

The Red Scare left many other casualties besides Sacco and Vanzetti. Panicky federal officials, overreacting to acts of terrorism, scapegoated groups of recently arrived immigrants. Thousands were sent to prison, suffered civil rights violations, or were deported. Dissent was stifled; critics were afraid to speak out. The give and take of free debate, essential to maintaining the health of democracy, was curtailed. Reformers no longer criticized institutions or proposed reforms. Radical movements in America were badly wounded by combined wartime and Red Scare repression. The government's campaign against its critics marred Wilson's otherwise excellent record as a war leader. His intolerance towards opponents of his war policies revealed both his lack of faith in democracy during wartime and a willingness to use repressive methods to stifle opposition. A legacy of repression, intolerance, and narrow conformity carried into the 1920s.

THE PEACE CONFERENCE

While the nation was in the throes of the Red Scare, President Wilson journeyed to Paris to try to implement his Fourteen Points. He faced many obstacles, some erected by his political rivals and some which he created himself by making political errors. Wilson was the first president to go abroad on a diplomatic mission during his term of office; his decision to go was controversial. Republican opponents suspected that Wilson desired to get all the credit for the peace settlement; they accused him of having a "messiah complex." He also left behind some serious domestic problems. Many farmers, businessmen, and trade unions were unhappy with some of his war policies.

Wilson erred by making a blatantly partisan appeal to the voters for the election of a Democratic Congress in 1918 on the eve of his departure for France. The voters, concerned with domestic issues, particularly inflation, promptly elected Republican majorities to both houses of Congress. The outcome of the 1918 elections meant that any treaty Wilson brought back from Paris would have to be ratified by a Republican-controlled Senate. Wilson also lost political stature in the eyes of foreign leaders with whom he would be soon be negotiating. He made further errors when he did not appoint any prominent Republican leaders to the delegation accompanying him to Paris, and he did not consult with the Senate Foreign Relations committee before he left for Paris.

At Paris he confronted more obstacles. The Allies were determined to impose a harsh peace on the defeated Germans. The French Premier Georges Clemenceau, the British Prime Minister David Lloyd George, and the Italian leader Vittorio Orlando, along with Woodrow Wilson, were the dominant voices at the conference. They had signed secret treaties during the war and they came to Paris intending to enlarge their empires at Germany's expense. They dismissed Wilson's liberal war aims as foolish and irrelevant. Clemenceau viewed Wilson's idealism as a species of political theology. Referring to Wilson's peace plan, Clemenceau said: "God gave us Ten Commandments and we broke them; Wilson gives us Fourteen Points. We shall see."

Most of the conference sessions were held at Versailles, a suburb of Paris. The delegates met behind closed doors, repudiating one of the Fourteen Points, which had called for open diplomacy. The victors demanded and got a clause in the treaty making Germany absolutely responsible for the war and creating a reparations commission to determine the huge bill Germany would have to pay. (The commission later set the figure at $33 billion!)

Wilson fought hard to decolonization and for self-determination, but he had to make many concessions to imperialism. Former German colonies were placed in a mandate system that gave the French, British, and Japanese access to their resources. Japan gained influence over Germany's former sphere in China at Shantung and many of its former Pacific island colonies. France occupied Germany's Rhineland. But Wilson was able to carve several newly independent nations out of the remnants of the Austro-Hungarian empire—Austria, Hungary, Yugoslavia, Czechoslovakia, and Poland. He also helped to erect a *cordon sanitaire* of new nations—Finland, Estonia, Latvia, and Lithuania—along the western border of Russia in order to contain communism.

Wilson also fought hard for the League of Nations charter. He was willing to sacrifice many of his Fourteen Points because he reasoned that the League would moderate the harsh peace terms, contain imperialism, and ensure collective security in the postwar era. He wrote most of the new international organization's charter. He created a League of Nations dominated by a permanent council of the major powers, an assembly for discussion and debate among the member nations, and a World Court. The heart of the League's covenant was Article X, the collective security provision. It provided for League members to "respect and preserve as against external aggression the territorial integrity and existing political independence" of all members. Wilson also insisted that the League of Nations charter be incorporated into the body of the peace treaty, forming an integral part of it.

German representations signed the Treaty of Versailles in June 1919 under protest, giving up chunks of their territory, 10 percent of their population, all their colonies, and a huge portion of their wealth. It was a vindictive, humiliating peace imposed on the defeated Germans. Its draconian terms violated the spirit and most of the specific terms of the Fourteen Points. Many commentators, including the famed British economist John Maynard Keynes, foresaw the seeds of another war sown in the harsh terms imposed by the peacemakers at Versailles. Their words proved prophetic when the Fascist demagogue, Adolph Hitler, came to power, in part by voicing German discontent with the Versailles system.

While the peace conference was still in session, Senator Henry Cabot Lodge, chairman of the Senate Foreign Relations Committee, circulated a resolution signed by thirty-nine senators, more than enough votes to block ratification, stating that the League charter did not protect American national interests. Wilson responded by writing language into the League covenant that exempted the Monroe Doctrine and U.S. internal matters from League jurisdiction.

FIGHT FOR RATIFICATION

As the terms of the treaty became known in the United States, criticism of it mounted from several sides. Many Progressives attacked Wilson's betrayal of so many of his Fourteen Points. There was nothing in the Versailles treaty about freedom of the seas, free trade, or disarmament. Other liberals attacked the closed sessions, the concessions to imperialism, and the huge reparations imposed on Germany. Senator La Follette said the treaty's provisions confirmed his view that World War I was nothing more than a struggle between rival imperialisms. Conservative critics such as Senator Lodge feared the League would limit American freedom of action in the postwar world. Isolationists feared Article X would obligate the United States to provide armed forces to preserve collective security in the postwar world.

Wilson returned home to face his critics and to defend the treaty. He defended his concessions as necessary compromises and pointed out that the League of Nations would eventually right all wrongs in the postwar era. Senator Lodge was unimpressed; he organized Senate opposition to the Treaty of Versailles. He introduced fourteen reservations, modifications that he wanted made in the League charter, before he would approve the treaty. These reservations included exempting U.S. immigration policy from League decisions and giving Congress the right to approve any League resolution which implemented Article X.

The forty-nine Republican senators formed three distinct factions in the debate over ratifying the impending treaty. Twenty-three shared Lodge's view that all fourteen reservations would have to be implemented before they could support the treaty. They were called "strong reservationists." Twelve would support the treaty if some of the reservations were implemented. This group was known as the "mild reservationists." Fourteen isolationists opposed the treaty in any form and determined to oppose it with or without reservations. These senators formed the "irreconcilables."

In the fall of 1919, President Wilson went on a nationwide speaking tour to rally public support for the treaty; he hoped to pressure the Senate into ratifying it. Speaking at Pueblo, Colorado, the president became ill following an eloquent speech that left his audience in tears. Taken back to Washington, he suffered a thrombosis that left him partially paralyzed. For several weeks, he was incapacitated, unable to perform his duties as president. Even after he made a partial recovery, his judgment still remained impaired. He refused to consider compromising with his Republican opponents in the Senate, and he demanded absolute loyalty from his Democratic supporters.

In November 1919, the Senate voted twice on the treaty. Before the votes were taken, the Senate Democratic floor leader, Gilbert Hitchcock, told the president that the treaty could not pass without reservations. He suggested that "It might be wise to compromise." Wilson responded curtly, "Let Lodge compromise!" The first vote taken was on the treaty with Lodge's fourteen reservations attached. The Senate rejected it by a vote of 39 for to 55 against. Then a vote was taken without the reservations. It also failed by a vote of 38 to 53. The "irreconcilables" voted against it both times. They absolutely opposed American entry into the League of Nations. Senators representing midwestern and eastern states voted against the unamended version of the treaty. Democratic senators from the South favored it. Western senators were divided.

A third vote was taken in March 1920, with the reservations attached to the treaty. Wilson continued to insist that all Democrats oppose the treaty in amended form, refusing all efforts at compromise. Although twenty-one Democrats defied Wilson's order, the third vote fell 7 votes short of the necessary two-thirds majority, 49 to 35. Had Wilson permitted Democrats to compromise with Republicans who favored mild reservations, he would have probably gotten the two-thirds majority required for passage and the United States would have joined the League of Nations. Wilson's refusal to compromise doomed the treaty. His refusal to compromise had many causes—his personal dislike of Lodge, his illness that had impaired his judgment, and partisan political considerations.

There is a more fundamental cause of President Wilson's refusal to compromise and the unwillingness of Republican senators to accept the treaty without amendments. The fundamental conflict between Wilson and Lodge concerned two competing conceptions of the national interest. Was the national interest best served, as Wilson believed, by endorsing collective security? Or was the national interest best served, as Lodge believed, by continuing to travel the traditional American path of unilateralism, as expressed in Washington's Farewell Address and the Monroe Doctrine? Looking out on the postwar world, many senators preferred *unilateralism,* which meant nonalignment and free choice over the binding commitments of collective security mediated through the League of Nations. Woodrow Wilson had a bold vision of a new world order based on internationalist collective security arrangements, but he was unable to find the arguments or concoct the formula that would enable him to bring the requisite number of senators along with him.

Historians have speculated on the long-run historical significance of the failure of the United States to join the League of Nations. The United States emerged from World War I the preeminent world power economically and financially; it also had the potential to be the world's number-one strategic power. Had the United States joined, the League of Nations would have been a stronger and more prestigious agency. During the 1930s, when revisionist nations began to disrupt the

Europe after Versailles.   *Source:* Moss, *Rise of Modern America*, p. 128.

world order, the League of Nations, bolstered by American membership, might have been more effective at maintaining collective security and curbing aggression. World War II might have been avoided or at least curtailed. If these speculations have the ring of truth, then the failure of the United States to ratify the Treaty of Versailles and join the League of Nations was a colossal world tragedy.

THE WAR EXPERIENCE

World War I was a brief, intense experience for the American people that had a profound and enduring effect on their lives and institutions. During the war, the federal government intervened in the economy and influenced the lives of Americans in unprecedented ways. The wartime cooperation of business and government stimulated the growth of trade associations that during the 1920s lobbied to protect their interests and to minimize competition. The suspension of antitrust laws in wartime fostered the growth of monopoly and oligopoly that flourished during the 1920s. War accelerated the emergence of the modern corporate economy with its complex, usually cooperative, relations with the central government. The war effort was a modernizing experience that ended forever the old laissez-faire, voluntaristic order that had emerged from the nineteenth century.

The war also afforded American businessmen many world economic opportunities. They reduced the outflow of capital from this country by purchasing billions of dollars of American stocks and bonds sold on the market by foreign belligerents desperate for cash. They also reclaimed many of the dollars spent repatriating these securities by selling huge quantities of foodstuffs and ammunition to the Allies. When the Allies had exhausted their dollar accounts, American banks advanced them billions in credits, which reversed America's historic credit dependency on European investors. And, Americans moved to take over markets previously dominated by Europeans, particularly in Latin America, at the expense of the British and Germans.

America emerged from the war as the world's preeminent economic power. In the 1920s, the United States produced about half of the world's coal and steel and over 70 percent of its petroleum. American trade accounted for about 30 percent of the world's commerce. American corporations opened subsidiaries in foreign lands. European companies, strained by the war, fell behind their U.S. rivals. America had also become the world's leading creditor. New York replaced London as the world's banking center. U.S. financiers and investors loaned billions of dollars to businesses and governments in Europe and Latin America.

Although the Versailles settlement disillusioned many Americans about the war and the United States did not join the League of Nations, the United States did not revert to isolationism after the war. American observers attended all League meetings, and America usually supported League actions. But the United States was wary about intervening in European affairs, given Europe's postwar economic and political disorder; America preserved its freedom of action.

The war changed the public mood. Photographs and films revealed the brutal, deadly reality of trench warfare, dramatically different from the soaring rhetoric of President Wilson's speeches. Veterans cared only to return home and forget about their war experiences. Americans wearied of idealistic crusades; they became cynical about their internationalist commitments. They turned inward, closing out the larger world. They claimed the baseball scoreboard was more important than news of the world, and it was a lot more fun.

The war split the Progressive movement, destroying the reform coalition. Most Progressive intellectuals ended up supporting the war, sharing Wilson's belief that it was a war to save democracy. A left-wing Progressive minority, led by Jane Addams, retained its pacifistic beliefs and opposed the war. Progressivism emerged from World War I shaken and much weaker. Progressives who had viewed the war as a grand opportunity for America to reform the world—a chance to bring peace, democracy, and progressive capitalism to Europe—also became disillusioned. Many lost enthusiasm for crusades both at home and abroad. Some reformers felt betrayed by European imperialists who had used the Paris conference to turn a glorious victory into a sordid settlement perpetuating world problems and sowing the seeds of future wars. Progressivism had lost its innocence.

IMPORTANT EVENTS

1900	U.S. troops join international expeditionary force to suppress the Boxer rebellion in China
1902	The Platt Amendment is imposed on Cuba
1903	The Panamanian revolution begins
1904	Construction of the Panama Canal starts
1905	Theodore Roosevelt mediates settlement of the Russo-Japanese war
1906	U.S. troops intervene in Cuba
1908	U.S. "Great White Fleet" sails around the world
1910	The Mexican revolution begins
1914	World War I begins
1914	U.S. troops intervene in Haiti
1914	Wilson sends U.S. sailors and marines to Vera Cruz, Mexico
1915	HMS *Lusitania* is sunk by a German submarine
1916	Mexican general "Pancho Villa" invades the United States
1916	Wilson orders the U.S. Army to invade Mexico
1917	The Russian revolution occurs
1918	World War I ends
1919	The Treaty of Versailles is signed
1920	The U.S. Senate rejects the Treaty of Versailles

BIBLIOGRAPHY

John Dobson's *America's Ascent: The United States Becomes a Great Power, 1890–1914,* charts the rise of the United States to world prominence during the Progressive Era. David McCullough's, *The Path Between the Seas: The Creation of the Panama Canal, 1870–1914* is a beautifully rendered account of the Panama Canal project. Howard K. Beale's classic *Theodore Roosevelt and the Rise of America to World Power* remains the best book on Progressive foreign policy. All facets of the American experience during World War I have been written about. The best account of the causes of U.S. entry into the war is Ernest R. May's *The World and American Isolation, 1914–1917.* Ross Gregory, in *The Origins of American Intervention in the First World War,* gives a short, lively account. A classic study of America and the war is Daniel M. Smith's, *The Great Departure: The United States and World War I, 1914–1920.* Wilson's official biographer, Arthur Link, has written a good account of the president's diplomacy, *Wilson the Diplomatist.* The best military history of the American involvement in World War I is Edward M. Coffman's, *The War to End All Wars.* A. E. Barbeau and Florette Henri have written *The Unknown Soldiers: Black American Troops in World War I.* The role of women in the war has been recorded by Maurine W. Greenwald's, *Women, War, and Work.* The best account of the home front in the war is David Kennedy's *Over Here: The First World War and American Society.* The attack on civil liberties in wartime is recorded in *Opponents of War, 1917–1918,* by H. C. Peterson and Gilbert Fite. The best account of the Red Scare and the man who led the attack on it is Stanley Coben's *A. Mitchell Palmer: Politician.* The best account of the fight over the League of Nations is by Thomas A. Bailey, a work entitled *Woodrow Wilson and the Great Betrayal.*

CHAPTER 4

The Twenties

The 1920s were a complex, vital, and divided decade; an era of conflict and contrast. Americans during the 1920s were forward-looking and reactionary, liberal and repressive, progressive and nostalgic. A majority of Americans enjoyed a life of unprecedented material abundance and leisure. But poverty plagued millions of small farmers, industrial workers, and nonwhite minorities. Prosperity eradicated neither poverty nor social injustice from the land.

The most important trend of the 1920s was the emergence of a new mass consumer culture that fostered changes in the ways many Americans worked, lived, and cared for one another. It also brought changes in manners, morals, and personal identities. Consumerism also shifted the American sense of community— from communities based on shared values toward communities based on shared styles of consumption. But beneath the surface unity of consumerism and mass participation in new games, sports, and recreations, cultural conflicts and tensions seethed. During the 1920s, American society was fragmented along many fault lines—urbanites versus rural folks, WASPs versus ethnics, white against black, and perhaps the most profound divide: between those who embraced a modernist culture and those who retained traditional values.

The 1920s were a decade of great accomplishments in art, science, and technology. Creative American writers, musicians, and artists flourished. It was also a decade characterized by stunts, fads, contests, and commercial promotions. Ballyhoo artists prospered, as did criminals who made millions from the illegal liquor trade. It was a time of prosperity, social change, and personal liberation. It was also an age that featured an upsurge in religious fundamentalism, the Ku Klux Klan, nativist immigration restriction, and repression of radicalism. Crime rates and church attendance both soared during the decade.

The 1920s also marked a beginning, a time when millions of Americans adapted to urban patterns of existence. They centered their new urban life styles around ownership of automobiles and participation in the new urban mass culture. While many urbanites abandoned their former rural, agrarian ways of life, they retained some of its values. It was a time of transition. During the 1920s the major historical developments of twentieth-century American life—technological change, urbanization, the growth of bureaucratic modes of organization, and the growth of the middle classes—accelerated rapidly. Between the end of World War I and the stock market crash, the shape of modern America emerged; the historical forces driving the rise of the urban nation accelerated. The New Era was the first recognizably modern decade.

A MOBILE PEOPLE

The 1920s census confirmed the major demographic trend underway in this country since the American revolution, that a majority of American families had left the countryside and moved to the city. Of the 106 million people living in America in 1920, 52 percent resided in towns and cities with populations of twenty-five hundred or more. America had become an urban nation. That movement, from the hinterlands to the cities, accelerated during the 1920s. By 1930, 69 million of the 123 million inhabitants of the United States resided in urban areas, compared with 54 million who lived in the countryside. The emigration of African Americans from the rural South to northern cities, spawned by the opportunities for work in war industries, continued during the 1920s. Sizable numbers of Puerto Ricans came to America during the 1920s, as did Mexicans fleeing poverty, oppression, and political instability in their native land.

Because the United States severely restricted immigration after 1921 and because the birth rate dropped sharply among middle-class families, the growth rate of the population during the decade of the 1920s slowed to the smallest rate recorded since the nation began taking censuses in 1790. While national population growth rates slowed, the rate of urban population growth accelerated, especially in the nation's largest cities. The five American cities whose populations exceeded 1 million in 1920—New York, Chicago, Philadelphia, Detroit, and Los Angeles—collectively increased their populations by 50 percent during the decade.

During the 1920s, for the first time in American history, the nation's farm population showed a net decline. During the decade, more than 13 million rural Americans left the countryside and moved to the urban frontiers. Construction of interurban highways and the advent of mass ownership of automobiles permitted rapid growth of suburban communities that sprung up around the nation's large metropolitan centers. During the 1920s, the other great demographic trend, as old as the republic itself, continued, as millions of families continued to move west, although during the 1920s they made the trek west in cars and passenger trains rather than in covered wagons and on horseback. California often appeared to be the favorite destination of these 1920s western migrants.

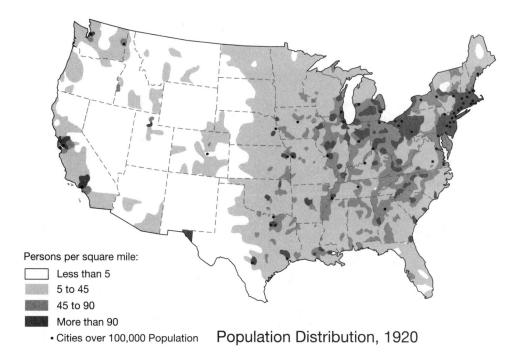

Population Distribution, 1920

Persons per square mile:
- Less than 5
- 5 to 45
- 45 to 90
- More than 90
- Cities over 100,000 Population

Population distribution, 1920.   *Source:* Moss, *Rise of Modern America,* p. 133.

THE CONSUMER ECONOMY

The decade is famed for its prosperity, but the "roaring twenties" economy began slowly. Along with postwar disorder and the Red Scare, Americans suffered severe economic difficulties during 1919 and 1920. The government's heedless decontrol of the economy and mass discharge of veterans in 1919 contributed to the economic downturn. High inflation continued to plague consumers. As 1920 ended, recession occurred. Consumer demand fell, exports dropped as war markets closed, and farm income plunged. Unemployment soared—from 2 or 3 percent to over 12 percent, the highest rate since the severe depression of 1892–1894. Railroads went bankrupt, coal mines closed, and many New England textile mills shut their gates. Americans had their first contact with "stagflation," or high prices combined with high unemployment. Recovery began in late 1922. Year One of the prosperity decade was 1923. The prosperity, although uneven, continued until the collapse of the securities industry in 1929, one of the longest epochs of good times in American economic history.

During these seven good years, industrial output nearly doubled and the gross domestic product (GDP) rose 40 percent. National per capita income increased by 30 percent, from $520 to $681. Prices remained stable, even dropping for some items during the late 1920s. In an economy with no inflation and no rise in the cost of living, increased GNP meant significant increases in consumer purchasing power and rapidly rising living standards. By the mid-1920s, a typical middle-class household owned an automobile, a radio, a phonograph, a washing machine, a vacuum cleaner, a sewing machine, and a telephone. A generation earlier only the rich could have afforded these possessions, and they would have used technologically inferior versions.

The key to the new prosperity lay in technology. The continuous-flow assembly line, pioneered by Henry Ford at his River Rouge auto factory near Detroit, became standard in most American manufacturing plants. Electric motors replaced steam engines as the basic source of energy driving factory machines. By the end of the decade, electricity supplied 70 percent of all industrial power. Efficiency experts broke down manufacturing processes into minute parts in "time-and-motion" studies to show how workers and machines could maximize output. Frederick W. Taylor, trained as a civil engineer, was the most prominent of these "time-and-motion" experts. Output per man-hour, the basic measure of productivity, increased an amazing 75 percent over the decade. In 1929, a workforce only slightly larger than the one employed in 1919 was producing almost twice as many goods.

Most of this explosive growth occurred in industries producing consumer goods—-automobiles, appliances, furniture, clothing, and radios. Dozens of new consumer products flowed from factories and shops. New alloys, chemicals, and synthetics such as rayon and cellophane became commonplace. People bought more preserved, processed, and canned foods; they bought more machine-fashioned clothing. Americans found a whole new spectrum of products to buy—cigarette lighters, wristwatches, heat-resistant cookware, and sheer rayon stockings. Service industries also expanded to accommodate the new affluence and leisure middle-class Americans enjoyed. Specialty stores, restaurants, beauty shops, movie theaters, and service stations proliferated. Henry Ford's slogan "Buy a Ford and Spend the Difference" best expressed the spirit of the New Era's rampant consumerism.

The automobile led the parade of technological marvels that made the American way of life the wonder of the world during the 1920s. During the decade, Americans bought 15 million new cars. Efficient production methods dropped the prices of new cars sharply, making what had been a plaything of the rich affordable for the middle class and for some working-class families. If many families could not afford a new car, they could buy a used one.

The man who put America on wheels was a Michigan farm boy who taught himself to be a mechanic. Henry Ford had two key insights: The first, in his words, was "Get the prices down to the buying power." He installed continuously moving assembly lines in his factories, which enabled him to manufacture nine thousand cars per day by 1925. The second insight was to pay his workers top wages. The assembly line increased worker productivity significantly. It also simplified jobs, making them boring and fatiguing. Absenteeism and high worker turnover became serious problems for Ford. In 1914, he raised wages to $5 per day, making Ford employees the highest-paid industrial workers in the world. Absenteeism

Henry Ford (right) beside the first automobile he built in 1896. His son, Edsel, inspects the ten millionth (!) "Model T" Ford car, which rolled off the assembly line in 1924. *Source:* National Archives.

and turnover practically disappeared. Ford's sales and profits soared. Between 1922 and 1927, more than half of all new cars sold in America were Model T's. During those years, Henry Ford netted $25,000 a day. He owned the entire Ford Motor Company and became the nation's second billionaire.

He also became a folk hero. His simple tastes, his dislike of bankers, and his disdain for society inspired mass affection for him. For millions of people, Ford's achievement symbolized the wonders of the American system. He had given the American people a marvelous machine at an affordable price. He was also an inspiring example of a poor boy's rise to riches, and he paid his employees well. A serious grass-roots boom promoted him for president in 1923.

Although uneducated and ignorant of most things outside the automotive business, Ford, because he was famous and successful, spoke out often on public issues. His views derived from his nineteenth-century rural roots. He condemned drinking, dancing, and the use of tobacco. He held nativist views and published anti-Semitic propaganda. He denounced modern art and once proclaimed that "History is bunk." Ironically, mass ownership of automobiles and road building was fast destroying the old-fashioned rural America that Ford cherished.

A new Ford Model T cost as little as $285 in 1925, and the joke went that you could get it in any color you wanted as long as it was black. New or used Fords could be purchased by factory workers who earned about $1,200 annually during the 1920s and by office workers who earned about $2,000 per year. For many car buyers, owning an automobile was more urgent than owning a home or the other consumer items of the era. An interviewer once asked a rural housewife why her family owned a car but not a bathtub. Her reply, "Bathtub? You can't go to town in a bathtub!"

Mass ownership of automobiles profoundly altered American culture. Traffic jams, speeding tickets, and auto accidents became permanent features of the American scene. The automobile catered to the American desire for individual autonomy. Young people out for a drive could escape the watchful eyes of parents. Moralists feared that automobiles were becoming "bedrooms on wheels." Most of all, the motor car symbolized a new age of social equality. The average man could own America's most important status symbol. Henry Ford, the man who had put America on wheels, had accomplished a capitalist revolution. The son of an east European peasant could now drive along the same highways, view the same scenery, and enjoy the same trip just as much as a rich man. Marxists would be hard put to convince an American factory worker at the wheel of his new Ford that he was being ground to dust by capitalist exploiters. The car became the supreme symbol of the 1920s version of the American dream with its promise of mobility, freedom, and social equality.

The automobile stimulated extensive road construction and spawned many service industries that catered to drivers. Congress enacted a Federal Highway Act providing federal money for states to build highways. The Bureau of Public Roads began planning a national highway system. Service stations and a new kind of hotel, a motor hotel, later shortened to "motel," made its appearance. Insurance companies, previously concerned with life insurance, added auto insurance to their policy lines.

The oil industry, which had sold mostly kerosene to light people's homes, shifted production to gasoline, an unimportant product before the advent of the automobile with its internal combustion engine. During the early 1920s, oil companies could not produce gasoline fast enough to meet the rapidly growing demands of a people taking to the roads. An "energy crisis" occurred. Long lines of angry motorists formed at the gas pumps. The price of a gallon of gas doubled, from 20¢ to 40¢. The crisis faded in 1924 when Standard Oil gained access to British-controlled oil in Iraq.

The automobile also altered urban residential patterns. People now drove downtown to work and shop instead of catching a trolley. Suburbs, previously located within the outer neighborhoods of cities, now evolved as satellite cities, often 10 to 20 miles away from central cities. Los Angeles was the first American metropolis to develop during the age of the automobile. It took shape as a series of neighborhoods and shopping districts sprawling over a large geographic area, all

Traffic jams that clogged the streets of all large cities by the 1920s and that even began spilling into the suburbs, as shown here, were a sign that Americans had entered the Age of the Automobile.   *Source:* Courtesy of the State of Michigan Archives.

connected by long streets and highways. One observer called the metropolis "a series of suburbs in search of a city."

The most distinctive feature of the new consumer economy was its stress on advertising. The advertising industry, which developed during the Gilded Age, centered on Manhattan's Madison Avenue, became big business during the 1920s. The earnings of ad agencies rose from $1.8 billion in 1921 to $3.4 billion in 1926. Clever ad writers manipulated public taste and consumer spending with increasing effectiveness. Advertisers sought to create consumer desires for new products by identifying them with the good life; sometimes they employed psychology to appeal to consumer needs, fears, anxieties, and sexual fantasies.

Advertisers viewed human beings as infinitely suggestible and infinitely manipulable. Edward Bernays, who became America's leading public relations expert during the 1920s, believed that opinions were formed by groups, not by individuals. He insisted that advertisers appeal to group leaders. Sell a new product by getting celebrities or socially prominent people to endorse it. Hire Babe Ruth to sell athletic equipment to kids. Hire a movie actress or debutante to sell cigarette smoking to women. Bernays believed strongly in the ability of an educated elite to use the persuasive power of advertising to sell the growing cornucopia of consumer goods to the gullible masses. Bernays once snorted: "The average person does not know what he wants until we tell him."

An adman became a best-selling author. Bruce Barton, who wrote *The Man Nobody Knows* (1925), expounded a new gospel of business. The man nobody knew was Jesus of Nazareth. According to Barton, Jesus was the greatest salesman who ever lived and "the founder of modern business." This Madison Avenue Jesus "picked up twelve humble men and created an organization that won the world." Advertisers encouraged credit buying to enhance sales. The new consumerism was enhanced by advertising and fueled by credit. Installment buying or time-payment plans flourished. Of the millions of new automobiles sold annually during the prosperous 1920s, over 80 percent were purchased on credit.

During the 1920s, a revolution in communications and the rapid expansion of advertising combined to create a consuming public that possessed up-to-date information about the latest products, services, fads, and fashions. People spent much time and energy learning about new products and the latest trends—of wanting what others had, of "keeping up with the Joneses." H. L. Mencken, one of the leading journalist-pundits of the decade, observed that advertisers employed the new communications media to create a new human species in America, *Homo consumerins.* Most middle-class Americans who sampled the wonders of the New Era pronounced them good and wanted more.

National chain stores advanced rapidly during the 1920s at the expense of small, local businesses. Atlantic and Pacific Tea Company (A & P) and Safeway dominated the retail food market. A & P had fifteen thousand stores as the decade ended. Woolworth's "five and dimes" and giant drug chains like Rexall's spread coast-to-coast. J.C. Penney opened thousands of clothing stores. As the 1920s ended, chain stores in many retail fields had opened outlets in nearly every town and city in the land. They offered their customers good value and courteous service, and generated huge profits from volume sales.

Corporations continued to be the dominant economic unit of the 1920s. Large corporations often had a million or more individual stockholders, and one individual rarely held more than a few percent of the stock. Most corporations generated large profits from volume sales during the 1920s, enabling them to finance their expansions out of revenues and freeing them from dependence on bankers and financiers. Professing a new ethic of social responsibility, professional corporate managers ran their giant firms independently of any external controls or restraints.

Big business grew bigger during the 1920s. The consolidation drive that had begun during the Gilded Age continued through the Progressive Era despite its antitrust activity, accelerated during the war years, and climaxed during the New Era. Another wave of mergers swept the corporate world. Over eight thousand mergers occurred between 1920 and 1928 as thousands of small firms, unable to compete with big companies, were taken over. As the decade ended, about two hundred giant corporations owned half of the nation's wealth. In almost every manufacturing sector, huge, integrated companies were in control—in automobile manufacturing, steel milling, oil refining, meat processing, flour milling, mining, railroading, and other industries. They dominated not only production, but also marketing, distribution, and financing. Antitrust activities faded in an age of economic giants and the continuing centralization of economic activity.

Organizational activities, fostered by Progressive reformers before and during the war, flourished during the 1920s. Business and professional associations worked to protect their members' interests. Retailers and small manufacturers formed trade associations to exchange information, to coordinate planning, and to promote their industries. Farm bureaus and farm cooperative associations lobbied for government help and tried to stabilize declining commodity prices. Lawyers, engineers, doctors, teachers, scientists, and other professionals formed associations and societies to promote their interests. The Progressive organizational impulse had turned to professionalism.

Uniformity and standardization, the dominant characteristics of modern mass production processes, became major cultural influences. An Iowa farmer bought the same kind of car that an auto worker in Detroit or a businessman in Los Angeles purchased. They also bought the same groceries, the same health and beauty aids, and the same underwear. They listened to the same radio programs, saw the same movies, and read the same comic strips. Regional differences in lifestyles and speech accents declined. Americans began to look, act, and sound more and more alike. Consumerism fostered conformity in manners and morals.

THE URBAN NATION

Between 1920 and 1930, cities with populations of 250,000 or more added 8 million more people. New York, America's great metropolis, grew 25 percent in the decade. Detroit, site of America's expanding auto industry, more than doubled its population during the same period. Iowans and other midwestern migrants moved to Los Angeles, the burgeoning metropolis of southern California. Southerners left their farms and hamlets for northern industrial cities. Miami was the one southern city that grew rapidly during the 1920s. Miami's flourishing real estate boom attracted thousands seeking retirement or vacation homes.

African American sharecroppers fled the deteriorating southern agricultural economy for northern cities, continuing a trend that had begun during the war. African American newcomers to city life were forced to squeeze into northern ghettos as they discovered that better neighborhoods were closed to them. The black populations of New York, Chicago, and Detroit doubled during the decade.

Thousands of northern African Americans during the early 1920s joined a black nationalist movement led by a Jamaican immigrant, Marcus Garvey. Garvey denounced all whites as corrupt and preached a doctrine of black separatism. He promoted race pride and black capitalism. He also fostered a "back to Africa" campaign and founded a steamship line to foster emigration. Garvey was attacked by African American leaders like Dubois. Later Garvey's steamship company went bankrupt, and he was deported for mail fraud. His movement quickly disintegrated, but Garvey had tapped a wellspring of black grievances and aspirations.

Hispanic emigrants also poured into America's cities during the 1920s. *Campesinos* from northern Mexico, fleeing rural poverty and revolutionary disorder, moved into California and the southwestern desert states. They flocked to the growing cities of Los Angeles, Tucson, and San Antonio. These Mexican immigrants also confronted residential segregation, and they crowded into low-rent, inner-city districts to form their own communities, or *barrios*. During the 1920s, thousands of Puerto Ricans moved to mainland America. They represented a surplus rural population attracted by economic opportunities in the states. Puerto Rican communities formed in Brooklyn and Manhattan. These migrants found work in hotels, restaurants, and domestic service.

Skyscrapers became a distinctive feature of every large American city during the 1920s. Skyscrapers were a uniquely American contribution to urban landscapes. The major cause of this massive building upwards was a sharp rise in land values generated by industrial expansion and rapid population growth. New York led the way. The Empire State Building, completed in 1930 and rising 1,250 feet into the sky, had 102 stories and space for twenty-five thousand offices. The skyscraper became a major symbol of the new American mass culture and the mighty metropolis on Manhattan Island was the dynamic center of American civilization, its commercial and cultural capital.

Suburban growth accelerated during the 1920s. Rising prosperity and the coming of automobiles made fringe areas surrounding central cities accessible. The greatest urban growth of the decade took place in middle- and upper-middle-class enclaves surrounding New York, Chicago, and Los Angeles. These suburbs often incorporated, developed their own city services, and resisted annexation to core cities. Suburbanites fought to preserve local control and to avoid the dirt, noise, crime, and high taxes of the big cities.

It was in the cities and suburbs of the "Roaring Twenties" that the new mass consumer culture flourished. Urbanites dined out, went to movies, and attended sporting events. Most "speakeasies" (illegal bars and clubs opened during Prohibition) were located in cities where patrons could drink, wear garish clothes, and listen to jazz. Cities were also the center of a growing social and cultural pluralism in American life. They were places where women, immigrants, racial minorities, and religious denominations all struggled to adapt and to succeed. America's towns and villages remained mostly homogeneous WASP (white Anglo-Saxon Protestant) enclaves.

WOMEN AND FAMILY LIFE

Family life changed. Birth control became more effective and more widely practiced during the 1920s. Birthrates and family size dropped sharply. Average family size shrunk from six or seven members in 1900 to four or five members by 1930. Divorce rates rose sharply. In 1920, there was one divorce for every eight marriages;

by 1929, the ratio of divorces to marriages was two to seven. Young people during the 1920s were spending more years in schools, lengthening adolescence and postponing the time when they would enter the workforce. High school enrollment quadrupled between World War I and 1930; by 1929, one-third of all high school graduates entered college. More women than men were going on to college as the decade ended.

Schools and peer groups played a much more important role in socializing children than before the war. Classes, sports, and social clubs brought young people of the same age together. A middle-class youth culture made its appearance with its own values, consumer preferences, and lifestyles, often conflicting with those of their parents. Prolonged adolescence led to strains on the family as youngsters rebelled against parental authority and their Victorian moral standards. Middle-class youngsters, freed from the necessity of having to go to work at an early age, went on a spree. Novelist F. Scott Fitzgerald recorded the heavy drinking, casual sexual encounters, and constant search for thrills and excitement among upper-class youth in *This Side of Paradise*. The theme of rebellion characterized this generation of "flaming youth."

Improved nutrition, health care, and easier lives caused average life expectancy to increase from fifty-four to sixty years during the decade. The number of people aged sixty-five and older increased by one-third between 1920 and 1930; the elderly were the most rapidly growing demographic group in the population. Retirement communities sprang up in the warm climes of Florida and southern California. It was also during the 1920s that median female life expectancy exceeded male life expectancy for the first time in history. Lengthened female life expectancy was caused mainly by reducing the dangers of pregnancy and childbearing. Infant mortality rates decreased by two-thirds during the 1920s also.

The elderly emerged during the 1920s as a large, growing population category with distinct needs and preferences. Many of the elderly were poor because of forced retirement and the lack of pensions. In the 1920s, few private employers and no government provided pension plans for its workers. Progressive reformers of the 1920s developed ways of meeting the economic needs of some of the elderly poor. Most states implemented old-age pensions during the decade, and the principle of old-age support through pensions, insurance programs, and retirement homes was established. Foundations were lain for a national program of old-age insurance that was subsequently implemented during the 1930s.

The new lifestyles of the 1920s had a major effect on the lives of women. Middle-class women had fewer children to rear. Their houses often had central heating and hot-water heaters. They used vacuum cleaners, electric irons, electric sewing machines, electric stoves, and washing machines to lighten domestic duties. They bought preserved foods, ready-made clothing, and mass-produced furniture. Women were no longer domestic producers or beasts of burden, as their mothers and grandmothers had been. But labor-saving devices and ready-made products did not allow most middle-class women to become women of leisure.

Performance standards were raised. Homes now had to be kept immaculate. Nurturing responsibilities towards children expanded even though there were fewer children to care for. Women were also household managers and responsible for much of their family's consumer spending.

Although domesticity remained the most common realm of women, millions joined the labor force during the 1920s. In 1920, about 8 million women worked outside the home. By 1930, about 11 million had jobs. But traditional patterns of gender discrimination continued during the 1920s. Women earned about half of what men did for comparable work; most women worked in "female jobs" in which few men were found—in jobs as teachers, nurses, typists, bookkeepers, clerical workers, department store salesclerks, waitresses, maids, and hairdressers. The number of women working in factories—2 million—did not increase during the decade. The number of women in some professions declined during the 1920s. Although women earned about one-third of all graduate degrees awarded during the 1920s, women made up only 4 percent of college faculties. The professions remained mostly all male bastions.

Before the 1920s, most women who worked had been young, single women from poor backgrounds who had to work. A few had been middle-class careerists, mostly unmarried doctors, attorneys, scientists, or academics. During the 1920s, married women entered the labor force in significantly increased numbers. Some married women were responding to the pressures of poverty; more were working to supplement family incomes and to enhance their family's lifestyles. Most married working women claimed they worked because of economic necessity, but their definition of need reflected new consumer values. Their families "needed" radios, a new car, and a larger home. But most married women did not work outside the home during the 1920s; only about 10 percent had jobs.

Feminists continued to be active during the 1920s. With the battle for the vote won, they concentrated on issues involving women in the workplace. Feminists pushed for greater economic opportunity and for equal pay. Alice Paul, leader of a new organization, the National Woman's Party, supported an equal rights amendment introduced in Congress in 1923. Some feminists, many of whom had fought for the vote such as the League of Women Voters, opposed the equal rights amendment because they believed that women needed special legal protections, particularly laws guaranteeing them a minimum wage and setting a ceiling on their hours of work. They feared the courts would nullify these protective laws for women if the equal rights amendment were ratified. The drive to enact the ERA during the 1920s failed. So did feminist campaigns to improve the economic status of women and to abolish child labor. Feminists succeeded in getting the Sheppard-Towner Act (1921) passed, which authorized federal aid to states to establish maternal and infant health care programs. Also, feminists continued to be involved in local and state progressive reform politics, pushing for consumer protection legislation and for the inclusion of women on juries.

A generational change had a major effect on feminism during the 1920s. New images of femininity emerged. Young women were more interested in individual freedom of expression than they were in political reform or social progress. Some adopted what H. L. Mencken called the "flapper image." Short skirts and bobbed hair, signals of sexual freedom, spread on college campuses and in offices. Young women rouged their cheeks, smoked cigarettes, swore, drank at parties, danced to the beat of "hot jazz" combos, and necked in the back seats of automobiles. Premarital sex increased and became less scandalous as Victorian inhibitions declined.

Popular female movie stars like Clara Bow, the "It Girl," and Gloria Swanson, a passionate screen lover, became role models for young women. The mass media promoted the flapper image as a new women whose manners and morals resembled her male counterparts. The androgynous aspects of the flapper image, particularly bobbed hair, small breasts, and short skirts, suggested that many young women in the Twenties equated liberation with emulating men. As one critic put it, "there was now a single standard for men and women, and that a low one." Women, especially young middle-class women, were liberated from many social restraints of the prewar era. Flappers competed with men on the golf course and in the speakeasies. They expected sexual fulfillment before and during marriage.

It is important not to exaggerate the extent to which women participated in the new trends and styles of the 1920s. A contemporary survey of over two thousand middle-class women found that only 7 percent of them had engaged in premarital sex. The typical American woman of the 1920s did not work outside the home and lived in a household that could not afford most of the new labor-saving appliances of the age. The average housewife-mother spent about fifty hours per week performing household duties. The typical girl continued to play with dolls and was socialized in traditional ways to become a housewife and mother as her mother had before her. Boys continued to play "cowboys and Indians" and grew up to head their families and compete in the marketplace as their fathers had done. According to feminist historian June Sochen, "In the 1920s, as in the 1790s, marriage was the only approved state for women."

POPULAR CULTURE

Even as they tried to preserve old values, many Americans were irresistibly attracted to the new order. During the 1920s, millions of Americans turned enthusiastically to varieties of recreation, as participants and spectators. In 1929, Americans spent over $4 billion on play, a figure that would not be surpassed until the 1950s. The entertainment industry became big business as promoters hurried to satisfy the great American need for fun. Fads flowered and ballyhoo flourished.

Fashions and fads flashed across the recreational landscape during the 1920s. Early in the decade, it was mahjong, a parlor game imported from China. In 1924 and 1925, crossword puzzles seized the popular fancy. Every newspaper and mass circulation magazine carried crossword puzzles. A new card game invented by a group of American socialites, contract bridge, became popular. In the late 1920s, it was miniature golf that was the rage. By 1930, an estimated thirty thousand miniature golf courses hosted millions of players each week. Throughout the decade, various dance crazes like the Charleston and Black Bottom attracted millions of enthusiasts.

THE MOVIES

Americans became avid moviegoers during the 1920s. Motion pictures became a mass medium, and big business. Movies also became a major American art form. Almost every community had at least one movie theater. Movie houses ranged from small-town storefronts to big-city luxury palaces. In 1925, 60 million people attended movies each week. By 1930, the figure had reached 100 million, nearly twice the average weekly church attendance.

The most popular movies were grand spectators such as *The Ten Commandments* (1923), slapstick comedies starring Charlie Chaplin, and adventure films like *Robin Hood* (1925), starring Douglas Fairbanks. Movie romances also had large audiences. John Gilbert and Greta Garbo were the most famous screen lovers of the silent film era, their passionate lovemaking enthralling audiences everywhere. Moviegoers idolized and often identified with film stars, who ranked among the reigning celebrities of the 1920s. Mass-circulation gossip magazines offered lurid details of their private lives to credulous fans.

The most ballyhooed movie star of the 1920s was Rudolph Valentino, an Italian immigrant whose passionate Latin machismo caused women in the audience to sigh and faint. Valentino's films played upon sexual fantasies and thrilling encounters with evil. In his most famous role he played an Arab Sheik, a combination kidnapper and seducer, who lifted women into his arms and carried them into his tent. When he died of ulcers at age thirty-one in 1926, his New York funeral turned into a public spectacle. Crowds lined up for over a mile to file past his coffin. Police had to fend off thousands of weepy women who tried to throw themselves on his corpse.

The 1920s was the great age of silent films. The beginning of their end came when sound was introduced in *The Jazz Singer,* starring Al Jolson, in 1927, although studios continued to turn out silent films into the 1930s. Sound had its hazards, however, for some of the great silent screen stars turned out to have squeaky or harsh voices unsuitable for talking films. John Gilbert was sound's most famous casualty. The great screen lover had to retire from movie making for want of a voice.

SPECTATOR SPORTS

Spectator sports also boomed in the 1920s. Each year, millions of fans packed stadia and arenas to watch college football, major league baseball, auto racing, boxing, horse racing, and tennis. Sporting events provided excitement, thrills, and drama. Sportswriters and radio sportscasters described athletic contests and reported results. Many sportswriters were also ballyhoo artists, promoting and hyp-

Rudolph Valentino was Hollywood's greatest romantic idol during the 1920s (pictured here with co-star Nita Naldi). *Source:* Museum of Modern Art, Film Stills Archive.

ing ballgames and boxing matches. The new media information technologies, such as the national wire services, radio, and film newsreels, disseminated box scores and outcomes of sporting events to huge national audiences. National sporting events also served to unite Americans divided along ethnic, racial, class, and regional lines.

Baseball was the most popular spectator sport of the 1920s. Attendance at major league games increased vastly in the early 1920s when owners introduced a livelier ball that enabled powerful hitters to belt home runs into the stands, and sometimes out of the park. More than 20 million spectators attended games in 1927. The most popular baseball player of the 1920s, the most famous athlete-celebrity of his era, was George Herman "Babe" Ruth. The Babe hit sixty home runs in 1927 and led his New York Yankees to a World Series sweep over the Pittsburgh Pirates. Ruth was legendary for his off-the-field exploits as well. He was a glutton for food, drink, and women. The Babe missed almost two months of the 1925 season because of a mysterious illness, which was publicly diagnosed as a stomach ache, but was in reality venereal disease picked up during a nightly adventure. People tended to forgive the Babe for his transgressions, for he was a remarkable athlete, and he spent a lot of his time visiting with youngsters and signing autographs.

Second in popularity only to Ruth was Jack Dempsey, a powerful fighter with a lethal punch who was heavyweight champion from 1921 until 1926. Dempsey's fights were often savage brawls and drew huge gates. In a fight with Luis Firpo, an Argentine slugger, Dempsey got knocked out of the ring. He managed to crawl back through the ropes and knock Firpo out in the third round. He lost his title to Gene Tunney, a skilled boxer, in 1926 via a decision. He failed to regain his title in a rematch with Tunney the following year at Soldier Field in Chicago. Dempsey's second fight with Tunney drew 145,000 fans, the largest crowd ever to see an athletic event in the United States.

Other athletes enjoyed celebrity status in the 1920s. William "Big Bill" Tilden was a champion tennis player. Earl Sande was the finest jockey. Man O' War was a great equine champion, considered one of the greatest race horses ever. Gertrude Ederle, a seventeen-year-old schoolgirl, became the first woman to swim the English Channel, and set a new record doing it. She returned to New York to receive a stupendous ticker tape parade. The greatest college football player of the decade was Harold "Red" Grange, a running back for the University of Illinois and three-time All-American player. Grange was a talented broken-field runner who thrilled spectators with his long touchdown runs. He was a celebrity when still in college, receiving lucrative offers from movie studios and real estate promoters. During his first year in professional football, fans urged him to run for Congress, although he was only twenty-two years old.

AN AMERICAN HERO

The greatest hero of the 1920s was neither a movie star nor a professional athlete: he was a young aviator named Charles Augustus Lindbergh. In May 1927, Lindbergh flew solo nonstop across the Atlantic from New York to Paris in thirty-three and a half hours in a small monoplane named "The Spirit of St. Louis." His feat was the greatest news story of the decade. President Coolidge sent the cruiser USS *Augusta* to bring Lindbergh home to the wildest celebration of the 1920s.

Lindbergh was a handsome, modest, middle-class midwesterner who did not try to cash in on his fame. His quiet personality, at variance with the frantic hype and ballyhoo of the decade, caused Americans to honor him more. Lindbergh's flight also represented a triumph of American industrial technology, a point that Lindbergh made repeatedly. It was the machine that had been specially configured for the long flight as much as the man that made the crossing possible. A contemporary observer also suggested that the intense emotional response Lindbergh provoked in this country was a reaction to his clean-cut appearance, WASP background, and moral character. In an age of ballyhoo and change, Lind-

In a hero-worshipping age, Charles A. Lindbergh was the greatest hero of all for his solo flight across the Atlantic in May 1927. Here, he stands before "The Spirit of St. Louis," the plane in which he made his historic flight.   *Source:* Library of Congress.

bergh affirmed traditional values. Will Rogers, an actor and humorist, said Lindbergh's flight proved that "someone could still make the front pages without murdering anybody."

THE ETHIC OF PLAY

In their heedless pursuit of fun, Americans in the 1920s became lawbreakers and supporters of organized crime. Americans had voted for Prohibition, which took effect January 1, 1920. The law was effective initially. Per capita liquor consumption dropped sharply. Prohibition was especially effective in the South and Midwest, where it had strong popular support. But the Prohibition Bureau, charged with enforcement of the law, had a small budget and only a few thousand agents, many of whom were inept, corrupt, or both. After 1925, enforcement declined in urban areas. Smuggling and home manufacture of liquor increased. Many people made beer, wine, and "bathtub" gin. Foreign booze was brought across the nation's long borders and shorelines. Local police stopped enforcing Prohibition in many cities.

Illegal drinking became a big business with millions of customers. Criminal organizations moved into the illicit liquor industry. The most notorious of these crooked businesses was headed by Al Capone, whose mob seized control of the

---

How to Make Bathtub Gin

Bathtub gin was usually made in gallon jugs, rather than in bathtubs. Juniper juice, which gives gin its distinctive flavor, was available at most drugstores or supplied as a gift with the alcohol by one's bootlegger. This recipe cost the maker about $.02 per ounce and was ready to drink upon mixing.

    2 parts alcohol (hospital alcohol or grain alcohol)
    3 parts water
    1 teaspoon juniper juice
    1 tablespoon glycerin to smooth it

Source: Moss, *America in the Twentieth Century,* 1st ed., p. 108.

liquor and vice trade in Chicago. Capone maintained his power for years through bribery, threats, and violence. During the 1920s, more than 500 gangland murders occurred on the streets of Chicago, many involving Capone's hired gunmen. Capone's organization took in an estimated $60 million a year. He was immune from local reprisals but ran afoul of the FBI. Capone was convicted of income tax evasion and sent to prison in 1931. He died years later of syphilis.

Americans during the 1920s were caught between two conflicting value systems. They retained traditional ethics of hard work, thrift, and sobriety; they also embraced the new ethic of play. They turned to mass entertainment provided by nightclubs, movies, sports, and radio. They also took up individual hobbies and amusements like photography, stamp collecting, playing and listening to music, and camping. Most such activities were neither illegal nor immoral, but millions of Americans were willing to break the law or reject traditional morality if such restrictions interfered with their pursuit of pleasure.

POPULAR WRITERS

During the 1920s, Americans read millions of books, but most readers did not read serious works of literature. Most critically acclaimed writers of the 1920s whose reputations have endured and whose books have become classics did not sell well during the decade. The most popular writers of the 1920s, whose books sold millions of copies and who perennially topped the best-seller charts included Geneva "Gene" Stratton Porter, Harold Bell Wright, Zane Grey, and Edgar Rice Burroughs.

Gene Stratton-Porter became rich writing novels that affirmed traditional values during a transitional era. Her books championed the virtues of optimism, a love for nature, and triumph over adversity. Harold Bell Wright, formerly a minister, was a prolific writer. He turned out a book every two years for twenty years. He used his novels as didactic vehicles to preach the gospel of hard work and clean living. Zane Grey was the most popular of the 1920s novelists. His books went on the best-seller lists every year during the decade, and total sales for the era exceeded 20 million copies. A dentist turned writer, Grey's novels were usually set in a highly romanticized version of the Old West. Author of more than fifty novels, many of which were transformed into Western movies, Grey was the most widely read novelist of his age. Edgar Rice Burroughs made his fame and fortune as the author of the Tarzan books. Burroughs' novels were purely escapist fare—writing about the adventures of a white man in Africa who had been reared by apes. Tarzan became the inspiration for cartoons, comic books, and dozens of films starring several different athletic actors playing the lead role.

Americans during the 1920s were also enthusiastic readers of newspapers. The trend toward consolidation occurring in the industrial economy also happened in the newspaper business. Ownership of newspapers was increasingly concentrated in the hands of a few media magnates such as William Randolph Hearst. Even though newspaper readership increased by millions during the decade, in 1929 there were two thousand fewer papers than in 1919. Tabloid newspapers made their appearance during the 1920s, led by the pioneer in the field, *The New York Daily News.* Tabloids sensationalized and simplified news stories, and also included lots of comics, sports news, features, and puzzles.

LITERATURE

The most impressive cultural achievement of Americans during the 1920s was a vast outpouring of serious literature. Urban America produced a generation of literary intellectuals who attacked the new consumer culture and its values. Many of the young writers had been involved in the war and came home traumatized and disillusioned by the great crusade to save democracy. The war experience shattered their lives and destroyed their progressive idealism. They were bewildered by rapid social change and appalled by the shallow materialism of the New Era. They condemned the excesses of the new business civilization and lamented the loss of American innocence.

The new writers included Ezra Pound, who developed new forms of poetic expression. He abandoned rhyme and meter to use clear, cold images that powerfully conveyed reality. Pound called the Western world that had waged four years of destructive warfare a "botched civilization, an old bitch gone in the teeth." He wrote of the hellish experience of American soldiers fighting on the Western Front and then coming home to a society they found empty and disillusioning.

T. S. Eliot, born in St. Louis, Missouri, moved to England, later becoming a British citizen. His greatest poem, published in 1992, is "The Waste Land." It is a long, difficult work expressing Eliot's profound despair about modern life and its loss of faith. He evoked images of sterility and fragmentation depicting contemporary civilization as a spiritual and moral wasteland. "The Waste Land" became an anthem for the disillusioned writers of the postwar generation. Eliot also composed "The Hollow Men" (1925), a biting description of the emptiness of modern man's existence.

From the depths of their profound disillusionment, this generation of young writers forged a major new literature. The symbol of this "lost generation" was F. Scott Fitzgerald. In a fine novel, *The Great Gatsby* (1925), Fitzgerald told the tragic story of Jay Gatsby, a romantic believer in the American dream who was destroyed by an unscrupulous millionaire, Tom Buchanan. Buchanan had Gatsby killed because he had fallen in love with Buchanan's wife, Daisy, a "vulgar, meretricious beauty" who did not deserve Gatsby's passion. Fitzgerald told his generation that innocent America where the dreams of men came true had been corrupted. Money and power had become the arbiters of fate.

Fitzgerald's own life was filled with sadness. He had married an attractive socialite, Zelda Sayre. He and Zelda lived extravagantly, beyond his means. He had to write popular stories to pay his bills. He later became an alcoholic and his wife, Zelda, had an emotional collapse and had to be institutionalized. Fitzgerald ended his days as a Hollywood script writer, dying of a heart attack in 1940.

Many young American writers and artists fled the United States. They lived and worked in Rome, Berlin, London, and especially Paris. In Paris, they lived along the left bank of the Seine. They lived cheaply and mixed with other writers, artists, and Bohemians. They wrote by day and talked, drank, and made love by night. Ernest Hemingway was the best writer of the young expatriates. He had grown up in the Midwest and worked as a newspaper reporter. During the war, he was an ambulance driver on the Italian front. He was seriously wounded by an artillery shell. After his recovery and return to America, he worked for a time as a reporter. In 1922, he settled in Paris to write. His first novel, *The Sun Also Rises* (1926), captured the amorality and sense of meaningless of life among expatriate drifters of the postwar era. *Farewell to Arms* (1929), his finest novel, portrayed the horrors and confusions of the war. Like Hemingway, the main character in the story, Frederick Henry, is wounded on the Italian Front and Hemingway uses Henry's wound to symbolize the disillusionment and the psychic damage done by a pointless war.

It was Hemingway's style—direct, terse, simple, a style that evoked powerful feelings—that made him the most important American writer of his generation. Hemingway was a muscular, athletic man who loved the outdoors and participated in strenuous sports. He boxed, fought bulls, and hunted lions in Africa. He survived a plane crash in Africa. The Hemingway lifestyle created a legend and made him a cult hero, the celebrity writer. Many people were more interested in the life of the artist than they were in his art.

Sinclair Lewis was the most popular serious writer of the 1920s. His first major work, *Main Street* (1920), sold well and drew critical acclaim. It depicted the ignorance, smugness, and mean-spiritedness of small-town life. Two years later, he brought forth *Babbitt*, his most famous novel. George Babbitt represented the archetypal businessman of the 1920s. Babbitt was a booster, gregarious, and narrowly conformist in his opinions. Beneath the noisy clichés hid a timid man who wanted to do better but was afraid to try. Both book titles passed into everyday language. "Main Street" symbolized the complacent bigotry of small-town life. "Babbitt" became a symbol of middle-class materialism and conformity. Lewis, a social satirist with great descriptive powers, masterfully depicted the sights and sounds of 1920s American life. His scathing satire skewered the fads and foibles of his era. In other words, he attacked the medical profession, religious evangelists, and manufacturers. His books sold well, making him rich and famous. Lewis became the first American writer to win a Nobel Prize for literature.

H. L. Mencken was another prominent American writer of the decade. Mencken was a middle-aged journalist and language scholar who founded the *American Mercury,* a sophisticated magazine that carried modern poetry, short stories, reviews, and satire. Mencken savagely satirized every aspect of American life. Anything sacred or significant to traditionalists was fair game for Mencken. At one time or another, he went after the Ku Klux Klan, Rotary Clubs, funerals, the Boy Scouts, motherhood, home cooking, Prohibition, democracy, and religious fundamentalism. He especially disliked religious people, all of whom he called "Puritans." He defined a Puritan as someone "who lives in mortal fear that somewhere, somehow, someone might be enjoying himself."

Mencken was at his best ridiculing politics and politicians. He regularly launched all-out assaults on the men in the White House and other prominent politicians. His readers laughed uproariously as he called Bryan "a charlatan, a mountebank, a zany without sense or dignity." He called Woodrow Wilson a "bogus liberal." Harding was a "numskull" and a "stonehead," and Coolidge was "a cheap and trashy fellow," a "dreadful little cad." Mencken's Hoover became a "pious old woman, a fat Coolidge." He coined a word—"booboisie"—to describe the complacent middle-class majority. He wrote about the great American "boobocracy" and the "boobocratic" way of life. Once when a young woman, upset by his diatribes, asked him why be bothered to live in the United States, Mencken replied, "Why do people go to zoos?"

Mencken was a professional iconoclast. His satires were amusing but never profound. His chief talent was his marvelous flair for language. He appeared to believe only in his own cleverness and a good turn of phrase. Mencken also very much reflected the spirit of the 1920s. When the Depression brought hard times in the 1930s, Mencken, in his accustomed way, satirized Franklin Roosevelt. No one laughed, and Mencken faded from public view.

The literary explosion of the 1920s was broad, rich, and diverse. It included the novelists Sherwood Anderson and John Dos Passos, who showed how the new technologies had undermined traditional values of craftsmanship and community. American dramatists Eugene O'Neill, Maxwell Anderson, and Elmer Rice created the modern American theater. Female writers made major contributions to the literature of the 1920s. Edith Wharton wrote a scathing indictment of wealthy easterners in *The Age of Innocence* (1921). Willa Cather and Ellen Glasgow wrote novels focusing on the problems besetting women in the Midwest and South.

THE HARLEM RENAISSANCE

African American writers also flourished during the 1920s. Harlem (a part of New York City), the largest black city in the world during the 1920s, became a cultural mecca, site of the "Harlem Renaissance." African American newspapers, magazines, and theater companies flourished. William E. B. Dubois was the dominant intellectual voice of Harlem. James Weldon Johnson, scholar, novelist, and poet, was another significant voice.

Langston Hughes, the leading poet of the Harlem Renaissance, wrote excitedly of the gathering of young African American poets, novelists, painters, and composers. Poets Countee Cullen and Claude McKay both wrote militant verses urging African Americans to challenge bigotry in all its forms. Jean Toomer was an outstanding realistic novelist and short-story writer. Alain Locke wrote of a "New Negro" coming into being who would shed his dependency and become a participant in American civilization. Zora Neale Hurston, the finest black woman writer of the Harlem Renaissance, turned out novels and short stories. Other writers addressed the issue of black identity—how to retain pride in their African heritage and come to terms with themselves as Americans. Hughes wrote

> We younger Negro artists who create now intend to express our individual dark-skinned selves without fear or shame. If white people are pleased we are glad. If they are not, it doesn't matter. We know we are beautiful.[1]

Art and music also thrived during the Harlem Renaissance. Plays and concerts were performed. All were part of the ferment. Historian David Lewis commented: "You could be proud and black, politically assertive, economically independent, creative and disciplined . . . ."Although Harlem was the center of African American intellectual and artistic life during the twenties, the new black cultural awareness spread to other cities where theater groups and poetry circles flourished.

THE JAZZ AGE

The Jazz Age, as the 1920s was sometimes called, owed its name to the music created by African American musicians working in New Orleans at the turn of the century. By the 1920s, this music had spread to the rest of the country. White musicians learned to play jazz and white audiences gathered to listen and to dance. Jazz was endlessly experimental, the best jazz musicians were inspired improvisers. Jazz also provided a way for African Americans to express symbolically their resentments and frustrations at the constraints imposed on their lives. Jazz also expressed their joy and a sense of community. Jazz also served as a call for freedom and rebellion. Jazz appealed to young middle-class whites rebelling against the Victorian restraints imposed by their parents.

---

[1]Quoted in Norton and others, *A People and a Nation,* p. 703.

Harlem was almost a city in itself—consisting of over one-half million people during the 1920s. Young black writers and artists gathered to celebrate a new pride in black people and black culture. Langston Hughes was one of the most gifted of the young black writers congregating in the black mecca. *Source:* Schomburg Center For Research in Black Culture, The New York Public Library. Astor, Lenox and Tilde Foundations.

Gifted African American jazz musicians such as trumpeter Louis Armstrong, trombonist Kid Ory, and blues singer Bessie Smith, became famous during the 1920s. Phonograph records and radiocasts popularized their music. Music recorded by African American artists and bought by millions of black purchasers gave African Americans a distinctive place in the new consumer culture. Jazz also gave a big boost to the pop record industry. Most important, jazz gave America its most distinctive art form.

Popular songwriters, some working in the jazz idiom or blending it with traditional musical forms, occupied a central place in the culture. Thousands of songs expressed the spirit of the age, the values, and the important personal concerns. Records, radio, and movies greatly expanded the availability of new popular music. Music could be heard everywhere. Some of the great masters of popular songwriting were active during the decade, including Irving Berlin, Jerome Kern, Ira Gershwin, Cole Porter, and Fats Waller. Many of their songs have endured, providing valuable historical clues to the inner life of the era.

It was during the 1920s that popular songs took on their modern form, a subjective, personal idiom expressing the singer's private feelings. A recurrent theme of 1920s songs was a man or woman singing of a lost love, a lost romance that he or she still feels. Another was the hope that true love will come along someday or of a love that was all-possessive. More songs were upbeat, happy, expressing the gaiety and fun-loving aspects of a decade in which many people devoted themselves to the serious business of going to parties. Cole Porter, the most talented of the lyricists of the 1920s, expressed the new morality of the era in witty verse. It is the popular songs of the decade that comprise one of its richest cultural legacies.

ART AND MUSIC

In all cultural realms, the 1920s were one of the most creative eras in American history. In addition to the literary outpouring, the evolution of jazz, and the wide circulation of popular songs, Georgia O'Keefe worked to develop a distinctive American style of painting. Composer Aaron Copeland built orchestral and vocal works around native themes and folk idioms. George Gershwin blended jazz, classical, and folk musical forms in compositions including "Rhapsody in Blue" (1924) and "Concerto in F" (1925). In architecture, the American skyscraper boom expanded. Midwesterner Frank Lloyd Wright built homes, churches, and schools in a distinctively American style, called the "prairie style," in which he merged the environment and the structure.

There is a paradox at the heart of the cultural flowering of the Roaring Twenties. All serious writers and artists railed against the conformity and materialism of the age. They wrote scathingly of the flawed promise of American life. They attacked technology, mass production, and the forced, frantic pace of modern existence. They were oblivious to politics and to social reform. They retreated into individualism, into writing, and into other forms of artistic expression. But despite their disillusionment and their alienation, or perhaps because of them, they created a first-rate body of artistic works. Ironically, contemporary critics of the 1920s wrote some of the finest American prose and poetry ever. Their best work suggested, despite their complaints and condemnations, that America had come of age artistically during the 1920s. Americans now ranked in the forefront of world literature and popular culture.

THE RISE OF RADIO

Radio hardly existed when the 1920s began, but within a few years, the new electronic medium enjoyed explosive growth. Over five hundred stations were launched in 1922. The Radio Corporation of America (RCA), which had begun the first commercial broadcast station to promote the sales of its radios, organized the first national radio network in 1926 and called it the National Broadcasting Company (NBC). In the early years of radio, music dominated the airwaves. It was radio that popularized jazz and the hit songs coming out of Tin Pan Alley.

Although musical programs continued to dominate the airwaves, radio diversified and expanded its programming as the 1920s developed. Radio began covering major sporting events during the 1920s, including the World Series and major

Radio had become a mass medium by the mid-1920s and brought urban popular culture to rural Americans. *Source:* National Archives.

college football games. Important boxing matches, especially heavyweight championship fights, were aired to the growing American radio audiences. Soon comedy shows, dramatic shows, soap operas, and quiz shows were added to the network repertoire of programs.

By the mid-1920s, most radio stations devoted a few minutes each evening to broadcasting national news. By 1930, about half of American households owned at least one radio. By the end of the 1920s, radio had become a mass medium and a big business. Advertisers were paying thousands of dollars for a minute's worth of prime-time advertising. The Radio Act of 1927 formally established the principle of federal regulation of the broadcast industry. The act also created the Federal Radio Commission to license stations.

RELIGIOUS FUNDAMENTALISM

Traditionalists opposed many of the modernist social and cultural trends of the 1920s. They were threatened by the secularist, hedonistic, and pluralistic tendencies of urban Americans, and they acted to defend themselves against these offending forces.

Millions of Americans turned to religious fundamentalism. They sought certainty in a rapidly changing society by joining evangelical Protestant churches, which embraced a literal interpretation of the Bible. Unquestioning faith in the revealed word of God brought fundamentalists both a means to salvation and protection against a materialistic and skeptical social order.

Fundamentalists, who were most numerous and politically influential in southern states, campaigned to have legislatures enact laws prohibiting the teaching of Darwinian evolutionary theory in public schools and colleges. They did not want young people learning a theory that stated human beings had evolved by natural processes over vast stretches of time from lower forms of life, a theory contradicting the Biblical version of Divine creation. Tennessee was one state that passed an antievolutionism law.

In 1925, scientific theory and revealed religion collided in a courtroom in Dayton, Tennessee. By teaching his class evolutionary theory, John Scopes, a young high school biology teacher, deliberately violated the state's antievolutionism statute to provide a test case. The trial became front-page news in the summer of 1925 when prominent public figures involved themselves on both sides of the controversy. William Jennings Bryan, three-time presidential candidate and long-time spokesman for traditional values, joined the prosecution. Clarence Darrow, the country's most successful trial lawyer and prominent reformer, headed a defense team of civil libertarians who had volunteered their services because they believed that an important constitutional issue was at stake. Journalists descended on the small farm community in the Tennesse hills to provided sensational coverage of the "Monkey Trial." It was also covered by radio, which was fast becoming a mass medium.

The emotional highlight of the trial came when Darrow cross-examined Bryan about his beliefs. Darrow exposed Bryan's ignorance of science and his fundamentalist religious views. The old Populist insisted that Eve had been created from Adam's rib and that a whale had swallowed Jonah. He told Darrow: "If God wanted a sponge to think, a sponge could think." He also quipped, "It's better to know the Rock of Ages than the age of rocks." Intellectuals and educated, secular people laughed at Bryan's simplistic ideas. H. L. Mencken, covering the trial, savagely satirized the old man's beliefs, delighting sophisticated readers on college campuses.

Bryan and the fundamentalists won their case in court. The Tennessee state prosecutor won a conviction against Scopes on the grounds that the legislature had the right to determine what was taught in public schools within the state. Darrow apealed the conviction, but the Tennesse State Supreme Court sustained the state's right to ban the teaching of unpopular theories even if they were valid scientifically. The state supreme court also outmaneuvered the defense attorneys when it overturned Scopes's conviction on a procedural technicality that prevented the defense from taking the case to the U.S. Supreme Court. Tennessee's antievolutionism law remained on the books, as did similar laws in other states.

Additional states soon passed antievolutionism laws. Publishers removed accounts of Darwinian theory from high school biology textbooks. By 1930, 70 percent of high school biology classes did not teach evolutionary biology, far fewer than in 1920, when the fundamentalists began their crusade. Modernists might scoff at Bryan's antiquated views, Darrow might reduce the old man's ideas to intellectual rubble, but Bryan and his fundamentalist cohorts won the battle to influence young people's minds, which was the most important issue at stake in the "Monkey Trial."

THE REVIVAL OF THE KLAN

Another reactionary movement of the 1920s, the revived Ku Klux Klan, also involved millions of Americans defending traditional values against the forces of change. The new Klan was founded in 1915 by William J. Simmons, an Atlanta insurance salesman. Simmons claimed he was reviving the terrorist organization that had intimidated and brutalized blacks during Reconstruction in order to purge southern culture of what he termed corrupting influences. The new Klan adopted the earlier organization's cloth hoods, mystical terms, secrecy, and vicious tactics, and it achieved a far larger membership than the old Klan.

It spread nationally and during the early 1920s, the "invisible empire" claimed 5 million members. If often allied itself with Protestant church congregations and lcoal leaders in southern and midwestern communities. It achieved significant political influence in various regions of the country and wielded power within the Democratic Party in several states. The revived Ku Klux Klan represented the sour side of progressivism. It was a species of reactionary populism that flourished in the early 1920s, a time of economic dislocation and moral confusion.

The new Klan also sought a broader range of targets than its predecessor. It tapped powerful nativist sentiments that asserted native, white Protestant

The "invisible empire" of Ku Klux Klan members marching in full regalia in the nation's capital in 1926.   *Source:* Library of Congress.

supremacy not only over blacks, but also over immigrants, Catholics, Jews, radicals, and anyone who violated their sense of moral order. They intimidated, beat up, and occasionally murdered blacks. They administered vigilante justice to bootleggers, prostitutes, and adulterers. They campaigned against Catholic and Jewish political candidates. They forced schools to adopt Bible readings and to stop teaching evolutionary theory. They beat up trade union organizers and harassed immigrant families. The 1920s Klansmen were essentially moral vigilantes. Although men dominated the Ku Klux Klan, they had many female supporters and collaborators.

During the mid-1920s, the Klan went into decline. Scandals helped undermine its appeal. Some members became involved in bootlegging and racketeering. One of its leaders was convicted of murdering a young woman whom he had kidnapped and raped. The economy revived and the Klan's brand of coercive, exclusive patriotism gradually lost much of its appeal within a pluralistic society. Some analysts have defined the 1920s Ku Klux Klan as an indigenous American Fascist movement, resembling the Italian *Fascisti* and German Nazis. These analysts ignore or misunderstand the ideological underpinnings of the KKK; they embraced traditional American republican values. They did not repudiate democracy; they embraced a narrow, cranky, and bigoted version of it.

CLOSING THE DOOR

Another powerful reactionary current flowing through the early 1920s sprang from native-born American prejudices against the "new" immigrants from southern and eastern Europe. Since the 1880s, nativist organizations, labor leaders, and some Progressive reformers had urged an end to unrestricted immigration. Nativists complained that these newcomers were inherently inferior, with alien habits and beliefs that they did not abandon, and that they polluted native stock. They also feared that Catholic private schools would undermine the American system of public education. Labor leaders charged the "new" immigrants with lowering wage levels, raising unemployment, refusing to join unions, and working as strikebreakers. Some reformers argued that the immigrants crowding inner-city slums exacerbated urban problems, supported corrupt political machines, and formed a permanent underclass of unassimilable aliens.

The drive to restrict immigration gained momentum during and after World War I. Congress enacted a Literary Test Act in 1917 over President Wilson's veto, which required immigrants to be literate in any language. The Red Scare strengthened anti-immigrant movements by heightening fears of radical aliens importing revolutionary ideologies and tactics. Businessmen, who had long been the most powerful champions of free immigration because it gave them a pool of low-wage workers, installed assembly line technologies that cut labor costs and decreased their need for workers.

Social scientists also joined the cause of immigration restriction when they misinterpreted the findings of intelligence tests the Army had given draftees during World War I. They found that recruits from southern and eastern European countries scored much lower than soldiers whose ancestors had come from the British Isles, northern, and western Europe. The tests really measured educational levels attained and the cultural opportunities experienced, but scientists assumed that they measured innate intellectual abilities, confirming the nativist assumption that the "new" immigrants were of lower intelligence than old-stock Americans.

When immigration after the war threatened to reach prewar levels despite the literacy test, Congress enacted restrictive legislation that reduced immigration generally, sharply curtailing immigration from southern and eastern Europe, and excluding Asians. In 1921, Congress enacted the Emergency Quota Act. According to its provisions, immigrants equal to 3 percent of the number of foreign-born residents of the United States could enter each year. This number amounted to about 350,000 people, since there were 11.7 million foreign-born Americans according to the 1910 census. Each country's portion of the 350,000 was determined by the number of its nationals already resident in the United States. For example, there were about 1.3 million Italians, which amounted to 11 percent of the foreign-born population in 1910. Italy, therefore, got 11 percent of the 350,000 slots, or 38,500 places, for the year 1922.

The Emergency Quota Act was a temporary measure. Following extensive study and hearings, Congress enacted a comprehensive measure in 1924, the National Origins Act, which would define U.S. immigration policy for the next forty years. The act phased in a more restrictive system that reduced the "new" immigration to an annual trickle and banned Asians altogether, but it allowed sizeable numbers of immigrants from northern and western Europe to continue to enter America.

By its terms, beginning in 1925, immigration equal to only 2 percent of the foreign-born population living in the United States in 1890 could enter the country. Since that population amounted to about 7.5 million, only 150,000 people could enter annually. This law both sharply reduced total immigration and further limited "new" immigration because most southern and eastern Europeans residing in the United States had arrived after 1890. For example, of the 7.5 million foreign-born residents in the country in 1890, only 450,000, 6 percent, were Italians. Hence Italy's 1925 quota came to only 9,000 slots compared to 38,500 under the Emergency Quota Act.

Congress amended the National Origins Act in 1927 to establish an immigration system that kept the 150,000 annual quota, but further reduced the number of "new" immigrants allowed to enter annually. Starting in 1929, each nation's quota was based not on a percentage of the foreign-born population living in the United States, but on the national origins of the entire European population of the country according to the 1920 census. For example, there were about 3.8 million Americans of Italian descent residing in the United States in 1920, counting both those born in Italy and their descendants born in America. They composed 4 percent of the total European population in 1920 of 96 million. So Italy got 4 percent of the 150,000 immigration slots available in 1929, or 6,000 openings. Between 1900 and 1910, before the country adopted restrictive immigration policies, about 1.6 million Italians had come to the United States, an average of 160,000 annually. All southern and eastern Europe nationalities suffered sharp reductions in their quotas. What had been a flood before World War I became a trickle after 1929.

In practice, the national origins quota system reduced immigration below the 150,000 allowed annually because it assigned large quotas to western and northern European nations that did not use all of their assigned slots each year. Great Britain had 65,000 slots annually, most of which went unused during the Depression years of the 1930s. The unused slots did not transfer to other nations. Meanwhile, in Italy and other southern and eastern European countries, which had small quotas, a huge backlog of potential immigrants built up.

The national origins system was designed to preserve the ethnic and racial status quo that prevailed during the 1920s. It also reflected prevailing nativist assumptions and prejudices. America sent a message to the world with its new immigration policy: If you were white, Anglo-Saxon, and preferably Protestant, you were welcome. If you were Catholic, Jewish, or Slavic, a few of you could come each year. If you were Asian, you were excluded. America, which had opened its doors to the people of the world as no nation ever had, now closed the "golden door" except to a few favored nationalities. The national origins system severely compromised the inspiring verse on the base of the Statue of Liberty, "give me your poor, your tired, your huddled masses, yearning to breathe free."

Religious fundamentalism, the Ku Klux Klan, and immigration restriction represented reactionary efforts by traditionalists to preserve an older, simpler, and (from their perspective) purer America against spreading modernism and urban-industrial values. Traditionalists attempted to sustain old values in the midst of a dynamic materialistic, hedonistic, and pluralistic society.

THE BUSINESS OF GOVERNMENT

With the upsurge in prosperity, most Americans shed their fears of big business and ceased complaining about the depredations of large corporations. John D. Rockefeller, previously denounced as a robber baron and an enemy of democracy, became a celebrity, praised for his generous philanthropy. Part of the new acceptance of oligopoly was attributable to the public's perception that big business contributed to rising productivity, higher wages, and improved living standards. Popular approval of big business was also encouraged by skilled business publicists who projected a corporate image of ethical concern and social responsibility. An ethic of service replaced the older predatory, "public-be-damned" attitudes of Gilded Age buccaneers. A spokesman applied the language of religion to corporate enterprise, "Through business, . . . the human race is finally to be redeemed."

Both Congress and the executive branch supported business during the 1920s. Congress lowered corporation taxes in 1921 and raised tariff rates a year later. Secretary of the Treasury Andrew Mellon got Congress to slash federal spending from a high of $18 billion in 1918 to $3 billion in 1925, generating a surplus used to retire part of the national debt. He persuaded Congress to reduce income taxes in 1926. In 1921, the government returned the railroads, modernized at taxpayers' expense, to their private owners. Government-built merchant ships were sold to private shipping companies at a fraction of their cost. Regulatory agencies such as the Federal Trade Commission and the Interstate Commerce Commission were staffed with businessmen who took a protective stance toward the industries they were regulating.

The federal government's role in the economy increased during the 1920s. Republicans widened the scope of federal activity and the number of government employees nearly doubled between 1921 and 1929. Herbert Hoover led the way in the Commerce Department, establishing new agencies to make the housing, transportation, and mining industries more efficient. Government encouraged corporations to develop welfare programs for employees. Agencies also devised new federal machinery to arbitrate labor disputes. Despite their use of the rhetoric of laissez-faire, the Republican administrations of the 1920s expanded the apparatus of the developing federal bureaucracy pioneered by progressive reformers. They applied Theodore Roosevelt's conception of business-government cooperation; although the 1920s' presidents viewed the role of government as a passive servant of business, rather than as the active regulator that Roosevelt had championed.

Progressivism declined during the 1920s. Antitrust activities and the commitment to social justice waned. But progressivism survived in Congress: A group of midwestern senators supported labor legislation and aid to farmers. Progressivism survived also at state and local levels. Several states enacted workers' compensation laws and old-age pensions. City planning and zoning commissions controlled urban growth in a professional manner. Social workers provided help for the urban poor.

The 1920s were lean years for organized labor. Public opinion was indifferent or hostile to trade unions, especially when they struck. Government hostility also hindered the growth of unions. The Justice Department used court injunctions against striking unions; the Clayton Act's provisions designed to protect unions proved useless. Corporations took actions to wean employees away from unions. Company unions, profit sharing, pensions, and company-sponsored social events were all expressions of welfare capitalism. Union membership fell from 5 million in 1920 to 3.6 million at the end of the decade.

The Supreme Court was dominated by conservative jurists during the 1920s, headed by Chief Justice, and former President, William Howard Taft. Many of its decisions protected business from rigorous regulation, weakened trade unions, and nullified social legislation. In *Bailey* v. *Drexel Furniture Company* (1922), the Court nullified a law restricting child labor. In *Adkins* v. *Children's Hospital* (1923) the court overturned a minimum wage law for women on the grounds that it infringed upon women's freedom of contract.

Electoral politics during the 1920s continually demonstrated the strong popular appeal of Republican candidates. At the 1920 Republican convention, a lightly regarded candidate, Senator Warren G. Harding of Ohio, got the presidential

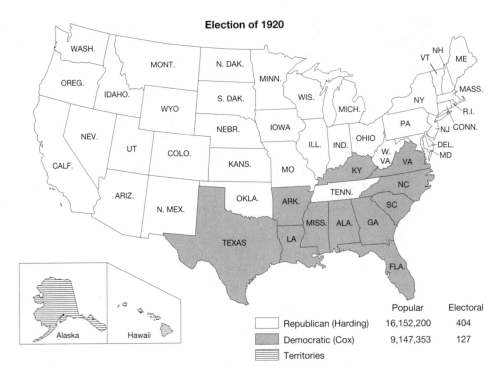

Election of 1920

	Popular	Electoral
Republican (Harding)	16,152,200	404
Democratic (Cox)	9,147,353	127
Territories		

Election of 1920. *Source:* Moss, *Rise of Modern America*, p. 144.

nomination because the leading contenders were deadlocked. His genial personality and lack of strong views made him an appealing compromise choice. He conducted a clever campaign tailored to the public mood, which had turned against both domestic reform and Wilsonian internationalism. Harding coined a new word to describe public yearnings; he told an audience that Americans wanted "not nostrums but normalcy." "Normalcy" was not good usage, but it made for good politics in the 1920 campaign.

Harding and his running mate, Calvin Coolidge, a journeyman professional politician made famous by his role in the crushing of the Boston police strike, easily defeated their Democratic opponents, Governor James Cox of Ohio and Franklin Roosevelt, formerly Assistant Secretary of the Navy and a distant relative of the late President Theodore Roosevelt. Cox was saddled with Woodrow Wilson's discredited administration and Cox's support for American membership in the League of Nations had become unpopular by the fall of 1920. Harding and Coolidge rolled to a landslide triumph. Harding received over 16 million votes, more than twice as many as any previous candidate had ever gotten. His 61 percent of the popular vote was also a historic high. His huge majority also came from women voters. The 1920 election was the first in which the Nineteenth Amendment, enfranchising women, was in force. Feminists were disappointed when only about 25 percent of eligible women voted and when most voted the way their husbands did.

President Harding was politically shrewd and hardworking. He selected capable men to serve in key cabinet positions. These appointees included Secretary of State Charles Evans Hughes, Secretary of Agriculture Henry C. Wallace, Andrew Mellon at the Department of Treasury, and Herbert Hoover at the Department of Commerce. Harding relied heavily on his cabinet advisers; he had a conception of government-by-cabinet in contrast to his strong-willed predecessor, President Wilson, who rarely sought advice from anyone.

Although a traditional Republican, Harding was responsive to reform concerns. He established a modern budgeting system for the government, supported an antilynching measure, approved legislation aiding farmers, responded to some labor concerns, and supported civil liberties. Harding pardoned Eugene Debs, the Socialist Party leader imprisoned for his opposition to the war, and invited him to the White House for a visit following his release.

Harding's administration is best remembered for its many scandals. Although honest himself, Harding inadvertently appointed many men to office who were crooks. Charles Forbes, who headed the Veterans Bureau, served time in prison for fraud and bribery. Attorney General Harry Daugherty, Harding's campaign manager in 1920, was tried for bribery but avoided conviction by refusing to testify. The most notorious case revealed that Secretary of the Interior Albert Fall had accepted bribes from oil companies in exchange for his leasing public oil lands to them illegally. It is known as the Teapot Dome Scandal, named for the site of a federal oil reserve in eastern Wyoming that had been turned over to the Mammoth Oil Company. After a congressional investigation unearthed the criminal activity, Fall was tried, convicted, fined $100,000, and sent to prison.

In the summer of 1923, neither Harding nor the American people knew about his administration's extensive corruption, although there is evidence suggesting Harding was becoming suspicious and fearful. He confided to journalist William Allen White, "I have no trouble with my enemies . . . .But my friends, . . . they're the ones that keep me walking the floor nights." Harding went on a speaking tour of the West, became ill, and died in San Francisco in a room on the seventh floor of the Palace Hotel on the evening of August 2, 1923. The cause of death was a coronary embolism, a blood clot that lodged in his brain. The sudden death of a popular president came as a great shock to the nation, and millions mourned the passage of a kindly, genial man who appeared to be the appropriate leader for a country seeking "normalcy" in the wake of world upheavals. In the years after his death, investigations and trials exposed the corruption and thievery riddling his administration; Harding's reputation plummeted. Historians rate him among the republic's least successful presidents.

Calvin Coolidge, a laconic Puritan from rural Vermont, succeeded the affable Harding. Coolidge purged the government of crooks and thieves. He replaced Daugherty with Harlan Fiske Stone, the respected dean of Columbia

Law School and future Supreme Court justice. But mostly he kept the Harding administration in place and continued Harding's policies. Coolidge admired successful businessmen and bankers; the new president was devoted to the principles of laissez-faire. He stated "if the federal government disappeared, the average citizen would probably never notice the difference." He also said, "the man who builds a factory builds a temple." Mellon became his mentor in fiscal and financial affairs.

Coolidge quickly took control of the Republican Party and easily gained his party's 1924 presidential nomination. His restoring of integrity to the national government and the nation's rising prosperity ensured his election. Coolidge was also aided by the Democratic Party, which nearly tore itself apart at its nominating convention. The party was split into an eastern, urban wing and a southern, rural wing. A motion to condemn the Ku Klux Klan was ferociously debated and defeated. Southern Democrats, dry (politicians who favored retaining Prohibition were called "drys"; politicians who favored repealing Prohibition were called "wets"), anti-immigrant, and pro-Klan, rallied to the candidacy of William Gibbs McAdoo. Eastern big-city Democrats supported Governor Alfred E. Smith, a Catholic Progressive with a background in machine politics. It took 103 ballots before the deadlocked convention could agree on a compromise candidate, John Davis, a conservative corporation lawyer associated with Morgan banking interests.

The old reformer warhorse, Robert La Follette, entered the 1924 presidential race as the head of a reborn Progressive Party. Progressives adopted a platform calling for government ownership of railroads, direct election of the president, and a host of labor and social reforms. His Progressive candidacy contrasted sharply with the probusiness platforms of the major parties.

The election results were predictable. It was 1912 in reverse. The two probusiness candidates got most of the votes. Coolidge won easily, defeating Davis and La Follette in the popular vote. He received 15.7 million to 8.4 million for Davis and a mere 4.8 million for La Follette. In the electoral vote column, Coolidge got 382 to Davis's 136. La Follette carried only his native Wisconsin. In an electoral contest characterized by a low voter turnout, "Coolidge prosperity" had received a strong popular endorsement. The Republicans also retained large majorities in both houses of Congress. Conservatism reigned. National progressivism appeared mortally ill, if not dead. It was time to "keep cool with Coolidge."

President Coolidge chose not to run in 1928 mainly for health reasons. Had he sought another presidential term, he would easily have been reelected. The country was prosperous, most people content, convinced that the wonders of the New Era would continue indefinitely. When Coolidge stepped aside, Herbert Hoover came forward to wear the mantle of prosperity. Hoover was an apt candidate for the Republicans. He combined the traditional ethic of personal success through hard work with a progressive emphasis on collective action. Born poor on an Iowa farm and orphaned at nine, he had worked his way through Stanford University. He graduated with its first class in 1895 amidst the worst depression in American history. By the time he was forty, Hoover was a multimillionaire mining engineer. He retired from business to begin a second career in government service. During and after World War I, Hoover distinguished himself as the U.S. food administrator and as head of general relief for Europe. He served as Secretary of Commerce under Harding and Coolidge. In both administrations, he was a highly visible, active cabinet officer.

Hoover was not a traditional Republican conservative; he was a Progressive who expanded Theodore Roosevelt's New Nationalist concept of business-government cooperation. As Commerce Secretary, he had promoted business, encouraged the formation of trade associations, held conferences, and sponsored studies—all aimed at improving production and profits. In his speech accepting the Republican nomination for President in the summer of 1928, the confident Hoover proclaimed that Americans would soon be the first nation in the history of the world to abolish poverty.

The Democrats nominated New York Governor Alfred E. "Al" Smith. Smith's background contrasted dramatically with Hoover's. Whereas Hoover had rural, Protestant roots and a business background, and had never run for office, Smith was from immigrant stock, raised on the streets of a Manhattan slum, and his political career was rooted in machine politics. Smith had risen through the ranks of New York City's Tammany Hall. He was also the first Roman Catholic to run for president on a major party ticket.

Hoover ran on a platform pledging to continue Republican prosperity for four more years. Unwilling to challenge the public's complacent view of Coolidge prosperity, the Democrats adopted a similar, conservative program. Smith appointed his friend John J. Raskob, the president of General Motors, to manage his campaign. The weak, "me too" strategy adopted by Smith and Raskob failed. Nothing Smith could say or do convinced businessmen or most voters that he was a better choice than Coolidge's heir apparent. Smith also lost votes in some regions because of his religious affiliation, his political machine connections, his urban background, and his attacks on Prohibition.

Smith waged a vigorous campaign. He struck back at bigots who charged that his Catholicism made him a servant of the Pope. But he was overwhelmed by the prosperity wave that Hoover rode to a landslide victory. It was the prosperous economy—not his Catholic religion—that defeated Al Smith. Hoover won the popular vote with 21 million votes to 15 million for Smith; and, in the electoral vote, Hoover received 444 to Smith's 87. Hoover even won a few states of the "solid south," the first Republican to carry Texas and Florida since Reconstruction. The Republicans also rolled up large majorities in both houses of Congress. It was a Republican sweep.

After this defeat, its third shellacking in a row, the Democratic Party appeared on the verge of extinction. But the epitaphs sounded were premature. Prosperity had defeated Smith; and, although no one in November 1928 could know, prosperity was about to end. Hoover's overwhelming victory concealed a significant political realignment taking form. Catholic working-class voters in the big cities, who were not sharing in the 1920s prosperity, were switching from Republican ranks to the Democrats. Coolidge had carried the twelve largest cities in 1924. All twelve had voted for Smith in 1928. Farmers in the Midwest, upset over continuing low prices for farm commodities, also voted for Smith in 1928. A new coalition of urban workers and dissatisfied farmers was in the making. This coalition waited upon the economic collapse that was just around the corner.

IMPORTANT EVENTS

1920	The first commercial radio station, KDKA in Pittsburgh, begins broadcasting
1920	Prohibition goes into effect
1920	The Nineteenth Amendment grants women the right to vote
1921	The first Miss America is crowned in Atlantic City, New Jersey
1921	Margaret Sanger founds the American Birth Control League
1922	"The Wasteland," by T. S. Eliot, is published
1922	*Babbitt*, by Sinclair Lewis, is published
1923	The Teapot Dome scandal exposed
1923	*Time* magazine is founded
1924	National Origins Act is passed
1924	George Gershwin composes "Rhapsody in Blue"
1925	*The Great Gatsby*, by F. Scott Fitzgerald, is published
1925	*The New Negro*, by Alain Locke, is published
1925	Scopes "Monkey Trial" in Dayton, Tennessee
1926	*The Sun Also Rises*, by Ernest Hemingway, is published
1927	The first sound motion picture, "The Jazz Singer," is released
1927	Charles Lindbergh flies solo across the Atlantic, from New York to Paris
1927	Babe Ruth hits sixty home runs
1927	Sacco and Vanzetti are executed
1928	Herbert Hoover is elected president
1929	The stock market collapses

BIBLIOGRAPHY

The best book ever done on the 1920s is Frederick Lewis Allen's famed *Only Yesterday: An Informal History of the 1920s,* a relatively brief, entertaining account that highlights the frivolity and disillusionment of the era. William E. Leuchtenburg's *The Perils of Prosperity* is the best scholarly history of the New Era. A fine recent account is Geoffrey Perrett's *America in the Twenties.* Isabel Leighton, editor of *The Aspirin Age,* offers a fine collection of essays on various events and personalities of the 1920s and 1930s. James J. Flink, in *The Car Culture,* gives us the best study we have of the impact of mass ownership of automobiles on American life. A fine study of young people in the 1920s is by Paula Fass, *The Damned and the Beautiful: American Youth in the 1920s.* Kenneth S. Davis's *The Hero: Charles A. Lindbergh* is a good biography of the preeminent culture hero of the times. In *Babe,* Robert Creamer has written the best biography of the greatest baseball player of the 1920s. Nathan I. Huggins has written the finest account of black culture during the 1920s, *Harlem Renaissance.* Ray Ginger's *Six*

Days or Forever is a marvelous account of the famous Scopes "Monkey Trial" that took place in 1925. Andrew Sinclair's *Prohibition: The Era of Excess* records the social consequences of the Noble Experiment. Roderick Nash, in *The Nervous Generation: American Thought, 1917–1930,* offers a fine intellectual history of the 1920s. Gilbert Seldes, in *The Seven Lively Arts,* has written the best cultural history of the 1920s. Frederick L. Hoffmann's *The Twenties: American Writing in the Postwar Decade* is the best general study of the great American writers of the 1920s. George Soule's *Prosperity Decade: From War to Depression, 1917–1929* is the best short economic history of the 1920s. Irving Berstein, writing in *The Lean Years: A History of the American Worker, 1920–1933,* presents the best 1920s labor history.

CHAPTER 5

The Great Depression

The prosperous 1920s gave way to economic disaster during the 1930s. The spectacular collapse of the securities markets in this country during the fall of 1929 catalyzed the process of economic disintegration historians label the Great Depression. The boosterism of the 1920s collapsed along with stock values, commodity prices, and real estate prices. President Hoover, who had ridden the last wave of 1920s prosperity to an overwhelming electoral victory in 1928, found himself confronting an unprecedented national crisis. Millions of his fellow citizens faced massive unemployment and underemployment, failing businesses, and farm commodity prices so low that it did not pay to harvest the crops. The American economic collapse of the early 1930s triggered a worldwide crisis of capitalism that gripped most of the leading industrial countries and Third World producers of raw materials for years. International trade declined sharply. Most nations devalued their currencies in vain efforts to maintain their export markets. Internationalism weakened, and aggressive nations such as Germany, Italy, and Japan took advantage of the situation to conquer weak and vulnerable countries. Within the United States, American voters during the election of 1932, perceiving Hoover's vigorous efforts to combat the effects of Depression as ineffective, turned to the Democratic candidate, New York's Governor Franklin Delano Roosevelt, to lead them out of the morass of depression.

THE HOOVER ERA

No American presidency ever began as favorably as Herbert Hoover's. His administration would crown one of the most successful careers in the history of the Republic. The poor orphan boy had risen to become rich, famous, and the most admired man in public life. His experiences as businessman, wartime food and general relief administrator, and cabinet officer had prepared him thoroughly for the presidency. Hoover's career combined the idealistic and the pragmatic; he was the utopian who got things done in business and government.

America in March 1929 was peaceful and prosperous. Its economy was pre-eminent in the world, and New Era living standards were the highest in human history. Poverty persisted in America, but Hoover had declared repeatedly during his campaign for the presidency that the United States was putting poverty on the road to extinction. He had proclaimed "we shall soon be in sight of the day when poverty will be banished from this nation." All families would soon have "two cars in every garage and a chicken in every pot." His inaugural address celebrated the American standard of living: "we have reached a higher degree of comfort and security than ever before existed in the history of the world."

Hoover also espoused an energetic philosophy of government firmly grounded in the Progressive tradition of Theodore Roosevelt: "The election has again confirmed the determination of the American people that regulation of private enterprise . . . is the course rightly to be pursued in our relations to business." He concluded his inaugural address with a ringing affirmation of his faith in American progress: "I have no fears for the future of our country. It is bright with hope." These words came from the heart of a man who knew no failure in life.

Some voices dissented from Hooverian optimism. They voiced concern about the rampant speculation in the stock market. Hoover himself had, at times, fretted about the speculative mania that siphoned off investment funds into unproductive channels, but he had done nothing about it. He regarded agricultural problems and tariff reform to be more pressing. He called Congress into special session to tackle farm and tariff problems. Congress enacted the Agricultural Marketing Act that Hoover had requested, but it failed to raise farm prices. His tariff proposals failed to pass during the special session.

But Hoover did get much of his legislative program enacted during the eight months of his presidency preceding the stock market collapse, many of them Progressive measures. Congress outlawed any further leases of public oil lands to private developers. Appropriations for Native American educational and health services were increased. Hoover created a commission to study ways of abolishing poverty in America and to usher in what he called a "Great Society." These and other Progressive measures suggest the direction in which Hoover was moving. They indicate what might have been had the stock market not crashed and plunged Americans into the long dark night of the depression that transformed the Hoover administration into an ordeal of frustration and failed policies.

THE GREAT CRASH

During the summer of 1929, the economy slipped. Construction starts declined as new building permits were down 65 percent. Business inventories increased sharply as consumer spending slackened. During August, industrial production and wholesale prices dropped. Unemployment rose. The economy was sliding into

President Hoover, shown here on the day of his inauguration, battled the Great Depression vigorously, but ultimately his efforts failed to rid the country of depression or to even arrest the downward spiral.   *Source:* National Archives.

a recession. Simultaneously, the Federal Reserve Board, responding to its critics who had called for a tighter monetary policy to discourage speculation in the stock market, raised its discount rate, hoping to dampen gently the speculative orgy. But higher interest rates did not slow the traffic in brokers' loans; unfortunately, they did contribute to the recessionary downturn because they reduced borrowing by consumers and investors.

The stock market ignored the recession; stock prices continued to climb during August and September as stock averages soared to historic highs. On September 3, the price of a share of AT&T common stock sold for $304 and General Electric was up to $396, triple its price eighteen months previously. The biggest gainer of the decade, RCA, reached $450. As the economy faltered, business leaders, blinded by the Great Bull Market, forecast a quick recovery.

The Crash began Wednesday morning, October 23, 1929, when millions of shares of common stocks were suddenly offered for sale at the New York Stock Exchange by brokers executing sell orders from their customers. Key issues slumped in heavy trading. Although no one panicked that day, brokers noted nervously that the market had lost $4 billion. Speculative stocks had taken a beating and many blue chips were off as much as 5 points.

No one knows for sure why thousands of investors chose that particular morning to sell their holdings. The national mood was confident. Hoover's presidency had been successful. There were no political or economic crises anywhere to frighten investors. The mild recession was not considered serious, nor likely to last long. There was no conspiracy to rig the market. There was no shortage of investment funds. Banks and corporations had plenty of money, which they were eager to lend despite the new tight money policy. Higher interest rates had not deterred speculators.

The market had shown weaknesses in September, but it had rallied and September ended a positive month. Sharp losses occurred the first week in October, but the market again rallied. Losses occurred during the week preceding the Crash, but had caused no alarm. On both October 21 and 22 the market closed on the upside. The selling and huge losses of October 23 caught everyone by surprise. That night optimism vanished at the world's most important financial center. The bulls all became bears. The floodgates opened on Thursday—"Black Thursday"—October 24. Prices fell and did not recover. Bedlam reigned on the floor. Brokers shouted themselves hoarse seeking vanished buyers. At times, there were no takers of stocks at any price. Hysteria and panic prevailed. People screamed, shouted, and wept.

Although the origins of the selling wave of October 23 remain mysterious, its consequences proved to be catastrophic. It generated the contagion of selling historians call "Black Thursday." That afternoon, a group of New York's leading financiers formed a pool to buy stocks and stem the panic. A pool member walked on the floor of the exchange and bid 205 for 25,000 shares of U.S. Steel then selling for 193. For a moment, that dramatic gesture worked. Selling stopped, prices steadied. Some believed the panic to be over.

A flood of reassuring statements came the next day. John Maynard Keynes, the world's foremost economist, declared the decline a good thing for it had eliminated speculators and money would now be channeled into productive enterprises. Governor Franklin Roosevelt of New York expressed confidence in the stock market. President Hoover declared, "The fundamental business of the country is on a sound and prosperous basis." These official optimists failed to restore confidence. Stock prices held for a few days only.

New torrents of selling occurred the following week. Many investors were forced to sell to cover their debts. Tuesday, October 29, was the worst. In one of history's greatest avalanches of panic selling, more than 16 million shares were dumped on the market. Stock averages lost almost 40 points. In a single day, as much money in capital values vanished as the United States had spent fighting World War I. The October 30 headline of *Variety* trumpeted "Wall St. Lays an Egg." By month's end, over $15 billion in stock values had been lost. At year's end, losses reached $40 billion, representing 60 percent of the total value of stocks listed on the exchange when the Crash began.

As 1930 began, some businessmen still exuded optimism because no one had yet connected the Wall Street disaster to the general economy. They believed that the market crash had merely ruined the lunatic fringe of margin speculators without harming the people who produced and distributed goods within the economy. The notion that the basic economy remained healthy after the securities collapse underlay Secretary of the Treasury Andrew Mellon's famed remark,

> Let the slump liquidate itself. Liquidate labor, liquidate stocks, liquidate the farmers, liquidate real estate. . . . Values will be adjusted, and enterprising people will pick up the wrecks from less competent people.[1]

CAUSES OF THE GREAT DEPRESSION

As 1931 began, the recession that had begun during the summer of 1929 had become a depression, the first to afflict America in forty years. 1931 was Year One of the Great Depression.

The Depression had multiple causes. They included several flaws inherent in the prosperous economy of the 1920s. A fundamental defect of the economy of the 1920s was the unequal distribution of wealth. Average per capita disposable income rose about 10 percent during the 1920s, but income of the wealthiest Americans rose 75 percent during the same period. The Federal Trade Commission reported that the richest 1 percent of the population owned 60 percent of the nation's wealth. The savings of the top 60,000 families exceeded the savings of the 25 million poorest families. Cuts in corporate and personal income taxes, which mainly benefited business and wealthy people, increased the inequality of income distribution. Because a rising portion of national income went to upper-income families, the economy became increasingly dependent on their spending and saving for continued growth. With wealth concentrated at the top, much income went into investments, luxury purchases, and stock speculation instead of spending for consumer durables. The wealthy had more money than they could spend; farmers, workers, and the bulk of middle-class families together did not have enough money to keep the economy growing in 1928–1929.

Because profits rose faster than wages, businessmen increased their production of goods by investing some of their profits for plant expansion at a greater rate than the slowly increasing capacity of consumers to buy the goods. The gap be-

[1]Quoted in Robert Sobel, *The Great Bull Market: Wall Street in the 1920s* (New York: Norton, 1968), p. 145.

tween production and consumption of goods widened in durable goods industries such as automobile manufacturing and housing construction, which had become the mainstays of the 1920s consumer economy because so many other businesses depended on them. Construction, autos, steel, and many other major industries had overbuilt. In 1928 and 1929, sales lagged, inventories rose, production decreased, and unemployment increased.

Farmers did not share fully in the expanding consumer economy. Farmers never recovered from the collapse of commodity prices after World War I. Most farmers had been in recession since 1921. They had received 16 percent of national income in 1919; ten years later, they received only 9 percent. Agricultural overproduction became chronic during the 1920s as farm income declined relatively. Farmers' purchasing power remained weak during the 1920s.

Industrial wages rose about 10 percent during the decade, but workers also earned a smaller share of national income at the end of the decade than they did when it began. Technological unemployment caused by businessmen installing new labor-saving machinery in their factories threw thousands of people out of work each year. Unemployment remained high throughout the 1920s, averaging about 7 percent. Since unemployment insurance and federally funded welfare payments did not exist during the 1920s, sustained unemployment meant poverty and severely curtailed purchasing power.

In the fall of 1929, there were about 3 million people out of work, many of them in textiles, coal mining, lumbering, and railroads. These "sick industries" all suffered from overexpansion, declining demand, and inefficient management. They could not compete with more efficient rivals. Impoverished unemployed workers could not participate in the consumer economy. The closing of a coal mine or a textile factory also blighted communities and regions that depended on them, creating depressed areas that further diminished purchasing power.

Another inherent weakness of the New Era economy lay in the realm of international economic policy. During World War I, the United States became the world's leading creditor nation because European nations incurred huge losses of wealth and borrowed billions of dollars from American banks and the U.S. Treasury. But the United States never adjusted its trade relations to accord with the financial realities of the 1920s. A debtor nation must export more than it imports to earn foreign exchange with which to pay its foreign debts. A creditor nation has to import more than it exports to provide those nations that owe it money an opportunity to earn funds with which to pay its debts. Throughout the 1920s, the United States annually ran trade surpluses with its major European and Latin American debtors. Also, America enacted higher tariffs to protect its industries and farmers from foreign competition. These higher import taxes made an equal exchange of goods between the United States and its debtors impossible. What kept these unsound commercial relations going was credit. American lenders, aided by the "easy-money" policy of the Federal Reserve Board, extended credits to foreign businesses and governments to enable them to pay off debts and to buy American goods.

When the Crash occurred, many American lenders who had suffered losses refused to make new foreign loans and called in existing ones as they matured. Credit cutoffs caused foreign debtors to default and to stop buying American exports. American exports dropped sharply. American farmers were hurt most because many of them sold a large part of their crops abroad. Sharply declining international trade following the stock market collapse was a major cause of the Great Depression.

Weaknesses within the corporate structure also helped cause the Depression following the Crash. Many holding companies (corporations created to own stocks in other corporations instead of owning physical assets) had been set up within the electric power, railroad, and securities industries. Promoters used holding companies to get control of many companies in a given industry and to sell huge stock issues. Holding company was pyramided upon holding company until a small company at the top of the pyramid controlled hundreds of companies at its base. Many of these elaborate holding company structures collapsed after the Wall Street panic because the operating companies at the bottom of the pyramids stopped earning dividends. When these dividends stopped, all the other "upstream" companies in the pyramid collapsed because they had issued bonds whose interest had been paid by dividends from the "downstream" operating companies. With their bonds defaulting, the holding companies collapsed. A flurry of lawsuits and investigations exposed some holding company promoters as con artists. Samuel Insull, who had built an elaborate holding company empire in electric utilities, fled the country to escape arrest for embezzlement. He later returned, had to stand trial, and was acquitted. A giant investment trust, Goldman, Sachs, and Company, sold $1 billion worth of securities in 1929. After the Crash, its portfolio dwindled to zero! Sometimes these disastrous liquidations engulfed banks who had invested heavily in pyramided holding companies. Speculative and sometimes fraudulent holding companies were a weak link in the business sector. Their collapse ruined thousands of investors and shattered confidence in the soundness of the American financial system.

Many banks, even if they never invested in holding companies, got into serious trouble during the 1920s. Long before the Crash, bank failures had reached epidemic proportions in the Midwest and Southeast. Between 1921 and 1928, over 5,000 mostly small rural banks had failed. There were several causes: mismanagement, fraud, inadequate regulation, and economic decline in their operating regions. Often a bank failure would set off a series of devastating runs on nearby banks, as depositors scurried to withdraw their funds, ensuring the banks' failures. These panicky runs often meant that formerly sound banks went down along with the weak, crooked, and mismanaged ones. Weaknesses in the U.S. banking industry were a major cause of the depression following the stock market collapse.

The most spectacular flaw in the economy of the 1920s was the stock market itself. The Great Bull Market, which began in 1924, rose continually for five years, peaking in September 1929. The stock market came to dominate American economic life. Newspaper headlines quoted stock numbers daily; nearly everyone followed the market. It became the greatest celebrity of a hero-worshipping age, a symbol of economic health and emblem of the superiority of the American way. Because the market occupied a central place in the public consciousness, its collapse had a profoundly negative psychological effect far greater than the immediate financial disasters it caused. It confused and frightened people, shattering their confidence in the economy and the men who managed it, even though most Americans did not own a single share of stock and suffered no direct loss from the Crash.

What had kept the market rising for years had been the continuous entry of new investors who bought mostly common stocks. Money to fuel the market became abundant and funds came from many sources, both foreign and domestic. Institutional investors dominated, but thousands of small investors also played the market. Banks speculated with depositors' funds. Businessmen invested their profits. The easy-money policy of the Federal Reserve Board kept credit readily available at low interest rates, encouraging investment in the market.

In 1928 and 1929, thousands of small speculators were lured into the market by low margin requirements. (*Margin* was the amount of down payment required for purchasing a portfolio of stocks from a broker.) Margins as low as 10 percent were available to clients. Brokers' loans increased spectacularly as people swarmed in to buy stocks on margin. These margin-account speculators helped drive stocks to their historic highs on the eve of the Crash.

The danger inherent in the market, which people overlooked or failed to perceive, was that the boom was always self-liquidating. It required a continuous inflow of new investors to generate the demand that bid up stock prices and created the capital gains which most investors sought. When, for reasons that are unknown and unknowable, on the morning of October 23, 1929, the customary buyers did not show up and thousands of investors telephoned in sell orders, the market dropped sharply. That day's selling was a signal for massive selling to begin, both for those who wanted to sell and those who had to sell because their stocks, purchased on credit, were no longer safely margined. The rout was on; prices plummeted. Prices roared downward because there was no one or no instrument to stop them. The Federal Reserve's tools proved helpless. Pooling failed. Only direct government intervention to close the markets might have stopped the panic, but no one proposed such a drastic measure.

In the weeks following the Crash, newspapers carried sensational stories of ruined speculators committing suicide by leaping from upper-story windows at their banks and private clubs. There was, in reality, no suicide wave in the aftermath of the collapse. More people killed themselves during the summer of the Great Bull Market than in the winter following the Crash. The myth probably arose because the suicides of businessmen, occurring at the time of the Crash, were attributed to financial losses whether valid or not; whereas in previous, more prosperous years, such deaths went unnoticed. It was during the years between 1932 and 1934, the worst years of the Depression, that the suicide rate rose; and most suicide victims of the Great Depression were ordinary working-class and middle-class people in despair, not bankrupt securities speculators.

If the suicide rate after the Crash did not rise, the embezzlement rate did, or at least the number of trials for business crimes rose sharply. Investors, smarting from their losses, demanded audits of company books and management policies. Audits often led to indictments and trials. Embittered investors discovered that formerly admired financial wizards had been crooks and swindlers.

The central question is what role did the market collapse play in causing the Depression? Did the Crash cause the Depression, or was the Crash only a symptom of the coming collapse? Although few could see it at the time, the panic on Wall Street was a major cause of the Great Depression, for it exposed many of the underlying weaknesses inherent in the 1920s economy. Deep-rooted faults surfaced, compounded by foreign influences, faulty economic knowledge, political errors, and irrational behavior.

The Crash curtailed the purchasing power and investing capacity of the wealthy classes upon whom the consumer economy had come to depend for growth because many rich people had lost money in the market. The collapse also shook their confidence in the economic system, making them less willing spenders and investors. Loans to foreign governments that had kept international trade and debt repayments flowing stopped, causing massive defaults on bond payments and loss of foreign markets for American exporters. Investors, exporters, and farmers who sold their crops abroad lost income and purchasing power. Jerry-built holding companies collapsed. Investment trusts depreciated to nothing. Bank failures escalated. Credit dried up. Corporations that had lost money in the stock market had to curtail investment, decrease production, and eventually lay off workers. As workers were fired, purchasing power dropped further, starting another round of cutbacks and layoffs. In sum, the stock market crash immensely damaged the economy in many ways and was both catalyst and major cause of the Depression.

Governmental financial policy also contributed to the coming of the Great Depression. Easy availability of credit and low interest rates encouraged speculation in the market, and the government did nothing to regulate these. After the Crash, the Federal Reserve Board raised interest rates and tightened credit, which weakened further a severely deflated economy. A more enlightened monetary policy might have shortened and ameliorated the downtown; instead, the "Fed" helped cause the Crash and then made the Depression worse with its bumbling policies.

Within a year after the Crash, the American economy passed from recession into depression. Business confidence spiraled down along with the business cycle. A nation of boosters had been transformed into anxious pessimists by a disastrous chain of events triggered by the collapse of the Great Bull Market.

THE AMERICAN PEOPLE IN THE GREAT DEPRESSION

As the Depression deepened, statistics embodied a litany of human disaster. Between 1929 and 1933, about 100,000 businesses failed. Investment declined from $7 billion to less than $2 billion. Corporate profits fell from $10 billion to less than $1 billion. The gross national product dropped from $80 billion to $42 billion as the economy shrunk to half its former size. Manufacturing also declined by half. Wholesale prices shrank by almost 40 percent. Almost six thousand banks went under during those four years, and they took with them millions of savings accounts representing $25 billion in savings. By 1933, the Dow-Jones average for industrial stocks stood at 32 points, about 10 percent of its value on the eve of the Crash.

When the Crash occurred, unemployment stood at about 2 million. It climbed steadily thereafter as an average of 100,000 workers lost their jobs every week during the first three years after the stock market crash. Some large corporate employers laid off all their full-time employees. By March 1933, unemployment had soared to 13 million, about one-fourth of the workforce. At least that many continued to work part-time and for reduced wages. During the depths of the Depression, about half the American workforce was either unemployed or underemployed. Labor income fell 40 percent during those four dismal years.

Public schools suffered serious damage because of Depression conditions. In 1931 and 1932, about five thousand schools closed across the nation for lack of funds. Thousands of others shortened the instructional day, shortened the school year, fired teachers, increased class sizes, and eliminated programs. Educational opportunities, especially in the rural Midwest and South, were curtailed. Across the land, thousands of teachers joined the swelling ranks of the unemployed.

Scenes of misery abounded in the industrial cities. A million unemployed men and women trudged the sidewalks of New York. Unemployed office workers sold apples on street corners, 5 cents apiece. People sat forlornly in employment offices, keeping watch for nonexistent jobs. Diets deteriorated, malnutrition became all too common, and weakened people easily contracted diseases. People stopped going to doctors. The incidence of epidemic diseases like tuberculosis, typhoid, and dysentery increased. People, unable to pay heating bills, huddled together in unheated tenements. Many doubled up in crowded apartments. Often those unable to pay rent were evicted. Homeless people built shanty towns on vacant lots, in gullies and canyons, and in forests on the edge of cities. Other wanderers slept in parks and doorways. Breadlines and soup kitchens manned by charities proliferated. People stole food from grocery stores, rummaged through garbage cans and city dumps, and begged for food. In 1932, New York City hospitals reported 29 victims of starvation and 110 people dead of malnutrition.

In rural areas, long troubled by economic difficulties reaching back into the 1920s, the Depression made conditions far worse. Between 1929 and 1933, farm income, already low in many regions, dropped by one-half. Farmers responded to falling prices by producing more. Their increased productivity depressed prices further, and their troubles were compounded by the loss of foreign markets because of tariffs and economic collapse in Europe. Falling income, droughts, plagues, bank failures, unpaid mortgages and taxes, bankruptcies, and foreclosures ruined farmers. In some regions of the rural South and Southwest, the economy collapsed from a combination of economic and natural

Unemployed workers during the Great Depression selling apples for 5 cents apiece.
Source: Library of Congress.

The Great Depression ravaged rural areas, many of which were poor before hard times hit.
Source: National Archives.

Bread lines were commonplace during the Depression years of the early 1930s. Here, unemployed workers wait in line for a free meal. *Source:* Library of Congress.

disasters, depriving the rural poor of an economic base. Many poor tenant farmers and their families became transients, hitting the roads in search of jobs or food. Those that remained on the land struggled to survive on cash incomes of $300 per year.

The Depression also brought ecological disaster to the Great Plains region. Between 1929 and 1933, scores of dust storms howled across the land each year. These black blizzards brought darkness at noon and transformed an area stretching from the Oklahoma panhandle to western Nebraska into a giant "Dust Bowl." Drought-parched fields and pastures turned into sand dunes. Searing summer heat killed thousands of people, cattle, fish, and birds. Millions of people were forced to flee the stricken regions. Nature alone was not to blame for the Dust Bowl. The arid lands west of the ninety-eight meridian were not suitable for intensive agriculture or livestock grazing. Sixty years of ecological abuse had stripped the Great Plains of its natural vegetation by the time the droughts struck. Denuded of its native sod, the land lay helpless when the hot dry winds came. One-third of the Great Plains just blew away during the early 1930s. Grit from the Nebraska plains collected on window sills at the White House. Sailors swabbing the decks of ships in New York harbor swept away bits of Montana.

Many Americans found Depression conditions difficult to understand. The nation's productive capacity was unimpaired. Factories were intact, farm productivity was higher than ever, and workers were desperately eager to work. Yet economic paralysis was everywhere. The contradiction of poverty amidst plenty made

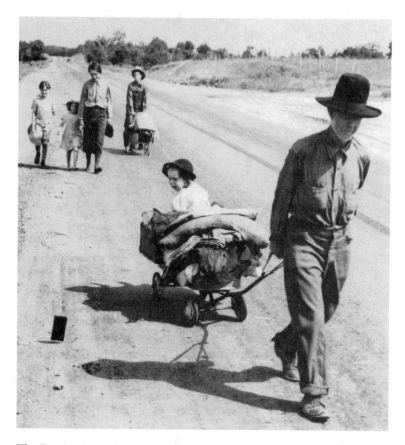

**The Depression savagely struck farm families. Farm commodity
prices plunged disastrously, and it was impossible for many tenant
farmers and sharecroppers to make a living. Families like this one hit
the road to join the thousands of other homeless wanderers.**
Source: Library of Congress.

little sense to a people reared on a gospel of hard work and self-help. Farmers
produced too much wool and cotton in the countryside and yet unemployed workers wore ragged clothing in the cities. Dairy farmers poured fresh milk on the
ground while people starved in the cities.

The Great Depression forever marked the generation of Americans who had
to endure a decade of deprivation. Years later, long after prosperity had returned
and most middle-aged Americans enjoyed affluent lives, many still retained vivid
memories of their Depression experiences. They remembered the shame and the
humiliation, but most of all they remembered the insecurity and fear. Deep down,
they also feared that it could happen again, that the bottom could once more fall
out and they would lose everything. The Depression left its invisible scars.

The Dust Bowl, triggered by years of poor land management and drought, brought ecological and economic disaster to the Great Plains region. *Source:* Library of Congress.

AFRICAN AMERICANS

Depression brought devastation to millions of African Americans. Black people, many of whom were poor when the depression began, sank deeper into poverty, disfranchisement, segregation, and deprivation. Most African Americans lived in the South during the 1930s, and most southern blacks resided in rural areas. The Depression exacerbated antiblack racism in the South. The Ku Klux Klan reported an upsurge in membership, and the number of lynchings tripled between 1932 and 1933. African American sharecroppers joined the Southern Tenant Farmers Union, which was organized in Arkansas in 1934. The union organized strikes in the fields and attracted national support from liberal and radical political leaders.

African Americans continued to migrate north, but during the Depression years they found that opportunities were no better in northern cities. Black unemployment was always far higher than white. Both employers and unions discriminated against African American workers. Black industrial unemployment rates ran between 40 percent and 50 percent in most cities. President Hoover was unconcerned about the problems African Americans faced during the Depression. Hard times meant a continuing struggle for survival for most African Americans within the confines of second-class citizenship.

WOMEN AND FAMILY LIFE

The Depression severely affected family life. Heads of families feared for the survival of their families and doubted their abilities to provide adequate shelter, food, and clothing for their children. Marriages were postponed. During the 1930s, the number of women aged twenty-five to thirty who never married increased 30 percent over the previous decade. Young married couples put off having children. The birthrate fell sharply. Although the divorce rate declined during the early 1930s, the desertion rate increased sharply. Young people dropped out of school or decided not to go to college. Family members, too poor to enjoy recreational pursuits outside the home, spent more time together. People found ways of amusing themselves and passing time without spending money. Church attendance dropped off but public libraries were heavily utilized.

When the Depression struck, most families had one income-earner, almost always the husband. Unemployment usually meant the man lost his job. After a few weeks of fruitless searching for another job, men often grew discouraged, lethargic, and began hanging around their homes. Many were demoralized by the experience of long-term unemployment. Traditional cultural values had defined them as society's producers and providers for their families. Unemployment deprived them of their accustomed social roles and robbed their lives of meaning and purpose. Within a culture that accentuated the traditional values of self-reliance and self-help, millions of unemployed men felt shame; they saw themselves as worthless, as failures. Feeling responsible for their children having to wear old clothes to school and to subsist on inadequate diets, they often felt intense guilt and self-hate.

Most of the nation's 30 million homemakers stayed at home during the Depression. Their daily routines were less disrupted than their spouse's. But pressures on them mounted because during hard times the role of homemaker became more important and their resources were often drastically limited. Managing a household on severely shrunken budgets often required enormous resourcefulness. Some families took in boarders, relatives, and in-laws. Some women started home businesses to supplement meager family incomes.

The Depression affected female workers differently from male workers. Female unemployment rates during the Depression were always lower than male rates because "men's jobs" in manufacturing were lost at a greater rate than were "women's jobs" in the service sectors. Assembly line workers were laid off more often than secretaries, teachers, social workers, or nurses. In some formerly two-income families, the wife continued to work after the husband had been dismissed. The proportion of women in the workforce rose during the 1930s from 20 to 25 percent. But traditional gender discriminations still dogged women in the Depression workforce. Over half of women workers were employed as domestic servants or in the garment trades. Pay in these jobs was low. Working women earned about 50 cents for every dollar that men earned. Few school districts would hire married women as teachers. During the 1930s, government employers prohibited more than one member of a family from working for the civil service, and if a spouse were forced to resign it was the woman who usually gave up her job.

POPULAR CULTURE

Popular culture flourished during hard times and also reflected the impact of the Depression. Games, hobbies, and fads, many of them carryovers from the 1920s, continued to be popular. Along with stamp collecting, contract bridge, and marathon dancing, came a new game, Monopoly, invented by an unemployed Atlantic City real estate salesman. Millions of Americans who had no money to invest in the real world accumulated a tidy fortune in Monopoly properties. In a generally depressed decade, Monopoly permitted vicarious accumulations of real estate and reinforced capitalistic values. Other people took a shot at the Irish Sweepstakes and got involved in chain-letter schemes.

Record sales increased during the Depression decade. Popular music generally gave expression to cheerful, sentimental, and romantic themes. In the later 1930s, "swing" and "big band" orchestras became enormously popular. A jazz clarinet player, Benny Goodman, became known as the "King of Swing" and his concerts inevitably played to sold-out audiences. Young couples learned an acrobatic dance, the "jitterbug," to keep pace with the fast rhythms produced by Goodman's and other Swing orchestras. Other dancers added exotic Latin American imports like the rhumba, the samba, and the beguin to their repertoires.

The 1930s coincided with the golden age of radio. Most middle-class families during the Depression managed to own at least one radio. People relied on radio for everything—for news, sports, weather, music, drama, comedy, adventure, murder mysteries, soap operas, religious inspiration, and advice. Radio provided some of the strongest cultural bonds holding Depression Americans together. Generally, this electronic mass medium functioned as a conservator of traditionalist values in a time of crisis.

Hollywood also entered its golden age during the 1930s. Eight large studios churned out most of the hundreds of feature films made each year. Technicolor made its appearance in 1935, although most motion pictures made in the late 1930s continued to appear in black-and-white. The major studios tended to serve up escapist fare that steered clear of depression realities and avoided raising serious social issues. Horror films such as *Frankenstein* and gangster films such as *The Public Enemy,* both made in 1931, were popular. The Marx brothers brought a kind of inspired anarchy to the cinema that entertained millions. Mae West used bawdy Western humor to become a box office star. Busby Berkeley's choreography and the dancing of Fred Astaire and Ginger Rodgers thrilled audiences in the best musicals of the 1930s. The two most popular movie stars of the Depression years were an animated cartoon character, Walt Disney's Mickey Mouse, and a child actress, Shirley Temple.

America's child sweetheart, child actress and movie star Shirley Temple, was one of Hollywood's biggest box office attractions during the Depression decade.   *Source:* National Archives.

Under pressure from religious groups, Hollywood instituted The Motion Picture Production Code of 1934 that strictly regulated the film industry. The code forbade filmmakers from depicting homosexuality, abortion, drug use, or sex. Actors could not utter profanities, not even a "hell" or a "damn." If couples were featured in bed, they had to wear clothes and both partners had to keep one foot on the floor during the scene. In the mid-1930s, about two-thirds of the nation's 135 million inhabitants went to the movies at least once a week. The top movie stars were among the highest-paid entertainers in the world. Both the film and radio industries boomed during the Depression decade.

Millions of Americans remained enthusiastic sports fans during the Depression. The most popular sport continued to be baseball, the "national pastime." Each year, millions of Americans clustered around their radios to listen to the World Series. College football was also very popular. One of the leading radio sportscasters during the mid-1930s was a young man from a small Illinois town destined for a political career one day, Ronald "Dutch" Reagan. Boxing was a major attraction during the 1930s, and the most popular fighter was heavyweight champion Joe Louis, the son of an African American sharecropper. Another African American athlete, Jesse Owens, starred in the 1936 Olympic Games held in Berlin, winning four gold medals in three days. Professional sports offered determined athletes an opportunity to make good money during the Depression, although professional baseball was closed to African Americans.

HOOVER BATTLES THE DEPRESSION

Far more than any previous president, Hoover committed the power and financial resources of the federal government to battling the Depression. Previous presidents had left fighting depressions to the private sector. Grover Cleveland confined his actions to maintaining the gold standard during the severe depression of the 1890s. Hoover, eschewing laissez-faire, accepted governmental responsibility for reviving the economy and saving the capitalist system. His actions paved the way for the New Deal of the mid-1930s; some New Deal proposals extended programs begun by Hoover.

Both Hoover and Franklin Roosevelt inherited the progressivism of Theodore Roosevelt and Woodrow Wilson. Franklin Roosevelt had been one of the Democratic Party leaders who had tried to persuade Herbert Hoover to accept his party's presidential nomination in 1920. At the time, Roosevelt said of Hoover, "He certainly is a wonder and I wish we could make him president of the United States. There could not be a better one."

A few weeks after the Crash, President Hoover began a series of antidepression measures. His approach reflected his Progressive faith in voluntary business-labor-government cooperation. He held meetings with prominent business, farm, and labor leaders; these leaders complied with his request to hold the line on production and wage levels to prevent the stock market collapse from spreading to the general economy. He requested and got an income tax cut from Congress to stimulate demand. He persuaded the Federal Reserve Board to lower interest rates to stimulate borrowing. Most important, the president expanded federal public works projects to stimulate regions with slack economies. Hoover was the first president to cut taxes, reduce interest rates, and use public works projects to try to stimulate the economy and spark an upturn in the business cycle. Roosevelt and his New Dealers would later make extensive use of all these inflationary devices.

Hoover's antidepression program, along with declining federal revenues caused by economic contraction, unbalanced the federal budget. Despite strong bipartisan pressure from Congress to keep the budget balanced, Hoover accepted deficit financing as necessary to combat the economic downturn. From 1931 to 1933, Hoover's budgets ran deficits totalling $6.5 billion; the national debt rose from $16 billion to $22.5 billion. Deficit spending in peacetime was unprecedented, and Hoover incurred much criticism for his efforts. During the 1932 presidential campaign, Roosevelt repeatedly attacked Hoover for his profligacy, saying, "I accuse the present administration of being the greatest spending administration in peace time in all our history." The Democratic candidate promised a 25 percent reduction in government spending and a balanced budget.

Hoover's antidepression program not only failed to generate economic recovery, it failed to arrest the downward spiral of the business cycle. Industrialists who had pledged earlier to hold the line were forced to cut production in the face of declining sales and mounting inventories. They also cut wages, hours, and discharged employees. Lowered interest rates failed to stimulate borrowing and tax cuts failed to stimulate spending. Public works projects offset only a portion of the decline in the construction industry. Although Hoover had made unprecedented use of federal power and battled the Depression across a wide front, there were limits to the actions he was willing to take. He opposed using federal funds for unemployment relief. He insisted that relief efforts remain in the hands of local governments, with supplemental aid from private charities such as the Red Cross and the Salvation Army. Despite his refusal to authorize federal funds for relief, Hoover's unprecedented use of the powers of the central state were advanced ideas for his time. But he lacked both political acumen and the power to turn the economy around without making use of massive deficit spending. Hoover could neither support nor get the Congress to support such action, which, according to the conventional economic wisdom of the era, appeared both heretical and irresponsible.

Amidst the rising tide of Depression, the 1930 elections occurred. The Democrats blamed the Republicans both for causing the Depression and failing to cure it. They also criticized Hoover for his refusal to allow federal unemployment relief. The Democrats won control of the House, but the Republicans retained narrow control of the Senate. The Republicans were clearly weakened by the Crash and the economic downturn which followed. The Democrats made a decisive comeback from their 1920s' doldrums and realized that they could win in 1932. In New York, Governor Franklin Roosevelt won reelection to a second term and positioned himself to win the Democratic presidential nomination in 1932.

THE COLLAPSE OF EUROPEAN ECONOMIES

During the first half of 1931, economic conditions improved. President Hoover confidently proclaimed the Depression to be over. But in July, the economy nosedived again, skidding to new lows. The summer decline coincided with the collapse of European economies, which was caused largely by the withdrawal of American credits and the loss of American markets. These effects of the American Depression dealt body blows to weak European economies only partially recovered from the ravages of World War I. Germany and Austria, the two weakest links of the continental economy, were the first to fail. The contagion of collapse spread to the rest of Europe, then to its colonies. Great Britain was forced off the gold standard, which destabilized all national currencies. The international free market was replaced by controlled national economies that instituted high tariffs, import and export quotas, and managed currencies. These devices were implemented to gain advantages over trading partners and to insulate national economies from the effects of worldwide deflation.

The American scene of mass unemployment, bankruptcy, and deprivation occurred on a world scale. In Britain, long lines of unemployed waited for relief benefits. German peasants starved in their fields. Millions of Frenchmen were reduced to one meal a day in a country famed for its abundant harvests and fine food. But in no other country were the effects of depression as severe as in America. Nowhere else did production decline so steeply, unemployment climb so high, currency deflate so severely, and recovery take so long. President Hoover, understanding the interrelatedness of the American and European economies, moved to combat the European crisis. He persuaded Congress to grant a one-year moratorium on all intergovernmental debt payments to try to save the international credit system. He failed. Germany defaulted on its reparations payments to France and Great Britain; both, in turn, defaulted on war debt payments to the United States.

The effects of default were devastating financially and psychologically because Americans viewed debt repayments as moral as well as contractual obligations. To Americans, default represented betrayal by former allies whom they had rescued from the brink of defeat in 1918. The United States became more isolationist, increasingly reluctant to join cooperative efforts to solve international economic and political problems. "America first" nationalistic attitudes were strengthened.

The European collapse further weakened the American economy, causing President Hoover thereafter to insist that the main causes of the American Depression were foreign. He believed that his antidepression program was working and that the American economy was on the road to recovery when it was derailed by the European Depression. It is true that an American upturn occurred during the spring of 1931, preceding the European collapse. But Hoover failed to see that it was the loss of U.S. credits and markets that had toppled the weak European economies. The main causes of the U.S. Depression were internal and can be found in the many imbalances of the economy of the 1920s, which were exposed by the stock market collapse. President Hoover only saw half of a central truth—that the international economic crisis of the early 1930s revealed how interdependent the capitalistic economies of the Western world had become. The Great Depression of the early 1930s was a worldwide capitalist crisis.

THE DEPRESSION DEEPENS

Sharp declines in foreign trade following the European collapse devastated the already depressed American farm sector. Declines in farm prices were greatest for wheat, cotton, and tobacco, which were the major U.S. export crops. Hoover spent much time trying to solve farm problems, but he could never solve the fundamental problem of overproduction. Programs extended credit to farmers. Emergency funds were allotted to feed starving livestock in drought-stricken states. The Federal Farm Board purchased surplus wheat and cotton and turned the surplus over to the Red Cross. The Red Cross processed the crops and then distributed flour and clothing to needy rural families. It was a generous gesture, but farmers needed higher commodity prices not handouts. But the Farm Board did not have the legal authority to order production cuts nor make cash payments to farmers. Neither the President nor Congress were willing to devise farm programs that would curb production or increase farm income with subsidy payments as demanded by rural spokesmen.

As farm income fell, and taxes and mortgage payments remained fixed, thousands of farmers lost their lands. Government's failure to raise farm prices or to prevent foreclosures provoked direct action among militant midwestern farmers. In Iowa during the summer of 1932, Milo Reno formed the Farmers' Holiday Association, which organized a farmers' strike. Members refused to ship their crops to market in order to force commodity prices up. They also blockaded highways to stop trucks from hauling nonmembers' produce to markets. Wisconsin dairy farmers dumped milk along roadsides and battled with deputy sheriffs. In Storm Lake, Iowa, farmers forcibly halted a foreclosure sale. In Bucks County, Pennsylvania, farmers forced an auctioneer to sell a farm for $1.18, bought it, and returned it to the former owner. These direct action tactics signaled the growing radicalism of farmers facing desperate economic circumstances and ineffective government programs.

Along with farmers, industrial workers suffered the ravages of the Depression. Detroit was especially hard hit as the market for new cars fell drastically. By the fall of 1932, approximately 350,000 people, half of the city's workers, were out of work. At Ford's River Rouge assembly plant, about one-quarter of the 1929 workforce was still on the job in 1933. The Communist Party organized a march of unemployed workers to the gates of Ford's factory to ask for jobs. Company guards opened fire on the marchers, killing four men and wounding others. Other industries sharply curtailed production and discharged workers by the thousands. Layoffs generally were by seniority. Young people, minorities, and unskilled workers were often the first fired and the last to be rehired. Many of the economic gains these groups had made during the prosperous years of the 1920s were undone by the Depression of the 1930s. For many still working, wages and hours were slashed severely.

By the fall of 1931, unemployment approached 8 million, representing 18 percent of the workforce. As unemployment reached massive proportions, private charities and municipal relief agencies proved inadequate to meet the ever-growing demands on their resources. States inevitably were forced to intervene. New York, under the leadership of Governor Roosevelt, took the lead among states in accepting responsibility for unemployment relief. The New York state legislature created an agency to help city and county governments handle their relief burdens. Other states followed. But in time, as the army of unemployed swelled to unprecedented size, state funding also proved inadequate. As 1931 ended, with the economy continuing to shrink, it was evident that only the federal government had the financial resources to provide adequate relief for unemployed workers and their families. In the winter of 1931 and 1932, New York City families on relief got $2.39 per week, which social workers admitted could not meet the needs of the smallest budget. In Houston, city officials no longer processed relief applications from black and Hispanic families, reserving what funds they had for whites only.

President Hoover, beset by a deteriorating economy and rising popular discontent, launched another recovery program in December 1931. Important measures included the Glass-Steagall Act (1932), which reformed the banking system, increasing the amount of money in circulation. The Federal Home Loan Bank enabled some homeowners to refinance their mortgages and save their homes. The heart of Hoover's second phase program was the Reconstruction Finance Corporation (RFC), a lending authority funded by $500 million from the U.S. Treasury and authorized to borrow an additional $1.5 billion from private sources. The RFC made large loans to banks, insurance companies, and railroads, many of whom were in financial difficulty during the Depression. The New Dealers would later expand the RFC and use it extensively to fight the Depression.

Hoover also tried to use psychological tools to fight the Depression and promote recovery. He tried to use publicity releases to stimulate optimism about American economic prospects. He stated "the worst has passed" and "prosperity is just around the corner." But, by 1932, the only thing around most corners were the lengthening breadlines of unemployed men and women. As the Depression lengthened, his upbeat statements made the president appear out of touch with reality, or worse, a cynical manipulator. Had Mr. Hoover been able to engineer a recovery, these efforts at ballyhoo and prophecy would probably have worked. President Roosevelt and his New Dealers used similar techniques to promote optimism successfully because they were accompanied by some improvement in business conditions during 1933 and 1934.

But Hoover continued to resist federal aid for the unemployed. He was not a cruel or insensitive man, nor did he embrace Social Darwinist tenets. He deplored the suffering that hard times inflicted on millions of his fellow citizens, but he deplored even more what he believed would be the consequences of federal relief: mass demoralization and the creation of a large class of welfare recipients permanently dependent on government handouts, which would undermine the American way of life. The president's ideological rigidity on this crucial matter of federal unemployment relief provoked bitter criticism from the Democrats and the opposition press. Hoover was denounced as the man who fed starving Europeans after the war but refused his countrymen funds with which to buy their families food. He could rush food to starving cattle but not to people. These charges stung the president and badly damaged his public image. He yielded a little in the summer of 1932, when he supported amendments to the RFC which allowed it to lend $300 million to state and local agencies for relief purposes. But large-scale federal unemployment relief had to await the New Deal.

Many other politicians of both parties and prominent Americans shared the President's concerns about relief. Franklin Roosevelt publicly worried that direct relief would undermine the characters of workingmen. Congress in 1932 voted down a measure to funnel federal relief funds to the states, with Democratic senators providing 40 percent of the votes that killed it. The traditional American view

The rout of the Bonus Marchers. In late July 1932, President Hoover ordered the U.S. Army to disperse the marchers and their families from public lands, where they had set up a shanty town in the nation's capital.   *Source:* National Archives.

of relief yielded slowly, even in the face of massive economic decline and vast human suffering.

As the president and his critics debated the relief issue, one group of unemployed sought to dramatize their plight and seek financial aid. In May 1932, about fifteen thousand World War I veterans converged on Washington. They came to support a demand veterans were making of Congress for early payment of an insurance bonus due them in 1945. They needed the money in 1932 to pay debts and feed their families. As their leaders lobbied on Capitol Hill, the veterans set up camps on marshy flats across the Anacostia River. Congress refused to grant the estimated $250 million required for early payment of the bonus, contending it was too costly.

After this defeat, most of the veterans went home, but about two thousand people remained. They lived in the Anacostia camp and occupied vacant public buildings. They were squatters, trespassers. They were a nuisance, maybe an embarrassment, but they posed no serious threat to public health or safety. On July 28, the President ordered the police to evict all squatters from government buildings. A conflict occurred at one site, several policemen were injured, and police shot and killed two veterans. Following this violence, President Hoover ordered the Army to drive the veterans out of Washington.

The Army deployed cavalry, infantry, tanks, tear gas, and machine guns. General Douglas MacArthur commanded the operation. The soldiers cleared the buildings and then attacked Anacostia Flats. Using overwhelming force, the Army forcibly dispersed the veterans and their families. They tossed tear gas at the defiant veterans and burned their shanties to prevent their return.

After the Army had completed its mission, General MacArthur called the veterans "a mob . . . animated by the essence of revolution." President Hoover claimed that most of the veterans were Communists and criminals. Neither a grand jury probe nor an exhaustive Veterans Bureau investigation found evidence to sustain these charges. More than 90 percent of the marchers had been veterans. Seventy percent had served overseas, and one in five was disabled. What they wanted was jobs and food for their families. The Bonus Marchers were mostly poor, unemployed, yet patriotic Americans petitioning their government for relief during hard times, hoping that their World War I military service gave them a claim for special treatment. They were at first rejected, and, later, some of them were attacked by their government. The *Washington News* editorialized:

> What a pitiful spectacle is that of the great American government, mightiest in the world, chasing unarmed men, women, and children with army tanks.[2]

THE 1932 ELECTION

President Hoover's callous handling of the Bonus Marchers hurt him politically, but the deteriorating economy and the failure of his antidepression programs did far worse damage to his reelection prospects. Hoover wanted renomination and no Republican rivals challenged him. He appeared confident that his program would soon bring recovery. But there was little enthusiasm for Hoover or his program at the Republican convention, although it was tightly controlled by the President's men and gave the incumbent a first-ballot nomination by acclamation. Many Republicans were frankly pessimistic about Hoover's reelection prospects with the millstone of depression hanging so firmly around his ample neck. Republican congressmen and senators, who did not want to be associated with a loser, ran independent campaigns.

The Democratic contest was much more exciting. New York Governor Franklin D. Roosevelt was the front runner for the nomination. He had formidable political assets—a famous name, a good record as a Progressive governor of the

[2]Quoted in Arthur M. Schlesinger, Jr., *The Crisis of the Old Order, 1919–1933* (Boston: Houghton Mifflin, 1957), p. 265.

most populous state, and strong support in all regions of the country. His princi-pal challenger was Alfred E. "Al" Smith, Roosevelt's former mentor who had pre-ceded him as New York's governor. Smith, whom Hoover had beaten decisively in 1928, fervently sought his party's nomination again, confident he could avenge his loss and lead the nation back to prosperity. He also had millions of supporters among the party faithful.

Roosevelt would come to the convention with a majority of delegates, but short of the necessary two-thirds required for nomination. Smith's strategy was to get enough votes (along with the votes pledged to other candidates) so that he could prevent Roosevelt getting a first-ballot victory. There were several candi-dates waiting in the wings if Smith succeeded in stopping Roosevelt and dead-locking the convention. The most important of these challengers was John Nance Garner, Speaker of the House, championed by William Randolph Hearst, a Demo-cratic Party titan because of his great personal wealth and his control of a vast me-dia empire. Garner was a small-town banker and realtor from Uvalde, Texas, who had worked his way up through party ranks via the seniority escalator. "Cactus Jack," as he was nicknamed, was a populist, a dry, and an isolationist.

Roosevelt had appeared unstoppable in the spring; he won all the early pri-maries. Then Smith beat him in Massachusetts; and Garner, with Hearst's help, beat him in California. Roosevelt's momentum slowed. When the convention opened in Chicago in late June, all was uncertainty. The stop-Roosevelt coalition, led by Smith, came within a whisker of victory. Through three ballots, Roosevelt fell about a hundred votes short of the two-thirds majority that he needed to nail down the nomination, and he could not break through that barrier. His support in several southern states was wavering. The convention recessed after the third bal-lot. Roosevelt's backers had a few hours in which to save his candidacy if they could. During those hours, a bargain was struck that saved the nomination for Roosevelt. The key figure in the deal was Hearst. He agreed to switch California's delegation from Garner to Roosevelt if Roosevelt would accept Garner as his vice-presidential running mate. James A. "Big Jim" Farley, Roosevelt's campaign mana-ger, accepted Hearst's offer. The convention reconvened and a fourth ballot was taken. The leader of the California delegation, William Gibbs McAdoo, rose to cast the Golden State's forty-four votes for Roosevelt. Within minutes, Roosevelt had the nomination.

He flew to Chicago to make his acceptance speech. It was an aggressive speech, peppered with criticisms of the Hoover presidency. He drew his loudest applause when he proclaimed "the theory that government helps the favored few" had been discredited and that his administration would do "the greatest good for the greatest number." Roosevelt called for economy in government, a balanced budget, and lower taxes, sounding more conservative than President Hoover. He also advocated progressive measures, including expanding public works, produc-tion controls for agriculture, and federal relief for unemployed workers. He pledged to help the "forgotten man" find meaningful work and regain his lost stan-dard of living. Near the end of his speech, Roosevelt told the delegates, "I pledge you, I pledge myself, to a New Deal for the American people." The press seized upon that figure of speech and the New Deal became a popular slogan for Roosevelt's antidepression program. As he finished, an organ blasted out the notes of "Happy Days Are Here Again;" Roosevelt's campaign had found its theme song. A radical journalist, unimpressed by the candidate or his speech, wondered if the country would be better off with a whole new deck of cards instead of just a new deal from the same old capitalist deck.

One feature of both conventions provides insight into the politics of Depression America. Prohibition remained a major issue with both parties. Both parties contained wet and dry factions, although there were more wets among the Democrats and more drys among the Republicans. After a ferocious debate over the issue, the Republicans adopted a plank keeping Prohibition, but they also proposed another constitutional amendment that would permit each state to determine whether it wanted to be wet or dry. The Democrats also had a rousing debate on the subject before adopting a plank calling for repeal of the Eighteenth Amendment. Walter Lippmann wondered why the delegates spent so much time on the Prohibition issue instead of addressing the many urgent economic problems created by the Great Depression. John Dewey grumbled,

> Here we are in the midst of the gravest crisis since the civil war and the only thing that the two national parties seem to want to debate is booze.[3]

Will Rogers quipped that the debate over Prohibition didn't matter much anyhow since "neither side could afford the price of a drink."

Both Hoover and Roosevelt began their campaigns in August. Both campaign organizations spent heavily for media exposure, mostly for radio time. Hoover had the support of most of the nation's newspapers and radio stations, and he had more money to spend than Roosevelt. But these advantages could not offset the fatal disadvantage of being the president in office when economic disaster struck the nation. The Democrats would have won the 1932 election with any candidate who could have been nominated. It was no contest from the outset.

Neither candidate succeeded in arousing the voters. Hoover's efforts failed completely. Roosevelt's speaking style was cool, controlled, and priggish. He conveyed no deep understanding of the economic crisis that was imperiling the American way of life. His cheerful confidence and statements of faith in the capacity of American institutions to revive and to prosper were superficial, uninformed by statistical data or economic theory. He appeared to lack understanding of complex economic and financial processes. He had no program to offer the American people, merely a collection of miscellaneous proposals. Many who heard him speak during the campaign must have shared Walter Lippmann's opinion of the candidate as "A pleasant man who, without any important qualifications for the office, would like very much to be president."

---

[3]Quoted in William E. Leuchtenburg, *Franklin D. Roosevelt and the New Deal* (New York: Harper & Row, 1963), p. 9.

Roosevelt's campaigning disappointed Progressive intellectuals, especially his habit of backing off from a position if it were attacked. A pattern emerged during the campaign: Roosevelt would attack Hoover in general terms; Hoover would strike back, refuting Roosevelt by citing statistical data; Roosevelt would beat a retreat, shifting the argument as he backed away. By the end of the campaign, Roosevelt had eaten so many of his own words that the voters had difficulty discerning any important issue differences between him and the incumbent. Hoover ridiculed Roosevelt's habit of waffling on the issues, calling him a political "chameleon." To those who sought a savior from the Depression in 1932, Franklin Roosevelt neither looked nor sounded like a Messiah.

Roosevelt did not offer the American people a New Deal during the 1932 campaign because it did not then exist. The phrase was merely empty rhetoric. He and his advisers concentrated on winning the election; programs to combat the Depression and promote recovery would come later, after victory and after he had forged his administration. It was also unnecessary for Roosevelt to offer specific programs; he knew that he was winning without them. So he played it safe. He blamed Hoover and his party for causing the Depression, condemned them for failing to solve it, and promised to solve all problems if elected.

Roosevelt understood that the central issue in the campaign was Hoover's failed program. Roosevelt avoided specific commitments and resisted all efforts by journalists and the embattled Hoover to pin him down. He did on occasion propose a few general programs—federal unemployment relief, more public works, production controls for farmers, and expansion of the Reconstruction Finance Corporation's lending authority to include small businesses. But the main purpose of these proposals was to attract votes, not solve Depression problems. The only specific commitments he made during the campaign were ones that he never kept: balance the budget, cut taxes, and reduce spending 25 percent. At times, his campaign utterances were contradictory, such as calling for spending for public works and unemployment relief at the same time he promised to cut taxes, reduce spending, and balance the budget. But always, Roosevelt's trump card was to deplore the effects of depression on the American people. His strategy worked brilliantly.

Compared to Roosevelt's clever performance, Hoover's reelection campaign was pathetic. No longer calm or confident, Hoover sounded harassed and peevish as he faced an increasingly skeptical and hostile electorate. He was an uninspiring speaker, reading his speeches in a nasal monotone that failed to arouse audiences or even to hold their attention. He failed to project much concern for the mass of ordinary citizens mired in Depression miseries. He did, in fact, care about them, but he lacked the emotional resources and rhetorical skill needed to convey sympathetic understanding to his audiences. He became defensive, lashing back at Roosevelt, journalists, and other critics.

Hoover was a proud, stubborn man, unaccustomed to failure or defeat. He could neither acknowledge the failure of his program nor devise alternatives, bound as he was by ideological blinkers. Long before election day, it was obvious to most observers that Hoover's reelection campaign had failed. He rarely left

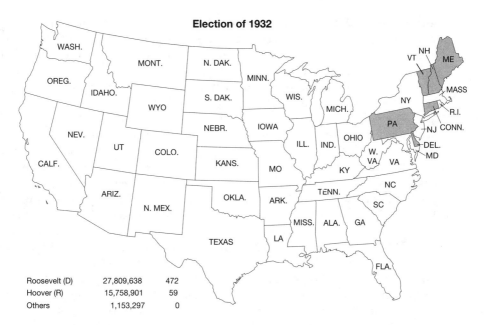

Election of 1932

Roosevelt (D)	27,809,638	472
Hoover (R)	15,758,901	59
Others	1,153,297	0

The election of 1932.   *Source:* Moss, *Rise of Modern America*, p. 207.

Washington during the final weeks, and, when he did, crowds frequently jeered and booed the harried leader. Much hostility toward him personally pervaded the stricken land. The Great Engineer, the Horatio Alger hero of 1928, now stood before the electorate in 1932 as the condemned killer of the American Dream. He became the butt of countless Depression-spawned jokes. Vaudeville comedians, upon hearing that business was improving, asked, "Is Hoover dead?" His name became a derisive prefix—Hoovervilles were shanty towns inhabited by the homeless; Hoover blankets were newspapers the unemployed wrapped themselves in for warmth; and Hoover hogs were jackrabbits put into hobo stew. On the final day of his campaign, Hoover's motorcade was stinkbombed.

On election day, the voters repudiated both Republicans and President Hoover by decisive majorities. In the popular vote, Roosevelt rolled up almost 23 million votes to Hoover's 15.8 million. In the electoral vote column, Roosevelt got 472 votes to Hoover's 59, and he carried forty-two of forty-eight states. No Republican incumbent had ever been beaten so badly except William Howard Taft in 1912; but Taft's decisive defeat had been caused by divisions within his party. The 1932 election also represented a party victory as well as a personal triumph for Roosevelt. The Democrats attained their largest majorities in both houses of Congress since before the Civil War, winning the House with 312 seats to 123 seats and the Senate with 59 seats to 37 seats. The 1932 election was the most dramatic turnabout in American political history. Roosevelt had beaten Hoover even worse than Hoover had beaten Smith. Hoover had won forty states in 1928; he got six in 1932. Roosevelt won millions of nominally Republican votes in northern and western states. About 3 million first-time voters cast ballots in the 1932 election, and Roosevelt got about 80 percent of them. These new voters were mostly young urban dwellers, many of them the children of "new" immigrants coming of age. These "ethnics" became an important voting block in the emerging Democratic coalition.

The political reversal of 1932 was both historic and long-lasting. The Republican Party had been the party of the normal majority since 1894 and had dominated national politics during the first three decades of the twentieth century. Since 1932, the Democrats have been the normal majority party, although their coalition has weakened since the late 1960s. Only three Congresses since 1932 have held Republican majorities. A major realignment of political parties occurred during the 1932 election, catalyzed by the Crash, the Great Depression, the Republican political failures, and demographic change.

The large majority who voted for Roosevelt and his party in 1932 could not know what programs they were voting for. Mainly, they voted for an attractive political personality who expressed faith in American institutions and the American people and who promised immediate action. Millions, including many who had voted for him in 1928, were repudiating Hoover, his party, and his failed policies, not endorsing a not-yet-existent New Deal. Republicans had been given three years to whip the Depression and they could not; conditions were worse than ever on election day 1932, and only President Hoover could see an upturn coming soon. Many voters felt that the Democrats could do no worse and maybe they would do better. American voters in 1932 were more certain of what they didn't want than what they were getting when they cast their ballots for the Hyde Park patrician, driving the fallen Horatio Alger hero from the White House.

For the United States, it was politics as usual amidst the severest economic crisis in the history of the Republic. Most Americans, despite enduring three years of economic depression with no end in sight, remained politically passive in 1932. Organized labor was quiet. Only Communists tried to organize the unemployed masses. The Communists, partially subsidized by Moscow, staged unemployment marches, rent strikes, and hunger riots. Party membership increased between 1930 and 1932, but Communism attracted few industrial workers, however hard-pressed they may have been. The Communist Party made special efforts to recruit African American workers, but could only attract a few. Probably in the view of most African Americans, it was tough enough being black in America without being a "Red" too. The most obvious achievement of the Communists was to frighten some conservatives who believed that a "Red" revolution was building in America. Despite hard times and government failures, there was little protest or rebellion in Depression America, and those few that occurred neither changed the conditions they challenged nor posed any threat to authorities. Neither the power nor legitimacy of government at any level was ever challenged by more than a handful of people. Discontent yes, but not even the preconditions for revolution had appeared in Depression America.

Both the Socialist Party and the Communists ran presidential candidates in 1932. Their candidates articulated radical indictments of the American capitalist system and offered socialist alternatives. Together, the two radical parties polled fewer than 1 million votes, less than 2 percent of the votes cast. Much more expressive of popular political views in the depths of economic depression were the 16 million voters who cast their ballots for Mr. Hoover, despite hard times, his failed program, and his lackluster campaign.

Far more Americans were demoralized by economic Depression than were radicalized by their searing experiences. Clinging to traditional individualistic values, they could not see economic collapse as a collective failure, as a crisis of institutions. They assumed personal responsibility for their predicaments, blaming themselves instead of the American system and its leaders for their impoverishment. Others, overwhelmed by disaster, were incapable of anger or rebellion. Dispirited, they remained at home or sat on park benches muttering to themselves. They suffered in silence, alone and isolated. Many hit the roads or rode the rails, joining 2 million other rootless individuals seeking a job, a meal, a shelter, or merely a sense of motion. Along with these homeless migrants of despair there were others who, rejecting all secular saviors, awaited divine deliverance from their earthly afflictions.

INTERREGNUM

The four-month interval between Roosevelt's election in November 1932 and his inauguration on March 4, 1933, proved to be the most painful winter of the Great Depression. Unemployment climbed past 13 million. Each month, thousands of farmers and businessmen went bankrupt. Across the land, destitute families shivered in darkened, heatless rooms without adequate food, clothing, or medical care. Recovery appeared nowhere in sight. A Roosevelt adviser, Rexford Guy Tugwell, wrote in his diary, "Never in modern times, I should think, has there been so widespread unemployment and such moving distress from cold and hunger."

As the Depression continued to deepen and its miseries multiplied, the search for scapegoats escalated. Who was to blame for the economic collapse? Inevitably, millions of Americans reached the same conclusion: If businessmen and Republican Party leaders were responsible for the prosperity of the 1920s, they were surely responsible for the poverty of the early 1930s. The reputations of financiers, industrialists, economists, and politicians plummeted. A Senate investigating committee, chaired by Ferdinand Pecora, probed the investment practices on the New York Stock Exchange. Pecora's committee discovered that Wall Street titans had rigged investor pools and often profiteered at the expense of their customers and their firms. Inside traders had frequently bought stocks below the market prices paid by the general public.

Pecora's committee failed, however, to prove its suspicion that a conspiracy of "short sellers" had caused the market to collapse, despite wide circulation of such rumors. (*Selling short* is an investment strategy used by speculators to profit from a declining stock market. They contract to sell stocks they do not yet own in the future at their current price. If the price of the stock drops before delivery date, speculators buy the stock at the lower price and deliver it to the buyer who has contracted to pay the previous higher price. The short seller pockets the difference as his profit for having guessed accurately that the market would drop.) But Pecora's committee succeeded in exposing many financiers as ruthless crooks who sold out their customers and their banks to save their own financial skins. The committee's investigations were one of the many Depression-era events that destroyed the American financier as folk hero.

The social irresponsibility of some prominent businessmen also contributed to the public's disillusionment with the business community. During a time when millions of families were living in dire poverty, many businessmen continued to collect large salaries and manipulated their investments to avoid taxes. Some falsified tax returns and others refused to pay taxes. Henry Ford, Detroit's largest employer and the richest man in America, refused to accept any responsibility for the army of jobless workers filling the city. A nation that had regarded its financial and business leaders with awe in 1929 turned on them furiously now that their abilities to generate wealth had vanished.

Congressional investigations, grand jury indictments, and trials of businessmen during the Depression paralleled the "witch hunts" for Communist subversives during the McCarthy era of the early 1950s. A similar need existed during the early 1930s to simplify and personify a grave disaster that, in reality, was vastly complex, and caused by a bewildering variety of forces and circumstances. It provided bleak comfort to confused and hungry citizens to believe that an evil conspiracy of greedy inside traders selling short had engineered the stock market crash for their own profit and then panicked when it got out of control, destroying the securities market and causing the Depression. In fact, no one planned the Crash and no one understood precisely why the market had fallen so sharply, why the Depression ensued, or why it was so severe and seemingly interminable.

Many who angrily scapegoated businessmen also despaired of the political process, which appeared incapable of coping with economic crises. During its "lame duck" session from December 1932 through February 1933, Congress failed to enact a single important piece of economic legislation. The national government appeared to have been reduced to farcical ineptitude at a time when there was an urgent need for effective measures to combat economic calamity.

NADIR

During that harrowing winter of 1932 and 1933, with the economy depressed and government paralyzed, some observers feared that the American system of political economy was dying. The European depression proved that the capitalist malaise was worldwide. Only the Soviet Union, undergoing rapid industrialization during the 1930s, had an expanding economy and labor shortages. During the Great Depression, over 100,000 unemployed Americans, responding to ads a Soviet company had placed in American newspapers, applied for work in the Soviet Union. About 6,000 obtained jobs and left the stagnant American economy to live and work in Stalinist Russia. Some American voices were heard calling for an end to political democracy and the creation of a directorate to make the "tough" decisions necessary to restore prosperity and order. These calls for "strong" leadership in time of crisis sounded the siren song of an American-bred fascism fearing economic collapse and the rise of radicalism. Perhaps it could happen here?

Meanwhile, President Hoover and President-elect Roosevelt were playing a political game. The outgoing president invited Roosevelt to attend a conference on European debt problems. They met on November 22, 1932. Hoover, believing that the main causes of the American Depression were foreign, gave foreign economic policy a higher priority than Roosevelt, who saw, correctly, that the Depression's main causes were domestic. Their meeting was unsuccessful. Roosevelt, suspecting Hoover was trying to get him to endorse his policies, avoided making any commitments. He did not want to be identified with the failed policies of a discredited leader. Hoover and Roosevelt had another inconclusive meeting in January 1933. Hoover believed that Roosevelt did not understand the economic situation and thought him a shallow demagogue. Both men, formerly good friends, had come to dislike each other intensely. The long delay between Roosevelt's election and his ascension to power in time of crisis brought about the enactment of the Twentieth Amendment, which moved up the inauguration date from March 4 to January 20.

Roosevelt spent most of the four-month interval between his election and inauguration meeting with advisers, forming his government, and drafting his legislative agenda. He was forging the New Deal. Many of his assistants were college professors recruited from the social science faculties at Columbia and other prestigious Ivy League universities. These scholars would form the "brain trust" of the Roosevelt Revolution that was about to descend upon Washington.

At a time when the political leadership of the nation appeared helpless, with a repudiated leader still holding office and the President-elect without power, there occurred an event that nearly eliminated the New Deal before it could begin. On February 15, 1933, three weeks before his scheduled inaugural, Roosevelt came to Miami to attend a reception. Sitting on the top of the back seat of an open car in a city park, Roosevelt was addressing a crowd of well-wishers. After finishing his informal speech, Roosevelt slipped down into the car seat. At that moment, the mayor of Chicago, Anton Cermak, came up to the car to ask a political favor of Roosevelt. Roosevelt leaned forward to hear what Cermak was saying. A short, dark man, standing on a box 35 feet away, began firing a pistol at Roosevelt. Cermak was fatally wounded, and four others were hit by bullets. Roosevelt escaped the deadly assault unharmed. The assassin was instantly captured and jailed. The man who had tried to kill the President-elect was Guiseppe Zangara, a little man with a consuming hatred of all rich and powerful people.

Roosevelt shrugged off the frightening incident. He believed that if fate intended him to die at the hands of an assassin, he would. This time was merely a near miss. He showed courage and poise, dismissing the murderous assault with jokes and smiles. Roosevelt also expressed remorse at the death of Cermak and sympathy for the others wounded during the shooting. It is sobering to reflect on what directions the history of the United States during the years of grave economic crisis at home and international disorder abroad might have taken had Zangara succeeded in killing Roosevelt. Would the American system of middle-class democracy and capitalism have survived?

As the spring of 1933 approached, the nation appeared to be heading for financial collapse. Another epidemic of bank failures swept the land. As February 1933 ended, banks all over the country closed their doors. They were either bankrupt or had closed to avoid bankruptcy. Panicky depositors stood in long lines for hours waiting to withdraw their money. They believed that their dollars would be safer in shoe boxes, under mattresses, or in tin cans buried in their back yards than in bank vaults. By March 3, the day before Roosevelt's inaugural, thirty-eight states had shut down all their banks and the remaining ten states were moving to close theirs. Normal business and commerce ground to a halt. People reverted to bartering for necessary goods and services. On that same day, the New York Stock Exchange suspended all securities trading and closed down. Financial paralysis crept across the nation; it was the lowest ebb of the commercial spirit in American history.

IMPORTANT EVENTS

1929	The Great Stock Market Crash occurs
1930	The Hawley-Smoot Tariff is enacted
1931	The Great Depression begins
1931	Weak European economies collapse
1931	Hoover declares a one-year moratorium on international debt payments
1932	The Bonus Marchers descend on Washington, D.C.
1932	The Pecora Committee investigates Wall Street
1932	The Reconstruction Finance Corporation is established
1932	The Farmers' Holiday Association is formed
1932	Franklin Delano Roosevelt is elected president
1933	Guiseppe Zangara tries to assassinate President-elect Roosevelt
1933	Franklin Roosevelt is inaugurated
1933	Black blizzards create the Dust Bowl in the Great Plains states
1933	An estimated 13 million Americans are out of work
1933	The Twenty-first amendment is ratified, repealing Prohibition
1934	The Southern Tenant Farmers' Union is organized
1934	Hollywood implements the Motion Picture Production Code
1936	Jesse Owens wins four gold medals in the 1936 Olympic Games
1937	Joe Louis becomes the heavyweight boxing champion of the world

BIBLIOGRAPHY

There are many good books written about the stock market crash, the causes of the Great Depression of the 1930s, and the Depression's impact on the American people. Robert Sobel's *The Great Bull Market* and John Kenneth Galbraith's *The Great Crash* are two short studies of the coming of the Great Depression. Gordon Thomas and Max Morgan-Witts have written a colorful social history of the Crash called *The Day the Bubble Burst*. The impact of the Depression on the lives of people is vividly expressed in Studs Terkel's *Hard Times,* a collection of interviews with hundreds of people who recall their experiences of hard times. David Shannon, editor of *The Great Depression,* offers an excellent collection of primary sources about life during the economic crisis. The finest economic history of the Great Depression, which explains why the Depression was so severe and lasted so long, is by Michael Bernstein and entitled *The Great Depression: Delayed Recovery and Economic Change in America, 1929–1939.* Another fine account of the Depression experience is Caroline Bird's *The Invisible Scar.* Two classic studies from the 1930s have endured: Robert S. and Helen Merrell Lynd's *Middletown in Transition,* a sociological study of a midwestern city in the Depression; and James Agee's and Walker Evans's *Let Us Now Praise Famous Men,* a powerful documentary in words and pictures of poverty-stricken Alabama sharecroppers. John Garraty, in *The Great Depression: An Inquiry into the Causes, Course, and Consequences of the Worldwide Depression of the 1930s,* presents a fine recent study that puts the Depression into comparative perspective. Two good recent biographies of Herbert Hoover are David Burner's *Herbert Hoover: A Public Life* and Joan Hoff Wilson's *Herbert Hoover: Forgotten Progressive.* Roger Daniels's *The Bonus March* and John Shover's *Cornbelt Rebellion* are fine accounts of 1932 radical protest movements.

CHAPTER 6

The New Deal

When Franklin Delano Roosevelt assumed the presidency on March 4, 1933, the United States and most of the world was gripped by the iron hand of the Depression. Roosevelt himself was largely an unknown quantity, and the New Deal existed only as upbeat political rhetoric. Over the next five years, Roosevelt and the New Dealers proceeded to design and implement an energetic legislative program to alleviate the effects of depression, restore prosperity and make the federal government responsive to a broad range of issues affecting most Americans. Although the New Deal only partially solved the grave problems of economic depression, Roosevelt and his program achieved a resounding political success. Roosevelt became one of the most powerful and popular leaders in the history of the Republic. His overwhelming reelection victory in 1936 demonstrated that the New Deal accorded with the hopes and dreams of most Americans. Before the New Deal ran its course, the basic American approach to governance had been redefined, and the role of the federal government in the lives of most Americans had been enlarged. The American welfare state had been forged and the federal government had committed itself to maintaining minimum living standards for those in need. The New Deal reshaped modern American politics.

FDR

Franklin Delano Roosevelt was a professional politician from a wealthy background. Born on an estate in Hyde Park, New York, in 1882, Franklin Roosevelt was the son of a middle-aged country gentleman of Dutch descent and a young mother who doted on her only child. He enjoyed all the privileges and luxuries that wealth could command, including extensive travel in Europe with his family. He was tutored by governesses at home until he was fourteen, then went away to Groton, a distinguished prep school near Boston. At Groton, he came under the influence of Headmaster Endicott Peabody, who implanted within young Roosevelt the "Christian gentleman's" ideal of service to the less fortunate, the conviction that privileged Americans should help solve national and international problems.

Franklin grew up to be an ambitious young man who believed himself destined to achieve distinction, and he already harbored political ambitions. He was much influenced by the achievements of his famous distant cousin, Theodore Roosevelt, whom he affectionately called "Uncle Ted," and Franklin apparently aspired to the presidency from an early age. After Groton, he enrolled at Harvard. He was fiercely competitive, trying hard to win distinction in athletics, but he had to settle for managing the baseball team and editing the college newspaper. From Harvard, he went to Columbia Law School. In the spring of 1905, he married his fifth cousin, Eleanor. In 1907, Roosevelt began a law career with a prominent Wall Street firm. Roosevelt at twenty-five was a well-educated, wealthy, athletic, handsome young man. He was widely traveled, already well acquainted with many men prominent in American life, and moved comfortably in high society. But corporate law could never satisfy his ambitions or his exalted sense of himself as a man of destiny. He yearned for a larger arena and found it in politics.

His political career began in 1910 when he got elected to the New York State Senate. He entered politics as a Progressive Democrat and worked for political reform, conservation, and aid for farmers. In 1912, he campaigned energetically for Woodrow Wilson. President Wilson rewarded his efforts by making him Assistant Secretary of Navy, a position he held for eight years. It was the job he most wanted, for it both advanced his political career and was closely tied to his favorite pastime, sailing. Sailing was Roosevelt's passion; he spent as much time as he could on his family's yacht, and later his own yacht. Most vacations were spent with friends who shared his love of ships and the sea.

In 1920, he was the Democratic vice-presidential candidate running with James Cox on a ticket that got buried by Harding and Coolidge. This experience did no harm to Roosevelt, however, and he emerged from the campaign a nationally known figure and party leader. In the summer of 1921, Roosevelt was felled by a severe attack of polio at age thirty-nine. His recovery was slow and exceedingly painful and left him a cripple with wasted legs. His wife Eleanor said that his suffering gave him a courage and strength that he never had before.

His illness slowed but did not deter his political career. He was never out of politics; he remained a party leader all through the 1920s. He supported New York Governor Alfred E. "Al" Smith's candidacy at the 1924 Democratic convention and attracted national attention with a brilliant speech endorsing Smith's nomination. Standing before the delegates on crutches, he urged the nomination of Smith, whom he called the "Happy Warrior." He supported Smith again in 1928 and also won election as governor of New York, succeeding Smith who had lost his bid for the presidency to Republican Herbert Hoover. Roosevelt's gubernatorial victory instantly made him a leading contender for his party's next presidential nomination. Roosevelt's tenure as New York's governor coincided with Hoover's presidency. As governor, he showed a greater commitment to unemployment relief than had Hoover and a greater willingness to experiment with innovative programs in time of crisis. Looking ahead to a possible presidency, he was also gathering advisers to develop programs that would combat the effects of depression nationally.

Roosevelt's political philosophy was anchored firmly within the Progressive tradition; and despite his association with Wilson, he was more of a New Nationalist than a Wilsonian. These views he shared with his leading advisers. Roosevelt favored a vigorous role for the federal government in regulating corporate enterprise and restoring purchasing power to farmers, workers, and hard-pressed middle-class citizens. He favored the application of scarcity economics; that is, of reducing production in order to raise prices and increase profits and wages as the best way to end the Depression and restore prosperity.

Roosevelt was an experienced, confident political leader, convinced that he could provide both the leadership and the programs to lead his nation out of its greatest economic crisis. As he prepared for his inauguration, he believed he could restore both confidence and prosperity. He was prepared to act boldly and to experiment. He was not afraid. He once told a friend that the hardest thing he ever tried to do was to wiggle his big toe after polio had destroyed his legs. After that ordeal, he said, all else was easy.

THE NEW DEAL BEGINS

On March 4, 1933, a man who could not walk began to lead a crippled country. Not since 1861 had a new president taken office amidst such ominous circumstances. With their economy mired in its deepest depression, their government paralyzed, and their financial system crumbling, Americans turned to Roosevelt with desperate expectations. "First of all," declared the new president in his inaugural address, "let me assert my firm belief that the only thing we have to fear is fear itself—nameless, unreasoning, unjustified terror." Speaking firmly, a tinge of anger in his voice, he denounced businessmen and bankers who caused the Depression and could find no cure for it: "Rulers of the exchange of mankind's goods have failed, through their own stubbornness and their own incompetence, have admitted their failure, and have abdicated. . . . The money changers have fled from their high seats in the temple of our civilization. We may now restore that temple to the ancient truths." The heart of his speech was a promise to fight the Depression with a bold program, to do whatever was necessary to restore prosperity. He also proclaimed his faith that "This nation will revive and will prosper."

His words electrified a people yearning for reassurance. He instilled hope and courage in millions of his fellow citizens. In one speech he had accomplished what Hoover had failed to do in four years: he convinced Americans that an effective leader with faith in the future had taken command. That night, instead of attending the inaugural ball, he met with financial advisers to face the nation's imminent

Mar. 4, 1933   THE   Price 15 cents

NEW YORKER

A *New Yorker* cover featuring a gloomy Hoover and a buoyant Roosevelt en route to the inauguration ceremony on March 4, 1993. *Source*: Franklin D. Roosevelt Presidential Library.

financial crisis. The next day he declared a four-day "bank holiday" and summoned Congress to a special session. Congress began its emergency session on March 9.

His first measures revealed a streak of fiscal conservatism in the early New Deal. An Emergency Banking Relief bill, drafted with the help of Hoover's Treasury officials who were still on the job, attacked the banking crisis. It outlawed hoarding and exporting gold. It also arranged for the reopening of solvent banks and the reorganization of failed banks under Treasury Department supervision. But it left the banking system essentially unchanged and with the same people in charge. Complained one Congressman, "The President drove the money changers out of the Capitol on March 4th—and they were all back on the 9th." Roosevelt then sent Congress an Economy Act to trim federal expenditures by $400 million and balance the budget, mainly by cutting veterans' benefits. Another measure raised federal excise taxes. These deflationary measures made the New Deal initially appear more conservative than Hoover's program.

Roosevelt's effective leadership in time of grave economic crisis depended crucially on his ability to communicate with average citizens. He made expert use of all available mass media. He adeptly handled photo journalists and newswriters. He held frequent news conferences and quickly mastered the format. He had a keen sense of humor and a master politician's sense of timing. No one has ever been better than FDR delivering a speech from a prepared text. He used radio to convey a sense of warm concern and to demonstrate a talent for explaining

Early in his presidency, Roosevelt hit upon one of his most popular devices—the "fireside chat," an informal radio address to the people in which he discussed important issues of the day. He conducted dozens of fireside chats during his long presidency. *Source:* National Archives.

complex socioeconomic policies in simple language intelligible to ordinary citizens. His demeanor, captured best by the newsreels shown in the nation's movie houses, reflected that of an optimistic, energetic, and capable chief executive who held a special concern for the welfare of those Americans hardest hit by the Great Depression.

Early in his presidency, he developed one of his most successful communicatory devices: a radio address directly to the American people, the "fireside chat." On Sunday evening, March 12, Roosevelt gave the first of the many fireside chats he would deliver over his long presidency. He spoke informally to an estimated 60 million Americans gathered around their radios across the nation. He talked about the banking crisis and the measures his administration had taken to end it. He assured his countrymen that the banks were once again sound and "would take care of all legitimate needs." He told them it was safe to put their money back in the banks, adding that "Hoarding has become an exceedingly unfashionable pastime." The next day, long lines once again appeared in front of banks, but this time customers were putting their money in. He had told the people the banks were sound and they had believed him. The banking crisis was over. Roosevelt had shown remarkable leadership. Raymond Moley, one of his advisers, observed, "Capitalism was saved in eight days."

During his presidency, Roosevelt relied on his wife, Eleanor Roosevelt, more than any previous president had ever relied on his wife. She redefined what it meant to be First Lady. She became a political force in her own right, one of the leaders of the liberal wing of the Democratic Party. She made public appearances, gave speeches, held press conferences, and made weekly radio broadcasts. She also wrote a newspaper column that was nationally syndicated. She traveled 40,000 miles a year as the eyes and ears of her husband's presidency. More progressive than Franklin, Eleanor functioned as a liberal conscience, as a kind of goad to take actions on behalf of the disadvantaged and downtrodden. She was enormously popular with most Americans and often got higher approval ratings than did the president.

THE HUNDRED DAYS

During the next several weeks, which became known as "The Hundred Days," the New Deal gathered momentum. Many legislative proposals were sent up the hill to the special session of Congress. These bills dealt with a wide range of depression problems. Congress quickly enacted relief measures to help unemployed Americans. One measure created the Civilian Conservation Corps (CCC). Young men were taken out of the cities and put to work in camps organized along military lines in national parks and forests. They planted trees, cleared campsites, built bridges, constructed dams, and made fire trails. The CCC was Roosevelt's favorite relief program; its conservation of both human and natural resources appealed to his patrician humanitarian instincts. During its ten-year lifetime, the CCC put over 2 million young men to work. Congress also passed the Federal Emergency Relief Act (FERA), a direct-relief measure that allocated $500 million to state and local governments to dispense to needy families.

The Agricultural Adjustment Act (AAA), an important early New Deal measure, was enacted in May 1933. Its chief purpose was to raise farm income by raising commodity prices. Defining the farm problem as one of overproduction, the measure reflected Roosevelt's commitment to scarcity economics. A domestic allotment program was established for seven major commodities—cotton, corn, tobacco, rice, wheat, hogs, and dairy products—whereby the government paid farmers to reduce their acreage and produce less. Subsidy payments came from a tax levied on the primary processor for each crop. For example, the wheat subsidy came from a tax on the companies that ground the wheat into flour. The subsidy payments were based on "parity," a system designed to allow farmers to regain the purchasing power they had enjoyed during the period between 1910 and 1914, a time of general agricultural prosperity.

Before the "Triple A" could be put into effect, the 1933 crops had already been planted. To forestall another year of overproduction, Secretary of Agriculture Henry A. Wallace ordered farmers to plow up millions of acres of cotton, corn, and

The Civilian Conservation Corps (CCC) was one of the most popular early New Deal programs and it was Roosevelt's favorite. Begun in 1933, it took unemployed young men off the streets where there was nothing for them to do and put them to work in the countryside. Here, workers check farmland erosion.   *Source*: The Franklin D. Roosevelt Presidential Library.

wheat, and to slaughter millions of baby hogs to be eligible for the subsidy payments. These drastic actions taken at a time when many Americans went to bed hungry each night provoked furious criticisms. Wallace called the actions he had ordered "a shocking comment on our civilization." It also raised food prices to consumers during a time of massive unemployment and underemployment. Other New Deal programs shared this Depression characteristic with the Triple A—that the price of helping a particular interest group was higher living costs borne by the general public. But the AAA did benefit those farmers who participated in its subsidy programs. For the first time since World War I, farm income rose.

A month after passing the AAA program for agriculture, Congress enacted a comprehensive program for industrial recovery called the National Industrial Recovery Act (NIRA). The NIRA expressed the early New Deal's commitment to economic planning and business-government cooperation as replacements for the Depression-spawned cutthroat competition raging in all industrial sectors. NIRA set up a planning agency called the National Recovery Administration (NRA) that exempted businesses from antitrust laws. Under NRA supervision, competing businesses within a given industry met with union leaders and consumer groups to draft codes of fair competition that limited production, divided it among various companies, and stabilized prices by establishing minimum price levels. Section 7(a) of NRA guaranteed workers' rights to join unions and to engage in collective bargaining. It also established minimum wages and maximum hours for workers. The NIRA, like the AAA, was based on the principles of scarcity economics. It was designed to promote industrial recovery by curbing production and raising prices that would generate higher profits and wages. The NRA, launched with much hoopla and great expectations, failed to promote much industrial recovery. Production increased only slowly and companies did not hire many additional employees.

The New Deal's first large-scale public works program got incorporated into the NIRA. Called the Public Works Administration (PWA), it carried a $3.3 billion price tag in order to build roads, public buildings, ships, and naval aircraft. Its purpose was to let contracts to idle construction companies, to put unemployed workers to work, and to stimulate local economies by pumping in federal funding for the projects.

Congress also created the Tennessee Valley Authority (TVA). TVA was a multipurpose regional developmental program for the Tennessee River Valley running through Tennessee, North Carolina, Kentucky, Virginia, Mississippi, Alabama, and Georgia—one of the poorest, most depressed areas of the nation. TVA spent billions constructing dams for flood control and to generate hydroelectric power. Other TVA projects reclaimed and reforested land and fought soil erosion. The TVA widened and deepened a 650-mile stretch of the river, making it navigable to river traffic. TVA also provided thousands of jobs for poor residents, both black and white, of the region. This striking example of Progressive enterprise was originally one of eight proposed regional development programs for the nation. But effective political opposition by power companies who charged the government with unfair competition killed all the other projects. The TVA still functions today. Like many New Deal programs it left a mixed legacy. It reclaimed millions of acres and enhanced the regional economy. But it also forced thousands of families from their lands and became one of the worst polluters in the nation.

Other significant early New Deal measures included the Federal Securities Act that grew out of Senator Pecora's exposures of wrongdoing on Wall Street. The new law gave the Federal Trade Commission power to supervise new securities issues, required each new stock issue to be accompanied by statements disclosing the financial status of the issuing company, and made misrepresentation a federal crime. A Banking Act created the Federal Deposit Insurance Corporation (FDIC) that insured depositor bank accounts through the Federal Reserve System. The

Tennessee Valley Authority.   *Source*: Moss, *Rise of Modern America*, p. 221.

Home Owners' Loan Corporation (HOLC) enabled homeowners to refinance their home mortgages at lower rates of interest and with smaller payments. Thousands of families were able to retain ownership of their homes through HOLC mortgages. Roosevelt also took the nation off the international gold standard in order to inflate the currency to complement his efforts to raise domestic price levels through the Triple A and the NRA.

Roosevelt also requested that Congress make good his campaign promise to repeal Prohibition. The lame-duck Congress, meeting in February 1933, had proposed a constitutional amendment repealing the Eighteenth Amendment. While the amendment was making its way through the states, the new Congress modified the Volstead Act by legalizing beer and wine with an alcoholic content of 3.2 percent. These beverages went on sale April 7, 1933, marking the first time in over thirteen years that it was legal to drink in America. The new amendment, the Twenty-first, was ratified in December 1933. Booze was back, although eight states remained dry. The Noble Experiment was over. Roosevelt supported repeal of Prohibition mainly because enforcement had failed, and repeal would reactivate a major industry, employ thousands of workers, and generate federal revenue in time of severe depression.

Congress ended its special session June 16. The "Hundred Days" were over. During this intensely busy congressional session, Roosevelt and his New Dealers had sent up fifteen major bills. All were enacted with few changes. Normal partisan rivalries and debate were suspended as both houses responded positively to Roosevelt's energetic assault on a wide range of Depression miseries. During the "Hundred Days," the public mood had been transformed. A nation of pessimists had reclaimed their characteristically American optimism, confident that they could whip the Depression and control their destiny. During the next year, many more New Deal measures became law. These laws gave further help to farmers, created additional relief projects employing thousands of workers, strengthened trade unions, aided small businessmen, and helped homeowners refinance their mortgages.

The New Deal of 1933 and 1934 represented interest group democracy at work, not the single-interest government characteristic of the 1920s. Government help went to business, agriculture, and labor. Also consumers, homeowners, local governments, and the unemployed benefited. And the New Deal seemed to work. Unemployment fell steadily from 13 million in 1933 to 9 million by 1936. Farm income doubled—from $3 billion in 1933 to $6 billion in 1936. Manufacturing wages rose from $6 billion in 1933 to $13 billion in 1937.

The 1934 elections confirmed the immense popularity of Roosevelt and his New Deal. Normally, the party in power losses seats in an off-year election. But voters in November elected 322 Democratic congressmen to only 103 Republicans, a gain of 13 seats for the Democrats. Never in its history had the Republicans held such a low percentage of House seats. In the Senate, the rout of the GOP was worse. The Democrats gained 9 seats, bringing their total to 69, and leaving the Republicans with only 37 seats. One of the new Democratic senators was an obscure county judge from Missouri named Henry Truman. Forty-one of the 48 states elected Democratic governors. The 1934 elections almost erased the Republican Party as a national force. It had no program and no national leader with any popular appeal. Arthur Krock of *The New York Times* exclaimed the New Deal had won "the most overwhelming victory in the history of American politics." William Allen White noted that Roosevelt "has been all but crowned by the people." Whatever its economic shortcomings, the New Deal made good politics.

CRITICS—LEFT, RIGHT, AND POPULIST

Although the 1934 elections demonstrated the immense popularity of Roosevelt and the New Deal, he and his programs called forth a barrage of criticism. New Deal critics spanned the political spectrum from radical left to far right, and some of them defied political categorizing. Many businessmen and conservative politicians attacked the New Deal. They denounced excessive taxation and government regulation of business. Others criticized deficit financing, public works, and federal relief payments to the unemployed. Conservatives denounced the growth in size and power of the federal government and its subversion of individual initiative. They worried that Roosevelt might be assuming dictatorial powers, and they suggested that the New Deal state resembled totalitarian Fascist and Communist regimes. The American Liberty League, formed in 1934, served as a vehicle for corporate anti–New Deal critics. Former President Hoover and former Democratic presidential candidate Alfred E. (Al) Smith both bitterly attacked the New Deal. Despite spending over $1 million, Liberty League orators failed to inflict any serious political wounds on Roosevelt or the New Deal. During the depths of the Great Depression, most voters were not terribly concerned about the plight of the wealthy.

Other critics attacked particular New Deal programs as inadequate and unfair. The National Recovery Administration attracted much criticism. Its detractors charged that corporate leaders had written NRA codes that favored big businesses' interests over the interests of workers, consumers, and small businesses. The AAA also came under attack. People were angry about the wasteful destruction of food crops to start the program at a time when millions were ill fed. Although the "Triple A" worked for landowners, it neglected tenants and sharecroppers. They rarely got subsidy money for cutting back production. In the South, plantation owners who took land out of production to collect the AAA subsidies, often turned their sharecroppers off the land, depriving them of their economic base. Thousands of these uprooted "Okies" and "Arkies" headed for California, victims of both hard times and New Deal politics.

Many people were disappointed by the partial recovery made under the New Deal in 1933 and 1934. Even though business was up and unemployment down, they remained well below 1920s predepression standards. Demagogues appealed to the dissatisfactions and frustrations of many Americans. Father Charles Coughlin, a Roman Catholic priest whose parish lay in a suburb of Detroit, developed a following of millions with his weekly radio broadcasts denouncing the New Deal. He organized a political movement called the National Union for Social Justice. He preached a curious blend of anti-Communism, anticapitalism, and anti-Semitism, which appealed mainly to midwestern farmers and ethnic city dwellers.

Another anti-New Deal movement that called attention to its shortcomings was the Old Age Revolving Pensions plan conceived by Dr. Francis E. Townsend, a retired dentist. Dr. Townsend proposed that everyone over sixty receive $200 per month on the condition that they spend the money during the same month they got it. The money for the pensions would be raised by a "transaction tax," a sales tax levied each time goods were sold. He claimed his plan would both provide for the elderly and would end the Depression by pumping billions of dollars of purchasing power into the economy. New Deal economists quickly demonstrated that the plan was fiscally unsound. The tax could raise only a portion of the money required to fund the plan and would have only a small impact on the Depression. Dr. Townsend's scheme attracted a huge following. Millions of elderly, whose savings and investments had been lost during the Depression, joined his movement. It also called attention to inadequate pensions and local relief for aged, retired workers. Social Security was enacted in part to undercut the appeal of the dentist's panacea.

The most significant challenge to the New Deal came from Huey Long, a brilliant, ambitious southern demagogue. Long, a left-wing populist, became governor of Louisiana in 1929 and a U.S. senator in 1932. Along the way, he crafted a corrupt political machine that gave him dictatorial control of Louisiana politics. He also enjoyed an immense popular following among workers and farmers of Louisiana because of his program of public works and public schools that were paid for by taxes on big businesses doing business in the state. He did much to improve the quality of life for ordinary people in one of the poorest regions in the country.

Long supported the New Deal when it began. He turned against it in 1934 because of its fiscal conservatism. He made a bid for national leadership with a program he called "Share the Wealth" and coined a slogan, "Every Man a King." "Share the Wealth" proposed using the tax power to confiscate all incomes over $1 million and all estates over $5 million. The money raised would furnish each family with $5,000 for buying a farm or home, an annual income of $2,000, a free college education for their children, a radio, and other benefits for farmers and industrial workers. Long's plan was also fiscally unsound. The funds raised by confiscatory taxes would not begin to pay for promised benefits. The Senate twice rejected his tax bills by large majorities. But Long's scheme appealed to the aspirations of poor people during the Depression, to their resentment of the rich, and to their disappointment with New Deal efforts. Even though he was a corrupt demagogue and his distributionist schemes were fiscally unsound, Long addressed a real problem: the uneven distribution of wealth in America that allowed mass poverty in a rich country. By mid-1935, he had built a national following of millions and was planning a presidential bid in 1936, challenging Roosevelt. Roosevelt and his advisers considered Long a serious threat. An assassin's bullet ended Long's career in September 1935, and his movement quickly disintegrated.

There were also many other left-wing critics of the New Deal. Both the Communist and Socialist parties attacked it. Minnesota elected a socialist governor. In California, the socialist muckraker, Upton Sinclair, captured the 1934 Democratic party gubernatorial nomination. He campaigned for governor on a program he called End Poverty in California (EPIC) that included establishing socialist enterprises within the state. Although he lost to a conservative Republican, Sinclair attracted over 800,000 votes.

The New Deal also came under attack from the Supreme Court. Most justices feared that many New Deal measures, which were hastily drawn up and enacted without debate or criticism by Congress, gave the executive branch too much power. On "Black Monday," May 27, 1935, the Supreme Court handed down three decisions that nullified key parts of the New Deal. In the most famous of these cases, *Schecter* v. *U.S.*, a unanimous court declared the NRA unconstitutional on the grounds that it gave excessive legislative power to the White

During the mid-1930s, Huey P. Long of Louisiana emerged as the most formidable challenger to Roosevelt and the New Deal.   *Source*: National Archives.

House and that the commerce clause of the Constitution did not give the federal government the authority to regular intrastate commerce. The Schecter decision killed the New Deal's most important program for industrial recovery. In *U.S.* v. *Butler* (1936), the Court also nullified the AAA when it declared the processing tax unconstitutional because it was not a legitimate use of the tax power. The Butler decision killed the New Deal's major program for agricultural recovery.

THE SECOND NEW DEAL

As 1935 dawned, despite its big victory at the polls, the New Deal faced trouble. Critics were attacking particular programs and its failure to bring complete recovery. Demagogues were offering alternatives and luring away supporters, and the Supreme Court was dismantling its major programs. Roosevelt burst forth again in the spring and summer of 1935 with a flurry of legislative initiatives known as the Second New Deal. The Second New Deal differed from early efforts in several significant ways. The first New Deal had emphasized relief and recovery measures; the second continued relief and recovery efforts, but was more concerned with reform. Earlier, Roosevelt had sought to cooperate with business; in 1935, he accused business of putting its interests ahead of the general welfare. He also proposed measures for increasing business taxes and tightening government regulation of some industries. The First New Deal had been most responsive to political pressures from established interests—bankers, large farmers, and big business. The Second New Deal responded to the rising power of organized labor, and included measures that reflected Roosevelt's concern about the emergence of demagogic critics of the New Deal. Together these factors combined to move Roosevelt to the left; the Second New Deal was more liberal than the first. FDR abandoned his alliance with the business community and more directly addressed the needs of the disadvantaged and the dispossessed.

In April 1935, Congress enacted the first major piece of Second New Deal legislation, the Emergency Relief Appropriation Act (ERAA). The new law empowered President Roosevelt to establish public works programs for millions of jobless Americans, including the Works Progress Administration (WPA). The WPA was the most important of the New Deal work relief programs. Before it was phased out in 1943, more than 8.5 million people were employed on more than 1 million different projects. WPA workers built over 650,000 miles of roads, 125,000 public buildings, 8,000 parks, and hundreds of bridges.

In addition to its construction projects, the WPA also funded many cultural efforts. A Federal Theater Project brought dramas, comedies, and variety shows to cities and towns across the nation. John Houseman and Orson Welles were among the young artists who acted and directed in the Federal Theater Project. Artists on WPA payrolls painted murals in post offices and other public buildings. Dance and music projects sponsored ballet companies and symphony orchestras that performed across the country. A Federal Writers' Project hired

First Lady Eleanor Roosevelt was a powerful political leader in her own right and an ardent liberal advocate for the poor and disadvantaged during the Depression. *Source:* Library of Congress.

writers including Richard Wright, John Steinbeck, and John Cheever to write guidebooks and regional histories. The WPA even hired unemployed historians for its writers' project.

In addition to the WPA, the ERAA also funded other relief and public works measures. The Resettlement Administration (RA) moved thousands of impoverished farm families from submarginal land and gave them a fresh start on good soil with adequate farming equipment and guidance from farm experts. Later the Farm Security Administration (FSA), which replaced the RA, granted long-term, low-interest loans to sharecroppers and tenants, enabling them to buy family farms. Another FSA program built chains of sanitary, well-run camps for migrant farm workers. Both the RA and FSA were New Deal relief agencies that attacked the problem of rural poverty.

The ERAA also established the Rural Electrification Administration (REA). No other New Deal measure improved the quality of rural life as much as the REA. Until 1935, rural America lacked electrical power. Kerosene lamps illuminated homes after dark, and farmers' wives lacked washing machines, refrigerators, vacuum cleaners, and radios. The REA subsidized the building of power lines in rural America. Where private power was unavailable or private companies refused to build lines, the REA financed the creation of nonprofit, cooperative electric companies. In 1935, fewer than 10 percent of rural homes had electricity. By 1940, 40 percent were electrified, and by 1950, 90 percent.

The ERAA also authorized the National Youth Administration (NYA), the most important New Deal relief measure for young people. Its director, Aubrey Williams, worked to find part-time employment for more than 600,000 college students and over 1.5 million high school students so that they could continue their studies. It also found employment for over 2 million jobless young people who were not in school.

In June 1935, Roosevelt sent Congress five major bills—a labor bill, a Social Security bill, a banking bill, a public utilities bill, and a tax measure. Congress responded with a "Second Hundred Days" and enacted them all. Out of this remarkable congressional session came some of the most important and enduring legislation in the history of the republic.

The first bill to pass was the National Labor Relations Act (NLRA), also known as the Wagner Act, after its principal sponsor, Senator Robert Wagner of New York. The NLRA reaffirmed the right of workers to unionize and to bargain collectively that had been guaranteed in Section 7(a) of the National Recovery Administration. But the Wagner Act was much stronger than the NRA, for it required management to bargain with certified union representatives. It also created the National Labor Relations Board to supervise plant elections and to issue "cease and desist" orders against companies that committed unfair labor practices such as refusing to permit union elections, refusing to allow union members to distribute union literature on company property, and firing employees engaged in union activities. The Wagner Act extended the realm of government regulation to include labor-management relations and created a legal framework within which labor-management activities could function. It strengthened the bargaining leverage of unions and reduced the power of companies to resist unionization. Additionally, its passage showed the growing political influence of organized labor within New Deal ranks.

After the NLRA came the Social Security Act, which created a series of programs, including a partial retirement pension for elderly workers. It also established three joint federal-state systems of unemployment insurance, disability insurance, and payments to mothers with dependent children. The pension supplement was a compulsory insurance program funded by a payroll tax paid jointly by the employee and his or her employer. Workers who had paid into the system for at least five years would be eligible to receive monthly payments starting in 1940.

Social Security pensions were created in part to deflect the challenge of the Townsendites as well to meet the pressing needs of the aged. Social Security also reflected the fiscal conservatism of President Roosevelt. It was the only social security system ever established that was self-funding; it was paid for not from general tax revenues, but from a trust fund paid into by workers and their bosses. It was also funded by a regressive tax, because the more a worker earned, the less tax he paid proportionally. Further, Social Security was a deflationary measure that took money out of a still-depressed economy and did not return any to it for five years.

Compared to social insurance programs implemented by European nations that were not as rich as the United States, Social Security appeared paltry. Initially, it excluded millions of workers—farm workers, domestics, and many categories of industrial workers. Because it excluded many low-wage occupations, it necessarily excluded large numbers of women and minority workers. But, for all its limitations, it was a historic measure. It established federal responsibility for helping the elderly, the temporarily unemployed, the disabled, and poor mothers with dependent children. A new social contract, however, narrowly defined, counterbalanced the gospel of self-help. For the first time in the history of the republic, the federal government acknowledged the social rights of its citizens and a responsibility to protect them. The American welfare state had arrived.

Next came the Banking Act of 1935, which overhauled the Federal Reserve System, bringing major changes to the nation's banking industry. The new law expanded the size of the Board of Governors of the Federal Reserve to seven members and lengthened their terms of office. It also gave the board greater control over regional banks, interest rates, and the setting of reserve requirements of member banks. Further, it gave the board control over open market operations, and it required that all state banks join the Federal Reserve System by July 1, 1942, if they wished to remain eligible for Federal Deposit Insurance Corporation (FDIC) coverage. The Banking Act of 1935 centralized the American banking system, giving the federal government much greater control over currency and credit, which was Roosevelt's aim. It was the most important banking measure since the Federal Reserve Act created the system in 1913.

The fourth Second New Deal law was the Public Utility Holding Company Act (PUHCA). This important measure revealed Roosevelt's growing hostility toward big business, and it was the first piece of antitrust legislation enacted since Wilson's first term. Its key provision provided for the elimination of utility holding companies, and, within three years of its passage, almost all of them had been extinguished.

The fifth of the major Second New Deal measures was a tax measure that proposed to redistribute wealth by "soaking the rich." It called for increased inheritance taxes, imposition of gift taxes, graduated income taxes on large incomes, and significantly higher corporate income taxes. Roosevelt also had a political motive for proposing his tax bill—to offset the rising power of Huey Long, who was trumpeting his "Share the Wealth" movement. Roosevelt's "wealth tax," the most radical of all New Deal proposals, provoked a firestorm of criticism from business and the media. William Randolph Hearst, the press baron who had helped Roosevelt get the Democratic nomination in 1932, attacked the measure furiously. Thereafter, he always called Roosevelt's reform program the "Raw Deal." Business and other interests lobbied Congress intensively to eliminate or reduce Roosevelt's tax proposals, and Congress proceeded to gut the measure. The tax measure passed by Congress eliminated the inheritance tax and reduced corporate tax rates sharply. The Wealth Tax Act of 1935 raised little revenue and did not redistribute wealth. Even though the wealth tax had little fiscal effort, no other New Deal measure provoked as much bitter criticism. Roosevelt, despite proposing the wealth tax, remained a fiscal conservative at heart. Most New Deal tax measures were regressive.

The Second New Deal was the culmination of Roosevelt's efforts to impose a welfare state on a capitalistic economic foundation in order to bring the American ideal of equality of opportunity closer to reality. Without challenging the system of private profit or redistributing wealth, New Dealers used the power of the federal government to regulate corporations, strengthen trade unions, provide pensions for the elderly, help the disabled, maintain the poor, and provide relief to the unemployed. The New Deal represented the fullest expression of the Progressive social vision to date.

A NEW DEAL FOR THE ENVIRONMENT

Franklin Roosevelt shared his cousin Theodore Roosevelt's love of nature and his concern to promote and develop national conservation policies. New Dealers did more to protect the American ecosystem and to develop national conservation policies than any administration since Theodore Roosevelt's presidency during the first decade of the twentieth century. Conservation was a top New Deal priority from the beginning. Franklin Roosevelt's main environmental concerns were protecting land and water resources.

Both the size of the U.S. Forest Service staff and its budgets were increased in 1933 and 1934, and its existing programs were expanded. Perhaps the most spectacular step to enhance ecology taken by New Dealers was the building of a "shelterbelt" on the Great Plains. Over 200 million trees were planted across a 100-mile-wide zone along the 100th meridian. Stretching from the Canadian border south to the state of Texas, the shelterbelt functioned as a giant windbreak and also prevented the disastrous dust storms that had blown away much of the Great Plains topsoil during the early 1930s. Congress enacted the Soil Conservation Act in 1935, which enabled the federal government to tackle the problem of soil erosion on a national scale. About the same time, Congress also enacted the Taylor Grazing Act, which set strict requirements for grazing cattle on the vast western rangelands owned by the federal government. CCC and many WPA projects also conserved natural resources as well as providing jobs for the unemployed during the Depression.

Conservation was a top New Deal priority from its beginnings. The New Dealers' most spectacular ecological step was the building of a "shelterbelt," the planting of millions of trees on the Great Plains states along the 100th meridian. *Source*: National Archives.

President Roosevelt also signed legislation that created the National Resources Planning Board, later known as the National Resources Committee. The board promoted local conservation planning and encouraged the development of regional plans for conserving natural resources. The board's long-range goal, a comprehensive national resource plan, was never fully realized, but the New Deal did much to increase public awareness of and promote resource planning.

THE 1936 ELECTION

Public opinion polls taken in 1936 showed Roosevelt and his New Deal programs enjoyed broad popular support in all regions of the nation. Over 100,000 frenzied partisans packed Franklin Field in Philadelphia to hear Roosevelt accept his nomination for a second term. Flashing his famed victory smile he told the crowd and a national radio audience that "this generation of Americans has a rendezvous with destiny."

The Republicans faced a strong uphill battle in their first campaign to oust the popular incumbent. To oppose the President, the GOP turned to Alfred M. "Alf" Landon, a former follower of Theodore Roosevelt who was then the Progressive Republican governor of Kansas. Landon was more liberal than most Republican party regulars. He had a good civil liberties record and favored regulation of business. He endorsed many New Deal programs, to the dismay of many conservative members of his own party. His support of much of the New Deal forced Landon to run a weak "me too" campaign against the charismatic incumbent.

Landon's campaign against Roosevelt never caught fire even though the Republicans outspent the Democrats $14 million to $9 million, and most of the nation's newspapers and radio stations endorsed Landon. He was a colorless individual and a poor public speaker. His radio delivery was also ineffective. He tried to make issues of Roosevelt's deficit spending and the huge increase in the size and power of the presidency, but neither carried much beyond the realm of those already converted to his political philosophy. He was hurt by his reactionary supporters who cost him votes because of their harsh anti–New Deal rhetoric. The Liberty League was so obviously a front for wealthy critics of New Deal tax and regulatory policies that Landon asked it not to endorse his candidacy. However, the Kansan did attract a number of disaffected Democrats including two former presidential candidates, Al Smith and John W. Davis.

There was another element in the 1936 election. Roosevelt's political advisers feared that popular demagogues might combine forces to mount a third party challenge. Huey Long's assassination had eliminated the most dangerous threat. The major challenge came from Father Coughlin and Dr. Townsend. They tried to join with the Reverend Gerald L. K. Smith, an anti-Semitic rabble-rouser who had inherited part of Long's forces, in support of the candidacy of Congressman William Lemke of North Dakota running as the candidate of the newly

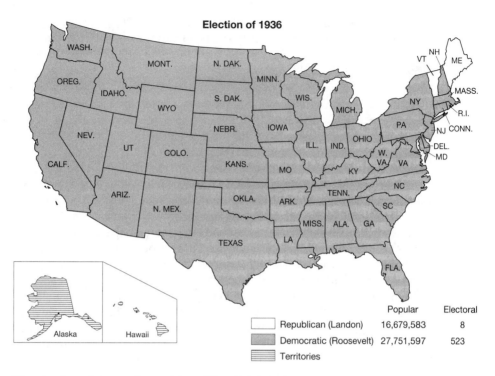

Election of 1936

	Popular	Electoral
Republican (Landon)	16,679,583	8
Democratic (Roosevelt)	27,751,597	523
Territories		

The election of 1936. *Source*: Moss, *Rise of Modern America*, p. 237.

formed Union party. These efforts failed as the extremists feuded among themselves and Father Coughlin went off on his own. Coughlin's radio speeches denounced Roosevelt's New Deal in vicious terms. He sounded anti-Semitic themes, called Roosevelt "anti-God," and also accused him of being a Communist. But the challenge posed by the demagogues in 1936 proved to be weak. They neither hurt Roosevelt's candidacy nor had any impact on the election's outcome.

When Roosevelt hit the campaign trail in 1936, he ran hard against the business classes. His opening speech attacked "economic royalists" who took "other people's money" to impose a "new industrial dictatorship." Roosevelt turned his reelection campaign into a great nonpartisan liberal crusade, a clash between the "haves" and "have-nots." For the rest of the campaign, he ignored the weak challenge of Landon, and ran against former President Hoover and "the interests." Hoover responded with a series of denunciatory speeches. The former president claimed that the New Deal philosophy rested on "coercion and the compulsory organization of men" and that it derived part of its program from Karl Marx.

In his final campaign speech, delivered at Madison Square Garden to a full house cheering his every word, and knowing that he was going to win, Roosevelt taunted his hapless Republican opponents:

Never before in history have these forces been united against one candidate as they stand today. They are unanimous in their hate for me—and I welcome their hatred! I should like to have it said of my first administration that in it the forces of selfishness and lust for power met their match. I should like to have it said of my second administration that in it these forces met their master.[1]

Roosevelt and the Democrats swept to a landslide victory. Roosevelt got 27.8 million votes to Landon's 16.7 million. Lemke attracted only 882,000 votes and the Socialist Party candidate Norman Thomas received a mere 187,000. Six million more people voted in 1936 than had cast ballots in 1932, and most of these new voters voted for Roosevelt. Most new voters were recruited from the ranks of the poor, people on relief, the unemployed, and the working classes who expressed their solidarity with the man who had forged the New Deal. They had perceived Roosevelt to be a candidate with a program and a conception of government that favored the common people. The Democrats carried every state in the union except Maine and Vermont and rolled up huge majorities in the House and Senate. The people had been given a chance to vote on the performance of Roosevelt and his program, and they had responded with an overwhelming vote of approval. Some analysts thought the Republican Party on the verge of extinction, about to go the way of the Federalists after 1801 and the Whigs after 1852. James "Big Jim" Farley, Roosevelt's campaign manager, quipped that the election proved that "as Maine goes, so goes Vermont." Reporter Dorothy Thompson suggested that if the campaign had lasted another week, Roosevelt would have carried Canada too.

THE NEW DEAL COALITION

By 1936, Roosevelt and the Democrats had forged a new political coalition firmly based on the mass of voters living in large northern cities and led in Congress by a new political type, the northern urban liberal. Whereas old-stock Americans in small towns and cities clung to the GOP, the newer ethnic groups in the cities joined the Democrats. These "ethnics" had benefited from New Deal programs and were delighted at the attention given them by New Dealers. Hard times and New Deal programs had also attracted the votes of most farmers and of the elderly. Organized labor was an integral part of the New Deal coalition, especially the new industrial unions being forged by the Congress of Industrial Organizations (CIO). These unions fused the interests of millions of workers both skilled and unskilled, native-born and foreign-born, white and nonwhite, male and female. Black voters in northern cities abandoned their historic allegiance to the Republicans and joined the new coalition. Many former Republican Progressive middle-class voters and thousands of former Socialists also joined the Roosevelt coalition.

A dramatic political realignment had taken place in America, as important as the one occurring in 1894 and 1896 that had made the Republicans the dominant party until the Great Depression. Now the Democrats had become the majority

[1]Quoted in Leutchenburg, *Franklin Roosevelt and the New Deal*, p. 184.

coalition and would retain their dominance for more than thirty years. A historic realignment, underway since the election of 1928 and forged in the crucible of the 1932 Depression election, was completed in 1936.

ROOSEVELT ATTACKS THE SUPREME COURT

Roosevelt's Second Inaugural Address, delivered on January 20, 1937, sounded a call for more radical reforms. He spoke feelingly of the plight of the poor: "I see one-third of a nation ill-housed, ill-clad, and ill-nourished." Observers wondered if he had a New Deal war on poverty in mind. Conservatives trembled at the thought of the new tax bills and antitrust measures Roosevelt might propose. The once-mighty Republican Party had been reduced to a legislative remnant in both houses of Congress, incapable of effective opposition.

As he began his second term, Roosevelt was at the height of his power and prestige; he was coming off an election in which he, his program, and his party had been given an emphatic endorsement. If he read the result as a mandate to continue on a reformist path, who would resist? If he had in mind an assault on the prerogatives of the rich in favor of the poor, who could prevent it? But when Roosevelt sent a specific legislative proposal to Congress two weeks later, he surprised everyone. He asked not for more social reforms, but for reform of the Supreme Court, an issue which he had never raised in the recent campaign.

The Supreme Court had already nullified several important New Deal measures including the "Triple A" and the NRA. Roosevelt and his advisers were afraid that it would soon invalidate recently enacted Second New Deal measures, particularly the Wagner Act and Social Security Act. Roosevelt was angry with the Court's conservative majority that had thwarted many New Deal efforts to promote recovery and to reform American society. He feared that the Court might kill more programs.

To prevent further damage to the New Deal, he proposed a scheme to reform the Court. Rejecting a constitutional amendment as too time consuming, on February 5, 1937, Roosevelt sent Congress his Judiciary Reorganization Bill. He requested authority to add a federal judge whenever an incumbent reached the age of seventy and failed to retire within six months. He proposed adding fifty federal judges, including six Supreme Court justices. He insisted that the current judiciary was understaffed, and additional jurists were required to relieve overworked, "elderly, feeble" judges. Six additional judges on the Supreme Court would help the "nine old men." Roosevelt's disingenuous proposal fooled no one. It was obvious that he would use court reform as a vehicle to liberalize the Supreme Court by appointing younger, more progressive members. At the time Roosevelt proposed reforming the Court, its lineup included four reactionaries who opposed the New Deal, three liberals who usually supported it, and two moderates—Chief Justice Charles Evans Hughes and Associate Justice Owen Roberts. Hughes and Roberts were the swingmen—they sometimes upheld New Deal legislation; more often, they opposed it.

Roosevelt's controversial proposal generated much opposition. Critics quickly dubbed his proposed court reform "Court packing." Two polls showed the public divided on the issue. Media editorials almost universally condemned it. Most Republicans opposed it, as did many Democrats, including some liberals. Roosevelt had attacked a national symbol that gave Americans a sense of identity and unity. He also threatened the constitutional principle of checks and balances with his blatant proposal to politicize the Court and to bend it to the executive will. There were limits beyond which many people did not want even this most powerful and popular of modern presidents to venture. The debate in Congress lasted for months and divided the Democrats.

As debate over the measure continued, the two swingmen, Hughes and Roberts, voted to sustain a state minimum wage law. In April 1937, in *National Labor Relations Board* v. *Jones and Laughlin Steel Corp.*, they voted with the majority in a five-to-four decision sustaining the National Labor Relations Act. A month later, they joined with another majority in a five-to-four decision to uphold Social Security. The conservatives had been eclipsed.

A few days after the Social Security decision, Justice Willis Van Devanter, a conservative judge, announced his retirement from the Court. Roosevelt would now have a six-to-three majority on the Court willing to approve New Deal legislation. The need for drastic Court reform had vanished. Hughes's and Roberts's conversions to New Deal liberalism, coupled to Van Devanter's resignation, doomed Roosevelt's bill. In a career hitherto marked by matchless political astuteness, Roosevelt committed a costly blunder. He refused to yield; he continued to battle stubbornly for what had become a hopeless cause. The Senate adjourned in July without passing his judicial reform proposal, handing Roosevelt his first major political defeat. The Court fight had consumed 168 days, during which no important legislation was enacted.

In later years, Roosevelt claimed that he had lost the "battle" but had won the "war" for judicial reform. In a sense he was correct. He appointed a liberal, Alabama Senator Hugo Black, to replace Van Devanter. Within two-and-a-half years after Congress had rejected his Court-packing scheme, Roosevelt had appointed four more liberals to the Supreme Court. The new "Roosevelt Court" greatly expanded the constitutionally permissible areas of government regulation of economic activity. Never again would a major Roosevelt bill be overturned. In fact, from 1937 to the present, the Supreme Court has never overturned a single piece of significant national or state socioeconomic legislation. Out of the political jumble of 1937, there occurred a veritable constitutional revolution.

But his success represented a classic Pyrrhic victory. In more important ways, Roosevelt lost the "war." The Court fight divided and weakened the Democratic Party, and it greatly strengthened the emerging conservative bipartisan coalition of southern Democratic and northern Republican opponents of the New Deal. The new coalition was composed largely of congressmen who represented safe, rural constituencies. The Roosevelt Court might uphold all new laws, but a divided Congress, no longer so responsive to Roosevelt's leadership, passed few measures

Roosevelt's proposal to reform the Supreme Court alarmed many Americans who feared that he was trying to impose one-man rule on the country. *Source*: The Franklin D. Roosevelt Presidential Library.

for the justices to consider. Shortly after the Court fight, a major administration bill to reorganize the executive branch was sent to Capitol Hill. Alarmed opponents denounced the measure as an effort to impose dictatorship on the American people. Congress rejected the bill, handing Roosevelt another stinging political defeat. Although Roosevelt would never acknowledge it, most historians date the beginning of the end of the New Deal from the repercussions of the fight he provoked over the Court. Ironically, a constitutional breakthrough coincided with the throttling of the very liberal reform impulse to which the constitutional barriers had been removed.

THE ROOSEVELT RECESSION

Roosevelt was also largely responsible for triggering a severe economic recession that began in 1937 and persisted until 1939. Never comfortable with deficit financing, the President decided that the economy had recovered to the point where it no longer needed stimulation from government spending and budget deficits. During the first half of 1937, Roosevelt ordered the WPA to cut its enrollment from 3 million to 1.5 million jobs. Other New Deal relief agencies slashed their enrollments drastically. To reduce the inflation rate that had reached 3.5 percent, the Federal Reserve System tightened reserve requirements and raised interest rates. The weak economy, deprived of billions in federal spending, declined sharply; within a year, the unemployment rate had risen 5 percentage points, approaching the 1933 and 1934 levels.

Confronted with the sharp economic downturn, Roosevelt reversed himself and revived deficit financing. The WPA, CCC, and other work relief agencies all increased their appropriations. But not until the end of 1939 did unemployment return to early 1937 levels. Leaders of both parties criticized Roosevelt for having unnecessarily subjected Americans to two years of increased hardship. The "Roosevelt recession" quickly erased gains that had taken four years to achieve and discouraged many people who believed that the Depression was behind them. The President's popularity and prestige sagged to new lows.

Occurring in the midst of a recession that Republicans could blame on the president, the 1938 elections severely damaged the Roosevelt coalition. Republicans picked up 81 seats in the House, 8 seats in the Senate, and they gained 13 governorships. Robert Taft from Ohio, son of former President and Chief Justice William Howard Taft, was one of the new Republican senators. Several prominent incumbent liberals went down to defeat. It was mainly the effects of the "Roosevelt recession" that hurt the Democrats and allowed the Republican comeback. Roosevelt also hurt himself politically by entering the 1938 elections. He intervened in several southern elections, trying to get rid of prominent conservative Senate opponents of the New Deal. All incumbents defeated the liberal challengers backed by Roosevelt, dealing him another serious defeat. The conservative coalition emerged from the 1938 elections as the strongest political force in Washington. From 1939 on, Roosevelt and the New Dealers were on the defensive, unable to enlarge the New Deal and at times forced to accept cuts in its programs. These contours would endure until the mid-1960s, until liberal reformers would once again be briefly ascendant under the leadership of Lyndon Johnson, one of FDR's most devoted followers.

By 1938, Roosevelt also was increasingly involved with conflicts in Europe and Asia. Japanese aggression in China and Germany's forced annexation of Austria threatened to send the world skidding toward another world war. Increasingly, the outer world claimed the President's attention. Domestic reform became a less urgent Roosevelt priority.

THE END OF THE NEW DEAL

Congress enacted the last two significant New Deal measures in early 1938. One was a new Agricultural Adjustment Act to replace the one nullified by the Supreme Court. Yielding to pressure from the farm bloc, the new AAA allowed unlimited crop production and larger subsidies. The government was required to store the inevitable surplus production and sell some of it overseas at low prices. Agricultural overproduction returned, but farm income was maintained by taxpayers providing new "Triple A" subsidies. The final New Deal reform was the Fair Labor Standards Act (FLSA), enacted in May, 1938. It established the first minimum wage at 40 cents per hour and set the standard work week at forty hours. The FLSA forced immediate pay raises for over 12 million workers who were making less than minimum wage at the time it became law. The act also abolished child labor and established rules for the employment of teenagers.

The New Deal had ended by the summer of 1938. It was a victim of recession, declining liberal support, political blunders by President Roosevelt, and the growing prominence of foreign affairs in a sullen world girding for war. But mainly it had been stifled by the growing assertiveness of the bipartisan conservative coalition comprised of northern Republicans and anti–New Deal southern Democrats. Ironically, Roosevelt's own political mistakes, especially his feckless effort to reform the Supreme Court, hastened the formation of the New Deal's nemesis that stopped it in its tracks.

THE RISE OF ORGANIZED LABOR

At the outset of the Great Depression, trade unions in this country were neither strong nor militant. Only about 3 million of the nation's 46 million workers belong to unions, and most of these unionists were skilled workers who belonged to the American Federation of Labor. AFL membership mainly consisted of members of craft unions. (Craft unions typically represented skilled workers in a particular trade, for example, plumbing or typesetting.)

The National Recovery Administration promoted union growth through its Section 7(a), which required that every industrial code grant employees "the right to organize and bargain collectively through representatives of their own choosing." The greatest increase was among industrial unions within the AFL. (Industrial unions represented all workers, skilled and unskilled, in a given industry, for example steelworkers or autoworkers.) The United Mine Workers added 300,000 workers within a few months. After one year of NRA, over seventeen hundred locals had been formed in the automobile, steel, rubber, aluminum, and other mass production industries, adding 1 million members to AFL rolls. But many companies resisted unionization through the NRA codes. They prohibited unions or formed company unions. Collective bargaining rarely occurred and NRA officials often went along with efforts to thwart independent unions. Disappointed labor leaders complained about the "National Run Around," and a wave of strikes spread across the country in 1934.

An important strike occurred on the San Franciscan waterfront in July 1934, when shipping companies rejected longshoremen's demands for union recognition, control of hiring halls, and higher wages. A violent confrontation occurred when police tried to clear five thousand pickets from the Embarcadero, the main waterfront street, to let strikebreakers work. Shots were fired from both sides. Scores were injured and two strikers were killed. The governor sent National

Guardsmen to occupy the waterfront. Organized labor responded with a general strike that nearly shut the city down for four days. Federal officials intervened to facilitate a settlement granting union recognition and control of hiring halls, a major victory for labor.

In 1935, the Supreme Court nullified the NRA; a few months later, Congress enacted the National Labor Relations Act (Wagner Act) which created a more hospitable environment for unionizing activities and strengthened union bargaining leverage with employers. Union organizing efforts increased dramatically. The Wagner Act also spurred the creation of a new labor organization, which originated as a faction within the AFL that was dissatisfied with the Federation's lack of sympathy for industrial unionism. Its leader was John L. Lewis, head of the United Mine Workers, who formed a Committee for Industrial Organizations within the AFL. In 1936, AFL leaders expelled Lewis and his industrial unions, who later formed their own trade union organization, renamed the Congress of Industrial Organizations (CIO).

The CIO launched major organizing drives in mass-production industries in the late 1930s. One of its first campaigns occurred in the steel industry, which had been a bastion of nonunion shops since the failed strikes of 1919. It created a Steel Workers Organizing Committee (SWOC) under the leadership of Philip Murray and four hundred organizers who descended upon the nation's major steel centers. "Big Steel," as the United States Steel Corporation was known, the nation's largest steel company, gave up without a fight. After secret negotiations, a contract was signed recognizing SWOC as the bargaining agent and granting workers an eight-hour day, a forty-hour week, and a large pay raise. It was an astonishing settlement from a major company that had been an antiunion bastion since its creation in 1901. USS's management cut the deal with SWOC because it did not want a strike that would disrupt its production schedules during a time of improving business.

"Little Steel," the four companies ranking from second to fifth, refused to surrender. Under the leadership of Republic Steel, the companies prepared to battle SWOC. In May 1937, the union called a strike against the companies and a fierce conflict occurred. "Little Steel" employed a variety of antiunion tactics, including intimidation and violence. The worst violence occurred on May 30 when Chicago police attacked pickets in front of Republic's main plant. They fired into the crowd, killing ten strikers and wounding dozens more. This brutal incident is known as the Memorial Day Massacre. It created widespread sympathy for strikers, but "Little Steel" broke the strike and defeated the CIO's organizing effort that year.

In January 1937, another CIO union, the United Automobile Workers (UAW) began a famous strike in Flint, Michigan, against General Motors, the world's largest industrial corporation. The strikers used a novel tactic, the "sit-down" strike, against the giant automaker. Instead of walking out of the plant at the end of a shift, the workers sat at their stations on the shop floor, shutting down the factory and preventing strikebreakers from working. Caught off guard by the sit-down tactic, company officials tried to dislodge the workers who were guilty of trespassing. They cut off the heat, letting wintertime temperatures drop to zero, but the workers built bonfires and stayed inside the factor. Police charged the plants, but were driven off by a barrage of coffee mugs, tools, lunch pails, and auto parts. Police then lobbed in tear gas, but the workers broke windows to let the gas out, and again drove the police back, this time using company fire hoses.

General Motors officials then demanded that the state militia be mobilized to remove the strikers, and they got a court order setting February 3 as a deadline for evacuation. The workers, who were risking fines, imprisonment, and possibly violent assaults, refused to yield. They demanded that the company engage in collective bargaining. When February 3 arrived, Michigan Governor Frank Murphy, a liberal Democrat elected with labor support, refused to call out the troops. President Roosevelt, who also sympathized with the strikers, appealed for negotiations. Faced with the prospect of class warfare and powerful political opposition, General Motors capitulated. Negotiations between company representatives and UAW leaders began. Within weeks, the UAW was recognized as the autoworkers' bargaining agent. Company and union representations negotiated a contract that provided substantial pay increases and a forty-hour week. Chrysler signed a similar agreement after a short strike. Ford, bitterly antiunion, held out until 1941, and there were several bloody encounters at Ford's River Rouge plant between UAW forces and company guards.

The sit-down strike proved an effective tactic, and all kinds of workers used it in the late 1930s—textile, glass, and rubber workers; dime store clerks, janitors, dressmakers, and bakers. Sometimes workers sat down spontaneously at the job and waited for CIO organizers to come sign them up. No large mass production or service industry was neglected. The sit-down tactic worked and expressed the rank-and-file militancy that activated the trade union movement in the late 1930s. Public opinion, generally sympathetic to the CIO union drives of the late 1930s, disapproved of the sit-down strike. It appeared too radical, too disrespectful of employer property rights. A liberal-dominated Supreme Court outlawed the sit-down strike tactic in 1939.

The CIO, aided by legislation, liberal politicians like Governor Murphy and President Roosevelt, and often favorable public opinion, added millions of union members during its organizing drives of the late 1930s. Hundreds of thousands of auto workers, coal miners, steelworkers, clothing workers, rubber workers, and others formed strong industrial unions. Most of the nation's major mass-production industries were organized. CIO membership reached 5 million by the end of the decade. The day of Big Labor in America had dawned.

A NEW DEAL FOR WOMEN

Many New Deal programs designed during the 1930s often helped women less than men. The National Recovery act allowed industries to structure gendered wage differentials into their codes of fair practices; women inevitably received the lower wages. Many New Deal programs resisted hiring women or hired far fewer women than men. Of the myriad of programs established by the WPA, the largest of the New Deal public works program, perhaps 10 percent of jobs went to women, and these jobs were largely limited to clerical work, library work, recreational activities, health and nutrition program work, and, most often, sewing projects. The Civilian Conservation Corps excluded women while providing work for over 2 million unemployed young men.

Women continued to improve their political status during the 1930s. Arkansas elected the first woman to serve in the U.S. Senate, Hattie Caraway. Middle- and upper-middle class women, led by First Lady Eleanor Roosevelt and Secretary of Labor Frances Perkins, the first female cabinet member, made significant political gains during the New Deal years. Josephine Roche served as assistant secretary of the treasury and Nellie Taylor Ross became the director of the U.S. Mint. Many women joined the staffs of newly created New Deal agencies. Franklin Roosevelt was the first president to appoint women to diplomatic posts. Women became important parts of the Democratic Party political machinery and the new Democratic Party coalition. There were over two hundred women delegates at the 1936 Democratic convention. Under the leadership of Mary W. "Molly" Dewson, a close friend of Eleanor's, the Women's Division of the Democratic National Committee played a major role in Franklin Roosevelt's landslide reelection victory in 1936.

During the New Deal Era, women significantly increased their influence in the nation's cultural life. The increasing cultural influence of women derived largely from the Depression-generated upsurge of cultural nationalism. Government patronage of the arts was more likely to be gender-neutral than was private patronage, and it involved a far larger number of women because it was publicly funded. Thousands of talented women participated in WPA artistic and cultural projects. Women writers participated in the Federal Writers Project.

Women also made their mark in the popular culture—in aviation, sports, and, above all, the movies. The greatest female athlete of the 1930s was a young Texan named Babe Didrickson. At the 1932 summer Olympics held in Los Angeles, she won four gold medals! Later she became the nation's finest women's golfer. Amelia Earhart was the most famous pilot of the 1930s. She was the first woman pilot to fly solo across the Atlantic, duplicating Charles Lindbergh's famed feat. Determined to prove that women aviators could equal or surpass the achievements of male pilots, Earhart set many new records. She disappeared while on a flight across the Pacific Ocean.

It was through the medium of the motion picture that female actresses exercised their greatest cultural influence on the American people: in the realms of styles of dress, speech, manners, mores, behavior, sexuality, and appearance. Female movie stars were the highest paid women in the country; in fact, salaries of top female film stars equaled or surpassed those of all but a few men. Each week, of the 80 million or more Americans who attended the movies, probably 60 percent were women.

During the 1930s, despite the hard times and the widespread suffering of women, they were often able to achieve greater economic independence, enter a wider range of occupations, join unions, enjoy greater personal and sexual freedom, enhance their political status, achieve greater cultural influence, and achieve a more serious and positive public image. In the words of Susan Ware, the leading historian of women during the 1930s, women "held their own," and even made modest advances.

THE EMERGENCE OF ETHNIC AMERICANS

During the 1930s, millions of ethnic Americans, the sons and daughters of the "new" immigrants who had poured into America during the first fifteen years of the twentieth century, came of age. The large majority of these first-generation Americans identified with Roosevelt and the New Deal. They saw Roosevelt as both a liberal leader who acknowledged their claims to full acceptance as Americans and their sense of entitlement to all the opportunities and challenges of citizenship. Ethnic Americans also perceived the New Deal as a response to their special concerns and also as an effort to preserve the modest social and economic gains that they had made during the 1920s. Roosevelt cemented his hold on the political loyalties of ethnic Americans by appointed their leaders in unprecedented numbers to important public offices. Nearly one-fourth of the federal judicial appointments made during the New Deal era were Catholics.

Most ethnic Americans during the 1930s resided in the large cities of the Northeast and the Midwest, especially New York and Chicago. During his 1936 electoral sweep, Roosevelt carried 104 of the nation's 106 largest cities. By 1936, northern ethnic Americans had acquired enough political clout within the Democratic Party to abolish the rule requiring the party's presidential candidate to win a two-thirds majority vote at its nominating convention. This rule, in place for more than one hundred years, had been used by southern Democrats to prevent any candidate they did not accept from getting the nomination. The anachronistic two-thirds rule had nearly cost Roosevelt the 1932 nomination. Bolstered by the support of northern ethnics, he got rid of it by the time of the 1936 convention.

Most Catholics supported the New Deal and the Democratic Party. In large eastern cities, Irish Americans and Italian Americans flocked to Roosevelt's banner. In the Midwest, Polish Americans and other Slavic groups likewise joined the New Deal coalition. A large majority of American Jews, most of them the sons and daughters of Russian or Polish Jews who had come to America during the first decade of the twentieth century, enthusiastically supported Roosevelt and the New Dealers. Jews perceived the Roosevelt administration as a special protector of Jews and also determined to extend their educational, economic, and social opportunities.

AFRICAN AMERICANS AND THE NEW DEAL

African Americans benefited from many New Deal programs and rallied to Roosevelt's leadership. New Dealers were more responsive to African American concerns than any administration had been since Reconstruction. Roosevelt invited many African American visitors to the White House and appointed an unofficial black cabinet to advise him on African American issues. He also appointed several African Americans to government jobs. William Hastie and Robert Weaver worked in the Department of the Interior. He appointed a prominent African American educator, Mary McLeod Bethune, to be Director of Negro Affairs of the National Youth Administration. African American social scientists, such as Ralph Bunche and Rayford Logan, served as government consultants. African American illiteracy declined and life expectancy for black people jumped about five years during the 1930s.

Several New Dealers were committed to undermining both segregation and African American disfranchisement. Eleanor Roosevelt was the leader of those New Dealers committed to equal rights for African Americans. She worked closely with Walter White, president of the NAACP, supporting its efforts to strike at the legal foundations of Jim Crow laws. In 1939, when the Daughters of the American Revolution refused to allow an African American opera singer, Marian Anderson, to perform in Washington's Constitution Hall, Mrs. Roosevelt arranged for her to sing on Easter Sunday from the steps of the Lincoln Memorial.

But President Roosevelt was never committed to black civil rights. Unwilling to risk alienating southern whites, he never endorsed two key African American political issues of the 1930s—a federal antilynching law and abolition of the poll tax. He also accepted discrimination and segregation against African Americans by many government agencies, as New Dealers acceded to prevailing racist practices. The Federal Housing Authority (FHA) accepted residential segregation by refusing to guarantee mortgages purchased by African American families in white neighborhoods. The CCC was racially segregated, as was the TVA, which constructed all-white towns and confined African American workers to low-paying job categories. Since waiters, cooks, janitors, domestics, and farm workers were excluded both from Social Security coverage and from the minimum-wage provisions of the Fair Labor Standards Act, millions of African American workers who held these low-paying jobs were denied benefits available to most white workers. One New Deal program harmed blacks. The first "Triple A" denied crop subsidies to African American tenants and deprived thousands of black sharecroppers of their livelihoods by forcing them off the land. Even though African Americans were worse off than whites during the Depression and their needs were greater, they received fewer benefits than whites. When African Americans did benefit from New Deal programs, it was more because they were economically distressed citizens than because they belonged to an oppressed racial minority.

Despite the shortcomings of the New Deal for African Americans, blacks supported it enthusiastically. African American voters abandoned their historical allegiance to the party of Lincoln and moved into the Democratic camp. Two-thirds of African American voters had voted for Hoover in 1932. In 1936, two-thirds voted for Roosevelt, joining the New Deal coalition. By the 1938 Congressional elections, 85 percent of African American voters had joined the Democratic Party. Since the New Deal Era, African American voters have been a loyal Democratic constituency, and the Democratic Party has been much more responsive to black concerns than the Republicans. Today African American politicians form one of the most powerful blocs within the Democratic Party.

HISPANIC AMERICANS DURING THE NEW DEAL

Many of the 1.2 million Mexican Americans living in the southwestern United States suffered extreme hardship during the Depression, but got no help from the New Deal. Mexican Americans had little political clout and official America was not much concerned about their welfare. Mostly uneducated and unskilled, they toiled at the economic margins. They were either beyond the reach of or fell through the cracks of many New Deal programs. U.S. government policy during the 1930s discouraged Mexican-Americans from living in the United States. The Mexican-born population declined substantially during the years of the New Deal as many families returned to Mexico because of U.S. government pressure and declining economic opportunities.

But despite poverty, hardship, and official indifference or hostility, the members of the Mexican American population who were politically active generally voted Democratic and supported Roosevelt's New Deal. In Texas, Arizona, and California, Mexican Americans enrolled in sizable numbers in the Civilian Conservation Corps and some of the WPA projects. One of the major reasons Hispanic Americans benefited to the extent that they did from New Deal social welfare programs and supported Roosevelt was because of the political influence of Senator Dennis Chavez of New Mexico, the only important U.S. political leader of Hispanic descent during the 1930s. Roosevelt frequently sought the advice of Chavez and regarded him as the national spokesman for the Hispanic American community. Chavez proved an effective advocate and he succeeded in channeling millions of New Deal dollars into programs that benefited Hispanic American populations.

During the 1920s, hundreds of thousands of Mexicans had moved to California and the Southwest. When the Depression struck the Golden State, Mexican Americans composed the bulk of the agricultural workforce. They reacted to hard times by engaging in strikes. Mexican American workers in Southern California formed a union that staged about twenty strikes from 1933 to 1936. About eighteen thousand Mexican American cotton pickers joined a union and struck the cotton fields of the San Joaquin Valley in 1933. Vigilantes fired on their union hall, killing two workers. The Immigration Service supported grower efforts to break the strike by deporting workers, some of whom were legal residents.

The arrival of dispossessed white tenant farmers and sharecroppers from the southern plains states undermined the economic position of Mexican American farm workers in California. Between 1935 and 1938, about 300,000 "Okies" came to California's Central Valley to work in the fields. Growers were happy to hire them as strikebreakers and replacements for the Mexicans. By the late 1930s, poor whites composed 90 percent of the state's migrant farm workers, and many of the

During the late 1930s, hundreds of thousands of farm families fled rural poverty in the southern plains states for California. This photo shows a family of "Okies" stalled by car trouble somewhere in New Mexico in 1937.   *Source*: Library of Congress.

Hispanic workers they had displaced had been forcibly taken or voluntarily returned to Mexico.

During the 1930s, a sizeable number of Mexicans emigrated to midwestern states such as Illinois, Michigan, and Ohio. Refugees from grinding rural poverty in their native land, they arrived uneducated and unskilled. They often found work as migratory farm laborers. Some found their way into the lower ranks of unskilled workers in some of the traditional industries, including railroad gangs, meat packing, steel, and autos. Many of the *barrios* of midwestern as well as southwestern and western cities were founded or greatly expanded during the Depression decade.

During the 1930s a relatively small immigration from Puerto Rico to the United States mainland continued. These Puerto Ricans, like the Mexicans, mostly refugees from a grinding rural poverty, settled in New York, Philadelphia, and a few other large eastern cities. Most lacked education, job skills, and did not speak English. Many Puerto Ricans discovered in Depression America of the 1930s that they had traded rural poverty in their homeland for urban poverty in America.

A NEW DEAL FOR NATIVE AMERICANS

Federal Indian policy was transformed during the 1930s. Although President Roosevelt had little firsthand knowledge of Native Americans or their problems, he relied on Harold Ickes, who did. Ickes arranged for John S. Collier to become commissioner of the Bureau of Indian Affairs (BIA). Collier, a social scientist who had been a director of the American Indian Defense Association, had long championed Native American causes. He had also edited *American Indian Life,* the most important journal devoted to Native American issues. Collier had become convinced that the federal government's integrationist policy had failed to work and that it was destroying Native American culture and ways of living. He believed that Native Americans required autonomy and self-determination to survive. During his long tenure as commissioner of the BIA from 1933 to 1945, Collier worked to promote cultural pluralism and cultural nationalism among Native Americans.

Collier fought for Indian tribal ownership of land. He championed the Indian Reorganization Act passed by Congress in 1934, which ended the allotment policy established by the Dawes Act nearly fifty years earlier. The allotment system had worked over decades to transfer much Indian land to white ranchers, miners, and farmers. Since 1887, Indian landholdings had dropped from 138 million acres to 48 million. When the Depression struck, Native Americans were the poorest, most deprived, and most depressed of all major ethnic groups in the country. Indian families on reservations earned an average annual income of about $100. Their infant mortality rate was the highest, their life expectancy the shortest, their educational attainment the lowest, and their rate of unemployment the highest of any major ethnic group in the nation.

The Indian Reorganization Act restored lands to tribal ownership. Collier also tried to get additional lands for many of the tribes via government grants, court actions, and private efforts. Other provisions of the reorganization act provided for Indian self-government and loans for economic development. Collier promoted efforts by Native Americans to develop their own business enterprises on reservations. Medical and educational services were expanded. Native American religious practices and traditional cultures were protected. Collier, deeply respectful of Indian ways, was committed to democratic pluralism: "The cultural history of Indians is in all respects to be considered equal to that of any non-Indian group. And it is desirable that Indians be bilingual." For the first time in its history, under Collier's leadership the Bureau of Indian Affairs hired many Native Americans for its own staff. Of the approximately five thousand employees of the BIA in 1938, thirteen hundred were Native Americans.

Native Americans also benefited from some New Deal relief programs. The Civilian Conservation Corps was especially appealing to young Native American men who got an opportunity to do important conservation work and earn money desperately needed by their families. Altogether, more than eighty thousand young Indian men participated in CCC projects in fifteen western states. During the 1930s, for the first time since Columbus "discovered" America, the Native American population showed a net increase.

Under Collier's enlightened leadership, the BIA promoted efforts by various tribes to develop governing councils to administer programs and formulate policies at the local level. At the same time, bureau officials sought to promote Native American cultural awareness and pride. Indians were encouraged to preserve their native religions, arts and crafts, languages, rituals, ceremonials, and traditions. Native Americans were urged to respect and celebrate the traditional Indian ways and to speak their native languages. Collier hoped that Native Americans would achieve both political and cultural autonomy, protected from the oppressions and depredations of Euro-American society. Collier also worked to end the practice of sending young Native Americans away to boarding schools. BIA officials built schools on reservations where Native American youngsters could learn both how to cope with mainstream America and to learn about their own culture and to develop a strong Indian identity.

FDR AND THE NEW DEAL PERSPECTIVE

The New Deal was an extension of the commanding personality at its center, Franklin Roosevelt. He began his presidency confident that he could lead the American people out of the morass of depression; that he could provide both the inspiration and the means to restore prosperity and confidence. His leadership proved effective. Feelings of despair, of imminent collapse, vanished. Partial recovery occurred and people regained their optimistic vitality. James MacGregor Burns, a Roosevelt biographer, found in Roosevelt "the lineaments of greatness—courage, joyousness, responsiveness, vitality, faith, and above all, concern for his fellow man." A poll of American historians taken in 1984 rated Roosevelt Number Two among all Presidents, behind Lincoln and ahead of Washington. During the New Deal years, neither his popularity nor his power were seriously challenged by spokesmen for the Left or Right. His smashing electoral victory in 1936 confirmed his popularity and the political success of New Deal programs.

But Roosevelt and the New Deal were controversial; and, he provoked legions of detractors. Most newspaper and radio editorials regularly attacked the man in the White House, often vehemently. Rightist critics called him a dictator, a Socialist, a Communist, and a Fascist. They denounced the New Deal as un-American, subverting the American way of life. They also insisted that deficit spending for New Deal relief programs would bankrupt the nation and that Roosevelt's usurpations of power would destroy democracy. None of these rightist criticisms are literally true: they were hyperbolic rhetoric that mainly expressed the feelings of intense fear, hostility, and hatred Roosevelt aroused among corporate executives and the wealthy elite, some of whose prerogatives had been modestly curtailed by New Deal reforms.

More thoughtful critics have faulted Roosevelt for being too pragmatic, too opportunistic. They assert he failed to formulate a coherent strategy for economic recovery and social reform. The New Deal was not planned; it evolved. It was a series of ad hoc improvisions. Roosevelt's grasp of economics was superficial; he did not understand economic processes or grasp economic theory. His ignorance of economics hindered his recovery efforts.

Other critics have cited flaws in the personality, character, and intellect of President Roosevelt. He had few close friends and lacked personal warmth. He was not close to his wife Eleanor nor was he a good father to his several children. He had a long-term affair with another woman, Lucy Mercer. He was not always truthful nor was he particularly loyal to many political associates. He seemed to enjoy setting his advisers against one another and having them compete for influence and power within his administrative circle. He had a petty, even vindictive, streak, and he appeared to delight in humiliating his political opponents, such as former president Herbert Hoover. He was a man of ordinary, perhaps slightly above average, intelligence. He had a lazy, undisciplined mind. He was poorly read and lacked the ability to think systematically or analytically about public policies and problems. He got most of his ideas and politics from picking the brains of his advisers during the New Deal era.

During the New Deal, the institution of the presidency was transformed. It vastly increased in size, power, and scope. Most New Deal agencies were created as bureaucracies within the executive branch. The national government, particularly its executive branch, became a major growth industry during the 1930s. During the New Deal era, the federal government became the focal point for civic life. People increasingly turned to Washington for solutions to problems; the importance of local and state governments withered. The New Deal was an ongoing civics lesson educating people in possible uses of federal power to stimulate the economy, change the money and banking system, provide jobs, aid farmers, supervise labor–management relations, and save homes and small businesses. The New Deal created the American welfare state. Many governmental agencies created during the New Deal function today to regulate business, stimulate the economy, and distribute benefits to millions.

Even though his capitalist critics never appreciated it, Roosevelt's moderate mix of reforms probably saved the capitalist system from self-destruction or socialism during its gravest crisis. Roosevelt, himself a wealthy man, had a sense that he was saving the American system. He was annoyed at shrill attacks leveled on him by other rich people that appeared to him both misguided and unfair. Capitalism not only survived, but the New Deal brought about some modest reforms that strengthened the underlying structure of capitalism. In particular, banking reform and securities legislation brought a greater degree of responsibility, safety, and stability to the American financial world. Profits and private property remained fundamental to the American system.

The wealthy survived as a class, although the New Deal accomplished a modest redistribution of wealth. In 1929, the top 5 percent of the population received 30 percent of national income. In 1938, at the end of the New Deal, the top 5 percent's share had dropped to 26 percent. The income lost to the wealthy mostly went to middle- and upper-middle-income families whose share increased from 33 percent in 1929 to 36 percent in 1938. The income share going to the poorest families rose slightly from 13.2 percent to 13.7 percent.

The New Deal also altered the distribution of political power. Business remained the single most powerful political interest, but during the New Deal it was forced to share power with other groups. Farmers gained political clout and so did trade unions. The New Deal also responded to consumers and homeowners.

Millions of unemployed workers benefited from New Deal relief programs. New Dealers created a broker state during the 1930s. New Dealers responded to organizations, to interest groups, to lobbies, and to trade associations. The web of power and influence expanded and diversified. Mediating claims of various groups pressuring the government became a complex art form. But the millions of Americans who were not organized to make claims upon the broker state got neglected. The reach of the New Deal rarely extended to minorities, to slum dwellers, to sharecroppers, and to other poor, unorganized, and powerless people. Those whose needs were greatest got the least help from the New Deal because they lacked the means to influence New Deal power brokers.

The New Deal helped to create a more just society by including farmers, industrial workers, particular ethnic groups, and a new class of intellectual-administrators. Yet it represented only a half-way revolution, swelling the ranks of the middle classes while continuing to exclude and marginalize millions of Americans—sharecroppers and tenant farmers, slum dwellers, most nonwhite minorities, and most women.

At the core the New Deal was an evolutionary centrist reform program. It drew upon ideologies that had been around for decades, principally the New Nationalism of Theodore Roosevelt and Wilsonian progressivism. Roosevelt and most other prominent New Dealers had previously been active Progressive reformers. New Dealers rejected socialism, fascism, and also eschewed indigenous radicalisms like the confiscatory tax schemes of the populist demagogue, Huey Long. Fundamentally, the New Deal tried to conserve the American capitalistic system by rescuing it from depression and reforming it to make it responsive to a broader range of interest groups. New Dealers were also concerned to reform the American economy to prevent a recurrence of a depression and to fend off more radical reforms.

But the New Deal was only a partial economic success. It proved politically invulnerable to the challenges of both radicalism or reaction. It succeeded politically, but it failed to solve the fundamental economic problem caused by the Great Depression—unemployment. As the New Deal ended in 1938, over 10 million men and women were still without jobs; the unemployment rate hovered near 20 percent. New Dealers failed to eliminate unemployment because they never solved the problem of underconsumption. Consumers and businesses never were able to buy enough to stimulate enough production to approach normal employment patterns. For example, in the pre-Depression year of 1929, new car sales totaled $6.5 billion. In 1938, at the end of the New Deal, the figure was $3.9 billion. Years after the New Deal had ended, massive unemployment persisted.

The most serious failure of the New Deal was its inability to promote economic recovery from the Depression. New Dealers enjoyed great success with most of their efforts to relieve distress and to reform the American system of political economy. But they failed to revive the American economy, restore prosperity, restore full employment, stimulate sufficient capital investment, or promote economic growth. Programs such as the National Recovery Administration (NRA) retarded economic recovery between 1933 and 1935. The NRA favored large corporations that were stagnating over small, dynamic companies. Only the gigantic federal spending and deficit financing required to pay the costs of World War II restored production, put everyone back to work, and regenerated prosperity. Prosperity only returned to America years after the New Deal was a spent force and was the adventitious by-product of the exogenous factor of the largest and most destructive war in the history of the world. Long before world war restored American prosperity, many other nations had shaken off the effects of the worldwide depression. But had war not come, economic stagnation in America would have persisted well into the 1940s, perhaps longer.

IMPORTANT EVENTS

1933	Franklin Delano Roosevelt is inaugurated as the thirty-second president
1933	"Hundred Days" legislation is enacted; the New Deal begins
1933	Frances Perkins, first female cabinet member, is appointed Secretary of Labor
1933	Prohibition is repealed
1934	The Securities and Exchange Commission is created
1934	The American Liberty League is formed
1935	The Indian Reorganization Act is passed
1934	The Supreme Court nullifies the NRA
1935	The WPA is created
1935	The Social Security Act is passed
1935	The National Labor Relations Act (Wagner Act) is passed
1935	Huey Long is assassinated
1936	The Congress of Industrial Organizations (CIO) is formed
1936	The UAW initiates the sit-down strike tactic
1936	The Supreme Court nullifies the first AAA
1936	Roosevelt is reelected
1937	The SWOC organizes U.S. Steel workers
1937	"Memorial Day Massacre" takes place in Chicago
1937	Roosevelt's efforts to "pack" the Supreme Court fail
1938	Fair Labor Standards Act (FLSA) is passed
1938	The New Deal ends
1939	African American singer Marian Anderson sings at the Lincoln Memorial

BIBLIOGRAPHY

There is vast historical literature on the New Deal Era and the commanding figure at its center. The best one-volume treatment is William E. Leuchtenburg's *Franklin D. Roosevelt and the New Deal, 1932–1940*. Arthur M. Schlesinger, Jr., in *The Age of Roosevelt*, has two lively volumes covering the 1933–1936 years. James MacGregor Burns, in *Roosevelt: The Lion and the Fox*, offers the best political biography of the most powerful and popular modern American president. Joseph P. Lash's *Eleanor and Franklin* is a graceful study of the president and his extraordinary First Lady. Lois Scharf's *Eleanor Roosevelt: First Lady of American Liberalism* is a recent first-rate biography of the greatest First Lady. Walter J. Stein, in *California and the Dust Bowl Migration*, presents the best study of the uprooted "Okies" who left the southern plains states for California during the Depression. Walter Galenson, in *The CIO Challenge to the AFL*, gives a good account of the rise of industrial unionism during the late 1930s. Alan Brinkley's *Voices of Protest: Huey Long, Father Coughlin, and the Great Depression* is a fine study of major New Deal critics. James T. Patterson, in *Congressional Conservatism and the New Deal*, charts the rise of the bipartisan conservative coalition of southern Democrats and northern Republicans that blocked New Deal reforms after 1938. Susan Ware's *Beyond Suffrage: Women in the New Deal* and Raymond Wolters's *Negroes and the New Deal* are fine studies of the impact of the Depression on particular groups. Kenneth Philip's *John Collier's Crusade for Indian Reform, 1920–1954* is a fine account of the New Deal for Native Americans. Richard H. Pells, in *Radical Visions and American Dreams: Culture and Social Thought in the Depression Years*, records the nation's artistic and intellectual life during the 1930s. A recent book by Alan Brinkley, *The End of Reform: New Deal Liberalism in Recession and War*, emphasizes the conservative nature of New Deal liberal reformism and explains why it failed to bring a greater measure of social justice and why it failed to cure the Great Depression.

CHAPTER 7

Diplomacy between Wars

The United States emerged from World War I an acknowledged world power with the most productive and prosperous economy in the world. American banks dominated the realms of international finance and investment. American diplomats understood that even had they desired it, America could not be a bystander in world affairs. It is true that during the interwar period, Americans tried to avoid foreign entanglements, but it is also true that American diplomatists pursued an activist foreign policy appropriate to that of a leading world power. During the 1920s and 1930s, American leaders sought a peaceful and prosperous world order by using nonmilitary means: treaties, disarmament conferences, and financial arrangements. The United States pursued isolationist policies between the wars only in the sense that it wanted to avoid war, reduce foreign military involvements, and preserve its freedom of action in international affairs. Historian Joan Hoff Wilson has characterized American interwar diplomacy not as isolationism but as "independent internationalism"—that is, actively involved in international affairs but preserving independence in actions. With differing degrees of success and sophistication, all the presidents who served between the wars pursued this uniquely American approach to international affairs called independent internationalism.

THE SEARCH FOR PEACE

President Harding came to office in 1921 committed to returning the nation to "normalcy." In foreign policy, "normalcy" meant repudiating Wilsonian internationalism and its commitment to collective security. Harding believed his landslide victory expressed deeply felt popular yearnings for ending overseas crusades, avoiding foreign entanglements, for curtailing huge military expenditures, and for healing domestic conflicts. He generously pardoned the Socialist leader, Eugene Debs, who was serving a ten-year prison sentence for having opposed American involvement in World War I. Harding also invited the radical leader to drop by the White House for a visit after his release from an Atlanta penitentiary and Debs obliged him.

In November 1921, Harding presided at ceremonies burying the Unknown Soldier in Arlington National Cemetery. In a moving speech, the president resolved that "never again" would the nation be led into another foreign war, and he called for "a new and lasting era of peace." That same month, Harding signed separate peace treaties with all Central Power nations that were still technically at war with the United States because of the Senate's rejection of the Treaty of Versailles. He also opened a major international conference in Washington hosted by the United States.

The Washington Conference, which convened in the nation's capital November 12, 1921, was the first important diplomatic gathering of the postwar era. It was called by the United States to show America's commitment to ensuring peace in the postwar world despite its refusal to join the League of Nations. It was also the first major international conference ever held in America, indicating the new prestige of the United States that had come out of the war as the world's preeminent power. Eight nations joined with the United States to discuss disarmament and Far Eastern diplomatic problems left by war.

Secretary of State Charles Evans Hughes seized the initiative at the conference with a bold speech calling for naval disarmament. After intense negotiations, the major naval powers accepted Hughes' proposals. A Five Power Treaty, signed February 6, 1922, by the United States, Great Britain, Japan, France, and Italy, established a ten-year moratorium on new capital ship construction. (*Capital ships* were battleships and cruisers exceeding 10,000 tons.) The treaty also required that the signatories scrap ships built or being built until their relative strength in capital ships reached a ratio of 5 to 5 to 3 to 1.75 to 1.75, in which a 5 would equal 525,000 tons of capital ships. The Americans and the British would have the highest ratio numbers of 5, allowing them 525,000 tons of capital ships each. The Japanese would have a ratio number of 3; the French and Italians would have ratio numbers of 1.75 each. To reach treaty limits, the major powers had to scrap seventy warships totaling nearly 2 million tons. The Five Power Treaty curbed a costly and dangerous postwar naval arms race among the major powers. It was a significant disarmament agreement, but the treaty had loopholes. There were no limits applied to submarines, destroyers, and cruisers under 10,000 tons.

A second treaty worked out at the Conference, the Four Power Treaty, signed by the United States, Great Britain, Japan, and France, required those four nations to respect each other's rights in the Pacific and to refer any disputes to a joint conference. This agreement bound the four powers to respect one another's island possessions in the Western Pacific. A third agreement, the Nine Power Treaty, bound all the nations attending the conference to observe the American Open Door policy toward China and to respect the "sovereignty, the independence, and the territorial and administrative integrity of China." The signatories formally affirmed the traditional American Open Door policy toward China promulgated by John Hay in 1899 and 1900.

The Washington Conference represented a major diplomatic achievement for the United States. Secretary of State Hughes provided the leadership that halted a naval arms race, saving taxpayers billions of dollars and easing international tensions. In the Far East, the Open Door was given a new lease on life, and a new balance of power emerged in Asia that reflected postwar realities.

Harding, unlike Wilson, had consulted with Senate leaders during conference negotiations and kept them informed of its proceedings. The Senate promptly ratified all three treaties, although isolationist senators attacked them during debates, especially the Four Power Treaty, which they saw as possibly involving the United States in a future war with Japan. Irreconcilable J. A. Reed of Montana called the Four Power Treaty "treacherous, treasonable, and damnable." As they ratified these agreements, the Senate, reflecting the isolationist sentiments of most Americans, declared "there is no commitment to armed force, no alliance, no obligation to join in any defense."

All three treaties would eventually prove to be toothless because neither the United States nor any other signatories bound themselves to defend the agreements with force or sanctions. Americans wanted peace, but they would not take responsibility for preserving peace. The treaties were gentlemen's agreements; their effectiveness depended on good faith compliance, which proved in time to be a frail prop. Beginning in 1931, the Japanese ultimately violated all the agreements, and for years America and the League of Nations reacted weakly to Japanese aggression, which went unchecked in China and the Pacific.

American peace societies during the 1920s advocated many strategies to preserve order in the world. They proposed cooperating with the League of Nations, joining the World Court, having additional disarmament conferences, signing arbitration treaties, curbing international business activity, and cutting military spending. The National Council for the Prevention of War kept alive ghastly memories of war carnage and reminded Americans of the suicidal folly of trying to settle international conflicts by war. *What Price Glory* (1926) and other antiwar films depicted the slaughter of World War I combat.

President Coolidge issued a call for another naval disarmament conference, which convened in Geneva in 1927. Coolidge wanted to extend the 5 to 5 to 3 to 1.75 to 1.75 ratios to all categories of warships to end a naval arms race developing in cruisers under 10,000 tons, destroyers, and submarines. After six weeks of angry debate, the delegates failed to find a formula they could accept. The conference broke up in complete failure.

Following the failure at Geneva, peace advocates shifted their emphasis from abolishing arms to abolishing war. Americans took the initiative in the movement to outlaw war. They approached the French Foreign Minister, Aristide Briand, who announced in April 1927 that France was prepared to sign a joint pact with the United States outlawing war. The drive generated wide popular support in both countries. The American Secretary of State Frank Kellogg suggested that the proposed bilateral agreement be expanded to include other powers, and the French agreed. The treaty was worded to permit defensive wars but to outlaw war "as an instrument of national policy." On August 27, 1928, the Pact of Paris was signed by fifteen nations, and in succeeding months another forty-five nations signed it, including Japan and Germany. The American public overwhelmingly supported the pact, which the Senate ratified by a vote of eighty-five to one. Kellogg was awarded the Nobel Peace Prize for 1929.

The Pact of Paris was a feeble document, a mere statement of principle requiring neither sacrifice nor the assumption of any responsibilities for keeping the peace. The pact reflected the delusions of Americans and others who believed that war could be eliminated by declaring it illegal. But the treaty did not outlaw war, it only outlawed aggressive wars and declared wars. Thereafter nations were to fight only "defensive" wars and only to become involved in "incidents." Even as they approved the treaty, most U.S. senators understood that the pact was nothing more than a pious gesture. Senator Hiram Johnson made fun of it, calling it "A helmless ship, a houseless street, a wordless book, a swordless sheath." Then he voted for it. On the same day that it ratified the treaty, the Senate also voted funds to build fifteen new cruisers.

Other disarmament conferences were held during the 1930s. The London Naval Conference (1930) extended the Five Power Treaty ratios to all categories of warships, closing a huge loophole in the previous treaty. But the French and Italians refused to accept these limits. The French refused because they feared for their security. The Italians refused because they had expansionist ambitions. The conferees then added an "escalator clause" that permitted any member to disregard the ratios if one of those nations not bound by the ratios, say Italy, began building ships that threatened the security of a nation that had accepted the ratios. Another disarmament conference met in Geneva in 1932 to try to reduce the size of armies. President Hoover strongly supported this conference, urging it to reduce the size of all armies by one-third and to abolish all offensive weapons. The conference failed completely, mainly because of Japanese aggression in Manchuria and the rise of Hitler to power in Germany. Security-conscious nations did not dare disarm in the face of these threatening developments. Another naval conference met in London in 1935, but no major agreements could be reached because the Italians still refused to accept any more limits on its naval forces and the Japanese, harboring expansionist ambitions in China and Southeast Asia, walked out. In 1936, the Japanese formally renounced all naval limitations. By 1938, all nations had abandoned them. Congress appropriated a billion dollars for U.S. naval construction in all ship categories. Disarmament ultimately failed to prevent World War II.

The League of Nations also failed to keep the peace, not only because the United States refused to join, but because its members usually chose not to use it to settle international disputes. Although the United States never joined the League of Nations, Americans participated in League activities during the 1920s and 1930s, attending meetings about public health, drug trafficking, and other

The League of Nations building in Geneva. The sphere in the foreground was a gift from the Woodrow Wilson Foundation.   *Source:* National Archives.

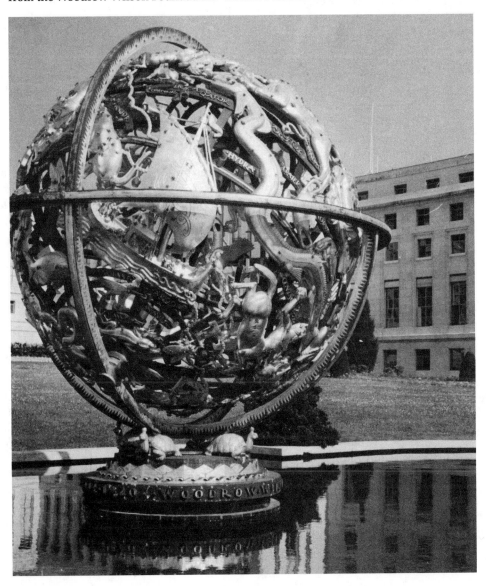

affairs not connected with international security. Eminent American jurists such as Charles Evans Hughes served on the World Court even though America had never joined it, either. But the League of Nations, the World Court, the Pact of Paris, and the disarmament conferences could not maintain world peace once the Great Depression of the 1930s and its disastrous economic effects upset the fragile world order.

FOREIGN ECONOMIC POLICY

During the early 1920s, the Harding administration and Congress both promoted American business activity overseas. Secretary of State Charles Evans Hughes believed that a prosperous world would be a peaceful world, free of political extremism, aggression, revolution, and war. He understood that in the modern world American international commercial and financial interests blended with traditional diplomatic concerns in the conduct of foreign affairs. The chief governmental agency actively promoting overseas business during the 1920s was the Department of Commerce, headed by Herbert Hoover, who had had a career as an international businessman.

Americans assumed a dominant role in international economic activity during the 1920s. The gigantic American economy produced nearly half of the world's manufactured goods. American traders had become the world's leading exporters and American bankers the world's foremost lenders. Between 1920 and 1929, American investments abroad increased from $6 billion to almost $16 billion, most of them made in Europe and Latin America. U.S. corporate investors led the way. General Electric invested heavily in various German enterprises. Standard Oil of New Jersey bought into Venezuela's rich oil resources. United Fruit Company was a huge landowner in several Central American countries. International Telephone and Telegraph built Cuba's communication network.

As American companies expanded their overseas activities, the American government moved energetically to collect war debts owed it by European nations, incurring their resentment. When war had begun in 1914, the United States was the world's largest net debtor; Americans owed foreigners $3 billion more than foreigners owed them. Huge European expenditures for war quickly transformed America from a net debtor to the world's leading creditor. By 1920, Europeans owed the U.S. Treasury $10.4 billion, of which the British owed $4.3 billion, the French $3.4 billion, and the Italians $1.6 billion. The smaller nations together owed another $1 billion to the United States.

These nations had borrowed the money mostly to buy war material, principally ammunition, from American suppliers. The money had been collected from American citizens who had bought Liberty Bonds. The government credited the money to European accounts opened in American banks who, in turn, paid it to businesses who had sold ammunition to the Europeans. These loan funds never left the United States, and, being spent in the United States, they contributed significantly to the wartime prosperity that most Americans enjoyed.

During the 1920s, Europeans tried to persuade Americans to cancel these debts. They used a variety of arguments to claim the loans were subsidies: As Europeans fought and died, neutral Americans prospered. The Allies had paid in blood and Americans should pay in dollars by canceling the loans. Had the Germans won, the United States would have had to spend far more than $10 billion building up its defenses. The Europeans also insisted that they could not repay the loans. They had no gold. American tourism did not begin to provide enough funds, and American tariff barriers prevented Europeans from earning export credits to apply against their loans.

Americans rejected all the European arguments and demanded repayment. They insisted that the loans were loans, and that they had been made in good faith with money borrowed from the American people. President Coolidge put the matter tersely: "Well, they hired the money, didn't they?" Americans also noticed that despite their pleas of poverty, the Europeans, especially the French, were quickly re-arming after the war.

Congress established a World War Foreign Debt Commission to set up repayment schedules with each of the debtor nations. The British were the first to sign up, agreeing to repay their $4.3 billion obligation in full over sixty-two years at 3.3 percent interest, a mortgage on the wealth of the next two British generations. An embittered Briton observed that for the next sixty years, "the American flag is going to look like the $tars and $tripes." Other Europeans grumbled about selfish "Uncle Shylock" profiting from war and demanding his pound of flesh.

Several European nations refused to pay their war debt unless they could be assured of collecting reparations from Germany with which to pay them. The Allied Reparations Commission, meeting in 1921, had saddled the hapless Germans with an absurdly inflated $33 billion reparations bill. Germany could not begin to pay that amount and soon defaulted. In response to Germany's defaulting, French troops occupied Germany's Ruhr Valley, its industrial heartland, and prepared to extract reparations in kind. The Germans foiled the French efforts by mounting a campaign of passive disobedience. Reparations dried up. Angry American officials denied any connection between German reparations payments to the Allies and Allied war debt payments to the United States, and they demanded that the French and others pay up.

Even though the United States officially rejected any tie-in between reparations and war debts, an American banker, Charles Dawes, worked out an arrangement, with Secretary Hughes' unofficial approval, to ease the payments crunch. The Dawes Plan encouraged U.S. bankers to lend the Germans $200 million, and it scaled down the size of German reparations payments to DM 1 billion ($250 million) per year, an amount the Germans could pay. Assured of reparations, the French and the other debtors all negotiated repayment plans similar to the British. In 1929, the Dawes Plan gave way to a plan devised by Owen Young, Chairman of the Board of General Electric, which was a major investor in German companies. The Young Plan called for Germany to pay reparations annually for fifty-nine years, at the end of which the Germans would have paid about $9 billion plus interest, a drastic reduction of the $33 billion originally demanded by the Allies.

With repayment of the Allied war debts owed the United States chained to German reparations payments to the Allies, a financial merry-go-round evolved. American investors loaned the Germans money; the Germans paid the Allies reparations; and the Allies, in turn, paid war debts to the United States. But war debt and reparations payments depended on the continuing flow of loan money from Americans. After the stock market collapsed in the United States in October, 1929, Americans loans to Germany dried up, German reparations payments ceased, and Allied war debt repayments to the United States stopped. The financial merry-go-round ground to a halt.

President Hoover and Congress contributed to the spreading depression by enacting the Smoot-Hawley Tariff Act (1930). Smoot-Hawley raised U.S. tariffs to historic high levels and triggered a chain reaction of economic miseries at home and abroad. Foreign traders, no longer able to sell their goods in the United States, stopped buying American exports. Twenty-six nations retaliated against the Smoot-Hawley tax schedules by raising their tariff rates, which closed their markets to American goods. Great Britain abandoned its historic free-trade policy and bound its empire more closely to its home market through an imperial preference system.

Worldwide depression wrecked international trade and finance. From 1929 to 1933, world trade declined 40 percent. American exports shrunk 60 percent during those four years. As the Great Depression deepened, economic nationalism intensified. Nations increasingly sought to insulate themselves from the virus of economic depression at the expense of other countries. Efforts at international economic cooperation failed. *Autarky,* a kind of international anarchy, became the rule of the day.

President Hoover tried to salvage the system of international debt payments before it collapsed completely. He declared a general moratorium for one year on all debt transactions, beginning in June 1931. Congress approved Hoover's proposal and the public applauded his efforts. During the one-year holiday, efforts were made to further reduce the size of both reparations and war debt payments, but these efforts proved unsuccessful. The moratorium ended in July 1932. When the first war debt payments came due in December 1932, six nations, led by France, defaulted. More nations defaulted in 1933, and all were in default by 1934, except Finland. Payments were never resumed. The Allied war debts owed to America joined the ranks of history's bad debts.

Resentment and disunity lingered on both sides of the Atlantic during the 1930s, facilitating Hitler's rise to power. The collapse of debt payments, the decline in trade, and the rise of economic nationalism were major causes of World War II. American efforts to use its vast economic and financial resources to promote international prosperity and peace failed in the face of international depression and anarchy.

LATIN AMERICA

By 1920, the Caribbean Sea had become a "Yankee lake." An informal American empire, including many countries within the sea and along its Central American coast, flourished. The United States maintained control of its client nations in this region through military occupation and economic domination, which American officials justified by evoking the Roosevelt Corollary to the Monroe Doctrine. In 1920, American troops occupied Cuba, the Dominican Republic, Haiti, Panama, and Nicaragua. There were also many benign effects of American imperialism evident in these countries—more schools and roads, improved public health, communication systems, irrigation networks, and higher national incomes.

During the 1920s, American military occupation of Latin American countries came under fire both at home and abroad. Domestic Progressive critics like Senator William Borah asserted that Latin Americans should have the right of self-determination; he also accused President Coolidge of violating the U.S. Constitution by ordering troops into Nicaragua in 1927 without a congressional declaration of war. Nationalistic Latin Americans claimed that U.S. military intervention in the Caribbean area violated both American democratic traditions and the spirit of Pan-Americanism. American businessmen worried that resentful Latin terrorists might attack Americans or their property.

President Hoover came to office in 1929 determined to improve U.S. relations with Latin America. As president-elect, he had gone on a goodwill tour of many Latin American nations, the first ever by an American leader. Many Latin Americans were delighted by Hoover's visit, especially when he stated that relations between Western Hemispheric nations should be governed by the principle of the "Good Neighbor." In his inaugural address, the new president made clear his determination to accelerate a "retreat from imperialism" in Latin America and to remove American troops. Hoover embraced a memorandum prepared in 1928 by Undersecretary of State Reuben Clark. The Clark Memorandum repudiated the Roosevelt Corollary, arguing that the many American interventions in the Caribbean had not been justified by the Monroe Doctrine, which had aimed at keeping European nations out of the Western Hemisphere, not promoting U.S. intervention in Latin America. President Franklin Roosevelt, who succeeded Hoover, embraced and enlarged the Good Neighbor policy during the 1930s.

The Great Depression severely tested Hoover's "Good Neighbor" policy during the early 1930s. Economic hardship weakened governments and provoked rebellions in many Latin American nations. Hoover refrained from sending in the Marines in all these uprisings, even when revolutionaries triumphed. The Depression also caused large reductions in U.S. investments and trade in Latin America, "dollar diplomacy in reverse." Congress pressured Hoover to withdraw troops stationed in Latin American as an economy measure, and, before he left office in March 1933, all U.S. forces were out of Latin America.

In small, poor countries like Nicaragua, Haiti, and the Dominican Republic, the withdrawal of American troops did not bring democratic governments to power. In these countries, the departing Americans trained national guards to maintain order. Dictators emerged from the ranks of these national guards to seize control of governments. In the Dominican Republic, a guard commander, Rafael T. M. Trujillo, became head of state in 1930 and ruled his country with an iron fist until he was assassinated in 1961. In Nicaragua, the head of the national guard, General Anastasio Somoza, became dictator in 1936. With American backing, he (and then his son) ruled Nicaragua like a medieval fiefdom for over forty years. In Haiti, government was in the hands of a series of military strongmen following U.S. troop withdrawals.

In Cuba, the scenario was somewhat different, but military dictatorships backed by the United States ruled Cuban affairs most of the time. By 1929, U.S. investments in Cuba had reached $1.5 billion. Americans owned about two-thirds of the Cuban sugar industry, the mainstay of its economy. With American troops withdrawn, Cuban rebels overthrew a military dictator, General Gerardo Machado. They installed a radical intellectual as president, Ramon Grau San Martin, in 1933. San Martin canceled the Platt Amendment and nationalized some American properties. Roosevelt, unhappy with San Martin, refrained from military intervention, honoring the Good Neighbor spirit. However, he supported a coup led by an army sergeant, Fulgencio Batista, that overthrew San Martin in 1934. Batista ruled Cuba, sometimes as president, sometimes from behind the scenes, with American backing for twenty-five years. The Batista era in Cuba ended in 1959 when the aging dictator was overthrown by Fidel Castro.

U.S. relations with Mexico during the depression years took a different turn. At the time of the Mexican revolution, from 1910 to 1917, American investments in Mexico were extensive—railroads, silver mines, timber, cattle, farmland, and oil. Over 40 percent of the capital wealth of Mexico belonged to American companies. Article 27 of the Mexican Constitution, proclaimed in 1917, stated that all land and subsoil raw materials belonged to the Mexican nation, placing in jeopardy about $300 million of U.S. investments in land and oil. In 1923, the two nations signed an agreement that permitted American companies that held subsoil rights before 1917 to keep them, and it required payment to Americans whose holdings were expropriated by the Mexican government.

In 1938, American business interests collided with Mexican nationalism when Mexican President Lazaro Cardenas nationalized all foreign oil properties, including extensive U.S. holdings. Secretary of State Cordell Hull angrily denounced the Mexican takeover. President Roosevelt suspended U.S. purchases of Mexican silver. American oil companies refused to transport Mexican oil. Standard Oil of New Jersey, whose Mexican subsidiary was the largest company to be nationalized, mounted a propaganda campaign in the United States depicting Cardenas as a Bolshevik bent on socializing Mexico's entire economy.

Roosevelt ruled out military intervention, opting for negotiations to gain compensation for expropriated U.S. oil properties. Roosevelt's restraint was caused partly by his desire to observe the Good Neighbor policy, and partly because Mexico threatened to sell its oil to Japan and the European Fascist powers if the American oil companies continued to boycott Mexican oil. After lengthy negotiations, the two nations reached an agreement. Mexico would retain ownership of its oil, but would pay the foreign companies for their nationalized properties. Mexico remained a major trading partner of the United States and joined the fight against the Axis powers in World War II.

Pan-Americans also flourished during the era of the Good Neighbor. Pan-Americanism had originated with Secretary of State James G. Blaine in 1889 to promote trade and political stability among Western Hemispheric nations. Pan-Americanism was later broadened to include cultural exchanges and to encourage inter-American unity and friendship. At a Pan-American conference held in Montevideo, Uruguay, in 1933, Secretary of State Cordell Hull supported a resolution that stated: "No state has the right to intervene in the internal or external affairs of another." At the 1936 conference held in Buenos Aires, Argentina, Hull again endorsed a nonintervention statement, which he understood to bar military intervention, but not political or economic pressure.

By the late 1930s, the United States was clearly worried about possible Axis inroads in Latin America. Nazi activists were present in Argentina, Uruguay, Chile, and Brazil. At the 1938 Pan-American conference held in Lima, Peru, the United States stressed continental solidarity and hemispheric security. All nations attending the conference signed the Declaration of Lima, which committed them to cooperate with one another in resisting any foreign activity which might threaten them. In 1939, these nations formed a security belt around the Western Hemisphere to prevent Axis intrusions. With the outbreak of World War II, the United States led a united band of Western Hemispheric nations against the Axis powers. The United States' Latin American policy of the Good Neighbor paid off: It increased hemispheric friendship, promoted American trade and investment, curtailed revolution, allowed the United States to retain its hegemony by nonmilitary means, and promoted regional solidarity in wartime.

THE TRIUMPH OF ISOLATIONISM

Franklin Roosevelt took office in March 1933, determined to concentrate his energies on rescuing the American economy from the Depression. When an economic conference convened in London in the summer of 1933 to grapple with urgent international economic problems, including war debts, tariff barriers, and monetary stabilization, Roosevelt opposed any changes in tariff policy and refused to discuss war debts. When the conference tried to commit the United States to a currency-stabilization system, Roosevelt, who had recently devalued the American dollar to promote American exports, rebuked the conferees for ignoring "fundamental economic ills." Roosevelt, the leader of the world's preeminent economic and financial power, refused to commit the dollar to any stabilization program that threatened to harm the weak American economy. His actions undermined the London Economic Conference. It collapsed shortly thereafter, its participants unable to reach an agreement on any important issues and also bitterly critical of the economic nationalism displayed by the new American leader.

Roosevelt also sought to undo the damage done to American trade by the Smoot-Hawley tariff. His Secretary of State, Cordell Hull, was a longtime advocate of lower tariffs. Congress enacted the Reciprocal Trade Agreements Act in June 1934. The act empowered the president to negotiate bilateral arrangements with nations to reduce tariffs up to 50 percent with each nation that was willing to make reciprocal concessions. The act also granted "most favored nation" status with the United States to any nation that joined the United States in negotiating a trading arrangement, entitling both nations to the lowest tariff rates on the commodities they sold each other. Hull actively sought reciprocal agreements among Latin American and European nations during his long tenure as Secretary of State (from 1933 to 1944). He negotiated agreements with over twenty nations, which reduced domestic tariffs covering nearly 70 percent of American imports. Smoot-Hawley tariff rates were reduced, and American exports, particularly to Latin American countries, increased.

The American peace movement, active in the 1920s, increased in strength during the 1930s. Led by women, clergy, and college students disillusioned by the outcome of World War I, it claimed 12 million members and reached an audience of 50 million. As the Depression deepened and international tension increased, and as disarmament conferences failed, peace advocates pushed for an arms embargo to be applied by the president in time of war against aggressors. Roosevelt supported this discretionary arms embargo, but opposition from arms manufacturers and isolationist congressmen killed it.

The lobbying of munitions makers who opposed arms embargoes provoked a Senate investigation of the arms industry. The chairman of the committee was a progressive isolationist, Gerald P. Nye of North Dakota. Nye believed that America had been pressured into entering World War I by a conspiracy of American business interests protecting their investments in an Allied victory. Committee hearings, held between 1934 and 1936, investigated the activities of bankers and munitions makers. Staff members found many instances of business profiteering and lobbying, which made headline news. They found that the DuPont Company had made huge profits from the war, a revelation that angered millions of Americans who were suffering from the deprivations of the Great Depression.

Senator Nye claimed his committee investigations proved that the bankers who had lent the Allies money, and the "merchants of death," who sold them ammunition, had conspired with President Wilson to take the country to war in 1917. In reality, his committee found no evidence to sustain his charge. Committee findings showed munitions makers profited more during the neutrality period than during the years of American participation in World War I. Nye also found no evidence that industry spokesmen had pressured President Wilson into a declaration of war, and committee investigators ignored the German submarine threat. But many Americans were willing to believe the worst about big business during the 1930s, and many accepted Nye's sensational charges. The Nye Committee hearings reinforced the popular conviction that American involvement in World War I had been a mistake, or worse, promoted by a sinister conspiracy of business interests. It also strengthened many people's determination to never again participate in a foreign war.

As the Nye Committee went after the munitions makers, revisionist journalists and popular historians wrote accounts of the American entry into World War I. The best of these books, Walter Millis's best-selling *Road to War* (1935) claimed that British propaganda, business and financial ties to the Allies, and President Wilson's pro-Allied bias combined to draw the United States into a war that it should have avoided. Charles Warren, a prominent authority on international law, asserted that the United States should never enter another foreign war "to preserve and protect . . . profits to be made out of war trading by some of its citizens." Historian Carl Becker argued that although the United States had gone to war in 1917 to defend its property and to make the world safe for democracy, it lost billions of dollars in bad debts and helped make the world safe for dictators. A 1937 public opinion poll found that 60 percent of Americans believed that U.S. involvement in World War I had been a mistake.

The activities of peace groups, the Nye Committee investigations, the writings of revisionist scholars and journalists, which reinforced the idea that American participation in World War I had been mistaken, led to the triumph of isolationism in the mid-1930s. As the threat of another war increased steadily in the world because of Japan, Italy, and Germany using force to achieve their expansionist aims, isolationist attitudes intensified. Americans tried to withdraw from world affairs and immunize themselves from the contagion of war. If, as many Americans believed, U.S. entry into World War I had been a mistake, they vowed not to blunder into another foreign war in the 1930s.

Isolationist sentiment was strongest in the Midwest, particularly among German Americans and Irish Americans, but isolationism cut across all regional, class, and ethnic lines, appealing to most Americans during the mid-1930s. Isolationism spanned the American political spectrum from left-wing New Dealers to right-wing Republicans. It also included Socialists like Norman Thomas, Communists, and neo-Fascists. Businessmen, scholars, scientists, ministers, publishers, and many other professionals could be found within isolationist ranks. What united these disparate groups was the shared conviction that involvement in another world war would be ruinous to America and must be avoided. They believed that the nation could pursue diplomatic and economic policies that would both avoid war and preserve American security and freedom. Although he remained a Wilsonian internationalist at heart, President Roosevelt expressed isolationist attitudes during the mid-1930s, as did most senators and congressmen. It was not until the late 1930s that Roosevelt and many other Americans, at last perceiving the danger of Axis aggression, cautiously distanced themselves from the noninterventionists.

EUROPE DISINTEGRATES

In 1933, Adolph Hitler came to power in Germany by promising to solve Germany's severe economic and security problems. Like Benito Mussolini, who had gained power in Italy in 1922, Hitler was the leader of a fascist movement. Hitler headed the National Socialist Party, nicknamed the Nazis. Hitler vowed to revive German economic and military power, crush the Bolshevik threat, and to purify the German "race" from the "contamination" of Jewish influence, whom he blamed for all of Germany's many severe problems.

In 1933 and 1934, Hitler withdrew from the Geneva disarmament conference, pulled Germany out of the League of Nations, and began to re-arm his nation, in violation of the Versailles treaty. He began secret planning for the conquest of Europe. Neither Western leaders nor Roosevelt perceived initially the mortal danger Hitler would pose to their interests. His fanatical doctrines and ambitions were not taken seriously for several years.

Hitler watched approvingly as Mussolini prepared to invade the African country of Ethiopia in 1935. This Italian threat of war caused American isolationists to impose a strict neutrality policy on the United States government. In August, Congress passed the Neutrality Act of 1935, which prohibited arms sales to either side in a war. President Roosevelt had wanted a law that allowed him to embargo arms sales only to aggressors, but the legislators, who recalled what they believed were President Wilson's unneutral maneuverings that had led America into World War I, wanted a law that strictly limited presidential action. Roosevelt signed the measure and kept his misgivings to himself.

In October 1935, Italy invaded Ethiopia. Roosevelt invoked the Neutrality Act. Most Americans sympathized with the Ethiopians who fought with spears against a modern, mechanized army using planes, tanks, and poison gas. The League of Nations imposed a limited embargo against Italy that did not curtail its war effort. Roosevelt, who wanted to curb Italian aggression if he could, called for an American "moral embargo" that would deny shipment of important raw materials to feed Italy's war machine. The moral embargo failed, American companies increased their shipments of strategic raw materials, especially oil, to the Italians. Italy conquered Ethiopia and turned it into an Italian colony. In February 1936, Congress enacted another Neutrality Law that tightened America's neutrality policy, adding a loan embargo to the arms embargo.

In the summer of 1936, civil war began in Spain when Francisco Franco, an army officer holding Fascist beliefs, led a revolt of Spanish army units against Spain's center-left republican government. Roosevelt adopted a policy of neutrality toward the Spanish Civil War and supported French and British efforts to confine the war to Spain, even if that meant a Fascist victory. Congress responded with a third Neutrality Law in 1937, applying the arms and loan embargoes to the Spanish Civil War.

Most Americans were indifferent to the outcome of the Spanish Civil War, favoring neither side. But some Americans passionately took sides, especially when the Fascist powers, Italy and Germany, intervened to aid Franco's Nationalist forces, and the Soviet Union aided the Spanish Republicans. American volunteers, many of them Communists, who called themselves the Abraham Lincoln Battalion, went to Spain to fight for the Republican cause. Franco's forces, with German and Italian help, eventually prevailed. General Franco took power in early 1939 and established an authoritarian government with Fascistic characteristics in Spain that lasted until his death in 1976.

As the Spanish Civil War raged, the aggressors became bolder. In 1936, Hitler sent his troops into the Rhineland, a region demilitarized by the Versailles Treaty. France, responsible for enforcing the treaty, accepted the German action. Later that year, Germany and Italy signed an agreement called the Rome-Berlin Axis. Germany and Japan united against the Soviet Union, forming the Anti-Comintern Pact. Great Britain and France responded to these moves by adopting a timid policy of appeasement, hoping to satisfy Germany's and Italy's expansionist appetites with territorial concessions that would avoid war.

In 1938, Hitler pressed Europe to the brink of war. In March, he forcibly annexed Austria. The democracies, pursuing appeasement, did nothing. In the fall, Hitler continued his "war of nerves" by threatening to invade Czechoslovakia when it refused to give him its Sudetenland, a mountainous region bordering the two countries whose inhabitants were mostly ethnic Germans. The Czechs mobilized their small but well-fortified army and turned to their allies, France and the Soviet Union, for help. Both the French and the Soviets refused to honor their treaties with the only democracy in eastern Europe. Britain and France both pressed the Czechs to give Hitler what he wanted in exchange for his pledge: "This is the last territorial claim I have to make in Europe."

To a hastily called conference at Munich on September 29, 1938, came Prime Minister Neville Chamberlain of England and Premier Edouard Daladier of France. There they met with the Fascist leaders, Hitler and Mussolini, to sacrifice Czechoslovakia upon the altar of appeasement. The hapless Czechs, isolated and vulnerable, surrendered. They demobilized their army and Germany sheared off the Sudetenland for annexation.

Although he had doubts about the effectiveness of the British and French appeasement policies, President Roosevelt hailed the Munich agreement as an act of statesmanship that had averted war. Upon his return to England, Chamberlain proclaimed: "I believed it is peace for our time." In Parliament, Winston Churchill rose to dissent: "England and France had to choose between war and dishonor. They chose dishonor; they will have war." Churchill perceived the folly and moral bankruptcy of appeasement embodied in the Munich agreement; it was merely surrender on the installment plan. Six months after Hitler solemnly promised to seek no more territory, German columns erased the Czech remnant from the map. A month after the rape of Czechoslovakia, Mussolini's legions conquered defenseless Albania. Two more dominoes had fallen to the Fascists. The Munich agreement could only postpone war, not prevent it.

German aggression, 1936–1939. *Source:* Moss, *Rise of Modern America*, p. 287.

The following labels appear on the map:

SOVIET UNION

German Aggression, 1936 - 1939

RUMANIA

Vilna

Memel’an reoccupied March, 1939

LITHUANIA

SUWALKIE

Kaunas

Bailystok

Niemen R.

Lvov

SUBCARPATHIAN RUTHENIA

Lublin

POLAND

Bug R.

EAST PRUSSIA

Warsaw

Cracow

SLOVAKIA

German protectorate, March, 1939

HUNGARY

Vistula

Memel

Danzig

POLISH CORRIDOR

Posen

Bratislava

Budapest

Baltic Sea

SWEDEN

Breslau

Oder R.

BOHEMIA

Prague

MORAVIA

Bohemia and Moravia annexed, March, 1939

Vienna

Berlin

Dresden

AUSTRIA

Austria annexed, March, 1938

DENMARK

HELIGOLAND

Hamburg

Elbe R.

GERMANY

Sudetan areas annexed, October, 1938

North Sea

Bremen

Rhineland reoccupied, March, 1936

Munich

Danube R.

ITALY

Essen

Cologne

Mainz

Rhine R.

SAAR

NETHERLANDS

BELGIUM

LUX.

FRANCE

SWITZERLAND

At last awakened to the Nazi peril, Britain and France abandoned appeasement. They quickly concluded security treaties with Poland, the next target on Hitler's list of intended victims. But the decisive factor in the European political equation that tense summer of 1939 was the Soviet Union. When the Western leaders rebuffed Stalin's offer of alliance against Germany, he turned to Hitler. On August 23, the Germans and Soviets stunned the West by concluding a cynical nonaggression pact that publicly proclaimed peace between them, yet secretly divided the spoils in eastern Europe. With his eastern flank secured by this adroit agreement with the Soviets, Hitler unleashed his torrents of fire and steel on the Polish people on September 1, 1939. Two days later, honoring their commitments to Poland, Britain and France declared war on Germany. World War II in Europe had begun. It was 3:00 A.M. in Washington when Ambassador William Bullitt, calling from Paris, awakened the President to tell him war had broken out. Roosevelt replied softly: "Well, Bill, it has come at last, God help us all."

The United States, as it had done when World War I began, promptly declared itself neutral. Unlike President Wilson in August 1914, Roosevelt did not ask the American people to be neutral in thought: "Even a neutral cannot be asked to close his mind or his conscience." He made clear that his sympathies lay with the victims of German aggression, as did those of nearly all Americans. Roosevelt also told the American people: "I hope that the United States will keep out of this war. I believe that it will," Most Americans shared the President's views.

Following his speech, he called Congress into special session to amend the neutrality legislation to permit British and French arms purchases. Isolationists loudly opposed his request and vowed to resist "from hell to breakfast." But the public supported Roosevelt. They wanted to stay clear of the war, but they also wanted to help the Allies. After six weeks of heated debate, Congress modified the neutrality laws to permit "cash and carry"; the Allies could buy American arms if they paid cash and hauled them in their own ships. Roosevelt was determined to help the Allies and to challenge the isolationists.

The Soviet Union posed a special problem for American foreign relations during the years when Europe lurched toward war. Starting with Woodrow Wilson in 1917, four consecutive administrations had refused to recognize the Moscow regime. They adhered to a policy of nonrecognition because in 1917 the Bolsheviks had repudiated wartime alliances and concluded a separate peace with Germany, imperiling the Allies. The Communist leaders also repudiated czarist debts to Washington and expropriated American properties in the Soviet Union without compensation. Further, from the time of their accession to power in 1917, the Bolsheviks had sought the overthrow of the American government through propaganda and subversion. But most other nations had recognized the Soviet Union by 1933, and America's policy of nonrecognition had neither isolated nor weakened the Soviets.

The Great Depression changed American attitudes toward the Soviets. American businessmen hoped that normalizing relations with the Soviet Union would open new markets in that vast country and reduce unemployment in the

United States. Japan was threatening China and Hitler was on the rise in Germany; Roosevelt hoped that recognition of the Soviet Union might serve to restrain those two expansionist powers.

After negotiations with Soviet representatives, the United States formally recognized the Soviet Union in November 1933. In exchange for U.S. recognition, the Soviets agreed to permit religious freedom in the Soviet Union and to stop spreading Soviet propaganda within the United States. The debt payment question and other claims were deferred.

United States recognition of the Soviet Union proved to be a great disappointment. The expected increase in trade did not materialize. The Soviets continued their anti-American propaganda and their denial of freedom of worship within the Soviet Union. The two nations did not coordinate their foreign policies to curtail Japanese or German expansionism, but continued to pursue independent foreign policies. Relations between the two countries were not notably friendlier following recognition; but now they could officially denounce each other. Relations with the USSR deteriorated further after the Nazi-Soviet Pact of 1939 and a Soviet attack upon its small neighbor, Finland, in 1940. As World War II began, many Americans could see little difference between the Nazis and the Communists: Both appeared to be aggressive totalitarian dictatorships bent on military conquest, and they were partners in aggression.

THE RISING SUN

United States–Japanese relations in the twentieth century were rarely cordial. United States officials viewed the Japanese as potential threats to American Far Eastern possessions, which included the Philippines, Guam, and other Pacific islands. The United States also retained a variety of interests in China—missionaries, trade, investments, and maintenance of the Open Door policy. The Japanese suspected the United States wanted to restrain Japanese expansionism and to deprive Japan of the fruits of empire that America and many European powers enjoyed. They resented U.S. criticism of Japanese imperialism, which they regarded as hypocritical and self-serving. The Japanese were also deeply insulted by the National Origins Act (1924), which excluded Japanese immigrants from the United States.

During the 1920s, despite the Washington treaties, naval competition continued between the two nations. Naval war planners in both countries conducted mock wars against the other's forces, preparing for a possible real war in the future. Trade rivalries strained relations between the two nations. In 1931, Japanese army units took control of Chinese Manchuria. The Japanese had been in Manchuria since they had defeated the Soviets in 1905. The region was valuable to them as a buffer against the Soviet Union and as a source of foodstuffs and raw materials. The seizure of Manchuria violated the Nine Power Treaty, but that treaty was toothless, having no binding enforcement provisions. The United States, powerless to force the Japanese out of Manchuria, resorted to moralistic denunciations of Japanese aggression and adopted a policy of nonrecognition. Secretary of State Henry

Stimson asserted that the United States would not recognize violations of the Open Door policy. Nonrecognition was a weak policy that merely annoyed the Japanese without deterring them. They installed a puppet regime in Manchuria, renamed the region Manchukuo, and turned it into a Japanese colony.

In July 1937, following a clash between Japanese and Chinese troops at the Marco Polo Bridge near Beijing, Japanese forces invaded northern China. Full-scale fighting erupted between Japanese and Chinese troops. World War II in Asia had begun. Japanese planes bombed Chinese cities, killing thousands of civilians. Japanese armies occupied many urban areas. Americans angrily denounced Japanese aggression and atrocities. In an effort to help the Chinese, President Roosevelt refused to declare the existence of war in Asia so that China could buy American arms. Roosevelt also spoke to the American people on October 5, 1937, from Chicago, the isolationist heartland. He tried to rally the Western nations to act against aggressors:

> The peace-loving nations must make a concerted effort in opposition to those violations of treaties and those ignorings of humane instincts which today are creating a state of international anarchy and instability from which there is no escape through mere isolation or neutrality.[1]

He called for a "quarantine" to curb "the epidemic of world lawlessness." Most Americans responded sympathetically to the president's words, but isolationist leaders such as Senator Nye warned that the president was edging towards war. Europeans ignored the President's call, viewing America as a minor player in world affairs. Roosevelt later confessed that he had no specific plan of action in mind to halt Japanese or Fascist aggression; he was only giving expression to an attitude.

Japan continued its war in China in 1938 and 1939. The United States sent military equipment to the Chinese and loaned them money. But the United States also continued its extensive trade with Japan, which included strategic raw materials. Roosevelt did not want to impose economic sanctions on Japan lest they provoke a war at a time when the president saw the more serious threats to U.S. interests coming from Europe. When war broke out in Europe in September 1939, United States–Japanese relations were strained further.

WAR IN EUROPE

World War II began in Europe with Germany's invasion of Poland on September 1, 1939. Poland fell within a month to German forces invading from the west and Soviet forces invading from the east. Following their conquests, the Nazis and the Communists partitioned Poland in accordance with their previous pact and settled in for a joint occupation.

Following Poland's destruction, an eerie silence descended upon Europe. German and French armies faced each other from behind their fortified Siegfried

---

[1]Quoted in James MacGregor Burns, *Roosevelt: The Lion and the Fox* (New York: Harcourt, Brace, 1956), p. 318.

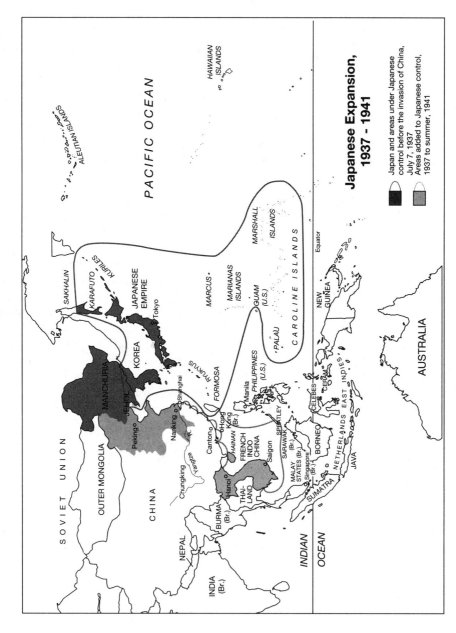

Japanese expansion, 1937–1941. *Source: Moss, Rise of Modern America, p. 291.*

and Maginot lines; neither moved. Isolationist Senator William Borah sniffed: "There's something phony about this war." Soon Americans talked of a "phony war" in Europe. Three thousand miles away, Americans viewed events in Europe with considerable detachment. Once war erupted, they believed, the British navy would strangle the Germany economy, and the French army, the largest in the world, would whip its upstart foe. Europe's latest conflagration could not reach the United States.

The American false confidence was shattered by German offensives launched in April 1940. Hitler's "blitzkrieg" (lightening war) overran Denmark, Norway, the Netherlands, Luxembourg, and Belgium within a month. Germany then attacked France. Hitler sent his Panzers (armored divisions) crashing through the Ardennes Forest. Within two weeks, German forces had shattered French defenses and swept behind the Maginot line. Paris fell June 16 and Germany soon occupied the northern two-thirds of the country. The unoccupied southern third of France was permitted a rump government at Vichy. Wherever the Nazis extended what they called their New Order, they established a barbaric reign of terror. Concentration camps, slave labor, extreme repression and brutality, mass execution of civilians, and wholesale looting of governments and private citizens became common aspects of German occupations.

The fall of France stunned and alarmed most Americans. Hitler had required only six weeks to achieve what Germany had failed to accomplish in four years of attrition warfare during World War I. The fall of France erased a lot of U.S. illusions; a majority of Americans now understood that Germany posed a potential long-term threat to the United States and the Western Hemisphere. Only the British survived to carry on the struggle against the Nazis. If England fell, Germany might gain control of the British Navy. The Atlantic Ocean would then no longer be a barrier shielding America from Europe's power struggles; it would become a watery highway for Nazi penetration of the New World.

The British, viewing the fall of France with dismay, prepared to battle the Nazis. Prime Minister Neville Chamberlain resigned in disgrace in May 1940 and was replaced by Winston Churchill. Following the Allied rout on the continent, the British managed to retrieve their army, which had been fighting in France and was cut off from land retreat, by evacuating 330,000 men from the beaches at Dunkirk in the north of France. The British also possessed a formidable fleet, a modern air force, and a indomitable leader who rallied his people to face the German war machine. Churchill offered the British people not only "blood, toil, tears, and sweat," but ultimate victory over the Nazi menace.

In the summer of 1940, Hitler hurled his *Luftwaffe* (air force) at the British. His goal was to achieve air superiority over England preparatory to launching an amphibious invasion of the islands. Night after night, waves of German bombers attacked British air bases. The Germans were on the verge of winning the Battle of Britain; they had destroyed or shut down almost all the Royal Air Force interceptor bases. One more raid would have given Hitler control of the English skies. At that moment, Hitler, impatient for victory, concerned to cut German aircraft losses, and anxious to retaliate for a British air raid on Berlin, suddenly switched tactics. He turned his bombers on British cites. He planned to bring England to its knees by terror bombing civilians.

Hitler's tactical switch saved England. The British people, though badly battered, refused to break. British air defenders used this time as a reprieve to repair their damaged bases and planes. Gradually, the tide turned in Britain's direction. Within three months, the battle was over. The Royal Air Force had won and Germany had lost the cream of its air force.

Hitler canceled his planned invasion of Britain and turned his attention to the Balkans and North Africa, where his ally Italy was engaged. German troops aided the Italians, who were losing battles to Greek forces and Albanian guerrillas. During spring, 1941, German armies conquered Yugoslavia, Greece, Hungary, Rumania, and Bulgaria. In North Africa, German forces put tremendous pressures on British armies protecting the approaches to the Suez Canal. These campaigns in the Balkans and North Africa preceded the German War to destroy Hitler's most hated foe, the Soviet Union, which began June 22, 1941.

Following the fall of France, and with the outcome of the Battle of Britain hanging in the balance, President Roosevelt committed the United States to a policy of "all aid to the Allies short of war," abandoning any pretense of neutrality. The U.S. military buildup accelerated. In July, Congress appropraited $8 billion for rearming the nation, an unprecedented sum for a peacetime mobilization. Bidding to form a bipartisan coalition in support of his policy, he appointed Republicans Henry L. Stimson Secretary of War and Frank Knox Secretary of the Navy. At his request, Congress enacted the first peacetime conscription in American history. U.S. industry, spurred by defense contracts, showed signs of life not seen since the late 1920s. By the end of the year, factories had produced seventeen thousand planes, seventeen thousand heavy artillery, and nine thousand tanks. Even though isolationists and peace groups denounced the military spending and draft bills, Roosevelt had committed the United States to pro-Allied nonbelligerency. U.S. neutrality amounted to no more than a legal sham. A Gallup poll taken at the time showed a majority of citizens favored all these measures; isolationist sentiments were losing their hold on many Americans in the face of the Nazi conquest of western Europe.

With the Battle of Britain raging, Churchill wrote Roosevelt requesting the United States transfer a portion of its destroyer fleet to the Royal Navy to protect the British home islands and to escort arms convoys across the Atlantic. Roosevelt, linking American security to the survival of Britain, responded promptly. On his executive authority, he offered the British fifty World War I–vintage destroyers in exchange for leases to eight British military bases stretching from Newfoundland to British Guiana. Churchill, needing the ships desperately, quickly accepted Roosevelt's proposal. Giving warships to a nation at war was clearly a violation of America's ostensible neutrality policy, but FDR stressed the importance of guarding the Atlantic approaches to U.S. territory. Before making his proposal, Roosevelt had consulted with a battery of constitutional lawyers who assured him that he did not need congressional approval to transfer the destroyers. Public reaction to the transaction was mostly favorable.

THE ELECTION OF 1940

Amidst the U.S. military buildup, the deteriorating world situation, and the destroyer-for-bases deal, the 1940 election occurred. It pitted Roosevelt, seeking an unprecedented third term, against the Republican challenger, Wendell Willkie. Willkie, a utilities magnate turned politican, was an internationalist and generally supported Roosevelt's foreign policy. But he attacked the New Deal for failing to lift the country out of economic depression. He also attacked Roosevelt's bid for a third term as contrary to the spirit of American democracy, and he denounced Roosevelt's failure to clear the destroyer transaction with Congress as "the most dictatorial action ever taken by an American president."

In late September, Willkie was running well behind Roosevelt in the polls. His attacks on Roosevelt for failing to end the Depression and to provide a proper defense had been ineffective. Desperate to find an issue that would enable him to gain ground, he abandoned his bipartisan approach to foreign policy and attacked Roosevelt as a warmonger whose policies would take the country to war. He struck a responsive chord among anxious voters in both parties. Polls taken in mid-October showed Willkie cutting into FDR's lead.

Roosevelt, who had avoided campaigning until Willkie's charges that he was a warmonger flushed him out, responded forcibly; but Willkie continued to gain. As election day approached, Democratic Party officials nervously watched the polls. On October 30, a poll showed Willkie had closed to within 4 percentage points of the president. On the same day, the Republican challenger charged that reelection of Roosevelt would mean American entry into the war by April 1941. That night, Roosevelt, speaking in Boston, offered unqualified assurances of peace. Answering what he termed his opponent's "verbal blitzkrieg," he told the mothers of America that

> I have said this before, but I shall say it again and again; your boys are not going to be sent into any foreign wars.[2]

FDR's reassurances worked. Roosevelt fended off Willkie's late surge and won reelection handily. The president got 27 million votes to Willkie's 22 million. Roosevelt had a decisive 449-to-82 margin in the electoral votes. But Willkie had gotten 5 million more votes than Landon had in 1936, and he had given Roosevelt his toughest election campaign to date. The Democrats retained large majorities in both houses of Congress, but the bipartisan conservative coalition continued to gain strength.

But neither candidate had leveled with the voters during the campaign. After it was over, Willkie confessed that his warmongering charges had been "just politics,"

---

[2]Quoted in *Ibid.*, p. 449.

and he strongly supported Roosevelt's policy of giving all-out aid to the Allies short of war. Roosevelt, bowing to political pressures, had given the American people false assurance of peace, knowing that his policies risked eventual entry into the European war. The 1940 election was neither the first nor the last in which presidential candidates dealt dishonestly with the crucial issues of war and peace. A young New Dealer congressman from Texas, Lyndon Johnson, observed Roosevelt's 1940 election tactics and remembered them. When Johnson ran for President in 1964, he too would give voters false assurances of peace in order to ensure electoral victory.

LEND-LEASE

Once reelected, Roosevelt soon confronted a new crisis in the Atlantic. Germany, failing to subdue England by air, turned to its submarines to try to sever Britain's oceanic lifeline and starve its people into submission. Great Britain also faced another threat to its survival besides German U-boats. Its dollar reserves depleted, England could no longer pay for its American supplies. Prime Minister Churchill wrote a personal letter to Roosevelt in which he urged the American president to continue to provide the supplies the British urgently required but for which they could no longer pay.

When that problem had arisen during World War I, American bankers had advanced credits to the British. But in this war, neutrality legislation prohibited bank loans to nations at war. Roosevelt himself devised a clever program to circumvent the Neutrality Act: Lend or lease to the British the guns, tanks, planes, ammunition, whatever they needed to win the war, and they would repay or replace these materials after the war ended. In a December 29, 1940, fireside chat, he explained Lend-Lease to the American people, stating that aiding the British was the best way to keep America out of the war:

> There is far less chance of the United States getting into war if we do all we can now to support the nations defending themselves against attack by the Axis than if we acquiesce in their defeat, submit tamely to an Axis victory, and wait our turn to be the object of attack in another war later on.[3]

He also urged the United States to "be the great arsenal of democracy." It was one of his most successful speeches; over 60 percent of the public approved the Lend-Lease proposal. Churchill pleaded: "Give us the tools and we will finish the job."

Isolationists in Congress battled to defeat Lend-Lease. They were convinced its passage would lead to entry into a war whose consequences would be ruinous to the United States. Senator Burton K. Wheeler compared Lend-Lease with the Agricultural Adjustment Administration's crop plough-up of 1933, calling it "the New Deal's triple A foreign policy: it will plough under every fourth American boy." But the isolationists did not have the votes. Lend-Lease passed easily, 60 to 31 in the Senate and 317 to 71 in the House. Public opinion polls showed a broad

---

[3]Quoted in Robert Dallek, *Franklin D. Roosevelt and American Foreign Policy, 1932–1945* (New York, Oxford University Press, 1979), p. 256.

national consensus favored the legislation. Roosevelt signed the measure, formally titled "An Act to Promote the Defense of the United States," into law on March 11, 1941. An elated Churchill hailed it as "a new Magna Carta."

Passage of Lend-Lease marked a point of no return for America. The United States had committed itself to the survival of Great Britain with an aid program that amounted to a declaration of economic warfare on Germany. Lend-Lease committed more than American economic resources to the British. It also expanded the naval battle in the Atlantic to include U.S. destroyers patroling for German submarines. In April 1941, U.S. Marines occupied the Danish colony of Greenland, and in August they took over Iceland. In August, Roosevelt also authorized U.S. destroyers to convoy British ships hauling Lend-Lease supplies as far as Iceland. At the time, German submarines were roaming the North Atlantic shipping lanes and were sinking cargo ships hauling Lend-Lease supplies at the rate of one or two a day. Roosevelt was inching America closer to war.

Roosevelt was determined to do everything necessary to ensure Germany's defeat even though it risked American entry into the war. By the spring of 1941, he had apparently concluded that American military intervention would be necessary to achieve victory over the Axis powers. He seized Axis shipping in American ports; he froze German and Italian assets in the United States. When Germany invaded the Soviet Union on June 21, 1941, Roosevelt promptly offered support to the embattled Soviets.

For four days in July, Roosevelt met with the British prime minister for the first time at a conference held off the Newfoundland coast abroad the USS *Augusta*. Their discussions focused on the means necessary to defeat Germany and to contain Japan. The meeting also produced the Atlantic Charter, a joint declaration of war aims. It reaffirmed the principles of self-determination, free trade, freedom of the seas, and called for the creation of a new postwar international organization to keep the peace. Roosevelt hoped that the Charter would educate Americans to what was at stake in the European war and to make them more willing to intervene if conflicts with Germany escalated. The Atlantic Charter also signaled the kind of postwar world that Roosevelt envisioned: A stable, unified international order in which all nations could enjoy freedom, equal economic opportunities, and prosperity; a world in which American power and wealth would dominate, for the benefit of all nations. Henry Luce, an influential publisher, in a 1941 editorial in *Life* magazine, wrote of the "American century" that was dawning, exhorting his fellow citizens "to assume the leadership of the world" for the good of people in every land. The Atlantic Charter gave ideological shape to the American century.

UNDECLARED NAVAL WAR

With American destroyers convoying British ships as far as Iceland, clashes between U.S. warships and German submarines became inevitable. On September 4, 1941, a U-boat, after being chased for hours by a destroyer, the USS *Greer*, turned

Roosevelt and Churchill first met in August 1941 off the Newfoundland coast during the Atlantic Charter meeting. *Source:* National Archives

and attacked the destroyer, but the torpedo the U-boat fired missed. The president used the *Greer* incident to announce an undeclared naval war in the North Atlantic. He ordered all ships engaged in escort duty to "shoot on sight" any German submarines appearing in waters west of Iceland. He called German submarines "the rattlesnakes of the Atlantic" and denounced their "piratical acts." He also misled Americans by reporting the *Greer* incident as if it had been an unprovoked German attack on a peaceful American ship. Polls showed most Americans supporting the "shoot on sight" policy and that they believed Hitler must be defeated "at all costs."

But most Americans also clung to the hope of staying out of the war. They hoped all aid, short of war, would prevent American entry. Roosevelt faced a dilemma, given the public's contradictory attitudes. Seventy percent wished to avoid the war. Seventy percent also wanted Hitler defeated at all cost, even if that meant America entering the war. President Roosevelt believed that if he asked Congress for a declaration of war, he would not get it and would lose popular support. The war declaration request would also trigger an angry, divisive debate between isolationists and interventionists. He decided to build incrementally a consensus for war by devious means, believing that it was essential to national security that America enter the war in Europe and defeat Germany. He would wage an undeclared war and look for incidents that would unify the country behind a war in Europe.

Having committed the country to undeclared naval war by the fall of 1941, President Roosevelt then asked Congress to repeal the remaining neutrality legislation in order to permit the arming of American merchant ships and to allow them to sail into war zones. On October 17, a U-boat torpedoed a U.S. destroyer, the USS *Kearny*, inflicting severe damage and killing eleven crewmen. Two weeks after the attack on the *Kearny*, a submarine sank an American destroyer, the USS *Reuben James*, killing 115 sailors. These two incidents strengthened public opinion supporting Roosevelt's request. Public opinion polls taken in October showed a large majority favoring repeal of the neutrality laws. Congress repealed the Neutrality Acts on November 13, 1941, although the vote was close. Isolationists were still a powerful minority. American merchant ships were armed and permitted to sail through war zones to British and Soviet ports. The last remaining restrictions on American actions had been removed.

While Roosevelt was taking these fateful measures in November 1941, his foreign policy of pro-Allied nonbelligerency, with its drift toward military intervention, continued to draw fire from various isolationist groups and individuals. Senator Wheeler belittled the Nazi threat and denounced Roosevelt as a warmonger. The All-American hero Charles Lindbergh, who did not see fascism as a threat to American interests, believed Roosevelt "could make a deal with Hitler" if he had to. An odd assortment of ethnic isolationists, religious pacifists, liberal intellectuals, Socialists, Communists, and Fascists opposed Roosevelt's foreign policies. The most prominent isolationist organization called itself the America First Committee. America First was chaired by Robert E. Wood, CEO of Sears, Roebuck, and Co., the world's largest retailer. America First spokesmen kept their views constantly before the public, and their agents formed a powerful lobby in Washington. Committee spokesmen denied that Germany posed any significant threat to American or Western Hemispheric security. They claimed America had sufficient military strength to defend itself regardless of who controlled Europe.

At the same time that isolationists accused Roosevelt of secretly plotting to take the country to war, interventionists believed that Roosevelt was moving too slowly and too cautiously in extending aid to the Allies and preparing for possible military intervention. Interventionists were recruited from the ranks of eastern Anglophiles, moderate New Dealers, and liberal Republicans like Thomas Dewey and Wendell Willkie. The most influential interventionist organization was the Committee to Defend America by Aiding the Allies, chaired by a prominent Progressive journalist from Kansas, William Allen White. White and his organization worked to increase the amount of military aid going to the Allies. They also tried to influence public opinion, to move the American people in the direction of supporting Roosevelt's foreign policy. Above all, interventionists rejected the isolationist premise that an aggressive Germany posed no threat to the security of the

The European Theater, 1939–1942. *Source: Moss, Rise of Modern America, p. 304.*

United States. White stated that, "The future of Western civilization is being decided upon the battlefield of Europe."

Neither the America First Committe nor the Committee to Defend America by Aiding the Allies had much influence on public opinion. It was the events themselves, the rapidly deteriorating military situations in Europe and the Far East, that swayed growing numbers of Americans to support Roosevelt's foreign policy, even though most Americans clung to the hope of avoiding war.

As November 1941 ended, the United States was at war unofficially with Germany. But Roosevelt could only wait upon events, hoping that German submarines would provide him with incidents that would allow a declaration of war and full-scale involvement against the Fascist powers. The initiative lay with Hitler and his submarine forces. Ironically, with all eyes upon the European conflict, Japanese military actions on the other side of the world rescued the United States from the uncertain drift of its European policy. American entry into World War II came first in the Pacific following the surprise Japanese attack on Pearl Harbor on December 7, 1941.

Many Americans have found in difficult to understand why the Japanese attackers caught the Americans in Hawaii by complete surprise. Revisionist historians have resorted to conspiracy theories to solve the riddle: President Roosevelt, wanting badly to get into war in Europe, but unable to generate popular support for a formal declaration of war, put economic pressure on the Japanese and forced them to fight. He then lured them to Pearl Harbor by exposing the American fleet and let the raid come without alerting American commanders in Hawaii. The surprise attack angered and united Americans in support of war. Revisionists, in effect, have accused Roosevelt of forcing America into the European war via the "back door" of Asia.

The case for conspiracy at Pearl Harbor is flimsy. It rests entirely on circumstantial evidence, a kind of simplistic plausibility, and on his accusers' willingness to believe that President Roosevelt was a Machiavellian leader capable of sacrificing the American Pacific fleet and thousands of lives to achieve his goal. No documentary proof of conspiracy has ever been found. No professional historian of World War II takes this devil theory seriously. It is easily refuted by knowledgeable scholars who can explain Japanese success at Pearl Harbor in non-conspiratorial terms.

IMPASSE OVER CHINA

War in the Pacific between the United States and Japan occurred fundamentally because of an impasse over China. Since 1937, Japan had been extending its control over China. But the Japanese, although able to conquer the populous coastal areas of China, had been unable to defeat Jiang Jieshi's Nationalist forces, who had retreated into China's vast interior regions. America supported the Chinese Nationalists and condemned Japanese aggression. The German defeat of the Netherlands and France in 1940 left these two nations' colonial possessions in Southeast Asia defenseless. Japan set out to incorporate these territories, rich in rubber, oil, tin, and rice, into their imperial orbit. President Roosevelt tried to use American economic pressure to pry the Japanese out of China and contain its expansion into Southeast Asia. American efforts at economic coercion ultimately failed and the Japanese struck first at Pearl Harbor.

Knowing that the Japanese were heavily dependent on the United States for shipments of petroleum as well as scrap iron and steel, on July 26, 1939, Roosevelt renounced the major commercial treaty between Japan and the United States as of January 1, 1940. This action would allow the United States to curb or halt Japan's access to American iron, oil, and other strategic goods. The President hoped that Japan would ease its pressure on China instead of risking an American embargo of essential raw materials. The threatened embargo did not deter the Japanese. They were determined to conquer China and to forge an empire they called the Greater East Asia Co-prosperity Sphere. But they did not want a rupture of relations with the United States that would dry up sources of needed commodities. Roosevelt also applied economic pressure on the Japanese cautiously. His first priority was the European war, where he perceived the threat to American interests to be much greater than that of Japanese imperialism in Asia. And, he had to be careful lest economic sanctions provoke the Japanese to war for which the United States was completely unprepared.

Japanese-American relations deteriorated further during the summer and fall of 1940. A more militant government came to power in Japan headed by Prince Konoye. A key official in his new government was war minister, General Hideki Tojo. Konoye and Tojo were determined to defeat China and to end the drain on Japanese men and material. The Japanese also intended to ally with the European Fascist powers and to expand into Southeast Asia. They planned to take advantage of German victories in Europe by seizing the lightly protected European Southeast Asian colonies and expropriating their rich resources.

In July 1940, the Japanese moved into northern Indochina, a lightly defended French colony in Southeast Asia. In September, Japan concluded a Tripartite Pact with Germany and Italy, creating the Rome-Berlin-Tokyo Axis. The treaty bound the three nations to help one another if attacked by a power not currently involved in fighting in Europe or Asia. The treaty clearly aimed to prevent the United States from joining either the British against the Germans or from directly opposing Japan's efforts to carve out an empire in China and Southeast Asia.

America responded to Japan's signing the Tripartite Pact by embargoing all shipments of scrap metal to Japan. Roosevelt also began coordinating U.S. Far Eastern policy with the British and increasing U.S. economic and military aid to China. He sent the Chinese fifty fighter planes and arranged for American volunteers to go to China to fly them. These volunteers, all military pilots, formed the nucleus of the famed "Flying Tigers," commanded by Claire Chennault. Roosevelt believed that aiding China was the most effective way of restraining Japanese expansion, keeping them tied down in that vast country. He also sent additional forces to Guam, the Philippines, and other American territories in the Pacific.

THE STRATEGY OF STALL

In February 1941, Japan sent a new ambassador to the United States, Admiral Kichisaburo Nomura. He and Secretary of State Cordell Hull held a series of talks that continued off and on until the Japanese attack at Pearl Harbor. Nomura urged America to restore trade with Japan and to stop supporting Jiang Jieshi, the Chinese Nationalist leader. These proposals were unacceptable to the United States, but Roosevelt told Hull to avoid outright rejection of Nomura's suggestions and to leave open the possibility of American concessions. Roosevelt hoped to encourage moderate elements within the Japanese government who might restrain the militant expansionists. He was also following a strategy of stalling the Japanese. He wanted to restrain Japan yet avoid a showdown with them because of the increasing danger of American entry into the European war. Roosevelt and Hull hoped that a combination of limited economic sanctions, the threat of additional sanctions, and aid to the Chinese might eventually force Japan to withdraw from China and refrain from further aggression in Southeast Asia.

These negotiations between American and Japanese officials did not have a realistic possibility of success; the two sides were too far apart and neither was willing to compromise. The Japanese wanted a free hand to continue their war of conquest against China and an end to U.S. economic sanctions. The United States demanded that the Japanese withdraw from China and not attack the Southeast Asian territories belonging to European colonial powers that had been beaten by the Germans.

Relations between America and Japan worsened in July 1941, when the Japanese forced the French to let them take over eight air and two naval bases in southern Indochina. Roosevelt, interpreting the action as the opening move in a campaign of conquest in Southeast Asia, froze all Japanese assets in the United States. The freeze order was a major step down the road to war. It became the American instrument for ending trade between the U.S. and Japan. A few days after the freeze went into effect, America embargoed all oil and steel shipments to Japan. The trade cut-off pushed the Japanese into a corner. Without these crucial commodities, their industrial economy and war machine would grind to a halt within a few months. Either a way had to be found quickly to restore trade with America, or Japan would have to get these necessary goods elsewhere.

Since all but the most extreme Japanese leaders opposed war with the American colossus at this date, Japanese diplomats sought to negotiate an arrangement with Washington that would restore the lost strategic trade. Nomura met several times with Hull. He also met with the President. Roosevelt told him that the United States wanted improved relations with Japan. He indicated that he was interested in meeting with Prince Konoye if Japan were ready "to suspend its expansionist activities" and the two countries could resolve their "fundamental differences." Even as he made these statements, Roosevelt was skeptical that a meaningful rapprochement was possible. He was mainly continuing to stall the Japanese in order to allow the American military buildup more time and to avoid a war in Asia when preparing to enter one in Europe.

High-level Japanese meetings held in early September proved that American-Japanese differences were irreconcilable. Convinced that they must move before American economic sanctions hindered their ability to fight, army militants insisted that Konoye settle differences with the Americans by mid-October. If no agreement was made, Japan would prepare for war with the United States. The conditions for a settlement agreed to on September 6 by an Imperial Conference set Japan firmly on the road to war: The United States would not interfere with Japanese efforts in China, would not increase its forces in the Pacific, and would restore trade with Japan. In return, Japan pledged no further moves into Southeast Asia and guaranteed the neutrality of the Philippines. In late September, Nomura conveyed these terms to Roosevelt and Hull.

Roosevelt found them unacceptable, confirming his sense that irreconcilable differences separated the two nations, especially regarding China, and that a meeting with Konoye would be pointless. He also read public opinion polls showing Americans firmly opposed to any appeasement of Japanese aggression in China. He and Hull continued negotiations, but made no concessions on China or agreements to restore trade. They continued the strategy of stalling, of trying to buy time in the Pacific to allow the United States to build up its air force in the Philippines, hoping the added striking power might deter Japan expansion into Southeast Asia. Roosevelt's top military advisers, General George Marshall and Admiral Harold Stark, cautioned the President against taking any actions that might provoke the Japanese to war, since the American forces in the Pacific were not ready and the United States could soon be at war in Europe.

In early October 1941, when it became evident that Prince Konoye could not achieve a diplomatic agreement with the United States, he and his cabinet resigned. General Tojo headed the new government, a military dictatorship committed to ending what Tojo called the "deadlock of indecision." On November 5, Japanese leaders, meeting in the presence of Emperor Hirohito, reached a crucial decision: They would continue diplomacy for three more weeks, but if no agreement were reached by November 26, Japan would go to war. The date for the attack was set for December 8, Tokyo time (December 7, Washington time).

Japan's final proposals offered no prospect of avoiding war. The proposals were divided into Plan A and Plan B, with B to be offered only if Plan A failed. Admiral Nomura presented Plan A to Roosevelt on November 10. Plan A made clear Japan's continuing refusal to get out of China and its refusal to leave the Tripartite Pact. Roosevelt rejected these terms. Tokyo sent another envoy to join Nomura, Saburo Kurusu, and together they presented Plan B to Secretary of State Hull on November 20. It was a more complex proposal but it still left Japan a free hand in China and called for a full restoration of American trade with Japan. Roosevelt and Hull both understood that diplomacy had failed. The United States rejected Plan B on November 26 and told Japan to "withdraw all military, naval, air, and police forces" from China and Indochina. The Japanese prepared to assault the Dutch East

Indies, Malaya, and the American territory of the Philippines. They also planned a surprise attack on Pearl Harbor to destroy the American Pacific fleet, the only military force that posed a serious threat to Japanese imperial ambitions in the Far East.

PEARL HARBOR ATTACKED!

Because a brilliant Army cryptanalyst, Colonel Lawrence Friedman, had cracked the principal Japanese diplomatic code, which the analysts called code "Purple," President Roosevelt knew that the Tojo government had set a November 26 deadline for a diplomatic solution, and that now war would soon follow. The decoding machines enabling Americans to read the coded Japanese messages were named "Magic." But "Magic" intercepts never contained specific information pinpointing where and when any attacks would occur.

On November 27, the day after the Tojo government's deadline for diplomacy, Washington sent a final alert to American military commanders in the Pacific. The message sent to Admiral Kimmel at Pearl Harbor read, in part:

> This dispatch is to be considered a war warning. . . . an aggressive move by Japan is expected within the next few days.[4]

On November 29, Tokyo learned that the European Axis powers promised to declare war on the United States if new Japanese actions in the Pacific provoked war. The Japanese now knew they would not be fighting America alone. The same day, Emperor Hirohito gave his assent for war.

In Washington, American leaders waited grimly for the Japanese blow, wherever it might come. "Why not attack first?" Roosevelt's top aide, Harry Hopkins, asked the President. "No," said Roosevelt, "we would have to wait until it came." Secretary of War Stimson, concerned about divisions of public opinion within the country, explained that the United States had to let Japan fire the first shot "so there should remain no doubt in anyone's mind as to who were the aggressors." Where would the Japanese strike? Roosevelt's guess, based on his analysis of information available from "Magic" intercepts and many other intelligence sources, was that Japan would strike somewhere in Southeast Asia. Neither Roosevelt nor any of his senior advisers anticipated an attack on U.S. military installations in Hawaii.

On the evening of December 6, "Magic" began decoding a long message from Tokyo to Nomura. Its final section announced that there was no chance of reaching a diplomatic settlement with the United States "because of American attitudes." Reading the intercept, Roosevelt said: "This means war." Another intercept received early Sunday morning, December 7, indicated an attack could occur any time. Another alert was sent to the commanders at Pearl Harbor; tragically, that message did not arrive until after the Japanese attack had begun.

---

[4]Quoted in John E. Wiltz, *From Isolation to War, 1931–1941* (New York: Thomas Y. Crowell, 1968), pp. 126–7.

December 7, 1941, a date which will live in infamy. . . . After the Japanese attackers have flown back toward their carriers, battered U.S. warships burn at their moorings. Left to right: the USS *Arizona*, USS *Tennessee*, and USS *West Virginia*. The USS *Arizona* later capsized and sunk, carrying 1100 sailors to a watery grave. *Source:* National Archives.

The Japanese naval task force assigned to attack Pearl Harbor had set sail from its home port in the Kurile Islands on November 26. To avoid detection sailing across more than 3,000 miles of ocean, all ships observed radio silence and sailed in lanes unused by commercial vessels. On December 2, the task force received final clearance to attack from imperial headquarters. Early morning, December 7, the task force reached the point from which it would launch air strikes. Shortly after 6:00 A.M. local time, the planes began taking off from four carriers. They were launched in two waves, 360 planes in all. Pearl Harbor lay 275 miles southwest, 105 minutes flying time.

Conditions for the attack were ideal. Visibility was perfect. The Americans were caught by complete surprise. The attackers encountered no antiaircraft fire and no interceptors rose to challenge them. Spread out before them in neat alignment was the American Pacific fleet. At 7:55 A.M., Hawaiian time, the first wave of dive bombers screamed to the attack. Their primary targets were the American battleships and the airfields. The assaults lasted about two hours. At 9:45, the planes withdrew and headed back to their carriers.

Although caught off guard, the Americans recovered quickly and fought courageously. Some pilots found planes not destroyed on the ground and took to the air after the swarming enemy. Many acts of valor and sacrifice were performed that day by the outgunned Americans. But the odds were hopeless and American losses were severe. The Japanese sank or crippled eighteen warships, destroyed or damaged 204 planes on the ground, extensively damaged five airfields, and killed 2,403 Americans—1,100 of whom were entombed in the USS *Arizona* when it exploded and sank. Japanese losses were light: twenty-nine planes, forty-five pilots and air crewmen, one regular submarine, and five midget subs.

The Japanese attackers exceeded even their most optimistic expectations. Their carrier task force escaped detection and returned to its home waters undamaged and with no casualties. On the same day, other Japanese forces attacked U.S. bases on Guam and Midway Island. Japanese planes also destroyed the American air forces in the Philippines, catching the planes on the ground. December 7, 1941, was the worst day in American military history.

American military blunders contributed to the smashing Japanese successes at Pearl Harbor and elsewhere in the Pacific. Intelligence analysts seriously underestimated Japanese military capabilities. The costliest error was the failure of the American commanders in Hawaii, Admiral Kimmel and General Short, to respond properly to the war alert from Washington they had received on November 27. Expecting the Japanese attack to come elsewhere, they had taken precautions only against sabotage.

The Japanese made serious errors carrying out their attacks at Pearl Harbor. They failed to destroy oil storage and ship repair facilities, which the Americans soon put to good use. Most of the eighteen ships left battered and helpless that day were restored, and they later got into the battles that would destroy Japanese sea power. The attackers also failed to seek out and destroy the two American aircraft carriers that were, as luck would have it, operating at sea that fateful December morning. One carrier was at sea on a training exercise; the other had been sent to Midway Island to ferry some aircraft back to Pearl Harbor. The war in the Pacific was principally a naval war, and naval aviation played a far more important role than battleships in determining the eventual American victory.

Put in a larger context, although achieving a decisive tactical victory, the Japanese committed a colossal strategic blunder by attacking Pearl Harbor. Had they attacked European colonial possessions in Southeast Asia as expected, Roosevelt would have had difficulty bringing America promptly into the war. Isolationists were still vocal on the eve of Pearl Harbor, and a sizable number of Americans would have strongly opposed a declaration of war against Japan following an attack on Borneo or Malaya. At the least, Roosevelt would have taken a badly divided nation to war. Roosevelt later told Churchill that if "it had not been for the Japanese attack, he would have had great difficulty in getting the American people into the war."

The Japanese solved Roosevelt's dilemma. Eager to destroy the American fleet at Pearl, the only military force in the Pacific capable of blocking their planned Pacific conquests, they directly attacked American soil and shed American blood. The surprise attack, and the death and destruction it caused, enraged and united nearly all Americans in support of an immediate declaration of war against Japan. Admiral Isoruku Yamamoto, the brilliant strategist who conceived the Pearl Harbor attack, upon learning that it had been a great success, felt no joy. Instead, he somberly told his colleagues: "I fear all we have done is to awaken a sleeping giant and fill him with a terrible resolve."

The next day, President Roosevelt, calling December 7, 1941, "a date which will live in infamy," asked a joint session of Congress to declare war on Japan effective from the moment the first bomb struck Pearl Harbor. All over the land, 60 million Americans gathered by their radios to listen intently to his speech. Within hours, Congress complied, with only one dissenting vote. Three days later, Germany and Italy declared war on the United States, honoring their commitments under the terms of the Tripartite Pact. America replied in kind on the same day. In four days, Americans had gone from peace to war in both Europe and the Pacific. The United States was now a participant in history's largest war. Isolation had ended, forever.

IMPORTANT EVENTS

1921	The Washington Naval Conference takes place
1924	The Dawes Plan is enacted
1928	The Kellogg-Briant Pact is negotiated
1929	President Hoover proclaims the Good Neighbor policy
1930	The Smoot-Hawley Tariff Act is enacted
1931	Japan invades Manchuria
1931	President Hoover declares a one-year moratorium on debt payments
1933	Cuba cancels the Platt Amendment
1934	Nye Committee hearings begin
1935	The first Neutrality Act is passed
1935	Italy attacks Ethiopia
1936	Germany reoccupies the Rhineland
1936	The Spanish Civil War begins
1937	Japan invades northern China; World War II in Asia begins
1937	President Roosevelt delivers his "quarantine the aggressor" speech
1938	The Munich Conference is held
1939	Germany occupies Czechoslovakia
1939	The Nazi-Soviet Pact is signed
1939	Germany invades Poland; World War II in Europe begins
1940	The fall of France occurs
1940	America and Great Britain complete a destroyers-for-bases deal
1940	The Battle of Britain takes place

1941   Roosevelt and Churchill sign the Atlantic Charter
1941   Pearl Harbor is attacked; the United States enters World War II

BIBLIOGRAPHY

The two best general studies of American foreign policy during the 1920s are L. Ethan Ellis's *Republican Foreign Policy, 1921–1933* and Joan Hoff Wilson's *American Business and Foreign Policy, 1920–1933*. Dana Munro's *United States and the Caribbean Republics, 1921–1933* and Irwin F. Gellman's *Good Neighbor Diplomacy: United States Policies in Latin America, 1933–1945* are good accounts of the United States' Latin American policies between the wars. Walter LaFeber, in *Inevitable Revolutions: The United States in Central America,* offers a fine recent study of American foreign policy in Central America and its consequences. Robert Dallek's *Franklin D. Roosevelt and American Foreign Policy, 1932–1945* is the best and most comprehensive treatment of Roosevelt's foreign policy that we have. Robert A. Divine, in *The Illusion of Neutrality,* presents a good study of 1930s isolationism. Arnold Offner's *The Origins of the Second World War* is excellent. John Wiltz, in *From Isolation to War, 1931–1941,* gives a good short account of United States entry into World War II. Waldo Heinrichs, in *Threshold of War: Franklin D. Roosevelt and American Entry into World War II,* has written an excellent recent study. William L. Langer and S. E. Gleason, in *The Undeclared War, 1940–1941,* offers a detailed account of the deteriorating relations between the United States and Germany. See also Basil Rauch's *Roosevelt: From Munich to Pearl Harbor.* The best study of the isolationists who were attacking Roosevelt's foreign policy in 1940 and 1941 is that by Wayne S. Cole, *America First: The Battle Against Intervention, 1940–1941.* Warren F. Kimball's *The Most Unsordid Act: Lend-Lease, 1939–1941* is a good study. David Reynolds's *The Creation of the Anglo-American Alliance, 1937–1941* is an important work. The attack on Pearl Harbor is the subject of many books. By far the best of these is Gordon W. Prange's *At Dawn We Slept,* the finest account of the Japanese surprise attack on U.S. military installations in Hawaii which plunged America into the vortex of war. Roberta Wohlstetter's *Pearl Harbor: Warning and Decision* is a brilliant study of intelligence information and misinformation and the best refutation of the Pearl Harbor conspiracy theories. Walter Lord's *Day of Infamy* is a popular account that vividly recreates the events of the day Pearl Harbor was attacked. Some scholars have accused Roosevelt of complicity in the attack. One of these is John Toland, who wrote *Infamy.* Charles DeBenedetti's *The Peace Reform Movement in American History* has good accounts of American peace activities during the 1920s and 1930s.

CHAPTER **8**

World War II

When the United States entered World War II immediately following the Japanese surprise attack on U.S. military installations in Hawaii, the vast conflict became history's first global war. The struggle constituted two wars waged simultaneously. In Europe, North Africa, and the Middle East, the United States, Great Britain, and the Soviet Union battled Germany and Italy, with both sides aided by minor allies. In the Pacific basin and along the East Asian perimeter, America, with help from the British, Australians, New Zealanders, Indians, and Chinese, fought the Japanese, who had no allies in Asia. World War II was also history's largest, costliest, and most destructive war. About 50 million people perished between 1939 and 1945, half of them civilians. The war also claimed about $2 trillion of the world's wealth.

From its entry into World War II, American armed forces played crucial roles in winning both the European and Pacific conflicts. In addition to supporting its own far-flung forces fighting around the world, the United States furnished its major allies with substantial amounts of food, equipment, ammunition, and weapons. The war revitalized the American economy. Lingering vestiges of the Great Depression were erased and an economic boom that was to last for thirty years began in 1942. When World War II ended in the summer of 1945 in total victory for the Allied cause, the United States strode the world as a new colossus. America emerged from the ashes of war as the richest, freest, and most powerful nation in the history of the planet.

WAR IN EUROPE

American industrial output largely determined the eventual Allied victory over the Axis. Hitler fatally underestimated U.S. economic power when he sneered that Americans "only know how to make refrigerators and razor blades." American industry undergirded the Allied war effort, producing millions of planes, tanks, trucks, rifles, howitzers, and ships. American military production more than doubled the Axis output, winning a war of attrition.

American and British leaders agreed on a "beat Hitler first" strategy for compelling reasons: Germany posed a potential threat to the Western Hemisphere; their military technology was more likely than the Japanese technology to achieve a breakthrough weapon that might enable them to win the war, and Germany, in late 1941, was putting tremendous pressure on the Soviet Union.

Determined to engage the Germans in decisive battle, American war planners proposed an invasion of France scheduled for the fall of 1942. The embattled Soviets, fighting for their lives against the best German armies, pleaded with their allies to open a "second front" in the west as soon as possible to ease the pressure on their forces. The British rejected the American invasion proposal. They preferred to strike initially at the periphery of Axis power and to delay a frontal assault until after German resistance had weakened. The British proposed an alternative campaign, a joint Anglo-American invasion of North Africa. President Roosevelt accepted the British offer with the understanding that the North African assault would be followed soon by an invasion of France.

On November 8, 1942, Anglo-American forces, under the command of a rising American star, General Dwight Eisenhower, stormed ashore at points along the coast of the French North African colonies of Morocco and Algeria. The operation succeeded tactically, but political complications soon developed. The invaded territories were controlled by the collaborationist French regime at Vichy, and its forces resisted the Allied invaders. General Eisenhower negotiated an armistice agreement with Admiral Darlan, the Vichy leader in North Africa, in exchange for Allied recognition of Darlan's authority. The arrangement outraged Charles de Gaulle's Free French government, backed by the British, which claimed authority in North Africa.

Hitler, surprised by the Allied thrust into French North Africa, rushed German troops to neighboring Tunisia. Eisenhower responded by sending his forces into Tunisia from the west. British forces from Egypt, under the command of General Bernard Montgomery, invaded Tunisia from the east, catching the German and Italian forces in a giant pincers. Tunisia proved a hard campaign. Its terrain was rugged and arid, vast deserts punctured by sheer cliffs. The Allies also came up against one of Hitler's best generals, Field Marshall Erwin Rommel. His veteran Afrika Korps defeated inexperienced American forces in early encounters. One of America's ablest generals made his debut as a field commander during the Tunisian campaign—General George S. Patton, Jr., whose flamboyant attire and severe discipline earned him his nickname, "Old Blood and Guts." After months of heavy fighting, the Axis forces surrendered. Although the North African diversion delayed opening a second front in France, it proved a significant victory. The Mediterranean was reopened to Allied shipping, the British lifeline through Suez was secured, and the Middle Eastern oil fields were saved. Victory in North Africa also opened up what Churchill called the "soft underbelly" of the Axis—Italy and the Balkans—to Allied attacks.

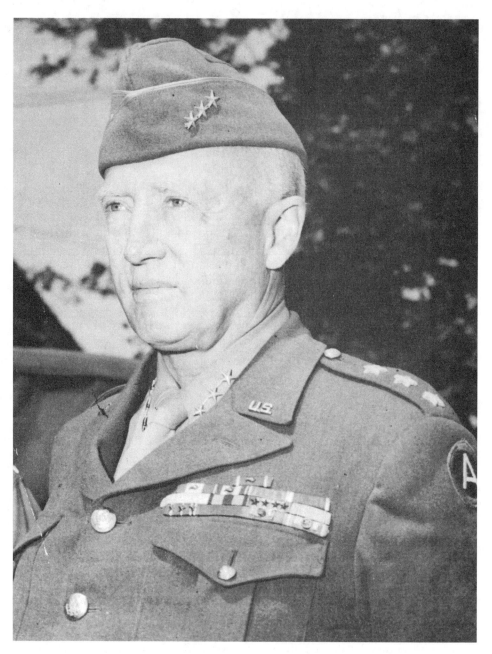

General George S. Patton, Jr.   *Source:* National Archives.

As fighting raged in North Africa, President Roosevelt met with the British Prime Minister at Casablanca to plot the next campaign. Roosevelt wanted to attack France; the absent Soviets pointedly endorsed his proposal. Churchill proposed instead a move into Sicily and southern Italy to maintain the Mediterranean initiative. Roosevelt reluctantly accepted Churchill's suggestion, and the French invasion was put off until after 1943.

Anglo-American forces invaded Sicily in July 1943, and southern Italy in September. These attacks toppled the shaky Mussolini government. General Eisenhower recognized a new Italian government formed by Field Marshall Pietro Badoglio, who promptly surrendered to the Allies. The invasions had knocked Italy out of the war, but German forces in Italy formidably resisted Allied invaders. Fighting continued in Italy almost to the end of the European war.

As the Allies were winning the North African campaign, Soviet forces began driving the Germans back from the gates of Moscow. Soviet armies also surrounded a large German force at Stalingrad, a city in the south of Russia. Both armies fought ferociously in the depths of winter. In January 1943, the Germans, having lost 300,000 men, surrendered. The Battle of Stalingrad was a turning point in the European war. Bolstered by Lend-Lease aid from the United States, by 1943 the Soviets had forged the largest army in the world. In summer offensives across a thousand-mile front, Soviet armies drove the Germans back. In July, near Kursk, occurred the greatest tank battle in history in which Soviet armor destroyed the once dreaded German Panzers.

At sea, Allied naval forces were winning the Battle of the Atlantic. By the end of 1943, Allied convoy tactics, teamed with antisubmarine forces, contained German submarines. Huge quantities of Lend-Lease supplies reached England and the Soviet Union, and hundreds of American troop ships arrived in Europe.

The air war also turned in favor of the Allies. By 1943, Allied strategic bombers flew both day and night over Germany and its Central European allies. U.S. Eighth Air Force planes flying from English bases pounded Germany's great industrial web. U.S. aerial war horses included the B-24 Liberator and the B-17, an indomitable flying machine called the Flying Fortress. By year's end, Allied planes controlled the air over Germany. American and British bombs destroyed German factories, railroads, and military installations. Air raids also destroyed many German cities including Hamburg, Berlin, and Dresden, killing thousands of civilians.

In the summer of 1944, the Allies, under the supreme command of General Eisenhower, launched the long-delayed second front. The invasion occurred early in the morning of June 6, 1944, "D-Day," with landings along the Normandy coast of France. It was the largest amphibious operation in history: an armada of landing craft spilling 150,000 American, British, Canadian, French, and Polish soldiers and seven thousand vehicles onto the French beaches. Thousands of fighter planes and bombers raced in over the French coast to take control of the air. Hundreds of warships stood offshore in the English Channel pounding German fortifications. By the end of the day, the Allies had secured their beachhead, but success had come at a terrible price in lives and material. Allied success was due as much to German

D-Day, June 6, 1944. American troops wade ashore at Omaha Beach in the face of fierce resistance from German gunners.   *Source:* U.S. Army.

blunders as to Allied initiative, particularly the German failure to build up their air forces. The successful landings and buildups on the beaches were only possible because the bulk of the German army and its best divisions were committed to the war against the Soviet Union.

Even so, the depleted German defenders kept the invaders pinned to the coast until July 26, when General Patton's Third Army broke through to Brittany. Racing through holes torn in the German lines, Patton's forces led a lightning advance through France. The German army began reeling backward. Allied forces liberated Paris August 25. General Charles de Gaulle strutted down the Champs Élysée in triumph. To the south, Allied forces captured Rome. The invaders reached German soil in September.

WAR IN THE PACIFIC

Although the European war had priority, the United States did not ignore the war in the Pacific. Victory at Pearl Harbor had marked the beginning of a period of rapid Japanese expansion in the Far East. One after another, the bastions of Western imperialism fell to their advancing forces: Guam, Hong Kong, Singapore, Java, and the Philippine archipelago. For six months after Pearl Harbor, the Japanese ruled the Pacific. The Japanese navy was the most powerful fleet in the world. American forces trying to stem the Japanese tide were hampered by the damage done at Pearl Harbor and by the priorities of war planners in Washington who gave the European war preference in men and weapons.

But the naval war in the Pacific turned against Japan in mid-1942. In two hard-fought battles, American fleets halted the Japanese expansionist thrusts south and east. From May 5 to May 8, in the Battle of the Coral Sea northeast of Australia, American and Japanese aircraft carrier task forces fought a series of engagements. It was history's first sea battle in which surface ships did not fire a shot at each other, the battle being entirely fought with aircraft from carriers. This battle represented a significant victory for the Americans because U.S. forces prevented Japanese control of the Coral Sea region and ended any possibility of Japanese attacks on northern Australia.

The most important naval battle of the Pacific war, the Battle of Midway, occurred a month after Coral Sea. The Japanese objective was to capture Midway Island, located 1,000 miles west of Hawaii, and to take islands in the Aleutian chain southwest of Alaska. These islands would then serve the Japanese navy as anchor points for an expanded defense perimeter for their island empire in the Pacific basin. Japanese control of Midway would also allow them to launch further attacks on Hawaii. The Japanese also intended to force the Americans to defend Midway in order to finish what the attack at Pearl Harbor had begun, the destruction of American sea power in the Pacific.

For the Midway campaign, the Japanese assigned four aircraft carriers; the Americans had three, one of which had sustained severe damaged during the Battle of the Coral Sea. Japanese naval aircraft, particularly their "Zeroes," were superior to American planes. The Japanese had hundreds of the finest navy pilots in the world. American naval aviators were mostly young, inexperienced pilots, fresh out of flight training in the states. It appeared only a miracle could give the United States victory over vastly superior Japanese forces.

American code breakers scored an intelligence coup when they intercepted and analyzed a Japanese message which enabled them to learn the exact date, time, and place of the Japanese attack, and the composition of their forces. Using this valuable information, Admiral Chester Nimitz, Commander of the Pacific Fleet, prepared a battle plan to surprise the Japanese attackers by attacking them early.

The crucial encounters during the Battle of Midway occurred on June 4, 1942, the most important single day's fighting of the entire Pacific war. Admiral Richard Spruance, commander of Task Force 16, boldly executed the American battle plan. His planes caught the Japanese carriers before they could launch their aircraft. American dive bombers sank all four Japanese aircraft carriers, destroying the heart of their mighty task force. American losses included a carrier, a destroyer, and dozens of planes and pilots, but the Americans scored a critical victory at Midway.

Following the victories in the Coral Sea and at Midway, American Marines and Army infantry invaded Japanese strongholds in the South Pacific. Guadalcanal, an island in the Solomon chain, was one of the most important campaigns

World War II: Japanese advances, 1941-1942. *Source: Moss, Rise of Modern America*, p. 335.

of the Pacific war. Both sides waged savage wars of attrition that went on for months. The turning point came during November 13–15, when the Americans won a decisive naval victory. In February 1943, after seven months of air and sea battles, and grueling combat in steamy jungles and rugged mountainous terrain, the Japanese abandoned the strategic island. Guadalcanal represented a catastrophic strategic defeat for the Japanese.

By mid-1943, American war planners had developed a strategy that would bring victory in the Pacific. It comprised two parallel offensives. Forces commanded by General Douglas MacArthur would advance from the South Pacific through New Guinea to the Philippines, and then to Japan. Other forces, commanded by Admiral Nimitz, would advance through the Central Pacific via the Marianas Islands to Formosa (Taiwan), along the China coast, and then to Japan. As these two forces battled toward Japan, Army Air Corps planes bombed and strafed Japanese shipping and their island garrisons. Battles at sea continued as carrier task forces encountered Japanese fleets. Under the sea, American submarines attacked both naval and merchant Japanese shipping. As the U.S. campaigns progressed, strategists discovered that they could bypass heavily fortified Japanese-held islands because American air and sea power could prevent the enemy from reinforcing them. Isolated and impotent, these bases posed no threat to American forces. This bypass technique, called "leap-frogging," saved thousands of American lives and accelerated the war effort across the Pacific toward Japan.

During 1944, the Pacific war turned decisively against Japan. Admiral Nimitz's forces advanced into the Marianas, an island chain located within 1,500 miles of Tokyo. The Japanese defenders were determined to destroy the American fleet and beat back the invaders. During the Battle of the Philippine Sea, June 19, 1944, waves of Japanese planes attacked the American task force off the coast of Saipan. U.S. Navy pilots massacred the Japanese aviators. At day's end, fewer than 100 of the 373 Japanese planes returned to their carriers. America lost 29 planes. One of the American navy pilots labeled the day's action "the Great Marianas Turkey Shoot." The air arm of the Japanese navy, once the finest in the world, was annihilated. The American victory in the Philippine Sea isolated the Marianas. Saipan fell after a bloody struggle on July 9. U.S. forces liberated Guam on August 10. In both these campaigns, Japanese defenders resorted to wild "banzai" charges, trying to frighten and overwhelm American invaders. U.S. Marines and Army infantrymen cut them down with deadly fire.

Conquest of the Marianas provided forward bases for American submarines, which cut off Japanese shipping to and from the home islands and the South Pacific. The Air Force got bases from which its new bomber, the B-29 "Superfortress," could strike Japan directly. On November 24, 1944, 144 Superfortresses left Saipan for a raid on Tokyo. The size and frequency of air raids steadily increased through the remaining months of war, devastating most of Japan's cities. A B-29, flying out of Tinian, another Marianas island, would one day carry an atomic bomb to Hiroshima.

Following the occupation of the Marianas, President Roosevelt approved a campaign to liberate the Philippines, which had been seized by the Japanese in 1942. A gigantic combined force of air, sea, and land units assembled. The

Japanese gathered their still formidable forces for an all-out defense of the vital archipelago linking Japan to Malaya and the East Indies.

Leyte, one of the central islands, would be the point of attack by the most powerful strike force in military history. The Battle of Leyte Gulf, the largest naval battle in all of history between the two mightiest fleets ever assembled, preceded the invasion. It was a series of engagements between various units of both navies that took place over several days. During one of these battles, the increasingly desperate Japanese first used a suicide attack unit known as the *Kamikaze.* Kamikazes trained to crash-dive their planes on enemy aircraft carrier decks. This unorthodox military tactic inflicted heavy losses on American naval forces before war's end. But Kamikazes could not prevent a crushing Japanese defeat in the battle for Leyte Gulf. In the end, U.S. naval air power proved decisive. On October 20, 1944, General MacArthur waded ashore on a Leyte Beach proclaiming: "People of the Philippines: I have returned!" Between October 25 and 27, the American fleets completed their destruction of the world's once mightiest navy. American sea power now controlled the Pacific. The once-powerful Japanese Imperial Navy had been reduced to an impotent rump. Leyte was liberated on Christmas Day, 1944.

The invasion of Luzon, the largest and most important Philippine island, began January 9, 1945. Japanese defenders numbered 250,000. The battle for Luzon proved to be a long, fierce campaign. Japanese troops occupying Manila refused to surrender, and much of the beautiful city was destroyed by weeks of vicious house-to-house fighting. Over 100,000 civilian residents of Manila lost their lives during the campaign to liberate Manila. It took six months to pacify Luzon. Brave Filipino guerrillas furnished valuable help to the American forces during the long, hard campaign.

President Roosevelt had hoped China could play a major role in the war against Japan. But Jiang Jieshi's Nationalist regime, exhausted from years of warfare, could not take effective action against the Japanese, even with extensive American aid and support. In 1941 and 1942, American pilots, flying from India "over the hump" of the Himalayas, ferried supplies to the Chinese government at Chungking. In 1943, Allied forces under General Joseph "Vinegar Joe" Stilwell constructed the Burma Road across northern Burma to the Chinese city of Kungming. Roosevelt then assigned Stilwell to Chungking with orders to maximize the Chinese war effort against Japan. But Stilwell discovered that Jiang was more concerned about fighting an enemy within China, the spreading Communist movement led by Mao Zedong. Frustrated, Stilwell fired off a report to Washington accusing Jiang of preventing the fulfillment of his mission to China. A furious Jiang then demanded that Roosevelt recall General Stilwell. Roosevelt complied with Jiang's request. China's military potential went down the drain of internal political conflict.

WARTIME DIPLOMACY

During the war, the Axis powers failed to coordinate their military and diplomatic strategies. The Allies, despite much tension and disagreement, maintained a wartime harmony of interests. The Americans and British forged a partnership even before the United States entered the war. In December 1941, the two nations created a Combined Chiefs of Staff to coordinate grand strategy in both Europe and Asia. Although they agreed on war aims, American and British leaders disagreed on the timing and location of a second front in Europe. Churchill also refused to apply the principle of self-determination, embodied in the Atlantic Charter, to the British empire. The Soviet Union, the third member of the Allied coalition, endorsed the Charter with reservations about its applicability to eastern Europe. Generally, the Soviets were willing to mute their strategic, political, and ideological differences with Western powers as long as military necessity bound them together. But Stalin protested bitterly the continual delays by the Western nations in opening a second front in France. The Grand Alliance remained a shotgun wedding; only the necessity of defeating Germany kept the unnatural marriage together. The immediate origins of the Cold War lay in the wartime tensions and conflicts of the Allies.

Wartime coalition required periodic meetings among the Allied leaders. Early in 1943, Roosevelt and Churchill met at Casablanca to plot strategy following the successful North African landings. Here they adopted the doctrine of "unconditional surrender," meaning they would press the war until the Axis leaders gave up without any assurances that they would remain in power.

The Big Three (Roosevelt, Churchill, and Stalin) met for the first time at Teheran in November 1943. A meeting in Cairo among Roosevelt, Churchill, and Jiang Jieshi preceded the Teheran conference, where the leaders discussed the Asian war in which the Soviets were not engaged at the time. The three allies agreed that Manchuria and Formosa would be returned to China after the war. The Teheran conference focused primarily on military strategy. Stalin got his long-sought commitment from the Western powers that a second front would be opened in France within six months. The three leaders also discussed postwar political questions involving Germany and eastern European countries. President Roosevelt, in his meetings with Stalin, used his talents at personal diplomacy to try to win the trust and cooperation of the Soviet dictator.

Another year of war occurred before the Big Three met again. As the end of 1944 approached, the Allies were winning both the European and Asian wars, although much bloody fighting remained. In December, the Germans mounted a counteroffensive in the Ardennes Forest region of southern Belgium. For three weeks, Nazi Panzers drove the Allies back, but the Germans could not sustain their momentum. This "Battle of the Bulge," named for the big bulge created in the Allied lines at Bastogne, ended on Christmas. The Battle of the Bulge was the largest military campaign in the history of American warfare. Approaching victory generated a host of related strategic and political questions that required the personal attention of the Big Three. They had to chart the final drives of the European war, discuss the Pacific war, talk about the postwar political status of eastern European countries, plan for occupying Germany, and arrange for the creation of a proposed United Nations. The three leaders met at Yalta, a Crimean resort on the Black Sea coast, February 4 through 11, 1945.

The first important matter discussed at Yalta involved the occupation policy for postwar Germany. Roosevelt and Churchill rejected a Soviet request to strip Germany of $20 billion worth of reparations. To prevent this dispute from dividing the conference, all parties accepted the principle of reparations and referred the matter to an appointed commission to determine specific amounts. The Big Three agreed to divide Germany into four occupation zones, with France assigned the fourth zone. They also agreed to a joint occupation of Berlin, which lay deep within the Soviet zone in eastern Germany, an arrangement both sides deeply regretted after the rise of the Cold War.

Roosevelt initiated discussions at Yalta on the pending formation of the United Nations. Vigorous U.S. participation in an international organization armed with power to maintain peace by using economic sanctions or military force was FDR's chief concern at Yalta. He wanted Stalin, without whose cooperation it could not succeed, to commit himself to full support for the new agency to be created at San Francisco in April 1945. To encourage Soviet cooperation, he accepted Stalin's demand for three votes in the General Assembly; he also accepted a veto designed to protect great power prerogatives within the UN.

The postwar political status of Poland caused the most controversy at the conference, particularly the composition of its new government. There were, at the time, two governments claiming to represent all Poles, one headquartered in London and championed by the British, and one in Lublin, backed by the Soviets. Stalin, who made it clear that Poland was a vital Soviet interest, proposed that the Communist-controlled government at Lublin become the government of a new Poland. Roosevelt proposed a government comprising representatives of Poland's five major political parties. The Soviets rejected it, but Stalin agreed to add "democratic elements" to the Lublin regime. To avoid letting differences over Poland undermine conference harmony, the Allies worked out an agreement that papered over significant differences with vague, elastic language. Stalin agreed to "free and unfettered elections" at an unspecified time in the future. Roosevelt settled for a reorganized Lublin regime that included "other" political leaders, language susceptible to many differing interpretations.

Roosevelt understood that the presence of Soviet troops in Poland, and elsewhere in eastern Europe, gave them controlling influence in determining the political future for these countries. He did not expect to achieve genuine democracy for Poland, but he hoped to convince American public opinion that he had succeeded in doing so. The best he privately hoped for was that the United Nations might be able to restrain Soviet actions in Poland in the future. Roosevelt also got Churchill and Stalin to sign a Declaration of Liberated Europe that committed the Big Three to help the liberated people of eastern Europe to form democratic governments through free elections.

Roosevelt also wanted to commit the Soviets to entering the Asian war against Japan as soon as possible. On February 10, Stalin and Roosevelt signed a secret treaty in which the Soviet Union agreed to enter the war within three months following Germany's surrender. In return, the Soviets were given several concessions includ-

The Big Three—Prime Minister Winston Churchill of Great Britain, President Franklin Roosevelt of the United States, and premier Joseph Stalin of the Soviet Union—held several wartime conferences. At Yalta, a Black Sea resort in the Crimea, they met for the last time in February 1945.   *Source:* U.S. Army.

ing a Soviet-controlled satellite in Outer Mongolia. They were guaranteed the return of the southern portion of Sakhalin Island. The port of Darien would be internationalized. A lease would be given the Soviets for the use of Port Author as a naval base. A joint Chinese-Soviet consortium would be established to operate the Manchurian railways, and the Japanese would cede the Kurile Islands to the Soviets.

Roosevelt and his advisers considered the price of Soviet entry into the Asian war reasonable at the time. The expectation that an atomic bomb would be ready in August did not alter Roosevelt's goal of getting the Soviets into the war. His military advisers told FDR that Soviet participation at the earliest possible moment would ensure the defeat of Japanese forces in Manchuria, and that Soviet air raids on Japan flown from Siberia would assure the disruption of Japanese shipping from the Asian mainland. Most important, Soviet intervention would shorten the war and save American lives. Roosevelt did not consult with Jiang Jieshi before granting the Soviets the concessions affecting China.

The atmosphere at Yalta was cordial, as befitted members of a wartime coalition who still needed one another to achieve victory over their enemies. Both sides made compromises and concessions. Roosevelt left the conference believing that he had attained Soviet cooperation in winning the war and building a postwar structure of peace. On March 1, Roosevelt told Congress that Yalta had been "a great success" and he asked the American people to support it.

But the Soviets achieved important diplomatic victories at Yalta. Stalin used the military situation favoring the Soviet Union at the time to achieve his objectives. The role of the Allied military in the ultimate defeat of the Germans was minor compared to the Soviet effort. Hundreds of Soviet divisions fighting the best Wehrmacht armies in the Soviet Union and eastern Europe eventually broke the spine of German power. As Red forces overran eastern and southern Europe, Stalin used military occupation to gain political control of countries within these strategic regions. Stalin also used the American desire for Soviet entry into the war against Japan to exact major diplomatic concessions in the Far East. Roosevelt did not "sell out" China to the Soviets at Yalta as Republican critics later charged, but the Yalta agreements amounted to a significant diplomatic victory for the Soviet Union.

VICTORY IN EUROPE

Shortly after Yalta, advancing American forces reached the Rhine River. With the Nazi regime approaching extinction, the Soviets installed the Lublin Communists in power in Poland, violating the Yalta agreement. Roosevelt warned Stalin that his actions jeopardized "future world cooperation." FDR also warned Churchill on April 6 that they would have to be firm in the dealings with the Soviets about Poland's political future. But on April 12, Roosevelt died of a cerebral hemorrhage at his vacation retreat in Warm Springs, Georgia.

Harry Truman, an unknown professional politician with an undistinguished record, succeeded Roosevelt. Truman initially doubted if he could handle the responsibilities of the world's most demanding job. After taking the oath of office, a shaken Truman told reporters that he felt as if "the moon, the stars, and all the planets had suddenly fallen on me." Fate had thrust Truman into the presidency, an office he had never sought and for which he was ill prepared. He had no background in foreign policy. During his brief vice presidency, Truman had never participated in policy decisions. The new president assumed office at a time when momentous strategic and political decisions had to be made.

As Truman struggled to take hold of the reins of office, the European war ground towards its inevitable conclusion. Churchill, reacting to Soviet political moves in Poland, advised Roosevelt just before his death that Anglo-American forces should "beat the Russians to Berlin" to stretch Western postwar political

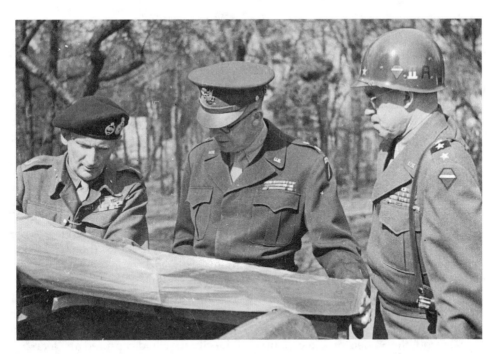

The Supreme Allied commander General Dwight D. Eisenhower, flanked by General Omar Bradley (right) and British General Bernard Montgomery. *Source:* National Archives.

leverage as far east as possible. FDR died before he could make a decision, and he was replaced by the inexperienced Truman. The Supreme Allied Commander in Europe, General Eisenhower, rejected Churchill's proposal and permitted the Soviets to capture Berlin. He ordered American advance forces to halt at the Elbe river, 50 miles from the German capital. The Joint Chiefs and President Truman both accepted Eisenhower's decision which he made for strategic reasons.

Some historians believe that Anglo-American forces could have beaten the Soviets to Berlin; had they done so, they would have gained advantages over the Soviets in postwar conflicts over Germany that were among the major causes of the Cold War. They argue that Berlin would have been a Western city and that there would have been no Berlin blockade and no Berlin Wall. Further, they believe that Germany would never have been divided and would have always remained within the Western orbit. In their view, Eisenhower, guided by short-term military considerations, made a grave political error by rejecting Churchill's advice, and the Soviets, guided by long-term political goals serving Soviet interests, took advantage of U.S. shortsightedness. Such views are invalid. Had U.S. forces taken Berlin and other territory in eastern Germany, they would have been withdrawn beyond the Elbe after the war to be in accord with the Yalta agreement. The Soviets would have then occupied their zone in East Germany and their sector of Berlin just as they did. After these arrangements were in place, events would have unfolded exactly as they did.

Eisenhower made his decision to stop at the Elbe because all his efforts were aimed at defeating Germany and ending the war as fast as possible. He feared that a Berlin campaign would enable remaining German forces in southern Germany to regroup into guerrilla units that could prolong the war and increase American casualties. Further, he knew that a U.S. drive on Berlin could result in military conflicts with the Soviets. American public opinion would have exploded at the prospect of substituting Soviets for Germans as enemies. His most important consideration was that America still had another war to win in the Pacific. Washington wanted to end the European war as quickly as possible so troops fighting in Europe could be sent to the Far East. It was also crucially important that the Soviets honor their commitment to enter the Asian war.

It is unlikely that American forces could have beaten the Soviets to Berlin had they tried. On April 11, General William Simpson had fifty thousand troops within 50 miles of the city. A weak Germany army and some water barriers stood between them and the capital. On that date, the Soviets were 15 miles closer, had 1.25 million men, and faced two weak Germany armies. The terrain was flat, dry land. It cost the Soviets over 100,000 casualties to take Berlin, more than America had suffered in fighting on German soil during the final months of war. After the war's end, the Soviets had to give up half the city they had captured at a fearsome price. The Allies got their Berlin sectors without losing a single man. As the Soviets took Berlin, Eisenhower's forces crushed remaining pockets of German resistance. Fighting ended on May 5, and Germany surrendered on May 7.

As Allied armies liberated Poland and conquered Germany, they discovered the death camps that revealed the radical evil at the heart of the Nazi regime. Battle-hardened soldiers started in disbelief at open mass graves filled with skeletons, and still-living, emaciated victims of Nazi savagery. Early in the war, Hitler had approved a plan prepared for "a final solution to the Jewish question": their systemic destruction. The Nazis built five extermination centers, the most infamous located near the Polish village of Auschwitz. For three years, trains of cattle cars from all German-occupied areas of Europe hauled doomed human cargoes to their final destinations. Jews were not the only Holocaust victims. Slavs, gypsies, criminals, homosexuals, mentally retarded people, resistance fighters, and even some Germans opposing Hitler's regime—all were liquidated, all victims of Germany's ferocious racism and technical efficiency. But Jews remained the primary targets, and before the victorious Allies halted the horrid process, an estimated 5 to 6 million of the 7 million European Jews were murdered, or died from starvation, disease, abuse, and overwork. Besides the Jews, the other victims together numbered about 6 million. As many as 12 million human beings were killed by a self-styled master race who had decreed whole races of people unfit to live. In a brutal war that featured many barbaric acts by both sides, the enormity of Nazi genocide overwhelmed all others. The Holocaust was the ultimate atrocity.

The European Theater, 1942–1945. *Source: Moss, Rise of Modern America, p. 322.*

VICTORY IN THE PACIFIC

As war ended in Europe, Japanese resistance in the Pacific stiffened. They made last ditch stands at Iwo Jima and Okinawa. Iwo Jima was a tiny volcanic atoll situated midway between the Marianas and Japan. American strategists determined that Iwo Jima had to be taken because Japanese interceptors based on the island attacked B-29 bombers flying to and from Japan. U.S. pilots needed the atoll as a haven for crippled planes unable to reach their bases at Tinian and Saipan. During March 1945, over six thousand U.S. Marines died in one of the most bitter and lethal battles of the Pacific war. The most famous photograph of the Pacific war came out of the Battle for Iwo Jima. It depicts four marines and a sailor proudly raising the American flag atop Mount Suribachi in the midst of battle.

Control of Okinawa, a large island located 325 miles from southern Japan, would give American forces a staging area from which to launch amphibious attacks against the China coast and Japan itself. The largest amphibious assault of the Asian war occurred at Okinawa; over 180,000 troops hit its beaches at various landing sites. The Japanese made extensive use of Kamikazes who inflicted severe damage on the American Fifth Fleet supporting the invasions. U.S. casualties exceeded 50,000 during a three-month war of annihilation ending on June 22. The Battle of Okinawa was the bloodiest campaign of the Pacific War. The capture of Okinawa secured the final stepping stone for the invasion of Japan, scheduled to begin in November 1945. The fanatic Japanese resistance at Iwo Jima and Okinawa foretold that the impending invasions of their home islands would be long, exceedingly costly, and bloody campaigns.

But an extraordinary new weapon radically altered the course of the Pacific war. In 1939, the noted scientist Dr. Albert Einstein had informed Roosevelt that it might be possible to build "extremely powerful [atomic] bombs." Einstein also warned FDR that German scientists might already be developing a nuclear bomb. Roosevelt, after conferences with scientific advisers, ordered work to begin to develop nuclear weapons, mainly to beat the Germans to the bomb.

Between 1941 and 1945, U.S. and British scientists, engineers, and technicians labored intensively to build atomic bombs. General Leslie Groves headed the secret, top-priority program, code-named the "Manhattan District Project." A brilliant scientific team gathered under the leadership of Dr. J. Robert Oppenheimer and working at Los Alamos, New Mexico, eventually solved the complex theoretical and technical problems involved in creating the immensely powerful new weapons.

The Manhattan District Project was so secret that congressmen who appropriated the vast sums of money for the bomb had no idea what the money was for. Harry Truman came to the presidency ignorant of the project. He was astonished to learn in April 1945 from Secretary of War Stimson that the United States would soon have "the most terrible weapon ever known in human history, one bomb of which could destroy a whole city." In July, the world's first atomic device, nicknamed "the Gadget," was exploded in the desert near Los Alamos. An awed Dr.

Oppenheimer, witnessing the enormous fireball created by the explosion, recalled a passage from Hindu scriptures, "I am become Death, destroyer of worlds."

Before the weapon was completed, Stimson convened an Interim Committee that recommended unanimously to the president that the atomic bomb, when ready, be used without warning against Japan. Truman concurred. Some scientists who had worked on the project opposed this recommendation at committee hearings and proposed instead that the Americans invite Japanese observers to witness a harmless demonstration of the bomb's power, perhaps inducing their surrender. Committee members unanimously rejected their recommendation and Truman never learned of their proposal. Other officials also urged holding back and trying to get Japan to surrender without having to use atomic weapons, perhaps by offering them better surrender terms. Truman consistently rejected such advice.

Meanwhile a new government took power in Japan. Its moderate civilian faction sought a way to end the hopeless war. Unaware of the secret Yalta agreements that would soon bring the Soviet Union into the war against Japan, a member of the peace faction sought Soviet mediation to get a modification of the unconditional surrender terms that would permit the Japanese to keep their emperor. The Soviets rebuffed the Japanese approach and informed Washington. American officials already knew of the Japanese peace feeler from reading "Magic" intercepts. They also knew that Japanese army officers, controlling the government, meant to fight on.

After discussions with advisers, Truman issued a final warning to Japan before dropping the bombs. The message urged Japan to surrender unconditionally or else face "the utter devastation of the Japanese homeland." But it made no mention of atomic weapons. The divided Japanese government, rejecting the ultimatum as "unworthy of public notice," ignored it.

Interpreting their silence as rejection, Truman saw no need to rescind an order given July 30 to proceed with the atomic bomb attack. Early on the morning of August 6, 1945, three B-29s lifted off the runway at Tinian bound for Hiroshima, Japan's eighth-largest city. The lead aircraft, the *Enola Gay,* carried a 5-ton atomic bomb in its specially configured bomb bay. The other two planes were escorts; they carried cameras and assemblages of scientific recording instruments.

At 8:16 A.M. local time, the sky exploded over Hiroshima: The world's first atomic bomb struck with the force of 12,000 tons of TNT. It killed or seriously wounded some 80,000 people instantly, many of them vaporized by the intense heat that exceeded 50 million degrees Fahrenheit at the center of the huge fireball. By the end of the year, 60,000 more people had died a dog's death from burns, wounds, and radiation poisoning. A city of 320,000 inhabitants was reduced to instant rubble. A few hours after the bombing, Truman announced to the world the existence and first use of the bomb. He also warned the Japanese that unless they surrendered unconditionally immediately, "they may expect a rain of ruin from the air, the like of which has never before been seen on earth." The Japanese did not surrender. Militarists urged death over defeat.

Bad weather delayed the dropping of the second bomb for a few days. On August 8, Red Army units invaded Manchuria and Korea. The next day, an atomic bomb was dropped on Nagasaki. Originally, the city of Kokura had been selected for the second bombing, but stormy weather made bombing that target impossible. Nagasaki was an alternative target. The bomb that devastated Nagasaki was a Plutonium bomb that yielded about 20,000 tons of TNT. It destroyed large sections of the city and killed twenty-six thousand people. It would have killed far more people and done far greater damage if it had not fallen off target and because of Nagasaki's terrain.

Even after the second atomic bombing and the Soviet entry into the war, Japanese military leaders wanted to fight on. Only the personal intercession of Emperor Hirohito induced them to surrender. Japan surrendered unconditionally on August 14, although President Truman did offer veiled assurances that the Japanese could retain their emperor providing that he was stripped of his status as a divinity. Surrender ceremonies occurred September 2 aboard the battleship USS *Missouri,* anchored in Tokyo Bay, with General Douglas MacArthur presiding.

Most Americans have accepted President Truman's justification for using the atomic bomb: "We have used it in order to shorten the agony of war, in order to save the lives of thousands and thousands of young Americans." But since the 1960s, a few radical critics have contended that the Japanese, perceiving their cause to be hopeless, would have surrendered soon without the atomic bombings. They argue that Truman had other, more important, motives for using nuclear weapons besides ending the war. He wanted to enhance American postwar diplomatic leverage against the Soviet Union. They accuse him of using the bombs on the already beaten Japanese to hasten their surrender in order to keep the Soviets from sharing in the postwar occupation of Japan and to make them more manageable. If these charges were to be proven true, the president of the United States would have been guilty of war crimes: the mass murder of over 100,000 Japanese civilians, in pursuit of postwar political goals.

It is impossible for any scholar, after examining the extensive available evidence, to determine with any degree of certainty, Truman's motives for ordering the atomic bombings. Besides, Truman never debated with his senior advisers whether or not to use atomic weapons on the Japanese. The atomic bomb project, started by Roosevelt years earlier, was nearing completion at the time Truman became president. FDR had understood that the bomb, when available, would be used on the Germans and the Japanese if the wars were still raging. Since Germany surrendered on May 8, 1945, Truman simply assumed that atomic bombs would be used on Japan as soon as they became available.

Truman and his advisers discussed where, when, and how to use atomic weapons, *they did not debate whether to use them or not to use them.* No one in Truman's circle considered the morality, strategic necessity, or wisdom of using those horrifically destructive weapons. Truman's role was basically a decision not to in-

The Atomic Age began on August 6, 1945, when a lone American bomber dropped the world's first atomic bomb on Hiroshima, a city of 320,000 people in southern Japan. Tens of thousands of people died, and most of the city was turned into instant rubble. *Source:* U.S. Army.

terfere with existing plans for the bombs' uses. Truman himself later said, "I regarded the bomb as a military weapon and never had any doubt that it would be used." There were additional considerations. Political leaders feared *post hoc* criticism if they did not use the weapons. Suppose it came out after the war that they had wasted $2 billion on a giant atomic boondoggle that was developed and never used? Suppose it came out that they had developed a powerful weapon that might have shortened the war and saved thousands of U.S. soldiers' lives and they failed to use it?

Although there can be no certainty in discerning Truman's motivation, it appears that his primary concern was to try to shorten the war and to save American soldiers' lives, just as he always claimed. He hoped to avoid a protracted and bloody campaign to conquer the Japanese home islands. Truman also hoped that American use of the powerful new weapon would make the Soviets more cooperative, that it would give the U.S. additional bargaining leverage with them. He also hoped that use of the bombs might induce Japanese surrender before the Soviet Union entered the war, but the Soviet Union intervened between the dropping of the bombs. Truman was also disappointed to discover that the U.S. possession and use of atomic bombs did not soften Russian diplomacy. The Soviet response was to become more intractable, not less.

American willingness to use the atomic bombs in war, coupled with Washington's failure to keep Stalin informed of the progress of the Manhattan project and with American refusal to share any broad scientific information about nuclear weaponry with the Soviets, contributed to the development of the Cold War. At a garden party held one afternoon following a Potsdam conference session, Truman told Stalin that the United States had recently tested an extremely powerful new weapon. He did not tell the Soviet dictator that it was a nuclear device. Stalin merely smiled and said that was fine and that he hoped that it would soon be used on Japan. Truman did not have to tell Stalin that the United States had developed an atomic bomb; the Soviet leader understood instantly what Truman was talking about. As soon as Truman walked away, Stalin hastily conferred with his top aides and decided on the spot to speed up a Soviet atomic weapons project that had been curtailed in wartime. The nuclear arms race began at that moment.

FBI files, subsequently made public, proved that a spy ring working for the Soviet Union whose most prominent members included an English physicist, Klaus Fuchs, and Americans David Greenglass, Harry Gold, and Julius Rosenberg, had penetrated the Manhattan District Project. By the time Americans had atomic-bombed the two Japanese cities, the spy ring had already delivered about ten thousand pages of classified government documents to their Soviet masters. These secret data significantly shaped the Soviet atomic bomb project. Experts have estimated that espionage accelerated the Soviet bomb project by as much as two years. At war's end, Soviet scientists already knew the technology required to process fissionable materials; they would build their own bombs within four years.

Scientists working at Los Alamos who built the bombs did not know how powerful they would be, nor did they anticipate the grave health problems posed by radiation poisoning to bombing victims. Perhaps the Japanese should have been forewarned. Perhaps a demonstration explosion should have been made. Perhaps the unconditional surrender terms should have been modified before the bombs were used in order to strengthen the peace party within the Japanese government. Any or all these measures might have induced Japanese surrender before the bombs were used, although no one can know for sure how the Japanese would have responded to any of these initiatives.

It is also important to remember that even if Japan could have been induced to surrender without having to endure the horrors of two atomic bombings, the conceivable alternative scenarios would have, in all probability, been worse. Had the war gone on for a few weeks more, the continuing fire bomb raids over Japanese cities would have killed more people and destroyed more property than did the two atomic bombs. Had invasions by U.S. forces been necessary, there would have been devastating losses on both sides, including millions of Japanese civilians. Hand-to-hand combat in Japan might have destroyed the country. While fighting went on in Japan between Americans and Japanese, Soviet soldiers would have annihilated the Japanese armies in Korea, Manchuria, and northern China.

So victory came to America and its allies. They had prevailed in the costliest, most destructive war in the planet's history. The war cost Americans about $350 billion. The war also claimed over 1 million American casualties, including 292,000 battle deaths. That summer of 1945, Americans could gaze into a future bright with hope because the Axis menace had been destroyed and democracy appeared to have no enemies in the world. They also gazed at a world darkened by the nuclear shadow that they had allowed to be cast over its future.

HOME FRONT USA

Americans in the late fall of 1941 drifted into history's largest war. As they faced and eventually defeated dangerous threats to the American way of life and democratic values, they got caught up in the greatest collective experience of their lives. Sharing a sense of common purpose under the inspired leadership of Franklin D. Roosevelt, Americans enjoyed greater national unity than any time in their history. Citizens who remained behind on the home front contributed in many ways, large and small, to the war effort. They gave blood, bought war bonds, planted victory gardens, and collected scrap metal, used tires, oil and grease, and tin cans. People worked as volunteers on civil defense, as school aides, in hospitals, in first aid programs, as volunteer firemen and police, and as airplane spotters.

The war effort involved many homefront sacrifices. Between the attack at Pearl Harbor and V-J Day (December 7, 1941 and August 14, 1945), about 300,000 workers died in industrial accidents and 1 million workers were permanently disabled. More workers were killed or crippled in homefront accidents than soldiers were killed or crippled in battle! Consumers had to do without many of the civilian goods and services normally churned out by the gigantic American economy. The nation's automakers ceased making new cars early in 1942; for the duration of the war they turned out trucks, jeeps, tanks, and planes. Major consumer items were rationed. People traveled less, dressed more informally, entertained more at home, and went to bed earlier. Hunting and fishing were banned for the duration of the war.

DEMOGRAPHIC CHANGES

World War II had a dramatic impact on the lives of nearly all Americans—on where they lived and what kind of work they did. It also affected family life, and patterns of leisure and recreation. The war experience set demographic patterns that would persist for the next half-century. Military bases and war industries transformed cities and revitalized entire regions of the country. The West Coast, especially California, which had been a relatively isolated and underdeveloped area of the nation, became the most dynamic region in the country. The western coastal states, with 10 percent of the nation's population, accounted for 20 percent of total wartime production. Economists estimated that the coastal states' economies did about fifty years of growing in less than four.

Between 1941 and 1945, approximately 16 million men, about 95 percent of whom were drafted, and 250,000 women served in the armed forces. About half of those who went into the military during the war never left the continental United States. But many of those servicemen who never left the states were assigned to bases in different parts of the country that they had never seen before. After the war had ended and they had been discharged, they returned with their families to become permanent residents of the locales were they had done military service. In

Internal migration in the United States during World War II.   *Source: Statistical Abstract of the United States, 1974 ed.*

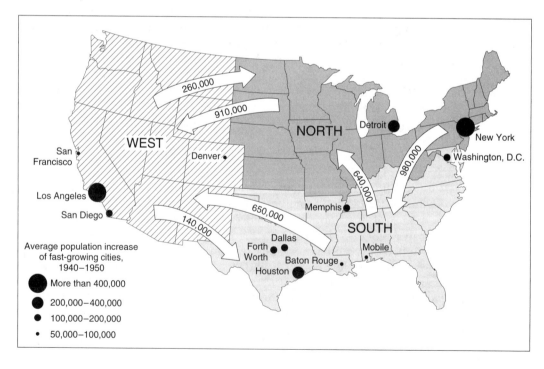

addition to service personnel, millions of civilian war workers moved from rural areas to the cities where jobs in war industries could be found. In many cases, those transplanted civilian war workers, refugees from rural poverty and isolation, did not go home after the war. They and their families joined the burgeoning postwar urban and suburban populations.

Several important population shifts occurred in wartime that would shape the demographic contours of postwar America for decades. Population flowed from the rural interior of the country outward toward the cities along the Pacific, Atlantic, and Gulf coasts. People also left inland farms and villages for the cities of the Upper Midwest because it was in the coastal and midwestern cities that the major military installations, shipyards, aircraft assembly plants, and other war industries were located. Population also made a major shift westward, particularly to California. California's population increased by 40 percent from 1940 to 1945, and millions of the military personnel and war workers who came to California in wartime remained or returned after the war to become permanent residents of the Golden State. The Sunbelt, that southern rim of states stretching from South Carolina to California, also began to grow rapidly during the war years. The Sunbelt states, especially Florida, Texas, and Southern California, would become the nation's most dynamic centers of population growth and economic expansion in the postwar decades.

Another important demographic trend induced by World War II: good-paying jobs in war industries lured over a million African Americans out of the Old South and on to New York, Chicago, Philadelphia, Detroit, and the rapidly growing cities along the West Coast. Many African Americans and their families also remained in these new locales after the war. They became permanent residents of New York, Pennsylvania, Illinois, Michigan, and California. The geographic mobility induced by the war resulted in permanent relocations for millions of American families. Rural America declined. Regional differences among Americans diminished; the demographic foundations for the postwar surge of urban and suburban communities were lain.

Despite the mobilization of America's vast human and economic resources for the war effort, there occurred more social reform affecting the quality of American lives during the war than had occurred previously during the years of New Deal reforms. Medical and dental care improved dramatically. Prepaid health insurance became available for the first time for working people. Some progressive employers such as Kaiser Shipyards offered medical care as a fringe benefit to its employees. Millions of young men from disadvantaged backgrounds drafted into the armed forces enjoyed a nutritious diet and adequate medical and dental care for the first time in their lives. Even with the nation at war and even with the dangers of war work, the overall health of the American people improved dramatically during the war years. Birth rates rose rapidly; death rates sharply diminished. Median life expectancy increased by five years!

A huge increase in the size of the American middle classes was the most significant demographic transformation of the war years. The United States became

American industry made a major contribution to eventual military victory. This ship was completed in ten days, a remarkable feat that brought FDR (in the foreground, left) to the Portland, Oregon, shipyard where it was accomplished. *Source:* Franklin D. Roosevelt Presidential Library.

for the first time in its history a middle-class nation in the sense that more than half of the nation's families enjoyed middle-class incomes and lifestyles. Personal income more than doubled during the war, and national income was more equitably distributed than ever before. Perhaps one-third of the nation's families remained poor during the war, but most of these families enjoyed relative improvements in their living standards. It was during the early 1940s that prosperity levels that had been reached in the late 1920s before the Great Crash were finally eclipsed.

ECONOMIC TRANSFORMATIONS

In addition to raising a vast military force, the United States had to gear its economy for global war. America's factories had to produce arms for ourselves and for our major allies, the British and Soviets. During the first half of 1942, the federal government placed orders for over $100 billion in war contracts, more goods than the economy had ever produced in a year. Converting the economy to a war footing challenged American industrialists and government bureaucrats. Initial government efforts to organize the war economy proved ineffective. But by 1943, the Office of Economic Stabilization, headed by James F. Byrnes, brought order to the gigantic wartime industrial effort. Byrnes used the immense powers granted his office to weave together the various strands of America's domestic war effort.

Fueled by federal expenditures that dwarfed all spending for New Deal Era programs, the gross domestic product more than doubled during the war years. The GDP grew from $95 billion in 1940 to more than $211 billion by 1946. During those years, economic expansion added 10 million new jobs. The federal government during World War II spent more than twice as much money than all previous governments combined had spent since the creation of the Republic.

To help pay for these prodigious wartime expenditures, Congress broadened and deepened the tax structure. The Revenue Acts of 1942 and 1943 created the modern federal income tax system. Most Americans had never filed an income tax return before World War II because the income tax, on the books since 1913, had been a small tax on upper-income families. Starting with 1942, anyone earning $600 or more annually had to file an income tax return. A withholding tax went into effect in 1943. Income tax revenues rose from $5 billion dollars in 1940 to $44 billion in 1945. Even so, tax revenues paid only 41 percent of the cost of the war. Government paid the rest of the bills by borrowing. War bonds, peddled by movie stars, war heroes, and professional athletes, added $100 billion. By war's end, the national debt had climbed to $280 billion, up from $40 billion when it began.

Vast federal spending for war ended the lingering depression that had afflicted Americans for a decade. The New Deal had failed to find a cure for economic depression. On the eve of war, over 7 million Americans were out of work, 14 percent of the labor force. Real wages in 1941 remained below 1929 levels. By New Year's day 1943, unemployment in America had vanished. Wartime economic expansion, fueled by unprecedented levels of government spending, combined with mass conscription to create severe labor shortages.

The discovery that government spending could banish the specter of depression confirmed the claims of the world's foremost economist, England's John Maynard Keynes. Keynes contended that government spending could cure economic depression. If private sector investment proved inadequate, government could cut taxes and begin large-scale spending programs to stimulate demand and restore the business cycle. During the New Deal of the mid-1930s, government spending was not large enough and taxes were generally regressive, so Keynes's theories could not be confirmed until the war years. The wartime success of eliminating the depression also gave American political leaders a confidence that they could regulate the economy—a confidence that lasted for the next thirty years. They believed they now possessed fiscal tools to monitor spending levels in order to maintain prosperity, keep unemployment low, and prevent the recurrence of recession, all the while controlling inflation. Americans also looked to government after the war to maintain and promote prosperity.

Farmers and industrial workers, two classes devastated by depression, prospered during the war years. Farm output rose 20 percent even though the farm population declined more than 50 percent, and farmers struggled with chronic labor shortages. Congress created the War Labor Board in 1942, which set guidelines for wages, hours, and collective bargaining. Employers, unions, and government officials generally cooperated during the war. Unions added over 6 million new members between 1940 and 1945; real wages for workers employed in manufacturing rose 50 percent from 1941 to 1945.

Some labor problems the War Labor Board could not resolve. The American Federation of Labor and the Congress of Industrial Organizations engaged in bitter, sometimes violent, jurisdictional disputes. Although organized labor had given a no-strike pledge for the duration of the war, it could not be enforced. In 1943, over 3 million workers went on strike, although most work stoppages only lasted a few days. These wartime strikes never caused serious production delays in the industries that cranked out the huge amounts of war materials required by the Armed Forces.

Increased federal spending also unleashed powerful inflationary forces. The shift from peacetime to wartime production sharply reduced the amount of consumer goods available to buy just when people had more money to spend. By 1943, production of new cars and other durable goods had stopped. A giant inflationary gap generated by "too much money chasing too few goods" threatened to drive prices way up and to rob Americans of their wartime economic gains. To clamp a lid on inflation, the government imposed price controls, joining them to a rationing system that used coupon allotments to consumers for scarce items such as sugar, butter, coffee, beef, tires, and gasoline.

Roosevelt created the Office of Price Administration (OPA) to administer the control apparatus nationally. The OPA had a daunting task. Business lobbyists, farm bloc politicians, and union leaders waged unceasing "guerrilla warfare" against the OPA for the duration of the war. Consumers chafed under rationing restrictions, particularly those on beef and gasoline. A ban on all "pleasure driving" and a 35-mile-per-hour speed limit accompanied gasoline rationing. The average motorist got 3 gallons of gas per week. Most people walked to work or took public transportation. Auto touring all but vanished. Black markets in gasoline flourished; racketeers had not had it so good since Prohibition. At times, motorists could get no gas, legal or illegal. Service stations often closed, stranding motorists and truckers. When a station could get gas, customers lined their cars up for miles waiting to buy it. Beef rationing also caused serious problems. Butcher display cases frequently emptied. Frustrated shoppers often abused butchers and occasionally rioted. Horsemeat and muskrat meat appeared in several places as beef substitutes. Despite grievances and injustices, the universally unpopular OPA maintained price stability and distributed scarce goods reasonably fairly. Most people complied with the system of controls, considering it both a wartime necessity and to their economic advantage. The OPA controlled wartime inflation; the cost of living rose only 3 percent in 1944 and 1945.

Despite shortages and rationing, people in wartime with money to spend found ways to spend it and to enjoy it. Wartime prosperity strengthened materialistic values and revived consumerism, largely suspended during the depression decade. Americans spent money on entertainment, going to movies, and going out to dinner. People resorted to black markets when rationed goods could not be found. Many people saved their money for new cars, new homes, new appliances, new radios, and new clothes they could buy after the war. Advertisers promised consumers new and better goods when civilian production patterns were restored following victory over the Axis. Consumerism, reborn during World War II, would become a powerful engine driving the postwar economy.

For millions of American families, hardship, danger, and social upheaval composed integral parts of their wartime experience. The sudden influx of hordes of war workers swamped the coastal cities. Trailer parks and shanty towns sprang up on the outskirts of towns and cities. Housing, schools, hospitals, maintenance services, and fire and police protection often could not meet the needs of new populations.

WOMEN IN WARTIME

Between 1941 and 1945, over 6 million women entered the labor force, about half of whom worked in the manufacturing sector. Women also joined the branches of military service open to them. They served in the WACS (Women's Auxiliary Army Corps), and the WAVES (Women Accepted for Voluntary Emergency Service). They also served in women's units in the Coast Guard and Marine Corps, and over a thousand women became noncombat military pilots.

Married women, many with children, made up three-quarters of working women in wartime. Before the war, typically, working women had been young and single. By 1945, more than half of working women had married, and their median age was thirty-seven. Before the war, women had been excluded from most manufacturing jobs. Employers considered them unsuitable for heavy labor amidst the masculine atmosphere prevailing in factories. Acute wartime labor shortages quickly changed those attitudes. Women learned skilled trades, joined unions, and earned high wages. Women performed certain jobs better than did men, such as those requiring close attention to detail and good manual dexterity. Women worked in munitions factories. They became riveters, welders, crane operators, tool and die makers, iron workers, and train engineers. Women increased their geographic and occupational mobility tremendously in wartime. Black women quit work as domestics to join the factory labor force. Millions of women moved from the rural South and Midwest to coastal cities where the war-generated jobs were located. In southern California and elsewhere, hundreds of thousands of women went to work in aircraft assembly plants.

Public opinion favored wartime work by women. Media campaigns portrayed women's work in shops and factories as both necessary and noble. "Rosie the Riveter" became a popular symbol, celebrated in a hit tune of the era. "Do the job HE left behind," exhorted the billboards.

But women's wartime factory work was considered only a temporary response to a national emergency. Once victory was achieved and the soldiers returned, women were supposed to surrender their jobs to returning GIs. The president of the National Association of Manufacturers intoned, "Too many

Three Native American Marine Corps Woman Reservists at Camp Lejuene, North Carolina, October 1943. They are (from left to right) Minnie Spotted Wolf (Blackfoot), Celia Mix (Potawatomi), and Viola Eastman (Chippewa).   *Source:* National Archives.

women should not stay in the labor force. The home is the basic American institution." But surveys showed most women wanted to continue working after the war. After the war, their war contracts canceled or phased out, employers fired their women employees. Others were pressured by their husbands to quit and return to the kitchen. Many single working women after the war could find only low-paying jobs in domestic service, restaurants, and department stores.

Traditional patterns of gender discrimination persisted in wartime. Women in manufacturing earned about 60 percent of what men got for comparable work. Factories offered limited promotional opportunities and supervisorial positions for women. Even though the war emergency opened up hitherto closed occupations to women, most jobs in the sex-segregated labor market remained classified as "male" or "female" work. Where women worked in factories, they often worked on all-female shop floors, under male supervisors and managers. The most serious problem faced by working mothers in wartime was the almost complete absence of child-care centers. During the war, juvenile delinquency, venereal disease, and teenage pregnancies rose sharply. "Latchkey children," children left alone while their mothers worked their shifts at a factory, became a national scandal. Children roamed the streets, were put in all-day or all-night movie houses, or were locked in cars. Police arrested many teenage girls for prostitution and apprehended boys for theft and vandalism.

Increased numbers of women got married at the same time they went to work in war industries. Marriage rates rose sharply in 1942. Many young couples got married to spend time together before the man got shipped overseas. The birthrate climbed sharply also. Many births enabled men to qualify for military deferments. Others conceived "goodbye babies" to perpetuate the family even if the father got killed in war. Returning prosperity provided the main reason for the increase in marriages and rising birthrates. A parent, often two parents with good jobs in a war industry, headed the new families. The population, which had only grown by 3 million during the entire decade of the 1930s, added 6.5 million people during the war years. The baby boom had begun.

AFRICAN AMERICANS AT WAR

World War II proved a mix blessing for African Americans: It provided both unprecedented economic opportunities and continuing encounters with the hardships and humiliations of racism. About a million black men and women served in the armed forces during the war, entering all branches of military service. Even though the American military was still segregated during World War II, African Americans attained far more opportunities than had been available in World War I. The Army Air Corps trained black pilots who flew in all-black squadrons. African American Marines, fighting in all-black units, fought heroically in savage island battles in the Pacific.

Black–white race relations within the military reflected the racist society it served. Many race riots occurred on military bases. White civilians often attacked

Over 6 million women entered the labor force during World War II. Many of them worked in industries as these two "Rosie the Riveters" helping to build military aircraft. *Source:* National Archives.

African American soldiers stationed in the South. The morale and motivation of black soldiers often suffered from encounters with racist whites. African American soldiers sometimes found enemy prisoners of war treated better than they were. But most black soldiers found reason to fight the Axis, even if at times they could see little difference between German racism and the homegrown kind. They planned to trade their wartime military service for improved educational and job opportunities after the war. African Americans fought for a double victory: over the Axis abroad and Jim Crow at home. Many returning black veterans could not celebrate the victorious end of the war as enthusiastically as white Americans could because they knew that they were coming home to face a segregated society and the attitudes that sustained it.

The war also opened many new employment opportunities for African Americans. In January 1941, A. Philip Randolph, angered because employers with war contracts refused to hire African American workers, threatened to stage a march on Washington to protest both employer discrimination and segregation in the armed forces. President Roosevelt, wanting to avoid the embarrassment of a

African Americans made a major contribution to American victories during World War II. Here, the Army Air Force's all-black 99th Fighter Group assembles at the beachhead of Anzio, Italy, in 1944. *Source:* National Archives.

protest march and possible violence, persuaded Randolph to call off the proposed march in return for an executive order establishing a President's Fair Employment Practices Committee (FEPC). It ordered employers in defense industries to make jobs available "without discrimination because of race, creed, color, or national origin." The FEPC was understaffed and underfunded, and proved to be of limited effectiveness during the war. It was acute labor shortages more than government policy that opened war employment opportunities for African Americans.

Over 2 million African American men and women left the South to find work in the industrial cities of the North and West. Many joined CIO unions. Black voters in northern cities became an important constituency in local and state elections. Most African American families who left the South during the war remained a permanent part of the growing northern urban population in the postwar era. Southern black migrants often encountered racist hostility as they struggled to adapt to their new lives in northern cities. They discovered there was little difference between northern and southern white racial attitudes. Many whites hated their new African American competitors for housing, jobs, and schools for their children. They resented coming into contact with African Americans at parks, beaches, and other public facilities.

These racial antagonisms flared violently during the summer of 1943. About 250 race riots occurred in nearly fifty northern cities, the largest riots happening in

Detroit and Harlem. The worst violence happened in Detroit. It had been building for years. The immediate provocation had been an angry struggle for access to a public housing project demanded by both African American and white workers during a time of acute housing shortages for everyone. One hot night in June, things got out of control. A full-scale riot exploded. It lasted several days. Twenty-five African Americans and nine whites died.

Despite these outbreaks of homefront racial violence, World War II proved to be a watershed for African Americans; the war experience aided the black struggle for civil rights and full citizenship. Military service gave most African American veterans greater self-esteem and a sense of empowerment. It raised expectations. Many black veterans did not return to the rural South after the war, but chose to settle in one of the northern or western states, perhaps one in which they had spent time while in the military. Others took advantage of the GI Bill to go to college or learn a skilled trade after the war. These educated black professionals and technicians formed a new and much larger African American middle class. The National Association for the Advancement of Colored People (NAACP) increased its membership from 50,000 members at the time of the Pearl Harbor attack to ten times that number at war's end. A new, more militant civil rights organization was created in wartime: the Congress of Racial Equality (CORE) was founded in 1942 in Chicago. In 1944, for the first time, President Roosevelt admitted black journalists to his press conferences. A combination of vastly improved economic opportunities and continuing encounters with racism generated a new militancy among black people. They were determined not to accept second-class citizenship after the war. These African American veterans and their children took the lead in challenging segregation in postwar America. The roots of the modern civil rights movement can be found in black experiences of World War II.

HISPANIC AMERICANS IN WARTIME

According to the 1940 census, about 2.7 million Hispanic people lived among the United States population. Most were of Mexican descent living in California, Texas, and the Southwest. Much of this predominantly rural population endured poverty, discrimination, and segregation. They lacked decent jobs, housing, educational opportunities, and they had no political influence. Many other Mexican Americans moved to urban areas to find work in war industries. The war created opportunities for Hispanic Americans. About 350,000 went into the Armed Forces, nearly all of them draftees. Although the military never segregated Hispanics in the systematic way that they did African Americans, many served in predominantly Hispanic units. Mexican American warriors joined elite units like the airborne rangers and often volunteered for dangerous missions. Eleven Mexican Americans won the nation's highest military award, the Congressional Medal of Honor.

At the same time, the war created acute shortages of farm workers. American growers persuaded the government to make arrangements with Mexico to import farm workers from Mexico. Under a program established in 1942, nearly 2 million

Mexican *braceros* (laborers) entered the United States. Because of lax government supervision, employers often ruthlessly exploited these imported contract laborers. The *braceros* often worked for 50 cents a day, had no fringe benefits, and were housed in shacks and converted chicken coops.

Hispanic Americans in the war labor force often suffered discriminations similar to those encountered by African Americans and women. They sometimes got paid less than "Anglo" employees for doing the same work. They found their problems most acute in the crowded cities. Many young Mexican Americans belonged to neighborhood gangs. They called themselves *pachucos* and favored a distinctive style of dress, called a "zoot suit." The "zoot suit" consisted of baggy trousers flared at the knees and fitted tightly around the ankles, complemented by a wide-brimmed felt hat. These costumes were an assertion of a distinct cultural identity and a defiance of Anglo values.

In June 1943, at a time when black–white racial tensions were erupting in cities, ethnic relations in Los Angeles were also strained. Hundreds of sailors and Marines on leave from bases in southern California assaulted Mexican Americans on the streets of Los Angeles and tore off their "zoot suits." Police either looked the other way or arrested only Mexican American youths during these encounters. The local media supported the attacks on the *pachucos*. Only after the president of Mexico threatened to cancel the *bracero* program did President Roosevelt intervene to stop the violence.

Despite the zoot-suit incidents, Hispanic American wartime experiences brought many advances. As was the case for African Americans, military service gave thousands of Mexican Americans an enhanced sense of self-worth. They returned from the war with greater expectations and enlarged views of life's possibilities. Many Hispanic veterans took advantage of the GI Bill. In the postwar years, Mexican American veterans led the fight against discrimination in southwestern states.

NATIVE AMERICANS IN WARTIME

In addition to the twenty-five thousand Native Americans who served in the armed forces during World War II, many thousands more left their reservations to work in war industries in various cities around the country. Most of these mobile people did not return to reservations after the war. They remained within the cities after the war industries had shut down and became part of the nation's rapidly growing postwar urban and suburban population. Some Native Americans did return to the reservations after the war and brought them new ideas and new technologies.

In 1944 in California, lawyers representing a group of Native Americans filed suit in federal court for $100 million. They sought compensation for lands taken illegally from their ancestors during the 1850s. Congress enacted legislation to pay them for their lands, but President Franklin Roosevelt vetoed the bill. Litigation on this matter continued off and on for the next thirty-five years. Finally, both parties reached a compromise agreement. The Native Americans accepted a settlement that brought them about 47 cents per acre.

ASIAN AMERICANS IN WARTIME

The war to save democracy featured many homefront violations of democracy. In some areas, civil liberties violations during World War II were not as severe as during World War I. Most conscientious objectors were permitted to serve in non-combatant roles in the military or else perform essential civilian work. Of the more than fifty-five hundred conscientious objectors jailed for refusing to serve in the military, most were Jehovah's Witnesses. They refused to cooperate with the Selective Service authorities. Further, they did not oppose all wars, only secular wars for mere political objectives. Some fascist publications were banned from the mails. In July 1942, a federal grand jury brought indictments against twenty-eight fascists for sedition. The cases continued off and on for the duration of the war. No one was convicted, and all charges against the twenty-eight defendants were dropped after the war ended. German Americans were not harassed or persecuted, as in World War I, nor were Italian American citizens. Congress never enacted repressive measures like the Espionage Act or the Sedition Act.

But during the spring and summer of 1942, about 110,000 Japanese Americans, two-thirds of them native-born American citizens, were uprooted from their homes along the Pacific Coast and taken to internment centers located in remote interior regions of the country. There they lived in tarpaper barracks behind barbed wire for three years. The internment of Japanese Americans for the duration of World War II represented the worst violation of civil liberties in wartime in American history.

The initiative was taken by the military commander in charge of security along the West Coast, General John Dewitt. Dewitt and other officials claimed relocation of Japanese Americans was necessary to guarantee military security along the West Coast. They argued that if the Japanese Americans were not relocated, some of them would aid the enemy in case of attack. Since the "disloyals" could not be separated from the "loyals," all would have to go. Their accusations were demonstrably false. FBI agents admitted that they never discovered a single proven act of disloyalty committed by any Japanese American. The real reasons for their removal included anti-Japanese race prejudice, wartime hysteria, and greed. The claim of military necessity was based on unfounded suspicion, not evidence. Relocation of Japanese Americans in wartime was also the culminating act of a half-century of anti-Japanese agitation and assaults in California, Oregon, and Washington.

Japanese American spokesmen asserted their loyalty to the United States, to no avail. No political leaders or newspaper editors defended the Japanese Americans, nor did any question the need for relocation. Earl Warren, California's Attorney General in 1942, strongly advocated removal. The removal order, Executive Order No. 9066, came from President Roosevelt and could not be challenged. In 1944, the Supreme Court placed the constitutional seal of approval upon relocation of Japanese Americans. In the case of *Fred Korematsu* v. *the United States,* the Court accepted the claim of Army lawyers that relocation was a wartime military neces-

U.S. soldiers uprooted about 110,000 Japanese Americans, most of them U.S. citizens, from their homes in early 1942 and imprisoned them in various internment centers. The move, spawned by panic and prejudice, was both unnecessary and wrong. Here, a family awaits a bus to haul them away. *Source:* National Archives.

sity. A five-to-three majority ruled that in time of war, individual rights could be sacrificed to military necessity. Associate Justice Frank Murphy filed a powerful dissenting opinion, stating that relocation of Japanese Americans fell "into the ugly abyss of racism."

Following the advice of their leaders, virtually the entire Japanese American population complied with the relocation order without resistance or protest. They submitted in accordance with the spirit of *Shikata Ga Nai* (realistic resignation). Because they were given little time to gather at assembly centers and allowed to take only what they could carry to the camps, families lost homes, businesses, farms, and personal property worth an estimated $400 million. They arrived at the camps to find hastily built tarpaper barracks amidst bleak desert landscapes that would be their homes for three years. The internment centers were de facto prisons. People were not free to come and go. The camps were under continuous surveillance by armed guards and enclosed by barbed wire fencing. During the course of the war, some internees were allowed to leave the camps, provided they agreed to settle in eastern states. By war's end, all were allowed to leave. A fortunate few families had friends who had saved their homes or businesses for them while they were incarcerated. But many internees had no homes or businesses to which to return. They found that interlopers now resided in their former residences and owned their former businesses.

Even though their families were imprisoned in camps, thousands of young men volunteered for military service. They were determined to prove their loyalty to a government that had betrayed them. Japanese American soldiers contributed much to the war effort. They fought in the European theater, and many served in the Pacific war as translators, interpreters, and intelligence officers. They proved themselves to be brave warriors, winning many medals and suffering severe casualties. One Japanese American unit, the 442nd Regimental Combat Engineers, was the most decorated unit in American military history.

The government refused to relocate Japanese Americans living in Hawaii. Thousands of them continued to work for the American military at Pearl Harbor and other installations following the Japanese attacks. Ironically, they were not removed because of military necessity. They made up one-fifth of the Hawaiian population, their labor was essential, and there was no place to put them, nor ships to transport them.

Loyal Americans were the victims of an egregious injustice. Congress authorized token restitution for Japanese Americans in 1948, and a total of about $38 million was paid to claimants during the 1950s. These payments amounted to about 10¢ for each $1 of loss. Years later, after much litigation and quiet political pressure, Japanese Americans belatedly received vindication and additional restitution. In 1983, U.S. District Court Judge Marilyn Hall Patel vacated Fred Korematsu's conviction. Judge Patel's action came after Korematsu's attorneys discovered secret documents proving that government officials knew that Japanese Americans posed no dangers to national security in wartime and withheld this evidence from the Supreme Court. On August 10, 1988, President Ronald Reagan signed legislation authorizing $20,000 in reparations to each of the estimated 60,000 survivors of wartime relocation. As he signed the historic legislation, President Ronald Reagan, speaking for all Americans, apologized to the Japanese American community: "We admit a wrong. Here we reaffirm our commitment as a nation to equal justice under the law." Although some embittered victims dismissed the money as "too little, too late," others were grateful and appreciated the symbolic significance of the gesture.

After the war, Japanese Americans did not protest the gross injustices they were forced to endure in wartime. They internalized the anger, hurt, and shame associated with the relocation experience. They rarely talked about those experiences even among close friends and family. Instead, Japanese Americans vowed to put their wartime experiences behind them and to go forward—to prove emphatically to the government and the white majority that had abused them that they were good citizens and productive members of society.

Their postwar record of achievement was astonishing. Japanese Americans, by any measure, are among the most successful and prosperous groups in the country. The have integrated themselves into the larger society. They have achieved distinction in the sciences, the arts, medicine, the law, engineering, academic life, business, finance, athletics, and politics. They are among the leaders in amount of education attained and annual per capita income. In the half-century following their harrowing wartime experiences, Japanese Americans and their descendants have powerfully demonstrated their individual capabilities as well as their loyalty to their country.

In contrast to persecution of Japanese Americans in wartime, Chinese Americans fared comparatively well. Chinese Americans enjoyed the sympathy and goodwill of most Americans because China was a wartime ally of the United States. Americans also felt much sympathy for China and the Chinese people, who were suffering terribly at the hands of the Japanese soldiers during the war years. Because of their status as allies and because of acute labor shortages in war industries, unprecedented opportunities for Chinese workers suddenly opened up. By the thousands, Chinese families streamed out of the Chinatown ghettos into the mainstream of American life. Most of these mobile Chinese families never returned to the Chinatowns and after the war they headed for the suburbs.

In 1943, Congress at long last repealed the Chinese Exclusion Act that had been in place since 1882. For the first time in over sixty years, it was now possible for people to emigrate legally from China to the United States. In addition, the government finally extended citizenship to thousands of Chinese, many of whom were quite elderly, who were longtime residents of the United States but had hitherto been ineligible for citizenship.

THE POLITICS OF WAR

War moved the country toward the Right. Resurgent Republicans gained seventy-seven seats in the House and ten seats in the Senate in the 1942 midterm elections. A conservative coalition of northern Republicans and southern Democrats, which had emerged following the 1938 elections, consolidated its control of Congress. Roosevelt, sensing the political drift and preoccupied with the vast tasks of running the war, put social reform on the back burner. Conservatives snuffed out many New Deal agencies in 1942 and 1943 on the grounds that wartime economic revival had rendered them obsolete. Among their most prominent victims were the WPA and the CCC. Federal spending for social programs declined sharply.

Antitrust activity ceased. Businessmen poured into Washington to run new wartime bureaucracies. Businessmen regained much of the popularity and prestige they had lost during the Depression years. Popular resentment of business greed and social irresponsibility gave way to a popular image of businessmen as patriotic partners providing the tools needed to win the war. Roosevelt, needing business cooperation for the war effort, cultivated a cordial relationship among his former adversaries. Populistic, antibusiness rhetoric vanished from the public dialogue. Secretary of War Henry Stimson observed: "If you are going to go to war . . . in a capitalist country, you have got to let business make money out of the process or business won't work." Many corporate leaders abandoned their bitter criticisms of Roosevelt and New Deal policies, having discovered that they could profit from the policies of the welfare state turned warfare state. Businessmen switched their political strategy from one of trying to dismantle big government to trying to use it to their advantage.

The war effort further centralized the corporate economy because 90 percent of the billions of dollars the government spent on war contracts went to 100 large corporations. Big business got bigger in wartime, and most companies enjoyed historic high profits, surpassing anything earned during the best years of the 1920s. Wartime politics showed that the positive state, erected by liberals to fight the Great Depression and promote social reform, could be manned by conservatives who would use its power to promote business interests, curtail reform, and attack trade unions—while winning a war.

During the 1944 election, President Roosevelt faced the challenge of Republican New York Governor Thomas E. Dewey. Roosevelt, to keep his party unified in wartime, dumped his vice president, Henry Wallace. Wallace, a fervent New Dealer, had alienated powerful big-city bosses and conservative southerners within the Democratic Party. Political insiders knew that Roosevelt's health was failing and he would probably not serve a full four years if reelected. They therefore understood that they were not just picking a vice president, but the possible successor to FDR. Thus the decision took on a greater urgency and significance than the normal jockeying for power in American politics. But because Roosevelt was very much a candidate for reelection despite his growing infirmities, the stakes involved in the battle for the vice presidency could not be discussed openly.

Roosevelt replaced Wallace with a candidate acceptable to all factions within the party, Missouri Senator Harry Truman. Truman had rendered valuable service to the country in wartime, heading a watchdog committee that had investigated government war contracts. Senator Truman's energetic, scrupulous efforts saved taxpayers billions of dollars and expedited delivery of crucial war materials. Despite his wartime service, though, Truman was still a relative unknown in 1944, an undistinguished journeyman politician, but acceptable to all the power brokers within the Democratic Party ranks.

The contest between Roosevelt and Dewey was a rather dull and one-sided affair. To many observers, Dewey did not appear presidential. He was a short, neat little man who came across as rather aloof, cold, and stiff. He hurt his chances of winning by failing to cultivate good relations with the working press covering the campaign. Alice Roosevelt Longworth asked, "How can we be expected to vote for a man who looks like the bridegroom on a wedding cake?"

Newly empowered, organized labor played a major role in the 1944 campaign. The CIO, through its Political Action Committee, circumvented laws restricting union activities and funneled millions of dollars into the campaign for the

Roosevelt ticket and many liberal congressional candidates. It also registered voters, circulated campaign literature, and got out the vote on election day.

Dewey's campaign strategy differed from previous Republican efforts. He accepted the New Deal welfare state but accused New Dealers of waste and inefficiency. He also refused to make Roosevelt's foreign policy a campaign issue, not wishing to revive isolationist issues amidst the war. By embracing the welfare state and internationalism, Dewey placed both the New Deal and the war beyond partisan debate.

Roosevelt, who did not campaign much, exploited his prestige as wartime commander-in-chief of a vast military effort that was winning everywhere. He called attention to legislation benefiting veterans, including the "G.I. Bill of Rights." During the campaign, friends, political associates, and perceptive journalists all noticed that Roosevelt had grown thin and frail. His hands trembled and there were dark circles under his eyes. His doctors knew that he was suffering from heart disease and hypertension. Most Americans, however, were not informed of his medical conditions and took no notice of FDR's failing health. In accordance with the journalistic practices of the era, reporters, even those hostile to Roosevelt, made no public mention of this rapidly deteriorating health.

Roosevelt easily won his fourth presidential election victory in November. His electoral vote count was 432 to 99, but his popular vote tally was only 25.6 million to 22 million for Dewey, his narrowest margin of victory ever. The 1944 vote revealed that the Democratic Party was becoming more urban as a result of the wartime migration that had lured millions of workers from rural regions into the cities, where jobs could be found. The Democrats regained 22 of the seats in the House that they had lost in 1942, but they lost another Senate seat. The conservative coalition retained its control of Congress.

The huge increase in the size and scope of the federal government, particularly the executive branch, represented the most important wartime political development. As government spent more money, it became more centralized. Federal bureaucracies assumed many economic functions previously performed by the private sector. The number of federal employees nearly quadrupled—from 1 million in 1940 to 3.8 million in 1945. Wartime agencies proliferated, generating an alphabetical avalanche that dwarfed the New Deal. FDR issued more executive orders during the war than all previous presidents had during the entire history of the republic. The most powerful politicians, after Roosevelt, were men he appointed to run the war agencies, most of whom he recruited from the ranks of business. During the war, politicians forged the permanent welfare and regulatory state by providing it with a permanent bureaucratic base and ample sources of tax dollars. There occurred a revolution in the size, cost, and power of federal government. The war played the dominant role in turning the national state into the behemoth that it has become today.

As the executive branch made a quantum leap in size and power, Congress suffered a relative decline in power and prestige. Through his active participation in foreign conferences and various domestic agencies coordinating the gigantic war effort, Roosevelt significantly enhanced the powers of the presidency and set an example followed by all postwar presidents. The "imperial" presidency had its origins in World War II.

The Supreme Court, dominated by Roosevelt's liberal appointees, refused to review any cases involving wartime extensions of federal power into economic affairs, an arena in which it had been especially active during the New Deal years. The Court also refused to intervene in cases involving wartime violations of civil liberties, except to affirm the relocation of Japanese Americans from the Pacific Coast. The FBI's force of special agents increased fivefold, from 785 in 1939 to 4,370 at war's end. The FBI in wartime also got enhanced authority to spy on Americans and to tap telephones in national security cases.

The war multiplied the points of contact between the federal government and its citizens. Millions were added to the social security rolls, and everyone who worked paid federal income taxes. War experiences strengthened the tendency to look to Washington for solutions to problems. This trend weakened social bonds and undermined local governments. People traded some of their personal freedom for greater government control and an enhanced sense of social security.

Washington became the biggest of all war boomtowns. In 1942, the Pentagon, the world's largest office building, opened. It housed over 35,000 bureaucrats and its offices consumed 30 tons of paper annually. Lobbyists stalked the corridors of political power seeking ever-larger shares of the vast expenditures flowing out of Washington into corporate coffers. The Pentagon also developed generous tax write-offs to motivate business participation in the war effort. It developed the cost-plus contract whereby the federal government underwrote all developmental and production costs plus guaranteed a percentage profit to contractors providing needed war material. The government also subsidized the creation of new industries required by the necessities of war. With supplies of natural rubber from Southeast Asia cut, Washington spent nearly $1 billion to create a synthetic rubber industry to provide substitute products.

Much basic research for new weaponry and war industries had come from universities and colleges, which became committed to meeting the needs of military research. Most colleges and universities suffered no loss of enrollment during the war despite the draft because the government utilized their campuses for training enlisted men and officers. After the war, the GI Bill, which paid for millions of veteran' college educations, assured continuing growth and expansion of higher education.

World War II created a wartime partnership among business, universities, Congress, and the Pentagon, engaged in the procurement of war contracts. This "military-industrial complex," as President Eisenhower would later call it, nurtured during the war, came of age during the Cold War. It became a powerful lobby for creating the permanent war economy. The military–industrial complex guaranteed that the vastly enhanced authority of government in American economic and scientific affairs would continue after the war.

CULTURE AND WAR

Popular culture flourished in vigorous variety during the war. Sales of books, both fiction and nonfiction, increased sharply. Many war novels and journalistic accounts of the war made the best-seller charts. The best and most popular war correspondent was Ernie Pyle, a quiet midwesterner who wrote with great insight and accuracy about ordinary soldiers in combat. His *Brave Men,* published in 1945 after he had been killed covering the Okinawa campaign, remains the finest account of GI life ever written. Bill Mauldin, a cartoonist whose panels portrayed two weary, dirty, unshaven GIs named Willie and Joe, also realistically recorded battlefield conditions.

Not everyone remained home at nights reading about the war. Ballroom dancing flourished in wartime. The popularity of jitterbugging, a carryover from the late 1930s, continued unabated, especially among young people for whom it offered a distinctive world with its own clothes, language, and ritual behaviors. Energetic, athletic youngsters spun, whirled, and tossed their partners to the pulsing rhythms of hot jazz. Older couples enjoyed the more sedate pleasures of fox trots and waltzes. Nightlife, particularly New York nightlife, sparkled. Patrons at the Copacabana or the Latin Quarter could spend $100 in an evening of drinking, dancing, and enjoying the singing of young crooners like Frank Sinatra or the sounds of Tommy Dorsey's Big Band. Spectator sports drew large crowds in wartime despite the loss of most skilled athletes to the war. Major league baseball continued its pennant races and annual World Series using mostly teenagers, castoffs, and overage players.

Hollywood was still king in wartime. Movies remained by far the most popular mass-entertainment medium, although the film industry had to adapt to wartime conditions. Most top male stars either got drafted or enlisted, and thousands of technicians and production personnel went off to war. Jimmy Stewart flew bombing missions over Germany. Henry Fonda joined the Navy and served in the South Pacific. Clark Gable, "The King," joined the Army Air Corps. A lesser star, Ronald Reagan, was assigned to an Army motion picture unit in Hollywood that made training and documentary films. Many actors not in the armed forces and top female stars like Dorothy Lamour, Rita Hayworth, and Betty Grable entertained the troops both in the states and around the world.

Wartime Hollywood mostly made war movies. The studios churned out a flood of war and spy stories. Many Chinese actors got work in Hollywood films for the first time playing Japanese villains in war movies. John Wayne starred in a series of war epics glorifying various branches of the military service—*Flying Tiger, Fighting Seabees,* and *The Sands of Iwo Jima,* the last about the Marine Corps. The best war film was *The Story of GI Joe,* adapted from Ernie Pyle's reporting. It contained no preaching, no propaganda, no hateful enemy stereotypes, and no heroes. It depicted American soldiers as skilled professionals doing a dirty job, trying mainly to survive and return home after the war. Hollywood also made several excellent war documentaries, the best a series produced by Frank Capra and John Huston.

Hollywood does its bit for the war effort . . . Pin-up photos of Betty Grable, famed for her "million dollar legs," adorned thousand of soldiers' foot-lockers around the world. *Source:* National Archives.

"Canteen films" represented another Hollywood wartime film genre. They were celluloid USO shows, hosted by a big-name star featuring celebrity guests who sang, danced, and told jokes—all promoting the war effort.

African American soldiers occasionally appeared in war films, usually as stereotyped "happy Negroes," jiving, dancing, and laughing. Jewish soldiers usually were stereotypically portrayed as guys named "Brooklyn" who looked forward to returning to Ebbets Field after the war and jeering at the Giants. American allies were shown as heroes in war films. Wartime movie Russians were hearty, simple people, and gallant fighters. In *Mission to Moscow,* a U.S. diplomat goes off to Moscow to meet the Russians. He is tailed by two jolly KGB agents who cheerfully inform the American star that the infamous purge trials of the 1930s were necessary to save the Soviet Union from a fascist coup.

One World War II film has become a classic. In 1942, Warner Brothers brought out a low-budget melodrama set in Morocco. It told a tale of an American nightclub owner, Rick Blaine, who hides patriotic idealism beneath a hard-boiled surface. In the end, Rick sacrifices both his business and the woman he loves to rescue an anti-Nazi resistance fighter. Humphrey Bogart played Rick Blaine in *Casablanca,* becoming a cult hero to millions of moviegoers.

Radio, more popular than ever, became a prime source of news about the war. World War II was the first war given live media coverage. War correspondent Edward R. Murrow described the Battle of Britain for American radio audiences in the summer of 1940. People listened to his deep, solemn voice, hearing shrill air raid sirens and the roar of exploding bombs in the background, as Murrow vividly described the "blitz" of London. He brought the European war into American living rooms. Foreign correspondents in Europe and Asia went everywhere the soldiers went to transmit firsthand accounts of battles to the folks back home. Never had war journalism been so direct or authentic. But censors often edited the news. Broadcasters often sacrificed factual accuracy for dramatic effect. War news had entertainment as well as informational value. Wartime radio remained essentially an entertainment medium. Programming continued much as usual: variety, sitcoms, and melodrama—and always incessant commercial messages urging listeners to buy cigarettes, soap, and chewing gum.

No great war songs came out of World War II, unlike the first war, which left a great musical legacy. The biggest hit of the war years was Irving Berlin's "White Christmas," introduced by Bing Crosby in a 1942 film, *Holiday Inn.* Its vast appeal was related to its mood—melancholy, expressing a yearning to be home; it caught the wartime homesickness felt by war workers and soldiers thousands of miles from home at Christmas.

WORLD WAR AND ITS CONSEQUENCES

World War II was an intense, transforming experience for most Americans. The war fundamentally changed American society in many ways. These war-induced changes were more profound and permanent than any occurring in this country since the industrial revolution. On the eve of war, Americans suffered from lingering effects of the Great Depression—high unemployment, low productivity, and massive poverty, accompanied by lurking doubts about the vitality of American institutions and the purpose of national life. They looked out at a threatening world engulfed in war, a world in which their nation played only a peripheral role. Within the nation, Americans quarreled bitterly among themselves over President Roosevelt's conduct of foreign policy, until the bombing of Pearl Harbor abruptly ended all arguments.

A unified, proud, and powerful nation emerged victoriously from war four years later. Its armed forces and industrial might had played decisive roles in destroying fascism, militarism, and imperialism around the globe. America had won the largest war in human history. War revitalized the American economy; it emerged far more productive and prosperous than ever. American faith in capitalism and democratic institutions had also been restored. Compared to other nations, American war casualties had been light, and Americans had been spared the devastations and terrors of a war fought outside its continental boundaries. Fewer than 12 percent of its population had served in the armed forces; over half of those who did never left the states, and many sent overseas never experienced a moment's combat.

At war's end, the United States strode the world as an international colossus; its armed forces, linked to its nuclear monopoly, made it the most powerful nation-state in the history of the planet. Its statesmen took the lead in creating a new international agency to preserve peace in the postwar era. Fittingly, the United Nation's permanent home would be New York, the greatest metropolis of the new imperium.

World War II ushered in a new age for the United States. The war was a watershed from which emerged the dominant patterns of postwar life. The war forced Americans to accept involvement with the world beyond national boundaries; there could be no reversion to isolationism after 1945. Their war experiences gave Americans new confidence that they could solve all serious problems, both internal and external. They had proved that they had both the will and the means to lick depression at home and aggression abroad.

The major contours of post-1945 American history originated in the war experience. The Cold War with the Soviet Union stemmed from the tensions and conflicts that strained the Grand Alliance. Postwar economic policies derived from the awareness that federal spending in wartime had finally ended economic depression. Political leaders during the postwar era assumed that similar fiscal practices could stabilize the business cycle and promote economic growth without inflation. New understanding of the role of consumerism in sustaining economic growth meant that government would promote spending instead of saving after the war. The struggles and achievements of women and minorities in wartime planted the seeds of their postwar drives for equal access to the American dream.

The war restored America's philosophic birthright, an optimistic sense of individual and national potential that would shape the national experience for the next three decades. The Axis powers were destroyed, the Soviet Union exhausted, and western Europe depleted. But America was strong, prosperous, and free. Its people felt ready for the "American Century" they knew lay ahead. America's economy was powerful, its resources abundant, and it had the scientific and technological talent to use them. Success in wartime gave Americans confidence and great expectations for an unbounded future.

Americans also soberly confronted a future that they feared could bring recurrence of the Great Depression. Could prosperity, growth, and full employment be sustained in a postwar era without the stimulus of the war economy? Could jobs be found for the millions of returning veterans and displaced war workers? Americans also worried about threats to their peace and security posed by the Soviet Union. Perhaps the war had not made the world safe for democracy? Perhaps there was not going to be an American century after all, or at least not an uncontested American century. Most of all, Americans were alarmed by the nuclear shadow they had cast over the postwar era.

And so Americans in the summer of 1945 faced the future with mixed feelings: with feelings of pride, and confidence, and hope. They also faced the future with feelings of fear—of the return of depression, of expanding Soviet power, and of a nuclear Armageddon.

IMPORTANT EVENTS

1942	Japanese Americans are interned
1942	The Battle of the Coral Sea occurs
1942	The Battle of Midway takes place
1942	Allied troops invade North Africa
1942	The Manhattan District Project begins
1943	Soviets win the Battle for Stalingrad
1943	FDR and Churchill announce unconditional surrender at Casablanca
1943	Allied forces invade Italy; Italy surrenders
1943	A race riot breaks out in Detroit

1943	The Big Three meet at Teheran
1944	D-Day: Allied invasion at Normandy
1944	Paris is liberated
1944	The Battle of Philippine Sea takes place
1944	The Battle of the Bulge takes place
1945	The conference at Yalta takes place
1945	The Battle of Iwo Jima occurs
1945	Roosevelt dies; Truman becomes president
1945	Germany surrenders
1945	The Battle of Okinawa takes place
1945	The Potsdam conference is held
1945	Japanese cities are atomic-bombed
1945	Japan surrenders; World War II ends

BIBLIOGRAPHY

There is vast literature on all facets of American involvement in World War II. The following books are recommended for those who want to know more about the war experience in general or to explore a particular aspect. Two good short surveys of World War II are Martha Byrd Hoyle's *A World in Flames: A History of World War II* and Mark Arnold-Forster's *The World at War*. Basil Collier's *The Second World War: A Military History* is a good short account of the U.S. military role in World War II. A recent book on the Pacific war is by Ronald H. Spector and entitled *Eagle Against the Sun*. Samuel Eliot Morison's *The Two Ocean War* (two vols.) is a naval history of World War II. A recent study that highlights the racial antagonisms that undergirded the war between the United States and Japan is John Dower's *War without Mercy: Race and Power in the Pacific War*. The best war journalism can be found in Ernie Pyle's classic, *Brave Men*. The best short study of U.S. wartime diplomacy is Gaddis Smith's *American Diplomacy During World War II*. The best account of the decision to build and use atomic bombs on Japan is Martin J. Sherwin's *A World Destroyed*. John Hersey's *Hiroshima* is an eyewitness account of the tragedy that launched the atomic age. The horrors of the Jewish Holocaust have been recorded by Arthur D. Morse in *Six Million Died*. The best studies of the Home Front are by Richard Polenberg (*War and Society: The United States, 1941–1945*) and John Morton Blum (*"V" Was for Victory: Politics and American Culture During World War II*). Susan M. Hartmann, in *The Homefront and Beyond: American Women in the 1940s*, offers an account of women and the war. Neil A. Wynn, in *The Afro-American and the Second World War*, has recorded the crucial experiences of black people in wartime. The best account of the wartime relocation of Japanese Americans is by Edward Spencer and entitled *Impounded People: Japanese Americans and World War II*. Jeanne Wakatsuki Houston and James D. Houston, in *Farewell to Manzanar*, give a compelling story of a Japanese family interned for the duration of the war. Richard R. Lingeman, in *Don't You Know There's a War On?*, presents a general account of popular culture in wartime. Joel Greenberg's *Hollywood in the Forties* is an account of wartime movies and their effects on the populace. John Brooks, in *The Great Leap: The Past Twenty-Five Years in America* (1966), offers an important book highlighting the immense changes brought about in this country by World War II, which have shaped the postwar era. The best novels about the war experience are Harriet Arnow's *The Dollmaker*, which movingly describes the disruptions and dislocations of war; James Jones's *From Here to Eternity*, which is about enlisted life in the Army on the eve of Pearl Harbor; Norman Mailer's *The Naked and the Dead*, a powerful novel which uses a platoon of infantrymen to symbolize American society, its class structure, and social values; and Herman Wouk's *The Caine Mutiny*, the dramatic story of a ship's officers rebelling against a mentally ill, tyrannical ship commander.

CHAPTER 9

The Rise
of the Cold War

When World War II ended, much of the world faced the daunting task of digging itself out from rubble. The world's first global war had left a large part of Europe and many nations of Asia and elsewhere in ruins and had shattered the old balance of power. Even most of the victors had fared badly. The Soviets had lost more than 20 million people, and much of their economy had been ruined by war. It would be years before the Soviets would regain the industrial and agricultural productivity they had enjoyed when Germany invaded them in 1941. The British, depleted economically and militarily, faced the imminent loss of much of their vast empire and the painful necessity of adjusting to the new status of a second-rate power in the postwar world. After 1945, Britain's ability to play a major role in world affairs would depend mainly on American friendship and support. France had been humiliated by defeat and occupation during the war. The French economy was weak, its government unstable, and the French Communist Party was a rising force.

The war had so weakened the British, French, and the Dutch nations that they could no longer control many of their rebellious colonies in Asia, Africa, and the Middle East. Throughout the postwar era, the decolonization process begun during World War II accelerated, presenting challenges to the United States in what became known as the Third World. In the Far East, China was sinking into the chaos of civil war, dashing any hopes that it would be a major factor in postwar Asian diplomacy. Only America emerged from war with its wealth and power enhanced, and with most of its citizens better off materially than they had ever been before. The United States, for the first time in its history, had become a global power.

Postwar American celebrations of victory and expectations of a peaceful and prosperous world order dominated by the United States quickly gave way to conflicts between America and its erstwhile ally, the Soviet Union. A multitude of challenging postwar political problems generated over forty years of tension, ideological warfare, and a thermonuclear arms race that historians have called the Cold War. The Cold War would remain the dominant international reality influencing the conduct of U.S. foreign policy for over four decades. Cold War preoccupations also played powerful roles in shaping American domestic politics during the 1940s and 1950s.

THE UNITED NATIONS

It was a grim world into which the United Nations was born. Roosevelt had made creation of a postwar international organization to prevent aggression in the world his major diplomatic objective. Most influential Americans shared his goal, determined not to repeat the mistake they believed Americans had made after World War I when they refused to join the League of Nations. They believed that the United States' failure to join the League had helped undermine international order during the 1930s, which had led to World War II.

The UN experienced significant birthing pains. Soviet and American delegates quarreled frequently over many features of the new organization. Delegates from many of the gathered nations all played politics as usual. Eventually they wrote and signed a charter. Despite some concessions to the Soviets to ensure their participation, the UN was largely an American creation. It was Woodrow Wilson's League of Nation's Covenant reborn, and slightly revised.

The UN Charter created an "upper house," the Security Council, and a "lower house," the General Assembly. It also fashioned a permanent administrative structure called the Secretariat, and many allied agencies including the International Court of Justice, the International Monetary Fund, the Export-Import Bank, and the United Nations Relief and Rehabilitation Agency (UNRRA). The Security Council comprised five major powers—the United States, the Soviet Union, Great Britain, France, and China—and six associate members elected from the General Assembly to serve for two years on a rotating basis. Action on all important matters required unanimous approval from the five permanent Security Council members, giving each an absolute veto of any UN action it found contrary to its interests. In the General Assembly, every nation was represented, but only for debate, not for decision. The United Nations was a federation of sovereign states. It had only the power the major nations permitted it to have. It had no tax powers, depending on member contributions for funds. It quickly proved to be powerless to prevent aggression by the major powers.

U.S. officials were mainly responsible for creating an international agency with only contingent powers. FDR had insisted upon devising an organization that would not impair national sovereignty and allowed the major powers to police their regional spheres of influence. There was a core of realpolitik underlying Roosevelt's commitment to internationalism. Neither the United States nor the Soviet

Union would have joined any postwar international agency that did not permit them to retain an absolute veto over its actions.

Immediately after the war, the United Nations provided relief to the war-ravaged populations of Europe and Asia. The United States funneled billions of dollars through the UNRRA for food, clothing, and medicines for needy people in Germany, Japan, China, and Eastern Europe. The British borrowed $3.75 billion from the United States in 1946, much of which was used to pay for food imports. Postwar Germany faced economic disaster. German industrial and agricultural production had shrunk to pitiful fractions of prewar levels. Germany's population had swelled from the addition of 10 million "displaced persons," German refugees who had either been expelled or had fled from Eastern Europe. Churchill called postwar Europe "a rubble heap, a charnel house."

The United States shared occupation responsibilities in Germany with the Soviets, the British, and the French; but it had sole authority in Japan. In Germany, the U.S. tried to eliminate all traces of Naziism. Special courts punished over 1,500 major Nazi offenders and over 600,000 minor Nazi officials. The most famous trial occurred at Nuremberg, former site of huge Nazi party rallies during the 1930s. An international tribunal put twenty-two former high Nazi officials on trial, nineteen of whom were convicted and twelve hanged for "war crimes and atrocities." In Japan, U.S. officials under the command of the American proconsul, General Douglas MacArthur, staged a Tokyo equivalent of Nuremberg. Twenty-eight former high Japanese officials were tried and all were convicted of war crimes. Seven were hanged.

Americans also completely remade Japanese society. They broke up industrial monopolies, abolished feudal estates, and implemented land reform. They introduced political democracy and established independent trade unions. They forced the Japanese to destroy all military weapons and to renounce war as an instrument of national policy. The Japanese have depended on America's nuclear shield to protect their national security ever since. Most important for the future of Japan, U.S. engineers modernized Japanese industry, introducing new management and quality control techniques, and modern technology. From the ashes of war, with help from their conquerors, the Japanese fashioned a working democratic and capitalistic system. By 1970, Japan had become both a major trading partner and potent commercial rival of the United States.

ORIGINS OF COLD WAR

During 1945 and 1946, American and Soviet leaders clashed over many issues. Their wartime alliance deteriorated. Even before war's end, the Allies had quarreled over the opening of a second front in western Europe and the future political status of eastern European countries. The proximate origins of Cold War conflict lay in these wartime strains within the Grand Alliance. Historians, concerned to put the origins of the Cold War into a larger framework, have traced the roots of Cold War to the American response to the 1917 Bolshevik revolution and Lenin's profound hatred of Western liberal capitalist culture. From 1917 until 1933, a succession of American presidents refused to recognize the Soviet state. Even after the normalization of U.S.–USSR relations in 1933, friendly relations between the two nations did not evolve. When Stalin concluded his cynical nonaggression pact with Hitler in August 1939, most Americans equated the Soviet Union with Nazi Germany. It was the wartime alliance between the Americans and the Soviets, born of strategic necessity, that represented a departure from the historic norm of mutual distrust and ideological hostility.

In March 1945, President Roosevelt perceived Soviet efforts to impose a Communist regime on Poland to be a violation of the Yalta accords and protested to Stalin. Roosevelt's successor, Harry Truman, inexperienced in the craft of diplomacy and lacking FDR's poise and style, rebuked the Soviet foreign minister, V. M. Molotov, over Yalta violations. But military force gave the Soviet Union control of Poland's and Eastern Europe's political destinies. Between 1945 and 1948, the Soviet Union imposed Communist-controlled regimes on these nations. Stalin, determined to protect his empire and its Communist system from future security threats, and perhaps also from Western cultural influences and U.S. investment, erected a ring of submissive client states along the Soviet Union's vulnerable western periphery.

American political leaders and prominent journalists strongly condemned Soviet domination of Poland and other Eastern European countries. American statesmen would not concede, at least for the record, that the new Soviet empire in Eastern Europe constituted a legitimate "sphere of influence." For several reasons: Besides the sense of betrayal felt over Yalta, there were domestic political considerations. Millions of Americans of Eastern European background were enraged at Russia's brutal domination of their ancestral homelands. Americans also anticipated having economic relations with Eastern European countries in the postwar era until Communist control sealed them off. American leaders also felt a sense of righteous, missionary power; that they could move Eastern Europe toward democratic capitalism. Soviet intrusions frustrated American good intentions and imposed an abhorrent system of political economy on the region that many Americans equated with fascism.

At a time when American–Soviet relations were strained because of Stalin's intrusions into Eastern Europe, the Soviets applied for a $6 billion loan from the United States to rebuild their wrecked economy. American officials tried to apply pressure on the Soviets to make them more receptive to American goals for Eastern Europe. The State Department refused to consider the loan unless, as U.S. Ambassador to the Soviet Union Averill Harriman put it, the Russians "work cooperatively with us on international problems in accordance with our standards." The Soviets refused U.S. terms, and Americans rejected the loan request. A later Soviet request for $1 billion was made contingent upon the Soviets permitting American trade and investment in Eastern Europe. Stalin also refused to accept those terms and the loan was denied. The Soviets rebuilt their economy using their own resources plus what they could extract from Germany and Eastern Europe. Although U.S. efforts to extract Soviet concessions in exchange for credits had failed to change Soviet behavior in Eastern Europe, they angered Stalin, reinforcing his distrust of Western capitalist powers. Stalin also resented America's refusal to accept Soviet domination of Eastern Europe while excluding the Soviets from Italian and Japanese occupations.

But there were clear limits to what actions the Truman administration would take to prevent Soviet domination of Eastern Europe. It could denounce Soviet actions; it could apply economic and diplomatic pressures. It could even use its temporary atomic monopoly as a veiled threat; but the United States never directly threatened the Soviets with either conventional or nuclear military action. When Stalin forcibly incorporated the eastern half of Europe into the Soviet empire between 1945 and 1948, the United States, in effect, grudgingly accepted the creation of a Soviet sphere of influence.

The Potsdam conference, held in late July 1945, the final wartime meeting of the Big Three, revealed the strains within the Grand Alliance. They often quarreled—over German boundaries and reparations, over the composition of the new Polish government, and over when the Soviet Union would enter the Pacific War against Japan. At Potsdam, the Soviets pressed their demand, made at Yalta, for $20 billion of reparations to be taken from the German occupation zones. The Americans and British refused to fix a dollar amount for reparations but permitted the Soviets to remove some industry from their zones. But in May 1946, the U.S. military governor suddenly halted all reparations shipments from the American zone. The Soviets denounced this unilateral action that canceled an agreement important to their postwar reconstruction. Continual conflicts between the Soviets and the Western powers over occupation policy in Germany were major causes of the Cold War. In fact, conflicts among former allies over Germany were the core causes of the Cold War, which originated in the heart of Europe.

At war's end, America was overwhelmingly the world's preeminent power. With about 5 percent of the world's population, the United States produced over 60 percent of the world's goods and controlled over half the world's wealth. Its $14 billion in gold reserves stored at Fort Knox represented about 75 percent of the world's gold supply in 1945. Despite its great wealth and power, the United States could not prevent the growing division of Europe nor bring stability to the Far East. When American, British, and Soviet foreign ministers met in London in September 1945, they quarreled bitterly over who threatened whom. Mutual suspicion and hostility rendered diplomacy impossible. The Western powers demanded that the Soviets ease their control of Eastern Europe. In response, the Soviet leaders accused the West of capitalist encirclement and atomic blackmail.

The former allies appeared to be on collision courses: The Soviets were determined to dominate the lesser states of Eastern Europe to erect a security sphere around their nation. The United States was determined to break down international trade barriers and rebuild Germany, policies that frightened the Soviet leaders. Further, American leaders shared a vision of national greatness and national mission. In the postwar era, America intended to build a prosperous new world order, a world order based on free governments and free trade. In the world's family of nations, given its great wealth and power, America would be *primus inter pares* (first among equals). Such arrogance, with an atomic holster hanging on its hip, frightened and angered the Soviet leaders.

From the American perspective, neither its great wealth nor its atomic monopoly guaranteed U.S. security in the postwar era. The destruction of German and Japanese power had removed historic barriers to Soviet expansion in Europe and northeastern Asia. Rising anticolonial rebellions against lingering Western imperialism also gave the Soviet Union opportunities to expand its influence. From the Soviet perspective, expanding American influence in Europe and Asia alarmed the Soviet leaders. They were skeptical that the capitalist West could work cooperatively with the Communists, and they were fearful of the vastly superior American wealth and military power. Instinctively, Stalin tried to isolate the Soviet Union and its newly acquired empire in Eastern Europe from contact with the Western powers.

In early 1946, both sides escalated their rhetoric. On March 5, 1946, former Prime Minister Winston Churchill, visiting in the United States, declared "From Stettin in the Baltic to Trieste in the Adriatic, an iron curtain has descended across the continent." He called for an Anglo-American effort to roll back the Soviet iron curtain. Stalin accused Churchill of calling for war against the Soviet Union. U.S. public opinion polls showed widespread disapproval for Russian actions in Germany and Eastern Europe. Stalin had also given a speech in February in which he reasserted the Leninist doctrine of the incompatibility of capitalism and socialism, and the necessity of revolutionary conflict in the world. Following this angry exchange, the Soviets rejected an American offer to join the World Bank and International Monetary Fund, the two principal agencies for promoting free trade and stable currencies in the postwar world. The Soviets refused to join because they saw the Bank and the Fund as instruments through which the United States intended to dominate the emergent world economy.

In an atmosphere of growing hostility and suspicion, Truman and his advisers tried to work out a plan for the international control of nuclear weapons through the UN. Bernard Baruch, the American delegate, proposed a plan calling for international control of atomic weapons to be achieved in stages, during which the United States would retain its nuclear monopoly. His plan called for inspections within the Soviet Union by a UN commission to ensure compliance. The Soviets, working feverishly to develop their own nuclear weapons, rejected on-site inspections within their territory. They proposed an alternative plan calling for the destruction of American nuclear weapons before any control system would be devised. The Americans rejected the Soviet plan. The United States then opted for its own internal control mechanisms. Congress enacted the Atomic Energy Act in 1946, which empowered the newly created Atomic Energy Commission (AEC) to control all atomic energy research and development in the nation under tight security restrictions.

Thus vanished the world's only chance, admittedly a slim one, to eliminate the nuclear arms race before it became a central feature of the Cold War. It was the nuclear arms race that added a terrifying dimension to the U.S.–USSR rivalry, making it unlike any previous great power conflict in history. Since about 1955, both sides possessed the technical capability to destroy the other. Ironically, nuclear weapons also functioned to keep the Cold War cold. Had it not been for nuclear weapons, the Americans and the Soviets would probably have had a war long ago, for there has been enough provocation on both sides. But neither side dared attack the other because it knew the other would resort to nuclear weapons before it would accept defeat. Mutual terror deterred both nations from combat.

The failure of Washington and the Kremlin to find a mutually acceptable formula for controlling atomic weapons technology highlighted the dawn of the atomic age. About the same time the UN was debating the weapons issue, the United States conducted a series of atomic bomb tests in the South Pacific at Bikini atoll. Radio accounts and dramatic photos of the tests forced Americans to the horrific realization that humankind had produced weapons of mass destruction that could destroy cities in an instant. Some jaunty folks tried to make light of the matter, laugh it off. Later that year, a French designer brought out a new type of women's bathing suit, which he named the "Bikini." It had an explosive impact on women's fashion because the new-style swimsuits exposed much more of the female body than had any previous model. Despite these brave efforts to laugh it away, fear of a nuclear holocaust had taken root. The American imagination in the postwar era was haunted by twin symbols of catastrophe—the mushroom cloud and nuclear missiles striking America's great cities. According to historian Paul Boyer, "A primal fear of extinction pervaded all society." The atomic age ushered in the age of anxiety that continually undercut celebrations of the affluent society.

There were many other conflicts—and misunderstandings—arising in 1945–1946 that poisoned the postwar U.S.–USSR diplomatic atmosphere. The major conflicts—over the postwar political status of Eastern Europe, over occupation policy in Germany, and over international control of atomic weapons—drove America and the Soviet Union apart. They were the major causes of the Cold War.

These disputes between America and the Soviet Union grew out of the war and the power vacuum created by the smashing of German power, a vacuum into which rushed the two expansionist powers: The United States, a global power; its leaders motivated by a sense of righteous power based on America's prosperous economy and atomic monopoly, by strong ideological convictions, and by important economic interests. The USSR, a strong regional power; its leaders motivated by a fervent Communist ideology, an urgent desire to protect vital security interests, and a pressing need to rebuild its shattered economy. The United States and

The mushroom cloud became one of the haunting symbols of catastrophe, proving that the age of affluence was also the age of anxiety.   *Source:* U.S. Navy.

the Soviet Union collided at many points in central and eastern Europe. Emotions flared as leaders on both sides struggled to solve challenging and frustrating problems. Given their fundamental differences, the intrinsic difficulties of their many problems, the pressures and antagonisms inherent in their many disputes, and their clashing goals and ambitions; in retrospect, it appears that conflicts between the Americans and Soviets were inevitable.

Perhaps the Cold War was also inevitable. But it is at least remotely possible that more adroit and patient diplomacy by leaders of both sides, especially by Truman and Stalin, might have prevented these disputes from hardening into the long-term conflicts of the Cold War. The Cold War occurred because of the tragic failure of the two most powerful nations emerging from World War II to resolve their disputes through the traditional processes of diplomacy, by negotiations and compromise. Instead, the leaders of the two nations, ready to read the worst intentions into the actions of their rivals and to anticipate worst-case scenarios, believed themselves compelled to resort to over four decades of ideological warfare. They also felt compelled, "like two apes on a treadmill," in analyst Paul Warnke's phrase, to engage in a costly and dangerous thermonuclear arms race without precedent in human history. The Cold War became an interlocking, reciprocal process, involving genuine differences of principle, clashes of interest, and a wide range of misperceptions and misunderstandings.

Division of Europe, 1945–1955.   *Source:* George D. Moss, *Moving On* (Englewood Cliffs, NJ: Prentice Hall, 1994), p. 38.

THE TRUMAN DOCTRINE

From the vantage point of Washington in early 1947, the world appeared to be sinking into chaos. A nearly bankrupt Great Britain prepared to abandon India, Palestine, and Greece. The Vietnamese refused to accept the return of French colonialism, and Indochina was engulfed in war. Likewise, the Indonesians refused to accept the return of the Dutch and ignited a war. In China, a civil war raged between the Nationalists and Communists. Amidst rubble-strewn cities and ruined economies, the Japanese and Germans struggled to avoid famine. American leaders feared that the Soviet Union would try to exploit the severe political and economic problems of Europe and Asia.

In 1947, crises arose in the Balkans involving Greece and Turkey. Greece was engulfed in a civil war that pitted Communist insurgents against a Rightist government backed by the British. Simultaneously, the Soviets were pressuring the Turkish government to grant them joint control of the Dardanelles, a vital link between the Black Sea and the Mediterranean. Stalin viewed joint control of the strait as vital to Soviet security. The Turks rebuffed the Soviets and Stalin threatened to take action against them. The British were backing the Turks in their dispute with the Soviets over control of the waterway. On February 21, 1947, citing economic problems, the British government informed Washington that it could no longer support Greece and Turkey.

President Truman wanted the United States to replace the British in the Mediterranean and to help the Greeks and Turks. But he had to convince the Republican-controlled and economy-minded Eightieth Congress that his initiative served the national interest. The principal architect of the American aid program to Greece and Turkey was Undersecretary of State Dean Acheson. Acheson evoked an early version of the "domino theory" to stress the need for American aid to the two countries. He stated that if Greece fell to the Communists and the Soviets gained control of the Dardanelles, North Africa and the Middle East would be endangered. Morale would sink in Italy, France, and western Germany; all would then be more vulnerable to a Communist takeover. Three continents would be opened to Soviet penetration. Acheson's alarmist presentation persuaded Senator Arthur Vandenberg, Chairman of the Senate Foreign Relations Committee, to support Truman's proposed aid bill for Greece and Turkey. George Kennan, a brilliant State Department Soviet expert, also furnished arguments supporting Truman's interventionist policy. Kennan wrote of the need to develop

> a policy of firm containment, designed to confront the Russians with unalterable counter-force at every point where they show signs of encroaching upon the interests of a peaceful and stable world.[1]

---

[1] George Kennan, *American Diplomacy* (New York: New American Library, 1952), p. 104. (Reprinted, by permission of the editor, from *Foreign Affairs*, XXV, no. 4 (July 1947), pp. 566–82.)

His analysis coincided with Truman's views of Soviet behavior; his recommendations accorded with the President's desire to get tough with the Soviets. Containment, stopping the spread of Communist influence in the world, became the chief operating principle of American foreign policy in the postwar era. It remained the cornerstone of U.S. foreign policy for forty years.

Truman also actively promoted the aid bill. In a speech given at Baylor University on March 6, 1947, he said the American system of free enterprise could survive only if it were part of a free world economic system. He contended that American aid to Greece and Turkey was part of his strategy for preserving economic freedom in the world. Only a peaceful and prosperous world ensured American security in the Cold War era. He warned his audience that the "seeds of totalitarian regimes are nurtured by misery and want."

Truman's Baylor University speech preceded his major address before a joint session of Congress, March 12, to ask Congress to appropriate $400 million for Greek and Turkish aid. In the most important foreign policy speech of his presidency, written for him by Acheson, Truman told the American people that the Communist threat to Greece and Turkey was Hitler and World War II all over again. History appeared to be repeating itself in southern Europe. Truman then spoke the famed words that became known as the Truman Doctrine. The Truman Doctrine became, in the words of historian Thomas G. Paterson, "the commanding guide to American foreign policy in the Cold War."

> At the present moment in world history, nearly every nation must choose between alternative ways of life.
>
> One way of life is based upon the will of the majority, and is distinguished by free institutions . . . and freedom from political oppression. The second way of life is based upon the will of a minority forcibly imposed on the majority . . . and the suppression of personal freedom.
>
> I believe that it must be the policy of the United States to support free peoples who are resisting attempted subjugation by armed minorities or by outside pressures. . . . If we falter in our leadership, we may endanger the peace of the world—we shall surely endanger the welfare of our own nation.[2]

Truman's speech amounted to a declaration of ideological warfare against the Soviet Union. He depicted a world engaged in a struggle between the forces of freedom and the forces of tyranny. The political fate of mankind hung on the outcome. In this mortal struggle, American aid to Greece and Turkey would serve the American mission of preserving freedom in the world and preventing World War III. Senator Vandenberg had told Truman that if he wanted to get bipartisan support for his aid program, he would have to "scare hell out of the American people." He did. The President also played to America's idealistic bent for moral crusades for universal causes. Polls, which had been negative before his speech, soon showed a large majority favoring the aid program.

---

[2]Taken from a printed copy of Truman's speech found in Armin Rappaport, ed., *Sources in American Diplomacy* (New York: Macmillan, 1966), pp. 329–30.

Not everyone accepted Truman's fervent invitation to join the anti-Communist crusade. Liberal and conservative critics both opposed aid to Greece and Turkey. Henry Wallace denounced it as a waste of money and provocative to the Soviets. Walter Lippmann, the nation's premier political journalist, also opposed it, observing that the United States could not police the world. But after a brief debate, large bipartisan majorities in both houses of Congress supported the aid bill. Truman's powerful rhetoric had carried his cause.

The Truman Doctrine defined a new foreign policy direction. Isolationism had been abandoned and the United Nations bypassed. Truman had committed America to resist actively Soviet expansionism in southern Europe. The Truman Doctrine proclaimed that the era of the containment of Communism had begun. Although the first application of the new containment policy was limited, the doctrine justifying it was unlimited. During the early 1950s, U.S. foreign policy based on the containment of Communism would expand to become a global commitment.

Congress fashioned several new government agencies to implement the containment policy. The National Security Act (1947) created the Department of Defense and established the Joint Chiefs of Staff. The act also made the Air Force a separate branch of military service and put administration of the Army, Navy, and Air Force under a single department. The first Secretary of Defense was a hard-line Cold Warrior, James Forrestal. The National Security Act also created the National Security Council (NSC), a cabinet-level advisory body to coordinate military and foreign policy for the President. Creation of the NSC indicated the growing influence of military considerations in the conduct of American foreign policy. The National Security Act also created the Central Intelligence Agency (CIA) as an agency directly under the authority of the National Security Council. The CIA, child of the Cold War, became a covert arm of American foreign policy during the early 1950s. The National Security Act institutionalized the Cold War.

THE MARSHALL PLAN

In 1947, European recovery from the devastation of war was flagging. Washington feared that continuing hardships could force cold and hungry Europeans to turn to Communism; particularly in France and Italy, which had strong Communist parties. A prostrate Europe also endangered American prosperity because of a huge "dollar gap" that had emerged. The dollar gap, totaling about $8 billion in 1947, represented the difference between the value of U.S. exports and the number of dollars European customers had on hand to pay for them. The dollar gap threatened to undermine overseas trade and erode U.S. postwar economic growth and prosperity.

Europeans could not buy U.S. products unless they received dollars from the United States. To offset the lure of Communism, to hold off the possibility of Soviet intervention in Western Europe, and to pump dollars into the impoverished European economy, American officials drafted a comprehensive European aid program.

Secretary of State George Marshall, speaking at Harvard University on June 5, 1947, formally announced the plan directed against "hunger, poverty, desperation, and chaos," which came to bear his name. Truman urged Congress to back up the proposed Marshall Plan with a $27 billion appropriation.

The Marshall Plan called for a cooperative approach in which Europeans would plan their recovery needs collectively and America would underwrite a long-term recovery program. All European nations were invited to participate in the Marshall Plan, including the Soviet Union and the Eastern European nations. With the British and French leading the way, Europeans responded immediately and enthusiastically. A general planning conference convened in Paris on June 26, 1947, to formulate a European reply. But the Soviets walked out of the conference, denouncing the Marshall Plan as an American scheme to dominate Europe. Stalin may have also feared that U.S. economic aid would undermine his control of Eastern Europe, so he forced these nations to abstain from the recovery program. On July 16, Europeans established a Committee on European Economic Cooperation, which drew up plans for a four-year recovery effort.

Within the United States, Senator Vandenberg led a bipartisan effort to get congressional approval for the plan. Support for the aid program increased when Americans learned of a Communist takeover in Czechoslovakia that occurred as Congress debated the bill. Stalin ordered the Czech coup as a response to the increasing integration of the western German economy into the liberal capitalist orbit. Congress enacted a slimmed-down version of the aid plan. The legislators appropriated $5.3 billion to implement the Marshall Plan in the summer of 1948. Congress also appropriated billions of dollars to rebuild Japan's shattered economy. When the Marshall Plan ended in 1952, the United States had provided over $13 billion for European economic recovery.

The Marshall Plan worked. European industrial production increased 200 percent from 1948 to 1952. The foundations for the West's later affluence were firmly laid. The appeal of Communism in the West diminished. The program worked because of its planned, long-term, cooperative approach. It succeeded also because Europe possessed the industrial base and skilled manpower needed to use the aid funds effectively. European economic recovery restored a region of crucial importance to the United States. It also provided a major stimulus to American economic activity and it accorded with Cold War ideological goals. George Marshall expected American economic aid to permit the "emergence of political and social conditions in which free institutions can exist." The Marshall Plan gave the U.S. policy of containment of Communism in Europe a sound economic foundation.

NATO

While furnishing the means for Europe's economic reconstruction, America also concerned itself with rebuilding western Germany. With the rise of Soviet power in Eastern Europe, there was a power vacuum in central Europe that America wanted to fill with a democratic and capitalistic Germany. Near the end of 1946, the Americans and British merged their German occupation zones and began to assign administrative responsibilities to German officials. By mid-1947, the effort to rebuild Germany's industrial economy had begun.

The Soviets reacted to Western efforts to rebuild the German economy and incorporate it into the European recovery plan by tightening their control of Eastern Europe. Perceiving that he had failed to prevent the restoration of the West German state, Stalin also tried to squeeze the Western powers out of Berlin. In June 1948, the Soviets suddenly shut down all Western access routes to their Berlin sectors, which lay deep inside the Soviet zone. The Berlin Blockade confronted the Truman administration with a serious crisis. Choices at first appeared to include only surrender or risk World War III. Truman ordered U.S. strategic bombers with the capability of hauling nuclear weapons to fly to bases in England. The Western powers also devised an Anglo-American airlift that flew food and fuel to 2.5 million West Berliners. The Soviets, not wanting war, did not interfere with the airlift. After 324 days, the Soviets canceled the blockade. It had failed to dislodge the Allies and it had failed to prevent the integration of the western German economy into the European recovery program. In American eyes, the Berlin airlift symbolized Western resolve to maintain an outpost of freedom in the heart of Soviet tyranny. Truman had outmaneuvered the Soviets and forced them to rescind the blockade. The airlift also appeared to confirm George Kennan's contention that only force could contain Communist expansionism. The Western powers created the Federal Republic of Germany (West Germany) soon after the blockade ended. In retaliation, the Soviets erected the Democratic Socialist Republic of Germany (East Germany).

The Czech coup, the Berlin Blockade, and other Soviet actions hostile to Western interests convinced Washington officials that containment required military as well as economic measures. The germ of the North Atlantic Treaty Organization (NATO) appeared in a Senate resolution passed in 1948 expressing American resolve to defend themselves through collective security if necessary. The Truman administration began planning for the defense of Western Europe.

NATO came to life on April 4, 1949; ten European nations, Canada, and the United States signed the treaty. The heart of the mutual security pact could be found in Article 5: "an armed attack against one or more members . . . shall be considered an attack against them all." Attack any NATO member and you have to fight them all. With the establishment of NATO, Soviet aggression against Western Europe would mean World War III. The Senate ratified the treaty eighty-two to thirteen on July 21, 1949, with little debate. Most Americans believed NATO was a necessary response to current Soviet actions and future threats. One of the few prominent figures to criticize NATO was the Republican Party leader Senator Robert Taft. He denounced the pact as unnecessary, provocative to the Soviets, too expensive, and likely to accelerate the arms race. He also noted that NATO gave the president the power to commit U.S. soldiers to battle without the customary constitutional or congressional restraints.

Congress followed its approval of American membership in NATO by voting to grant military aid to its allies and to contribute American troops to NATO defense forces. By early 1950, a NATO command structure had been created. American forces stationed in Europe would function as a "tripwire" in case of Soviet aggression, guaranteeing that American strategic bombers would attack the Soviet Union if Western Europe were invaded. The Soviets responded to the creation of NATO by creating the Warsaw Pact among Eastern European countries.

Because U.S. forces were not sent to Europe until 1952, the creation of NATO did not immediately alter the strategic balance of power in that critical region. At the time of NATO's creation, there was no imminent threat of war in Europe. Few senior American civilian or military advisers believed that the Red Army was poised to invaded Western Europe. America appeared to be winning the Cold War in Western Europe and Japan. The Marshall Plan nations and the Japanese were both well on the road to economic recovery. The new state of West Germany under the leadership of Konrad Adenauer had been firmly established. Soviet efforts to keep Japan and Europe weak and divided, and isolated from the United States, had obviously failed. By 1949, Stalin was clearly on the defensive.

Given the geopolitical situation in Europe, it is evident that NATO had other uses besides giving containment of Communism in Europe military muscle. NATO was less about giving Europeans arms and more about giving them the confidence to combat internal subversion and the will to resist Communist pressure. NATO conveyed a sense of security that encouraged Western European economic recovery under the Marshall Plan. NATO also served as a means to bind Western Europeans more tightly into an American sphere of influence and to discourage any tendencies to make deals with or to appease the Soviets. Ironically, NATO later proved useful in providing a way to re-arm West Germany. By integrating the new West German military forces into NATO, the United States could allay French alarm at a re-armed Germany.

From 1947 to 1949, American leaders made many crucial decisions that shaped American Cold War policy for decades. First came the formulation of containment ideology, the declaration of principles embodied in the Truman Doctrine. Then the Marshall Plan offered economic aid, enabling Western Europeans to stay clear of the iron curtain and rebuild their war-shattered economies. NATO added a strategic component. NATO also represented a historic departure for the United States: America joined its first binding military alliance in modern history. Foreign entanglements now appeared necessary to ensure U.S. security in the nuclear age.

Soon after Senate ratification of NATO came the alarming news that the Soviets had developed an atomic bomb. The American nuclear monopoly, which had functioned as a security blanket to dampen Cold War anxieties, had vanished. Soviet possession of nuclear weapons prompted President Truman to consider ordering development of a hydrogen fusion weapon, a "superbomb" many times more powerful than atomic fission weapons. In January 1950, an intense secret debate occurred between scientific supporters of the H-bomb, led by Edward Teller, and its opponents, led by J. Robert Oppenheimer, the leader of the scientific team that had created nuclear weapons in 1945. Teller carried the debate with his argument that if the United States failed to develop the weapon and the Soviets did develop it, they could blackmail the United States. Truman agreed with Dr. Teller and ordered the hydrogen bomb to be built.

After obtaining permission to built the new superweapon, U.S. scientists exploded a hydrogen bomb in November 1952. But the American technological edge in the spiraling arms race against the Soviet Union proved short-lived. The Soviets tested their own hydrogen bomb in August 1953. These thermonuclear weapons were a thousand times more powerful than the bombs that had destroyed Hiroshima and Nagasaki in August 1945. With the advent of the hydrogen bomb, the potential thermonuclear threat to world survival had taken a quantum leap.

THE CHINESE REVOLUTION

Since the Cold War began, the Truman administration had pursued a Europe-oriented foreign policy. But the collapse of the Chinese Nationalist government in 1949, after years of civil war between its forces and Communist troops, brought American Asian policy to the fore. As the Communist leader Mao Zedong established the People's Republic of China, the American people were disheartened at the loss of a favored ally. Conservative critics of the Truman administration went on the warpath.

America's China policy had been in disarray since the end of the World War II. The long civil war between the Nationalists and the Communists, suspended during the war with Japan, resumed soon after the Japanese surrendered. Between 1945 and 1949, the United States had provided the Nationalist government $2 billion in economic and military aid. In 1946, Truman had sent General George Marshall to China to try to arrange a political compromise with the warring parties. Both sides, each believing that it could win a military victory over the other, refused to share power. Marshall gave up his futile efforts in January 1947, pronounced a plague on both their houses, and returned to America.

In 1947, the Nationalist leader Jiang Jieshi, using American logistical support, launched a major offensive designed to destroy his Communist foes. His armies captured the major cities of China, but in doing so, Jiang's forces spread themselves thin. The Communists controlled the countryside, which contained over 85 percent of the vast Chinese population and provided food for the cities. The Maoist armies besieged the Nationalist troops in the cities. By the summer of 1949, Nationalist forces had lost their will to fight and surrendered en masse. As 1949 ended, Jiang, with a remnant of his government, sought refuge on the island of Formosa (Taiwan).

Washington cut itself loose from the failing Nationalist government in August 1949, a few months before Jiang fled China. A State Department White Paper maintained that the United States had done all it could for the Nationalists. They had lost the civil war because they had not used American assistance properly.

Communist victory in China triggered an intense debate within the United States over foreign policy in general and Asian policy in particular. Bipartisanship, which had prevailed during the years of containing Communism in Europe, disintegrated as Republican leaders attacked Truman's Far Eastern policy. The Asia-first wing of the Republican party and the China Lobby led by Senator Styles Bridges and Congressman Walter Judd charged the Democratic-controlled Congress and the Truman administration with responsibility for Jiang's fall. They insisted that U.S. military involvement in the Chinese civil war could have saved Jiang's government. They asked the rhetorical question: If the essence of U.S. foreign policy was containing Communism without geographical limit as stated in the Truman Doctrine, why did the United States not intervene in China? If Greece and Turkey, why not China?

But China was not America's to lose. Jiang and his corrupt and inept government lost China. The U.S. failure in China was not because of insufficient aid or lack of concern. American leaders never understood the dynamic force of a peasant society ripe for change and the strong appeal of the Maoist land reform program among the Chinese peasants. The mistake the Truman administration made was to continue to cling to Jiang until it was much too late. As historian Barbara Tuchman has observed: "there is little virtue in a client being anti-Communist if he is at the same time rotting from within." But millions of Americans believed the charges brought by the Asia-firsters and the China Lobby. Such beliefs stemmed from a false assumption many Americans made about U.S. foreign policy during the early Cold War era— that the rich and mighty United States could control political events around the globe if only leaders took the right actions. They could see no limits to American power. China had fallen to Communism only because U.S. leaders had blundered, or worse, as Joseph McCarthy and others charged, because disloyal American officials, secretly favoring the Communist forces, had subverted America's China policy.

If the Chinese revolution could have been thwarted, it would have taken a massive and sustained U.S. military intervention. In 1949, the United States lacked the ground troops to intervene in China. Had Truman confronted Congress with the hard choices of either large-scale military intervention or Communist victory in China, they would most likely have opposed direct American involvement in an Asian civil war. The American people did not want to fight a major land war in Asia. But Truman tried to hide the declining status of the Nationalist regime until near the end, hence its collapse came as a sudden shock. His own actions left him vulnerable to Republican accusations that his administration had lost China. Whereas containment of Communism had worked in Europe, it failed in China. The Maoist victory in China was a devastating diplomatic defeat for the United States and a political disaster for the Truman administration.

After the Maoist victory, Secretary of State Dean Acheson wanted to grant diplomatic recognition to the Communist regime, but he changed his mind after Maoists seized American property, imprisoned American citizens, and signed a pact with the Soviet Union. Instead, the United States implemented a policy of nonrecognition and clamped a trade boycott on the world's most populous nation. American officials insisted that Jiang's government now ensconced in Formosa constituted the legitimate government of China. Nonrecognition of mainland China would represent official U.S. policy for the next twenty years, until Richard Nixon made his famous journey to Beijing in February 1972.

VIETNAM: THE BEGINNINGS

The success of the Chinese Communist revolution also had a major influence on U.S. foreign policy in Southeast Asia. Since 1946, the French had been trying to reimpose colonialism on the Vietnamese people. The Vietnamese, led by Ho Chi Minh and General Vo Nguyen Giap, leaders of a nationalist front organization known to the West as the Viet Minh, refused to accept the return of their former imperial masters and waged a guerrilla war that the French could not suppress. U.S. views toward the war in Indochina had been ambivalent. Publicly, the United States took a neutral stance; the Americans did not wish to align themselves with European colonialism in Southeast Asia and were skeptical that the French could defeat the Vietnamese nationalists. But since Ho, Giap, and most of the other Vietnamese leaders were Communists, Americans strongly opposed the idea of another country joining the Communist world. Hence Americans covertly supported the French effort in Vietnam. America also supported the French war in Vietnam because Washington feared that a French defeat in Indochina might weaken Paris's resolve to resist Soviet expansionism in Europe. In 1949, the French made their cause in Southeast Asia more palatable to the Americans when they set up a puppet government in Saigon under the nominal leadership of Bao Dai, a descendant of the last Vietnamese royal family. Now the French could claim, disingenuously, that they were fighting to preserve Vietnamese national independence from the threat of Communism.

The Communist victory in China had a major impact on the Indochinese war. Hitherto the Vietnamese had been fighting alone against the French. Now they had a powerful friend and ally in the Chinese Communists with whom they shared a common border. Soon Chinese economic and military aid flowed to the Viet Minh and the war began to go badly for the French. In February 1950, China and the Soviet Union formally recognized Ho's revolutionary government. Alarmed, the French appealed to the United States for help. Dean Acheson, who had become Secretary of State in 1949, succeeding Marshall, responded by formally recognizing Bao Dai's pseudo-government. In May 1950, the United States began to send economic and military aid to the French forces fighting in Vietnam. A small group of U.S. military advisers arrived in Vietnam during the summer of 1950. On a modest scale, the Truman administration began an American involvement in Vietnam during the summer of 1950 that would last for twenty-five years, include a major war, and ultimately end in disaster for the United States and the people in Southeast Asia whom it tried to help.

NSC-68

Truman's response to the news that the Soviets had developed atomic weapons and the fall of China was to direct Secretary of State Acheson to conduct a full-dress review of American foreign and military policy. Under Acheson's guidance, the review was conducted by the State and Defense Departments, coordinated by the National Security Council. Six months later, analysts produced National Security

Council Document Number 68 (NSC-68), an important top-secret paper that shaped American foreign policy for the next twenty years.

Truman received NSC-68 in April 1950. NSC-68 was mostly written by Paul Nitze. Nitze and his associates assumed continual conflict in the world between the United States and the Soviet Union. It depicted this struggle in stark terms—what was at issue was no less than the survival of America, its free institutions, and its ideals. It assumed that the Soviets would achieve the nuclear capability to destroy the United States within a few years. Hence NSC-68 called for a massive buildup of American military force to resist the Soviet menace anywhere in the world it might arise. It recommended defense budgets of $50 billion per year, a fourfold increase over the $13 billion earmarked for 1950. NSC-68 called these huge expenditures "the necessary price of freedom." The outbreak of the Korean war would give President Truman the opportunity to implement many of the recommendations contained in NSC-68, which militarized containment and transformed it from a regional into a global policy.

WAR IN KOREA

After the fall of China, the Administration forged a new Asian policy. Secretary of State Acheson delineated a new defense perimeter in the Far East, incorporating Japan, Okinawa, and the Philippines. It excluded Formosa, Korea, and Southeast Asia. The new line suggested that nations located within the excluded regions would have to defend themselves against Chinese aggression, or they would have to seek help from the United Nations. Republican leaders vigorously attacked Truman's Asian policy. Senator Joseph McCarthy said it proved that the State Department was riddled with Communists and their fellow-travelers. Senator Robert Taft called it a policy that promoted Communism in China.

As partisan political controversy over American Asian policy continued, the Truman administration confronted another Far Eastern crisis—North Korea's invasion of South Korea. The invasion was rooted in divisions within the country stemming from World War II. As the war ended, Soviet and American troops had occupied Korea. The two nations arranged for Soviet soldiers to accept the surrender of Japanese troops north of the thirty-eighth parallel of north latitude and for American soldiers to accept the surrender of Japanese forces south of that line. Efforts to unify Korea failed and the nation remain divided at the thirty-eighth parallel. North of the boundary, the Soviets created a Communist state and trained an army to defend it. South of the border, the United States supervised the creation of a government headed by Syngman Rhee. The Soviet Union and America removed their troops from the divided land in the late 1940s. Both Rhee and Kim Il-sung, the North Korean leader, sought to unify Korea—one under capitalism and the other under Communism.

Kim moved first. With direct assistance from the Soviets, North Korean forces invaded the South on June 25, 1950, in an effort to unify Korea under Communist control. Kim expected to win an easy victory having calculated that the United States would not intervene given the recent policy statements out of Washington that Korea lay outside the boundary of American vital interests. Kim had received

Stalin's permission to invade South Korea and Mao Zedong concurred. They anticipated a quick victory for the North Koreans and saw the move as advancing their diplomatic interests.

President Truman, surprised by the invasion, conferred with advisers. He understood that if the United States did not intervene quickly, North Korea would overrun the South. He decided to send American troops to try to save South Korea from Communism. He called Korea "the Greece of the Far East." He compared Communist aggression in Korea with Fascist aggression during the 1930s. He said that if the United States let aggression go unchallenged, as the democracies had done in the 1930s, "it would mean a third world war." Truman viewed the conflict in global terms. He assumed the Soviets had masterminded the attack and he believed that U.S. national security and world peace were threatened. Truman also believed that the Soviets were using the invasion as a feint to suck American troops into Korea, leaving Western Europe vulnerable to Soviet attack just at the time that NATO was being implemented. He further shared a concern about Japanese security. Conquest of South Korea would give the Communists airfields within thirty minutes flying time of Japanese cities. Finally, Truman dared not serve up the loss of Korea to the Republicans in an election year that followed so soon after the "loss" of China.

When Truman committed the Armed Forces to the Korean war, he failed to seek a declaration of war from Congress. He claimed he lacked time and he relied on what he called his "inherent war-making powers" as commander-in-chief of the Armed Forces. But the United States did obtain UN endorsement for its Korean intervention. The Security Council approved U.S. military intervention because the Soviet delegate was absent from its sessions. The Soviet representative had been boycotting the Security Council sessions to protest its refusal to replace the Chinese Nationalist delegate with a Communist delegate following Mao's victory. Officially, the Korean war was a United Nations' "police action" to repel aggression against South Korea. In reality, UN sanction furnished a cover for what was mainly an American effort. The United States provided 90 percent of the ground forces and all the sea and air power aiding the South Koreans. All battlefield commanders came from the United States, not from the UN. General MacArthur, whom Truman appointed to head the Korean campaign, took orders from the American Joint Chiefs of Staff.

The war was nearly lost at its beginning. North Korean troops overran most of South Korea except for a small area around Pusan, a seaport at the southern tip of the peninsula. For a time, Washington feared the defenders would be pushed into the sea. But American and South Korean forces finally halted the invaders at Pusan in August 1950. General MacArthur then turned the war around with a brilliantly executed amphibious landing at Inchon 150 miles north of Pusan. American forces moved south from Inchon as other forces broke out at Pusan and headed north. They caught the North Koreans in a giant pincers, and a rout was on. By the end of September, the UN forces had pushed the retreating North Koreans back across the thirty-eighth parallel.

Within three months, the UN mission had been accomplished. The aggressors had been cleared from South Korea. But with the North Korean army in disarray, and the USSR and China apparently not inclined to intervene, Truman decided to go north across the thirty-eighth parallel. General MacArthur enthusiastically approved. Truman's decision to cross the border transformed the war. Containment became rollback, an effort to liberate North Korea from Communism. UN forces set out to destroy a Communist satellite and to unify Korea under a pro-Western government. The Security Council obediently endorsed Truman's decision to transform the war.

At first, all went well. The American forces drove their foes north. Meanwhile the general American military buildup in accordance with NCS-68 continued. The draft had been reinstated. Congress doubled the Pentagon's budget, from $13 billion to $26 billion. Additional troops were earmarked for NATO. The Seventh Fleet was stationed between the Chinese mainland and Formosa to shield Jiang's forces from a possible Communist attack. The war effort enjoyed strong bipartisan support and broad popular approval. The UN forces appeared headed for victory. The North Korean army verged on destruction.

As the UN forces advanced northward, the Chinese issued a series of warnings. When General MacArthur ignored their warnings, the Chinese stated publicly that if UN forces continued their advance, they would intervene. On October 15, 1950, President Truman flew to Wake Island in the mid-Pacific to confer with General MacArthur. MacArthur assured the president that the Chinese would not intervene, and if they did, they would be slaughtered. He also told Truman that he would win the Korean war and "have the boys home by Christmas." Truman accepted MacArthur's assessment and discounted the Chinese warnings. MacArthur launched what he assumed would be the final Korean offensive on November 24. UN forces advanced along two widely separated routes toward the Yalu River border with China and towards Pyongyang, the North Korean capital. Two days later, the Chinese sent more than 300,000 troops swarming across the frozen Yalu. Fighting in terrible winter weather, the Chinese armies split the UN forces and sent them reeling backwards. In two weeks, they drove MacArthur's forces back across the thirty-eighth parallel and down the Korean peninsula.

U.S. officials, who had walked into disaster together, now divided over how to respond to it. MacArthur wanted to expand the war and strike at China. He was supported by many Republicans and some Democrats. He believed the Chinese made the decision to invade Korea on their own. Truman and Acheson assumed the Chinese were carrying out Soviet policies. If they were correct, going to war with China meant going to war with the Soviet Union in Asia. Washington was not prepared to fight World War III. President Truman opted for a return to the original limited UN mission of restoring the prewar status quo in Korea and for continuing the U.S. military buildup in accordance with NSC-68.

In December, the U.S. field commander, General Matthew Ridgway, brought in reinforcements and rallied the American forces. Heavy artillery slaughtered the Chinese forces advancing in massed formations. American naval and air forces helped to blunt the Chinese drive. Ridgway's Eighth Army fought its way back to a point near the thirty-eighth parallel and held that line for the rest of the war. Truce negotiations began on July 10, 1951, but were unproductive for a long time. A seesaw war of trenches and fortified hills would continue for two more years.

During the first months of 1951, as Ridgway's troops held the line in Korea, Truman continued his implementation of NCS-68. Annual military spending reached $50 billion. America committed additional forces to NATO and obtained additional over-seas bases. The Army expanded to 3.6 million men, six times its size when the Korean war began. Military aid was sent to Jiang's Nationalist forces on Formosa. The United States also began to supply military aid to French forces fighting to reimpose colonialism in Southeast Asia. Washington signed a peace treaty with Japan that ended the occupation and restored Japanese sovereignty. The treaty permitted America to maintain military bases in that country. The Truman administration embraced the general strategy of ringing China and the Soviet Union with U.S. military might. Containment had become a global commitment and now packed potent military muscle.

The huge American military buildup did not satisfy Republican critics supporting General MacArthur's proposal to take the war to China. He did not want to hold the line at the thirty-eighth parallel and negotiate; MacArthur wanted a military victory over China and a unified, pro-Western Korea. Ordered by Truman to make no public statements, he defied his commander-in-chief. On April 5, the House Republican leader, Joseph Martin, read a letter from MacArthur to Congress calling for an alternative foreign policy. If victory in Asia required bombing

U.S. soldiers serving in the 2nd Infantry Division, fighting in Korea near the Cmongchon River, December, 1950. *Source:* Dept. of Defense/Acme/UPI/Corbis-Bettmann.

Manchurian bases, blockading Chinese ports, and using Nationalist forces from Taiwan, so be it: "In war there is no substitute for victory." MacArthur's letter also stated: "Here in Asia is where the Communist conspirators have elected to make their play for global conquest." MacArthur rejected Truman's Europe-first orientation, his effort to achieve limited political goals in Korea, and his containment policy. He had issued a fundamental challenge to the administration's foreign policy. Truman dismissed MacArthur and ordered him home. Truman's actions provoked one of the great emotional events of modern American history. The White House was swamped with letters and phone calls, mostly supporting MacArthur. Polls showed 75 percent of the people supported the general. Republican supporters of MacArthur heaped abuse upon the embattled Truman. Many newspaper and magazine editors called for his impeachment.

Much of the uproar over Truman's firing of MacArthur reflected popular disenchantment with the war. Many Americans neither understood nor accepted the concept of limited war for particular political objectives. After all, when an easy military victory appeared possible, Truman himself had tried to take all of Korea, only to revert to the original, limited objective following Chinese intervention. The president wanted to avoid a major war that he feared could escalate into World War III. But MacArthur's contempt for half measures and his stirring call for victory appealed to a nation of impatient idealists. The United States had the power to destroy North Korea. Why not use it?

MacArthur returned to America to a hero's welcome. About 500,000 people turned out to greet him when he arrived in San Francisco on April 16, 1951. Three days later, he addressed a joint session of Congress. His moving speech was interrupted thirty times by applause. Millions of his fellow Americans who watched or heard his speech were equally moved.

As MacArthur basked in public acclaim, Congress investigated the circumstances of his removal. Hearings were held before the combined Senate Armed Services Committee and Foreign Relations Committee. At first, the senators favored MacArthur; but the testimony of the Joint Chiefs, particularly of General Omar Bradley, put the case for containment in Korea forcibly and clearly: Russia, not China, was America's main enemy; Europe, not Asia, was the most important region of American interest. General Bradley stated that fighting China in Asia "would be the wrong war in the wrong place at the wrong time against the wrong enemy." There was also MacArthur's refusal to follow orders and his efforts to make foreign policy over the president's head. The constitutional principle of civilian control of foreign policy and military strategy was at stake. Truman had fired an insubordinate general. Gradually, the tumult subsided and MacArthur faded into quiet retirement. A MacArthur-for-president movement in 1952 never got off the ground.

Meanwhile, in Korea, the truce talks between the Americans on one side and the North Koreans and Chinese on the other dragged on inconclusively and fighting continued. Fighting and talking would continue for two more years, and thousands more American soldiers would die. The main reason for the impasse at the

The Korean War, 1950–1953. *Source:* Moss, *Moving On,* p. 50.

talks was Chinese insistence that captured North Korean and Chinese soldiers be returned to them even though these soldiers wanted to remain in South Korea. The United States refused to return them against their will. An armistice was finally reached on July 27, 1953, when President Eisenhower threatened the Chinese with an expansion of the war. The Chinese yielded and the prisoners remained in the South. The thirty-eighth parallel was restored as the boundary between North and South Korea. To appease Syngman Rhee, who was unhappy with the settlement, the United States furnished his government military aid and kept fifty-thousand American troops in South Korea.

Although it has been forgotten by many Americans, Korea was a major land war in Asia. It lasted for three years and involved over 3 million U.S. military personnel. Its costs exceeded $100 billion. About fifty-four thousand Americans died

General Douglas MacArthur.   *Source:* National Archives.

in Korea, and another 150,000 were wounded. Millions of Koreans and Chinese perished during the war. Korea proved to be an unpopular, frustrating, and confusing war, which ended in a draw. No celebrations greeted its end. Returning Korean veterans melted into society to became part of the 1950s "silent generation." In the summer of 1995, nearly a half-century after their war, elderly Korean veterans attended ceremonies held in the nation's capital to dedicate a memorial to their valiant service.

The Korean conflict significantly influenced U.S. foreign policy. In Korea, the Cold War suddenly turned hot. Containment was transformed from a regional policy to a general global stance. U.S. foreign policy shifted from its Eurocentric focus toward increasing concern in the Far East. War with the People's Republic of China ensured that the United States and China would remain bitter Cold War adversaries for decades. The image of an aggressive Soviet Union commanding a centralized, worldwide Communist movement fastened itself on the American mind. China was seen to be but an extension of Soviet power. Truman incorporated the defense of Formosa and French interests in Southeast Asia into the larger pattern of American containment of Communism in the Far East.

The Korean War transformed the Cold War from a political and ideological conflict into a military struggle. Prior to the war in Korea, containment primarily represented an effort to eliminate the political and economic conditions that spawned Communism. After Korea, containment consisted of setting up military frontiers behind which free societies could develop. America committed itself to maintaining a huge permanent military force in peacetime, although given the crisis atmosphere prevailing during much of the Cold War, the traditional distinction between peace and war was blurred. The military-industrial-complex expanded rapidly as a major component of the permanent war economy. Foreign aid was militarized and the power of the presidency expanded. Truman also extended the draft, raised taxes, and imposed wage and price controls during the Korean War. Although it failed to take hold of American emotions and imprint itself indelibly on the national memory, the Korean War transformed the Cold War and influenced U.S. foreign policy for decades.

THE COLD WAR CONSENSUS

From war's end to the spring of 1947, the Cold War between the United States and the Soviet Union emerged as the major reality shaping America's foreign policy in the postwar world. Containment of Communism evolved as the major American foreign policy response to the emergence of the Cold War. Beginning as a response to perceived Soviet threats to the security of small nations in Southern Europe, containment expanded to include the periphery of East and Southeast Asia in 1950 following the Maoist triumph in China, the U.S. decision to support the French in Indochina, and the outbreak of the Korean War.

As the world split between the former allies widened, most Americans came to support President Truman's "get tough" approach to the Soviet Union. Influenced by the media, Americans increasingly viewed the Soviet Union as the aggressive successor of the destroyed Third Reich. Communism was equated with Fascism, and Stalin was seen as a Red Hitler, a despotic ruler with megalomaniacal ambitions to dominate the new postwar world order. Soviet leaders were depicted as Marxist-Leninist zealots in the service of a master plan for imposing Communism on the world. The great lesson of World War II appeared to be that aggressors could not be appeased. As the Soviet leaders came to be seen as the New Nazis in the world, American leaders vowed to contain them, to prevent aggression and to ensure that there would be no World War III.

Some Americans dissented from Truman's new foreign policy approach. These critics were unprepared for the pressures and pitfalls of the world leadership role that Truman and his senior advisers had designed for America in the postwar world. They opposed the enormous costs of re-armament and foreign aid. They disliked the new internal security controls clamped onto American life, the complexities and tensions of great power rivalries, and the domination of public life by foreign policy issues. Some idealistic Americans did not relish having to support reactionary governments just because they appeared to be threatened by Communism. Liberals such as Henry A. Wallace and conservatives such as Senator Robert Taft of Ohio opposed the Truman Doctrine and the Marshall Plan.

But the dramatic events of the early Cold War years—the Soviet takeover of Eastern Europe, Soviet pressures on Turkey, the civil war in Greece, the Communist coup in Czechoslovakia, the Berlin Blockade, Soviet acquisition of nuclear weapons, the "fall" of China, and the Korean War worked on the American public consciousness to create a consensus supporting the Truman administration's policy of containment. During World War II, cooperation with the Soviets had been a strategic necessity. By 1947, the world had changed dramatically. A revolution in world affairs brought about by World War II necessitated a revolution in U.S. attitudes and approaches to foreign policy. Containing the expansionist tendencies of the Soviet Union had become the new American strategic imperative.

Despite continuing criticism from both Left and Right, a bipartisan consensus in support of the main direction of U.S. foreign policy had emerged in this country by 1947. There was broad agreement spanning all but the fringes of the political spectrum that the major objective of American foreign policy would be the containment of Communism. The American bipartisan foreign policy consensus in support of containment of Communism would remain intact until the Vietnam War cracked it during the late 1960s and provoked the first major debates over American foreign policy goals in nearly twenty years.

COLD WAR AT HOME

As a result of growing hostility between the United States and the Soviet Union, frustrations, tensions, and anxieties gripped American society. The Cold War hit home in early 1950 when millions of Americans were alarmed by charges that Communists had infiltrated their government and many other institutions. Fears of internal threats posed by Communists long preceded the Cold War era. Following World War I, jittery Americans worried lest a Bolshevik-style uprising occur in America. The Red Scare of 1919 and 1920 had culminated in the Palmer raids and mass deportations of radical aliens. In 1938, southern opponents of New Deal agricultural policies established the House Committee on Un-American Activities (HUAC), chaired by Martin Dies. Dies and his colleagues accused New Deal farm officials of marching to Moscow's beat. In 1940, Congress enacted the Smith Act, which made it a federal crime for anyone to advocate the overthrow of the government.

Neither the Palmer raids nor HUAC's accusations of the late 1930s were justified, but fears of Communist subversion arising after 1945 had a basis in reality. During the late 1930s and early 1940s, government security procedures had been lax. Communists had infiltrated government agencies, some of whom spied for the Soviets. Unfortunately, during this Second Red Scare, opportunistic politicians exploited the popular fear of Communism to enhance their power. They vastly exaggerated the menace, harmed innocent people, divided Americans, and undermined basic political freedoms.

The drive to root Communists out of government agencies began in 1945. The Office of Strategic Services (OSS), a wartime intelligence agency, discovered that some of its classified documents had been delivered to Soviet agents. The next year, a Canadian investigating commission exposed the operation of Soviet spy rings within Canada and the United States, and documented subversion that had occurred during the war. These spy revelations, coming at a time when United States–Soviet relations were deteriorating, energized Washington. President Truman established a loyalty program for federal employees in March 1947. Truman also directed the Attorney General to publish a list of ninety organizations considered disloyal to the United States. Truman's efforts resulted in 2,900 resignations and 300 dismissals from various federal agencies. The people dismissed were considered "security risks," among them alcoholics, homosexuals, and debtors thought to be susceptible to blackmail. In most cases, there was no question of employee loyalty. Although federal investigators found no Communists and no spies, the Truman loyalty program heightened public fears of subversion.

Congress was also active. In October 1947, HUAC, with Richard Nixon its junior member, launched a sensational two weeks' long investigation of Hollywood to see if the film industry had been subverted by Reds. Actor Ronald Reagan, president of the Screen Actors' Guild, appeared before the committee to defend the loyalty of his industry. HUAC found little evidence of "celluloid" Communism. But in the aftermath of its investigation, the major studios blacklisted ten writers, directors, and actors who had been uncooperative witnesses during committee hearings. The studios later added others to the blacklist for alleged Communist affiliations. The blacklist spread to radio and television and eventually affected hundreds of people.

As the Cold War escalated into a tense, unrelenting, occasionally terrifying struggle, a great fear of anyone thought to be disloyal spread across the land. Teachers and professors were fired for expressing dissenting views. Books were removed from library shelves. Parent Teacher Association (PTA) leaders were attacked as subversives. Liberal ministers were harassed. Trade unions purged their ranks of Communist influences. Ironically, those who waged the domestic Cold War in the name of national security often undermined the democratic rights and intellectual freedoms for whose sake the United States waged the Cold War against the Soviet Union. The idea that a free and open society, tolerant of wide-ranging discussions and rigorous criticism of American institutions, might be the best defense against the spread of Communism in the United States, was an alien notion to those engaged in the urgent quest for internal security. To many an enthusiastic Red hunter of the early 1950s, it had become necessary to destroy freedom in order to save it.

The domestic Cold War also engulfed the American trade union movement. Within the ranks of the CIO, Communist Party members or individuals supportive of the Communist Party program, held leadership positions in many of the affiliated unions. Often these Communist labor leaders had been skilled organizers who had helped to build the CIO unions into strong institutions. The Communists had risen to positions of power within the ranks of labor because they were committed trade unionists, not because they belonged to the Communist Party. Most of the rank-and-file members of these Communist-led unions were either indifferent or hostile to Communism.

In 1948, Philip Murray, head of the CIO, fearing his organization's vulnerability to attack by powerful antiunion forces for having Communist leaders, began to purge the CIO of its Communist influences. Within a year, eleven unions had been expelled from the CIO. CIO membership fell from 5.2 million to about 3.7 million.

In 1948, the Truman administration went after the leadership of the American Communist Party. The Justice Department put the top leaders of the party on trial for violating the Smith Act. They were convicted and the Supreme Court upheld the verdicts. After the Court had sustained the convictions of the top leaders, the Justice Department prosecuted dozens of lesser figures within the Communist movement over the next several years.

Truman's loyalty program did not quiet popular fears of Communist subversion nor prevent Republicans from exploiting the Communists-in-government issue. One event severely damaged the reputation of the Truman administration and hurt liberal Democrats. In 1949, after the most famous political trial in American history, Alger Hiss was ostensibly convicted of perjury, but in reality, for having been a Communist spy. Hiss, a participant in a Soviet espionage ring during the late 1930s, had risen to become an assistant secretary of state. Hiss had been an adviser at Yalta and had chaired the founding sessions of the United Nations in San Francisco. He had left the State Department in 1947 to become president of the Carnegie Endowment for International Peace. Outwardly, Hiss's public career had been that of a brilliant bureaucrat and model New Dealer.

Hiss's downfall came in 1948 when Whittaker Chambers, a confessed former courier in the same spy ring to which Hiss had belonged, appeared before the HUAC in closed session to accuse Hiss of having been a Communist spy while working for the State Department in 1937 and 1938. He offered no evidence to substantiate his charges. In a later HUAC session, Hiss confronted Chambers and threatened him with a libel suit if he dared make his accusations public. Chambers appeared on a television show, *Face the Nation,* and repeated his charge that Hiss was a former Communist spy. Hiss denied the charge and filed his libel suit. Many prominent public figures backed Hiss and dismissed the charges against him. Among HUAC members, only Richard Nixon, who believed that Hiss was lying, initially backed Chambers's unsubstantiated charges.

To defend himself against Hiss's libel suit, Chambers produced evidence: microfilm copies of sixty-five classified State Department documents which Chambers claimed Hiss had passed to him in 1937 and 1938 to give to the Soviets. A federal grand jury could only indict Hiss for perjury because the statute of limitations on espionage had expired. Hiss was tried twice, his first trial having ended with a hung jury. During the second trial, the prosecution established that many of the documents had been copied in Hiss's handwriting and others had been typed on a typewriter that had belonged to Hiss at the time. Experts dated the microfilm as being from 1937 and 1938. Hiss was convicted and sentenced to five years in prison.

Hiss was HUAC's greatest catch and vaulted Richard Nixon into national prominence. Many liberals believed that Hiss was innocent; they believed that he had been framed by a conspiracy of vindictive conservative political forces. But the Hiss conviction, more than any other event of the domestic Cold War, convinced millions of Americans that there was truth to the oft-made Republican charges that Roosevelt and Truman had not been sufficiently alert to the dangers of Communist infiltration, subversion, and espionage. Americans worried about other undetected

Communist agents who might still be working at the State Department and other government agencies. The Hiss case boosted the anti-Communist crusade at home and legitimated the witch-hunts which followed.

Other events shook the Truman administration. The FBI caught Judith Coplon, a Justice Department employee, passing information to a Soviet agent. In 1949, the Soviets exploded an atomic device, ending the American nuclear monopoly. Soon after this shock came the Communist victory in China. Over 600 million people passed behind the "bamboo curtain." The stage was set for the emergence of a demagogue: widespread fear of a hidden enemy thought to be everywhere, and frustration that victory in the Second World War had brought not eternal peace but only the nightmare possibility of nuclear holocaust.

Enter Senator Joseph McCarthy. In 1950, casting about for an issue that might get him reelected, the first-term senator from Wisconsin decided to see if he could get any political mileage out of the Communists-in-government issue. He had previously used the issue effectively in Wisconsin political battles. McCarthy was by no means the only politician who practiced the politics of anti-Communism; in fact, he was something of a late-comer to the issue. But McCarthy quickly became the political star of the domestic Cold War, and he retained his top billing until his Senate colleagues destroyed his power in late 1954.

McCarthy opened his anti-Communist campaign February 9, 1950, in Wheeling, West Virginia. He told the Ladies' Republican Club of Wheeling that the United States found itself in a weak position in the Cold War because of the actions of disloyal officials in the State Department. Holding up a piece of paper in his right hand, he apparently told his fascinated audience that "I have in my hand" a list of 205 names of Communists working at the State Department. Further, he charged that some of them were in policy-making positions and their names were known to the Secretary of State. An unknown rookie Senator had dared accuse Dean Acheson of permitting known Communists to hold high-level positions in the State Department! A Senate committee, convened to investigate McCarthy's sensational charges, quickly demonstrated that McCarthy not only did not have 205 names, he didn't have even one name. It dismissed his charges as a "fraud and a hoax." Undaunted, McCarthy then accused Owen Lattimore, a prominent expert on Far Eastern affairs, of being the leader of "the espionage ring in the State Department." The charges against Lattimore also collapsed.

Such setbacks at the outset of his campaign might have discouraged a less nervy politician, but McCarthy persisted. He sensed he had a vast following among a public primed by the Hiss case and frustrated by the Korean war. He kept on the offensive. He kept making unsubstantiated charges and naming names. He implied guilt by association and he told outright lies. It was impossible to keep up with his accusations or to pin him down. He called Secretary of State Acheson the "Red Dean of the State Department." He denounced George Marshall, a man with a distinguished record of public service, as a liar and traitor. McCarthy was always careful to make his charges when shielded by his senatorial cloak of immunity that

The pre-eminent practitioner of the politics of anti-Communism, Senator Joseph McCarthy of Wisconsin. For a few years during the early 1950s this ruthless and clever demagogue was the second most powerful politician in Washington. *Source:* National Archives.

prevented his victims from suing him for libel. His smear tactics and use of the "big lie" technique added a new word to the American political lexicon: "McCarthyism."

Several factors accounted for McCarthy's spectacular success. The ground had been prepared by years of Cold War conflict with the Soviet Union and by politicians who had dramatized the issue, frightening Americans with their accounts of the enemy within. J. Howard Mcgrath, Truman's Attorney General, had alarmed the nation in 1949 with his vivid warning:

> Communists . . . are everywhere—in factories, offices, butcher shops, on street corners, in private business. . . . At this very moment (they are) busy at work—undermining your government, plotting to destroy the liberties of every citizen, and feverishly trying, in whatever way they can, to aid the Soviet Union.[3]

Alarms raised by politicians were seconded by prominent media editorials. McCarthy's sense of timing, his ruthless tactics, and his ability to voice the fears of many ordinary American citizens all strengthened his cause. He made skillful use of the news media. Radio and television newscasts carried his charges. Newspapers headlined his accusations. Millions of Americans, frightened by revelations of real espionage, found McCarthy's lies plausible. McCarthy's appeal also came from his being the man with the simple explanation for America's Cold War setbacks: Communists and liberals who secretly supported the Communists had undermined U.S. foreign policy from within. Traitors working within the State Department bureaucracy and other government agencies were responsible for Soviet Cold War triumphs. When he showed popular support during the 1950 elections, his Republican colleagues encouraged McCarthy to go after the Democrats.

---

[3]Quoted in Athan Theoharis, *Seeds of Repression: Harry S. Truman and the Origins of McCarthyism* (Chicago: Quadrangle Books, 1971), p. 136.

Events also played into McCarthy's hands. Two weeks after his Wheeling speech, British intelligence agents discovered the Anglo-American spy ring that had penetrated the atomic bomb project at New Mexico in 1944–1945. The key man in the ring had been a nuclear physicist, Dr. Klaus Fuchs, a German-born, naturalized British citizen assigned to the bomb project. He was arrested and confessed everything. He told the British that he had succeeded in delivering complete information on the bomb to Soviet agents. Using information from Fuchs' confession, FBI agents arrested his American accomplices, Harry Gold and David Greenglass. They, in turn, implicated Julius and Ethel Rosenberg. The Rosenbergs were tried for espionage, convicted, and executed in 1953. The stalemated Korean war also aided McCarthy significantly. As American morale sagged, he attacked those whom he called "the traitors and bunglers in the State Department who were losing the Cold War to the Communists."

POSTWAR POLITICS

Harry S. Truman assumed the presidency in April 1945 ill-prepared and nearly unknown. He brought a mix of talents to the office. He could make and implement decisions; he became famous for placing a sign on his desk that read "the buck stops here." He worked hard, could withstand pressure, and never feared unpopularity. He expressed his views and opinions openly, a trait that a later generation of Americans, sickened by the lies and evasions of Vietnam and Watergate-era politicians, would admire in retrospect.

Truman had difficulties early in his presidency because of his inexperience and because he inherited an administration many of whose members viewed him as an inferior successor to Roosevelt. They lacked confidence in him and he did not trust them. Prominent New Dealers departed and Truman replaced them with more conservative, sometimes mediocre or even corrupt men. Honest and able himself, Truman tolerated cronies belonging to the "Missouri gang," led by an obese politician named Harry Vaughn.

When the war ended, Truman's first major domestic issues involved demobilizing the armed forces and reconverting the war economy to peacetime production. The rush to disarm after the war was irresistible. The Armed Forces were quickly dismantled. When the Army and the Navy could not bring servicemen home fast enough, they rioted overseas. A force that had numbered 12 million at its peak quickly shrank to 1.5 million and the draft was canceled. As the Cold War heated up in 1946 and 1947, the United States had only a small arsenal of nuclear weapons with which to protect Europeans or Asians from Soviet expansion.

As it demobilized its military forces, the nation also confronted the tasks of economic reconversion. Most Americans in 1945 shared a persistent fear that the American economy, no longer stimulated by war spending, would regress to massive unemployment and depression. They feared that millions of suddenly released war workers and veterans could not be absorbed by a peacetime economy. Worried about the economic future, New Dealers called for the federal government

Harry Truman takes the oath of office the evening of April 12, 1945, in the Cabinet Room at the White House. Swearing him to office is Chief Justice Harlan Fiske Stone. Standing between them is the new First Lady, Elizabeth "Bess" Wallace Truman. Standing behind Chief Justice Stone are, from left to right: Speaker of the House Sam Rayburn, Office of War Mobilization Director Fred Vinson, and House Minority Leader Joseph Martin. *Source:* National Archives.

to assume responsibility for full employment by enhancing purchasing power and spending for public works. "Full employment after the war" had been a Democratic campaign pledge in 1944, reaffirmed by Truman after the war. Congress enacted a measure in 1946 called the Employment Act. It established the government's responsibility for maintaining prosperity without prescribing the means to achieve it.

The economy shrank during the first year after the war, mainly because the government abruptly canceled $35 billion in war contracts. The GDP for 1946 was slightly smaller than for 1945, the last year of the war. Unemployment, which had vanished in wartime, rose to 4.5 percent in 1946. But the feared reversion to depression never happened; most war workers and veterans were absorbed into the postwar economy. Many factors accounted for the economy's unexpected resiliency. The GI Bill provided low-interest loans to help veterans buy homes, farms, and businesses. It granted billions of dollars of educational benefits, permitting millions of veterans, many with families, to attend college. Tax cuts strengthened consumer purchasing power and stimulated business activity. Government also aided the business sector by transfering over $15 billion worth of government-owned plants to the private sector, adding some 20 percent to industrial capacity. Further, government spending, although much reduced from wartime levels, remained far higher than prewar levels. But the most important reason for the economy's transition from war to peace without depression lay in an unforseen powerful force. American consumers came out of the war with billions of dollars in savings and with long-frustrated desires to buy new homes, cars, and appliances. Consumer power kept factories humming and people working after war ended.

But unleashed consumer demand, which voided the danger of depression, ignited runaway inflation as the economy was decontrolled. By early 1946, the Office of Price Administration had removed most rationing restrictions, but had kept wage, price, and rent controls. Inflation soared. Desired goods like new cars and refrigerators remained scarce. Businessmen, farmers, and trade unionists demanded removal of all remaining restrictions on their economic activity. A rash of strikes broke out in the auto, meat packing, electrical, and steel industries, idling productive capacity and delaying fulfillment of consumer demands. President Truman tried and failed to ensure a gradual, orderly phaseout of controls by restraining all interest groups.

In the spring of 1946, the bipartisan conservative coalition controlling Congress battled the president over extending the life of the OPA. Congress enacted a weak control measure that Truman vetoed, causing all controls to expire July 1. There followed the worst surge of inflation since 1919. Congress, deluged with angry complaints, hastily passed another, even weaker bill, that Truman signed. Prices continued to soar amidst the politics of confusion. Thereafter, the OPA lifted all remaining controls and faded away. The cost of living rose 20 percent in 1946 and shortages persisted.

Strikes threatened in railroads and coal, two primary industries. Walkouts in both of these industries might have paralyzed the economy. The railroad strike was averted, but not before the president had asked Congress to grant him authority to draft striking railroad workers into the Army. John L. Lewis took his coal miners off the job in April 1946, over wage and pension fund disputes with mine owners. Industrial production dropped. Efforts to settle the strike failed. On May 21, with the nation's supplies of coal exhausted, President Truman ordered the government to seize the mines. The coal mines were administered by Julius Krug, the Secretary of the Interior, who promptly began negotiations with Lewis. They reached an agreement within two weeks and the coal strike ended. The mines were returned to their owners. Truman's bold efforts to prevent the strikes hurt him politically; he and his party lost support among resentful workers that affected the upcoming elections.

As the 1946 elections approached, Truman and his party faced serious political trouble. The Democrats split into their northern and southern wings, with southern conservative Democrats often joining northern Republicans to block liberal measures. Many liberal Democrats still yearned for Roosevelt, dismissing Truman as an inept successor. Truman and his party were blamed both for shortages and for skyrocketing prices. Organized labor, sullen over Truman's threat to draft strikers, made only token efforts to support the Democrats.

Republican congressional candidates attacked the failures of the price control program. They jeered, "to err is Truman." When beef disappeared from meat markets, housewives rioted. When beef was back on the shelf a week later, they were shocked to discover prices had doubled. "Had enough?" chorused Republicans. On the eve of the elections, polls showed Truman's popularity had dropped to 32 percent. The election results mirrored the popular mood. Republicans won majorities in both houses of Congress for the first time since before the Great Depression. Many working class voters deserted the Democrats, shattering the labor bloc that had been solidly Democratic since 1932.

THE EIGHTIETH CONGRESS

A lot of new faces appeared in Washington as members of the Eightieth Congress. Many were veterans, representing a new generation of politicians come of age. One congressional rookie, Republican Richard Nixon, hailed from southern California. Another, Democrat John F. Kennedy, represented a working-class district of the south side of Boston. To the Senate came a conservative Republican from Wisconsin, Joseph McCarthy.

The Republicans took charge of the new Congress. So long out of power, the GOP set out to reassert the authority of Congress and to trim the executive branch. They proposed the Twenty-Second Amendment, which limited future presidents to two elected terms. They wanted to ensure there would be no more presidential reigns such as Franklin Roosevelt's. The Eightieth Congress tore to shreds Truman's liberal domestic program to extend the welfare state. They rejected all his important proposals. Although it did not abolish basic New Deal programs, the Eightieth Congress certainly trimmed its edges.

Senator Robert Taft of Ohio, son of a former president and intellectual leader of the GOP, spearheaded the Republican assault on the New Deal. Taft, who had been in the Senate since 1938, hoped to create a record that would vault him into the White House one day. Taft believed the voters had given the Republicans a mandate to cut the New Deal. He said most Americans wanted lower taxes, less governmental interference in business, and, especially, curbs on the power of organized labor. Twice in 1947, Congress enacted tax cuts. Truman vetoed both measures. A third tax cut was passed over his veto in 1948.

In 1947, Taft led the fight to enact a measure, passed over Truman's veto, modifying the National Labor Relations Act (Wagner Act), the nation's basic labor law and centerpiece of the Second New Deal. The new law, the Labor Management Relations Act, popularly called the Taft-Hartley Act, made many changes in the Wagner Act. It extended the concept of "unfair labor practices," previously confined to management, to unions. Among forbidden union practices were the closed shop, which required a worker to join a union before working. It required unions

Class of 1946: A group of freshman Congressmen introduce themselves in January, 1947. Standing to the right rear of this gathering of rookies are two future presidents, John F. Kennedy and Richard M. Nixon.
Source: National Archives.

to file annual financial statements with the Department of Labor. Cold War concerns could be seen in the requirement that all union officials file affidavits showing they were not members of the Communist Party or any other subversive organization. It prohibited union contributions to national political campaigns, and it forbade strikes by federal employees. In cases of strikes that "affected the national welfare," the Taft-Hartley Act empowered the Attorney General to seek a court injunction ordering an eighty-day delay in the strike. During this eighty-day "cooling off period," federal mediators would try to settle the conflict. If, after eighty days, union members rejected the mediator's final offer, the strike could occur. One section of the new law, Section 14(b), permitted states to legalize the open shop, making union membership voluntary.

Organized labor vigorously attacked the Taft-Hartley Act. William Green, head of the AFL, charged that the bill was forged "in a spirit of vindictiveness against unions." Many workers condemned what they called the "slave labor law." President Truman claimed it was both unworkable and unfair. In addition to general denunciations, labor leaders attacked particular provisions of the new law such as the mandatory eighty-day strike delay feature. Repeal of the new law became the major political goal for organized labor.

The Taft-Hartley Act was the most important social legislation enacted during Truman's presidency. It did not undermine the basic strength of American trade unions which conservatives hoped and liberals feared might happen. The Communist registration requirement was nullified by the Supreme Court. Union membership increased from 14 million at the time of passage to 16 million five years later. During the 1950s, collective bargaining between teams of labor and management representatives generated wage increases and improved fringe benefits that made American industrial workers members of the most affluent working class in history. Later congresses never repealed the Taft-Hartley law, nor even amended any of its major provisions.

THE 1948 ELECTION

As the 1948 election approached, Truman appeared to have no chance for reelection. At times he was discouraged by his inability to lead the country and his low ratings in the polls. In the fall of 1947, he even sent a member of his staff to talk to General Eisenhower, then Army Chief of Staff, to see if Ike might be interested in the Democratic nomination for 1948. Eisenhower was not. Truman then decided to seek reelection. At the Democratic convention held in Philadelphia in July, delegates, convinced Truman could not win, tried to promote a boom for Eisenhower—it fizzled. Disappointed Democrats then held up signs that read "I'm just mild about Harry."

To add to his woes, Truman's party was fragmenting. Splinter groups formed on the left and the right. At the convention, northern liberals forced the adoption of a strong civil rights plank over the furious objections of southern leaders. With its adoption, delegates from Mississippi and Alabama marched out in protest. These renegade southerners later formed their own party, the States' Rights, or "Dixiecrat," party. At their convention, delegates from thirteen states nominated South Carolina Governor J. Strom Thurmond as their candidate for President, who ran on a segregationist platform. These southern defections appeared to remove any remaining Democratic hopes for success. The Solid South, a Democratic stronghold since the end of Reconstruction, had vanished.

The liberal wing of the Democratic party also threatened to split off. Back in 1946, Truman had fired his Secretary of Commerce, Henry Wallace, for publicly criticizing his "get tough" foreign policy toward the Soviet Union. In 1948, Wallace became the presidential candidate of a leftist third party, the Progressive Party. Many New Dealers considered Wallace, whom Truman had replaced as Roosevelt's vice president in 1944, the true heir to the Roosevelt legacy and supported his candidacy. Polls taken that summer showed Wallace could cost Truman several northern industrial states. It appeared that the remnants of his party had given Truman a worthless nomination. But the gutsy leader told the assembled Democrats, "I will win this election and make those Republicans like it—don't you forget that." Few believed him.

The confident Republicans, eager to regain the White House after a sixteen-year Democratic hold on the presidency, again nominated New York Governor Thomas E. Dewey and adopted a moderate program. Dewey, soundly beaten by Roosevelt in 1944, was determined to avenge that defeat this time around. All polls showed him running far ahead of Truman. Dewey opted for a safe, restrained strategy to carry him to the executive office. He raised no controversial issues and he never mentioned his opponent by name.

Truman, with the help of a young assistant named Clark Clifford, had devised an electoral strategy he believed could win. He would stress his adherence to the New Deal tradition, advocating an advanced program of liberal reform. As soon as he got the nomination, he called the Eightieth Congress into special session and reintroduced all his reform programs that the Congress had failed to pass in regular sessions. Again the Congress rejected them. This bold move set the tone for the campaign.

Truman took off on a transcontinental train tour in search of an electorate. He traveled over 32,000 miles and made hundreds of speeches, talking directly to about 12 million people. He repeatedly blasted what he called the "do nothing, good for nothing" Eightieth Congress, blaming all the ills of the nation on the Republican-controlled legislature. He called the Republicans "gluttons of privilege" who would destroy the New Deal if elected. He evoked dire images from the Great Depression and depicted Dewey as Hoover reborn. He insisted that a Republican administration would bring back the grim days of depression. Speaking in an aggressive, choppy style, he delighted his crowds: "Give 'em hell, Harry!" they would yell. "I'm doin' it!" Truman would yell back. Despite his strenuous campaign, he apparently faced certain defeat. Two weeks before the election, fifty political experts unanimously predicted Dewey to win. Pollsters stopped interviewing a week before the election, assuming that Dewey already had it wrapped up.

On election day, Truman scored the biggest upset in American political history. Truman beat Dewey in the popular vote, 24.2 million to 22 million, and 303 to 189 in the electoral college. His party also regained control of Congress by a 54-to-42 margin in the Senate and a whopping 263-to-171 margin in the House. Wallace's campaign fizzled. Most liberals ended up voting for Truman. The Dixiecrats carried only four Deep South states. In reality, a trend toward Truman had surfaced in the final week of the campaign, but the pollsters missed it, since they had already quit taking opinion samples.

How could Truman score such a surprising victory? Republican overconfidence helped. Many Republicans, assuming victory, did not bother to vote. Truman's spirited, grass-roots campaign effort was a factor. But mainly, Truman won because he was able to hold together enough of the old New Deal coalition of labor, northern liberals, blacks, and farmers to win. Truman successfully pinned an anti-New Deal label on the Republicans and identified them with depression memories. Ironically, the splits within his party helped Truman. It sheared off the Democratic left and right and allowed Truman to concentrate on the political center where most of the votes were.

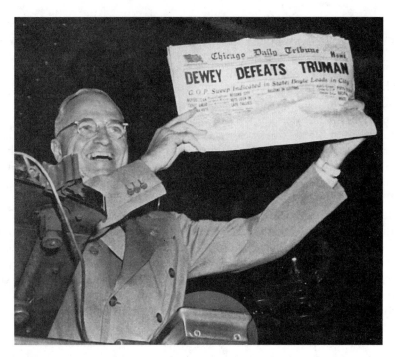

How sweet it was! A jubilant Harry Truman holds up a Republican
paper whose prediction of victory for Thomas Dewey, was to say the
least, a bit premature.   *Source:* Mercantile Library, St. Louis. Used with
permission.

THE FAIR DEAL

Now president in his own right, Truman moved to expand the New Deal as he had
promised during his campaign. In the fall of 1945, Truman had sent an ambitious
package of legislative proposals to Congress only to see them shunted aside during the political scrambling over decontrol and inflation. His January 1949 program
began " . . . every individual has the right to expect from our government a fair
deal." The Fair Deal included controlling prices, improving civil rights, expanding
public housing, raising the minimum wage, expanding Social Security, repealing
the Taft-Hartley law, supporting farm prices, providing federal aid to education,
and implementing national health insurance.

The Eighty-first Congress enacted only a small portion of the Fair Deal. It
raised the minimum wage. It also extended Social Security to 10 million additional
workers and increased benefits 77 percent. The most important Fair Deal measure
to pass in 1949 was the National Housing Act. It provided funds for slum clearance
and construction of 810,000 units of low-income housing over a period of six years.
Most of the Fair Deal never cleared Congress. Truman's civil rights proposals were
thwarted by the threat of a southern filibuster. Federal aid to education was op-

posed by the Catholic church for not including funds for parochial schools. Truman's controversial proposal for compulsory health insurance provoked opposition from the American Medical Association, a powerful doctors' lobby that blocked what it called "socialized medicine."

Most of the measures that passed only extended existing programs. Truman's efforts to expand the boundaries of the welfare state were defeated by a combination of lobbyists, the congressional conservative coalition, and public opinion, which had drifted toward the center. By 1950, the Fair Deal had lost momentum, submerged by Cold War concerns and growing complacency about domestic institutions. Truman, after an initial push for his program, retreated. He spent the rest of his presidency on foreign policy and defending his administration against mounting Republican attacks.

CIVIL RIGHTS

After the war, Americans wanted to re-create the prosperity of the Roaring Twenties, the prosperity they remembered before the long interludes of depression and war. But postwar economic dislocations, particularly rampant inflation and shortages of consumer goods, delayed achieving the goal of affluence. By the late 1940s, middle-class Americans enjoyed the benefits of the greatest industrial power ever. And, disadvantaged groups had begun their long, slow struggle to achieve their share of the American dream.

African Americans continued the struggle against discrimination that had gained momentum during the war. The NAACP pushed court cases that chipped away at the judicial foundations of segregation. Starting in 1947, the Justice Department began to submit friend-of-the-court briefs on behalf of civil rights cases involving public schools and housing. A dramatic breakthrough occurred in 1947 when Branch Rickey, the general manager of the Brooklyn Dodgers, broke the color line of major league baseball by adding a gifted black athlete, Jackie Robinson, to his team's roster. Robinson quickly became an all-star player and future hall-of-famer on a team that won six National League pennants in the next ten years. His success paved the way for other gifted African American athletes, previously confined to segregated black leagues, to play major league ball.

The Cold War brought additional pressure for integrating African Americans and other nonwhite minorities into the mainstream of American life. The United States was now seeking the support of African and Asian nations whose leaders resented American mistreatment of its racial minorities. Jim Crow laws also made the United States vulnerable to Soviet propaganda that sought to highlight the inequities of American democracy and win influence among Afro–Asian peoples.

Truman was the first modern President to promote civil rights causes. His involvement came from both moral and political considerations. He passionately felt a strong need for justice for African Americans. He was also aware of the growing importance of the black vote in northern cities and wanted to offset efforts by

Republicans to regain African American support that they had enjoyed before the Great Depression. Truman had supported creation of the Fair Employment Practices Commission (FEPC) in 1941, and he wanted to extend it after the war. But Congress refused to renew it. In December 1946, President Truman established a Committee on Civil Rights to draft a program. In February 1948, Truman sent Congress the first civil rights message since Reconstruction calling for enactment of a federal antilynching law, creation of a permanent FEPC, the abolition of segregation in interstate commerce, and federal protection of voting rights. Congress rejected Truman's civil rights proposals. Republicans generally ignored the proposals and southern Democrats denounced them.

Truman acted where he had the power to do so. He issued an executive order in February 1948, barring discrimination in all federal agencies. He also began the desegregation of the armed forces. Progress was slow at first in desegregating the military. Segregation persisted in the Army until the Korean War. Integration of the Army occurred during that conflict. Army officers discovered that African American soldiers fought more effectively in integrated units than in segregated ones. It was Truman's most important civil rights victory. The U.S. Army became the most integrated American institution, and many African Americans found opportunities in the military during the 1950s and 1960s not available to them in civilian life. Truman played a major role in bringing civil rights issues to the center of the American political stage. It was his greatest domestic political achievement.

IMPORTANT EVENTS

1945	Harry Truman becomes president
1945	The United Nations is founded in San Francisco
1945	Two atomic bombs are dropped on Japanese cities
1945	World War II ends
1946	Nuremberg war crimes trials begin
1946	The Atomic Energy Commission is created
1947	Truman Doctrine is announced
1947	Major League baseball is desegregated
1947	HUAC investigates Hollywood
1947	The Marshall Plan for European recovery is inaugurated
1947	The National Security Act is enacted
1947	The Taft-Hartley Act is enacted
1948	Berlin Blockade is established
1948	Truman orders the Armed Services desegregated
1948	Truman is elected
1949	NATO is created
1949	The Soviets explode an atomic device
1949	The Chinese revolution succeeds
1949	Alger Hiss is convicted of perjury

1950	Truman orders work to begin on the hydrogen bomb
1950	Senator Joseph McCarthy launches his anti-Communist campaign
1950	The Korean War begins
1950	NSC-68 is implemented
1951	Truman dismisses General MacArthur from his command

BIBLIOGRAPHY

Dean Acheson's *Present at the Creation* is a superb account of the origins of the Cold War by a former high State Department official who was one of the principal architects of U.S. Cold War foreign policy. Stephen Ambrose's *Rise to Globalism: American Foreign Policy, 1938–1980* is an excellent account of the origins of the Cold War. Another good study is by John L. Gaddis, entitled *The United States and the Origins of the Cold War*. Walter LaFeber, in *America, Russia, and the Cold War*, gives a classic account of the Cold War conflict between the United States and the Soviet Union. A fine recent interpretive study of the Cold War is by Thomas J. McCormick: *America's Half-Century: United States Foreign Policy in the Cold War*. John Gimbel's *The Origins of the Marshall Plan* and R. E. Osgood's *Nato: Entangling Alliance* are two important studies of major American postwar foreign policy initiatives in Europe. Akira Iriye's *The Cold War in Asia* is a good account. The best short history of the Korean War is Burton I. Kaufman's *The Korean War*. Robert H. Ferrell, in *Harry S. Truman and the Modern Presidency*, offers a recent short biography of the American leader who presided over the rise of the Cold War. Alonzo L. Hamby's *Beyond the New Deal: Harry S. Truman and American Liberalism* is an account of Truman's Fair Deal programs and their underlying political philosophy. Eric Goldman, in *The Crucial Decade and After: America, 1945–1960*, presents a lively account of the Truman and Eisenhower years. Two good studies of Senator Joseph McCarthy are by Richard Rovere, *Senator Joe McCarthy* and Robert Griffith, *The Politics of Fear*. Allen Weinstein, in *Perjury: The Hiss-Chambers Case*, argues persuasively that Hiss was a secret member of the Communist Party and was guilty of espionage. Richard Freeland's *The Truman Doctrine and the Origins of McCarthyism* is an account of the Second Red Scare. Stephen J. Whitfield's *The Culture of the Cold War* recreates the atmosphere of the 1950s when fear of Communist subversion pervaded American culture.

CHAPTER 10

The Age of Consensus

At the middle of the twentieth century, a majority of Americans enthusiastically participated in a culture of abundance and leisure. The world's most productive economy generated a cornucopia of consumer goods that crowded the shelves and display racks of supermarkets and department stores everywhere. Millions of working-class families owned those twin symbols of American affluence—a home in the suburbs and a gleaming new automobile.

In the larger world, the Cold War conflict between the United States and the Soviet Union raged unrelentingly throughout the 1950s. During the 1950s, the focus of the U.S.–Soviet rivalry shifted to the Third World, to those nations of Africa and Asia emerging from long periods of colonial domination by fading European imperial powers. At home, a bipartisan consensus spanning the American political spectrum supported the American global commitment to contain Communism. The domestic Cold War climaxed in 1954 when the Eisenhower administration combined with the Senate leadership to destroy the power of the preeminent Red-hunter in Washington, Senator Joseph McCarthy. After 1954, the Cold War at home receded; fears and tensions calmed.

At home, critics took a closer look at the affluent society and discovered base metal beneath the glittering surface. Millions of American families were mired in poverty amidst plenty. Many young people were growing up alienated and rebellious. They did not fit in; they refused to join the ranks of organization men. Millions of middle-class Americans, many with all the outward trappings of affluence, found achieving their versions of the American dream insufficient. Some of these anxious souls sought comfort and meaning in religion; some sought escape in popular music, sports, alcohol, and a frenetic social life. Others continued to live lives of quiet desperation. For many Americans in the 1950s, the age of affluence could also be an age of anxiety.

DEMOGRAPHIC PATTERNS

The postwar "baby boom" caused a tremendous population increase as returning veterans and their wives made up for lost time. The American population grew from 153 million in 1950 to 179 million in 1960, the largest decennial increase ever. In 1957, 4.3 million births were recorded, the highest one-year total in American history. That year, demographers discovered that over 50 million Americans were aged fourteen or younger. These young baby boomers created powerful demands for new houses, appliances, toys, and diapers. During the decade of the 1950s, the number of youngsters enrolled in schools from grades kindergarten through twelve increased from 28 million to 42 million. More new schools were constructed during the 1950s, mostly in the burgeoning suburban communities surrounding central cities, than had been built during the first fifty years of the twentieth century. As the U.S. birthrate shot up, the death rate fell. Americans added five years to their life expectancy during the 1950s. Death rates among young people declined dramatically. New "miracle drugs" such as penicillin and cortisone took much of the misery out of life. Polio vaccines tamed a cruel childhood disease that often had left its victims crippled and helpless for life.

Suburban growth, underway in the late 1940s, exploded during the 1950s. Millions of families, seeking new homes and jobs, or just fleeing a myriad of urban problems, moved from metropolitan centers to outlying communities. By the end of the decade, the suburban population of 60 million equaled that of the rest of urban America. During the 1950s, most large cities within the United States lost population. Of cities with more than 1 million people, only Los Angeles grew significantly during the decade. The flight to the suburbs transformed living patterns for millions of middle-class families at mid-century.

Americans in the 1950s were not only the richest and healthiest generation ever, they were also the most mobile. Regionally, the American population continued its shift west and south. By the millions, people poured into the South, the Southwest, and the West. California, Florida, and Texas added millions of new residents. Soon the sunbelt encompassed most of the southern rim of the nation from southern California to the Florida coast. Americans moved in search of better jobs and business opportunities, as well as the more spacious lifestyles possible in Sunbelt suburbs. The economic foundations of the Sunbelt's spectacular population boom included agribusiness, aerospace, electronics, oil, real estate, and a large infusion of military spending. Low taxes and right-to-work laws also attracted industry to the southern rim. Rural America continued to lose population during the 1950s. The depopulation of the countryside, a demographic trend that had accelerated during the years of World War II, continued into the postwar era and the Fifties.

AN ECONOMY OF ABUNDANCE

War spending restored American prosperity in the early 1940s, ending a decade of depression and beginning an era of sustained economic expansion and rising living standards lasting until the 1970s. Between 1945 and 1960, the gross domestic product (GDP) doubled. During the 1950s, the American economy grew at an average rate of 4.0 percent per year, despite enduring periodic recessions. Between 1946 and 1960, the American workforce grew from 54 million to 68 million jobholders. Median wages in manufacturing industries rose 60 percent, and median family income rose from $3,000 to $5,700 during that same period. Since the rate of inflation remained low, about 2 percent per annum for the decade of the 1950s, wage increases translated into significant gains in purchasing power and rising standards of living. Unemployment rates remained low, averaging around 4 percent for the decade. During the 1950s, millions of Americans could afford goods and services that would have been beyond their means in previous decades. The rapidly growing American economy generated an abundance that became the envy of the world. During the 1950s, the United States, with about 5 percent of the world's population, consumed over one-third of its goods and services.

Credit enhanced consumer purchasing power. Short-term installment credit, mainly for new cars, increased fivefold from 1946 to 1960. A revolution in spending patterns got underway in 1950 when the Diners' Club introduced the general credit card, followed soon by American Express. During the decade, oil companies and department stores issued millions of revolving credit cards. Private debt within the affluent society climbed from $73 billion to $200 billion during the decade of the 1950s. Consumer demand stimulated huge private sector investment in new plant capacity and new technology, an average of $10 billion per year. Automation, the use of self-regulating machines to control manufacturing operations, enhanced the nation's industrial productivity.

Big business grew bigger during the postwar era. Another wave of mergers swept the industrial economy. By 1960, America's 200 largest industrial corporations owned over half the nation's industrial assets. But, unlike the merger waves of the 1890s and 1920s, which joined businesses within the same economic sectors, the 1950s mergers brought together businesses in unrelated fields. Conglomerates like International Telephone and Telegraph (ITT) united a car rental company, a home construction company, a retail food outlet, a hotel chain, and an insurance company under the same corporate roof.

THE CAR CULTURE

Automobiles remained the most important American industry during the 1950s. New car and truck sales averaged 7 million units annually during the decade. By 1960, there were 70 million vehicles on the nation's roads and highways. Two-thirds of the nation's employees commuted to work by car. The number of service stations, garages, and motels all increased rapidly.

The growth of suburbia and the automobile boom occurred together. Suburbia required automobiles. Mothers driving station wagons piled full of kids on their way to school, to shopping centers, or to team practice became the reigning symbol of the 1950s suburban lifestyle. In the late 1950s, the federal government undertook to build an interstate highway system funded mainly by gasoline taxes. Summer traveling vacations became the great American pastime. The huge highway building project also included the construction of thousands of miles of freeways connecting the new suburbs to the central cities. Government road building amounted to a subsidy for the American car culture that promoted suburban growth and urban decay.

As the numbers of cars on the roads multiplied, they became longer, wider, more powerful, and gaudier. Detroit reached its pinnacle in the late 1950s. Automakers outdid themselves creating chromium ornaments, two- and three-tone color combinations, soaring tailfins, and gas-guzzling V-8 engines. The buying public was delighted with Detroit's offerings, which also included wrap-around windshields, power steering, automatic transmissions, air conditioning, and hi-fi radios. Advertisers stressed the power, the flashiness, even the sex appeal of these elaborate machines. Popular entertainers such as Pat Boone appeared on television to sing: "See the U.S.A. in your Chevrolet." Advertisers linked owning a new car with participating in the very essence of what it meant to be a successful American: What was more American than apple pie, mom, and your new Ford or Chevrolet? Domestic automakers had the American market all to themselves;

A big gleaming new car was one of the supreme status symbols of the affluent society. Here a 1954 Buick Super Riviera shines in all its glory. *Source:* National Archives.

imports accounted for less than 1 percent of sales in 1955. Gas was cheap and plentiful at 25¢ to 30¢ per gallon. A big gleaming new car was one of the supreme status symbols of the affluent society, a shining testament to America's technological world supremacy. It would be left to later generations of urban planners to worry about the decay of mass transit, the decline of smog-choked inner cities, and freeway gridlock.

GROWTH INDUSTRIES AND OTHERS

The chemical industry grew even faster than the auto business during the 1950s. DuPont's slogan, "Better things for better living through chemistry," became known to every television viewer. DuPont, Dow, and the other chemical giants turned out a never-ending feast of new synthetic products—aerosol spray cans, dacron, and new plastics like vinyl and teflon.

Electricity and electronics also grew rapidly in the postwar era. A horde of new electric appliances sprang forth—air conditioners, electric blankets, automatic clothes washers, clothes dryers, and hair dryers. The electronics industry expanded mainly because of the advent of television. By the early 1950s, dealers were selling 6 million new TV sets each year. Other popular electronic products enjoyed wide sales during the 1950s. Almost every one of the nearly 60 million new cars sold in the decade had a radio. Transistors made possible the development of new computer technologies. International Business Machines (IBM) marketed its first mainframe computers, inaugurating the postindustrial age. In 1960, the Xerox corporation marketed its 914 copier, thereby inaugurating a revolution in document copying. The aerospace industry kept pace with other growth industries, stimulated by multibillion dollar contracts to supply the Pentagon with sophisticated military hardware. Air travel increased rapidly after 1945 and took a quantum leap forward in 1958 with the introduction of regularly scheduled commercial jet travel.

Although postwar growth industries flourished, some traditional heavy industries and manufacturing declined, such as railroads, coal mining, and textiles. Long-haul trucking and air travel cut heavily into railroad freight and passenger business. Coal could no longer compete with oil, natural gas, and electricity. Cotton and woolen manufacturers succumbed to synthetic fibers spun out by the chemical companies. Americans increasingly wore clothes made of nylon, orlon, and polyester. Industrial decline brought permanent depression to New England mill towns and Appalachia, creating pockets of poverty amidst general affluence.

Agriculture changed drastically in the postwar years. Farmers produced more foodstuffs than consumers could buy; commodity prices dropped. Profits could be made in farming only by reducing unit costs of production through intensive use of fertilizers, pesticides, expensive farm machinery, and sophisticated managerial techniques. Larger farms prospered from a combination of greater efficiency and government subsidies. Small farmers got squeezed out and joined the rural exodus to the cities. The nation's farm population dropped from 25 million at the end of the war to 14 million in 1960. The number of agricultural workers dropped to just 6 percent of the workforce. In regions of Arizona, Florida, and California, huge corporate farms dominated many agricultural sectors. These "agribusiness" enterprises were replacing the family farm.

THE MIXED ECONOMY

The federal government stimulated economic growth during the 1950s in many ways. Washington dispensed billions of dollars annually as welfare payments, social security checks, and farm subsidies. Congress funded over half the nation's industrial research and development, and over half of all university scientific research. The Federal Reserve Board regulated the money supply and interest rates. Other government bureaucracies regulated the securities industry, interstate transportation, aviation, and the communications industry. During the 1950s, military budgets pumped $40 billion to $50 billion per year into the economy. During the 1950s, government spending as a percentage of the gross national product increased steadily. The number of Americans working for government at all levels increased 50 percent in the decade. The prosperity of many locales became dependent on government purchases or government payrolls.

Americans at mid-century celebrated what they were fond of calling the American free enterprise system. But economic reality was more complex and ambiguous than their simplistic rhetorical labels implied. Out of their efforts to battle the Great Depression and to produce the materials needed to win World War II, Americans had fashioned a mixed economy that blended public and private enterprise. Government spending and regulatory activities had become integral elements of the mixed economy. The mixed economy conformed to no economic model or theory. Most Americans did not understand its nature or how it worked. But they were delighted with its prime creation—the culture of abundance.

LABOR AT MID-CENTURY

Organized labor prospered during the 1950s as trade unions won wage increases and new fringe benefits from corporate employers. The United Auto Workers and General Motors agreed to a clause in their contract calling for automatic annual cost-of-living adjustments in wages. That agreement set a pattern soon copied in other industries and occupations. Corporate managers discovered that it was more profitable to negotiate wage increases with union representatives and pass their increased costs on to consumers than to engage in lengthy strikes with strong unions. Organized labor remained a powerful force within the Democratic Party, which normally controlled Congress during the 1950s. George Meany declared in 1955, "American labor never had it so good." Labor's major accomplishment came with the merger of the AFL and CIO in 1955. Creation of the AFL-CIO brought 90 percent of America's 18 million unionists into a single national labor federation, headed by George Meany.

Labor also faced serious problems during the era. Corruption riddled several unions. Senator John McClellan of Arkansas chaired a Senate committee that investigated union racketeering in 1957. The McClellan committee exposed widespread corruption in the Teamster's Union. Robert "Bobby" Kennedy served as chief counsel for the committee and his brother, Senator John F. "Jack" Kennedy, also served on the committee. They found that Teamster officials had involved themselves in a wide range of crooked activities including misappropriation of union funds, rigged elections, extortion, and association with members of organized crime. Committee investigations led to the enactment of the Landrum-Griffin Act in 1959. This labor reform measure expanded the list of union unfair labor practices. It also contained anticorruption provisions to safeguard democratic election procedures within unions and to make misuse of union funds a federal crime.

Trade unions also confronted a more fundamental problem than racketeering during the late 1950s. Union membership peaked in 1956 at 18.6 million and declined thereafter. The American economy continued to grow and prosper after 1958, but organized labor could not keep pace. Many industries moved to the South to take advantage of lower wage levels and greater numbers of nonunion workers. But even where unions remained strong, workers were less inclined to join unions than before, primarily because, without joining, they received the higher wages and benefits union negotiators had obtained. Most important, the economy was shifting from a production orientation to a service orientation, which meant a shift from blue-collar occupations to white-collar jobs. White-collar workers generally resisted efforts of union organizers in the 1950s. As white-collar jobs multiplied in the growth sectors of the economy, technological innovations eliminated jobs in mining, manufacturing, and transportation.

POVERTY AMIDST PLENTY

Millions of American families lived beyond the boundaries of abundance. In 1960, according to the Bureau of Labor Statistics, about 40 million Americans representing 25 percent of the population were poor. The elderly, people over sixty-five, made up one-fourth of the poor. A fifth were nonwhite, including 45 percent of the black population. Two-thirds of the poor inhabited households headed by a person with an eighth-grade education or less. One-fourth of poor people lived in a household headed by a single woman. The poor congregated in the inner cities as middle-class people moved to suburbia. Between 1945 and 1960, over 3 million black people, most of them unskilled and many of them illiterate, moved to northern and western cities from the rural South. Poor whites from Appalachia joined blacks in this migration from the country to the cities. Many poor people also inhabited rural America in the 1950s. Both white and black tenant farmers and sharecroppers were mired in a life cycle of poverty and hard work. A famous television documentary shown in 1960, the "Harvest of Shame," narrated by Edward R. Murrow, depicted the poverty and hopelessness of the migrant farm workers.

Some of the poverty in mid-century America could be attributed to the failure of the welfare state forged during the New Deal era to provide for poor people. Its benefits had gone to groups who were organized to pressure Congress. The Wagner Act did nothing for nonunion workers. Minimum wage laws and Social Security benefits did not extend to millions of low-income workers in dozens of occupations. Welfare programs available to poor people maintained them at subsistence levels.

Woman made up a large percentage of poor Americans at midcentury. Few well-paying jobs were open to women in the 1950s. A greater portion of women's jobs than men's jobs were not covered by minimum wage or Social Security protections. Also, divorced women usually were saddled with major child-rearing responsibilities. Ex-husbands often failed to make child-support payments. Many divorced women with children slipped into poverty.

Few officials showed any interest in the plight of poor Americans during the 1950s. Publicists focused on celebrating the achievements of the affluent majority. The poor themselves were silent. They lacked organization and leaders to call attention to their problems. They inhabited another America, neglected and suffering in silence, beyond the boundaries of affluence, an invisible minority amidst a rich society.

THE RISE OF SUBURBIA

America experienced the greatest internal population movement in its history in the fifteen years following World War II when 40 million Americans fled the cities for the suburbs. Young, well-educated, white middle-class people led the flight to the suburbs. Many factors combined to create this mighty exodus from the inner cities to the outlying areas. Families fled traffic jams, high taxes, contact with racial minorities, overcrowded schools, high real estate prices, and high crime rates. Suburbia beckoned for many reasons: The obvious attraction of open country where spacious houses could be built for a fraction of what big-city construction would cost. People wanted homes with yards where, as one father put it, a kid could "grow up with grass stains on his pants." Suburban homes also promised privacy and quiet not found in crowded city apartments. Many suburbanites sought a community of like-minded people and accessible local government.

The rapid rise of suburbia in the postwar era was made possible by an alliance between the central government and the private sector. Government subsidies permitted millions of families to move into suburbia who otherwise could not have afforded to do so. Low-interest mortgages requiring little or no down payments and tax subsidies produced a postwar housing boom. A burst of federally funded highway construction connected the central cities with surrounding bedroom communities.

During the 1950s, contractors built an average of 2 million new homes a year. Across the country developers busily tossed up new housing tracts, replacing forests, bean fields, fruit orchards, and grazing lands. By 1960, over 60 percent of American families owned their homes, the most significant accomplishment of the affluent society. Businesses also moved to the suburbs in response to the growing demands of suburbanites. Suburban shopping centers multiplied; by 1960, there were 3,840 such centers sprawled across the nation. They transformed shopping patterns throughout the nation. Suburban dwellers needed no longer to shop in the central cities; they bought whatever they needed in suburban stores.

Some suburban developments were tossed up virtually overnight. Using mass production and merchandizing techniques, William Levitt built Levittown on Long Island, 30 miles east of New York. Between 1947 and 1951, Levitt built seventeen thousand homes, along with seven village greens and shopping centers, fourteen playgrounds, nine swimming pools, two bowling alleys, and a town hall—on land where farmers had only recently grown potatoes. Other Levittowns soon appeared in Pennsylvania and New Jersey.

The Levittowns were immediate successes; tens of thousands of young families, many of them headed by veterans, left their urban neighborhoods and joined the rush to the suburbs. But social critics made Levittown stand as a metaphor for the postwar failings of American suburban society. They condemned Levittown for its uniform houses lined up on uniform roads in a treeless communal waste. According to critic Lewis Mumford, Levittown homes were inhabited by people of the same class, the same income, the same age group, watching the same fare on

Levittown, Long Island, New York, USA, during the 1950s.
Source: National Archives.

television, eating the same tasteless prefabricated foods from the same home freezers. Both inwardly and outwardly, in every aspect of their lives, the denizens of Levittown conformed to the same common mold.

Mumford's indictment was exaggerated and wrong in many of its particulars. Although suburbs tended to be internally homogeneous, they were typically differentiated along social and economic lines. Suburbs were identified as working-class towns, middle-class areas, or elite enclaves of upper-middle-class families. Analysts of suburban culture observed that ethnic identities attenuated in suburbia; in that sense, suburbs tended to make people more homogeneous. Suburban community identities were based more on shared styles of consumerism than on ethnic ancestry or culture.

While ethnicity declined in mid-century America, suburbanization separated Americans racially. Most African American families remained in the big cities as white families headed for the suburbs. The national metropolitan pattern became one of predominantly black cities encircled within white suburbs. The 1960 census showed suburbia to be 98 percent white; it also showed that some of the nation's larger cities—Washington, D.C., Newark, Richmond, and Atlanta—had black majorities. As the white middle classes moved out, the central cities declined. Urban tax bases shrunk, social services shriveled, and crime rates soared. A consequence of the white flight to suburbia that left black inner city populations entrapped in deteriorating ghettos would be the fiery urban riots during the summers of 1965–1968.

THE CULTURE OF AFFLUENCE

A vast increase in the size of the middle classes was the most important characteristic of the affluent society. The postwar class structure resembled a "diamond" instead of a "pyramid," with the "bulge" of the diamond composing the 60 percent of the population that had become middle class. A large increase in college enrollments accompanied the growth in numbers of middle-class households. A college education became accessible to young people from average American families. As the 1950s ended, nearly 4 million young people were enrolled at more than two thousand colleges and universities across the land. This large college population sought the conventional goals of family, career, and a home in the suburbs. College campuses were quiet, businesslike places during the 1950s. Students shunned politics, radicalism of any kind, and intellectual adventure. Observers labeled these careful young men and women of the 1950s the "silent generation."

American teenagers often set popular cultural trends during the 1950s. A teen culture flourished as a result of teens having money to spend and clear consumer preferences. Merchandizers responded synergistically to these teenage consumers. Ray Kroc, a traveling salesman from Chicago, observed a small drive-in restaurant in San Bernardino, California, that was doing a thriving business. It sold only hamburgers, french fries, and milk shakes, and it sold them fast. Its owners, Dick and Mac McDonald, had applied assembly-line, mass-production technology to the preparation of food, and in the process had invented the fast food restaurant. With borrowed money, Kroc concluded a business arrangement with the McDonalds that permitted him to establish a chain of fast food restaurants using their name and modeled on their format. The first McDonald's, complete with twin golden arches, sprang out of the prairie soil of Des Plaines, Illinois, a suburb of Chicago, on April 15, 1955. By the end of the decade, there were hundreds of McDonald's restaurants spreading across the country selling hamburgers for 15¢, french fries for a dime, and milk shakes for 20¢.

In the same year that Ray Kroc opened the first McDonald's fast food restaurant in the midwestern heartland, Walt Disney offered Disneyland to American consumers. Disneyland, located in Anaheim, California, a suburb that lay 30 miles southeast of Los Angeles, immediately attracted hordes of visitors, mostly families with children. It featured combinations of fairy tale images derived from Disney's earlier animated masterpieces and sanitized historical images from his live-action films. Some areas of the park—Main Street, Frontierland, and Adventureland—featured vast displays of the totems of Americana. Young people could also take a Jungle Cruise and conquer the "dark continent." They could take a cruise on the steamboat *Mark Twain* down a man-made river. They could enter the Enchanted Tiki Room where mostly white visitors mingled with friendly ethnic stereotypes. They could be inspired by a larger-than-life robotic Abraham Lincoln who, in a deep, rumbling voice, declaimed the virtues of constitutional democratic governance.

Much teenage spending centered around fads and pop music. The most popular musical style to emerge in the 1950s was rock 'n' roll, an amalgam of black rhythm-and-blues and country-and-western idioms. Elvis Presley, the first rock 'n' roll superstar, shot to the top of the hit parade in 1956 with a series of superhits, "Heartbreak Hotel," "Blue Suede Shoes," and "Hound Dog." Crowds of teenage girls screamed hysterically at Presley's highly suggestive stage performances, particularly his gyrating hips that kept time with the frenetic chords he banged out on his electric guitar. Presley's performing style became a symbol of youthful rebellion. His concerts provoked criticisms from parents, teachers, and ministers. The Presley rebellion was implicit in his music, in its rhythms, which excited youngsters and provoked sexual fantasies. Presley himself was anything but a rebel. He was an artist and showman, a champion of traditional values. Student radicals of the 1960s outraged him.

Controversy over the moral threat to young people posed by rock 'n' roll music in the late 1950s was closely linked to a taboo subject, sexual behavior. An Indiana biology professor, Dr. Alfred Kinsey, had published *Sexual Behavior in the Human Male* (1948) and its sequel, *Sexual Behavior in the Human Female* (1955). Kinsey interviewed thousands of subjects and used statistical analyses to produce the first scientific study of American sexual behavior. Among his most important findings, Kinsey discovered that premarital sexual relations, adultery, and homosexuality were more widespread than previously thought.

Elvis Presley with fans.
Source: Mercantile Library, St. Louis.
Used with permission.

WOMEN: FAMILY LIFE AND WORK

The immediate postwar years were a time of transition, frustration, and confusion for many American women. *Life* magazine ran a feature in 1947 entitled "The American Woman's Dilemma." Its author found that many women were torn between the traditional expectations that they stay home and their desire to work outside the realm of domesticity. Millions of women continued to work outside the home, mostly because they had to. Whether they wanted to work or not, more and more women married and gave birth to children in the postwar era. During the late 1950s and the decade of the 1960s, the family was the most rapidly growing social institution. It was these new families, which held down well-paying jobs, purchased suburban homes, reared children, and made the consumer purchases, that kept the mighty U.S. economy growing and prospering.

America became more child-oriented after the war. Dr. Benjamin Spock published the first edition of his *Baby and Child Care* in 1946, which strongly influenced child-rearing practices in the postwar era. Dr. Spock advised women to make child-rearing their most important task, to put their children's needs first. Early editions of his book also advised women to stay home and not work outside the home so they would be available to meet all their babies' needs. Some psychiatrists, influenced by Sigmund Freud's writings, criticized working women. They claimed women could only be fulfilled and happy through domesticity. They considered women who held jobs outside the home to be neurotic feminists trying to be "imitation men." They argued that a women's gender determined her role in life. Anatomy was destiny.

In 1956, *Life* magazine published a special issue on American women. It profiled housewife Marjorie Sutton as a successful woman who fulfilled her feminine potential. She was mother, wife, home manager, and hostess. She was active in PTA, Campfire Girls, and charity work. Married at sixteen, Sutton had four children, and she did all the cooking, cleaning, and sewing for her family. She also helped her husband's career by entertaining his business clients.

Films of the 1950s highlighted sex symbols like Marilyn Monroe or wholesome heroines like Doris Day. They became role models for women to follow. Women's fashions stressed femininity at the expense of practicality or comfort. In *Modern Woman: The Lost Sex*, one of the authors called feminism a "deep illness." There were strong pressures on women to conform to the prevailing sexual stereotype. During the decade, no organized feminist movement existed to challenge the prevailing feminine mystique.

Mid-century women were caught in a dilemma. According to the prevalent ideologies, the ideal role for women was found in the home. Her fulfillment lay in creating an island of love and security for her children and husband, with scant regard for her own needs. But millions of women, continuing the wartime trend, worked outside their homes during the 1950s. The female labor force expanded from 17 million in 1946 to 22 million by 1958. By 1960, 40 percent of women were employed full- or part-time. Millions of working women had to work, being their family's only source of income. Others worked to supplement family income. Despite the burgeoning cult of motherhood, most new entrants to the female job market after the war were married women with children. The feminine mystique collided with economic reality and caused confusion and stress.

Another factor strongly influenced family life and the roles of women during the 1950s, a consequence of American social history. Millions of American families during the 1950s were headed by men and women who had grown up amidst the economic deprivations of the Great Depression of the 1930s. They had been young adults during World War II, experiencing the loneliness and physical separation from friends and family inherent in military service in wartime. After experiencing fifteen years of economic and emotional insecurity, they were determined to enjoy the material security of the affluent society, and they were equally determined to have the emotional security found in cohesive family life. These men and women made the baby boom and championed "togetherness." The term "togetherness" first appeared in a 1954 *McCalls* article. It meant a happy family melded into a team; specifically, the woman fusing herself with her husband and children. Family life was oriented around shared activities—television watching, backyard barbecues, outings to parks and beaches, and vacation trips.

THE ADVENT OF TELEVISION

By 1953, two-thirds of American households owned television sets. Television entered politics. It became an all-encompassing cultural force. Art and culture came free, and with an ease of accessibility never before available. Mostly television brought popular entertainment and commercials. Prime-time television entertainment included situation comedies, action-suspense thrillers, family drama, variety shows, and Westerns. Tuesday night belonged to the king of comedy, "Uncle Miltie" Milton Berle. Other comedic stars included Phil Silvers as *Sergeant Bilko*, Lucille Ball in *I Love Lucy*, and Sid Caesar and Imogene Coca in *The Show of Shows*. *Dragnet*, a detective series starring Jack Webb, was popular year after year. Family togetherness was the theme of *Father Knows Best*, starring Robert Young. The most popular television shows during the 1950s proved to be Westerns. At one time, there were thirty-nine Western shows on each week. CBS showed most of the top Westerns, including *Have Gun Will Travel*, which starred Richard Boone as "Palladin," a hired gunman from San Francisco who killed wicked men in the Old West. The most durable of the 1950s television Westerns turned out to be *Gunsmoke*, starring James Arness as Marshall Matt Dillon enforcing the law in Dodge City, Kansas. But television functioned mostly as a commercial instrument, an advertising conduit, the most intrusive yet invented. Television quickly became the vital center of the consumer culture, a vast educational enterprise teaching American consumers about the latest styles of mass consumption and creating wants and needs for the multitudinous products of consumer civilization.

RELIGION REVIVED

Religion enjoyed a revival during the 1950s. President Eisenhower tied religion to patriotism when he observed recognition of God was "the most basic expression of Americanism." With America locked in Cold War with godless Communists, religious worship became one of the crucial dimensions of Americanism. Religion was also promoted as bonding family members together in worship: "The family that prays together stays together." The Bible topped the best-seller list every year during the 1950s. Congress inserted the words "under God" in the Pledge of Allegiance to the American flag recited in classrooms. Hundreds of new suburban churches appeared during the 1950s. From 1945 until 1960, church attendance in this country increased 50 percent. A Baptist evangelist, Billy Graham, emerged as the major leader of a mass movement back to Bible fundamentalism. Bishop Fulton Sheen became a prominent television personality talking to millions about ethical and spiritual issues. A minister with training in psychology, Dr. Norman Vincent Peale, was the most popular preacher of the 1950s. His landmark book, *The Power of Positive Thinking*, sold millions of copies. Peale preached a gospel of reassurance. He told anxious listeners that God watched over Americans, assuring individual success in careers and victory over Communism in the Cold War.

A public opinion poll taken in 1955 showed that 97 percent of Americans believed in God and two-thirds claimed to attend church regularly. America remained the most religious nation in the West. Religion played a serious role in the lives of millions of American families. For others, religious belief became intermixed with patriotism, family togetherness, and Thursday night bingo. Religion could also serve as a means of establishing ones social identity, of becoming a member of the American community.

SOCIAL CRITICS

Suburban society, mass culture, and the consumer economy generated a new American social character. William Whyte, author of the best-selling *The Organization Man,* claimed that Americans no longer followed the traditional individual success ethic. They embraced what Whyte termed on "organizational ethic" that stressed belonging to a group and being a team player. Corporations employed more and more Americans. Within these large companies, bureaucratic management styles prevailed. Businesses encouraged their employees to look, dress, and act alike. Each appeared to be The Man in the Gray Flannel Suit, the title of a best-selling 1950s novel by Sloan Wilson.

The urge to conform spread to the general society. A classic study of the postwar social character, sociologist David Riesman's *The Lonely Crowd,* highlighted the lonely individual lost within mass society. Riesman observed that mobility had uprooted people from their traditional moorings. Old values no longer offered guidance or meaning. People were cast adrift morally. Young people adapted to the new social environment by embracing peer group norms and turning to television for guidance. They consumed their values as they did their breakfast cereals. Unpopularity with peers was more to be feared than violations of personal standards, which were often confused. People valued success in the personality market more than retaining their integrity.

Riesman called this new American character type "other-directed" in contrast to the traditional "inner-directed" American who internalized individualistic success values early in life from his parents and thereafter follows his destiny. Other-directed men preferred to join the lonely crowd, not lead it. Other-directed workers were better adapted to fill the niches of the consumer economy. The American workforce at mid-century was predominately white-collar. New jobs were mostly generated in service sectors—sales, advertising, customer service, clerical, accounting, and the like. Organization men, whose tickets to employment were high-school diplomas or college degrees instead of union cards, proliferated.

REBELS

Not everyone was caught up in the culture of conformity during the 1950s; rebels, especially young people, rejected the manners and mores of the affluent society. Juvenile delinquency increased, and violent gangs of brawling teenagers staged gang fights in the streets of New York and Chicago. Bands of motorcyclists roamed the streets and highways. Some middle-class youngsters dropped out of the college-career "rat race." They joined Bohemian enclaves in Greenwich Village and San Francisco's North Beach district. Herb Caen, a San Francisco columnist, dubbed these dropouts "beatniks"; they preferred to call themselves the "beat generation." "Beats" confronted the apathy and conformity of American society; they went out of their way to defy prevailing norms of respectability. They abandoned materialistic values to embrace poverty. They lived in cheap flats, didn't work or study, listened to jazz, drank wine, smoked marijuana, and indulged in casual sexuality. The beats were harbingers of the hippie rebellion of the 1960s.

Beat writers wrote poems and novels espousing the values of their rebellious generation. Jack Kerouac wrote the best novel, *On the Road* (1958). It told a tale of two young men without any money, Sal Paradise and Dean Moriarty, traveling across America and into Mexico in frantic search of emotionally engaging adventures, what Kerouac and his buddies called "kicks." Poet Allen Ginsberg wrote the most famous beat poem, "Howl," that scathingly indicted a conformist and materialistic age that destroyed sensitive souls:

> I saw the best minds of my generation destroyed by madness, . . . burned alive in their innocent flannel suits on Madison Avenue. . . . [1]

In addition to the beat writers, there were individual authors who expressed alienation from the conformist culture. Novelist J. D. Salinger expressed the theme of personal alienation in one of the finest 1950s novels, *The Catcher in the Rye.* Salinger's hero, Holden Caulfield, is a schoolboy trapped in a world populated by adults with whom he cannot communicate and who do not understand him. Holden rebels, runs away, and has a weekend fling in New York, desperately trying to find an island of integrity amidst a sea of conformity. His efforts fail, and, in the end, the system triumphs. He returns to home and school. Salinger's novel was especially popular among 1950s college students, for he expressed their discontent with a culture that masked a painful reality—not everyone fitted easily into the "silent generation."

THE ELECTION OF 1952

President Dwight D. "Ike" Eisenhower was an appropriate political symbol for the 1950s. He was the reigning hero not only for his great accomplishments, but because he had established himself as the embodiment of the cardinal values of American culture. He had risen from humble farm folk, a self-made man whose extraordinary personal success affirmed the chief myth of America, that talented individuals can rise from the depths to the pinnacles of power, wealth, and fame.

Shaped by the late-nineteenth century into which he had been born, he accepted its values without question; in the words of historian Alonzo Hamby, "he

---

[1]From Allen Ginsberg, "Howl," (New York: Harper & Row, 1956), p. 12.

merely layered the requirements of the present century over them, and thus combined the reassurance of old tradition with the needs of the contemporary world." He projected an image of confidence and optimism. He shared the views and values of the executive elite who dominated the corporate world with which he identified. He admired efficiency and organization, had a contempt for politicians and politics, and generally distrusted mass democracy. He was the ultimate organization man.

At heart, Ike was also a determined anti-Communist, committed to maintaining American strength during continuing Cold War conflicts with the Soviets. British writer Godfrey Hodgson wrote that Americans in the 1950s were "confident to the verge of complacency about the perfectibility of American society, anxious to the point of paranoia about the threat of communism." Americans embraced a consensus in the 1950s that America was the greatest nation in the world, and they also agreed that the American dream required thermonuclear defenses in the Cold War era.

Eisenhower and the Republicans had swept to power in 1952. Korea had boosted their chances. The Republicans also capitalized on many scandals unearthed within Truman's administration. As the Republican presidential race shaped up in 1952, Senator Robert Taft, leader of the conservative heartland, appeared to have the inside track to the nomination. But the powerful eastern, internationalist wing of the party promoted the candidacy of the war hero, General Eisenhower, commander of the NATO forces in Europe. At the Republican convention held in Chicago in July, Eisenhower won a close first-ballot nomination. He chose Richard Nixon, a fast-rising political star who had nailed Alger Hiss and raised Red-baiting to a high art, to be his running mate. The Democrats chose Illinois governor Adlai Stevenson to challenge Eisenhower.

Eisenhower launched the Republican drive for the White House by announcing a "great crusade" for honest, efficient government at home and freedom abroad. Republican campaign strategists devised what they called their winning formula: K^1C^2 = Korea, Communism, and corruption. Nixon and Senator Joseph McCarthy turned their rhetorical siege guns on the Democrats. They convinced millions of voters that Communist infiltration of government agencies posed a serious threat to internal security for which the Democrats were mainly responsible. Eisenhower's genial smile caused crowds to shout "We like Ike!" His Horatio Alger background offset the Republican image as an elite party. He proved an adroit campaigner. His most dramatic move came when he took up the Korean War, the chief issue of the campaign. In a speech given in Detroit, he declared that "an early and honorable" peace required a personal effort, and he pledged, "I shall go to Korea."

In September, a hitch developed that threatened briefly to derail the Republican campaign. Reporters discovered that Richard Nixon had benefited from a secret fund raised by wealthy southern California businessmen to pay his political expenses. The party that had been scoring points from its moral crusade against its scandal-plagued opposition suddenly had a scandal of its own. A wave of anti-Nixon sentiment swept the land. Stevenson had a glimmer of hope. Eisenhower appeared to be considering dumping Nixon from the GOP ticket.

But the Republican National Committee purchased airtime and Nixon went on television and radio to defend himself successfully before the bar of public opinion. He convinced most of his huge television audience that he had not broken the law or done anything wrong. The emotional highpoint of his speech came when he referred to a cocker spaniel puppy a supporter had sent the family that one of his daughters had named "Checkers":

> And you know the kids, like all kids, love the dog, and I just want to say this right now that regardless of what they say about it, we're going to keep it.[2]

The "Checkers" speech outmaneuvered the Democrats and turned a potential disaster for his party to political advantage. He stayed on the ticket and the Republican campaign rolled on.

On election day, Eisenhower scored a landslide victory. Victory was in large measure a personal triumph for the popular general. But, in defeat, the Democratic Party showed considerable strength. The Republicans managed only a narrow majority in the House and broke even in the Senate. Eisenhower ran far ahead of his party despite Korea, Communism, and corruption. Issue differences between the parties appeared slight. The politics of consensus prevailed.

DYNAMIC CONSERVATISM

President Eisenhower projected an image of bland, moderate nonpartisanship. He came across as the amateur in politics, a disinterested leader serving the nation. He appeared happy to leave the details of government to energetic subordinates. But in reality, Ike embraced a strong conservative philosophy. He believed in fiscal restraint, balanced budgets, and devout anti-Communism. Beneath the mask was an able, effective politician who controlled his administration and its policies. Eisenhower was also a skilled, precise writer. Both his best-selling book, *Crusade in Europe*, which made him rich, and his memoirs, written after his presidency, show a talent capable of lucid, exact, and occasionally elegant prose. His writing stands in sharp contrast to the rambling, incoherent utterances characteristic of his press conference responses to reporters' questions. Liberal intellectuals made fun of Eisenhower's apparent muddleheadedness and ignorance without realizing they had fallen for one of his ploys. Eisenhower often feigned ignorance or resorted to gobbledegook to avoid premature disclosures of information or policy decisions. Eisenhower's frequent hunting and fishing trips, and his passion for golf, masked a hard-driving, domineering chief executive.

Eisenhower began his presidency proclaiming a new "dynamic conservatism," which he said meant "conservative when it comes to money, liberal when it comes to human beings." Adlai Stevenson quipped that Ike's dynamic conservatism meant that the Republicans would call for building a school then refuse to

---

[2]Quoted in Stephen E. Ambrose, *Nixon: The Education of a Politician, 1913–1962* (New York: Simon & Schuster, 1987), p. 289.

appropriate the money for it. Most of Ike's leading advisers came from the ranks of big business. Charles E. Wilson, the president of General Motors, became Secretary of Defense. The Treasury Department went to George Humphrey, a wealthy industrialist. Secretary of State John Foster Dulles was a corporation lawyer.

The new administration tried to implement conservative policies in several important policy areas. Humphrey put conservative fiscal policies in place. Income taxes and federal spending were both cut 10 percent. Interest rates were raised and credit tightened to reduce inflation which had averaged 10 percent between 1950 and 1953. Republicans tried hard to balance the budget but usually failed. Republican efforts to reduce the role of the federal government and to strengthen local and state governments failed. In addition, Eisenhower tried to reduce the role of the federal government in developing electrical power sites and offshore oil wells. On the electric power issue, his efforts usually failed. On the offshore oil issue, Congress enacted legislation giving states access to submerged coastal lands. For agriculture, the administration pushed for more flexible and lower price supports for farmers. Crop production increased, farm income dropped, and farmers protested the new policies.

But it soon became evident that "dynamic conservatism" was not an effort to repeal the New Deal. Although a fiscal conservative, Eisenhower accepted the expansion of several New Deal programs. Congress expanded Social Security coverage, raised the minimum wage, and extended unemployment insurance. Congress also created a new Department of Health, Education, and Welfare to coordinate government social programs. The size and scope of the federal government continued to expand during the Eisenhower years.

Eisenhower proposed the largest domestic spending program in American history in 1955, a federal-state highway construction program. Congress enacted the Federal Highway Act in 1956. It projected a 42,000-mile network of freeways linking all major urban areas. The federal government provided 90 percent and the states 10 percent of the estimated $27.5 billion cost. Funding came from a users' tax paid into a highway trust fund. Construction of mammoth freeway systems continued into the 1970s and the government spent billions of dollars annually on them.

Eisenhower's moderation accorded with the public mood of the 1950s. Most Americans felt smugly complacent about their society. They believed that economic growth would solve all social problems, gradually enlarging the economic pie until poverty vanished. There was no need for higher taxes, special programs, or sacrifices by anyone. The 1950s were a time for holding the line against inflation, recession, and social disorder—of balancing liberty and security within a moderate framework acceptable to all.

The New Deal was legitimated during the reign of Ike. It became the status quo undergirding consensus politics. The pragmatic accommodation that the conservative Eisenhower made by protecting and expanding the welfare state signaled the breakdown of traditional political categories. Politicians no longer battled one another over fundamental issues; they merely quarreled over which interest got how much. Previously, big government had been linked to liberalism, and limited government tied to conservatism. In the 1950s, except for a few traditional ideologues on the Left and Right, the real issue was no longer whether government was large or small, but whose interests it served. Conservatives often voted for huge spending programs like highway programs and social security extensions. Liberals often voted for huge defense budgets in the name of Cold War bipartisanship and to protect national security in the nuclear age.

MCCARTHY: ZENITH AND RUIN

National alarm over Communist infiltration of government agencies persisted well into Eisenhower's presidency. Joseph McCarthy quickly resumed his investigations of alleged subversion in government. For eighteen months, McCarthy was the second most powerful politician in Washington. He dominated the news with his spectacular accusations. A 1954 poll showed 50 percent of Americans approved of his activities and only 29 percent opposed them. Many of his Senate colleagues, knowing that he was a fraud, despised him. But they feared him even more, and refused to challenge him openly, having seen what McCarthy could do to an opponent at election time. Eisenhower also refused to confront him because he did not want a party rupture over the controversial demagogue.

The State Department continued to be McCarthy's favorite hunting ground, even though it was now controlled by Republicans. In 1953, McCarthy went after the State Department's overseas information service. Secretary of State John Foster Dulles ordered department personnel to cooperate fully with McCarthy's investigation. Supposedly subversive books were dutifully removed from the shelves by State Department functionaries and some of them were burned.

In 1954, McCarthy went after the United States Army. His subcommittee investigated alleged Communist subversion at Fort Monmouth, New Jersey, site of sensitive communications technology. During the inquiry, McCarthy discovered that the Army had promoted a dentist, Irving Peress, to the rank of major and then given him an honorable discharge when it learned that he had once invoked the Fifth Amendment when asked about Communist affiliations. An angry McCarthy bullied and humiliated General Ralph Zwicker, Peress's commanding officer, when he refused to give him Peress's file.

The army mounted a counterattack against McCarthy, accusing him of trying to blackmail the Army into giving preferential treatment to a former McCarthy staffer who had been assigned to Fort Monmouth. McCarthy retorted that the Army was holding his former staffer hostage to keep his committee from investigating the Army. McCarthy's subcommittee voted to hold hearings on the charges made by the two adversaries, with Senator Karl Mundt of South Dakota temporarily assuming the chairmanship. On April 22, 1954, the famed Army–McCarthy hearings began. For six weeks they were telecast daily to 15 million viewers.

McCarthy starred in the televised political drama. He interrupted the proceedings frequently. The hearings also made a star out of Joseph Welch, a soft-spoken trial lawyer who was the Army's chief counsel. At one point, Welch left McCarthy temporarily speechless by asking rhetorically, "At long last, sir, at long last, have you left no sense of decency?" The hearings ended inconclusively. It is not true that television exposure or Welch's dramatic remark undermined McCarthy's popularity. Polls taken shortly after the hearings showed McCarthy still retained his 50 percent approval ratings.

It was McCarthy's methods, his unruly behavior, which proved his downfall. He went too far when he attacked the Army; ironically, McCarthy himself was becoming a security risk. In August 1954, the Senate established a committee to study a set of censure charges brought against McCarthy by Republican Ralph Flanders of Vermont. Chairing the committee was conservative Republican Arthur Watkins of Utah. The committee recommended the Senate censure McCarthy. After noisy hearings, the full Senate voted to "condemn" McCarthy for contempt of the Senate and for abuse of Watkins committee members. The vote was sixty-seven to twenty-two.

Senate condemnation destroyed McCarthy's power. He still made accusations, but his attacks no longer made headlines. He had lost the spotlight even faster than he had found it. His health failed and he did not live out his Senate term. He died in May 1957 of infectious hepatitis, aggravated by heavy drinking, at the age of forty-seven. McCarthy could perform only as long as his colleagues were willing to support his Red-hunting and tolerate his unruly behavior. The most significant fact about the career of the nation's premier Red-hunter was that in four years of investigations, McCarthy never unearthed a single Communist in any federal agency.

THE POLITICS OF CONSENSUS

The 1954 elections were the last in which the Communist-in-government issue had any force. Anti-Communism as a major issue in American domestic politics died with McCarthy. But anti-Communism remained a staple of American political culture, far outliving its foremost practitioner. Most Americans regarded as axiomatic the notion that the Soviet Union headed an international conspiracy unrelentingly hostile to the United States. The Cold War bipartisan consensus on the conduct of American foreign policy remained intact.

Political alignments during the 1950s remained unstable. Eisenhower's 1952 victory signaled the breakup of the Roosevelt coalition of labor, farmers, ethnics, and southerners forged during the 1930s; but the Republicans could not form a majority coalition to replace it. As traditional political allegiances declined during the 1950s, a large independent "swing" vote emerged, varying in size with each election. Millions of citizens voted a split ticket, supporting a man or an issue instead of a party, and shifting sides in response to particular situations. The two major parties attained a rough equality for the first time since the early 1890s. An unstable equilibrium prevailed.

National elections held during the 1950s reflected the unstable balance of political forces. Except for 1952, the Democrats won the congressional elections and the Republicans the presidential elections. The 1956 election was a dull replay of 1952. Ike was at the peak of his popularity and almost immune to criticism. Stevenson campaigned tentatively, groping for an issue and never finding one. He tried to make issues of Ike's age and health. Eisenhower had suffered a serious heart attack in September 1955, and had been incapacitated for weeks. But he recovered, and in 1956 the sixty-five-year-old leader enjoyed good health, and he was obviously fit to run again. In 1956, the Democratic arsenal contained no political weapons to match the Republican slogan of "four more years of peace and prosperity." Eisenhower won reelection by a larger margin than his 1952 landslide victory. But the Democrats carried both houses of Congress. The year 1956 was the first time in American political history that a party won both Houses while losing the presidency.

But the nominal Democratic congressional majorities were undercut by the conservative bipartisan coalition of southern Democrats and northern Republicans who could gut or block most liberal legislation. During the 1950s, moderate Texas politicians led the Democrats in Congress. Speaker Sam Rayburn led the House and his protégé, Lyndon Johnson, led the Senate. Both leaders pursued a strategy of compromise and cooperation with the Republican White House.

CIVIL RIGHTS

Soon after taking office, President Eisenhower appointed Governor Earl Warren of California Chief Justice of the Supreme Court. The Court had been chipping away at the constitutional foundations of racial discrimination since the 1940s in two areas, denial of voting rights and school segregation. It was in the realm of education that the Court chose to nullify the "separate but equal" principle that had provided the constitutional basis of Jim Crow.

Several cases challenging school segregation were before the Court. With Warren providing the leadership that spurred his associates to action, the justices decided a representative case, *Brown* v. *the Board of Education of Topeka,* on May 17, 1954. A unanimous Court ruled that public school segregation was unconstitutional under the Fourteenth Amendment, reversing the "separate but equal" doctrine established in *Plessy* v. *Ferguson* (1896). The Court's decision incorporated much of the legal brief filed by Thurgood Marshall, chief counsel for the NAACP:

> In the field of public education, the doctrine of 'separate but equal' has no place. Separate educational facilities are inherently unequal.[3]

---

[3]Quoted in Anthony Lewis, *Portrait of a Decade: The Second American Revolution* (New York: Bantum Books, 1965), p. 26.

A year later, the Supreme Court instructed federal district courts to order school desegregation to begin in their areas, and to require "good faith compliance with all deliberate speed." Having destroyed the legal basis of school segregation, the courts proceeded to undermine Jim Crow everywhere. Federal court decisions nullified segregation in public housing, recreational facilities, and interstate commerce. The *Brown* decision was the most important Supreme Court decision of modern times.

The South defied the *Brown* decision. In 1956, a group of 101 congressmen and senators from eleven southern states that had composed the Confederacy almost a century before signed the Southern Manifesto. It pledged to "use all lawful means to bring about a reversal of this decision which is contrary to the Constitution." The Southern Manifesto also encouraged southern officials to try to prevent implementing the law. The crucial confrontation between federal and state authority over school desegregation came at Little Rock, Arkansas, where Eisenhower faced the most serious domestic crisis of his presidency.

In September 1957, Central High in Little Rock planned to enroll nine African American students under court order. But Arkansas governor Orville Faubus prevented integration by ordering National Guardsmen to block the school entrance. A federal court ordered the troops to leave, and the African American students enrolled. But white students threatened them, and they were removed from the school. Faced with clear defiance of the law, Eisenhower acted. For the first time since Reconstruction, a president sent federal troops into the South to protect the rights of African Americans. Paratroopers entered Central High and the National Guardsmen were placed under federal command. Guarded by soldiers with fixed bayonets, the nine teenagers enrolled.

There is a close interrelationship between the Supreme Court decision outlawing segregation and the southern civil rights campaigns of the mid-1950s. Civil rights activists were tremendously encouraged by the Court's ruling. They responded by escalating their attacks on racial injustice. When state and local jurisdictions refused to obey the *Brown* decision, activists took to the streets in an effort to pressure white southerners into compliance with the Constitution or provoke federal interventions to enforce the law. Civil rights activists were essentially using radical tactics such as civil disobedience and boycotts to bring about enforcement of federal law. The civil rights revolution was a very conservative sort of revolution.

Eighteen months after the *Brown* decision, in Montgomery, Alabama, Rosa Parks refused to surrender her seat at the front of a bus to a white man and ignited the modern civil rights movement. A charming myth has risen about Ms. Parks as the seamstress who was simply too tired to move to the back of the bus and whose arrest set off a spontaneous demonstration that ended happily with integrated bus service. Such an account misrepresents a carefully planned and well-organized movement for social change. It also omits Parks' long prior career as a community leader and social activist. Her action brought to prominence a young Baptist minister who, for the rest of his tragically short life, would be the foremost leader of the civil rights revolution. He was Dr. Martin Luther King, Jr., and he declared:

> Integration is the great issue of our age, the great issue of our nation and the great is-sue of our community. We are in the midst of a great struggle, the consequences of which will be world-shaking.[4]

Under Dr. King's leadership, Montgomery African Americans organized a boycott of the city's bus lines. Helped by a Supreme Court decision declaring bus segre-gation unconstitutional, after an arduous campaign lasting 381 days, they eventu-ally forced the city to integrate its bus service and to hire African Americans drivers and mechanics.

At the same time, the NAACP mounted an intensive legal campaign against segregation. Victorious in forty-two of forty-six appeals to the Supreme Court, the NAACP advanced voting rights and integrated housing, transportation, public ac-commodations, and schools in many parts of the South. While Thurgood Marshall and the NAACP fought their civil rights battles in the federal courts, Dr. King and his followers fought theirs in the streets of southern towns and cities.

A drive to guarantee African American voting rights also started. A civil rights bill moved through Congress mainly because of the leadership of Eisen-hower and Senator Lyndon Johnson. The Civil Rights Act of 1957, the first since Re-construction, created a Civil Rights Commission and gave the Attorney General power to take local officials to court in cases in which they denied African Ameri-cans the right to vote. Johnson was also instrumental in getting a stronger civil rights law enacted in 1960. It provided legal penalties against anyone interfering with the right to vote. The civil rights movement made a powerful beginning during the 1950s. Most progress came from the efforts by African Americans them-selves, aided by Supreme Court decisions that nullified the legal foundations of segregation.

THE NEW LOOK

During the 1952 campaign, Republicans charged that the Truman–Acheson policy of containing Communism had failed, especially in Asia with the loss of China and stalemate in Korea. John Foster Dulles insisted that the United States, instead of pursuing containment, should make it "publicly known that it wants and expects liberation to occur." But in office, Eisenhower and Dulles continued the contain-ment policies that they had condemned during the 1952 campaign. They had no choice. The logic of liberation led inescapably to one conclusion—Americans would have to fight to free the captive nations because the Communists would never voluntarily set them free. Freedom for Eastern Europe meant war with the Soviet Union. Further, Eisenhower had committed himself to cutting military

[4]Quoted in *Ibid.*, p. 62.

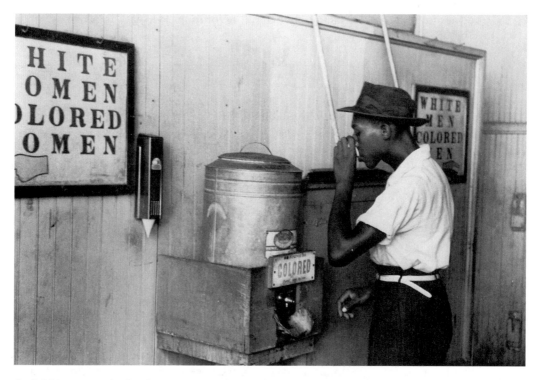

A vivid instance of "Jim Crow" segregation in the South during the 1950s.
Source: Library of Congress. Photo by Russell Lee.

expenditures. Liberation, far costlier than containment, could never be carried out by fiscal conservatives. Republicans hid their failure to liberate anyone from Communism behind tough talk.

Republicans called their foreign policy the New Look. It relied on strategic air power to destroy the Soviet Union with nuclear bombs if Communist aggression occurred anywhere in the world. Dulles believed the threat to obliterate the Soviets would "deter" them from hostile actions. The New Look strategy allowed the Administration to reduce outlays for conventional forces. Dulles described their approach as "massive retaliation." Secretary of Defense Wilson observed that the New Look provided "more bang for the buck." President Eisenhower insisted cuts in defense spending were necessary to preserve the American way of life. In a speech given April 16, 1953, he said,

> Every gun that is made, every warship launched, every rocket fired signifies, in the final sense, a theft from those who hunger and are not fed, those who are cold and are not clothed.[5]

[5]Quoted in Charles C. Alexander, *Holding the Line: The Eisenhower Era, 1952–1961* (Bloomington: Indiana University Press, 1975).

Critics of the New Look strategy charged that "massive retaliation" locked America into an all-or-nothing response to Communist aggression. A Communist-led uprising in a small country would not warrant an attack on the Soviet Union, hence the revolution would probably succeed. The Soviets could also see the limitations of massive retaliation and would not be deterred from helping small-scale insurrections. Freedom would be nibbled away at the periphery.

Ike defended his foreign policy by contending that the United States could not afford to police the entire world. It must concentrate on defending its vital interests. If NATO nations or Japan were attacked, the United States response would be swift and overwhelming. Dulles also tried to compensate for the limitations of the New Look strategy by forging regional security pacts with allies in which the United States would furnish the military hardware and the allies the troops if the Communists attacked. By 1960, the United States had committed itself to defend forty-three countries.

VIETNAM: GETTING IN DEEPER

Dulles described his diplomatic method as the willingness to go to the brink of war to achieve peace. "Brinkmanship" was more threatening as rhetoric than as action. Dulles never used brinkmanship on the Soviets. Nor did the United States become embroiled in any major wars during the Eisenhower–Dulles tenure. Brinkmanship was tried mainly in Asia, with mixed results. It worked in Korea. The President told Dulles to warn the Chinese that if they did not accept a settlement the United States might use nuclear weapons in the war. That threat broke a two-year-old deadlock and ended the conflict on American terms.

Dulles then applied brinkmanship to Southeast Asia where, since 1946, the French, trying to reimpose colonialism in Indochina, had been fighting Vietnamese guerrillas. In 1950, the Truman administration had begun sending economic and military aid to support the French efforts to contain Communism in Asia following the Maoist triumph in China. Eisenhower expanded American aid to the French; by 1954, the United States was paying 78 percent of the cost of the war. Eisenhower, like Truman before him, applied Cold War ideology to this struggle between Asia nationalists and European imperialists. Washington viewed the Indochina War as part of the global conflict between Free World forces and Communism. They viewed Ho Chi Minh as an advance agent of Beijing and Moscow.

Despite U.S. help, the French were losing the war. By 1954, Viet Minh forces held most of Vietnam. French generals tried to retrieve the military initiative. They put eleven thousand of their best troops in a remote fortress deep within guerrilla-held territory at Dien Bien Phu and dared them to fight an open battle. The French believed that Asians could not defeat European forces in a conventional battle. Superior Vietnamese forces besieged the garrison. Within weeks it was on the verge of surrender. With war weariness strong in France after eight years of war, the fall of Dien Bien Phu would mean victory for the Vietnamese and the end of French Indochina.

Facing imminent ruin in Southeast Asia, the French appealed to the Americans to save them. President Eisenhower considered air strikes to relieve the siege around Dien Bien Phu, but he insisted that American allies join the effort and that Congress support it. Prime minister Winston Churchill rebuffed Dulles's efforts to enlist British support. Senate leaders told the President that without British involvement the Senate would not approve U.S. military intervention. Lacking support from allies or Congress, Eisenhower rejected the French request. On May 7, 1954, Dien Bien Phu fell to the Communists.

Meanwhile, an international conference had convened in Geneva to find a political solution to the Indochina war. Conferees worked out a settlement in July 1954. By its terms, the French and Viet Minh agreed to a cease-fire and a temporary partition of Vietnam at the seventeenth parallel of north latitude, with French forces withdrawing south of that line and Viet Minh forces withdrawing to the north. Free elections were to be held within two years to unify the country. During the interim, the French were to help prepare southern Vietnam for independence and then leave.

The United States opposed the Geneva accords but could not prevent them. The American delegate refused to sign them, but he agreed to accept them and pledged not to use force to upset the arrangements. But at the time, President Eisenhower announced that the United States "has not been party to or is bound by the decisions taken by the conference." Ho Chi Minh, whose forces verged on taking all Vietnam, settled for just the northern half of the country at Geneva because he was confident of winning the forthcoming elections over the French-backed regime in the south.

After Geneva, Dulles salvaged what he could from what Washington regarded as a major Communist victory that threatened all Southeast Asia. In September 1954, Dulles arranged for Great Britain, France, Australia, New Zealand, Thailand, Pakistan, and the Philippines to create the Southeast Asia Treaty Organization (SEATO). It was not a mutual security pact. Members agreed only to "meet and confer" if one of them were attacked. A separate agreement covered Laos, Cambodia, and "South Vietnam"—that is, Vietnam south of the seventeenth parallel. SEATO tried to project U.S. power into Indochina in the aftermath of the French defeat.

The United States also supported a new government emerging in southern Vietnam, headed by Ngo Dinh Diem. Americans trained and equipped Diem's army and security forces. The Eisenhower administration promoted the diplomatic fiction that the seventeenth parallel had become a national boundary separating two states, "South Vietnam" and "North Vietnam." America also backed Diem when he refused to allow the scheduled elections to unify the country to take place in 1956.

Eisenhower believed if southern Vietnam fell to the Communists, all Southeast Asia would be imperiled. He compared the nations of Southeast Asia to a row of dominoes: knock one over and the rest would fall quickly. After Geneva, America committed its resources and prestige to creating a new nation in southern

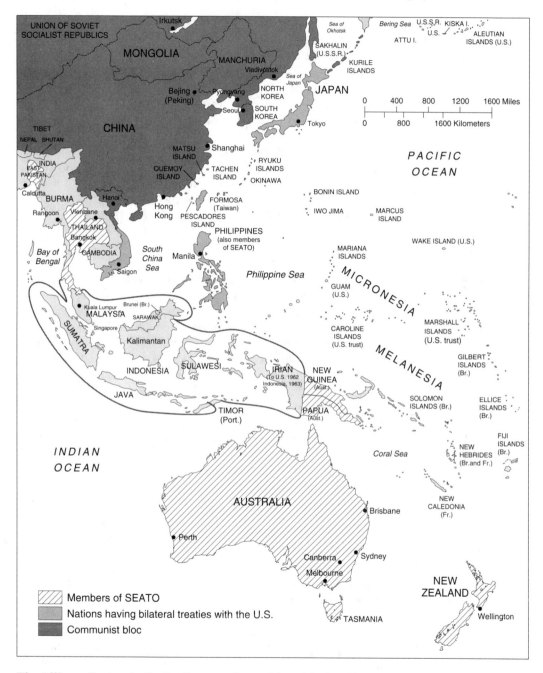

The Alliance System in the Far East.   *Source:* Moss, *Moving On,* p. 119.

Vietnam that would "serve as a proving ground for democracy in Asia." The survival of the new South Vietnam would sabotage the Geneva settlement that assumed the emergence of an unified, Communist-controlled Vietnam within two years.

With U.S. backing during the late 1950s, Diem attempted to suppress all opposition to his regime among religious sects, Viet Minh remnants, and other groups of dissidents. His repressive actions provoked violent opposition. Local officials and Diem informers were assassinated by Communist and non-Communist opponents, all of whom Diem called "Viet Cong," meaning Vietnamese who are Communists. The Viet Minh infiltrated men and supplies south of the seventeenth parallel to take control of the anti-Diem insurgency. Small-scale civil war had begun. By 1959, the Second Indochina war was underway. Without intending to, the Americans and the North Vietnamese had launched themselves on collision courses.

THE CHINA CRISIS

While Americans were trying to build a nation in Southeast Asia, they faced a crisis with mainland China over Formosa. Nationalist Chinese pilots, flying from Formosan bases in U.S. planes, had bombed mainland shipping and ports since 1953. The U.S. Seventh Fleet patrolled the waters between China and Formosa, protecting the Nationalists from Communist reprisals. In September 1954, Communist Chinese artillery began shelling Quemoy and Matsu, two small islands sitting in the mouths of two mainland ports about 100 miles from Formosa. These islands were held by Nationalist forces. Eisenhower was determined to hold these islands because he believed that they were essential to the defense of Formosa.

Washington reacted to the shelling by increasing the American military presence in the Taiwan Strait, strengthening Nationalist defenses, and issuing stern warnings to Beijing. In December 1954, Washington and Taiwan signed a mutual defense treaty. The following year, Congress gave President Eisenhower the authority to use military force if necessary to defend Taiwan and the offshore islands. If the Communist Chinese had invaded the islands, the United States probably would have bombed Chinese military targets. But the Chinese, lacking nuclear weapons and getting no help from the Soviets, reduced the shelling and offered to negotiate "a relaxation of tensions." The United States, which did not recognize the legitimacy of the mainland Chinese government, refused to negotiate with Beijing, but it stopped its war preparations and the situation calmed. Beginning quietly at Geneva in the summer of 1955, Chinese and U.S. officials held talks about Taiwan, trade, and other topics.

American problems in Asia highlighted the emergence of Third World nations as a major force in world affairs during the 1950s. These nations, many of them recently independent former European colonies, increasingly became the focus of the Cold War conflict between Russia and the United States. Third World nations were sources of raw materials, they attracted foreign investment, and they provided markets, particularly for American exports. Many Third World nations wanted to remain neutral in the Cold War. But to U.S. Secretary of State Dulles, neutralism in a bipolar world dominated by two superpowers, one of which was "immoral," was wrong. He opposed a conference of twenty-nine African and Asian nations held at Bandung, Indonesia, in April 1955, during the height of the Quemoy–Matsu crisis. Leaders of the Afro-Asian nations called for these nations to form an alternative to the two superpowers and their alliance systems. Chinese Premier Jou En-lai played a prominent role at Bandung; China assumed leadership of the emerging Third World nations.

AT THE SUMMIT

When the U.S. considered using nuclear weapons during the Formosan crisis, it highlighted a frightening world reality. Thermonuclear weapons of the mid-1950s were a thousand times more powerful than the two bombs which had devastated Hiroshima and Nagasaki in 1945. An American strategic bomber in 1955 carried more destructive power than all the explosives previously detonated in world history! Both the Russians and Americans possessed hydrogen bombs; both were developing intercontinental missiles. Both sides had to face the possibility of a nuclear exchange if they went to war. They agreed to hold a "summit conference" to try to reduce the possibility of nuclear catastrophe.

The conference convened at Geneva July 18, 1955. President Eisenhower, Premier Nikolai Bulganin of the Soviet Union, Prime Minister Anthony Eden of England, and Premier Edgar Faure of France attended. Geneva signaled a turning point in the Cold War. Both sides conceded in effect that the Cold War could not be won militarily. The atmosphere at the summit was cordial. A "spirit of Geneva" emerged, symbolized by a photograph of Eisenhower shaking hands with Bulganin. President Eisenhower also scored a propaganda victory when he offered, and the Russians rejected, his "Open Skies" proposal to the Soviets that would permit aerial surveillance of both countries' nuclear development and testing facilities. The conference yielded no substantive agreements and the arms race continued after the summit ended. But thermonuclear stalemate had forced a relaxation of tensions. Both sides agreed to start arms control negotiations and later suspended atmospheric testing of nuclear weapons.

THE CIA AT WORK

In 1953, Ike appointed Allen Dulles, younger brother of the Secretary of State, director of the Central Intelligence Agency (CIA). Together, the Dulles brothers became known to insiders as "The Cold War, Inc." Allen Dulles recruited Cold Warriors eager to fight Communism. Under his leadership, paramilitary covert operations became a secret arm of U.S. foreign policy. The CIA's first major triumph came in Iran in 1953. A nationalist government led by Mohammed Mossadegh had nationalized oil fields controlled by the British and forced the young Shah of Iran into exile. The United States, fearing that Mossadegh might sell oil to the Soviets and align himself with Iranian Communists, sent CIA operatives to Iran. Working with the British and Iranian army officials, they helped overthrow Mossadegh and restored the Shah to power. Iran then made a deal that gave U.S. oil companies 40 percent of Iranian oil production, the British 40 percent, and the Dutch 20 percent. The CIA helped to subvert a popular government and the United States now controlled a major share of Iranian oil production.

The CIA also helped overthrow a leftist government in Central America. Jacob Arbenz Guzman had been elected president of Guatemala in 1951. Arbenz was not a Communist, but Communists supported his government and held offices within it. In 1953, the government expropriated 234,000 acres of land belonging to an American corporation, the United Fruit Company, Guatemala's largest landowner, for a land reform program. The company claimed Latin America was being threatened with Communism.

The United States cut off economic aid and sent CIA forces to Guatemala to overthrow Arbenz. They recruited an army of exiles in neighboring Honduras led by Colonel Carlos Castillo Armas. Faced with a military threat to his power, Arbenz turned to the Soviet Union for weapons. When Armas's forces were ready for attack, CIA pilots airlifted their supplies and bombed the Guatemalan capital. Arbenz, facing military defeat, fled into exile. Armas established a military dictatorship and returned the expropriated lands to the company. Bouyed by their success in toppling a leftist government perceived to be hostile to U.S. economic and strategic interests in Guatemala, CIA officials would try to replicate their efforts in Cuba in 1961, with disastrous results. U.S. intervention in Guatemala intensified resentment toward U.S. foreign policy throughout Latin America. When Vice President Nixon travelled to Venezuela in 1958 as part of a goodwill tour of Latin America, he was met by angry mobs in the streets of Caracas who stoned his car.

TROUBLE IN SUEZ

The Cold War spread to the Middle East after World War II, deeply involving the United States in a region that had previously been of only peripheral interest. The Middle East was a compound of many parts: Arab nationalism, political instability, regional rivalries, religious fanaticism, superpower penetration, and most of all the intractable Arab-Israeli conflict. It is the presence of a Jewish state of Israel on land that was formerly Palestine that lies at the core of many Middle East conflicts.

The modern Arab–Israeli conflict dates from the end of World War II. Most of the European Jews who survived the Holocaust wanted to go to Palestine where a sizable Jewish population had been built up since 1900. Palestine was administered by the British who tried to prevent Zionist refugees from entering Palestine in order to safeguard their Anglo-Arabian oil interests. But the British, weakened by losses in World War II, withdrew from Palestine in 1947, turning it over to the United Nations. At that time, the United States and the Soviet Union united to carve an Israeli homeland out of the western portion of Palestine. The UN partitioned Palestine to create a Jewish state, Israel, along the Mediterranean coast. On

May 14, 1948, Israel proclaimed its independence. America recognized Israel immediately and the Soviet Union did soon afterwards.

Instantly, Arab armies attacked, determined to drive the Jews into the Mediterranean Sea, to destroy the new Jewish state, and to preserve all of Palestine for the Palestinian Arabs. At first, the outnumbered Israelis were driven back. Their cause appeared lost. They asked for a truce, and the Soviets and Americans imposed one. During the cease-fire, the Soviets flew in quantities of heavy arms, violating the truce. Soviet military aid at that critical juncture saved the fledgling Israeli state. When fighting resumed, the well-armed Israelis routed the Arab forces. Israeli forces also advanced far beyond the original boundaries assigned by the UN partition. The beaten Arabs sued for peace in 1949.

An African American diplomat, Dr. Ralph Bunche, arranged an armistice ending the first Arab–Israeli war. Israel survived because of Soviet arms and American diplomatic support. Its inflated borders included thousands of Palestinians. Another 700,000 Palestinians fled or were driven from their homes by the advancing Israeli forces, creating a Palestinian refugee problem that has never been solved. The Soviets supported Israel until 1955 when they switched to the Arab side. The United States continues to be Israel's major supporter while trying to maintain friendly relations with moderate Arab nations.

With U.S. assistance, Gamal Abdul Nasser came to power in Egypt in 1952, the first of a new generation of Arab nationalists. America offered him $270 million to build a huge dam on the Upper Nile to control flooding and to generate hydroelectric power. The aid money for the Aswan dam represented an American effort to tilt its Middle East policy in a more pro-Arab direction. In 1955, Dulles arranged the signing of the Baghdad Pact linking Britain, Turkey, Iran, Iraq, and Pakistan in an agreement to strengthen the Middle East against Soviet penetration. The Pact angered Nasser, who viewed it as an effort to bring the Cold War to the Middle East and to strengthen Iraq, Egypt's rival for Arab leadership. The Soviet Union reacted to the signing of the Baghdad Pact by becoming more active in Arab affairs, particularly in Egypt and Syria.

Egyptian and Israeli forces clashed along the Gaza Strip, territory both nations claimed, inhabited mainly by Palestinian refugees. The Israelis suddenly attacked in force in 1955, inflicting a major defeat on the Egyptians. Nasser, angry and humiliated, asked the United States for arms. Washington refused him. Nasser then turned to the Soviet bloc and concluded an arms deal with the Communists. Dulles, fearing Egypt was becoming a Soviet client, withdrew U.S. aid for the Aswan dam. Nasser responded by nationalizing the Suez Canal. He used its $30 million annual revenues to finance the Aswan dam. He also closed the canal to Israel shipping. The Soviets supported Nasser's actions.

Britain and France, dependent on Persian Gulf oil shipped through the Suez Canal, proposed overthrowing Nasser and returning the canal to its former owners. The United States, afraid such actions would involve the Soviets and lead to war, rejected the Anglo-French proposal. The British and French decided to overthrow Nasser and incorporated the Israelis into their plans. On October 29, 1956,

Israel invaded Egypt. A week later, the French and British landed troops in Egypt to seize the canal. The United States condemned the Anglo–French–Israeli actions before the United Nations. America also cut off oil shipments to France and Britain and threatened to wage financial war against the British pound sterling. The French and British, reeling from a combination of U.S. and UN opposition, Soviet threats to intervene, and an Arab oil boycott, withdrew without occupying the canal. The Soviets used the occasion to provide funds for the Aswan project in return for which the Egyptians granted the Soviets use of a former British military base at Suez.

U.S. efforts to avoid war in the Middle East had several mostly negative consequences for American foreign policy interests. Administration efforts weakened NATO, humiliated America's major European allies, alienated Nasser, angered the Israelis, helped the Soviets get a military base in Egypt, and failed to improve relations with other Arab countries. But Nasser eventually paid the French and British $81 million for the Suez canal, and Middle Eastern oil supplies remained in Western hands.

While the Suez crisis raged, crises erupted in Eastern Europe. Early in 1956, the new Soviet leader, Nikita Khrushchev, promised to ease Soviet restrictions in satellite countries. Ferment spread quickly through Eastern Europe. Riots in Poland forced the Soviets to grant the Poles substantial concessions. Hungarian students and workers overthrew a Stalinist puppet. He was replaced by Imre Nagy. Nagy demanded removal of Red Army forces and implementation of democracy; the Soviets conceded both of these demands. Dulles promised the Hungarians economic aid if they broke with the Soviets. On October 31, Hungary announced it was leaving the Warsaw Pact. Liberation appeared at hand; a captive people was freeing itself from Communist tyranny.

The Soviet Union, unwilling to let the Warsaw Pact disintegrate, invaded Hungary. Soviet tanks crushed the Hungarian revolution and killed thirty thousand Hungarians. Radio Budapest pleaded for help, but no help came from America or elsewhere. Eisenhower had never considered sending troops, nor would he have had there been no Suez crisis. Neither he nor any other U.S. president would ever risk World War III to help liberate an East European country. American talk of liberation for Eastern Europe had always been a sham. American forces were not strong enough to defeat the Red Army in Hungary, except with the use of nuclear weapons that would have ruined the country and killed millions of people. Hungarians learned the hard way that East European nations would have to make deals with their Soviet masters while Americans would go on mouthing pious rhetoric about the evils of Communist imperialism.

After the Suez incident, America announced the Eisenhower Doctrine to try to offset Soviet influence and militant Arab nationalism in the Middle East. It offered military aid to any country requesting it to resist Communist threats. The Eisenhower Doctrine extended containment to the region. Twice it was implemented. In 1957, U.S. troops were sent into Jordan to protect its government from Egyptian threats. In 1958, about fourteen thousand Marines landed in Lebanon to protect its government from an insurgency supported by Nasser.

As the 1950s ended, America enjoyed good relations with traditional Arab states like Saudi Arabia, the region's major oil producer, which had become a U.S. client through economic aid and arms sales. Middle Eastern oil continued its flow through the Suez Canal. But U.S. influence in the Middle East was declining. Arab nationalism and Soviet influence were growing. Egyptian and Syrian armies were equipped with Soviet weapons, and the Soviets were financing the Aswan project. Arab hostility toward Israel, combined with the U.S. commitment to the survival of the Jewish state, allowed the Soviets to champion Arab nationalism. American efforts to balance Arab and Israeli interests failed. No conceivable diplomatic formula promised a long-term solution to Middle East conflicts unless the Arab-Israeli impasse were overcome.

SPUTNIK

After the Suez crisis, the military balance appeared to shift toward the Soviet Union. In September 1957, the Soviets test-fired an intercontinental ballistics missile (ICBM) over a year ahead of the United States. A month later, they launched the first space satellite, which they called Sputnik. Sputnik's strategic implications were ominous. It proved the Soviets had powerful rockets and had solved guidance problems essential to delivering a thermonuclear warhead to its target. America appeared to face both a missile "gap" and a space "lag" with the Soviets.

At first the president played down Soviets achievements, trying to reassure anxious Americans. But he was not convincing. He offered no new programs to catch the Soviets in either the arms or the space race. For the first time, Ike was vigorously attacked in Congress and in the media. The attacks were reinforced by the sluggish performance of the economy, which slipped into recession, and the revelation of a scandal in the Administration. Eisenhower's special assistant, Sherman Adams, was forced to resign for accepting favors from a businessman who needed help from the federal government. The Soviets had scored a tremendous ideological victory over their rivals. American technological superiority over the supposedly backward Soviets, a source of security during the Cold war, was wiped away. Senator Lyndon Johnson conducted a thorough investigation of the nation's missile and space programs, thereby establishing the Democrats as favoring stronger national defense and space efforts than the administration.

Critics faulted American public schools for not demanding excellence from students and for stinting on basic education, math, and science training. There had been persistent criticisms of public schools preceding Sputnik. Dr. Rudolf Flesch, in his best-selling *Why Johnny Can't Read* (1955), had attacked overcrowded schools that used obsolete teaching methods and offered diverse, aimless curricula to bored students. After Sputnik, educational shortcomings became a national security issue. Educators insisted that Americans must put greater emphasis on mathematics, foreign language study, and science to regain its technological edge over the Soviets. Eisenhower and Congress responded in 1958 by enacting the National

Defense Education Act (NDEA) that funded high school math, language, and science programs; and, it offered fellowships and loans to college students entering these fields.

Initial American efforts to match Soviet rocketry embarrassed the nation. Two months after Sputnik's launching, an American rocket blew up on its launch pad; a U.S. journalist promptly dubbed it "kaputnik." Not until January 1958 did an Army rocket team manage to get a small American satellite into orbit. But the Russians then hurled aloft a 3,000-pound satellite. Khrushchev claimed that Soviet leadership in rocketry demonstrated the superiority of socialism over capitalism and boasted to alarmed Americans that "we will bury you."

CUBA AND CASTRO

Eisenhower, preoccupied with the arms race with the Soviets and conducting Cold War diplomacy in Europe, Asia, and the Middle East, usually gave relations with Latin America a low priority. Latin American politics during the 1950s swung between the extremes of leftist democracies and rightist military dictatorships. Washington, while paying lip service to democracy, preferred military regimes that maintained order, protected private property, supported U.S. foreign policy, and suppressed Communists. Latin Americans envied U.S. wealth, feared U.S. power, and resented U.S. diplomacy.

In the 1950s, U.S. economic interests dominated the Cuban economy, a result of the neocolonial relationship between the countries dating from the Spanish-American War. American companies owned Cuba's oil industry, 90 percent of its mines, 80 percent of its utilities, 50 percent of its railroads, 40 percent of its sugar plantations, and 40 percent of its cattle ranches. Most of Cuba's major export crop, sugar, was sold on U.S. markets and two-thirds of Cuban imports came from the United States.

At the end of 1958, Fidel Castro overthrew Fulgencio Batista, a corrupt dictator who had protected U.S. economic interests in Cuba. Castro implemented a social revolution. He broke up the large cattle ranches and sugar plantations, distributing the land to peasants. He established summary courts that condemned former Batista supporters, thousands of whom were shot or imprisoned. Communists took over Cuban trade unions and infiltrated Castro's army.

Although alarmed by Castro's radical actions, the United States quickly recognized his regime. Castro had considerable support within the United States; he was viewed as a liberal reformer who would restore Cuban democracy. He visited the United States in April 1959. In meetings with American officials, he spoke reassuringly about future relations with the United States. He promised that any future expropriations of American property would be legal and the owners compensated, but these were pledges he failed to keep. He tried to borrow money from U.S. bankers, but rejected their terms because they conflicted with his plans for

Cuban economic development. He then returned to Cuba and began nationalizing more U.S. property.

Relations between the United States and Cuba continued to deteriorate as Castro's revolution continued its left-wing tack. Cuban liberals, many of them former Castro supporters, fled Cuba for Florida. Castro, who had come to power with only vague notions about implementing an economic program once in power, joined the Communists in mid-1959. By the end of the year, his government had confiscated about $1 billion in U.S. properties. In February 1960, Castro signed an agreement with the Soviet Union in which the Soviets traded oil and machinery for sugar, and they also loaned Cuba $100 million. Khrushchev pronounced the Monroe Doctrine dead and said Soviet rockets would defend Cuba from U.S. "aggression." Washington responded by cutting the import quota on Cuba's sugar sharply.

Eisenhower decided by mid-1960 that Castro would have to be removed from power by whatever means necessary. The president preferred to work through the Organization of American States (OAS), but that route proved ineffective. Castro had supporters among OAS members; they admired him as a nationalist who had defied the United States. Others feared to oppose Castro lest he foment unrest among their people. Frustrated by OAS inaction, Ike approved a CIA project to train Cuban exiles for an invasion of Cuba to overthrow Castro. The CIA established a training site in Guatemala and began preparations. The United States then embargoed all trade with Cuba and severed diplomatic relations.

Cuban agents meanwhile spread Castroism elsewhere in Latin America and Washington tried to blunt Castro's appeal by promoting social reform. Administration officials, working through the OAS, promoted a reform agenda including tax reform, improved housing and schools, land reform, and economic development. Congress appropriated $500 million to launch the ambitious program. President John Kennedy, upon assuming office, endorsed the effort, increased the funding, and supplied an upbeat title, "The Alliance for Progress." The aid program failed to get off the ground. Administered by corrupt officials, opposed by ruling elites in every country, it was also too closely tied to the status quo to be effective.

CONTROVERSY IN EUROPE

During the late 1950s, the Cold War in Europe intensified, erasing any lingering "spirit of Geneva." The Soviets used the psychological advantage gained by their space exploits to put pressure on the United States. In November 1958, Khrushchev, unhappy with the integration of West Germany into NATO and the unresolved German question, announced that within six months he would sign a separate peace treaty with East Germany, thereby ending Western occupation rights in West Berlin. Another Cold War crisis was at hand.

Ike stood firm. He refused to abandon West Berlin, but he also used diplomacy to avoid a confrontation with the Soviets. Khrushchev extended the Berlin

On July 7, 1959, Vice President Richard Nixon, accompanied by the Soviet leader, Nikita Khrushchev, made an official visit to the American pavilion at an exhibit in Moscow. Moments later, the two leaders staged their famous "kitchen debate," arguing over the merits of their respective systems of government. The debate was one of the dramatic moments of the Cold War. *Source:* National Archives.

deadline following Eisenhower's invitation to him to visit the United States. Khrushchev spent two weeks in the United States in the summer of 1959, the first Soviet leader ever to set foot in America. Following meetings with Eisenhower at Camp David, an ebullient Khrushchev announced the cancellation of his Berlin ultimatum. At the same time, Ike suggested that the troubling question of West Berlin ought to be speedily resolved. Once again, a Cold War crisis over Berlin receded. A month after Khrushchev's American tour, Eisenhower announced that there would be another summit meeting in Paris scheduled for May 1960, and he invited the Soviet leader to attend. Khrushchev accepted and invited the President to visit the Soviet Union following the summit. Ike accepted Khrushchev's invitation. The Cold War appeared to be thawing once again.

But the Paris summit never met. Two weeks before its scheduled opening, the Soviets shot down an American U-2 spy plane over Soviet soil. Initially, the United States stated that a weather reconnaissance plane had flown off course and inadvertently violated Soviet air space. An angry Khrushchev then revealed that the aircraft had been shot down 1,200 miles into the Soviet Union and that the Soviets had captured the pilot who admitted that he had been on a spy mission. When President Eisenhower took full responsibility for the flight and refused to repudiate it, Khrushchev angrily denounced Eisenhower, canceled the summit, and withdrew Ike's invitation to visit the Soviet Union. Eisenhower deeply regretted the breakup of the summit, seeing all his efforts for peace dashed because of the U-2 incident. Khrushchev, having spurned Eisenhower, waited for the Americans to select a new president.

END OF AN ERA

The U-2 incident, the launching of Sputnik, and the seemingly endless crises of the Cold War took their toll on the American people in the late 1950s. American prestige and power in the world declined. This sense of declining power to control events in the world spurred a rising debate in this country over national purpose. Social critics wondered if Americans retained the same drive to achieve goals that had motivated previous generations. Did Americans still want to be great? Did they have the will to face future Soviet challenges? Had Americans gone soft from technology and affluence? Aldai Stevenson said the nation suffered from a "paralysis of will"; Americans appeared committed only to "pleasure and profit" and the "pursuit of ease."

In the spring of 1960, both *Life* and *The New York Times* published a series of commentaries on the national purpose written by prominent authors. All agreed that something was lacking in the national spirit. President Eisenhower established a National Goals Commission to develop national objectives. The commission brought out a book, *Goals for Americans,* in which it recommended an increase in military spending to meet the Soviet challenge, a government commitment to an expanding economy, a college education available to all, the promotion of scientific research and the arts, and a guaranteed right to vote for all citizens. The commission's suggested goals expressed a need felt by many Americans to restate the meaning of national existence; to reaffirm the American identity in a dangerous world; and to point the direction in which American society should be heading. John Kennedy later adapted many of the National Goals Commission's recommendations to his New Frontier agenda.

As Eisenhower prepared to leave office, the United States faced crises in Cuba, Berlin, and Southeast Asia. All were bequeathed to his young successor. On January 17, 1961, Ike spoke to the American people for the last time as president. His Farewell Address consisted of a series of warnings, as had George Washington's famed address of 1797. He warned of the Communist menace, he warned of squandering the nation's resources, and he warned about spending too much on either welfare or warfare. The most famous part of his valedictory warned about the power of the military establishment and its corporate clients:

> We must guard against the acquisition of unwarranted influence, whether sought or unsought, by the military-industrial complex.[6]

Ike asserted that the military–industrial complex could endanger basic liberties and democratic processes. In light of Vietnam and Watergate, the old general's warnings proved to be prophetic. He understood more clearly than any other modern president the dangers the Cold War posed to his people's wealth and freedom.

Eisenhower presided over a peaceful and prosperous interlude in American history. But as he exited public life, the nation faced many foreign crises and

[6]Quoted in *Ibid.,* p. 289.

unsolved domestic problems. The civil rights movement was gathering momentum and other disadvantaged groups would soon challenge the status quo. Although the United States remained the world's wealthiest and most powerful nation, its prosperity and power had suffered relative decline in the late 1950s. Western Europe and Japan prospered. Russia's military power and diplomatic influence were expanding. Anti-Western nationalism intensified among Third World countries. Eisenhower's successors in the 1960s would increase American military power and intensify the Cold War. They would also propose a broad range of social reforms. Troubled times lay ahead.

IMPORTANT EVENTS

1950	*The Lonely Crowd,* by David Riesman and others, is published
1950	J. D. Salinger's *Catcher in the Rye* is published
1952	Dwight D. Eisenhower is elected president
1953	Eisenhower appoints Earl Warren Chief Justice of the Supreme Court
1954	The Supreme Court rules on *Brown* v. *Board of Education of Topeka, Kansas*
1954	The Geneva conference partitions Vietnam at the seventeenth parallel
1954	Army–McCarthy hearings result in Senate condemnation of McCarthy
1955	Bus boycott in Montgomery, Alabama, ignites the modern civil rights movement
1955	The AFL and the CIO merge
1955	"Summit" conference is held at Geneva
1956	Elvis Presley's first superhit, "Heartbreak Hotel" is sold
1956	The Federal Highway Act passed
1956	The Suez Crisis erupts
1956	Soviet tanks crush the Hungarian revolution
1957	School desegregation crisis occurs in Little Rock, Arkansas
1957	The first modern Civil Rights Act is enacted
1957	Jack Kerouac's *On the Road* is published
1957	The Soviets launch "Sputnik"
1958	NASA is established
1958	U.S. Marines hit the beaches in Lebanon
1959	Castro comes to power in Cuba
1959	Nikita Khrushchev visits the United States
1960	U-2 incident causes impending summit meeting to be canceled
1961	Eisenhower makes his farewell address

BIBLIOGRAPHY

There are many fine books written about American economic, social, and cultural history during the 1945 to 1960 period. John Kenneth Galbraith's *The Affluent Society* is a good analysis of the postwar prosperity. John B. Rae, in *The American Automobile,* writes about the car culture of the 1950s. Landon Y. Jones's *Great Expectations: America and the Baby Boom Generation* is the best study of the most important demographic developments of postwar America. One of the finest accounts of suburbia is John Keats's *The Crack in the Picture Window.* Will Herberg, in *Catholic–Protestant–Jew,* writes about the important role of religion in mid-century American society. C. Wright Mills's *White Collar: The American Middle Class* is an account by a radical critic of the affluent society. Two classic studies of the social and cultural history of the 1950s are by David Riesman and others (*The Lonely Crowd: A Study of the Changing American Character*) and by William H. Whyte, Jr. (*The Organization Man*). Myron Matlaw's *American Popular Entertainment* has sections on television, pop music, and films of the 1950s. Erik Barnouw's *Tube of Plenty* is a fine study of television during its "golden age." Bruce Cook, in *The Beat Generation,* writes about the beat writers who flourished in the late 1950s. Juan Williams's *Eyes on the Prize: America's Civil Rights Years, 1954–1965* is a stirring account of the civil rights movement. The political history of the 1950s is generally well covered by Charles C. Alexander in *Holding the Line: the Eisenhower Era, 1952–1961.* Stephen E. Ambrose, in *Eisenhower the President,* offers the best account of the Eisenhower presidency. Robert A. Divine's *Eisenhower and the Cold War* is the best diplomatic history of the Eisenhower years. Michael A. Guhin, in *John Foster Dulles: A Statesman and His Times,* gives the fullest treatment of Eisenhower's energetic Secretary of State. Using recently released documents and records, Keith Kyle, in *Suez,* has written a good account of that crucial episode in U.S.–Middle Eastern diplomatic history.

CHAPTER 11

New Frontiers

In the early 1960s, Americans regained the confidence in their national destiny that had faltered in the late 1950s when the economy went slack and the Soviets appeared to have gained a strategic advantage in the Cold War. The economy revived. Most middle-class American families enjoyed unprecedented affluence and their children's prospects never looked better. An energetic and articulate young president kindled this resurgent optimism. John Fitzgerald Kennedy voiced national goals in language that Americans, particularly young Americans, could understand and accept. He told Americans that they could face the challenges of mid-century life, hold their own in world affairs, and solve nagging social problems at home. A new activist spirit surged across the land. For a few years, a spirit of "Camelot" reigned, a belief that anything was possible, that nothing was beyond the grasp of Americans.

A PATH TO THE PRESIDENCY

John F. "Jack" Kennedy inherited a rich political legacy. Both of his grandfathers, second-generation Irish immigrants, had been prominent ethnic politicians in Boston. His father, Joseph P. "Joe" Kennedy, a Harvard graduate, made a fortune estimated at $150 million in banking, real estate, and other enterprises. Joe Kennedy, a conservative Democratic supporter of Franklin Roosevelt, served as the Security and Exchange Commission's first chairman and later as Ambassador to Great Britain. Jack's political career began successfully when he won election to Congress in 1946 representing a working-class section of Boston. His father played a major behind-the-scenes role, providing both money and influence to help his son win. During Jack's congressional career, he represented his constituents' interests and he remained popular in his "safe" Democratic district.

    While in Congress, Kennedy introduced no important legislation nor identified himself with any major issue. He usually took liberal positions on domestic issues. He worked to purge Communists from union ranks, and he opposed the Taft-Hartley Act. On foreign policy, he sometimes aligned himself with conservative Republican critics of Truman's Far Eastern policy. He supported General MacArthur's call for war against China in 1951, and Truman's firing of the old general outraged him. He formed political friendships with two rising Republican stars, Congressman Richard Nixon and Senator Joseph McCarthy.

    Jack sought to move up to the Senate in 1952, even though it was clearly a Republican year. The GOP ran the popular war hero, General Dwight Eisenhower, for president. Richard Nixon and Joe McCarthy drew blood with their supercharged attacks on corruption and Communism in the Truman administration. Jack Kennedy faced a formidable challenge and began his campaign against the incumbent, Henry Cabot Lodge, Jr., as the underdog. He ran as a moderate Democrat and dissociated himself from the Democratic national ticket, which was obviously losing that year. In a close race, his father's money and Kennedy's superb campaign organization, led by his younger brother Robert, proved to be the decisive factors. His election to the Senate in November 1952 signaled the arrival of a new-style Democratic politician. Kennedy was the leader of an emergent generation of postwar Democrats who were less liberal, less idealistic, and less partisan than the traditional New Deal–Fair Dealers who had rallied to Adlai Stevenson's failed presidential bid.

    The election also represented a major turning point in Jack Kennedy's political journey. The young senator-elect began his career as a national leader that would carry him to the presidency. In the Senate, Kennedy could devote more attention to foreign affairs, always his major interest. He consistently advocated a strong Cold War policy and called for increased defense spending. He became a critic of the Eisenhower–Dulles New Look foreign policy. Kennedy thought their cuts in defense spending unwise, and he criticized their approach to the emerging nations of the Third World. He opposed giving aid to the French in Southeast Asia unless the administration prodded them to grant the people of Indochina independence. Senator Kennedy also became more partisan and liberal, and he held ambitions for higher office.

    Early in his Senate career, Kennedy had to confront his relationship with Senator Joseph McCarthy. He was caught in several binds when the Senate moved to censure McCarthy in late 1954. At the time, Kennedy was recovering from back surgery and a postoperative infection that had nearly killed him. He was living at his parent's mansion in West Palm Beach, Florida, when the vote was taken that ruined McCarthy. Kennedy faced a dilemma. Nearly all Democrats, President Eisenhower, and many Republican Senators favored censuring the irresponsible demagogue. Yet McCarthy was his friend and Jack had supported some of his earlier investigations of Communism. McCarthy was also a friend of his father's, and Joe Kennedy had contributed money to McCarthy's cause. Jack's younger brother Robert had worked for a time on McCarthy's staff. His former congressional district was McCarthyite and McCarthy had a strong following in Massachusetts. Even though ill and absent from the Senate when the vote was taken, Kennedy could have voted to condemn McCarthy. Instead, he used his illness as an excuse to abstain. He was the only northern Democrat who didn't vote to condemn McCarthy, an evasion that caused him trouble with the Democratic party's liberal elders when he sought the presidency in 1960.

At the 1956 Democratic convention, Jack Kennedy made a strong bid for the Democratic vice-presidential nomination. He lost narrowly to Senator Estes Kefauver of Tennessee. Many Americans got their first look at Kennedy during his fight for the vice presidency, and they liked what they saw. As it turned out, it was to his political advantage to be defeated at the convention. Had he got the vice-presidential nomination and run with Adlai Stevenson, he would have shared the humiliation of another lopsided electoral defeat at the hands of the popular incumbents, Eisenhower and Nixon. Such an outcome could have derailed his future presidential bid.

THE 1960 ELECTION

A Democratic resurgence began with the 1958 midterm elections. A series of events had shaken public confidence in the Eisenhower administration: Sputnik and the apparent missile and space race gaps, crises in the Middle East, and a sharp recession at home that had driven unemployment above 7 percent, the highest since 1941. And, the Sherman Adams scandal tarnished the antiseptic image the Republicans had enjoyed since coming to office. The Democrats increased their majorities 64 to 34 in the Senate and 283 to 153 in the House, their largest margins since the New Deal heyday of 1936. In Massachusetts, John Kennedy won a lopsided reelection victory. His impressive performance made him the Democratic front-runner for 1960.

Many Democratic leaders entered the race for their party's 1960 presidential nomination. With the popular Ike forced to resign because of the Twenty-second Amendment, prospects for a Democratic victory looked better than at any time since the glory days of FDR. Other candidates included Senator Hubert Humphrey, Senator Stuart Symington, and Senate majority leader Lyndon Johnson. Adlai Stevenson was still a contender even though he had lost twice to Eisenhower.

Two obstacles blocked Kennedy's path to the nomination. First, he would have to dispel the myth that a Catholic could never be elected President. The second obstacle was the candidacies of his powerful rivals, all of whom had longer, more distinguished political careers than he. Kennedy was an upstart among seasoned veterans of the political wars. Many informed observers believed that Kennedy lacked the experience, confidence, and stature necessary to run the country in the 1960s.

Victories in the early primaries gave him momentum that carried him to the nomination. Only Humphrey challenged him in these popularity contests. Symington and Johnson took the organizational route to the nomination, seeking delegates from the thirty-four states that did not hold primaries. Stevenson did not campaign, relying on his liberal followers to orchestrate his nomination at the convention if Kennedy's bid fell short. Jack eliminated Humphrey early. He beat him decisively in New Hampshire, Wisconsin, and West Virginia. Kennedy demonstrated he could win and put the Catholic issue to rest. His organization contained a Stevenson boom that developed at the convention, and Kennedy won a close first-ballot nomination. Kennedy chose Lyndon Johnson, who had come in second to Jack in the balloting for president, to be his vice-presidential running mate. He needed Johnson to win Texas and to hold the South if he was to have any chance of winning the presidency in November.

In his acceptance speech, Kennedy attacked the Eisenhower administration's handling of Cold War issues; he claimed the Republicans had been too soft in responding to Communist threats, and he pledged a stronger approach. He set forth an agenda of unfinished business facing the nation in the 1960s:

> We stand today at the edge of a New Frontier—the frontier of the 1960s—a frontier of unknown opportunities and perils—a frontier of unfulfilled hopes and threats.[1]

When the Republicans gathered in Chicago a week later, Richard Nixon had the nomination sewn up. The nearest thing to a challenge came from Nelson Rockefeller, governor of New York. He had no chance and withdrew long before the convention. But Rockefeller influenced the party platform. Two days before the convention opened, Nixon accepted Rockefeller's proposals calling for stronger defense programs, faster buildup of missiles, stronger civil rights measures, and government stimulation of the economy to promote economic growth. The Republican platform came out similar to the Democratic one and amounted to an implicit indictment of Eisenhower administration policies. Conservative Republicans reacted angrily to the Rockefeller platform. Arizona Senator Barry Goldwater called it "The Munich of the Republican Party." Nixon had to use all his clout to keep the unhappy conservatives in the party fold.

The 1960 presidential campaign broke all records for money spent and miles traveled by candidates. Nixon campaigned in all fifty states. Kennedy traveled over 100,000 miles in a jet airplane leased by his family for the campaign. It was the toughest, closest presidential election in modern American political history, and it generated tremendous interest among the electorate.

Despite the candidates' dramatically different backgrounds—Nixon, the poor boy from rural Southern California who had fought his way up the political ladder; and Kennedy, the privileged aristocrat whose political career depended largely on his father's wealth and influence—they shared similar political views. Nixon was a moderate conservative with liberal tendencies. Kennedy was a moderate liberal with conservative tendencies. Both were Cold Warriors. Both accepted the basic structure of the New Deal welfare state. Both advocated civil rights and

---

[1]Quoted in Herbert Parmet, *JFK: The Presidency of John F. Kennedy* (New York: Penguin Books, 1984), p. 31.

believed in a strong presidency. Both were young men, Nixon 47 and Kennedy 43. Because they shared similar political views, the campaign featured few substantial debates over the issues; they quarreled over details and means. Each challenged the other's capacity to govern and insisted that he was the better man. Because the electorate perceived their views to be so similar, the outcome of the election turned on personal image and the voter's feel for one or the other, not on the issues.

Even though he was only a few years older than Kennedy, Nixon tried to portray his opponent as immature and inexperienced, a dangerous man to have at the helm in the nuclear age. Kennedy linked Nixon to what he called "the horse and buggy" policies of Eisenhower that had let the nation fall behind the Soviets in missile and space technology and had let the economy stagnate. Jack promised "to get the country moving again" by providing strong leadership. He reminded audiences that although Richard Nixon might act the role of statesman in 1960, behind that facade lurked the real Nixon, the mudslinger of the early 1950s, the man who belonged to the party of Lincoln, but unlike Lincoln, showed "charity to none and malice toward all."

Nixon began the campaign with some liabilities. The sagging economy was the most serious. And, Eisenhower gave him only lukewarm support. Ike made matters temporarily worse for the candidate when a reporter asked him what decisions Nixon had helped him make and the old general quipped: "If you give me a week, I might think of one." Even so, the early advantage clearly lay with Nixon. He was far better known to the American people because of his active role in Eisenhower's administration, and he used this role to make his point that he was better qualified for presidential leadership than Kennedy, Eisenhower's quip notwithstanding. September public opinion polls gave Nixon the lead. The election appeared to be Nixon's to lose.

Kennedy's religious affiliation was an important campaign issue and he met his detractors forthrightly. He clearly stated his views: There was nothing in his religion that would prevent him from obeying his constitutional oath and governing the nation; he supported the First Amendment's separation of church and state; he opposed federal aid to parochial schools; and he favored birth control. He appeared before a gathering of prominent Protestant leaders in Houston and he told the ministers, "I am not the Catholic candidate for president, I am the Democratic party's candidate for president, who also happens to be a Catholic." As he neared the end of his short speech, he told the assembled divines:

> If this election is decided on the basis that 40 million Americans lost their chance of being President on the day they were baptized, then it is the whole nation that will be the loser in the eyes of history, and in the eyes of our own people.[2]

Kennedy won his audience. When he finished, the ministers gave him a warm, standing ovation. His performance could not remove anti-Catholicism from the

[2]Quoted in *Ibid.,* p. 43.

campaign, but it defused the religious issue and freed Kennedy to concentrate on attacking Nixon.

The highlight of the campaign occurred when the candidates staged four nationally televised debates between September 26 and October 21, the first televised debates between presidential candidates. The debates reflected the growing influence that television was now playing in the nation's political life. The first debate was decisive and Kennedy won it. Nixon looked haggard; he was weakened by a knee infection and tired from a day's campaigning. He was victimized by a poor makeup job that did not hide his dark stubble. On camera under hot lights, the makeup powder streaked as Nixon sweated noticeably. He faltered answering some of the questions. Kennedy, by contrast, was fresh and primed for the encounter. He exuded cool, cheerful confidence. He displayed a sure grasp of the issues, an agile intelligence, and a sharp wit. He dispelled any lingering doubts about his maturity or his ability to be President. Nixon did much better in the three subsequent debates and had a slight advantage overall. But he could not completely overcome the disadvantage of his appearance and performance during that first debate.

In none of the debates did the candidates explore issues in depth, and no clear issue distinctions between them surfaced. The debates were essentially popularity contests, whose outcomes depended on the cosmetic factors of personality and appearance. Kennedy won the one that counted most. October polls showed Kennedy taking the lead for the first time. In the final month of campaigning, Kennedy attracted large, excited crowds. He appeared along a beach in Southern California and was mobbed by excited followers behaving like rock 'n' roll or movie star fans. He had momentum and the Democrats sensed victory.

But in the final week of the campaign, the Republicans almost pulled it out. Nixon strongly defended the Eisenhower record and hammered away at Kennedy's inexperience in international affairs. Republicans staged a media blitz across the nation. Eisenhower entered the fray. He campaigned energetically for Nixon in those final days. On election day, Ike went on national television to exhort the American people to elect Nixon and to reject Kennedy. The old campaigner nearly eliminated Jack's lead.

Kennedy's 303-to-219 edge in electoral votes marked the closest presidential election in American history. In some states, the outcome was in doubt for days. Kennedy, by narrowly winning populous states such as New York, Pennsylvania, Michigan, and Texas squeezed out victory. Out of a record 68 million votes cast, Kennedy's margin of victory was about 118,000. Kennedy got 49.7 percent of the popular vote to Nixon's 49.5 percent. In congressional elections, Republicans picked up twenty-two seats in the House and two seats in the Senate, leaving the Democrats with large majorities in both. Most Democratic candidates ran better than Kennedy. His party was more popular than he. There were no presidential coattails in 1960.

It is impossible to say precisely what factor determined Kennedy's hairline victory. In such a close election, many variables could have determined the outcome,

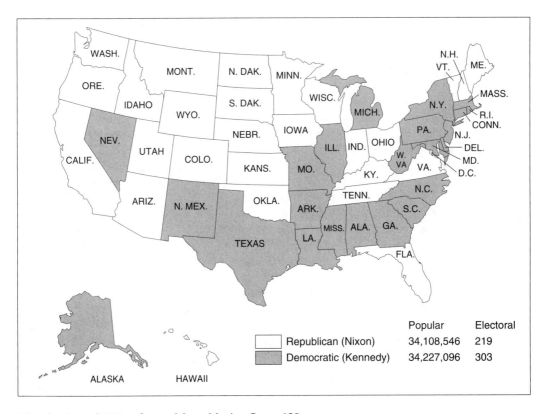

	Popular	Electoral
☐ Republican (Nixon)	34,108,546	219
▨ Democratic (Kennedy)	34,227,096	303

The election of 1960.   *Source:* Moss, *Moving On*, p. 138.

and there are too many imponderables involved. Suppose Eisenhower had entered the campaign a week earlier? Kennedy's religion cut both ways: In rural, Protestant areas of the South, Southwest, and West it cost him votes, but in northeastern, mid-western, and western urban states, it gained him votes. On balance, he may have gained more votes than he lost from his religion, for the states where people voted for him because of his religious affiliation contained the largest clusters of electoral votes. Kennedy benefited from the televised debates, particularly the first one. A poll showed 57 percent of voters felt that the debates had affected their choice, and, of these, 75 percent voted for Kennedy. Kennedy himself said, "It was TV more than anything else which won it." The winner also ran well among black voters, getting more of them than Stevenson had in 1956. Kennedy had followed a bold strategy during the campaign of relying on Johnson to hold white southerners while he appealed for black voters. He responded to an appeal to help Dr. Martin Luther King, Jr., gain release from a Georgia jail where his wife feared he would be killed. Kennedy promised to sign an executive order forbidding segregation in federally subsidized housing. Black votes provided his winning margin in Texas and North Carolina, and he got most of the northern, black, inner-city vote.

A new generation comes to power. . . . John F. Kennedy chats with outgoing President Dwight D. Eisenhower on the way to the inauguration ceremony January 20, 1961.   *Source:* National Archives.

The 1960 election signaled the end of the Solid South. Nixon got about half the southern vote in 1960. After the race, Nixon noted that had he concentrated his efforts on the South in the final week, he might have won the election. He would put that knowledge to good use in 1968. Kennedy did well in traditional Republican strongholds in New England, the Midwest, and the suburbs everywhere. Sectional, class, and party loyalties continued to erode. Many voters split their tickets in 1960. Millions of Republicans, many of them Catholics, voted for Kennedy. Millions of Democrats, mostly Protestants, voted for Nixon. The 1960 election further blurred the distinctions between the major parties and their candidates. The politics of consensus still prevailed.

THE KENNEDY STYLE

Kennedy's inauguration occurred on a clear, cold day in Washington, January 20, 1961. The inaugural ceremony vividly expressed the fresh start his administration intended to make. Consciously emulating Franklin Roosevelt, who had roused the country from depression torpor in 1933, Kennedy intended to "get the country moving again." Black singer Marion Anderson sang the national anthem. Poet Robert Frost read from his works. Kennedy's speech stirred the nation:

> Let the word go forth from this time and place, to friend and foe alike, that the torch has been passed to a new generation of Americans. . . .[3]

He called for a global alliance against the common enemies of mankind, "tyranny, poverty, disease, and war itself." It was high noon in the Cold War and Kennedy welcomed the challenge: "In the long history of the world, only a few generations have been granted the role of defending freedom in its hour of maximum danger. I do not shrink from this responsibility, I welcome it." He sent a warning to the Kremlin: "Let every nation know, whether it wishes us well or ill, that we shall pay any price, bear any burden, meet any hardship, support any friend, oppose any foe to assure the survival and the success of liberty. . . ." As he approached the end of his splendid speech, he spoke his most famous line. He appealed to his countrymen, especially to young Americans, to

> ask not what your country can do for you—ask what you can do for your country.[4]

The new Administration accented youth, brains, action, and glamour. Kennedy and his beautiful young wife, Jacqueline, exuded stylish charm. Intellectuals were frequent visitors to the White House. Kennedy hosted a dinner for Nobel Prize winners. Distinguished musicians performed there. The Kennedys and their friends played touch football on the White House lawn, conveying the youthful energy and exuberance characterizing the new government. Kennedy's salient presidential traits included energy, enthusiasm, confidence, and intelligence. He was the author of two books and he represented himself as the man of action comfortable in the world of ideas.

Kennedy believed in a strong, centralized presidency that operated free of the restraints of Congress, public opinion, and the media. He thought that the major problems he had inherited from the outgoing administration—a sluggish economy at home and Cold War crises abroad—stemmed from Eisenhower's failure to assert his power and to streamline the executive office for action. Kennedy was determined to energize the presidency. He would be at the center of action.

He selected able advisers to assist him; men who had compiled impressive dossiers as tough, energetic, and pragmatic managers who got things done. Secretary of State Dean Rusk came from the Rockefeller Foundation. For Secretary of Defense, he chose Robert S. McNamara, the president of Ford Motor Company. McGeorge Bundy, an administrator from Harvard, was appointed National Security Advisor. Bundy managed foreign policy. Kennedy's talented young staffer who had served with him in the Senate, Theodore Sorensen, took charge of domestic issues and wrote many of his speeches. Kennedy's younger brother Robert became Attorney General. When critics complained that "Bobby" was too young

[3]Quoted in Arthur M. Schlesinger, Jr., *A Thousand Days* (Greenwich, CT: Fawcett Publications, 1965), p. 13.
[4]Quoted in *Ibid.*, p. 14.

John F. Kennedy projected a vision of national renewal. He encouraged Americans, especially young people, to "ask not what your country can do for you—ask what you can do for your country." *Source:* Library of Congress.

and inexperienced for the job, the President quipped, "I thought my brother might as well get some experience before beginning the practice of law." He appointed several Republicans to try to reassure the business community that his administration would not be antibusiness nor an inflationary spender.

THE COLD WARRIOR

Kennedy gave top priority to the conduct of American foreign and military policy that centered on America's global rivalry with the Soviet Union. Cold War ideology shaped his view of the world. He viewed the Communist system itself as the Free World's main enemy:

> . . . implacable, insatiable, unceasing in its drive for world domination. For this is not a struggle for supremacy of arms alone—it is also a struggle for supremacy between two conflicting ideologies: Freedom under God versus ruthless, godless tyranny.[5]

Kennedy and his advisers made their major goal the development of policies and means to restore American primacy in world affairs. They would reverse the

[5]Quoted in Herbert Parmet, *Jack: The Struggles of John F. Kennedy* (New York: Dial Press, 1980).

decline that they believed had occurred under the cautious leadership of Eisenhower. They viewed the Third World as the key to winning the Cold War. It was among the underdeveloped countries of Asia, Africa, and Latin America where the battle against Communism would be joined and won. He told an audience at the University of California in Berkeley that "freedom and diversity," the essence of the American way, would prevail in the "lands of the rising people" over the Communist monolith. He had a bold vision, rooted in a deep faith in the American system, confident that American technology and expertise could prevail in the long, twilight struggle with the Soviet menace.

THE BAY OF PIGS

The new Administration encountered its first Cold War crisis in Cuba. Kennedy no more than his predecessor could tolerate the existence of a Communist state in the Caribbean that expropriated American property, developed close ties with the Soviet Union, and tried to foment revolution in Latin America. The CIA project to overthrow Castro, begun by Eisenhower six months earlier, readied for action. Anti-Castro Cuban exiles, many of them former liberal supporters of the Cuban dictator, had been trained for an amphibious assault on Cuba at a secret camp set up in the Guatemalan mountains. CIA officials believed that an invasion of Cuba would activate a general uprising within Cuba that would overthrow Castro. Kennedy, after consultations with senior advisers, gave the operation the green light. The invasion would be risky, but Kennedy and his New Frontiersmen were eager to strike the Communists.

About 1,450 invaders, debarking from a Nicaraguan port in ships provided by the CIA, landed before dawn on April 13, 1961, at the Bay of Pigs, a remote area on the southern Cuba coast. Castro quickly deployed his forces to meet them. The invaders, lacking adequate artillery support and air cover, were pinned on the beach and overwhelmed. All but about one hundred of them were killed or captured within three days. The invaders never made contact with Cuban underground elements, and the expected anti-Castro uprising never occurred.

The Bay of Pigs disaster humiliated the Kennedy administration. The United States' European allies sharply criticized its actions, and Third World spokesmen took turns condemning the United States at the United Nations. Within the United States, liberals attacked Kennedy for undertaking the invasion, and conservatives condemned him for failing to overthrow Castro. America stood exposed as both imperialistic and inept, a pathetic combination of wickedness and weakness.

The U.S.–backed invasion had violated the Organization of American States (OAS) charter that prohibited any Western Hemispheric nation from intervening in another's affairs. Latin American nations, resenting the thinly disguised American reversion to gunboat diplomacy, refused the United States' request to quarantine Cuba from inter-American affairs. Castro and Khrushchev enjoyed a propaganda harvest. Castro emerged from the affair stronger than ever. Both Soviet aid to Cuba

Cuban dictator Fidel Castro reviews Cuban troops with his brother Raul, the commander of the Cuban armed forces. Looming behind them is a statue of Jose Marti, Cuba's first president. *Source:* National Archives.

and the pace of Cuban socialization of private properties accelerated in the aftermath of the failed invasion.

The invasion project had been ill conceived and mismanaged from the start. The CIA victimized itself with faulty intelligence data and wishful thinking. It underestimated Castro's military strength and exaggerated the extent of anti-Castro sentiment in Cuba. Kennedy ensured the mission's failure when he curtailed CIA air strikes preceding the landings and then refused all requests for naval air support that might have salvaged the failing operation. Kennedy had concluded that the invasion had failed and that air cover could not save it, so he decided to cut his losses. He also did not want a war with Cuba, and he wanted to preserve the fiction that the invasion was a Cuban affair.

Kennedy got a rough baptism of fire and his first serious criticism as president. He assumed full responsibility for the fiasco, but afterwards, ordered an investigation of the CIA. He forced its aged director, Allen Dulles, into retirement and replaced him with John McCone, a conservative California oilman. Kennedy also made an aggressive speech before a convention of newspaper editors in which he reaffirmed his determination to be rid of Castro.

According to the findings of a special Senate investigating committee that later examined CIA covert operations, Kennedy ordered the CIA to eliminate Castro following the failure of the Bay of Pigs invasion. Robert Kennedy took charge of Operation Mongoose, which included efforts to disrupt the Cuban economy and to support anti-Castro elements. During 1961 and 1962, CIA operatives tried various schemes to kill the Cuban dictator. These efforts included cigars laced with explosives and deadly poison and an attempt to spear him with a harpoon while he was snorkling at a Caribbean resort. CIA agents also plotted with Mafia elements to get rid of Castro but had to abandon the project because of opposition from FBI director J. Edgar Hoover. Castro knew about Operation Mongoose and he was aware of some of the CIA plots to assassinate him. He appealed to his allies in Moscow for help. The Soviets responded by sending troops to Cuba. In October 1962, they would try to station nuclear-capable, intermediate-range missiles in Cuba, which provoked the most dangerous crisis of the Cold War.

THE THIRD WORLD

During his campaign for the presidency, Kennedy had repeatedly criticized the Eisenhower administration for failing to promote economic development and the growth of political democracy among the nations of Latin America, Asia, and Africa. Kennedy insisted that such neglect had given the Soviet Union opportunities to get ahead of the United States in the race for influence among the strategically important developing nations of the Third World. Kennedy pledged to help these nations modernize their societies and to restore American influence among them.

For Latin America, the Kennedy administration developed a multifaceted assistance program called the Alliance for Progress. Kennedy proposed the Alliance in a dramatic speech given in Mexico City in May 1961. The Alliance built upon and expanded Eisenhower's previously announced aid program for Latin America. Congress appropriated $500 million to start the program designed to eradicate poverty and social injustice in the Western Hemisphere. Over the life of the program, billions of dollars in loans and grants from both public and private sources were fed into the Alliance for Progress. In most Latin American countries, the results were disappointing. Conservative governments refused to reform their tax systems, grant land reform, or democratize their politics. Economic growth was sluggish throughout the 1960s in the region. Unemployment rates, mortality rates, literacy rates, and years of schooling did not improve in most Latin American countries. Perhaps the elite classes who held power in these lands feared Castroism as much as Kennedy, but they preferred to rely on repression rather than take their chances with social reform. If the Alliance for Progress could have succeeded, it would have required far more funds than were made available and mechanisms would have to have been created to bypass the governing elites and get money directly to poor people most in need.

In the summer of 1961, the Kennedy administration launched the Peace Corps, a much more successful initiative to help people in Third World countries. The Peace Corps derived from the same Cold War concern to involve the United States more directly in Third World countries and to give idealistic young Americans an opportunity for public service. Over the next two years, about seventy-five hundred Peace Corps volunteers, mostly young people, were sent to forty-four nations in Asia, Africa, and Latin America. Most of them worked as teachers; others found jobs in health care, agricultural reform, and community development. Many of the young people who served in the Peace Corps not only found an opportunity to help poor people but also returned to America with a greater appreciation of the diversity of the world's cultures. Most recipients of Peace Corp assistance were grateful and admired the young Americans that they got to know.

Although Africa remained a relatively low priority with the Kennedy administration, the United States did intervene in Zaire, formerly the Belgian Congo, in 1961, to support an anti-Communist leader as head of the government. The CIA maneuvered to block more radical candidates from coming to power whom Washington feared might have the backing of the Soviet Union. Amidst chaotic conditions civil war broke out and the United States pulled out. Washington then backed ultimately successful United Nations efforts to end the civil war and to prevent Zaire from disintegrating.

BERLIN

At the beginning of his Presidency, Kennedy and Secretary of Defense McNamara began a crash program to expand and diversify America's military forces. They believed that Eisenhower's reliance on massive retaliation and his refusal to engage the Soviets in a missile race had set dangerous limits to the American ability to counter Soviet-backed insurgencies in Third World countries. The United States rapidly increased its strategic nuclear forces that included ICBMs, missile-launching Polaris submarines, and long-range bombers. They also built up conventional war capabilities, adding a Kennedy favorite, counterinsurgency forces. The President sought strategic versatility, which he termed "flexible response"—the ability to intervene anywhere in the world with flexible force levels in response to Soviet or Soviet-backed initiatives.

The Kennedy military buildup had broad bipartisan congressional and popular support. At the same time the United States expanded its military capacities, Kennedy repeatedly urged the Soviets to join in arms limitation talks aimed at reducing the arms race. But Khrushchev responded by increasing Soviet military spending for more ICBMs, the backbone of the Soviet strategic system. The American arms buildup triggered another upward spiral in the nuclear arms race.

Having been burned badly by the Bay of Pigs fiasco, Kennedy was more determined than ever to respond strongly to Communist threats. He worried lest his administration appear weak-willed and lose prestige in the eyes of the world and its own people. Three months after the invasion, he met for a series of private talks with Khrushchev in Vienna in June 1961. The two leaders exchanged views on a wide range of issues, and used the occasion to size each other up. Kennedy was calm, rational, and polite in these conversations. Khrushchev's moods varied. At times he talked warmly of peaceful coexistence between Communism and capitalism. At other times he got angry, even threatening. He turned ideologue, asserting the inevitable triumph of socialism in the world. He bullied the young president, coming away from these meetings with the mistaken impression that Kennedy could be pressured. Khrushchev misread the young aristocrat's civility as weakness. His misjudgment would later contribute to the most dangerous moment in modern history.

The major issue discussed at Vienna was the long-standing problem of Berlin. The German question had never been formally settled after World War II because of Cold War conflicts. At war's end, Germany had been divided into occupation zones by the victorious nations. In 1948 and 1949, the Western zones were merged into one zone, which became the Federal Republic of Germany (West Germany), a Western liberal state. The Soviet zone in eastern Germany became the Socialist Democratic Republic of Germany (East Germany), on which the Soviets imposed a Communist system. By 1950, there existed two de facto German states. Neither state accepted the other as legitimate, but most Germans clung to the hope that someday Germany would again be a unified nation.

Berlin, lying deep within East Germany, also remained divided between East and West, causing periodic crises during the Cold War. Tensions had flared in 1948 when the Soviets had tried to drive the Western nations out of Berlin and Truman thwarted them with the Berlin airlift. Khrushchev pressured Eisenhower in 1958 over Berlin and then backed off when Ike stood firm. Now, with Kennedy in office, the Soviet leader pressed for a peace treaty between the two German states that would legitimate the de facto division of the country, remove the possibility of reunion, and deprive the West of any legal basis for its occupation of West Berlin. Khrushchev told Kennedy that he wanted the Berlin issue settled by year's end; and, if it were not settled, he threatened to conclude a separate peace treaty with East Germany, forcing the West to negotiate with a government that none of the Western states recognized. Khrushchev and the East German rulers also wanted to stop the flow of East Germans into West Berlin. Thousands of East Germans fled poverty and tyranny each month to enter free and prosperous West Germany.

Kennedy rebuffed Khrushchev's proposals and reaffirmed the Western presence in West Berlin. Kennedy told the American people on July 25: "We cannot and will not permit the Communists to drive us out of Berlin. . . ." He also asked Congress to increase military appropriations by $3 billion, tripled draft calls, called up reserves, and extended enlistments of military personnel on active duty. He also asked for $207 million from Congress to expand civil defense fallout shelters, dramatizing the implications of the Berlin crisis.

The Soviet response came August 13 when workers suddenly erected a wall across Berlin imprisoning East Germans in their own country and staunching the flow of refugees. Before the wall, nearly 3 million East Germans had escaped to the West since 1945. During the first twelve days of August 1961, about forty-six thousand had fled Communism. The Soviet action caught the Americans by complete surprise. Some of Kennedy's hawkish advisers urged him to tear the wall down. Kennedy never considered doing that because he did not want to risk war. To reassure West Berliners that accepting the wall did not presage eventual allied withdrawal from the divided city, Kennedy sent an additional fifteen hundred combat troops to West Berlin. In June 1963, he visited West Berlin and told a huge crowd, *"Ich bin ein Berliner"* ("I am a Berliner") to dramatize the U.S. determination to stay.

Months of tension followed the building of the Berlin Wall. East Germans tried to escape over the barrier and were shot by military police. The Berlin Wall quickly became a potent Cold War symbol of the impasse between East and West and of the division of Germany and its major city. It was also a stark admission of Communism's failure to win the hearts and minds of East Germans.

But the wall also provided a practical solution to the Berlin question. It stopped the flow of refugees, which was Khrushchev's immediate goal, and it allowed West Berlin to remain in the Western orbit, which was Kennedy's main goal. German reunification was deferred to the indefinite future. Khrushchev announced in October that he would no longer insist on Western withdrawal from West Berlin. The crisis ended and Berlin was never again a major source of Cold War conflict. But the wall endured for nearly thirty years as the most vivid symbol

President Kennedy goes to the Berlin Wall in June 1963 on a visit to West Berlin. The wall, erected in August 1961, quickly became a stark Cold War symbol of the impasse between the Communist World and the Free World, and it perpetuated the division of Germany in the heart of Europe. *Source:* National Archives.

of European Cold War divisions—until the people of East Germany themselves tore the wall down in November 1989 as they began the process of dismantling the Communist system imposed on them after World War II.

MISSILE CRISIS

Following the Bay of Pigs, the Soviets sent technicians and weapons to Cuba to protect that Communist satellite from American hostility. By the summer of 1962, American intelligence sources estimated that there were between ten and forty thousand Soviet troops stationed in Cuba. Castro also supported guerrilla actions and subversion in other Latin American countries. Republicans, looking for election-year issues, attacked the Kennedy administration for allowing the Soviet arms buildup in Cuba. Kennedy opposed attacking or invading Cuba as long as the Soviets placed only defensive weapons in Cuba that posed no threat to the United States or any other hemispheric nation. But Khrushchev and Castro decided on a daring move to deter any further U.S. action against Cuba and to score a Cold War coup. The Soviets secretly tried to install medium-range and intermediate-range nuclear missiles and bombers in Cuba. These missiles and bombers were offensive weapons capable of carrying nuclear payloads to American cities and military installations.

On October 14, 1962, a U-2 reconnaissance plane photographed a launching site for an intermediate-range missile nearing completion in western Cuba. Kennedy immediately determined that the missiles and bombers must be removed from the island. His sense of strategic and political reality told him that they had to go. But how to get the missiles out of Cuba? How, without triggering a nuclear war? The most dangerous Cold War crisis ever had begun.

Kennedy convened a special executive committee of thirteen senior advisers to find a way to remove the missiles and planes. The committee met secretly for the next twelve days. Their duty was to propose tactics that would force the Soviets to remove the missiles from Cuba without igniting World War III. The president's brother and closest adviser, Robert, chaired the committee sessions.

Beginning with their initial session, all members of the committee agreed that the missiles had to be removed, but they disagreed on tactics. Some members, led by the chairman of the Joint Chiefs of Staff, Army General Maxwell Taylor, wanted to take the missile sites out with surprise air strikes that were likely to kill both Soviet technicians and Cuban soldiers. Robert Kennedy, who proved to be the most influential member of the executive committee, rejected that idea, saying he wanted "no Pearl Harbors on his brother's record." The Taylor-led faction then proposed an invasion to get rid of both the offensive weapons and the Castro regime. The President rejected this suggestion as too risky; it could involve a prolonged war with Cuba, provoke a Soviet attack on West Berlin, or even bring nuclear war. Secretary of Defense McNamara proposed a naval blockade to prevent further shipments of weapons to Cuba. The blockade would allow both sides some freedom to maneuver. The United States could decide to attack or negotiate later, depending

Medium-range ballistic missile base in Cuba. The United States detected Soviet efforts to install missiles in Cuba when reconnaissance aircraft photographed missile bases under construction on the island. Here is an example of the photographic evidence shown President Kennedy in October 1962. *Source:* U.S. Air Force.

on the Soviet response to the blockade. A majority of the committee member's endorsed McNamara's proposal. The President accepted the blockade tactic.

President Kennedy attended few of the committee sessions, and, when he did attend, he said little so as to allow free deliberations by the committee members. With the 1962 midterm elections only three weeks away, he was on the campaign trail, acting as if everything were normal. He campaigned mostly about domestic issues, trying to build support for his New Frontier reform programs that were stalled in Congress. Neither the media nor the public had any inkling of the serious crisis that was building. The Soviets did not know that the missile sites had been detected, nor that Kennedy was planning his response.

On Monday morning, October 22, the blockade began. That evening, Kennedy went on television to inform the nation and the Soviets about the missile crisis. He bluntly told his audience around the world: "unmistakable evidence has established the fact that a series of offensive missile sites is now in preparation on that imprisoned island." He spoke of the naval blockade, which he called a "quarantine," that was in place around Cuba. He demanded that the Soviets dismantle and remove all missile bases and bombers from Cuba immediately, and he stated that the quarantine would remain in place until all offensive weapons had been removed. Then he spoke these chilling words:

> It shall be the policy of this nation to regard any nuclear missiles launched from Cuba against any nation in the Western Hemisphere as an attack by the Soviet Union on the United States, requiring a full retaliatory response upon the Soviet Union.[6]

Kennedy confronted Khrushchev with the risk of nuclear war if he did not remove the missiles. For the next five days, the world hovered at the brink of catastrophe. Khrushchev denounced the United States and denied that he was installing offensive weapons in Cuba. Meanwhile, work on the missile sites continued. The first sites would be operational in a few days. The Air Force prepared strikes to take them out before they could fire missiles at targets in the United States. Soviet merchant ships hauling more weapons continued to steam toward Cuba. The U.S. Navy positioned its blockade fleet to intercept them. American invasion forces gathered in Florida. B-52 strategic bombers took to the air with nuclear bombs on board. U.S. strategic missiles went to maximum alert. The moment of supreme danger would come if a Soviet ship tried to run the blockade, for American ship commanders had orders to stop them.

The first break came on October 24. Soviet ships hauling offensive weapons turned back. Two other Soviet freighters, hauling no offensive weapons, submitted to searches and were permitted to steam on to Cuba. Two days later, Khrushchev sent a letter to President Kennedy offering to remove all offensive weapons from Cuba in exchange for a U.S. pledge not to invade Cuba. Kennedy accepted the offer, but before he could send his reply, Khrushchev sent a second letter raising the stakes: America would have to give a no-invasion-of-Cuba pledge plus remove its Jupiter missiles that were stationed in Turkey, which were targeted at the Soviet Union. Kennedy refused to bargain. It was his view that Khrushchev's reckless initiative had threatened world peace, and it was the Soviet leader's responsibility to remove the missiles from Cuba quickly.

As the point of no return neared, Kennedy, heeding the advice of his brother, made one last try to avoid the looming catastrophe. The president sent a cable to Khrushchev accepting the offer in the first letter and ignoring the second letter. The next night, October 27, Robert Kennedy met with the Soviet ambassador to the United States, Anatoly Dobrynin, to warn him that the United States had to have "a commitment by tomorrow that those bases would be removed." He told Dobrynin this was the Soviets' last chance to avoid war: If the Soviets "did not remove those bases, we would remove them." He also indicated to Dobrynin that the American missiles in Turkey, although not part of any quid pro quo, would be removed soon after the Cuban missiles were removed.

While these tense negotiations were in progress, a U-2 spy plane was shot down over Cuba and the pilot, U.S. Air Force Major Rudolph Anderson, was killed. Angry hawks on the executive committee wanted to launch air strikes and invade Cuba, to not only destroy the missile sites but to overthrow Castro's regime and to send the Soviet troops back home. Robert Kennedy, McNamara, and others re-

---

[6]Quoted in Elie Abel, *The Missile Crisis* (New York, Bantam Books, 1966), p. 106.

strained them, pleading that a few more days were needed to allow the president to work out a diplomatic solution to the crisis.

American officials learned years later that their restraint avoided certain nuclear war with the Soviet Union! Unbeknownst to the Americans at the time, the Soviet field commander in Cuba had six tactical nuclear surface-to-surface missiles in his arsenal and had been authorized to use them if he judged it necessary to protect Soviet soldiers and to save the Cuban government. He is on record as having stated that if the Americans had invaded, he would have used the nuclear missiles on them. Secretary of Defense McNamara has stated that if any American troops had been killed by Soviet nuclear missiles, "it is a 100 percent certainty" that the United States would have retaliated with their own nuclear weapons.

The next morning, October 28, Khrushchev agreed to remove the missiles and bombers in return for the president's promise not to invade Cuba. He claimed that he had achieved his goal of protecting Cuba from American attacks. The United States suspended its blockade. The United Nations supervised the dismantling and removal of the Cuban bases. American missiles were removed from Turkey a few weeks later. The missile crisis had been resolved without war. Kennedy received high praise for his actions. The Democrats gained in the fall elections. Kennedy's standing in the polls soared to new heights. Americans who had been on the defensive in the Cold War for years, were elated. National pride soared along with Kennedy's popularity. America had stood up to the Soviets and forced them to back down.

Although Kennedy was showered with praise for his handling of the missile crisis, it proved humiliating to Khrushchev. The Soviet leader fell from power within a year, and his actions during the crisis contributed to his demise. The missile crisis had exposed the Soviets as strategic inferiors to the Americans. An angry Soviet official told his American counterpart, "Never will we be caught like this again." The Soviets embarked on a crash program to expand their navy and to bring their missile forces up to parity with the United States.

Foreign policy analysts have raised serious questions about the missile crisis. Why had Khrushchev tried to put the missiles in Cuba? There are several possible factors. He wanted to strengthen Cuban defenses against possible U.S. attacks, but he miscalculated, a dangerous thing for a superpower leader to do in the nuclear age. He did not expect Kennedy's strong response, having sized him up as weak under pressure. Kennedy's behavior in previous crises had fed Khrushchev's suspicions that he lacked courage. During the Bay of Pigs invasion, Kennedy had backed off from a war with Cuba, let the invasion fail, and allowed Castro to consolidate a Communist revolution right in America's backyard. He had let the Berlin Wall stand. These acts of restraint sent the wrong signals to the adventurous Soviet ideologue. Khrushchev was not looking for a confrontation with the United States over Cuba, and he certainly did not want a war. Khrushchev may also have been trying to appease Kremlin hawks and to silence Chinese criticisms that Soviet foreign policy was not protecting Third World countries from American imperialism.

Critics have accused Kennedy of manufacturing the missile crisis to silence Republican critics and to promote his party's chances in the fall elections. Even if the Soviet Cuban missile caper appeared to give the Soviets an advantage, the president knew that the presence of Soviet missiles in Cuba did not appreciably alter the strategic balance of power. America had over four times as many missiles as the USSR, and the Cuban missiles would have given the Soviets only forty-four more. Did President Kennedy unnecessarily take the world to the nuclear brink for the sake of Cold War appearances and domestic politics?

The missile crisis forced both sides to tone down their Cold War rivalry. Khrushchev shifted back to emphasizing peaceful coexistence. Kennedy stressed the need for arms reductions. Direct communications, a "hot line," were established between Moscow and Washington so that the two leaders could talk to each other in time of crisis to reduce the chances of miscalculation and war. A mutual desire to control nuclear testing gave the two leaders an opportunity to improve relations.

President Kennedy, hoping to move arms negotiations forward, spoke at American University on June 10, 1963. He called upon Americans to reexamine their attitudes toward the Soviet Union and the Cold War. He called peace between the superpowers "the necessary end of rational men." He spoke of "making the world safe for diversity," conceding that every world problem did not require an American solution. Following the speech, he sent Undersecretary of State Averell Harriman to Moscow to negotiate an agreement. The Soviets proved eager to conclude a treaty. The agreement, signed July 25, banned all atmospheric and underwater testing of nuclear weapons. The Senate promptly ratified the treaty. The Nuclear Test Ban treaty was the first agreement that imposed a measure of control on the nuclear arms race. Soon after signing the treaty, the United States and the Soviet Union concluded an agreement for Soviet purchases of U.S. wheat. A year after the showdown in Cuba, Americans and Soviets enjoyed relations friendlier than any time since World War II.

VIETNAM: RAISING THE STAKES

Throughout the Kennedy years, the United States continued its involvement in Indochina. The president first turned his attention in that region to Laos, which had been the scene of conflict for years. Neutral under the terms of the 1954 Geneva Accords, Laos was engulfed in a three-way civil war among pro-Western, pro-Communist, and neutralist forces. Kennedy, inheriting the conflict from Eisenhower, sought a political solution involving the Soviets that guaranteed a "neutral and independent Laos." Another Geneva conference worked out a settlement. On June 12, 1961, the leaders of the three Laotian factions formed a neutralist coalition government. But in southern Vietnam, Kennedy significantly escalated U.S. involvement in response to the Communists' stepped-up efforts to topple the American-backed government of Ngo Dinh Diem.

Kennedy viewed the civil war in southern Vietnam as a crucial part of the global cold war struggle between the United States and the Soviet Union. Ironically, Kennedy, when he had been a senator, often criticized the Eisenhower administration's Third World foreign policy for failing to understand the powerful appeal of nationalism in countries emerging from long periods of colonial domination by Western imperial powers. Kennedy had criticized American backing of French efforts to reimpose colonialism in Indochina by suppressing a nationalist revolution. But as president, Kennedy apparently failed to understand that Ho Chi Minh's Communist ideology also expressed Vietnamese nationalistic aspirations, or that many Vietnamese viewed the American presence in Vietnam supporting Diem as a continuation of Western imperialism. Kennedy also applied the domino theory to Vietnam:

> Vietnam represents the cornerstone of the Free World in Southeast Asia, . . . Burma, Thailand, India, Japan, the Philippines and obviously, Laos and Cambodia are among those whose security would be threatened if the red tide of Communism overflowed into Vietnam.[7]

Kennedy and his leading foreign policy advisers all shared the ideological fundaments of the Cold War with Eisenhower and Truman. They believed that it was imperative to contain Communist expansionism in Southeast Asia. The legacy of McCarthyism also stalked the Democrats in power. Since the early 1950s, they had been politically vulnerable to charges that they were "soft on Communism" at home and abroad. Kennedy dared not appeared to be irresolute in Southeast Asia, lest his administration suffer political reprisals at the hands of Republicans.

Further, the Kennedy team shared a faith in American power, technical expertise, and national goals. They believed that the Americans would succeed in southern Vietnam where the French had failed. To them, Vietnam furnished a bright opportunity for nation building. They believed that aid programs, military support, and use of America's counterinsurgency forces would show the world that Moscow-backed wars of national liberation could not succeed. Kennedy also deployed the Army Special Forces, the Green Berets, in Southeast Asia. They represented a key component of the flexible response capability to counter Communist insurgencies in peripheral regions without risking confrontations with China or the Soviet Union. Kennedy believed that the Special Forces, using counterinsurgency techniques, would neutralize the Communist threat and win the hearts and minds of the Vietnamese people for Diem and the West.

In 1961, there were about six hundred U.S. military advisers in South Vietnam assisting Diem's forces. Kennedy sent Vice President Lyndon Johnson to Saigon to emphasize the American commitment to Diem and to assess his needs. Johnson called Diem "the Winston Churchill of Southeast Asia." Upon his return, Johnson

---

[7]Quoted in George C. Herring, *America's Longest War*, 2nd ed. (New York: Knopf, 1986), p. 43.

advised Kennedy to increase American aid to South Vietnam. He told the president that the United States had to "help these countries to the best of our ability or throw in the towel and pull back our defenses to San Francisco." During the next eighteen months, Kennedy sent some sixteen thousand American troops to South Vietnam. Even though the soldiers went officially as advisers, some units occasionally engaged Viet Cong forces in combat.

Despite the huge increase in American support, Diemist forces were losing the civil war to the Viet Cong insurgents and their North Vietnamese backers. American officials tried to persuade Diem to implement social reforms, including land reform, and to curb his repressive police forces. Diem refused to do either. Diem's decline stemmed mainly from the inability of his military forces to fight effectively and his failure to win the loyalty of the peasants who comprised 85 percent of the South Vietnamese population. At the "rice roots" level, Diem was losing the battle for hearts and minds.

Diem provoked a political crisis in June 1963 that led to his downfall, when he ordered Buddhists to obey Catholic religious laws. When they refused and took to the streets to protest, Diem's police, led by his brother Nhu, brutally crushed their rebellion. In response to this repression, an elderly Buddhist monk immolated himself by fire at a busy intersection in downtown Saigon. Other monks followed suit as opposition to Diem's government mounted. Observing that Diem's political base had been reduced to family members and a few loyal generals and bureaucrats, and fearing that his army was losing the civil war, the Kennedy administration decided that Diem had to go. On November 1, an army coup, acting with the foreknowledge and support of the CIA, overthrew Diem. American officials backed a directorate of generals who formed a new government and continued the war. Three weeks later, Kennedy was assassinated.

At the time of Kennedy's death, U.S. Vietnam policy was in disarray and his advisers divided over what to do. Although he had increased the U.S. stake in Indochina significantly, Kennedy hinted that he might reappraise his commitment to South Vietnam because of Diem's political failures. In September 1963, Kennedy had attempted to warn Diem:

> "I don't think that unless a greater effort is made to win popular support the war can be won out there. In the final analysis it is their war. They are the ones who have to win it or lose it." But in that same speech, Kennedy also reaffirmed the American commitment: "For us to withdraw from that effort would mean a collapse not only of South Vietnam but Southeast Asia, . . . so we are going to stay there."[8]

Kennedy had inherited a deteriorating situation in Southeast Asia; his actions ensured that the United States would remain there a long time. Had Kennedy lived and been reelected in 1964, he probably would have reacted as Lyndon Johnson did in 1965 and committed the United States to war in Vietnam.

---

[8]From the transcript of a televised interview with Walter Cronkite broadcast on CBS news, September 2, 1963.

The pattern of Kennedy's foreign policy fitted that of an orthodox Cold Warrior striving to fulfill the extravagant rhetorical claims of his inaugural address. Undeniably, Kennedy had the intelligence and the insight to see that the world was changing, that Third World independence movements were redrawing the map of the world. He also understood that the old bipolar world was being replaced by a more polycentric one. He knew that the American-Soviet rivalry had to be replaced by détente. But the main thrust of his foreign policies was to escalate the arms race, sustain a tense relation with the Soviet Union for most of his presidency, and, at one terrifying point, push the world perilously close to nuclear disaster. He built up the American presence in Vietnam, assuring the debacle that followed. In the summer of 1963, he improved relations with the Soviets and the two powers signed a nuclear test ban treaty.

THE SPACE RACE

In mid-April 1961, at the time that the United States was being humiliated at the Bay of Pigs, a Soviet cosmonaut, Yury Gagarin, became the first human to orbit the earth. Once again the Soviets boasted of their accomplishments in space technology; the rest of the world was impressed and Americans were dismayed. Even though NASA scientists assured the president that American space science was superior to Soviet efforts, it had been the popular perception in this country since Sputnik that the United States trailed the Soviets. Media editorialists fretted that the United States had fallen behind in the Cold War and was losing the propaganda battle to the Soviets. Maybe the Soviets were right: the world would go to sleep under a Communist moon.

Not according to President Kennedy. He was determined to beat the Soviets in the space race; he was also determined to rally the American people to face a Cold War challenge he believed America could win. He put Vice President Lyndon Johnson in charge of the Space Council and told him to do whatever had to be done to defeat the Soviets. Kennedy also persuaded Congress to vote a large increase in NASA's budget to develop a space program "to put a man on the moon in ten years." He went before Congress in May 1961 to push the moon project:

> No single space project in this period will be more impressive to mankind or more important for the long-range exploration of space . . . than putting a man on the moon.[9]

To fulfill Kennedy's vision, NASA created the APOLLO program. Soon complexes of aerospace facilities mushroomed from Southern California to Texas to Florida. NASA employed thousands of technicians, engineers, and scientists. Private sector subcontractors hired thousands more. Within five years, upwards of a half-million people were employed on the vast and costly APOLLO project.

As scientists worked towards the goal of putting a man on the moon, they also tried to match the Soviet Union's space achievements. Seven military test

---

[9]Quoted in Tom Wolfe, *The Right Stuff* (New York: Bantam Books, 1979), pp. 228–29.

pilots were recruited for Project MERCURY, and they became the nation's first astronauts. After months of rigorous training, the astronauts readied for their flights. On May 5, 1961, Commander Alan B. Shepard, Jr., abroad a space capsule, was rocketed from a launch pad at Cape Canaveral, Florida, into a fifteen-minute suborbital flight 116 miles aloft. On February 20, 1962, nearly a year after the Soviets had put a man in space, Marine Colonel John H. Glenn, Jr., was blasted into orbit aboard his space capsule, *Friendship 7*. During his five-hour flight, Glenn orbited the earth three times. Americans were delighted by Glenn's remarkable achievement. Spirits were lifted: Maybe American's could win the space race with the Soviets. Glenn made an attractive hero. He was a much-decorated jet fighter pilot from the Korean War; an All-American boy grown up to become the first American to reach outer space. After his epic flight, President Kennedy invited Glenn to the White House. Glenn also addressed a joint session of Congress. He later received a frenzied ticker tape parade down Manhattan's famed Broadway. Following Glenn's flight, other astronauts rocketed into space and orbited the earth. At the time of Kennedy's death, the American space program was gaining momentum, the seven MERCURY astronauts had all become national heroes, and project APOLLO was ahead of schedule.

Three American heroes: Project Mercury astronauts John Glenn (left), Gus Grissom (center), and Alan Shepard (right) are shown during their training for manned space flights. *Source:* NASA.

SOCIAL REFORM

President Kennedy had more successes in the diplomatic arena than in the realm of domestic reform legislation. Although espousing liberal goals and calling for social justice for all Americans, he failed to get enacted most of his ambitions New Frontier program of medical care for the elderly, tax reform, federal aid to education, housing reform, aid to cities, and immigration reform. His New Frontier faced many political obstacles. In Congress, the bipartisan conservative coalition could block any effort to expand the welfare state and could often thwart measures designed to broaden existing programs. Kennedy's thin electoral victory in 1960 carried with it no mandate whatsoever for social reform. The Democrats had lost seats in both the House and Senate.

Two years later, Kennedy tried to focus the 1962 midterm elections on New Frontier issues, but the dangerous Cuban missile crisis forced him to curtail his campaign efforts. The new Congress of 1962 was similar to its predecessor. Public opinion in the early 1960s reflected the complacency toward unsolved social problems that had been characteristic of the 1950s. Kennedy's efforts to make most Americans share his sense of urgency for social reform through televised speeches and remarks at press conferences failed. Most New Frontier proposals never made it out of committee. Those few that did were either defeated on the floor of the House or cleared Congress in diluted form.

Kennedy also failed to assert effective legislative leadership. Congress questioned the depth of his commitment to social reform, understanding that he gave higher priority to foreign policy, military matters, world trade, and strengthening the economy. In addition, Kennedy wanted to maintain bipartisan support for American foreign policy initiatives and was reluctant to strain the unity of Congress with battles over divisive reform measures. Kennedy was not given to rhetorical speeches and making excessive demands on Congress in the name of high-flown principles. He disliked using political muscle and he disliked losing political battles. He could see the votes simply were not there for many New Frontier measures and thought it unreasonable to battle in a losing cause: "There is no sense in raising hell and not being successful."

A major defeat came early when Congress rejected Kennedy's $2.3 billion education bill. It foundered over the issue of federal aid to parochial schools. A Catholic himself, Kennedy knew that he would be accused of showing favoritism toward his coreligionists if he favored federal aid to Catholic schools. His bill excluded federal aid for private schools with a religious affiliation that he claimed would violate the First Amendment principle of separation of church and state. Opposition to the bill from the Catholic lobby was intense. The education bill never got out of the House Rules Committee. Members of Congress, observing that Kennedy had little leverage with its members, understood that they could go their own political ways on important White House measures without fear of reprisal. The failure of the education bill foreshadowed the defeat of the rest of the New Frontier agendum.

Although Kennedy failed to achieve his broad program of reform, he scored a few small victories. Congress enacted an Area Redevelopment Act in 1961 to provide funds for economically depressed areas. The Manpower Retraining Act of 1962 provided $435 million over three years to train unemployed workers in new job skills. Congress raised the minimum wage from $1.00 to $1.25 an hour and extended coverage under the minimum wage law to 3.6 million more workers.

THE ECONOMY

When Kennedy took office, the American economy was stagnant and suffering from lingering recession. The new president tried to work with the business community to restore prosperity. He consulted with several of his cabinet advisers recruited from the business world. He held meetings with corporate leaders to get their policy suggestions. He tried to reassure them that he was not a reckless spender nor a liberal ideologue, and that he was committed to a stable price structure. He told them that the age of ideology had ended and the time had come for government, business, labor, and academic leaders to combine their expertise in seeking solutions to complex technical problems that afflicted the economy. Corporate leaders, apparently wedded to a Republican approach, refused their cooperation, angering the president. They insisted on blaming the Kennedy administration for all their problems and rejected his technocratic approach to problem solving.

A major confrontation with business came in the spring of 1962. Earlier in the year, a strike in the steel industry had been averted when Secretary of Labor Arthur Goldberg had persuaded the steel workers to accept a modest pay increase that eliminated the need for a steel price rise. At the time, the president had praised both labor and management for their "industrial statesmanship." Ten days later, Roger Blough, the head of United States Steel, announced that his company was raising the price of steel $6 per ton. Other major steel producers announced identical increases.

Kennedy, feeling betrayed, denounced the steel companies. At a press conference, he said he was shocked that "a tiny handful of steel executives can show such utter contempt for the interests of 185 million Americans." He promptly mobilized all the considerable powers of the federal government to force the steel companies to rescind their price hikes. The Federal Trade Commission announced that it would investigate the steel industry for possible price fixing. Robert Kennedy hinted that he might open antitrust proceedings against the steel industry. Secretary of Defense McNamara announced that the military would buy steel only from companies that had not raised their prices. Under an all-out assault from the White House, the steel companies quickly surrendered. U.S. Steel and the other companies canceled their price increases. Kennedy had won, and his was a popular victory. But he paid a political price for winning: The business community remained intensely hostile towards his administration.

Kennedy proposed innovative economic policies to end the business slump of the early 1960s. Aware that huge budget deficits during World War II had promoted prosperity, he reasoned that deficit financing would also work in peacetime. In June 1962, he proposed a deliberately unbalanced budget to promote economic growth. Six months later, he asked Congress to enact a $13.5 billion cut in corporate and personal income taxes over the next three years. The tax cuts, coupled to increases in spending for military and space programs already in place, would guarantee budget deficits. Kennedy insisted that these applied Keynesian economic strategies would generate capital spending that would stimulate economic growth, create new jobs, and provide increased tax revenues—all without rampant inflation. But Kennedy's tax bill never cleared Congress.

Even though Kennedy failed to get his new economic policy enacted, the economy recovered from recession in 1962 and 1963 and began an extended period of growth. Recovery mainly occurred because the Kennedy administration sharply increased military and space spending. Kennedy's first defense budget called for spending $48 billion, a 20 percent increase over Eisenhower's final budget. Kennedy's economic foreign policies also contributed to the economic rebound of 1962 and 1963. Most of his foreign aid requests were approved, including increased spending for technical assistance and economic development for Third World countries. The Senate ratified a treaty in 1961 making the United States a member of the newly created Organization of Economic Cooperation and Development (OECD), comprising the United States, Canada, and eighteen European nations. Congress also enacted Kennedy's proposed Trade Expansion Act in 1962, his most important legislative victory. It established closer ties with European Common Market countries, America's most important trading partners. The Trade Expansion Act allowed the president to reduce tariffs on commodities in which the United States and European nations accounted for most of the world's trade. American overseas trade increased significantly during the years of Kennedy's presidency.

LET FREEDOM RING

During the 1960 presidential campaign, Kennedy came out strongly for civil rights to prevent Nixon's siphoning of African American voters, but at the same time he had also sought the votes of southern whites. His campaign rhetoric was bold: "If the President himself does not wage the struggle for equal rights, then the battle will inevitably be lost." He promised to issue an executive order ending racial segregation in federally funded housing. During the campaign, he helped get Dr. Martin Luther King, Jr., released from jail. African Americans appreciated these gestures from the candidate and gave Kennedy a large black majority in 1960, which helped him win his narrow victory.

But Kennedy in office proved to be a cautious leader on civil rights for much of his presidency. He delayed introducing civil rights legislation, fearing that it would fail and also alienate southern Democrats, whose votes he needed on other measures. He appointed some African Americans to federal offices, the first president to do so. Robert Weaver became head of the Housing and Home Finance Agency, and Thurgood Marshall became a Circuit Court judge. But Kennedy also appointed many segregationist judges to southern courts, and he delayed issuing his promised housing desegregation order for nearly two years.

At the beginning of his administration, the official lead in civil rights was taken by the president's brother, Attorney General Robert Kennedy. The Justice Department worked to end discrimination in interstate transportation and supported the voting rights of African Americans in the South. President Kennedy believed that the best civil rights policy would be a gradual achievement of integration over the years without disruption and violence. Dr. Martin Luther King, Jr., the foremost civil rights leader, pointedly observed: "If tokenism were our goal, this Administration has moved us adroitly towards its accomplishment."

But from the outset of his presidency, Kennedy had to respond to pressures created by civil rights activists and their segregationist foes. In the spring of 1961, the Congress of Racial Equality (CORE) sponsored "freedom rides." Groups of black and white travelers rode through the South deliberately entering segregated bus terminals and restaurants. Local mobs often attacked the "freedom riders." In Anniston, Alabama, the Greyhound bus in which one group had been riding was burned. In Mississippi, "freedom riders" were jailed *en masse.* Responding to the "freedom riders" and their violent encounters, the Interstate Commerce Commission (ICC) ordered bus companies to desegregate all their interstate routes and facilities. The companies complied and black passengers began entering previously "whites-only" restaurants, waiting rooms, and restrooms. The Justice Department persuaded thirteen of the nation's fifteen segregated airports to desegregate and filed suit against the two holdouts.

The following year, Mississippi became a civil rights battleground. In September 1962, an African American Air Force veteran, James Meredith, attempted to enroll at the all-white University of Mississippi. Although he met their entrance requirements, university officials refused to admit him. Meredith then obtained a court order from Supreme Court Justice Hugo Black enjoining the university to admit him, whereupon Governor Ross Barnett personally intervened to prevent his enrolling. President Kennedy responded to Barnett's defiance of federal authority by sending federal marshalls and troops to the university. They were met by a mob who treated them as if they were foreign invaders. Violence ensued in which vehicles were burned and destroyed. Tear gas covered the campus, and it took several thousand troops to restore order. During the mayhem, two men were killed and hundreds were injured.

Another confrontation occurred on April 12, 1963, Good Friday, when Dr. Martin Luther King, Jr., led a demonstration into the heart of white supremacy, Birmingham, Alabama, whose leaders boasted that it was the most segregated city in the South. Dr. King and his followers sought to end discrimination against African American customers in shops and restaurants and in employment and hiring policies. Their protests were nonviolent; the city's response was not. City officials declared that the marches violated city regulations against parading without a permit. During the next month, Birmingham police arrested over two thousand African American demonstrators, many of them school children. The police commissioner ordered his police to use high-pressure fire hoses, electric cattle prods, and police dogs to break up the demonstrations. Newspapers and television news broadcasts conveyed the brutal police assaults on African Americans to the nation, which watched in horror. Dr. King was jailed. During his stay in jail, he composed his famed "Letter from Birmingham Jail," an eloquent defense of the tactic of non-violent civil disobedience.

The Justice Department intervened during the Birmingham demonstrations. Government officials and city leaders worked out an agreement calling for desegregation of municipal facilities, hiring of African Americans, and creation of a biracial committee to keep channels of communication between the races open. Kennedy called the African American quest for equal rights a "moral issue," and he asked:

> "We preach freedom around the world . . . and we cherish our freedom here at home, but are we to say to the world, . . . and to each other that this is the land of the free except for the Negroes?"[10]

A few months after the Birmingham encounter, two young African Americans, Vivian Malone and James Hood, tried to enroll at the University of Alabama. Governor George Wallace pledged to the white people of his state that "he would stand in the doorway" to prevent African Americans from enrolling at the university. President Kennedy, hoping to avoid a replay of the Mississippi violence, federalized the Alabama National Guard. He confronted Wallace with an overwhelming show of force using native Alabama white and black soldiers. Wallace stood in the doorway only long enough to have his picture taken, then stepped aside. Malone and Hood enrolled peacefully.

That night, June 11, 1963, President Kennedy gave the first civil rights speech ever delivered by a president. Part of his speech was extemporaneous, and he conveyed a sense of moral urgency, an emotional concern for civil rights:

> If an American, because his skin is black, cannot eat lunch in a restaurant open to the public; if he cannot send his children to the best public school available; if he cannot vote for the public officials who represent him; if, in short, he cannot enjoy the full and free life which all of us want, then who among us would be content to have the color of his skin changed and stand in his place?
>
> One hundred years of delay have passed since President Lincoln freed the slaves, yet their heirs, their grandsons, are not fully free. They are not yet free from the bonds of injustice; they are not yet freed from social and economic oppression. And this nation will not be fully free until all its citizens are free.[11]

A week later, the president, stating "the time has come for this nation to fulfill its promise," proposed the most comprehensive civil rights bill in American history. It called for the desegregation of all public accommodations, the protection of

---

[10]Quoted in Schlesinger, *A Thousand Days,* pp. 880–1.

[11]From the transcript of Kennedy's televised speech over the three major television networks, June 11, 1963.

On August 28, 1963, supporters of the pending civil rights bill staged a march on Washington to show their support. Over 200,000 people rallied in front of the stately Washington Monument to sing songs and hear speeches. *Source:* National Archives.

voting rights for African Americans, and the end of job discrimination. Congress did not show a similar enthusiasm and gave no indication that it would enact the measure any time soon.

To show support for the pending legislation, civil rights leaders organized a march on Washington. Over 200,000 people gathered in front of the Washington monument on August 28. Black and white people joined in a peaceful, festive occasion. Adults chatted and sang songs. Children played, got lost, and were usually found. Dogs barked and chased frisbees. The highlight of the gathering came when Dr. King, the leader of the growing civil rights movement, passionately affirmed his faith in the decency of man and in the ultimate victory for his cause:

> I have a dream that one day this nation will rise up and live out the true meaning of its creed: We hold these truths to be self-evident; that all men are created equal. I have a dream that one day on the red hills of Georgia, the sons of former slaves and the sons of former slaveowners will be able to sit together at the table of brotherhood."[12]

[12]Quoted in Lewis, *Portrait of a Decade*, pp. 218–19.

Dr. Martin Luther King, Jr., preparing to deliver his most famous speech in front of the Washington Monument August 28, 1963. He inspired the huge crowd with his vision of a color-blind America: "I have a dream. . . ."
Source: National Archives.

The crowd was caught up in the power of his fervent rhetoric. Each time he shouted "I have a dream," the massive crowd roared its support. Dr. King concluded his stirring speech with a magnificent peroration:

> When we let freedom ring, when we let it ring from every village and every hamlet, from every state and every city, we will be able to speed up that day when all of God's children, black men and white men, Jews and Gentiles, Protestants and Catholics, will be able to join hands and sing in the words of the old Negro spiritual, "Free at last! Free at last! Thank God almighty, we are free at last!"[13]

Immediately following the demonstration, Dr. King and other civil rights leaders met with President Kennedy. But Congress continued to stall; southern Senators threatened to filibuster any civil rights bill to death. Three weeks after the march on Washington, white terrorists bombed an African American Sunday school in Birmingham, killing four little girls. Two months later, President Kennedy was assassinated, his civil rights legislation still pending. The South remained segregated; Dr. King's dream remained unrealized.

TRAGEDY IN DALLAS

In the fall of 1963, President Kennedy was giving much thought to next year's election. He traveled to Texas in late November to mend some political fences. With the help of Vice President Johnson, who accompanied him on that fateful rendezvous,

[13]Quoted in *Ibid.*

he came to unify warring factions of Texas Democrats who had feuded over policies and patronage. Texas was a populous state with a large bloc of electoral votes that Kennedy and Johnson had carried narrowly in 1960 and hoped to win again in 1964. Kennedy arrived at the Dallas airport on the morning of November 22. Texas Governor John Connally and his wife Nellie joined the president and his wife Jacqueline in an open-air limousine for the trip into the city. The presidential motorcade proceeded from the airport into downtown Dallas. The motorcade route had been published for days in the local papers to ensure a large turnout. Thousands of people lined the motorcade route; most of them smiling, waving, and cheering the president as he passed by. Kennedy responded warmly to their enthusiasm, waving, frequently flashing his million-dollar smile, and stopping the motorcade twice to shake hands with well-wishers.

At 12:30 P.M., the motorcade turned onto Elm Street and drove by the Texas Book Depository Building. At 12:33 P.M., three shots rang out. The president clutched his neck with both hands and slumped downward. The first bullet, deflected by a tree limb in the line of fire, had missed. The second bullet had passed through his throat and the third had struck the back of his head, blowing off part of his skull. Connally, sitting beside the president, had also been hit by the second bullet after it had passed through Kennedy's throat. The president's limousine quickly pulled out of the motorcade and raced the mortally wounded leader to nearby Parkland Hospital, where, in its emergency room, he was pronounced dead at 1:00 P.M.

Within two hours of the shooting, police captured the apparent assassin, twenty-four-year-old Lee Harvey Oswald, who worked in the book depository building. Oswald was an isolate, a drifter, with a troubled, confused past. He had recently moved to Dallas after spending two years living and working in the Soviet Union. He had previously served in the Marine Corps. He held leftist political views and was a Marxist sympathizer. Earlier in the year, he had tried to go to Cuba, but the Cuban embassy in Mexico City refused to grant him a visa.

Aboard the presidential plane still on the ground at the Dallas airport, ninety-nine minutes after Kennedy's death, Lyndon B. Johnson was sworn in as the thirty-sixth president of the United States. The former president's widow, Jacqueline, stood at Johnson's side. Two days later, a Dallas nightclub owner, Jack Ruby, shot and killed Oswald at point-blank range in the basement of the Dallas police station in full view of a national television audience. Ruby's murder of Oswald eliminated the possibility of ever knowing for sure Oswald's political beliefs, his motives for killing the president, and whether he was part of a conspiracy.

From the moment of Kennedy's death, many people doubted that Lee Harvey Oswald had acted alone. A public opinion poll taken within a week of the president's murder showed only 29 percent of Americans believed that Oswald was a lone killer. Within two weeks of Kennedy's murder, President Johnson appointed a special commission, headed by Chief Justice Earl Warren, to investigate the assassination and to report its findings to the American people. Ten months later, the commission published its conclusion: "The Commission has found no evidence that anyone assisted Oswald in planning or carrying out the assassination."

The commission's findings failed to satisfy those who felt others had to be involved in a plot to murder the president. Critics undermined the credibility of the Warren Commission's analysis of evidence and its findings, which were seriously flawed and limited. Many people have proposed conspiracy theories to account for Kennedy's death and millions of people have found them credible. These theories have implicated both pro- and anti-Castro Cubans, leftists, rightists, Texas oilmen, segregationists, Vietnamese, rogue elements within the Pentagon, the FBI and the CIA, the Mafia, the KGB, and even Lyndon Johnson. Most historians of the assassination do not believe that a conspiracy was involved in the murder of the president and they accept the Warren Commission's finding. The few historians who believe that a conspiracy might have killed Kennedy think that Cubans and elements within organized crime were involved.

The most important critique of the Warren Commission came in 1979 when a special congressional investigating committee released the results of a two-and-one-half-year examination of the deaths of both President Kennedy and Dr. Martin Luther King, Jr. Its key finding: "The scientific evidence available to the committee indicated that it is probable that more than one person was involved in the president's murder." But FBI experts demonstrated that the committee's evidence was flawed.

In all the time that has passed since Kennedy's murder, no tangible evidence has been found that proves that the Warren Commission's conclusion was incorrect, despite its flawed and limited investigation of the murder. Nor has any evidence turned up that links any particular group to the assassination. If a group of conspirators killed the president, which is doubtful, their identities remain unknown and will probably never be known.

The persistence of the belief, especially among young people, that a conspiracy killed Kennedy mainly represents an effort to make sense out of a horrific act that frightened Americans and shook their faith in the decency and viability of American political institutions. The notion that a sociopath, an utterly insignificant wretch acting alone, could bring down a great leader and wreak such havoc made the crime seem senseless and devoid of political meaning. Novelist Norman Mailer has suggested that many Americans cling to conspiracies to explain the president's death because they refuse to recognize the irrationality, the absurdity of historical events. The belief that a great and good man had been destroyed by powerful evil forces lurking in the dark underside of American politics made sense in a bleak, rueful sort of way to many people.

In the years following Kennedy's death, Americans watched other leaders die at the hands of assassins—Malcolm X, Martin Luther King, Jr., and Robert Kennedy. These assassinations reinforced a growing sense among Americans in the 1960s that they inhabited a violent and dangerous country where criminal conspirators thought nothing of snuffing out the lives of idealistic leaders. For them, the age of innocence ended November 22, 1963, and they have found it difficult to trust and support government leaders since.

The young president's murder gouged a deep wound in the nation's psyche. People around the world wept openly at the horrid news. A weeping woman on a Moscow street grabbed an American reporter by the arm and shouted, "How could you let it happen? He was so young, so beautiful!" A stricken nation watched numbly the solemn aftermath of the absurd tragedy. The president's body lay in state on the rotunda of the Capitol on the same catafalque that had held the body of Lincoln. Kennedy's funeral was held on November 25, a clear, cold day in Washington. At St. Matthew's Cathedral, Kennedy's friend, Richard Cardinal Cushing, Archbishop of Boston, said a funeral mass. The funeral train slowly wound its way past national monuments to Arlington Cemetery. There, on a knoll overlooking the capital of the nation, John Fitzgerald Kennedy was buried. Adlai Stevenson, in a moving eulogy, observed that

> Today we mourn him, tomorrow we shall miss him. . . . No one will ever know what this blazing political talent might have accomplished had he been permitted to live and labor long in the cause of freedom.[14]

THE LEGACY OF CAMELOT

Kennedy's violent death instantly transformed the man into a myth. After conversations with Kennedy's widow, Theodore White wrote an essay in which he compared Kennedy's presidency to "Camelot." Camelot had recently been popularized in this country by the successful Broadway run of a musical of that same name. Kennedy had seen "Camelot," and loved to listen to the recorded sound track. Camelot referred to the Arthurian legend, to the mythical kingdom of Arthur and the Knights of the Round Table. Because the country soon after Kennedy's death got caught up in a full-scale war in Southeast Asia and in violent domestic rebellions, followed in a few years by the sordid Watergate scandals, people viewed the Kennedy years as a brief golden age. Those who came of age during his reign felt an especially painful loss. For them, the Kennedy years had been a glorious interlude between the dull days of Eisenhower and the dark days of Johnson and Nixon. It had been a time when talent and idealism reigned, when the world appeared young and all things seemed possible:

> The World's great age begins anew, The golden years—[15]

For those who believed in Camelot, Kennedy had been the democratic prince whose achievements symbolized the American dream of success, both personal and national. His family history had been a saga of upward mobility from humble immigrant origins to the upper reaches of wealth, power, and fame. Then, in an instant, a loser's bullets had turned spectacular achievement into tragic loss. The death of the president shattered their dreams of glory.

---

[14]Taken from a documentary film, *The Age of Kennedy,* part 4.

[15]The verse is quoted in John Agar, *The Price of Power: America Since 1945* (Chicago: University of Chicago Press, 1957), p. 56.

The historical record belies the myth. Kennedy's record of accomplishment is mixed. Much of his New Frontier agenda failed of passage in his lifetime. He was usually a cautious leader on civil rights issues. He only belatedly sensed the moral passion that motivated civil rights activists like Dr. King. He got only a portion of his economic program enacted. Posthumous revelations about his extramarital affairs, drug use, serious health problems, and other Kennedy family scandals tarnished his moral stature and diminished his reputation. It was discovered that the book, *Profiles in Courage,* which established Kennedy as a scholar in politics, was mostly written by his aide, Theodore Sorensen.

His foreign policy achievements were more significant. America's putting a man on the moon in 1969 was a belated triumph. The Peace Corps and The Trade Expansion Act succeeded. But the Alliance for Progress flopped, neither undercutting the appeal of Castro nor promoting democracy and economic growth in most Latin American countries. Kennedy's "crisis managing" in Cuba was a disaster at the Bay of Pigs, and he risked nuclear war to pry Soviet missiles out of Cuba. The Berlin issue was defused after years of tension, but its resolution owed more to Khrushchev's Berlin Wall than to any initiatives taken by Kennedy. The test ban treaty and détente with the Russians in 1963 decreased the danger of nuclear war, but Kennedy had previously ordered major increases in American military spending, particularly for strategic thermonuclear weapons, that had escalated the arms race. Kennedy also significantly expanded American involvement in Vietnam, putting the country on course for war in Southeast Asia.

Kennedy's best speeches proved that he had the imagination and courage to see beyond the confines of the Cold War. But he spent the greatest part of his presidency fighting it. The man who could see the necessity of developing new relations with Third World people nevertheless applied counterrevolutionary Cold War ideologies to all nationalistic insurgencies. He remained a Cold Warrior at heart to the end.

Any full and fair accounting of his leadership must include intangible dimensions. He was a superb politician. His intelligence, wit, and immense personal charm contributed to his personal style and set a high tone for his presidency. Many of his countrymen felt great admiration and affection for him, viewing him as a fine symbol of the nation he had been elected to lead. He was devoted to the ideal of national service. His administration cultivated the arts. He paid high tribute to science and scholarship. He sought always to bring out the best in Americans; to challenge them to seek excellence in all things, especially young people with whom he felt a special bond. Whatever the failings of the private man, the public image that Kennedy cultivated was positive, energetic, and effective. Always, there must be the rueful speculation, what if he had lived? Any fair historical judgment must take into account the brutal fact of his abruptly abbreviated career, a young man in his prime cut down before he could make his full mark on his times. The Kennedy presidency was not a great one; historians rate him "above average" for his thousand days in office. Given a second term, an eight-year presidency, it is possible that he would have attained distinction.

IMPORTANT EVENTS

1960	Kennedy-Nixon televised debates take place
1960	John F. Kennedy is elected president
1961	Bay of Pigs fiasco occurs
1961	CORE "freedom rides" to the South take place
1961	The Berlin Wall is built
1961	The Peace Corps is created
1961	The Alliance for Progress is implemented
1962	James Meredith desegregates the University of Mississippi
1962	The Cuban Missile Crisis takes place
1963	Martin Luther King, Jr., leads demonstrations in Birmingham
1963	The Nuclear Test Ban Treaty is signed
1963	The March on Washington to support the civil rights bill takes place
1963	Ngo Dinh Diem is assassinated in Saigong
1963	John F. Kennedy is assassinated in Dallas

BIBLIOGRAPHY

There is a large and growing literature on John Fitzgerald Kennedy, his family, and all facets of his political career. The best and most balanced biography is Herbert Parmet's two-volume study, *Jack: The Struggles of John F. Kennedy* and *JFK: The Presidency of John F. Kennedy.* The best recent scholarly history of the Kennedy presidency is by James N. Giglio, *The Presidency of John F. Kennedy.* Two highly favorable insider accounts of his presidency are by Arthur M. Schlesinger, Jr. (*A Thousand Days*) and by Theodore C. Sorensen (*Kennedy*). Kenneth P. O'Donnel and David F. Powers, two political associates of Kennedy, have left an affectionate account in *Johnny, We Hardly Knew Ye.* Bruce Miroff's *Pragmatic Illusions: The Presidential Politics of John Kennedy* and Garry Wills's *The Kennedy Imprisonment* are both negative assessments of his presidency. The best account of the exciting and significant election of 1960 is found in Theodore H. White's *The Making of the President, 1960.* The best account of Kennedy's World War II career is found in Robert J. Donovan's *PT 109: John F. Kennedy in World War II.* Carl M. Brauer's *John F. Kennedy and the Second Reconstruction* is a favorable assessment of the president as civil rights leader. See also Peter Wyden's *Bay of Pigs: The Untold Story,* the best account of Kennedy's most embarrassing foreign policy venture. The best short account of the missile crisis is Elie Abel's *The Missile Crisis.* Two critical accounts of Kennedy's conduct of foreign policy include Richard J. Walton's *Cold War and Counterrevolution* and David Halberstam's *The Best and the Brightest.* A fine recent critical account of Kennedy's foreign policy is Michael R. Beschloss's *The Crisis Years: Kennedy and Khrushchev, 1960–1963.* Anyone who cares to know about the assassination must start by reading the *Report of the Warren Commission on the Assassination of John F. Kennedy.* Readers might also want to read one of the responsible accounts of the assassination such as the one by Michael L. Kurtz, *Crime of the Century: The Kennedy Assassination from a Historian's Perspective.* Gerald Posner, in *Case Closed: Lee Harvey Oswald and the Assassination of JFK,* does an effective job of demolishing the leading conspiracy theories and providing reasonable answers to the lingering questions about the assassination.

CHAPTER 12

Reform, Rebellion, and War

The consensus that had united most Americans in support of domestic reform at home and containment of Communism abroad fragmented following Kennedy's assassination. But for a time under Kennedy's successor, Lyndon Johnson, the cracks in the American system remained below the surface. Johnson was able to score a decisive electoral victory in 1964 over the ineffective challenge of Senator Barry Goldwater. Following his victory, Johnson pushed through Congress a broad range of social legislation. Soon the escalating Vietnam War combined with militant domestic insurgencies to collapse the American consensus. America appeared to be coming apart as the late 1960s witnessed the most violence and disorder within the United States since the early 1890s.

THE TALL TEXAN

The new president was a brilliant politician. He had been born August 27, 1908, near the village of Stonewall, in a cabin on his daddy's ranch. His family, long time residents of the hardscrabble southwest Texas hill country, were poor but prominent people. Lyndon's father and grandfather had both served in the state legislature. Politics appear to have been bred into Lyndon Johnson's bones, plus a driving ambition to someday become rich and famous. He attended Southwest Texas State College at San Marcos. Following graduation, he taught elementary school for a couple of years in a one-room schoolhouse where most of his students were the children of Mexican farm workers.

Johnson's political career began in 1932 when he joined the staff of his district's congressman. In 1935, the young politician became state director of the National Youth Administration (NYA), an important New Deal agency whose prime mission was to help young people finish high school and attend college during hard times. At a time when it was politically risky to do so, Johnson saw to it that NYA funds were made available to African American students, schools, and colleges. He got elected to Congress in 1937, where he quickly made a name for himself as an ardent populist and New Dealer. He impressed President Roosevelt as an avid fund-raiser and future leader of the Democrat Party. In 1948, Johnson moved up to the Senate, winning election by a scant eighty-seven votes. His squeaky-thin margin of victory coupled to charges of voting irregularities earned him his senate sobriquet of "landslide Lyndon."

Johnson's rise in the Senate was meteoric. He quickly made himself indispensable to senior Democratic leaders such as Richard Russell of Georgia. Russell and his colleagues saw to it that Johnson became Senate minority leader in 1953. When the Democrats regained control of the Senate in 1955, Johnson became majority leader. From 1955 to 1960, as Senate majority leader, Johnson was the second most powerful politician in Washington. He sometimes supported liberal measures, more often he took a moderate stance on issues. Johnson worked cooperatively with the Eisenhower administration. The key to his power was his mastery of the Senate legislative process. He did his best work behind the scenes; he was a skilled negotiator and dealmaker. He always seemed to know just the right mix of carrots and sticks required to put together winning coalitions of diverse groups in support of important legislation.

Johnson was in his element in the Senate. He was the consummate professional politician. Although a southerner, he transcended his regional roots by identifying with the West. As he became more powerful, he increasingly took national positions on important issues. In 1960, he made a bid for the presidency, finishing second to Kennedy in the balloting at Los Angeles. During his vice presidency, he had an active and visible role in governance. He and President Kennedy respected each other. When Kennedy was gunned down, Johnson was ready to take his place.

JOHNSON TAKES COMMAND

The new president assumed office under horrendous circumstances. The nation's papers all carried the photo of a somber Lyndon Johnson being sworn into office by a federal judge on board Air Force One less than two hours after the president's murder. Also on board was Kennedy's body, awaiting its mournful flight back to Washington.

Johnson's immediate duty was to preside over an orderly transition of power that assured continuity in government and restored the people's shattered confidence in the political order. He handled this delicate task with great skill and remarkable sensitivity. He persuaded almost all of Kennedy's key White House staff and cabinet officials to remain at their jobs. His first speech to Congress and to the American people, given five days after the assassination and probably the most important speech of his presidency, demonstrated that a sure hand was at the helm.

Less than two hours after President Kennedy's murder, a somber Lyndon Johnson was sworn into office aboard Air Force One, still parked on the ground at the Dallas airport. He is flanked left by Kennedy's widow, Jacqueline Bouvier Kennedy, and on the right by his wife, and new first lady, Clarisa "Lady Bird" Johnson. Federal Judge Sarah T. Hughes (foreground) officiated. *Source*: National Archives.

The words that counted most in his speech were the following: "Today, in this moment of new resolve, I would say to my fellow Americans, let us continue." Johnson pledged to continue what Kennedy had started. He made it clear that stalled New Frontier legislation would be the top priority on his domestic agenda. He called specifically for Congress to enact swiftly the stalled civil rights act and tax reduction bill.

Johnson possessed tremendous abilities and energy, and he was driven by an intense ambition. He was brighter than most of the Harvard intellectuals who trailed Kennedy to Washington. But he always felt inferior to these poised and articulate men because of his lowly social origins and second-rate education. He never read anything but newspapers and had no interests outside politics. He acquired his intricate knowledge of government from experience, shrewd observation, conversation, and picking the brains of associates, much as Franklin Roosevelt had mined his advisers for ideas and programs.

Johnson had a passionate concern for the welfare of poor people, the elderly, and minorities, especially African Americans. Considering his humble, essentially southern origins, he was remarkably free of racial prejudices. He believed that the federal government could be a major instrument for improving the lot of America's disadvantaged citizens, and he would use it if he could. Much more than his patrician predecessor, Lyndon Johnson was the inheritor of the New Deal commitment to achieving social justice for all Americans.

During his first six months in office, President Johnson used a successful strategy for getting Congress to enact much previously blocked New Frontier legislation. He evoked memories of the deceased Kennedy as a moral lever to pry bills out of congressional committees. He also sought to overcome conservative resistance to social reform by insisting on balanced budgets and reducing government expenditures. He obtained congressional passage of Kennedy's long-stalled tax cuts, which reduced personal and corporate income taxes about 5 percent across the board. Enactment of these tax cuts represented the first deliberate use of Keynesian fiscal policy to stimulate demand and to promote investment to keep the economy prosperous and expanding, thereby generating the tax revenues to pay for proposed reforms.

LBJ also persuaded Congress to enact the most comprehensive civil rights bill in American history. It passed the House in February 1964, but it ran into a southern filibuster in the Senate that delayed its passage until June, when a bipartisan effort broke the filibuster and passed the measure by a vote of seventy-seven to eighteen. The Civil Rights Bill of 1964 went well beyond Kennedy's initial proposal. It was the most sweeping affirmation of equal rights and the strongest commitment to their enforcement ever made by Congress. Its key provision guaranteed equal access to all public accommodations such as restaurants, bars, hotels, theaters, and casinos. Other provisions strengthened federal machinery for combating discrimination in hiring and promotions. The bill also empowered the federal government to file school desegregation suits, and it further strengthened voting rights. It further required corporations and trade unions to ensure equal employment opportunities to all applicants.

In addition to promoting tax cuts and civil rights, Kennedy was considering an antipoverty program at the time of his death. He had ordered his chief economic adviser, Walter Heller, to draft a plan for an assault on poverty. Heller informed Johnson of the plan and the new president eagerly adopted it. In his first State of the Union address delivered in January 1964, Johnson declared "unconditional war on poverty in America." Congress a few months later enacted the Economic Opportunity Act, authorizing the spending of $1 billion over three years beginning in 1965. The act created an umbrella agency called the Office of Economic Opportunity (OEO) to administer antipoverty programs. Johnson appointed Sargent Shriver, formerly director of the Peace Corps, to run OEO. The most radical feature of the new antipoverty law created "community action programs" (CAP) that involved the poor themselves in devising the kinds of programs they wanted in their communities. CAP quickly generated controversy as poverty advocates fought with local politicians for control of OEO funds and programs.

THE 1964 ELECTION

As Lyndon Johnson established himself as an effective president during the first six months of 1964, the Republicans sought a candidate to run against him. Within Republican ranks, angry conservatives, unhappy with their party's tendency, ever since the New Deal, to nominate nonideological centrists for the presidency, were determined this time to nominate one of their own. Conservatives represented diverse groups: midwesterners, southerners, westerners, far-right groups such as the John Birch Society, and New Right newcomers to the GOP such as former screen actor Ronald Reagan and an activist attorney from Illinois, Phyllis Schlafly. These aggressive conservatives supported the candidacy of Arizona Senator Barry Goldwater. Goldwater's political philosophy blended traditional conservatism with New Right ideological discontent with the restraints imposed on American system by the welfare state and the Cold War. Goldwater, a product of Sunbelt politics, favored both free enterprise and unilateral military action against the Communists.

Moderate eastern Republicans mounted an all-out effort to stall Goldwater's drive for their party's nomination in the California primary in June. Nelson Rockefeller challenged Goldwater in a bruising battle that split the California Republican Party. Goldwater scored a narrow victory, and with it he secured his presidential candidate nomination.

At the Republican nominating convention held in the Cow Palace near San Francisco in August, moderates hoped to tone down Goldwater's strident rhetoric and to persuade the party to adopt a moderate platform. But Goldwater's people were in no mood to compromise with the hated moderates, especially now that they had them on the run. Goldwater's acceptance speech was a New Right manifesto. He denounced government, especially the federal government. In memorable words, he read the moderates out of the GOP:

> Those who do not care for our cause, we don't expect to enter our ranks. . . . Extremism in the defense of liberty is no vice! Moderation in the pursuit of justice is no virtue![1]

The election campaign between President Johnson and his challenger was a dull, one-sided affair. Goldwater never had a chance. Early in the campaign, Goldwater urged that NATO field commanders be given control of tactical nuclear weapons. His proposal frightened most Americans who thought it made nuclear war more likely. The democrats hired an ad agency that ran a television commercial showing a little girl picking petals from a daisy; then the image of the little girl faded as an ominous voice counted down from ten. As the voice reached one, the screen suddenly filled with a mushroom cloud. Johnson is then heard in a voiceover saying "These are the stakes. We must learn to love one another, or surely we shall die."

Goldwater often did not need Democratic help to drive away voters. He told an audience of elderly people in Florida that he favored making Social Security voluntary. He chose Memphis, Tennessee, the cotton capital, to attack farm subsidy programs. He then journeyed to Knoxville, located in the center of a region made prosperous by the Tennessee Valley Authority, to tell voters that the TVA must be sold to private power companies. At Charleston, West Virginia, located at the edge of Appalachia, one of the poorest regions in the nation, he announced that the impending war on poverty was unnecessary.

Johnson refused to debate Goldwater on television. Because the polls all showed him holding a big lead, Johnson did not bother to do any campaigning until the final month. When he did enter the fray in October, he campaigned as a unifier. He forged a broad electoral consensus including much of the business

[1]Quoted in Michael Schaller, Virginia Scharff, and Robert D. Schulzinger, *Present Tense: The United States Since 1945* (Boston: Houghton Mifflin, 1992), p. 250.

community, trade unions, farmers, most middle-class voters, liberals, intellectuals, the elderly, the poor, blacks, and other minorities. A sizable part of Johnson's support came from Republican voters fleeing Goldwater's extremist campaign. Goldwater showed strength among white southerners and hard-core Republicans.

On election day, Johnson won his predicted landslide. In the popular vote, he got 43 million votes to Goldwater's 27 million, and 486 electoral votes to Goldwater's 52. Johnson carried forty-four states and received 60.7 percent of the popular vote. Democrats added 37 House seats and 2 more in the Senate. The new House of Representatives would have 295 Democrats to 140 Republicans. The new Senate would have 68 Democrats to only 32 Republicans.

In the aftermath of the Goldwater debacle, some analysts spoke of the impending demise of the Republican Party as a major political force. Such epitaphs proved premature; it turned out that Goldwater was merely ahead of his time. Ronald Reagan, inheriting Goldwater's cause, would ride it to the White House in 1980. While celebrating their landslide victories, some Democratic Party leaders nervously noted that five of the six states carried by Goldwater were southern. The Solid South was disintegrating as white voters, perceiving the Democratic Party to be increasingly identified with the drive by African Americans for full participation in public life, abandoned their historical allegiances and voted Republican.

GREAT SOCIETY

Soon after his overwhelming victory, Johnson, backed by the most liberal Congress since 1936, set out to create Great Society. He organized task forces made up of his staffers, social scientists, bureaucrats, and activists to draft legislative proposals to send to Congress. Johnson and his liaison people also worked closely with the Congress during all stages of the legislative process to get passage of the programs that became the Great Society. Dozens of programs poured from the most cooperative Congress since the "First Hundred Days." Among the most important measures enacted during 1965 was the Appalachian Regional Development Act. Appalachia, a mountainous region extending from Pennsylvania to northern Alabama that contained 17 million people, was a vast pocket of poverty. The act provided over $1 billion in subsidies for a variety of projects stressing economic development of the region.

Congress also attacked the problem of America's decaying central cities. The Housing and Urban Development Act of 1965 provided funding for 240,000 units of low-rent housing. It also authorized spending $2.9 billion over four years for urban renewal projects. Federal rent supplements for low-income families were added in 1966. Congress also created a new cabinet-level Department of Housing and Urban Development (HUD). President Johnson appointed Robert Weaver to head the new agency, the first African American cabinet member.

In addition to attacking urban problems, Congress enacted both the Medicare and the Medicaid programs in 1965. Medicare provided health care for people aged sixty-five and over, while Medicaid provided health care for low-income people not eligible for Medicare. Both programs would be funded through Social Security. At the time of the passage of these programs, the United States was the only industrial democracy in the world without some form of national health insurance. Organized physicians, working through their powerful lobby, the American Medical Association (AMA), had blocked all efforts to enact national health insurance since Truman first proposed it back in 1945. President Johnson, determined to add medical insurance in some form to the Great Society, overcame the opposition of the AMA and conservative legislators by limiting the insurance program to the elderly and the poor and by funding it through the Social Security system.

One of the most important achievements of Great Society was enactment of federal aid to education. The Elementary and Secondary Education Act of 1965 ended a long debate in Congress over the use of federal funds to support public schools. President Kennedy had made federal aid to public schools a top New Frontier priority and had suffered a serious defeat because of Catholic opposition to his bill, which did not fund parochial schools. On the other hand, Protestant and Jewish leaders strongly opposed funding parochial schools. Kennedy could never resolve the impasse. President Johnson also believed that providing federal funding for education was the primary way that the federal government could promote equality of opportunity in America, overcame the religious roadblock. He convinced Cardinal Spellman, the Reverend Billy Graham, and Jewish leaders to accept an aid program that provided federal funds for states based on the number of low-income students enrolled in their schools. The funds would be distributed to both private and public schools to benefit all children in need.

Johnson rescued another stalled New Frontier reform when he secured Congressional passage of the Immigration Act of 1965, the first comprehensive overhaul of U.S. immigration policy in forty years. The new law abolished the discriminatory national origins quota system implemented during the 1920s that had restricted immigration to this country on the basis of ethnic and racial background. Under the new legislation, each country would have an annual quota of about twenty-thousand slots. Eligibility would be based on the skills and education of the individual immigrant, as well as close family ties to people already here.

Additional civil rights legislation joined the Great Society agenda in 1965. Many African Americans could not yet vote in the Deep South states, despite the enactment of three previous civil rights bills and voter registration drives by civil rights groups. Hundreds of student volunteers working in Mississippi in the summer of 1964 to register African American voters encountered stubborn, often violent opposition from white segregationists. The Mississippi "Freedom Summer" dramatized the continuing disfranchisement of southern African Americans. In the spring of 1965, Dr. Martin Luther King, Jr., prepared to lead a 50-mile march of demonstrators from Selma, Alabama, to the state capitol in Montgomery to publicize continuing denial of African American voting rights. A few days before the march was scheduled to begin, President Johnson made a nationally televised speech to a joint session of Congress calling for a voting rights bill that would close all remaining loopholes in civil rights laws. Near the end of his speech, Johnson raised his arms in the style of a country preacher and recited the words from an old black spiritual that had become the anthem of the civil rights movement, "And we shall overcome!" The demonstrators in Selma, poised to begin their march, listened to his speech through tears of joy.

As they began their march for the right to vote, they were attacked by Alabama state troopers who gassed, clubbed, and whipped them. These vicious attacks on nonviolent protesters marching on behalf of a fundamental democratic right were televised nationally to a shocked nation. An angry president, viewing the attacks, federalized the Alabama National Guard and ordered it to provide protection for the marchers all the way to Montgomery. Johnson then maneuvered the Voting Rights Bill through Congress. The Voting Rights Act of 1965 gave the Attorney General power to appoint federal registrars to register voters in districts where historical patterns of disfranchisement prevailed. Empowered by the new law, federal officials registered hundreds of thousands of African American and Hispanic voters in six southern states during the next three years. The 1966 election was the first one held in this country in which most adult southern African Americans could vote.

There were many more Great Society measures. The first session of the Eighty-ninth Congress approved ninety administration-sponsored reform bills. The legislative pace slowed in 1966, but more measures continued to flow from Congress. Two important pieces of consumer-protection legislation passed, a "Truth-in-Packaging" bill and a "Truth-in-Lending" act. The former required sellers to label accurately the contents of packages sold for household use. The latter required detailed information about the true rate of interest charged on bank loans

The impact of the Voting Rights Act is shown in the percentage of adult white and black registrations in the South in 1964 and 1969.

	1964		1969	
	White	*Black*	*White*	*Black*
Alabama	69.2	19.3	94.6	61.3
Arkansas	65.6	40.4	81.6	77.9
Florida	74.8	51.2	94.2	67.0
Georgia	62.6	27.4	88.5	60.4
Louisiana	80.5	31.6	87.1	60.8
Mississippi	69.9	6.7	89.8	66.5
North Carolina	96.8	46.8	78.4	53.7
South Carolina	75.7	37.3	71.5	54.6
Tennessee	72.9	69.5	92.0	92.1
Texas			61.8	73.1
Virginia	61.1	38.3	78.7	59.8
Total	73.4	35.5	83.5	64.8

SOURCE: U.S. Department of Commerce, *Statistical Abstract of the United States, 1970* (Washington, D.C., 1970), p. 369; and Steven Lawson, *Black Ballots, 1944-1969* (New York: Columbia University Press, 1976), p. 331.

and credit purchases. Conservation and wildlife preservation laws were enacted. Congress added a new cabinet-level Department of Transportation in 1966 and enacted a series of highway safety laws. Consumer advocate Ralph Nader did more than anyone to secure passage of these new safety laws. His book *Unsafe at Any Speed* (1966), documented hazardous design defects in Detroit-made automobiles, promoting public awareness of these problems.

Great Society measures enacted between 1964 and 1966 represented the most far-reaching assault ever mounted on a vast array of social problems by the federal government. Reform measures left over from the New Deal and Fair Deal eras were enacted during the mid-1960s. Most of the problems that Great Society tried to solve had been around for years. They were challenged during the mid-1960s because of a confluence of circumstances that gave liberal reformers opportunities normally unavailable within the American political system. The nation was prosperous and there existed a widespread sense that Americans could afford the costs of social reform. Large liberal majorities prevailed in both houses of the Congress, breaking the bipartisan conservative bloc's control. Johnson's smashing victory in the 1964 election had given the activist liberal reform leader a mandate for social change. Most of all, Johnson's special political skills made the Great Society a reality. He formed broad-based coalitions supporting reform, and he used his remarkable abilities to steer complex legislation through the congressional minefields of special interest groups. President Lyndon Johnson ranks along with Franklin Roosevelt and Woodrow Wilson as one of the great liberal reform leaders of modern American history.

For a time, many Great Society programs worked. In part stimulated by tax cuts, the economy grew rapidly. The GDP increased 25 percent between 1964 and 1966, providing billions of dollars of additional tax revenues to fund the new programs without incurring budget deficits, raising interest rates, or igniting inflation. Unemployment dropped below 4 percent in 1965, the lowest rate since World War II. The number of poor people declined by millions; this reduction came from both antipoverty programs and new jobs generated by the strong economy. Medicare and Medicaid improved the quality of health care available to the elderly and to the poor. Students at all educational levels benefited from federal programs and African Americans in the South at long last had the vote.

But the Great Society immediately incurred a flurry of criticism from both Left and Right. Conservatives assailed its high costs, its centralization of government authority, and its proliferation of new federal bureaucracies. They insisted that social problems could not be solved by creating new federal agencies and throwing money at them. A few articulate radicals charged that most Great Society programs were woefully inadequate. A young militant, Tom Hayden, observed "the welfare state is more machinery than substance."

Johnson's war on poverty, which was launched in 1965 with much fanfare, came under heavy fire. Some of its programs worked well, particularly those that helped prepare poor minority youngsters for school and those that furnished job training for disadvantaged young men and women. But radical critics insisted that if government officials were serious about eradicating poverty in America, then a few billion dollars could not begin to meet the needs of the nation's 40 million poor people. In their view, the poverty program was both oversold and underfunded. It generated unrealistic expectations among poor African Americans and fierce resentments among working-class whites who perceived antipoverty programs as favoring militant protesters over hardworking people. Michael Harrington, whose book *The Other America* (1962) had helped President Kennedy to discover poverty in America, observed: "What was supposed to be a social war turned out to be a skirmish, and in any case, poverty won."

After 1966, Congress, concerned about rising crime rates, violence, and inflation, was reluctant to vote more funds for reform and welfare programs. Johnson had expected to finance the Great Society from increased tax revenues derived from an expanding economy. He believed that affluent Americans could continue to prosper without having to make any sacrifices to help the poor. He believed that the Great Society would enable the one-fourth of Americans who were disadvantaged to join the affluent three-fourths without requiring any tax increases or redistribution of wealth. He promised much more than the Great Society could deliver. He both exaggerated American wealth and underestimated the profound barriers to achieving affluence for all. He believed that America could fight a major war in Vietnam and continue to build the Great Society at home. Ironically, the leader who wanted to achieve his place in history as the man who fulfilled the social vision of the New Deal escalated the war in Vietnam and strangled his beloved Great Society. Liberal reformers lamented the fact that by 1967, except for token gestures, the Great Society was dead. The fight for civil rights, the struggle to save the cities, and the efforts to improve the public schools—all were starved for the sake of the escalating war. The Great Society turned out to be the last major reform spasm of social liberalism in modern times.

Poverty, 1969.   *Source:* U.S. Bureau of the Census, *Current Population Reports,* series P-60, No. 194, and unpublished data.

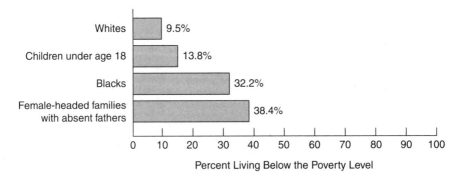

THE WARREN COURT

Led by its energetic Chief Justice, Earl Warren, the activist liberal majority controlling the Supreme Court during the 1960s rendered a series of landmark decisions that struck down the last remnants of the segregation system. The Court also protected the right of dissent, expanded the freedom of the press, regulated obscene materials, and restricted the role of religion in public schools. It further altered criminal legal procedures, expanded the right to privacy, and made the American political system more inclusive.

In *Bond* v. *Floyd* (1966), the Court ordered the Georgia House of Representatives to admit an elected representative, civil rights activist Julian Bond, who had been denied his seat because of his opposition to the Vietnam War and the conscription system that sustained it.

In *New York Times* v. *Sullivan* (1964), the Court ruled that people in the public eye—elected officials and celebrities, could not win a libel suit against a publication solely because its editors had published untrue statements. Under the Court's reading of libel laws, plaintiffs had to prove that the statements were "recklessly false" and made with "malice and aforethought." Since motivation was extremely difficult to establish within a court of law, the practical effect of *New York Times* v. *Sullivan* was to make it unlikely that a public figure could win a libel suit against a newspaper or magazine publisher.

In *Roth* v. *United States* (1957), the Court defined obscenity as material "without any redeeming social importance." The Court also defined as obscene material that "the average person, applying community standards, regarded as appealing to prurient interests." However, the Court found it impossible to come

The Warren Court. Photo taken Nov. 22, 1965. (L-R) (Standing) Byron White, William Brennan, Potter Stewart, and Abe Fortas. (Seated) Tom Clark, Hugo Black, Earl Warren, William Douglas, and John Marshall Harlan.   *Source*: National Archives.

up with objective criteria to determine what materials were obscene under its definitions. The problems were twofold: community standards varied and any definition of obscenity involved inherently subjective judgments. Associate Justice Potter Stewart acknowledged the Court's dilemma when he asserted that while he could not give a precise legal definition of obscenity, he knew it when he saw it.

The Court also broadened the First Amendment's ban on the establishment of religion. In *Engel* v. *Vitale* (1962), the Court banned prayer in public schools. In a later decision, the Court banned Bible readings from public school classrooms. The Court also nullified an Arkansas law that mandated the teaching of "creation science" as an alternative to Darwinian evolutionary theory. The cumulative effect over the years of these decisions was to remove religious observances from public schools.

In two controversial five-to-four decisions, the Supreme Court also enhanced the procedural rights of citizens accused of crimes. In the first case, *Gideon* v. *Wainwright* (1963), the Court ruled that Clarence Gideon, a professional criminal, had never gotten a fair trial because he never had had an attorney to defend him in court. The Court, in effect, ruled that the right to a fair trial included the right to be represented in court by a lawyer. As a consequence of the Court's rulings in *Gideon* v. *Wainwright,* all cases in the country in which defendants had been convicted of felonies without the benefit of attorneys to represent them had to be retried. If the defendant could not afford an attorney, the state—that is, taxpayers—had to furnish one. In the second case, *Miranda* v. *Arizona* (1966), the Court enhanced citizens' Fifth Amendment rights against self-incrimination. In this case, the Court ruled that Ernesto Miranda, a suspect charged with burglary, had been coerced by the Phoenix police into confessing. The police questioning Miranda had told him that if he did not confess, the judge would give him a longer sentence. According to the new rules implemented in *Miranda* v. *Arizona,* police were required to inform a suspect of their rights at the time of arrest: their right to remain silent, that anything they said could and would be used in a court of law to convict them, the right to have an attorney represent them in court, and, in the event that they could not afford a lawyer, the state would provide them one for free.

In 1965, the Warren Court struck down a Connecticut law that forbade the sale or use of contraceptives. In *Griswald* v. *Connecticut,* Associate Justice William O. Douglas, writing for the majority, found the law to be an unwarranted invasion of privacy. Nowhere in the Bill of Rights is there delineated a specific right to privacy; Douglas apparently inferred a right of privacy. Years later, another Supreme Court justice would ground the right of women to have an abortion on demand during the first trimester of pregnancy on that same inferred right of privacy.

Warren Court rulings also affected political practices in this country. In *Baker* v. *Carr* (1962), the Court declared that it could determine whether state legislative districts had been fairly drawn. The principle that the courts used during the 1960s to determine whether state legislative districts had been fairly drawn was "one person, one vote," derived from the equal protections clause of the Fourteenth Amendment. During the 1960s, as a consequence of *Baker* v. *Carr,* several states in which rural voters were overrepresented in state legislatures at the expense of urban residents, had to redraw the boundaries of their legislative districts to make them equal in population.

The cumulative effects of these landmark court decisions were to enhance significantly the rights of individuals, to curtail the arbitrary powers of government, and to make the political system more democratic. Ironically, the least democratic branch of the federal government, and the only one beyond the reach of the voting majority, had done much to strengthen American democracy and to validate the growing pluralism of the political culture. In the process, the Warren Court provoked many powerful enemies. Conservatives were enraged by what they considered judicial usurpations of the lawmaking process. Law enforcement officials complained that Court decisions made their jobs more difficult, allowed obviously guilty people to avoid punishment, and seemed to place the law on the side of criminals rather than their law-abiding victims. Devoutly religious people were often offended by the Court's proscriptions of religious observances in the public schools. Loud calls to impeach Earl Warren resounded across the South and Midwest. As the conservative revolt gathered momentum in this country during the 1970s, one of their salient issues was curtailing the judicial activism of the Supreme Court.

LYNDON JOHNSON AND THE WORLD

Johnson tried to conduct foreign policy using the same methods and skills that worked so well for him in domestic affairs. But he was handicapped by inexperience, and he lacked the depth of knowledge of world affairs required for effective diplomacy. His early ventures in world affairs met with mixed results. In time, his efforts to achieve an American military victory in Vietnam would destroy his presidency and bring his nation, and those whom he had tried to help in Southeast Asia, to disaster.

In Europe, Johnson could not prevent relations with NATO allies from deteriorating. His chief difficulties came with Charles de Gaulle, who wanted France and Western Europe to rid themselves of U.S. domination. The French leader spurned Johnson's offer to create a multilateral nuclear force and directed France to accelerate development of her own nuclear forces. In early 1966, the French withdrew their forces from NATO and ordered the United States to remove all its military installations and personnel from France. They also expelled the NATO headquarters. France's dramatic actions signaled that de Gaulle believed the Cold War in Europe was waning. European countries no longer feared Soviet aggression. Hence, they no longer felt dependent on U.S. support, nor were they inclined to passively support all American foreign policies.

As de Gaulle challenged American influence in Europe, tensions in the Middle East caused Johnson persistent problems. The president perceived Egyptian leader Gamal Abdul Nasser's efforts to promote Arab nationalism to be the chief threat to American Middle Eastern interests. The Soviet Union, backing Nasser, was gaining influence in the region. Then came another Arab-Israeli war. It occurred in June 1967, following border clashes between Israelis and Syrians in the

Golan Heights area. Nasser, backing Syria, mobilized his forces and blockaded Israel's Red Sea port of Elath. Egypt also worked out an agreement with Jordan that placed its forces under Egyptian command. The Israelis, concluding that an Arab attack was imminent, launched an offensive on June 5. Israeli forces quickly destroyed the Egyptian air force, decimated Jordan's army, and defeated Syrian forces. Israeli tanks routed the Egyptian army. Israel won the war in six days. When a UN-proposed ceasefire went into effect, Israel occupied the Sinai and that part of Jordan west of the River Jordan (the West Bank). Israeli forces also held Syrian territory in the Golan Heights. Egyptian military power was shattered, Nasser humiliated, and Soviet interests set back. Israel, now a major power in the region, kept all occupied territories, determined to use them to enhance her territory and to guarantee her security. Israeli imperialism intensified already powerful Arab anti-Zionist animosities.

Nasser survived the debacle of the Six Day War. He remained popular with the Egyptian people, and the Soviets quickly rebuilt his military forces. The Soviets also expanded their naval forces in the eastern Mediterranean to challenge the U.S. Sixth Fleet. America remained Israel's chief supporter. As LBJ's presidency ended, the danger of another Arab–Israeli war remained great. It now carried with it the ominous potential of a U.S.–USSR confrontation.

Johnson also had to face crises in the Caribbean, where he made preventing further Castro-like insurgencies his top priority. His first crisis came in Panama, long a U.S. protectorate. Violent conflicts erupted between Panamanians and American citizens living in the Canal Zone in January 1964. The violence began when Panamanian students demanded that their national flag be flown alongside the American flag at a high school located in the Canal Zone. American authorities rejected the students' demand. U.S. soldiers killed twenty-one Panamanians, and three Americans died in riots. Panama severed diplomatic relations with the United States. The Organization of American States (OAS) mediated the dispute. Normal relations between the two countries were quickly restored. American and Panamanian negotiators then produced a series of agreements allowing Panamanian participation in management of the Panama Canal and granting Panama a share of canal revenues.

Another crisis occurred in the Dominican Republic, which also had a long history of American domination. A right-wing director, Rafael Trujillo, was overthrown in 1961 by a military coup, ushering in years of political instability in that poor island country. President Kennedy, delighted to see Trujillo go, sought free elections in the country. The elections brought Juan Bosch to power in 1962. Bosch, a social democrat, was overthrown by another military coup seven months later. In early 1965, a coalition of liberals, radicals, and young army officers launched a revolution to restore Bosch to power.

President Johnson, fearful that pro-Castro elements might come to power and turn the country into another Cuba, sent troops to suppress the insurgency. U.S. Marines and Army infantrymen prevented Bosch's return to power. U.S. spokesmen announced that American intervention had prevented a Communist takeover of the Dominican Republic. An occupation force was set up to maintain order. Elections were held in 1966, and Joaquin Balaguer defeated Bosch. Balaguer was able to establish an effective government that protected U.S. interests, and Johnson withdrew the American forces. But the Bosch movement was an independent, nationalistic movement, not a Communist conspiracy. U.S. intervention violated the OAS charter and canceled the U.S. pledge not to intervene militarily in the affairs of other Western Hemisphere countries. American public opinion supported Johnson's intervention. Liberals and foreign critics attacked his actions, but he ignored them. The campaign was limited in duration and few American lives were lost. Johnson achieved his objectives and his success silenced his critics. Success in the Dominican operation encouraged Johnson to try more of the same in Vietnam, expecting U.S. military success there to also silence any detractors who might emerge.

VIETNAM: GOING TO WAR

The roots of U.S. intervention in Southeast Asia could be traced back to Truman's presidency, but it was not until the Kennedy years that the United States became inextricably involved in a war in Vietnam. At the time Johnson replaced Kennedy, the political situation in South Vietnam was deteriorating. A succession of inept military governments had followed Diem, none of which governed or fought effectively. National Liberation Front forces, the "Viet Cong," supported by supplies and troops from North Vietnam, extended their control in southern Vietnam.

Johnson did not concern himself greatly with Vietnam during his first year in office; he continued Kennedy's policy of supporting the South Vietnamese government. He retained Kennedy's top advisers, sharing their commitment to contain the spread of Chinese Communism into Southeast Asia. LBJ, just as Truman, Eisenhower, and Kennedy had before him, embraced the Cold War ideology. His primary foreign policy objectives were to contain the two Communist powers, the Soviet Union and the People's Republic of China, and to prevent revolutionary change in the Third World. Johnson dismissed any possibility of an American withdrawal from Vietnam or any political solution that did not guarantee the survival of an independent, non-Communist state in southern Vietnam. He increased both the number of American advisers in Vietnam and the level of economic aid. He also approved a series of covert operations against North Vietnam, including commando raids along the North Vietnamese coast and infiltration of CIA operatives into the North. This subtle shift toward the North opened the way to a wider war.

In the summer of 1964, as the presidential campaign was getting underway in the United States, there occurred a relatively minor event in the developing Vietnam war that had major consequences. On August 1, while engaged in electronic espionage off the coast of North Vietnam, the American destroyer USS *Maddox* was attacked by North Vietnamese torpedo boats. *Maddox* returned the fire and repulsed the attackers with the aid of U.S. naval aircraft. *Maddox* resumed its spy operations and was joined by another destroyer, *Turner Joy.* On the night of August 4, as they operated in heavy seas about 50 miles off the coast of North Vietnam in the

Gulf of Tonkin, both ships reported that they were under attack. No one on either ship sighted any attackers; their initial reports were based on radar and sonar contacts. Later, the *Maddox*'s captain reported that weather effects and a misreading of sonar data may have been responsible for the reported attacks.

Even though evidence of a second attack was not certain, Johnson authorized retaliatory air strikes against North Vietnamese naval bases. Johnson also asked Congress to approve a resolution authorizing him to take "all necessary measures to repel any armed attack against the forces of the United States and to prevent further aggression." Johnson's use of force, coupled with his appeal for public support, silenced his Republican challenger, Barry Goldwater, who earlier had called for the bombing of North Vietnam. In presenting their case for the resolution, administration officials misled the Congress. Congressmen and Senators were not told that the *Maddox* was on a spy mission when it was attacked nor that the second attack may not have occurred. Secretary of Defense McNamara characterized both incidents as mindless acts of aggression against American ships on routine patrol in international waters. Congress quickly gave the president what he wanted without serious debate. The House passed the resolution unanimously and the Senate enacted it by a vote of eighty-eight to two.

During the final month of the 1964 presidential campaign, Johnson said little about the war in Vietnam. Goldwater did not make an issue of it, and most Americans did not concern themselves much about a dirty little war in a faraway place. But at times, Johnson did appear to be telling the American people that he did not want to get involved in a war in Vietnam and that Americans would not be sent to fight there. At Akron, Ohio, on October 21, he stated "we are not about to send American boys nine or ten thousand miles away from home to do what Asian boys ought to be doing for themselves."

At the time he made those remarks, Johnson had not yet committed himself to further bombing of North Vietnam nor had he decided to send U.S. combat troops there. But he knew the situation in southern Vietnam was deteriorating, despite his own public assurances to the contrary. He was also involved with advisers who had developed contingency plans that could be implemented in the future, including bombing the North and sending American combat troops to South Vietnam. During his reelection campaign, he deliberately misled the American people, conveying the impression that he would limit American efforts in Vietnam to helping one side in a civil war. He offered himself as a peace candidate who did not seek a wider war in contrast to the hawkish Goldwater who called for an unlimited American military effort in Vietnam. Voters, who thought they were voting for peaceful restraint in November 1964, soon got war.

As the new year began, the South Vietnamese government verged on defeat and Johnson confronted a dilemma that was largely of his own making. Since he had ruled out American withdrawal from Southeast Asia, there remained only the options of negotiation or escalation. But negotiations with Hanoi in early 1965, given military realities in southern Vietnam, could only mean having to accept a neutral coalition government for South Vietnam with National Liberation Front (NLF) participation. Johnson feared, rightly, that such a government would soon be dominated by the NLF since the Saigon regime could only survive with strong American support. He therefore ruled out negotiations until the military situation was more favorable, and he made his decision to escalate the war.

Johnson authorized a sustained, gradually expanding bombing campaign against North Vietnam beginning February 13, called Operation Rolling Thunder, and he significantly expanded the much larger air war in southern Vietnam. There was a direct connection between the air war against North Vietnam and Johnson's decision to send combat forces to South Vietnam. Within two weeks, General William Westmoreland, the U.S. commander in Vietnam, requested Marine combat units to defend a large U.S. Air Force base at Da Nang because he could not rely on South Vietnamese security forces. Johnson quickly approved his request. On March 8, two Marine battalions in full battle gear waded ashore at Da Nang.

In July 1965, Johnson and his advisers made a series of fateful decisions that set the United States on a course in Vietnam from which it did not deviate for nearly three years, and from which also began seven years of war. They approved General Westmoreland's requests for saturation bombing in southern Vietnam and for expanding the war against North Vietnam. They also authorized sending an additional 100,000 combat troops. Most important, President Johnson gave General Westmoreland a free hand to assume the major burden of fighting in the South. These decisions, made during the last week of July, represent a conscious decision to conduct an American war in Vietnam.

When he committed the United States to war in Southeast Asia, LBJ refused to tell the American people what he had done and he refused to seek a formal declaration of war against North Vietnam. He claimed that the Gulf of Tonkin resolution granted him authority to wage war. Since the Supreme Court never ruled on the matter, it remains a moot question whether the resolution amounted to a declaration of war against North Vietnam. Senator Fulbright, along with other legislators who later turned against the war, believed that Johnson had tricked them into supporting a war. At the time, Johnson felt confident that he could win the war and persuade Congress and most Americans to support it.

Washington's decisions for war were based on two fundamental errors in judgment. The U.S. seriously underestimated the capacity of the NLF and the North Vietnamese to resist large-scale applications of U.S. military power over a long period of time. Johnson and his advisers assumed that within a year or two, North Vietnam would "break" from the ever-increasing punishment inflicted by American bombers, and that they would accept U.S. terms for settlement. Johnson could not conceive of a poor Asian country about the size of New Mexico standing up to the power of the United States. The second error was to underestimate drastically the cost of the war in both lives and dollars and to overestimate the willingness of Americans to go on passively paying those costs year after year.

THE AMERICAN WAY OF WAR

The United States relied heavily on air power to win the war. Air Force and Navy pilots had two primary missions—to check infiltration of men, equipment, and supplies coming south from North Vietnam along the "Ho Chi Minh Trail," and to punish the North Vietnamese from the air until they abandoned the insurgency in the South and came to the bargaining table on American terms. Bombing failed to achieve either objective, even though the Americans waged the largest aerial war in history. The bombing slowed the rate of infiltration down to the Ho Chi Minh Trail, although never enough to hamper seriously the NLF war effort. Bombing disrupted North Vietnam's agriculture, destroyed its industry, and damaged some of its cities. Thousands of civilians were killed or wounded. But bombing never appreciably reduced North Vietnam's war-making ability nor broke their morale. Although it failed to achieve its objectives, the air war proved very costly: Between 1965 and 1968, America lost nearly a thousand fixed-wing aircraft, and hundreds of flyers were killed or captured. The bombing also handed the Communists a propaganda weapon. Opponents of the war denounced the air war. "Stop the bombing" became a rallying cry for antiwar activists.

American ground combat operations also escalated drastically between July 1965 and the end of 1967, when the United States deployed nearly 500,000 troops. General Westmoreland used a strategy of attrition against the enemy. He believed

Vietnam was primarily a small unit war in which squads of American troops engaged the NLF forces in jungles, swamps, and rice paddies. Here, a wounded U.S. soldier is being evacuated. *Source:* U.S. Army. Photo by SSG Paul Halverson.

that "search and destroy" operations would eradicate the enemy and force them to the negotiating table. U.S. troops used their technological superiority to counter the enemy's guerrilla warfare tactics. Herbicides were used on a wide scale to deprive the Viet Cong of forest cover and food crops. These chemicals caused widespread ecological devastation and posed health hazards within southern Vietnam. Americans also relied on artillery, helicopter gunships, and bombing to destroy enemy bases and to drive the guerrillas into open country. Since all of South Vietnam became a combat zone, American soldiers found themselves fighting an unconventional war without fronts or territorial objectives. The only measure of progress toward victory in a war of attrition was the number of enemy supplies captured or destroyed, the number of enemy weapons and ammunition captured or destroyed, and most of all, the number of enemy soldiers captured, wounded, or killed.

The American takeover of the war in early 1965 had prevented certain South Vietnamese defeat. But the United States could only achieve a stalemate, not victory. The attrition strategy was based on the assumption that U.S. forces, using their superior firepower, could inflict irreplaceable losses on the enemy while keeping their own casualties low. Even though the Americans inflicted heavy casualties, both the NLF and the North Vietnamese replaced their losses and matched each American escalation with one of their own during the years between 1965 and 1967. They retained the strategic initiative, and the NLF political structure in the South remained intact.

American artillery and bombing campaigns below the seventeenth parallel disrupted the southern Vietnamese economy. Large numbers of civilians were killed; millions more were driven into the arms of the Vietcong or became refugees. The violent American assault undermined the social fabric of a fragile nation and alienated villagers from the South Vietnamese regime that had never enjoyed much support from the rural population. The American takeover of the war further weakened the resolve of the South Vietnamese forces, who became more dependent than ever on American combat forces.

In 1967, with firm prodding from Washington, the South Vietnamese government, headed by General Nguyen Van Thieu, attempted to build popular support among the rural population. They focused on pacification and rural development. Government cadres moved into villages providing medical supplies and social services. They tried to insulate the villagers from both Vietcong appeals and reprisals. They sought to promote a national rebirth while American forces tried to defeat the Communists militarily. These pacification efforts sometimes succeeded, but they more often failed for many reasons. Americans occasionally bombed or shelled pacified villages by mistake. Vietcong terrorists assassinated many rural development leaders. Often, the cadres were inept or corrupt. The inability of the South Vietnamese military government to win and to keep mass allegiance, or to solve their country's massive social problems, was a major reason for the eventual failure of the American effort in Vietnam.

The Thieu government survived not because it was strong, because it was popular with most South Vietnamese, or because its soldiers fought well, but because it was backed by massive American firepower. But relations between American advisers and their Vietnamese clients were often ambivalent. The Vietnamese resented American arrogance and inability to understand them. The Americans were frustrated by pervasive Vietnamese corruption and inefficiency. American soldiers, fighting in the steamy jungles and swamps of an alien land, not always able to tell a friendly Vietnamese from a deadly enemy, often expressed hostility and mistrust toward the people they were defending. Many American soldiers felt they were risking their lives in fighting to save a people that did not deserve to be saved.

The steady escalation of the war between 1965 and 1967 generated both international and domestic pressures for a negotiated settlement. But the continuing stalemate on the battlefields ensured that neither side wanted negotiations. For political reasons, both sides had to appear responsive to peace initiatives, but neither side would make concessions necessary to get negotiations started. Hanoi's strategy was to get maximum propaganda value out of peace initiatives while matching U.S. escalations until the Americans wearied of the war and pulled out. President Johnson continued to believe that the steadily expanding American military effort would eventually break Hanoi.

Hanoi maintained that the American military presence in South Vietnam violated the 1954 Geneva Accords and that the bombing of North Vietnam was unprovoked and criminal aggression. The North Vietnamese refused to negotiate until the United States ceased all acts of war against their country and withdrew its forces. Hanoi also insisted that the government in Saigon would have to be replaced by a coalition government including the NLF. The Americans refused to withdraw their forces until a political solution could be reached in the South that excluded the Viet Cong. It also refused to stop the bombing, which it maintained was necessary to keep the Communists from overrunning the South. The United States remained committed to achieving a non-Communist South Vietnam. So the war went on and numerous peace initiatives from various sources failed in 1966 and 1967.

WAR AT HOME

While the expanding military stalemate continued, within the United States, supporters and opponents of the war engaged in debates of rising intensity. On one side were the Hawks, mostly conservative Republicans and Democrats, who were strongly supportive of the war and wanted to increase the U.S. war effort. On the other side were Doves, who challenged both the effectiveness and the morality of the war. Doves represented a more diverse group: old-line pacifists, student radicals, civil rights leaders, some college professors, and liberal politicians. The most prominent Dove was Senator Fulbright. Initially a supporter of the war effort, Fulbright had turned against it by 1966.

Opposition to the war took many forms. Senator Fulbright held hearings on the conduct of the war before his Senate Foreign Relations Committee, providing a forum for war critics and helping to legitimate opposition to the war. Doves staged many rallies and protest demonstrations during 1967, the first year of extensive antiwar activity. On October 21, about fifty thousand opponents of war demonstrated in front of the Pentagon. Thousands of young men resisted or evaded the draft. Some fled America and its war to Canada or Sweden.

Most Americans in 1967 were neither Hawks nor Doves. Nearly all citizens had supported the initial escalations that Americanized the Vietnam war. Confident of quick victory, they had rallied around the flag. But after two years of rising costs and casualties, with military victory still elusive, popular frustration with the Vietnam war had mounted. Polls taken in August showed for the first time that a majority of Americans believed that sending American combat troops to Vietnam had been a mistake. But opponents of Johnson's war policy in 1967 formed no consensus on Vietnam. They divided over whether to escalate the war drastically and win it or to negotiate an American withdrawal. But the growing divisiveness, married to declining confidence in the integrity and competence of government officials, strained the social fabric. A housewife in Iowa summed up the dilemma facing the average American: "I want to get out, but I don't want to give up."

The president, trying to dampen growing criticism within the Congress of his war policy, brought General Westmoreland to Washington in November. Speaking before the National Press Club on November 21, Westmoreland gave an optimistic appraisal of the war. He said that Pacification was going so well that the Viet Cong could no longer mount a major offensive anywhere in South Vietnam. He stated, "We have reached an important point where the end begins to come into view." Johnson stressed the theme of impending military victory in Vietnam. Popular support for the war increased as the year ended.

TET-68 AND ITS CONSEQUENCES

Then came Tet. On January 30, 1968, choosing the Lunar New Year, the most important Vietnamese holiday, as a time to strike in order to catch their opponents by surprise, about eighty thousand NLF and North Vietnamese troops suddenly brought the war to the cities and towns of South Vietnam. They simultaneously attacked provincial capitals, district towns, and a dozen major U.S. military bases all over the country. At most attack sites, the Viet Cong were beaten back within a few hours or a few days and sustained heavy losses. Within a month, they had lost all of the cities they had originally taken.

Hanoi had planned the Tet Offensive carefully; it was designed to give them a smashing victory over the Americans, to demoralize the Army of the Republic of Vietnam (ARVN) forces, and to bring the urban population of South Vietnam over to their side. They would show the urban populations of the South that neither the Americans nor the South Vietnamese forces could protect them. The Communists hoped their assaults would provoke popular uprisings against the South Vietnamese government, forcing Americans to leave and hastening the end of the war. But Tet turned out to be a major tactical defeat for the Communists; they failed to achieve most of their goals and suffered heavy losses.

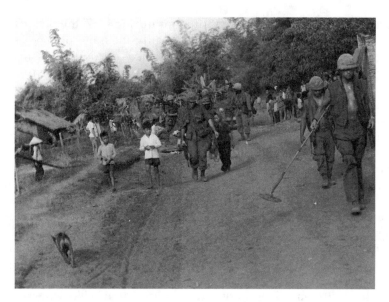

Soldiers from Rifle Co. "D," 2nd Battalion, 28th Infantry, fighting in the Mekong Delta, December, 1969.   *Source:* U.S. Army Photograph. Photo by SP5 Dennis L. Viets.

Within the United States, the Tet Offensive had a tremendous impact that was not anticipated by its North Vietnamese planners. Tet turned out to be a crucial political victory for the Communists. It had caught the South Vietnamese and Americans by surprise, although they had responded quickly to counteract it. President Johnson, too, was surprised and confused by the ability of an enemy he thought was verging on defeat to stage coordinated attacks against supposedly secure sites all over South Vietnam.

Although General Westmoreland talked confidently of having anticipated and suppressed the Tet offensive while inflicting heavy losses on the enemy, he shortly thereafter requested an additional 206,000 combat troops to be able to follow up and win the war. The Chairman of the Joint Chiefs, General Earl Wheeler, gave the president the first pessimistic appraisal of the war he ever heard from a military adviser. Wheeler hinted that Tet had "been a very near thing" and that the Americans could lose the war unless the requested reinforcements were sent. Johnson, confused by events and conflicting military opinions, asked his new Secretary of Defense, Clark Clifford, to conduct a thorough review of the troop request before the president responded to the military's request for more troops.

Clifford formed a committee whose investigations ranged far beyond the troop request issue; they conducted the first full review of the American war effort in Vietnam. Clifford demanded precise answers to fundamental questions: What were the ultimate objectives of the United States in Vietnam? How would additional forces contribute to attaining these goals? What would be the impact of a major escalation of the war on the public and on the economy? Was there a definable limit to the American commitment to Vietnam? Was there a point at which the price became too high? How would General Westmoreland deploy these troops and exactly what results could we expect from this additional manpower?

The answers he got from both military and civilian officials in the Pentagon discouraged him. To provide 206,000 more troops for Vietnam required further reductions of U.S. military commitments elsewhere, which were already stretched dangerously thin. America's ability to meet its major strategic commitments in other parts of the world and its capability to respond to challenges to its vital interests elsewhere would be compromised. Meeting these troop requests would require calling up reserves, increasing draft calls, and raising taxes. Casualties would rise and domestic opposition would intensify. Civilian analysts in the Pentagon told Clifford that the current war strategy could not bring victory even with the proposed escalation; they recommended that the United States should start phasing back its military involvement and try to get a negotiated settlement. They also proposed turning over more of the fighting to the South Vietnamese forces. Clifford recommended to the president that he reject Westmoreland's request for additional troops, assign the ARVN a greater fighting role, and seek a negotiated settlement.

The Tet Offensive also influenced the way the media, particularly television news, covered the Vietnam War. Previously, television had usually presented a well-ordered vision of the war—on the scene reports of combat operations that were usually reported as American victories, along with periodic analytical reports of the war's progress and of pacification programs. With Tet, viewers saw the results for the first time of a major Communist offensive striking all over South Vietnam. A rush of violent and confusing images flooded television—fighting in the streets of Saigon and Hue. The chaos in Vietnam viewed on television appeared to contradict all the official reports and media coverage of the past three years, which had conveyed the idea of steady progress toward military victory. The fact that the enemy could stage surprise attacks all over South Vietnam caused a growing number of Americans to wonder if all that three years of escalating war had achieved in Vietnam was unending stalemate. In the months following the Tet Offensive, public opinion polls recorded increases in the number of people expressing dovish sentiments.

Congressional opposition to the war also escalated after Tet. Antiwar sentiment on Capitol Hill boosted the candidacy of an obscure Minnesota Senator, Eugene McCarthy, who had announced in December 1967 that he would challenge Lyndon Johnson for the presidency as an antiwar candidate. In the New Hampshire primary on March 12, 1968, McCarthy got 42 percent of the vote, almost as many votes as Johnson, indicating more widespread opposition to Johnson's war policy than previously thought. Johnson appeared to be unpopular and politically vulnerable. Four days after the New Hampshire primary, a more formidable antiwar candidate, Robert Kennedy, announced that he, too, would seek the Democratic nomination.

CHINA

NORTH
VIETNAM

Red River

Hanoi

BURMA

Mekong River

LAOS

Gulf of
Tonkin

Hainan

Vientiane

Vinh

Donghoi

DMZ

17th Parallel

HO CHI MINH TRAIL

THAILAND

Nan River

Quang Tri
Hue

Demarcation Line
of 1954

Danang
Tamky
Chulai

I CORPS

Quangngai

Kontum

Bangkok

CAMBODIA

Tonle
Sap

Mekong River

Pleiku

Quinhon

SOUTH
VIETNAM

II CORPS

Nhatrang

Phnompenh

III CORPS

Dalat

Bencat

Gulf of Siam

Bienhoa
Saigon

Tan Son Nhut

Vinhlong

SOUTH
CHINA SEA

Cantho

Camau

Mekong Delta

★ Tet attacks, 1968

⊙ Provincial capital

0   100   200 Miles

Source: U.S. Army.

At the White House, Johnson struggled with his failed Vietnam policy. He convened a panel of distinguished civilian and military advisers who had previously endorsed his war policy. But in March these "wise men" told the president that the Vietnam War could not be won "save at unacceptable risk" to national interests at home and abroad. Their advice influenced Johnson. He accepted Clark Clifford's recommendations to scale back the war. On March 31, 1968, Johnson told the American people that he would reduce the bombing of North Vietnam in an effort to get negotiations underway. As he neared the end of his speech, he stunned the nation by stating "I shall not seek, nor will I accept, the nomination of my party for another term as your president." To restore unity to America, he would remove himself from politics and seek peace in Vietnam. To end the war at home that was tearing the nation apart, he would abandon the strategy of gradual escalation in Vietnam that he had begun three years earlier. Vietnam had claimed its most prominent victim.

YOUNG RADICALS

The insurgencies that characterized the mid- and late 1960s began on the campuses of some of America's leading universities, the prestigious Ivy League schools and the great public universities such as the Berkeley campus of the University of California and the University of Michigan at Ann Arbor. A new generation of politically committed young people had already became involved in the civil rights movement and had also tried to organize poor people at the community level. After 1965, many of these youthful insurgents, most of them from affluent middle-class families, became involved in protests against the Vietnam War. In 1960, a group of young activists organized Students for a Democratic Society (SDS). In 1962, one of its leaders, Tom Hayden, wrote a manifesto for the new organization, "The Port Huron Statement." He criticized apathetic college students and attacked the military-industrial complex. Hayden called for an end to poverty in America and for the creation of "a democracy of individual participation" in which all members subject to the authority of a governmental institution would participate in its decision-making processes. Until it disintegrated in 1969, SDS led the emergent New Left.

The first student uprising occurred on the Berkeley campus of the University of California in the fall of 1964. A group of students, many of them civil rights activists who had spent the previous summer registering voters in Mississippi, protested university efforts to prevent their using a campus area for rallying support for off-campus political activities. Student leaders Mario Savio and Jack Weinberg, both veterans of the Mississippi "Freedom Summer," formed the Free Speech Movement (FSM) to lead the resistance. When university officials attempted to discipline leaders of the FSM, about six hundred students and nonstudents occupied Sproul Hall, the university administration building. After university efforts to persuade the protesters to leave failed, Governor Edmund G. "Pat" Brown ordered state police to remove and arrest them. The forced removal of the demonstrators provoked a student strike, which was supported by a large majority of the faculty.

After two months of turmoil on campus, university officials permitted "free speech" on campus.

Leaders of the Free Speech movement aimed their attacks at the university itself. They saw it as a willing servant of a corporate order that controlled society and maintained an economic system which oppressed blacks and poor people. In their view, Berkeley had become an "impersonal machine" serving the established power structure, preparing students for careers as corporate functionaries. Cards designed by IBM and used to classify and identify students became for young radicals symbols of an educational system that had lost sight of its primary goals of making people better and improving society.

The rebellion that began at Berkeley soon spread to other campuses around the country. Insurgents attacked university complicity with racial injustice and the Vietnam War. They also attacked the universities themselves. Protesters demanded the right to sit on governing boards with power to veto faculty appointments. Curricula and methods of instruction came under fire. Students objected to taking "irrelevant" courses, mostly required science and language classes. They called for fewer required courses, more electives, and fewer tests and grades. Other protesters demanded the elimination of college parietal rules, which set curfews and visiting hours for university housing.

SDS became prominent on many college campuses by organizing opposition to the expanding war in Vietnam. By the mid-1960s, the stalemated Vietnam War had become the main student protest issue. Since the military draft was the prime way the war could reach young people, opposition to the draft brought thousands of new recruits into radical protest politics. When SDS launched a national draft resistance program, new chapters proliferated as thousands of recruits rushed to join. SDS organized a Stop the Draft Week for October 16 to 21, 1967. It staged sit-ins at army induction centers, held meetings for draft card burnings, opposed campus ROTC programs, demonstrated against corporations known to be prime Defense Department contractors, and harassed military recruiters. Thousands of protesters besieged the Oakland, California, Army Induction Center, blocking busses hauling in draftees. Between 1965 and 1968, SDS led or joined hundreds of demonstrations at over a hundred colleges and universities involving about fifty thousand students. As the Vietnam War escalated, the protest tactics used by SDS and other antiwar groups grew more militant. SDS also joined other groups opposed to the continuing and expanding war.

SDS also joined the most violent student uprising of the turbulent 1960s, which occurred at Columbia University during the first four months of 1968. The issues that sparked the conflict were two potent catalysts of student militancy, civil rights and Vietnam. Antiwar radicals and civil rights activists joined forces to attack one of the nation's leading universities. SDS sought an end to university ties with a military research institute on campus. The Black Student Union opposed university plans to construct a gymnasium on land adjacent to Harlem. Both groups occupied campus buildings to force the university to sever its ties with the military and to abandon the gym project. When negotiations between administration officials and radicals failed, police stormed the buildings to remove the protesters, who had barricaded doors and windows. Hundreds of students were injured and about seven hundred were arrested. Following the arrests, SDS organized a campus strike that forced the university to close early that spring. American student protests in 1968 were part of a larger web of student militancy around the world. While students barricaded buildings at Columbia, French students battled police in the streets of Paris.

At its 1969 annual meeting, the New Left split into warring factions. Its left wing, calling itself the "Weathermen," went off on its own. In October, hundreds of Weathermen staged "the days of rage" in Chicago, which they intended to be the opening campaign of a new American revolution. They broke windows in buildings and smashed automobile windshields. Police arrested and jailed most of them. About a hundred Weathermen went underground, forming terrorist bands that carried out sporadic bombings of public buildings and corporate headquarters during the early 1970s.

The New Left radicalized only a small portion of the millions of young people attending college during the 1960s. Most students attended class, pursued their social lives, worked part-time, and sought conventional goals. They never participated in radical protests on or off campus. Student rebels were mostly clustered on the campuses of major metropolitan universities like Berkeley and Columbia. Because they were a highly visible and articulate group that received extensive media coverage, especially television news coverage, the public perception was that student radicalism was much more extensive than demographic data confirmed. Most of the nation's twenty-three hundred community colleges, state universities, private liberal arts colleges, and campuses with religious affiliations, which educated the vast majority of the nation's collegians, remained quiet, orderly, businesslike places during the 1960s. The young radicals of the 1960s came mostly from upper-middle-class backgrounds; they were mostly the children of college-educated, liberal, affluent, and often influential parents. They formed a radical elite who rebelled against some of the institutions and practices of the affluent society. But these comparatively few privileged insurgents provoked a rebellion that spread beyond politics to challenge the entire culture. This cultural rebellion posed a more fundamental challenge to the values and mores of the comsumerist culture than did the New Left, and it had far greater appeal to young people of the 1960s.

THE GREENING OF AMERICA

Far more young people who felt alienated and frustrated by the affluent liberal society of the 1960s fled from it rather than radically confronted it. These "hippies" took a path previously traveled by Bohemians during the Roaring Twenties and the Beats during the 1950s. In fact, the best of the Beat poets, Allen Ginsberg, was a prominent member of the 1960s counterculture. The hippies embraced a new youth culture that ran counter to much that was cherished by middle-class Americans—affluence, economic growth, high technology, and, according to historian William Leuchtenburg:

> the institutions and value systems associated with the Protestant ethic of self-denial and sexual repression and more modern premises of the consumer culture and the meritocracy.[2]

The discipline of parents, schools, and jobs was abandoned for a free-flowing existence expressed by the hippie motto "do your own thing."

Hippies grew long hair and donned a uniform of jeans, tank tops, and sandals. These refugees from the "uptight, straight" world of parents, schools, and eight-to-five jobs flocked to havens in the Haight-Ashbury section of San Francisco, the Sunset Strip in Hollywood, and New York's East Village. They joined communes that cropped up in both urban neighborhoods and rural retreats. Communes varied considerably in their creeds and customs, but all were founded on hippie notions of extended family and collective property ownership. The appeal of the commune movement lay in a romantic urge to return to the land: to take up a simpler life, to regain physical and mental health, and perhaps to seek spiritual renewal.

The counterculture repudiated science, systematic knowledge, and rationalism. It embraced a notion of organic, mystical consciousness in which the Self merged seamlessly with Community and Nature. Infinite "being" supplanted linear boundaries of time and space. Feeling and intuition replaced thought and knowing. Hippies explored ancient Asian and African religions. Saffron-robed skinheads on San Francisco street corners chanted the "Hare Krishna." Others found the Age of Aquarius in astrology. Some hippies turned to witchcraft and demonology. They also flocked to religious revivals to participate in the emotional exaltations of passionate worship. Nature was valued as superior to society and technology. A wide array of synthetic consumer products were rejected as artificial—"plastic." Hippies prized being natural, using nature's products, and eating natural foods. The hippie ideal was personal authenticity: to live a life free of conflict, exploitation, and alienation; a life in harmony with society, nature, and one's true self.

Hippies also repudiated the restrictive sexual practices of "Puritan" America. Although sexual behavior in this country had become more liberal, hippies moved far beyond middle-class proprieties and inhibitions. The freer sexuality of the hippie lifestyle became one of its main attractions and also provoked the wrath of their elders. Casual sex often tied in with countercultural music as flocks of teenage "groupies" sought out rock musicians. English groups, especially the Beatles and the Rolling Stones, expressed the central themes and ideals of the hippie worldview. Bob Dylan was the main American countercultural band. He sang "The Times They Are A-Changing" and "Blowing in the Wind." In San Francisco, "acid

---

[2]William E. Leuchtenburg, *A Troubled Feast*, rev. ed. (Boston: Little, Brown, 1983), p. 179.

The Beatles.... (L-R) John Lennon, Paul McCartney, George Harrison, and Ringo Starr.   *Source:* Mercantile Library, St. Louis. Used with permission.

rock" appeared. Promoter Bill Graham staged concerts at Fillmore West featuring the psychedelic sounds of San Francisco's homegrown bands, the Grateful Dead and the Jefferson Airplane. A young white blues singer from Port Arthur, Texas, Janis Joplin, became the queen of San Francisco's psychedelic music scene. Drugs intertwined with music to form the vital center of the counterculture. "Tune in, turn on, and drop out" urged the high priest of LSD, Timothy Leary, a former Harvard psychologist who had been fired for conducting psychedelic drug experiments on his students. Song lyrics like the Beatles' "Lucy in the Sky with Diamonds" spelled out "LSD." Steppenwolf sang "Magic Carpet Ride," celebrating drug tripping. Many of the prominent musical stars of the counterculture were heavy drug users, and several died of drug overdoses, including Joplin.

Drugs reached into the countercultural literary scene, continuing a beat generation tradition. A gifted young writer, Ken Kesey, wrote part of his best-selling first novel, *One Flew Over the Cuckoo's Nest,* under the influence of LSD. With money earned from its sales, he purchased a bus and named it "Further." He painted it in psychedelic Day-Glo colors, wired it for stereo; and he and his friends, who called themselves the Merry Pranksters, toured up and down the West Coast. Everywhere they went, they conducted "acid tests," wild parties featuring LSD-spiked orange juice, loud rock music, and light shows.

Marijuana use was far more widespread than LSD. "Pot" became the common currency of the counterculture and spread into mainstream society. Marijuana turned up at high school and college parties during the 1960s. Older people with a yen for experimenting or a desire to be "with-it" also tried marijuana. Hippies also experimented with other drugs, including mescaline and methedrine. Counter-cultural drug use provoked a pathetic debate over whether smoking marijuana was less harmful than smoking cigarettes or drinking alcoholic beverages. All of these substances could be harmful, but that fact was beside the point because the debate was really about values and lifestyles, not the pharmacological properties of marijuana, tobacco, and alcohol.

One of the major events in the life of the counterculture occurred in the summer of 1967 in San Francisco's Haight-Ashbury district, "the summer of love." Hippies sought a cultural counterpart to the SDS's proclaimed summer of protest against the Vietnam War. Young people would flock to the Haight from all over the country; just as radical politics was transforming American political life, the summer of love would transform society by creating a community of young dropouts uninhibitedly enjoying the pleasures of the flesh. The reality of what occurred was dismal. Thousands of youngsters showed up, most of them runaways from troubled homes, utterly unprepared to support themselves. Many of them were poorly educated and lacked any job skills; they were often reduced to panhandling, drug-dealing, and prostitution to survive. Sexual promiscuity and rampant drug use led to epidemics of venereal disease and drug overdoses. Far from fleeing the social problems of the larger society, the runaways brought them with them. Racial tensions between hippies living in the Haight-Ashbury and a nearby African American community in the Fillmore district added a hateful dimension to the summer of love. Writer Joan Didion, who visited the Haight-Ashbury during the summer of 1967, depicted in a famous essay, "Slouching Toward Bethlehem," the squalor and aimlessness of hippie existence.

The hippie triad of "drugs, sex, and rock music" came together at rock festivals, the most important ritual of the countercultural community. The greatest of these "happenings" occurred at Woodstock in August 1969. At a site in New York's Hudson River valley, between 300,000 and 400,000 young people gathered to hear music, enjoy drugs, and engage in casual sex.

Intellectuals fashioned ideologies for the counterculture. Charles Reich wrote in *Greening of America* about a new consciousness that would renew America, forming the basis of another American revolution, one without tears or violence. The new order would just happen. But the counterculture's expected new utopia never arrived. Instead, it turned sour and disintegrated. Hard drugs replaced marijuana. Violence, most of it connected with illegal drug traffic, destroyed much of what had been attractive in the hippie culture.

Greed and selfishness also pervaded the counterculture, contradicting its presumptions of innocence. Another rock festival, promoted by the Rolling Stones and held at Altamont Raceway in northern California, revealed the crass commercialism of the rock music business. The Altamont concert ended in violence when the Hell's Angels, an outlaw motorcycle gang, hired by promoters to provide security, savagely beat people and even killed a person.

One commune turned pathological. A deranged ex-con who had spent more than half his life behind bars, Charles Manson, drifted into the Haight-Ashbury demimonde and gained control over a small commune. Manson, who was a paranoid psychopath, relocated his "family" in an arid mountainous region north of Los Angeles. On April 12, 1969, three female members of the Manson family, on the orders of their leader, murdered actress Sharon Tate and four of her jet-set friends at her expensive Bel Air home. The next day, they killed two more wealthy people. Manson and the three women were all convicted of first-degree murder. No coherent motives for the gruesome murders were ever established. Manson apparently had the insane notion of fomenting revolution in America by inciting a race war. He selected rich white people at random for his disciples to murder and hoped to pin the blame on militant blacks.

The counterculture lasted half a decade, then it simply evaporated, quickly becoming only an exotic memory. It had sprung to life because of some special circumstances prevailing during the 1960s. The postwar baby boom had created a large population cluster of young people between the ages of fourteen and twenty-five. Such a huge youth population created, for a moment, a consciousness of a separate culture. Permissive child-rearing practices also contributed to the formation of the counterculture. These children of abundance confronted a complex world of protracted education, large-scale corporate and government bureaucracies, an intricate and powerful technology, severe social conflicts and inequities, and, most of all, the military draft and a controversial war in Vietnam. Young people recoiled in fear and loathing at a world they never made, and they became "flower children" who urged others to "make love, not war."

But only a minority of young people ever joined the counterculture. Most youngsters went about the difficult enterprise of growing up and entering the adult world without visible alienation or protest. The greatest gap in the 1960s social fabric was not a generation gap between children and parents, but between different segments of the youth population. The more significant gap was intragenerational, not intergenerational. Value conflicts between middle-class and working-class young people were profound and occasionally violent. Upper-middle-class campus radicals scoffed at bourgeoise sensibilities and burned their draft cards. Young workers, for whom middle-class respectability remained a cherished ambition, defended their ways of life and patriotically supported the Vietnam war. Long-haired hippies and antiwar demonstrators infuriated working-class youth who regarded them as privileged cowards and traitors. One of the most violent riots of the era occurred in New York when hard-hat construction workers attacked a crowd of antiwar demonstrators.

Although short-lived and engaging only a fraction of young people during the 1960s, both the New Left and the counterculture left their marks. They heightened consciousness of war and racial injustice. They called attention to the negative ecological and human consequences of technology. They forced some people to confront the disparities between their professed ideals and the lives they lived. The most enduring impact of the counterculture came in lifestyle realms—

in diet, dress, decorative art, music, and sexual practices. People became more concerned to develop their inner selves, to achieve their "human potential," than to seek the external trappings of success.

THE FIRE THIS TIME

The civil rights movement crested in 1965 when Dr. Martin Luther King, Jr., led the Selma march and Congress passed the Voting Rights Act. Five days after President Johnson signed that historic measure, the Watts section of Los Angeles went up in flames. It ushered in the first of several successive "long, hot summers." The Watts riot, a week-long orgy of burning and looting, claimed thirty-four lives, injured eleven hundred people, and destroyed $40 million worth of property. The Watts explosion dismayed civil rights reformers because the residents of Watts generally lived much better than most African American slum dwellers in America. Watts was not physically a ghetto since families did not live in crowded, dilapidated tenements; they lived in single, detached houses with lawns located along palm-shaded, curving boulevards. Three African Americans sat on the Los Angeles City Council; Watts was represented by a black congressman and two black state assemblymen. Economically, African Americans living in Watts were better off than blacks in any other large American city.

Watts revealed a depth of antiwhite bitterness and alienation that few civil rights workers of either race even knew existed. African American progress in recent years and the promise of more to come had only raised exaggerated expectations and intensified the rage of many Watts residents. A special commission investigating the Watts upheaval warned if the breach between the races were not healed, the riot might be a curtain raiser for future racial blowups. The commission's warning proved prophetic. Between 1965 and 1968, hundreds of inner cities exploded into major riots. The worst violence occurred in Newark and Detroit within a week of each other in July 1967. In Newark, twenty-six people died and twelve hundred were injured. In Detroit, forty-three people died and another two thousand were hurt. Fires burned out the center of the nation's fifth-largest city. For two weeks that summer, Detroit was a war zone with tanks rolling through the streets and the sounds of machine-gun fire piercing the air.

Detroit's riot was the most alarming, not only because of the extensive destruction of life and property, but also because it occurred in a city governed by a coalition that included extensive African American participation. Great Society reformers had lavished extensive antipoverty and urban renewal programs on the Motor City. One-fourth of all workers employed in the automobile industry, Detroit's major business, were black; the UAW was a progressive, integrated union. Forty-five percent of Detroit's African American families owned their own homes.

Analysts of the Detroit riot drew a portrait of the typical rioter—a young adult black male, a high school graduate, employed, often an auto worker and a union member, veteran, married, with an annual income slightly below the national median for his age group. These data suggest that the typical Detroit rioters were neither juveniles out on a spree nor despairing members of a black underclass. The rioting did not occur in the worst neighborhoods, but in black working-class neighborhoods containing a high percentage of owner-occupied homes and intact families. Black rage and violence in Detroit was apparently provoked more by insensitive police tactics than by deprivation and despair.

Nearly all major race riots started from minor episodes, often from incidents growing out of white police arresting African Americans. Watts blew up when a crowd gathered to protest the arrest of a drunken motorist. Newark exploded after police arrested an African American taxicab driver named John Smith for following a police car too closely. Smith protested and was beaten by the arresting officers; news of the beating provoked the riot. Detroit erupted when police raided an after-hours bar hosting a party for two Vietnam veterans.

Studies revealed a general pattern prevailing in the urban riots. Most rioting occurred within ghetto confines. Most of the destruction was inflicted upon ghetto homes and businesses; most of the violence occurred between rioters and law enforcement personnel. Over 80 percent of the fatalities were rioters, shot either by the police or by soldiers. Studies of all major riots also suggested that the underlying causes of the uprisings were chronic slum conditions, aggravated by rough police tactics and hot weather. The National Advisory Commission on Civil Disorders called attention to a crucial reality about the black ghetto: "White institutions created it, white institutions maintain it, and white society condones it."

BLACK POWER

Urban riots were the most dramatic and destructive display of black militancy. The slogan "black power" made its appearance in 1966 when James Meredith attempted to march from Memphis, Tennessee, to Jackson, Mississippi, to inspire African Americans of his native state to assert their rights. He got only 10 miles into Mississippi when a sniper severely wounded him. Dr. King and other civil rights leaders quickly arrived to complete his march. Two of the marchers, young leaders of the Student Non-Violent Coordinating Committee (SNCC), began chanting "black power." Soon, most of the marchers were chanting it. Initially, "black power" was a cry of outrage and defiance that alarmed and bewildered white liberals. It later became political doctrine, although remaining diffuse, meaning different things to different people. For SNCC leader Stokely Carmichael, black power in essence meant that African Americans should take control of the civil rights movement, developing their own institutions and instruments of power. Implicit in these actions were rejection of integration, scorning white allies, and approval of violence. At the extremes, black power became an expression of African American separatism. Separatist doctrine traced its roots to a long tradition of black nationalism in this country.

The Black Muslims articulated the most important expression of 1960s' black nationalism. Founded during the 1930s in Detroit by Elijah Poole, who called himself the Prophet, Elijah Muhammad, it remained a small, obscure religious sect with about 100,000 members until the 1960s. Black Muslims had recruited many of their followers from the bottom ranks of ghetto society—street hustlers, drug addicts, and ex-cons. Their most famous recruit was world heavyweight boxing champion Cassius Clay, who changed his name to Muhammad Ali following his conversion to the Black Muslim sect in 1965. Their most articulate spokesman was Malcolm Little, an ex-con who took the name of Malcolm X. During the early 1960s, he offered an alternative to civil rights. He jeered at Dr. King's tactics of nonviolent Christian love: "You need somebody who is going to fight, you don't need any kneeling in and crawling in." He both angered and frightened whites with his tirades against integration with "white devils."

In 1964, he was expelled from the Black Muslim organization after a dispute with Elijah Muhammad. He moved to New York and founded his own movement. His political ideas were still evolving in the spring of 1965. He appeared to be groping for an integrationist strategy when he was murdered. Apparently his assassination had been ordered by Elijah Muhammad, or by members of his inner circle. Malcolm X's book, written with Alex Haley, *The Autobiography of Malcolm X*, became a posthumous best-seller. The book established Malcolm X as one of the foremost prophets of black liberation. The distinguished film actor Ossie Davis said of the fallen leader: "Malcolm expressed what was in all our hearts; he redeemed our manhood."

Black power also expressed African American pride; it became a celebration of African American history and culture, of "blackness itself." African American students in high schools and colleges demanded courses be added to established curricula in African American history, literature, and languages. Black hair and dress styles appeared. Black power encouraged young blacks to seek success and remain "black," to avoid emulating white role models. The popular soul singer James Brown sang: "Say it loud. I'm black and I'm proud."

During the late 1960s, as the civil rights movement became radicalized and fragmented, Dr. King, who remained committed to the tactic of nonviolence and the goal of an integrated, color-blind society, remained the foremost black leader. But he found that his methods did not work in the North. He tried and failed to desegregate Chicago. Tactics that had been effective against the de jure segregation of southern towns could not overcome the de facto segregation of northern cities. Dr. King also became increasingly involved in protesting the Vietnam War because it drained away funds for civil rights and Great Society reforms. His attacks on the war alienated President Johnson and cost him the support of the NAACP. The civil rights movement, politically successful in the South but an economic failure in the North, was faltering by 1967. In the spring of 1968, trying to regain momentum, Dr. King prepared to lead a poor people's march on Washington. He also took time to go to Memphis to lend support to a garbage workers' strike. While standing on a Memphis motel balcony, he was shot by James Earl Ray, a white drifter and ex-con.

News of King's murder provoked race riots across the land. The worst occurred in the nation's capital. Buildings burned within a few blocks of the White House and soldiers mounted machine guns on the capitol steps.

RED AND BROWN POWER

Other minorities, spurred by the example of African American insurgents, rebelled during the 1960s. Puerto Rican students in New York demanded that courses in Puerto Rican studies be added to high school and college curricula. Native Americans demanded respect for their cultural traditions and called attention to their severe economic needs, particularly repayment for their ancestral lands that had been illegally taken from them by white men. Red power militant Vine Deloria, Jr., wrote *Custer Died for Your Sins*, which emphasized the historical injustices European settlers in the New World had committed against Native Americans.

Mexican American militants also waged campaigns for recognition and for self-assertion. Brown Power militants took to calling themselves "Chicanos," turning a term of opprobrium into a badge of pride and an assertion of ethnic identity that did not depend on a relationship with the "Anglo" world. The most prominent Chicano militant of the 1960s was labor leader Cesar Chavez. A migrant farm worker turned labor organizer, Chavez founded the National Farm Workers Association (NFWA) in 1963. NFWA joined other farm worker unions to form the United Farm Workers Organizing Committee (UFWOC), affiliated with the AFL-CIO. Chavez organized lettuce workers and grape pickers using techniques developed by civil rights organizers, including marches, rallies, songs, and symbols that stressed the Chicano cultural heritage. Chavez led successful strikes in California's Jan Joaquin valley in the 1960s. His movement obtained crucial assistance from urban liberal middle-class support groups, who raised funds for the strikers and staged consumer boycotts that made table grapes picked by "scab" (nonunion) labor forbidden fruit.

Cesar Chavez (checked shirt, right) leads striking grape pickers. Most of the pickers working the grape fields of California in the 1960s and 1970s were of Mexican origin.   *Source:* National Archives.

GAY-LESBIAN LIBERATION

Another expression of the 1960s insurgent spirit was the open avowal of homosexuality by formerly deeply closeted gays and lesbians. If people could mobilize for political action around the issues of race, ethnicity, and gender, so, too, could they fight for their rights on the basis of their sexual identities and preferences. A dramatic event created the gay liberation movement: On June 29, 1969, police raided the Stonewall Inn, a gay bar located in Greenwich Village. Instead of meekly submitting to arrest, patrons defiantly hurled bottles at the police. They sent a message: there was a new militancy and pride growing among members of the gay community; they were no longer willing to accept passively police abuse and society's condemnations.

Gay and lesbian intellectuals developed ideologies that defined homosexuality as a legitimate sexual preference; they insisted that it was not abnormal, it was not sick, and it was not perverse. Gay and lesbian theorists attacked the psychoanalytic establishment for diagnosing homosexuality as a form of mental illness. Within gay and lesbian communities, a debate occurred over whether homosexuality was innate or a consequence of socialization. Although gays and lesbians could not resolve the debate over nature versus nurture, the gay liberation movement enabled millions of homosexuals to make their claim for acceptance into the larger society. Militant homosexuals marched in gay liberation parades chanting: "Say it loud, gay is proud." Gay and lesbian activists organized for political action, seeking an end to legislative and job discrimination against homosexuals, and a diminution of massive homophobic prejudices.

THE REBIRTH OF FEMINISM

The social and cultural ground was being prepared during the 1950s for a rebirth of feminism. By 1960, it had become the norm for middle-class white married women to be doing paid work outside the home. By 1962, married women accounted for nearly two-thirds of the female workforce. At the same time that they were entering the paid workforce in ever greater numbers, more and more women were going to college and earning degrees. In 1961, women received over 40 percent of all baccalaureate degrees awarded.

Despite such progress, women still entered a sex-segregated job market. They mostly took "women's jobs" such as nursing, clerical work, teaching, and domestic service, jobs that paid less than men's jobs and offered few prospects for promotion. In 1960, the median compensation for women working in full-time year-round employment was 61 percent of men's earnings. Traditional assumptions about the proper roles of men and women in the society remained deeply ingrained. There was no organized feminist alternative to challenge the established order or male hegemony. The wife who worked was perceived to be helping her family achieve a middle-class status and lifestyle, not pursuing a career of her own. As the 1960s began, there existed an ideological lag; feminine consciousness lagged behind social reality. Even though cultural norms remained unquestioned, there was increasing evidence that many college-educated middle-class women were restive, frustrated, and unfulfilled by lives that increasingly diverged from pre-scribed roles.

Because women, as women, did not share a common social experience, they tended to view their problems as individual rather than as socially derived. It was left to the founder of the modern women's movement, Betty Friedan, author of the best-selling *Feminine Mystique* (1963), to show women that what they had previ-ously understood to be their individual problems were in fact women's problems. They were caused not by personal inadequacies but by deeply rooted attitudes that would have to be changed before women could achieve equality and fulfillment. Friedan, giving eloquent voice to the discontents of middle-class women, called the suburban split-level home "a comfortable concentration camp." She called atten-tion to the "problem which has no name": feelings of emptiness, of being incom-plete, of wondering who am I? She asked: "What is the cause of the identity problem which bothers so many women who have ostensibly fulfilled the Ameri-can dream?" She urged women to listen to that still small voice within which de-mands "something more than my husband and my children and my home."[3]

The civil rights movement of the early 1960s catalyzed a sense of grievance among women. Women witnessed, and often joined, civil rights demonstrations. The civil rights movement also offered a model for political activity. Women made connections between black demands for freedom, equality, and dignity and their own lives; they saw possibilities for acting for themselves, of mobilizing for group political action. Women perceived that the same society that oppressed blacks also oppressed women; both groups had been assigned separate and unequal spheres and told to stay in their place. Any efforts at self-assertion or challenges to the sta-tus quo were considered deviant and were punished. Women reasoned if it was wrong to deny opportunity to one group because of skin color, it was wrong to deny it to another group because of gender.

The Great Society inadvertently helped the cause of women's rights. When the bill that eventually became the Civil Rights Act of 1964 was being drafted in committee, conservatives tried to kill it. Title VII contained a provision banning discrimination in hiring and promotion on the basis of race. Howard Smith, a pow-erful conservative Democrat from Virginia, introduced an amendment to Title VII banning job discrimination on the basis of sex. Smith believed that his amendment would defeat the proposed Title VII by reducing the whole matter of civil rights to an absurdity. He and his conservative colleagues were mistaken. Supporters of Ti-tle VII pushed it through along with Smith's amendment, and it became the law of the land.

Initially, the Equal Employment Opportunity Commission (EEOC), which had responsibility for enforcing Title VII of the Civil Rights Act, did not enforce the provision against sex discrimination. In response to EEOC's failure to enforce Title

[3]Betty Friedan, *The Feminine Mystique* (New York: Dell, 1963), *passim.*

VII on behalf of female workers, Betty Friedan and other women's rights activists formed the National Organization of Women (NOW) in 1966 to pressure the commission to take sex discrimination in hiring seriously. Other groups soon mobilized and the women's rights movement was reborn. These women's organizations were political pressure groups that sought to mobilize public opinion and obtain litigation on behalf of their cause. They sought change from within the existing structure. In part, the new feminism was a species of liberal reform. It called for equal pay for equal work and demanded that women have equal access to all professional schools and occupations. To allow women to compete equally in the job market with men, feminists demanded publicly funded child-care centers for women with preschool-age children and they sought legislation ending all forms of gender discrimination.

WOMEN'S LIBERATION

There was also a radical dimension to the emerging feminism of the 1960s that grew out of the experiences of young women in the New Left, in SNCC and SDS. Mary King and Casey Hayden, both civil rights activists within SNCC, had come to resent the arrogance of male activists who expected the women to work hard, take responsibilities and risks, and leave leadership and policy making to the men. When they raised these issues at an SNCC convention, the male leaders responded by laughing at them. The SNCC chairman, Stokely Carmichael, quipped, "The position of women in our movement is prone."

These radical women gradually found a language to express their grievances. They defined the problem as "sexism" or "male chauvinism." Having diagnosed the illness, they proposed a cure—"women's liberation." While liberal feminist reformers in NOW fought for equal pay for equal work, radical feminists like King and Hayden demanded control over their own bodies. They called for wider distribution of birth control literature, tougher enforcement of rape laws, sharing of housework and child-rearing duties with husbands, and the right to abortion on demand. They met in small groups for intense "consciousness raising" sessions. These sessions also allowed women to understand that their personal problems connected to the larger realms of social power, of "sexual politics." Feminist writer Robin Morgan contributed the defining slogan of the women's liberation movement: "The personal is political." Some radical feminists like Ti-Grace Atkinson and Susan Brownmiller expressed hostility toward men, considering the sexual act a form of male domination. They rejected such revered institutions as family and home, spurned childbirth, and advised women to seek lesbian relationships.

The reborn feminist movement encountered a formidable array of obstacles from the beginning. Many women as well as men rejected radical feminist demands. A 1970 Gallup poll showed that 70 percent of American women believed that they were treated fairly by men. Feminist leader Gloria Steinem acknowledged that she spoke for only a minority of women but attributed that reality to cultural conditioning. She asserted that women had been brainwashed to accept their oppression; they required "consciousness-raising" sessions to ignite a sense of grievance. Many men worried about the loss of male prerogatives that had long been givens in the culture. Many women feared that men would respond to the new assertiveness of women by abandoning their roles as providers and protectors. Fundamentalist Christians were incensed because feminist demands violated biblically ordained roles for women.

The most serious obstacle faced by feminists trying to build a movement based on women's common problems and concerns was the diversity of the women the movement was trying to organize. Women were differentiated on the basis of race, ethnicity, class, age, education, occupation, and sexuality. Feminists quickly discovered that they had sharp differences among themselves on many matters. There were disagreements over priorities, over long- and short-term goals, over methods and tactics. Was the most pressing problem economic—a capitalist system that oppressed women? Or was it cultural—male chauvinism? Because of the diversity prevailing among women activists, the reborn feminist movement of the 1960s spawned a proliferation of organizations, tactics, ideologies, and goals.

BACKLASH

By 1967, it seemed as if some unspoken signal had been sent coursing through the culture; the message had been received by SDS radicals, by black, brown, and red militants, and by activist women. Those who perceived themselves to be oppressed, disadvantaged, to have been denied their full measure of freedom, equality, opportunity, and dignity, rose in rebellion. To borrow a phrase from the days of trade union organizing—these people vowed that they weren't taking it any more. Perhaps they sensed their time had come: that the system was vulnerable, that it would be more responsive to their claims of justice and inclusion in the American dream; that it would not, perhaps could not, strike them down, repress them, or deny them their due. These militants were no longer willing to play the game by the old rules. Never in the history of the republic had so many groups mounted such a radical assault on cherished national values, morals, and institutions.

The radical insurgencies of the late 1960s provoked a furious response from the middle-class majority of Americans determined to uphold traditional American ways. The media dubbed their response the "backlash." Millions of citizens had worked hard all their lives and played the game by the rules. They had raised their families, attended church, voted, paid taxes, obeyed the law, and sent their sons to fight in the Vietnam War. The militant minority of blacks who rioted in the cities, of students who opposed the Vietnam War and carried Vietcong flags, and of long-haired hippies who openly flaunted their sexuality infuriated the middle-class majority.

The rise of black power provoked a response from hitherto passive groups. White working-class ethnics felt especially threatened by African American militants and were galvanized into action. These people had worked hard to achieve a modest piece of the American dream: a decent home, a secure job, and perhaps to see a bright son or daughter graduate from college. To them, it appeared that ghetto blacks were demanding that the government give them these same things; that they were entitled to them now—without having to work for them; without a struggle. White ethnics especially resented the antipoverty programs that appeared to reward black militants while law-abiding whites got nothing except higher tax bills. "Middle Americans"—those earning between $8,000 and $15,000 a year (in 1968 dollars), who constituted the rank-and-file blue-collar and white-collar workforces of the country—generally opposed and resented the challenges posed by the insurgents.

Analysts have discerned a mix of forces driving the backlashers. In part, it was simply residual antiblack racism. Many northern white ethnics and southern white working-class people had been taught to hate and fear black people and to consider them inferior. They did not want to associate with them, they did not want their children attending school with them, and they surely did not want to have to compete with them in the workplace. Economic insecurities also drove the backlash. By the late 1960s, many Middle Americans were feeling the effects of inflation, heavy indebtedness, and declining real income. A lot of these Americans, while not poor, enjoyed at best a marginal prosperity. Black demands for employment, rising taxes, and expensive government programs appeared to be direct threats to the economic well-being of hard-pressed Middle Americans.

Most of all, it was a sense of cultural crisis that activated the backlash response. The demands of the militants—antiwar protesters, black power advocates, and feminist radicals, all magnified by extensive media coverage and commentary, represented an attack on the American way and its most cherished values and institutions: patriotism, the work ethic, mobility, family, and religion. While the sons of Middle America were fighting and dying in Vietnam, the sons of upper-middle-class families were opposing the war from safe havens of prestigious university campuses and denouncing American society. To many parents of soldiers, and to the soldiers themselves, these antiwar protesters appeared to be a privileged corps of impudent cowards and traitors.

IMPORTANT EVENTS

1963	Lyndon Johnson accedes to the presidency
1964	The Civil Rights Act is enacted
1964	The Beatles hold their first American concert
1964	Johnson announces the beginning of a "war on poverty"
1964	Gulf of Tonkin incidents occur
1964	Johnson is elected president
1964	The Free Speech movement at the Berkeley campus of the University of California inaugurates an era of student protest
1965	Malcolm X is assassinated
1965	The Voting Rights Act is enacted

1965	The United States intervenes in the Dominican Republic
1965	A race riot occurs in Watts
1965	The United States goes to war in Vietnam
1965	Federal aid to public education is enacted
1965	Medicare and Medicaid are enacted
1965	The Immigration Act is enacted
1967	Major race riots occur in Newark and Detroit
1968	Communists launch the Tet Offensive
1968	Johnson announces that he will not seek reelection
1968	Martin Luther King, Jr., is assassinated
1968	Robert Kennedy is assassinated
1968	Richard Nixon is elected president
1969	The Woodstock festival takes place

BIBLIOGRAPHY

There are two substantial biographies of Lyndon Johnson in progress. Robert Caro has completed two volumes of his magisterial study, *The Path to Power* and *Means of Ascent.* Caro's researches have given him encyclopedic knowledge of the details of Johnson's life and he writes well. His books are marred by his remorseless hostility to his subject. Robert Dallek's first of two volumes, *Lone Star Rising: Lyndon Johnson and His Times, 1908–1960,* is a more balanced and more sophisticated treatment. Doris Kearn's *Lyndon Johnson and the American Dream* is an insightful study of Johnson's political career. Eric Goldman's *The Tragedy of Lyndon Johnson* is a sympathetic account of his presidency. Michael Harrington's analysis of poverty in the United States, *The Other America,* helped start the war on poverty. James C. Harvey, in *Black Civil Rights During the Johnson Administration,* offers a good account of this important issue. Johnson's foreign policy is studied by Philip L. Geyelin, in *Lyndon B. Johnson and the World.* The best general military and diplomatic history of the U.S. involvement in Vietnam is George Donelson Moss's *Vietnam: An American Ordeal.* For an assessment of student radicalism during the 1960s, see Irwin Unger's *The Movement: A History of the American New Left, 1959–1972.* The best biography we have of Dr. Martin Luther King, Jr., is by Stephen Oates, *Let the Trumpet Sound: The Life of Martin Luther King, Jr.* Reading *The Autobiography of Malcolm X* will provide understanding of a major source of black nationalism during the 1960s. Alfredo Mirande, in *The Chicano Experience,* documents militancy in the Mexican American world. Vine Deloria, Jr., in *Custer Died for Your Sins,* documents centuries of white mistreatment of Native Americans. Barbara Deckard's *The Women's Movement* is a fine account of the revived feminist movement. Theodore Roszak's *The Making of a Counter Culture* is a nicely written, sympathetic account of the hippie movement. Julian Messner's *The Superstars of Rock: Their Lives and Their Music* has insight into the pop music of the 1960s. Richard Krickus, in *Pursuing the American Dream: White Ethnics and the New Populism,* gives us a fascinating study of blue-collar culture and their resentment of liberal welfarism, student radicals, hippies, and black militants. William O'Neill, *Coming Apart: An Informal History of the 1960s,* is a lively account of that tumultuous decade.

CHAPTER 13

The Nixon Era

In November 1968, Richard M. Nixon was elected president by a narrow margin amidst the worst domestic violence and disorder in nearly a hundred years. He made his top priorities restoring national unity and phasing out the American war in Vietnam. He partially succeeded in calming the country, although the American Vietnam War continued for four more years. Nixon's greatest accomplishments came in the realm of foreign policy, particularly the opening to China and reaching détente with the Soviet Union. He was greatly aided in these foreign policy achievements by his chief adviser and special envoy, Henry Kissinger. Reelected by a landslide margin in November 1972, President Nixon never exercised the full powers of the presidency nor achieved all his political goals because of the developing Watergate scandals. Watergate became a public issue early in 1973 when the men caught during the burglary went on trial. Thereafter, the remainder of Nixon's presidency was increasingly preoccupied by his efforts to contain and survive Watergate. Ultimately, the president and his men were overwhelmed by media investigations, federal grand jury probes, the Congress, the courts, and public opinion. Richard Nixon resigned the presidency in disgrace August 9, 1974, mainly to avoid impeachment, trial, and probable conviction for "high crimes and misdemeanors" committed while president.

THE ELECTION OF 1968

The 1968 election occurred against a backdrop of the worst conflict and violence within American society since the Civil War. The Democratic Party, closer to the social pulse than was the Republican Party, was splintered by divisions seething within the deeply troubled nation. The antiwar candidacies of Senators Eugene McCarthy and Robert Kennedy gained momentum in the spring primaries. Party

regulars backed Vice President Hubert Humphrey, a Cold War liberal who supported Johnson's Vietnam policy. It was a wide-open race, with public opinion
polls giving Kennedy an edge over Humphrey and McCarthy. In the California primary, Kennedy and McCarthy waged a decisive showdown battle.

Kennedy, cashing in on his remarkable ability to attract black, Hispanic, and
white working class voters, narrowly defeated McCarthy. With his California victory, Robert Kennedy appeared to have the Democratic nomination within his
grasp. But on victory night, he was shot and killed in Los Angeles. His assassin was
Sirhan Sirhan, an Arab nationalist who hated Kennedy for his strong support of Israel. Robert Kennedy's murder destroyed any chance that antiwar forces could win
at the Democratic Party's Chicago convention. Humphrey won an easy first ballot
nomination. Convention delegates, after a lengthy, emotional debate, adopted a
pro-administration plank on the Vietnam war. The rest of the platform focused on
liberal domestic issues, such as providing consumer protection, increasing farmers' incomes, and strengthening trade unions. Humphrey chose Senator Edmund
Muskie of Maine as his running mate.

As the Democratic delegates gathered in Chicago to nominate a presidential
candidate, antiwar radicals gathered in the Windy City to protest the war. Most
came to support the efforts of antiwar Democratic politicians. More militant groups
came to disrupt the convention and provoke confrontations with the police. The
antiwar demonstrators came up against Mayor Richard Daley, the convention host,
who had vowed that there would be no disruptions. Police cordoned off the convention site and staked out the parks of Chicago where protesters had gathered.
Daley also had thousands of National Guardsmen and federal troops available if
he needed them.

The night Hubert Humphrey was nominated, violence reigned in the streets
of Chicago. Protesters, attempting to march on the convention, were blocked by police. They sat down in the street, blocking traffic. Police then moved in to remove
them by force. They clubbed and gassed demonstrators, newsmen, and bystanders
indiscriminately. Television cameramen brought the violence into millions of living rooms. Many liberal Democrats were everlastingly horrified by the actions of
the Chicago police. But millions of other Democrats in white-collar suburbs and
blue-collar neighborhoods cheered the police, seeing in the radical politics and
countercultural lifestyles of the youthful protesters an intolerable threat to order
and morality. The different reactions to the televised violence reflected the profound divisions seething within the American political culture created by Vietnam,
race riots, and domestic insurgencies. Hubert Humphrey emerged from the political ruins as the candidate of a profoundly divided party.

The divisive Democratic convention helped the Republicans meeting in
Miami. They nominated Richard Nixon, who had made a remarkable come-
back. Nixon had retired from politics following a disastrous defeat in the 1962
California gubernatorial election. But he had worked hard for Republican
candidates in 1964 and 1966, building support among party regulars. He came to
Miami the front-runner and easily repelled his only serious challenger, California

governor Ronald Reagan, who was making the first of his several runs at the presidency. Nixon chose Spiro T. Agnew, the governor of Maryland, who had a reputation for talking tough on law-and-order issues, to be his running mate. The Republican platform resembled the Democratic slate. On the war issue, Republicans called for peace, but not peace at any price.

Behind the Republican platform rhetoric and the choice of Agnew for vice president, lay a shrewd political strategy. Nixon perceived that southerners had become a power within his party. He also understood that Americans had become more conservative since 1964. Nixon cut his ties with declining northeastern liberal Republicans to forge an alliance with conservative southerners led by Strom Thurmond. Nixon promised Thurmond that he would never abandon the South Vietnamese government and that he would slow the pace of school desegregation. He also promised to crack down hard on demonstrators who broke the law. This "southern strategy" stopped Reagan's bid for the presidency. The only reason it did not give Nixon the entire South was because a strong third-party candidate who had a southern base entered the campaign.

George Wallace, governor of Alabama and leader of the American Independence Party, mounted a presidential campaign with popular appeal in all sections of the nation. He articulated the frustrations and resentments of his followers, who were upset by radical disruptions in the country and by upper-middle-class liberals who appeared to sanction them. Wallace attacked liberal intellectuals, black militants, antiwar protesters, and hippies. His main issue was playing to the white backlash against civil rights measures and antipoverty programs. He called for "law and order," code words for suppression of black power militants. Although his message was never a purely racist one, most of his strength derived from white anxieties about integration. Opposition to race-related federal initiatives was always at the center of his message.

Wallace championed free enterprise, traditional moral values, and the war in Vietnam. He was a political force to be reckoned with. A mid-September survey gave him 21 percent of the vote, almost as many as supported Humphrey. Had he held that 21 percent to November, he would have denied any candidate an electoral college majority and thrown the election into the House of Representatives. He hoped to play the role of "spoiler" and force Nixon and Humphrey to bargain for his support to win the presidency.

Meanwhile, Nixon's campaign was running smoothly. His acceptance speech had sounded his principal theme, a promise to heed the voice of "the great, quiet forgotten majority—the non-shouters and the non-demonstrators." He called for peace, unity, and a lowering of voices. His appeal reached millions of voters yearning for an end to years of discord. Nixon projected an image of maturity and inner tranquility; commentators spoke of a "new Nixon," who had replaced the fiery Red-baiter of 1950s. His campaign featured slick television commercials and short speeches filled with patriotic generalities. His vice-presidential running mate, Spiro Agnew, took the offensive. Agnew attacked the media for promoting radicalism, and he took a hard law-and-order line. Journalists dubbed him "Nixon's

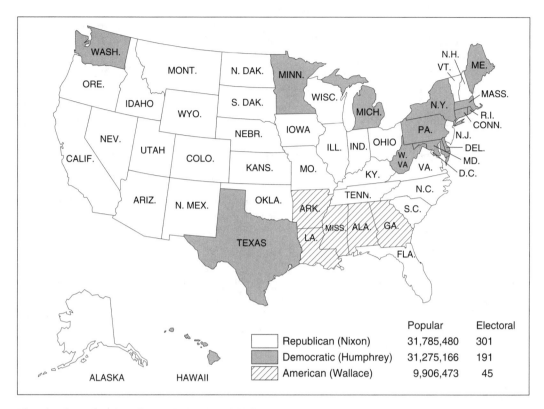

	Popular	Electoral
Republican (Nixon)	31,785,480	301
Democratic (Humphrey)	31,275,166	191
American (Wallace)	9,906,473	45

The election of 1968.   *Source:* Moss, *Moving On,* p. 215.

Nixon." Polls taken in early October showed Nixon well ahead of both Humphrey and Wallace.

Humphrey's campaign floundered along, disorganized, short of both money and campaign workers. McCarthy's followers initially refused to support Humphrey. He was hurt badly by his identification with an unpopular administration and its unpopular war. Millions of nominally Democratic voters were turning to Nixon and Wallace. But in October, Humphrey's campaign came to life. He distanced himself from Johnson's war policy by calling for a bombing halt. Union leaders campaigned hard for Humphrey and antiwar liberals drifted back into his fold. McCarthy endorsed Humphrey on October 29, and Johnson helped his chances by halting all bombing of North Vietnam and talking as if the war were about to end. Humphrey cut into Nixon's lead. Wallace's popularity declined. On election eve, pollsters said the election "was too close to call." But Humphrey's late surge fell just short. Nixon held on for a narrow victory. He got 43.4 percent of the popular vote to Humphrey's 42.7 percent and Wallace's 13.4 percent. Nixon carried thirty-two states with 301 electoral votes. The Democrats retained control of Congress with sizable majorities in both houses.

On the surface, the electorate appeared to speak in many voices, reflecting the acute political divisions within the country. The old Democratic coalition had fractured, split by civil rights issues and divisions over the war. Humphrey retained urban and union voters, although in reduced strength, and he got most of the African American vote. But his appeal was confined largely to the northeastern industrial states. The rest of the country voted for Nixon, except for five Deep South states that went for Wallace. The 1968 election revealed that the Democratic "Solid South" had vanished. Humphrey got only 31 percent of the Deep South vote, mostly from newly enfranchised African Americans. Ninety percent of southern whites voted either for Nixon or Wallace. Racial attitudes were significant vote determiners in 1968, the year of the backlash.

Although they cannot be certain in such a close election, most analysts believe that the Vietnam War gave Nixon his narrow win. In the final weeks of the campaign, Nixon attracted support with his talk of a plan to end the war, the details of which he refused to divulge because he said its prospects for success depended on its remaining secret until after the election. Humphrey might have won had he disavowed Johnson's war policy sooner. Nixon won and radicalism was contained because the large "silent majority" of American voters, as political analyst Richard Scammon observed, constituted "the unyoung, the unblack, and the unpoor." American political institutions had faced their most severe test in over a hundred years and had survived.

THE POLITICIAN

Richard Nixon's political career began with his election to Congress in 1946. His role in exposing Alger Hiss quickly brought him into prominence, which he parlayed into a Senate seat in 1950 and the vice presidency in 1952. After eight years as Eisenhower's active vice president, Nixon was beaten narrowly by John Kennedy in the 1960 presidential election. Apparently destined for the political scrap heap following his 1962 loss in the California gubernatorial campaign, Nixon returned in 1968 to beat Humphrey and gain the White House.

Nixon's political career was characterized by relentless ambition and sustained effort to achieve his personal goals. He combined incisive intelligence with hard work to master the art of politics. But Nixon was in many ways ill suited for the public career he chose. Shy, introverted, and a loner, he lacked the easy charm and affability characteristic of most American politicians. He armored himself for politics by imposing a tight discipline on his behavior and emotions. Many people intuitively regarded Nixon's public personality as a fabrication; they wondered who the "real Nixon" was.

The real Nixon inhabited a complex and conflicted personality. He prized hard work, tenacity, self-reliance, and seriousness of purpose. But Nixon had also used "smear" tactics to identify his political opponents with Communism in order to win elections. His ruthless tactics appeared to serve no larger political cause than his own advancement. He held a cynical view of politics as a process in which all politicians advocated principles and ideals as a cover for self-interest. Politics was never for Richard Nixon a friendly game. His opponents were not rivals to be defeated, but enemies to be destroyed. Nixon's blend of moral self-righteousness married to dirty campaign tactics accounts for his most singular quality—his ability to inspire strong loyalty among Republican supporters and intense loathing among Democratic opponents. He was a complete partisan who divided everyone into two political groups—"us against them," the foremost modern practitioner of the politics of division. Nixon combined in one complex personality an unusual mix of admirable and despicable traits. His tragedy was rooted in a paradox—the qualities that enabled him to win the presidency and made him a world statesman also rendered him arrogant, insensitive to the American preoccupation with political means, and susceptible to the corruptions of power. These character flaws ultimately destroyed his presidency and tarnished his place in national history.

PRAGMATIC CENTRISM

Nixon came to office determined to restore the consensus politics that had prevailed in this country during the 1950s and early 1960s before being shattered by the Vietnam war, civil rights, and other domestic insurgencies. To achieve his goal, he moved in different policy directions simultaneously. His general thrust was towards the center; but he also struck out in conservative directions in pursuit of his southern strategy, and he proposed far-reaching reforms to co-opt liberal causes. He failed to restore the lost consensus during his first term because he could not end the American War in Vietnam. His pursuit of his southern strategy perpetuated the divisions he hoped to end. Various activists and reformers continued to press their causes despite his efforts to co-opt or suppress them.

His cabinet selections and choices for leading advisory positions comprised a mix of conservatives, moderates, and liberals recruited from business, academia, and politics. The key men in Nixon's administration included Attorney General John Mitchell, a former law partner and his chief political adviser, and Henry Kissinger, a Harvard professor and chief foreign policy adviser. Nixon's chief of staff, Harry R. "Bob" Haldeman, came from the world of advertising. Attorney John Erlichman became Nixon's chief domestic affairs adviser.

Like Kennedy, Nixon always considered domestic affairs secondary to foreign policy concerns. His own lack of enthusiasm, the fact that 57 percent of the voters in 1968 preferred another candidate to him for president, and Democratic control of Congress all diminished his influence over domestic affairs. Liberal Democrats in control of Congress extended the Voting Rights Act of 1965, increased spending for food stamps, increased Social Security benefits, and increased federal aid to education. Congress also proposed the Twenty-sixth Amendment enfranchising eighteen-year-olds which was ratified in 1971. The new amendment added 12 million potential voters to the rolls. Nixon was not enthusiastic about these measures, but he did not oppose them.

Nixon proposed policies reflecting the growing conservatism of voters opposed to solving social problems by expanding the powers of the federal government and spending more money on them. A major target was the welfare system. He proposed a work-incentive program to replace the Aid to Dependent Children Program. Called the Family Assistance Plan, it guaranteed a family of four with no income $1,600 per year plus food stamps and Medicaid. It further required all heads of households on welfare, except for single mothers with pre-school-age children, to register for job training. Congress passed only the "Workfare" feature, requiring heads of households to register for job training. Nixon's other innovative proposal, revenue sharing, was part of what he called the "New Federalism," designed to reduce the power of the federal government and to strengthen state and local agencies. Congress enacted a revenue-sharing program to begin in 1972, when $30 billion in federal funds would be split over five years on a basis of two-thirds to local governments and one-third to the state.

NIXONOMICS

Nixon had to spend much of the time that he devoted to domestic affairs trying to manage an increasingly erratic American economy. The economic difficulties stemmed mainly from the Vietnam War and former president Johnson's fiscal irresponsibility. Johnson had drastically increased spending for the war in the midst of a booming economy without raising taxes. Prices rose 5 percent in 1968, the highest inflation rate since the Korean war. Nixon initially applied the monetarist theories of economist Milton Friedman, who claimed prices could be lowered by reducing the money supply. The results were disastrous. The stock market suffered its worst crash since 1929. The federal deficit increased and the GNP declined for the first time since 1958. Unemployment doubled, from 3 percent to 6 percent, and prices continued to rise. Monetarism generated both inflation and recession, creating "stagflation."

Appalled by its disastrous results, Nixon abandoned monetarism for a new economic approach, "jawboning," which amounted to pressuring both business and trade unions to keep down prices and wage demands. Jawboning produced only continuing stagflation. Nixon then decided that economic decline was a greater evil than inflation. Reverting to Keynesian practices, he deliberately unbalanced the budget to stimulate demand and increase employment. These efforts also failed. Stagflation stubbornly persisted as unemployment and inflation both remained high. The economy also ran its first trade deficit since 1893.

Still searching for an effective policy, Nixon again revamped his economic strategy. On August 15, 1971, he froze wages, prices, and rents for ninety days; asked Congress for tax cuts to promote business expansion, devalued the dollar, and clamped a 10 percent tax on imports. At the end of ninety days, he replaced the freeze with more flexible guidelines, allowing annual price increases of 2.5 percent and wage increases up to 5.5 percent. These drastic measures worked for a time. The trade deficit vanished and inflation was halved. The economy snapped out of a recession and the GNP rose sharply. But within a few months, pressures from business and labor undermined the controls and the inflation rate soared.

THE SOUTHERN STRATEGY

Despite his appeals for unity and peace, Nixon only partially succeeded in reuniting and quieting the American people. Discords inherited from the Johnson years continued, and, at times, intensified. A rash of terrorist bombings damaged government and corporate buildings in various cities. The bloodiest prison riot in U.S. history occurred in September 1971 at Attica, New York: prisoners rebelled, taking thirty-nine hostages, mostly guards. When the warden refused their demands, they threatened to kill the hostages. Governor Nelson Rockefeller then ordered an army of police to assault the prison barricades. Thirty prisoners and ten guards died in the ensuing violence.

Nixon's most divisive actions occurred when he implemented his southern strategy. It aimed to outflank George Wallace and secure the Middle American vote comprising southern whites, northern ethnics, and suburbanites. He also sought to attract the voters from the Sunbelt, the most dynamic region of the country. Middle America and the Sunbelt composed what political theorist Kevin Phillips called the new Republican majority. The southern strategy involved stressing "law and order," phasing out most antipoverty programs, and slowing the rate of school desegregation in the South.

Nixon's efforts to slow the pace of school desegregation involved his administration in a controversy over busing to achieve school integration. The Justice Department filed suits prohibiting transporting children to desegregate public schools. The busing issue had risen in 1971 when the Supreme Court ordered the Charlotte-Mecklenburg school system in North Carolina to use busing to achieve school integration after its efforts at voluntary desegregation had failed. Soon many other southern school districts were under court orders to bus children to achieve school integration. It was effective and within a few years the southern public school system was largely desegregated. Ironically, the South soon achieved a more integrated public school system than the North.

Court-ordered busing spread to the North, where resistance was fierce, and occasionally violent. The worst incidents occurred in Boston in 1974 when a federal judge ordered busing to integrate its public school system. Over half the public schools in Boston had student bodies which were 90 percent black. White pupils boycotted South Boston High School rather than accept integration. Buses hauling in African American students were stoned and several youngsters were injured. Racial conflict in South Boston and other northern cities led to a flight of white students from the public school system.

Administration efforts to thwart busing in order to slow the pace of school integration infuriated civil rights leaders. But the Supreme Court upheld busing, which infuriated Nixon and Mitchell. Despite Nixon's and Mitchell's efforts, many northern and southern cities used busing to achieve desegregation. Far more schools integrated during Nixon's presidency than during the administrations of Johnson and Kennedy. African Americans progressed in other areas as well. The size of the African American middle class increased rapidly, and black college enrollment nearly doubled between 1968 and 1972. Thirteen black congressmen and eighty-one black mayors held office in 1971. Nixon tried to steer a middle course between what he termed "instant integration and segregation forever." He also wanted to please his growing Middle American and white southern supporters. Many African Americans and white liberals viewed Nixon as an enemy of their cause.

Nixon's southern strategy also influenced his choices to fill Supreme Court vacancies, four of which opened up during his first term. He tried to appoint a Deep South conservative, but the Senate rejected both of his choices. His four appointees, including the new Chief Justice Warren Burger, who replaced the retired Earl Warren in 1969, were all strict constructionist conservatives. But the more conservative "Nixon Court" did not overturn any of the controversial decisions of its activist predecessor, and many of its decisions went against the Nixon administration grain. It upheld busing, the right of women to have an abortion on demand, and the publication of the Pentagon Papers. It struck down death penalty laws and limited Justice Department efforts at electronic surveillance. It did sustain laws banning pornography where those statutes reflected "community standards." The Nixon court proved to be an unpredictable, politically independent agency, whose decisions often angered conservatives.

Nixon used Vice President Agnew to implement part of the southern strategy. Agnew campaigned extensively during the 1970 election on behalf of Republican congressional candidates. During the election, he tried to link his Democratic opponents to campus upheavals, race riots, bombings, rising crime rates, drug use, and pornography. Agnew's verbal onslaughts had little noticeable impact. Republicans gained two Senate seats, but lost nine in the House. Nixon's southern strategy had yielded meager political dividends, and Agnew's extravagant rhetoric perpetuated divisions within the nation.

As part of its law-and-order campaign, the Justice Department prosecuted antiwar activists. The most important trial occurred in Chicago in 1971. It involved a group of radicals known as the "Chicago Seven." The trial turned into a farce because of the disruptive antics of the defendants and the extreme bias against them of the judge, Julius Hoffman. Six of the seven activists were convicted of various charges stemming from their parts in demonstrations at the 1968 Democratic convention in Chicago. But all of the convictions were overturned on appeal because of Judge Hoffmann's procedural errors and bias.

DÉTENTE

Nixon applied most of his considerable political talents to the conduct of U.S. foreign policy, where he often proved to be an able diplomatist. Nixon, who had built his political reputation as a hard-line Cold Warrior, with help from Kissinger, launched a new era of détente with the Soviet Union, built on a relaxation of tensions and realistic diplomacy. The development of new relations with the Soviets reversed the direction American foreign policy had taken since 1945. A glimmer of détente had surfaced in 1963 in the aftermath of the Missile Crisis with the signing of the Nuclear Test Ban Treaty, but Lyndon Johnson had been unable to sustain it. Relations between the United States and the Soviet Union were strained at the time of Nixon's accession to office, and ongoing efforts at arms control negotiations were unproductive.

Since the beginning of the Cold War, U.S. foreign policy had been premised on the necessity of responding to threats to American interests posed by expansionist Communist states. Both Nixon and Kissinger knew that the model of a world dominated by a bipolar struggle between Communism and the Free World had been rendered obsolete by the late 1960s. They understood that other power centers had arisen. Power now flowed along a pentagonal axis representing the United States, Western Europe, the Soviet empire, China, and Japan.

Nixon and Kissinger also understood that U.S. power had suffered relative decline since the late 1950s. America no longer dominated its major allies. They also understood that the unity of the Communist world had been fatally sundered. In early 1969, the most serious international conflict pitted the two major Communist states, the Soviet Union and the People's Republic of China, against each other. Kissinger and Nixon perceived that, in the case of the quarreling Communist giants, questions of conflicting national interests overrode their ideological kinship. The Soviets and Chinese engaged in skirmishes along border territories long claimed by both, and the two nations prepared for major war. Nixon and Kissinger set out to use this rift between the two Communist powers to improve U.S. relations with both, and to enhance American power in the world.

Nixon and Kissinger had many reasons for seeking détente with the Soviets. They hoped to persuade the Soviets to help them achieve a satisfactory peace in Indochina by linking Soviet willingness to persuade the North Vietnamese to accept U.S. terms with improved relations between the two superpowers. The U.S. diplomats also expected détente to enable America to maintain control over its NATO allies who had recently shown a distressing tendency to make deals of their own with the Soviets and with the Eastern bloc countries. Prosperous and no longer fearful of Soviet aggression, the French and West Germans had been pursuing their own détentes with the Communists and were no longer automatically supportive of U.S. foreign policy initiatives such as the Vietnam War. The West Germans, led by their new chancellor, Willy Brandt, had loaned the Soviets money and concluded a series of joint business ventures with them worth billions of dollars potentially. Another powerful motive for détente was the desire of American industrial and financial interests to move into Soviet and Eastern European markets. Powerful U.S. agricultural interests saw the Soviets as major customers for their wheat and other commodities. Most importantly, Nixon and Kissinger had to be concerned by the everpresent danger of nuclear war arising from the spiraling arms race. Both sides strongly desired to bring a measure of control to the arms race that would significantly reduce the threat of nuclear catastrophe engulfing both and much of the rest of the world.

In 1969, Nixon signed a Nuclear Nonproliferation Treaty with the Soviets. At Nixon's initiative, U.S. and Soviet delegates began strategic arms limitation talks (SALT) in April 1970 at Helsinki and Vienna. At the same time, Kissinger began talks with the Soviet Ambassador to the United States, Anatoly Dobrynin. Nixon wanted nuclear weapons agreements with the Soviets to be the key to détente and to an expanding network of agreements with the Soviets. As he pushed for SALT to begin, Nixon expanded America's nuclear arsenal, believing that the United States had always to negotiate from strength with the Soviets. At the time, both nations possessed roughly equal nuclear arsenals, and both were refining and expanding their nuclear weapons systems. Nixon wanted to add two new weapons systems to the U.S. arsenal, an antiballistics missile (ABM), which would protect U.S. missiles from a possible first strike, and a multiple, independently targeted reentry vehicle (MIRV) that would make it possible for multiple nuclear warheads to be fired from a single missile in flight at several targets simultaneously. The Soviets were also at work on ABMs and MIRV missiles.

Nixon also began a phased reduction of U.S. conventional military forces. These military cutbacks coincided with a general scaling back of American global commitments. In August 1969, the president proclaimed a new Asian policy, called the Nixon Doctrine. According to this new doctrine, America would no longer provide direct military protection in the Far East. Asian nations must henceforth assume greater responsibility for their strategic security. The United States could furnish economic and technical assistance and logistic support, but not troops. There would be no more Vietnams or Koreas. The Nixon Doctrine also had applications for other regions and other conflicts outside Southeast Asia. The new doctrine also signaled that a new dynamic U.S. policy of negotiation and maneuver was supplanting the essentially static policy based on military containment of Communism.

While SALT negotiators representing both sides grappled with the intricate technical questions involved in controlling the asymmetric nuclear weapons systems of the United States and the Soviet Union, other negotiators concluded a series of important economic agreements. In November 1971, representatives of both governments signed agreements whereby the United States would sell the Soviets $136 million worth of wheat and $125 million worth of oil drilling equipment. Arrangements were also concluded on a joint venture, the building of a large truck factory. These, and many other smaller deals, led to a threefold increase in U.S.–Soviet trade over the next three years.

In March 1972, Nixon sent Kissinger to Moscow to make preparations for a summit meeting between the American president and Leonid Brezhnev, General Secretary of the Soviet Communist Party. Nixon later journeyed to Moscow where he and Brezhnev met for a series of talks. From these talks came three major agreements signed by both leaders in May 1972. The first agreement limited each country to two ABM sites, and it also set a ceiling on the number of ABMs per site. The second agreement, an interim agreement called SALT I, froze the number of strategic missiles in both arsenals at 1972 levels for five years, but it put no limit on MIRVs, which both sides continued to build. Neither the ABM treaty nor SALT I ended the thermonuclear arms race, but the arms agreements did bring a measure of stability and control welcomed by both powers. The third agreement, called "Basic Principles of U.S.–Soviet Relations," committed both sides to accept strategic equality as the basic premise for future arms control negotiations. Americans no longer sought nuclear superiority over the Soviets; they had accepted sufficiency. Congress subsequently approved all three agreements. These breakthrough agreements fundamentally altered American-Soviet relations in the world and constituted the bedrock of the new superpower relationship founded on détente, a relaxation of tensions.

Other significant diplomatic agreements between the United States and the Soviet Union were concluded. The Berlin question, a recurring flash point in the Cold War, was resolved. Both sides signed the Berlin Agreement of 1971, which defined clearly the political status of Berlin and created mechanisms for the peaceful resolution of any conflicts that might arise. The next year, the two German states normalized relations and America recognized East Germany as a legitimate state. The United States and the Soviet Union even settled the longstanding question of the Soviet Lend-Lease debt left over from World War II. The Soviets agreed to pay a portion of a scaled-down debt annually for the next twenty years.

All these agreements forged during the most productive era in U.S.–USSR relations since World War II did not make the two superpowers allies. They remained political and ideological adversaries. But détente had created the opportunity for realistic agreements between the two countries that stabilized the arms race, reduced the risk of nuclear war, and resolved several longstanding political problems which had divided them. Competition and rivalry between the superpowers would continue, especially in the Third World, but "peaceful coexistence" had become a reality.

The Nixon and Kissinger policy of détente with the Soviet Union came under attack from liberal Democratic Cold Warriors who controlled Congress. Senator Henry "Scoop" Jackson, from the state of Washington, emerged as the leader of the Democratic opposition to détente. Jackson attacked SALT I as giving the Soviets a dangerous advantage over the United States because it allowed them to keep more land-based ICBMs. Jackson's criticism missed the mark because he ignored the fact that the United States relied for strategic deterrence on a triad of land-based missiles, submarine-launched missiles, and strategic bombers. The Soviets, lacking equivalent submarine and bomber forces, required additional ICBMs to offset the American advantage. Jackson also criticized the Nixon administration for its tolerance of Soviet human rights violations, particularly Moscow's refusal to let Soviet Jews emigrate.

Jackson's criticism was valid, although the Soviets liberalized their emigration policy and permitted thirty thousand Jews to leave the country during 1973, the largest number ever. Jackson, who harbored presidential ambitions, helped push the Jackson-Vanik Amendment through Congress that denied the Soviet Union "most favored nation" trading status with the United States until they stopped human rights abuses and allowed unlimited emigration. Jackson-Vanik effectively prevented Washington from granting equal trading rights to the Soviet Union, hindered the developing commerce between the two nations, weakened détente, angered President Nixon, and disappointed Brezhnev.

THE CHINA OPENING

Nixon's most dramatic foreign policy achievement was the famed opening to China. Since the Chinese revolution in 1949, the United States had insisted that Jiang Jieshi's regime on Taiwan was the true government of China and had refused to recognize the government in Beijing. For twenty years, America and China had had no commercial, diplomatic, or cultural relations, and the United States had successfully prevented China from joining the United Nations. Americans were forbidden to travel to China. The United States also maintained a trade boycott and loan ban against China and attempted to prevent other nations from trading with the Chinese. When Nixon took office in 1969, China was emerging from years of internal upheaval caused by Mao Zedong's "Cultural Revolution," and Chinese leaders, worried about threats to China's security posed by conflicts with the Soviets, sought contacts in the West. Mao was hopeful that friendly relations could be developed with the United States, a country he had long admired.

Beijing sent friendly signals to Western nations. Nixon, sensing possibilities for rapprochement with the People's Republic, responded. Trade and travel restrictions between the two countries were eased. In April 1971, the Chinese invited an American table tennis team to visit China to play Chinese athletes. This "ping pong gambit" preceded the major breakthrough that came in July when Henry Kissinger secretly visited China. Nixon then stunned the American people when he suddenly announced on July 15 that Kissinger had made arrangements for him to visit China in early 1972. By deploying their secretive style of diplomacy, Nixon and Kissinger were positioned to stage one of the most significant diplomatic transformations of modern times.

Nixon sought to improve relations with China for several reasons. He knew the American policy of nonrecognition was unrealistic. China was an established major power in world affairs. He also knew pressures were mounting within the United Nations to evict Taiwan and seat China in its stead. Further, Nixon expected to use friendly relations with China as a diplomatic weapon against the Soviets; he wanted to be able to play the "China card" to incline the Soviets to conclude arms control and other agreements with the Americans. Improved relations with China were also part of Nixon's and Kissinger's strategy for freeing America from its Vietnam entanglement. Perhaps the Chinese would be helpful in persuading Hanoi to negotiate a settlement of the war. A relationship with China would also help America reassert its power in Southeast Asia and develop a wider network of interests in that important region. Most of America's European allies had long since normalized relations with China; the current U.S. ban obviously had failed. Domestic politics also figured in Nixon's decision to go to China. He knew his impeccable anti-Communist credentials protected him from right-wing attacks about his being soft on Communism. He also knew that media coverage of the dramatic trip would boost his political stock at home during an election year.

The announcement that Nixon was going to China was greeted with tremendous enthusiasm and support by almost all Americans regardless of their political leanings. Media commentary was overwhelmingly favorable. Many Democratic political leaders put aside their usual criticisms of Nixon's and Kissinger's diplomacy to praise both men effusively. Kissinger returned to China in November 1971 to finalize the arrangements. While he was in Beijing, the United Nations expelled Taiwan and awarded its seat on the Security Council to China. There was no protest from President Nixon, who was willing to sacrifice the Taiwanese on the altar of détente with the major Communist powers. Some critical voices, mostly on the Republican Right, were raised in protest over Washington's quick abandonment of its long-time ally and friend.

President Nixon arrived in China on February 22, 1972, accompanied by advisers and a host of U.S. journalists. Back in America, millions of fascinated viewers watched spectacular live television coverage of Nixon's arrival at the Beijing airport, his journey into the Forbidden City, and many other highlights of his five-day visit. Nixon's party and the journalists were the first Americans to go to China officially in over twenty years! The video images beamed back to America via a communications satellite were the first live U.S. television pictures ever shot in China. Nixon met with Premier Jou En-lai several times for hours of discussion. Nixon and Kissinger also had a lengthy meeting with the legendary Mao ZeDong. The American delegation were guests of honor at a lavish banquet hosted by the Chinese leaders inside the Great Hall of the People. Nixon and his wife Pat were photographed at the Great Wall of China.

At the conclusion of the historical visit, Nixon and Jou En-lai issued a joint statement, known as the Shanghai Communique, that defined the terms of the new U.S.–Chinese relationship. Each country agreed to open a legation in the other's capital, offices that could evolve into embassies in time. America removed its restrictions on trade and travel to China. America acknowledged that Taiwan was part of China. Both sides criticized the Soviet Union. There was no agreement on the Vietnam war; both China and the United States reaffirmed support for their respective sides in that ongoing war. But the joint communique itself, the fact that it was being promulgated jointly by former adversaries, signaled that the United States had moved beyond Vietnam, beyond the war, toward a larger role in Southeast Asia. U.S.–Chinese relations would go forward regardless of the war in Indochina. Both nations affirmed a commitment to work towards normalizing relations. Within a year of Nixon's visit, American travelers flocked to China. Trade between the two nations increased rapidly. Both countries exchanged diplomatic missions. The China opening was the high point of Nixon's presidency and perhaps the most significant diplomatic achievement of any modern American president.

Nixon's greatest achievement was the opening to China, achieved when he journeyed to that great country in February, 1972. Here, he is greeted by the legendary Mao Zedong at the latter's apartment in Beijing. *Source:* National Archives.

During their historic visit to China, President Nixon and first lady, Catherine "Pat" Ryan Nixon posed for a picture at the famed Great Wall. *Source:* National Archives.

VIETNAM: A WAR TO END A WAR

The most pressing international problem confronting Nixon was extricating America from Vietnam. He tried new approaches to end the war, including implementing the plan announced during his presidential campaign. But his policies suffered from the same flaw as Johnson's. Nixon still sought to achieve an independent non-Communist South Vietnamese state, which the North Vietnamese refused to accept. Therefore, the war went on.

Even though Hanoi had consistently rejected any settlement that would leave a non-Communist government in the South, Nixon and Kissinger believed they could compel Hanoi to accept one. They planned to use the improved relationship between the United States and the USSR by linking increased trade and arms agreements with the Soviets to their willingness to pressure Hanoi into accepting U.S. terms in Vietnam. Nixon also escalated the war by removing the limits Johnson had placed on the use of military force in Southeast Asia. In the spring of 1969, Nixon ordered a bombing campaign to begin against the Viet Cong and North Vietnamese sanctuaries in Cambodia. Because Cambodia was a neutral nation, the bombing was illegal. It was kept secret from Congress and the American people. In addition, Nixon, through Soviet intermediaries, offered the North Vietnamese more realistic peace terms. He proposed withdrawing both American and North Vietnamese troops from the South and reinstituting the demilitarized zone as the boundary between North and South Vietnam. At the same time, to appease American public opinion, which had turned against the war, Nixon announced a phased withdrawal of American combat troops from Vietnam.

But Hanoi was neither intimidated by threats nor lured by concessions into changing its terms. The Paris talks remained deadlocked. Hanoi continued to demand the unilateral withdrawal of all U.S. forces from South Vietnam and creation of a coalition government in the South excluding General Thieu. Nor did the Soviets cooperate. The linkage strategy proved a failure in 1969. With the failure of his plan, Nixon faced a dilemma. Unable to extract the slightest concession from Hanoi, he had to choose between a major escalation of the war or a humiliating withdrawal. Unwilling to make concessions and unable to use greater force because he did not want to arouse domestic opponents of the war and because of doubts about its effectiveness, Nixon offered what he called "Vietnamization"— the United States would continue gradually to withdraw its troops while building up South Vietnamese forces in order to enable them to prevent a Communist takeover following the U.S. pullout. At the time Nixon announced his Vietnamization plan, it had already been in place for a year. He had inherited it from Johnson and given it a new label. While U.S. forces battled the North Vietnamese and Viet Cong, American advisers built up the South Vietnamese forces. Pacification and rural development programs accelerated. In March 1970, President Nixon announced that 150,000 U.S. combat troops would be withdrawn that year.

In neighboring Cambodia, a neutralist leader, Prince Sihanouk, was suddenly overthrown by his pro-American Prime Minister, Lon Nol. Nixon, fearing that the North Vietnamese might take over Cambodia following the coup and responding to an Army request to attack North Vietnamese sanctuaries in that country, ordered American troops into an area of Cambodia about 50 miles northwest of Saigon. The Cambodian incursion produced mixed results. It relieved pressure on Saigon and bought more time for Vietnamization. It also widened the war and provoked Hanoi into full-scale support of Cambodian insurgents fighting Lon Nol's forces. America now had two fragile client states in Southeast Asia to defend against insurgents backed by North Vietnam. The Vietnam war had been widened; it had become an Indochina war. The Cambodian campaign proved to be the last major campaign of the Indochina war involving U.S. ground combat forces.

Nixon did not anticipate the furious domestic reaction to the Cambodian invasion. College campuses across the land exploded at the news of an unexpected widening of a war he had promised to phase out. At Kent State University, tragedy occurred when Ohio National Guardsmen opened fire into a crowd of student protesters, killing four of them and wounding nine others. Following these shootings, hundreds of student strikes forced many colleges to shut down. More than 100,000 demonstrators gathered in Washington to protest the Cambodian invasion and the "Kent State massacre." The Cambodian initiative also caused the most serious congressional challenge to presidential authority to conduct the war. The Senate repealed the Gulf of Tonkin resolution and voted to cut off all funds for Cambodia. But the fund cutoff failed to clear the House. Both the North Vietnamese and the Viet Cong broke off negotiations in protest, confident that domestic and international pressures would eventually force U.S. withdrawal from both Cambodia and South Vietnam.

To appease Dovish critics at home, the President accelerated the timetable for troop withdrawals in 1971. He also expanded the air war by ordering more bombing missions into Cambodia and along the Laotian panhandle. He also authorized an ARVN raid into Laos to disrupt enemy supply routes and staging areas, but the raid failed to achieve its objectives. The South Vietnamese forces retreated after taking heavy casualties. Within the United States, Doves attacked another widening of the war.

During the spring and summer of 1971, two events at home shocked the war-weary nation. On March 29, a military court convicted Lieutenant William Calley of multiple murders and sentenced him to life imprisonment for ordering his infantry platoon to kill over a hundred Vietnamese civilians at My Lai-4. Calley's men had been brought in to destroy the hamlet, which was suspected of harboring Viet Cong. But instead of evacuating the population beforehand or eliminating the village with long-range artillery and bombs, Calley's men had massacred the villagers at close range with machine gun and automatic rifle fire.

Calley claimed that he only followed orders. Army attorneys insisted that Calley had misunderstood his orders. No one else was convicted of war crimes. Many Americans felt sympathy for Calley and his men; a public opinion poll showed a majority of Americans blamed the media for reporting the incident, which had exposed Army efforts to cover up the affair. Hawks denounced the verdict, arguing that no soldier should ever be convicted in wartime for doing his duty. Some Doves condemned the verdict because they believed a junior officer was being scapegoated while his superiors got off free. Responding to the angry outcry over Calley's conviction, President Nixon reduced Calley's sentence. Some Americans wondered how many other My Lai–type massacres had gone undetected. Others found cold comfort in the fact that Viet Cong and South Vietnamese army forces had murdered thousands of civilians. There was also the troubling inconsistency of convicting one young junior officer for mass murder in a war in which long-range artillery fire and aerial bombing had killed thousands of villagers since the Americanization of the war in 1965. What My Lai revealed above all was that the hellish circumstances of combat, which could generate intense confusion, fear, rage, and hate, sometimes brought out the worst in men.

No sooner had the uproar over Calley's conviction subsided than *The New York Times* began publishing excerpts from the "Pentagon Papers," secret government documents stolen from files of the RAND Corporation by a former employee, Daniel Ellsberg. The papers revealed that American leaders had deliberately escalated the war, had ignored peace offers, and had often lied to the public about their actions. These revelations further undermined the credibility of government officials and weakened support for the war.

An increasingly frustrated president fought back against the mounting opposition to his war policy. He ordered wiretaps placed on National Security Council staffers and journalists suspected of leaking secret information to the media. He ordered illegal surveillance of antiwar groups by both the FBI and CIA. He accused congressional Doves of encouraging the enemy and prolonging the war. The Nixon administration tried to prevent *The New York Times* from publishing the Pentagon Papers by securing a court injunction against their publication on the grounds that their release compromised national security. An appellate judge quashed the injunction and the Supreme Court sustained his ruling, finding only the reputation of some public officials compromised by its publication. Blocked by the Supreme Court, the president approved the creation of a special White House undercover unit, the "plumbers," to prevent leaks from within the government and to discredit Ellsberg. Under stress, Nixon developed a siege mentality, feeling beset by enemies in Congress, the media, the bureaucracies, and the streets; all of whom, he believed, were working to undermine his authority to govern. These paranoid attitudes, which drove him to order his men to commit illegal acts, were one of the prime causes of the Watergate scandals.

By the summer of 1971, polls showed public support for Nixon's war policies had dropped to 31 percent. Another survey revealed that two-thirds of Americans approved withdrawing all American troops from Vietnam by the end of the year even if that meant a Communist takeover in the South. Twice the Senate passed resolutions setting a deadline for withdrawal of all troops as soon as North Vietnam released U.S. prisoners of war. Nixon responded to those signs of war-weariness by making new, secret peace proposals to Hanoi: In exchange for release of the

American prisoners, the United States would withdraw all its troops within six months, and America would no longer insist that Hanoi withdraw its troops. These new U.S. concessions started the first serious negotiations since talks had begun in 1968, but deadlock continued because Washington insisted that Thieu remain in power in the South, whereas Hanoi insisted that his removal was a precondition of any settlement.

The war entered its final phase in 1972. Knowing there were only six thousand American combat troops remaining in the South, North Vietnam launched its largest offensive of the war. One hundred and twenty thousand North Vietnamese regulars struck directly at ARVN forces across several fronts. Simultaneously, Viet Cong guerrillas resumed their attacks in rural areas to disrupt pacification efforts. The U.S. retaliated with massive B-52 bombing raids against targets in the Hanoi-Haiphong area. Tactical bombers pounded the North Vietnamese invaders and their supply lines. The North Vietnamese and Viet Cong continued to press their attacks. Nixon then carried out his boldest escalation of the war. He ordered a naval blockade of North Vietnam, the mining of Haiphong harbor, and escalated the bombing campaigns. In addition to his military responses, Nixon also approached the Soviets again about persuading Hanoi into accepting a diplomatic settlement of the war.

Nixon's decisive response to the North Vietnamese assault got strong support at home. Congress and most Americans supported Nixon's moves. The bombing and blockade disrupted North Vietnamese supply lines sufficiently to enable the hard-pressed ARVN forces to stabilize their lines around Hue and Saigon. The North Vietnamese offensive was stalled by summer. South Vietnam managed to survive the assaults, thanks to the strong response by the United States. Both the Soviets and the Chinese, while loudly condemning the U.S. response publicly, privately exerted pressure on Hanoi to end its war with the United States. Détente with the two Communist powers at last bore fruit and helped Nixon bring the U.S. war in Southeast Asia to a belated end.

With the onset of the summer rains in 1972, the war stalemated once more. The North Vietnamese had expected its spring offensive, combined with the approaching American election, to force Nixon to accept their terms and remove Thieu. But the president's powerful response had neutralized their assault and inflicted heavy losses. Soviet pressure on Hanoi pushed them towards a diplomatic settlement. George McGovern, the Democratic challenger for the presidency in 1972, proved to be a weak candidate who posed no threat to Nixon or his war policy. A combination of military losses, economic strains, and diplomatic isolation finally forced Hanoi to seek a settlement with the United States, as long as it did not conflict with its long-range goal of achieving a unified Vietnam under Communist control.

Secret negotiations resumed in Paris. Hanoi dropped its demand that Thieu must go before any settlement could be reached. Kissinger and the North Vietnamese emissary, Le Duc Tho, bargained intensively. By October 11, 1972, they had forged an agreement: Within sixty days after a cease-fire, America would remove all its remaining troops and North Vietnam would release the U.S. POWs. The Thieu government would remain in power pending a political settlement in the South. North Vietnamese troops would remain in the South and the National Liberation Front, now calling itself the People's Revolutionary Government (PRG), would be accorded political status in southern Vietnam.

But General Thieu, who had the most to lose from these arrangements, refused to accept them. Nixon supported Thieu. The North Vietnamese, believing themselves tricked, began stalling. The October agreement was placed on hold and the war went on. Nixon, reelected by a landslide, tried to secure peace terms more favorable to the South Vietnamese government that could ensure its survival. He ordered unlimited air attacks on North Vietnamese military targets in the vicinity of Hanoi and Haiphong. There ensued the most powerful attack in the history of aerial warfare against North Vietnam. This "Christmas Bombing" lasted from December 18 to 29. Nixon was determined to pound Hanoi into resuming negotiations. At the same time he turned the Air Force loose on the North, Nixon significantly increased U.S. aid to South Vietnam and bluntly told General Thieu to accept U.S. peace terms or the United States would settle without him.

The Christmas Bombing provoked worldwide criticism and a storm of protest at home. Congress moved to cut off all funding for the war. With time running out on his options, Nixon told the North Vietnamese that if they agreed to resume negotiations, he would halt the bombing. The battered North Vietnamese accepted his offer and the talks resumed. Kissinger and Tho reached an agreement signed by all parties on January 27, 1973. The January agreement was similar in all major provisions to the suspended agreement of October 11. This time, Nixon imposed the agreement on Thieu, who signed reluctantly. In order to make the treaty more palatable to Thieu, Nixon pledged in writing that the United States "would respond in full force" if North Vietnam violated the agreement.

Although Nixon insisted that the peace agreement had brought "peace with honor" to Indochina, the January Accords represented a disguised defeat for the United States, which permitted the Americans to extricate themselves from a war they no longer believed in and to retrieve their POWs. It also permitted North Vietnamese forces to remain in the South, and it granted the PRG political legitimacy. It allowed the Thieu regime to survive in the South for a time. The treaty was essentially a deal between Washington and Hanoi. The major question over which the war had been fought for nearly a decade, who would govern in the South, was deferred, to be resolved by political means in the future. But that question would be finally settled by force of arms in two years.

THE END OF THE TUNNEL

The war went on even as Kissinger and Tho signed the agreements; there never was an effective cease-fire because neither side made a sincere effort to stop fighting or resolve their differences via negotiations. Nixon continued to support the Thieu government after the U.S. withdrawal, but his efforts were limited by the terms of the Paris Accords, by a lack of public and congressional support, and by his own deepening involvement in Watergate. Between 1973 and 1975, Congress restricted the president's power to involve America in the ongoing war and reduced the amount of aid going to Saigon. When North Vietnam mounted a spring offensive in 1975, South Vietnam suddenly collapsed. The invaders overran its territory. President Ford wanted to honor U.S. commitments to intervene, but lacking congressional support, he did nothing. On April 23, President Ford told a cheering audience at Tulane University that the Vietnam war "is finished as far as America is concerned" thereby making U.S. abandonment of the South Vietnamese official. Saigon fell to the Communists six days later.

The twenty-year-long American effort to prevent a Communist takeover in southern Vietnam had ended in disaster for the United States and the people it tried to help. It had been the longest, least popular war in U.S. history. It had divided Americans to a greater degree than any conflict since their own Civil War. It was the first major war Americans ever lost. Its aftermath refuted every Cold War assumption upon which American involvement had been based. American security was not threatened. American alliances elsewhere were not weakened, nor were American allies disheartened by the outcome. American power and prestige in the world community was not significantly diminished. There was no unified Communist takeover of Southeast Asia because the victorious Communist states fell to warring among themselves. A vicious Marxist regime, which overthrew Lon Nol in Cambodia about the time the North Vietnamese conquered Saigon, was responsible for the death of at least a million of its own people. Communist Vietnam invaded Cambodia, now called Kampuchea. China, supporting the Kampuchean regime, attacked Vietnam. The Soviets backed Vietnam in these intramural Communist wars. America, which had gone to war in Southeast Asia ostensibly to stop the spread of Chinese Communism, found itself quietly backing Chinese efforts to contain Vietnamese expansionism. Southeast Asian national interests turned out to be a stronger force than Marxist ideology in determining the behavior of nations. There was no bitter "who lost Vietnam" debate in the United States or a resurgence of McCarthyite Red-baiting. Instead, amnesia set in; no one wanted to talk about Vietnam for years, much less indulge in recriminations over it.

The harm done to the United States and Vietnam by the long, losing war was severe and lasting. George Kennan, the principal theorist of containment, called the Vietnam war "the most disastrous of all America's undertakings over the whole two hundred years of its history." The war killed perhaps 2 million Vietnamese and turned a fourth of its population into refugees. It left 58,000 Americans dead and another 300,000 wounded. There were few parades for returning Vietnam veterans. Except for the POWs, they were not welcomed home. A people who had carelessly sent them off to fight in Vietnam for a cause they no longer believed in were embarrassed by their presence and sought to ignore them, or worse, denounce them.

The war experience for many veterans had been an ordeal. In addition to facing the ravages of war, many soldiers returned home disillusioned by their combat experiences. To these veterans the war appeared futile, pointless, and wrong. The rejection of the war by the civilian population made it more difficult for many soldiers to justify their efforts or derive any meaning from them. The large majority of returning veterans were neither war criminals nor victims. They did not suffer from drug addiction nor have acute psychological or physical disabilities. But most veterans had to struggle to come to terms with their war experiences, readjust to civilian routines, and reintegrate into American society. In addition to the human costs of the war, the economic costs were also high. The Vietnam War cost more than any other war in U.S. history except World War II—$150 billion. President Johnson's efforts to finance both the Great Society and the war ignited inflation. His refusal to trim domestic spending, to raise taxes, or to apply economic controls, because he was trying to hide the costs of war, brought economic decline to the nation.

There were other costs of war. A bitter controversy erupted over whether draft evaders and deserters should be granted amnesty or severely punished. This nasty debate perpetuated the war-sown divisions between Doves and Hawks. The war also undermined public faith in the competence and honesty of elected officials. Military service was discredited for years.

The war shattered the bipartisan ideological consensus that had guided U.S. foreign policy since the late 1940s. The losing war also proved that American technology and wealth could not defeat a poor Third World nation determined to prevail, nor could America support forever an ineffective regime. Americans discovered that there were limits to U.S. power and there were limits to the burdens Americans were willing to bear in pursuit of foreign policy aims. For the first time since the Cold War began, many Americans questioned the validity of their global mission to contain Communism. The ordeal of Vietnam also marred the American spirit. The ultimate domino was America's vision of itself as a powerful and benevolent nation. That lofty self-image perished in the jungles, swamps, and rice paddies of Vietnam.

ACTIVISTS AND REFORMERS

Many of the insurgencies that had risen during the 1960s continued into the 1970s. The women's movement gained momentum as more women changed their perceptions about themselves and their roles in society. Women opted for many new career choices. The number of American women in medical schools, law schools, and graduate business programs doubled between 1970 and 1974. New magazines devoted to women's issues emerged. The most successful of these publications was *Ms.* magazine, edited by Gloria Steinem. *Ms.* focused on the emotional and political needs of women and gave liberated women a forum of their own. The women's movement of the 1970s continued to be divided between reformers in the National Organization of Women (NOW), who sought equality before the law, no-fault divorces, equal pay for equal work, child-care centers, and abortion rights; and radical feminists, who wanted fundamental changes in the structure of society and changes in sexual identity.

Political opposition to feminism in the 1970s came from a conservative leader, Phyllis Schlafly, head of the Eagle Forum. Schlafly led an effort to defeat the Equal

Rights Amendment (ERA). She insisted that its passage would not help women and would take away rights they already had, such as the right to be supported by a husband, the right to be exempted from conscription, and the right to special job protections. Schlafly succeeded when ERA fell three states short of the thirty-eight needed for ratification.

While feminists organized for action, so did Native Americans. Militant Indians occupied Alcatraz Island in San Francisco Bay in November 1969. The protesters wanted to highlight their demand that the Bureau of Indian Affairs respond more effectively to a myriad of Native American social problems. One of the prominent supporters of the Indian cause was a popular movie actress, Jane Fonda, who soon became involved in radical anti–Vietnam War activities.

In 1973, the most important militant Native American group, the American Indian Movement (AIM), seized the South Dakota town of Wounded Knee, the site of an 1890 massacre of Sioux Indians by the U.S. Seventh Calvary. AIM activists wanted to call attention to the misery of the impoverished Indian inhabitants of Wounded Knee and to the hundreds of Indian treaties broken by the federal government. Armed federal agents reclaimed the town, killing an AIM member in the process. In negotiations that followed, government officials agreed to examine conditions among the Indians and their treaty rights. The Second Battle of Wounded Knee signaled a new era of Indian militancy and activism.

Hispanic organizations were also active in the early 1970s. Young Chicanos formed a militant organization that called itself the Brown Berets, active in the Midwest and Southwest. Brown Berets also joined the antiwar movement. Spokesmen called attention to Chicano casualty rates in Vietnam that were higher proportionally than those of the general population. Aware of the political activity of some Mexican Americans, President Nixon set out to win their support. He offered them political appointments and programs. The effort paid off; in the 1972 election, Nixon received 31 percent of the Chicano vote, which helped him carry California and Texas. In 1974, the Supreme Court responded to another Chicano concern when it ruled that public schools had to meet the learning requirements of youngsters with limited English language skills. That decision led to federal funding of bilingual education programs.

ECOLOGY AND CONSUMERISM

Environmentalism was one of the many movements that emerged during the 1960s and grew rapidly during the early 1970s. The origins of the modern ecology movement lay in a book written by Rachel Carson called *Silent Spring* (1962). When there was almost no concern about ecological issues, Carson wrote about environmental damage done by chemical pesticides, particularly DDT. Her writings spawned a cause; by 1970, a broad-based, diverse environmentalist movement was active on a variety of fronts.

Congress responded to growing environmental concerns. Legislators enacted the Water Quality Improvement Act in 1970, tightening existing safeguards against threats to water quality. The National Air Quality Standards Act required automakers to reduce exhaust emission pollutants significantly by 1975 and required the federal government to set air quality standards. The Resource Recovery Act provided $453 million for resource recovery and recycling systems. In 1971, Congress created the Environmental Protection Agency, which combined federal agencies concerned with pesticides, radiation, auto exhaust emissions, air and water quality, and waste disposal under a single cabinet-level department. Nixon appointed former Deputy Attorney General William Ruckelshaus to head the new agency, who proved to be an energetic director. The EPA quickly initiated action on several fronts. It provoked a reaction from Detroit automakers, who insisted that EPA emission and safety standards were too expensive and beyond their technological capabilities. Nixon's Secretary of the Interior, Walter Hickel, a conservative, self-made oil millionaire, also turned out to be an energetic environmentalist who protected the public domain.

Ecology was not a major Nixon priority and at times he opposed the environmentalists. He pushed hard for funds to construct a supersonic jet transport in 1970, only to have the Senate kill the project because the design of the plane was too noisy and expensive. Nixon also vetoed a mammoth $24.7 billion measure to clean up America's polluted rivers and lakes, but Congress enacted the law over his veto. Environmentalism was a political issue that cut across party, class, and ideological lines. Most everyone endorsed in principle the need for clean air and water and the protection of scenic landscapes and wilderness areas. But not everyone was willing to pay its high costs.

Related to the ecology movement and sometimes overlapping with it was a strong consumer movement that developed during the early 1970s that concerned itself with protecting consumers from unsafe and shoddy products and with making business more responsive to consumers. Ralph Nader, whose attacks on the auto industry during the mid-1960s had led to enactment of federal safety laws, headed the consumer movement of the 1970s. From an office in the nation's capital, Nader organized task forces of volunteers called "Nader's Raiders," who examined many industries and governmental agencies. They followed up these investigations with critical reports about their operations and proposals for their reform.

Nader's Raiders attacked governmental regulatory agencies for being more protective of the businesses they were supposed to regulate than protective of the consumers. These latter day muckrakers also attacked the multibillion dollar processed food industry, accusing it of serving American consumers a "chemical feast" of harmful food additives. They also attacked agribusiness for its use of chemical fertilizers and pesticides that harmed the environment and put toxic substances into the nation's food supplies. In their most radical finding, they reported on the impact of land-use monopoly in some states. As a consequence of the consumer movement, millions of Americans became much more concerned about product safety and quality and more assertive of their rights as consumers.

THE ELECTION OF 1972

The president and his men prepared carefully for his 1972 reelection campaign. Attorney General John Mitchell resigned his office to devote full time to directing the newly formed Committee to Reelect the President (CREEP). CREEP fund-raisers accumulated a $60 million war chest to finance his campaign. CREEP also recruited men who were fiercely loyal to the president and who shared his siege mentality of "us against them." They appeared ready to do anything to ensure his reelection, including breaking laws and violating the ethical norms of democratic electoral practices. Nixon had always campaigned with fierce determination to win. He remembered his narrow loss to John Kennedy in 1960 and that he had barely beaten Humphrey in 1968. The 1970 midterm election results had shown strong continuing support for congressional Democrats. In 1972, Mr. Nixon was determined to leave nothing to chance to secure his reelection.

The Democratic Party was still in disarray from the upheavals of 1968, and its members remained deeply divided over emotional issues such as the war, busing, and "law and order." Nevertheless, many Democrats sought their party's nomination at the outset of the 1972 campaign. They included Senators Edmund Muskie, impressive as the vice-presidential candidate in 1968; Hubert Humphrey, around for another go; and George McGovern, an outspoken critic of the Vietnam War. After them came two formidable possibilities, Senator Edward "Ted" Kennedy and George Wallace. Kennedy's appeal had been tarnished by his behavior following an auto accident in which a young woman had been killed; but he still retained the vote-getting magic of the Kennedy name. Kennedy insisted that he was not an active candidate; however, he could accept a convention draft. George Wallace, returned to the Democratic fold, also remained a major factor.

Muskie flamed out early, in part the victim of Watergate "dirty tricks," as the nation would discover a year later. A would-be assassin eliminated Wallace by

George McGovern on the campaign trail in 1972.
Source: National Archives.

wounding him severely and forcing him out of the campaign in May. With Muskie and Wallace eliminated, McGovern moved strongly ahead. He won a series of primary victories, including one in California where he beat Humphrey, and rolled on to a first-ballot nomination. State delegations at the Democratic convention in Miami contained high proportions of women, blacks, and young antiwar activists. Taking advantage of new party rules governing delegate selection, these insurgent practitioners of a "new politics" replaced party regulars. They took control of the convention and forged McGovern's victory.

McGovern had pulled off a major political upset. His victory was largely a triumph of organization. He had borrowed savvy political professionals from the Kennedy organization, and his aides had enlisted young enthusiasts who rallied to McGovern's call for ending the war in Vietnam. He chose Thomas Eagleton, a young liberal senator from Missouri, as his running mate. His supporters drafted a platform calling for an "immediate total withdrawal of all American forces in Southeast Asia." It also supported busing to achieve school integration, full employment, tax reform, and various social reforms. McGovern made a stirring acceptance speech in which he sounded the theme of "come home America:" get out of Vietnam and attend to the nation's unfinished social agenda. His campaign began on a high note of enthusiasm and moral principle.

Meeting in Miami after the Democrats, the Republicans unanimously chose Nixon and Agnew to run again. The Republican platform staked out a clear strategy. It called for a "new American majority" to repudiate the "far-out goals of the Far Left," meaning McGovern's program. It also called for arms limitations with the Soviets, full employment, and tax reform. It opposed busing. On the crucial war issue, Republicans insisted that America could not withdraw from Vietnam until all the prisoners of war had been returned.

The presidential campaign was boring and one-sided, reminiscent of the election of 1964. McGovern never had a chance and most Americans quickly lost interest in the contest. The Democrats remained divided. Most Wallace supporters and about half of Humphrey's followers voted for Nixon. Organized labor, the strongest power bloc within the party, refused to support McGovern. McGovern's campaign suffered serious damage at the outset when the public learned that Senator Eagleton had undergone psychiatric care in the past. At first, McGovern stood behind Eagleton, but after a week's adverse publicity, he panicked and forced Eagleton off the ticket. McGovern then began a search for a substitute and suffered six embarrassing turndowns before finally persuading Sargent Shriver, former director of the War on Poverty, to accept. McGovern's inept, expediential handling of the Eagleton affair managed to alienate both young idealists and party regulars. To many of the new politics enthusiasts, McGovern appeared to be just another unprincipled politician; to the regulars, he appeared to be something worse, an incompetent bumbler.

The qualities that brought McGovern the nomination proved to be political liabilities in the contest against Nixon. His left-of-center appeal to the new politics cost him the political center inhabited by most voters. Republicans put McGovern on the defensive early in the campaign by depicting him as a radical even though he was a mild-mannered preacher's son, a World War II hero, and a former college professor. McGovern was a midwestern liberal, in the New Deal–Fair Deal–Great Society mold, with perhaps a whiff of 1930s Prairie Populism. But in the conservative political atmosphere of 1972, McGovern's advocacy of traditional liberal reforms sounded radical to many voters. He alienated far more voters than he attracted with his stands on emotion-laden issues such as his calls for amnesty for Vietnam draft resisters, and for liberalizing abortion laws and marijuana laws.

Nixon campaigned very little. He stayed in Washington and concentrated on appearing presidential while the hapless McGovern struggled futilely to get the monkey of radicalism off his back. Nixon possessed formidable political assets that made him practically unbeatable even if the Democrats had run their strongest possible ticket of Kennedy and Wallace. The president had achieved impressive diplomatic victories, capped by détente with the Soviets and the opening to China. The American war in Vietnam was winding down and most U.S. troops had been withdrawn. At home, the economy was reasonably strong and society had calmed. Nixon also stood four-square against all those features of American life that so upset Middle Americans and given liberalism a bad name—busing, hippies, the coddling of criminals and welfare chiselers, antiwar activists, drug use, and sexual permissiveness. He also employed, it came out later, an under-

President Nixon confers with his top aides in the Oval Office. Standing in front of Nixon is Henry Kissinger, national security adviser. Sitting to Kissinger's right is Harry R. "Bob" Haldeman, chief of staff. To Kissinger's left is John Erlichman, chief adviser for domestic affairs.   *Source:* National Archives.

cover army of political hirelings, using their arsenal of "dirty tricks" to sabotage the Democratic campaign.

There was a potential chink in Nixon's political armor—corruption. McGovern attacked it hard; he called Nixon's administration "the most morally corrupt in history." He cited several seamy deals in which corporations and trade associations had given the GOP large campaign donations in exchange for political favors. The most blatant case of corruption involved a break-in at Democratic Party national headquarters at Watergate Towers in Washington on June 17, 1972. Seven men, including two former White House aides and a member of CREEP, had been caught trying to photograph and steal documents, and to install electronic bugging equipment. It appeared that members of the Republican campaign organization and even members of the president's staff had engaged in espionage against their opponents. But news of the burglary excited little public concern at the time and the prominent mass media exhibited little sustained interest in the bizarre event after a day or two of sensational headlines. Republicans denied all McGovern's charges and dismissed the Watergate break-in. Nixon categorically denied that any member of his administration was involved. Even though he tried, McGovern failed to generate much voter interest in Watergate or the corruption issue. Within less than a year, it would turn out that McGovern had touched only the tip of the corruption iceberg.

Nixon scored a landslide victory in November. He carried forty-nine of fifty states and rolled up an electoral vote of 521 to 17. Nixon tore huge holes in the Democratic coalition. He swept the South. He even got a majority of the urban vote. The "silent majority" whom the President had courted—middle- and lower-middle-class whites, blue-collar voters, ethnics, Sunbelt inhabitants, and westerners—all voted for him. The 1972 election was the first in which newly enfranchised eighteen-to-twenty-one-year-olds could vote. McGovern spent much of his time campaigning for their vote, considering the youth vote his secret weapon. Only one-third of them voted and half of them opted for Nixon.

Despite Nixon's sweep, Democrats retained control of Congress, even gaining two seats in the Senate while losing twelve in the House. Such ticket-splitting suggested that millions of voters had cast their ballots for Nixon because they could not abide McGovern, not because they wanted to endorse the president or his party. Voter turnouts were lower than for any election since 1948. Clearly, the political environment had become more conservative by 1972; however, except for the South, results gave no indication that political realignment was occurring or that a new Republican majority was emerging. American voters mainly repudiated a candidate they saw lacking in leadership qualities and opted to keep the incumbent whom they perceived to be a successful leader.

WATERGATE

President Nixon began his second term in January 1973, convinced that his landslide victory was a mandate for conservative policies. His new budget cut spending for welfare and education. He removed all remaining controls from the economy and impounded billions of dollars appropriated by Congress for purposes he opposed. Nixon also began reorganizing the federal government to make the bureaucracies more efficient and subject to his control. His attitude toward the Democratic Congress was belligerent and contemptuous. He believed that the great mass of Americans supported him; that the tides of history were flowing in the direction he wanted to take the country. Richard Nixon was riding high that spring of 1973. Then his administration began to self-destruct.

Watergate, latent since the break-in, suddenly erupted with a rash of disclosures and confessions that made it one of the most serious political scandals in American history. Watergate activities fell into two categories—those occurring before the June 17, 1972 break-in, and those following. The break-in turned out to be only one event in an extensive dirty-tricks campaign developed by CREEP and White House staffers to prevent news leaks, to spy on radicals, and to ensure Mr. Nixon's reelection. Investigators eventually unearthed an astonishing web of illegal activities and abuses of power that had begun early in Nixon's presidency. These activities include illegal wiretaps placed on government bureaucrats and journalists suspected of leaking embarrassing information about administration policies to the press, using the Internal Revenue Service to harass political opponents, raising millions of dollars in illegal campaign funds, and ordering a break-in of Daniel Ellsberg's psychiatrist's office.

The burglars caught inside the Democratic Party national headquarters had previously tried unsuccessfully to break into McGovern's campaign headquarters. Other dirty tricksters circulated literature slandering Democratic candidates and disrupted their meetings. All dirty tricks were cleared with the president's top advisers. Nixon's defenders argued that many of the dirty tricks had been used by previous administrations and were part of the political process. That was true, but the extent of Nixonian dirty tricks vastly exceeded any previous administration's efforts. More seriously, these practices flowed from a mind-set that was contemptuous of law and fair play, viewed politics as war, and saw political opponents as enemies to be destroyed.

Dirty tricks proved to be only the beginning. The Watergate burglars had been caught red-handed. CREEP officials and White House staffers who sent them in could have confessed and resigned. Such actions would have embarrassed the Nixon administration, but the President would still have been reelected easily. But White House officials chose instead to cover up its and CREEP's complicity. They moved to destroy all evidentiary links between the burglary, themselves, and CREEP, and to concoct denials and alibis. An FBI investigation of the break-in and testimony before a grand jury were carefully limited so they could not uncover any tracks leading to CREEP or the White House. The president soon joined the cover-up activities and put White House Counsel John Dean in charge. At times Nixon himself directed the cover-up activities. From the moment the cover-up efforts began, a process was set in motion that would strain the constitutional system of government, cause many Americans great anguish, provide some of the most bizarre political theater in American history, and eventually destroy Nixon's presidency.

The cover-up orchestrated by Nixon, Dean, and other top White House aides succeeded for a time. In September 1972, a federal grand jury indicted only the seven men directly involved in the burglary. The cover-up also held through the November election in which Nixon won a landslide victory. The cover-up was still holding as the trial of the seven burglars began in March 1973. Meanwhile it was business as usual for the president and his men, confident that they had contained the incident and remained in the clear.

Theirs proved to be a foolish confidence. Too many people were involved in the cover-up. Too many connections among the burglars, CREEP, and the White House survived. Too many investigators were looking for answers to puzzling questions. The *Washington Post* had assigned two young reporters, Carl Bernstein and Bob Woodward, to find answers. They were able to trace some of the illegal campaign funds to CREEP. The Senate created a Select Committee on Presidential Campaign Activities, soon to be known as the Watergate Committee, chaired by Senator Sam J. Ervin, to investigate the burglary and other dirty tricks that may have influenced the outcome of the 1972 election. Federal prosecutors, continuing the federal grand jury probe, continuously investigated the burglary, other dirty tricks, violations of campaign spending laws, and the cover-up. The Watergate trial judge, John J. Sirica, who did not believe the burglars when they told him that they alone had planned the break-in, pressured them to tell the truth.

The cover-up began to come unglued when one of the convicted burglars, James McCord, hoping to avoid a long prison term, wrote a letter to Judge Sirica implicating CREEP and prominent White House officials in the planning of the Watergate burglary. After McCord cracked, the whole cover-up edifice crumbled. The accused officials hired lawyers and promptly implicated other prominent officials in the hopes of getting immunity from prosecution or a lighter sentence. Federal prosecutors often entered into plea bargaining arrangements with accused lesser officials to gather evidence against the ringleaders, including President Nixon.

In April, President Nixon was forced to fire several key advisers implicated in the cover-up—L. Patrick Gray III, Acting Director of the FBI, Erlichman, Haldeman, and Mitchell. Nixon fired John Dean, the White House counselor, for telling the Watergate Committee that the president had been involved in the cover-up from the beginning. President Nixon maintained publicly that he only learned about the cover-up from Dean in March, and since then had done everything he could to cooperate with investigators, to get out the truth about Watergate, and to punish wrongdoers. Nixon also tried to discredit Dean's testimony by suggesting that he had directed the cover-up without the president's knowledge. To reinforce the image of a president concerned to get to the bottom of the scandal, Nixon appointed a Special Prosecutor, Harvard law professor Archibald Cox, to investigate the cover-up.

On May 17, 1973, public interest in the scandal picked up when the Senate Watergate committee began holding televised hearings. The committee started with low-level hirelings, CREEP minions who did the dirty work and delivered illegal payments. Gradually they worked their way up the chain-of-command in

CREEP and the Nixon White House. On the way, the millions of viewers who watched the proceedings daily got a fascinating tour through the dark underside of American politics. They learned about political dirty tricks and the details of the cover-up. They learned about shredding documents, blackmail, bribery, forgery, perjury, and "laundered money." They also learned about the misuse of government agencies including the FBI and IRS. They also learned about fund-raising techniques that violated election laws and often amounted to blackmail. The televised hearings also made a folk hero out of the committee's chairman, seventy-nine-year-old Sam Ervin. Ervin's folksy manner and good humor cloaked a keen intellect and a fierce moral outrage at the steady stream of criminals and unethical politicians who appeared before his committee.

By mid-June, the key question had become whether President Nixon had been involved in the Watergate cover-up: In the words of Senate Committee member Howard Baker, "What did the President know and when did he know it?" On June 25, John Dean appeared before the committee. For two days, he read a lengthy 250-page statement describing the details of the cover-up: Nixon knew all about it, had approved it, indeed had played a central role in it from the outset. Despite efforts by the White House to discredit Dean, the fired counselor came across as credible to members of the committee and to the large television audience. He displayed a phenomenal memory. He knew too much; he had too many details at his command. The testimony of Nixon loyalists before the committee further damaged the president's position. Men like Haldeman, Erlichman, and Mitchell often gave rambling, incoherent, evasive answers to direct questions.

But Dean's testimony, while sounding plausible and authentic, was legally inconclusive. It depended entirely on his ability to recall the events and conversations that he described before the Committee. He had no corrobative evidence or documents to back it up. Only John Dean had implicated Nixon. The president had denied all charges and fired Dean. Dean himself was a suspect source. He was deeply involved in the cover-up. To a man, all of the Nixon loyalists insisted on the president's innocence and accused Dean of being the evil mastermind of the cover-up who was wickedly trying to pin the blame on Nixon in order to save himself.

THE DECLINE AND FALL OF RICHARD NIXON

Then on July 16 came a sensational discovery. The Watergate committee found out that President Nixon had recorded White House conversations and phone calls on a secret tape recording system installed in the Oval Office in 1970. If the disputed conversations between Dean and Nixon were on tape, it would be possible to find out which one of them was telling the truth and if the president had been involved in the cover-up. From that date on, the Watergate drama focused on the tapes and the prosecution's efforts to get them from the president, who was determined not to surrender them.

Immediately, both the Watergate Committee and the Special Prosecutor subpoenaed the tapes of the Nixon–Dean conversations. Nixon rejected both subpoenas. Both investigators then asked Judge Sirica to force Nixon to honor their sub-poenas. Nixon's attorneys defended his right to refuse to surrender the tapes on the grounds of "executive privilege." Judge Sirica rejected the argument and ordered Nixon to release the tapes. Nixon's attorneys appealed his ruling. The appeals court upheld the ruling saying "the President is not above the law's commands."

While the battle for control of the tapes was raging, another White House scandal surfaced, unrelated to Watergate, involving Vice President Agnew. Justice Department investigators learned that Agnew, when governor of Maryland during the 1960s, had taken bribes from construction companies in return for favorable rulings on their bids. In August 1973, Agnew was charged with bribery, extortion, conspiracy, and income tax invasion. Nixon, convinced of his guilt, pressured Agnew to resign. To get rid of him, Nixon offered him a deal: resign and plead "no contest" to a single count of tax evasion, and the other charges would be dropped. The other charges and evidence sustaining them would be published so people would know why Agnew resigned. Knowing that federal prosecutors had hard evidence against him, Agnew accepted Nixon's offer. Otherwise, he knew that he would be going to prison. He resigned, was fined $10,000, and given three years' unsupervised probation. The evidence released to the public showed the case against Agnew amounted to fifty indictable offenses. Even so, Agnew, displaying considerable gall, toured the country, making speeches and appearing on talk shows. Everywhere he insisted on his innocence and claimed that he only resigned to avoid embarrassing the embattled president.

Shortly after Agnew's forced resignation, President Nixon chose House minority leader Gerald R. Ford of Michigan to succeed the fallen vice president. Ford was a conservative, a Nixon loyalist, and popular with his colleagues. Further, there were no political or personal scandals in his life. This last factor was crucial because many senators who voted to confirm Ford knew that if the tapes substantiated Dean's charges, Mr. Nixon was not only selecting a vice president, he was choosing his successor. Ford had to be squeaky-clean.

Meanwhile, Archibald Cox was pressing the Nixon administration for more tapes. Release of these tapes posed a mortal danger to the president, which he knew better than anyone. Nixon decided on a bold move to avoid surrendering them: Unless a compromise were arranged permitting the president to keep custody of the tapes, Nixon would dismiss Cox and prepare his own summaries of the tapes for Judge Sirica. Efforts to forge a compromise failed. On Saturday evening, October 20, Nixon ordered Attorney General Elliot Richardson to fire Cox. The Attorney General refused and resigned. Nixon then directed Deputy Attorney General William Ruckelshaus to fire him. Rucklehaus also refused and Nixon fired Rucklehaus. Finally, the third-ranking officer at the Justice Department, Robert Bork, dismissed Cox. Nixon also abolished the special prosecutor's office and ordered the FBI to seal all of the office files.

Journalists dubbed these actions taken by Nixon the "Saturday Night Massacre." The firings provoked a dramatic outpouring of public protest. During the next forty-eight hours, over a million letters, telegrams, and phone calls poured into

Senate and congressional offices, nearly all of them denouncing the Saturday Night Massacre. Eight resolutions of impeachment were introduced into the House of Representatives. Nixon's approval rating in the polls dropped to 27 percent. Polls also revealed that most Americans suspected that the president was trying to hide his involvement in criminal activities. In addition to his Watergate actions, Nixon also came under attack for questionable financial dealings involving his real estate holdings in California and Florida. The IRS also investigated him for tax evasion.

Nixon tried hard to repair the damage with a public relations campaign. He agreed to release the original tapes ordered by Judge Sirica. He replaced Cox with another special prosecutor, Leon Jaworski, a Houston corporation lawyer. Nixon met with congressmen and senators to reassure them of his innocence. He released a detailed financial statement to dispel doubts about his personal finances. He went on a national speaking tour to reclaim his lost reputation. Before an audience of newspaper publishers, he insisted that he was "not a crook." His efforts failed. Except for hard-core loyalists, the public, the media, and Congress remained skeptical of Nixon's efforts at reassurance. The president's lingering credibility was further undermined when White House officials admitted that two of the nine subpoenaed tapes, covering important conversations with Dean, did not exist. Even worse, an eighteen-and-one-half-minute segment of a crucial conversation between Nixon and Haldeman, held three days after the break-in, had been erased. Calls for impeachment grew louder.

With the failure of his public relations campaign, Nixon grew defiant. He refused Jaworski's requests for more tapes. On March 1, 1974, the grand jury indicted several key players in the cover-up, including Erlichman, Haldeman, and Mitchell. It would have indicted Nixon as well if Jaworski had not told them that a sitting president was not indictable under the law. At about the same time the grand jury issued its indictments, the House Judiciary Committee began impeachment proceedings against the president. When its staff sought tapes and documents from the White House, Nixon refused its requests as well. Both Jaworski and the House Judiciary Committee then issued subpoenas to obtain the desired evidence and to overcome the president's "stonewalling" tactics.

Nixon was caught in a serious bind. He knew that refusal to comply with subpoenas would not work; he also knew that conversations on several of the requested tapes would ruin him if released. He tried to escape the trap. He decided to release edited transcripts of the requested tapes. In a speech to the American people delivered April 29, dubbed by the media "Checkers II," he made a final effort to retrieve his political reputation. He told his audience of his intent to release the transcripts. "These materials will tell all," he said. Next day the transcripts were published in full.

The public response to Nixon's ploy was again emphatically negative. House Judiciary Committee members, comparing the edited versions with tapes already released, discovered many discrepancies. The contents of the edited tapes were even more damning to the president's cause because of the impression they conveyed of Nixon's conduct of the presidency: Crude, vulgar language; the use of racial and ethnic stereotypes; wheeling and dealing; and the complete lack of scruples or morality. Nixon evidently failed to understand that the inner workings of his government could not stand public exposure. Conservatives as well as liberals were appalled by Nixon's way of governing. Senate Republican leader Hugh Scott called the transcripts "deplorable, disgusting, shabby, and immoral." House Republican leader John Rhodes of Ohio called upon Nixon to resign. Both the House Judiciary Committee and Jaworski continued their demands for more tapes from the White House. Nixon refused all their requests. Jaworski subpoenaed sixty-four additional tapes. Nixon tried to quash the subpoena, but Judge Sirica upheld it and ordered Nixon to release the tapes.

When the White House announced it would appeal the ruling, Jaworski asked the Supreme Court to decide the matter. It agreed to do so. The question before the Court was clear: Who had the final authority to decide whether a president had to obey a subpoena, himself or the courts? The Court heard arguments by both sides in July. Nixon's attorneys argued that the president had the right to decide; the only way the law could be applied to the president was via the impeachment process. Jaworski countered with the argument that if the president decides what the Constitution means, and "if he is wrong, who is there to tell him so?"

In the case of *The United States of America* v. *Richard M. Nixon*, the Supreme Court ruled unanimously that Nixon had to surrender the subpoenaed tapes to Judge Sirica. On the same day the Court announced its verdict, the House Judiciary Committee began voting on articles of impeachment against the president. Within a week, it voted to send three articles of impeachment to the full House. Article I accused the president of obstructing justice. Article II accused the president of abusing power. Article III accused the president of refusing to honor the Committee's subpoenas. Two other proposed impeachment articles were defeated. If the full House of Representatives adopted at least one of the three approved articles, Nixon would become the second president in United States history to be impeached. (Andrew Johnson had been the first in 1868.) Nixon would then go on trial before the Senate who would sit as a jury of 100 members. The Senate would decide whether the evidence warranted conviction and removal from office.

The evidence that destroyed Nixon's presidency was a taped conversation between Nixon and Haldeman held July 23, 1972, six weeks after the Watergate burglars had been caught: Nixon can be heard ordering Haldeman to tell the CIA to fabricate a national security operation to keep the FBI from pursuing its investigation of the burglary. Here was the "smoking gun," proof of criminal acts, conspiring to obstruct justice and abuse of power. The taped conversation also proved that Nixon had been lying about his Watergate involvement. He had known of the cover-up and had been involved with it from the beginning.

For several days, Nixon wavered between resigning and fighting the impeachment process. On August 7, Republican congressional leaders told Nixon that he faced certain impeachment, conviction, and removal from office. Some of the president's advisers worried about Nixon's mental health; they believed that he had been broken by the stresses of the long Watergate ordeal. Both Secretary of

Defense James Schlesinger and White House Chief of Staff Alexander Haig informed all U.S. military commanders around the world to check with them before carrying out any unusual orders that might come from President Nixon. That night he decided to resign.

On the evening of August 8, he spoke to the American people for the last time. He told the nation that everything he had done he believed had been done with the best interests of the country in mind. He expressed regret for any harm that he might have done others. He admitted to making "errors in judgment." But he could not bring himself to admit to breaking the law or any wrongdoing. He claimed that he was resigning only because he had lost his political base and could no longer govern effectively. His resignation became effective at 12:00 noon, August 9, 1974. At that point in time, Mr. Nixon was aboard the *Spirit of 76* flying over Middle America en route to "exile" in Southern California. At 12:00 noon, Gerald R. Ford took the oath of office as the thirty-eighth president of the United States. The new president began his short acceptance speech by saying, "our long national nightmare is over."

Ford was right; Watergate had been a long national nightmare, its impact accentuated by extensive media coverage for over a year. Americans reacted differently to the Watergate scandals. For well-educated, well-informed citizens who understood that the integrity of the American system of governance was at issue, the events of Watergate were the stuff of high drama. For less well-informed people, the revelations of Watergate appeared confusing, and perhaps much ado about not very much. For millions of Middle Americans who had voted for Nixon in 1972 in good faith, Watergate was a series of painful disillusionments. For young people, especially, Watergate was traumatic. Many of these youngsters sought refuge in a pathetic cynicism. They shrilly insisted that Watergate was what all politicians did; Nixon and his minions merely got nailed. And, even to the bitter end, Nixon retained many defenders. These sturdy souls insisted that the only mistake Nixon made was to not burn the tapes. It was the tapes that ruined him because they made him vulnerable. They gave his enemies among the liberal political and media establishments, the people who hated him because he had proved them wrong so often, the opportunity to destroy him. And then there were the professional Nixon haters. These liberals rejoiced in his humiliation and fall from power. They pointedly observed that Watergate only revealed the dark side of the man that they had known was there all along.

Thoughtful analysts searched out the multiple causes of the Watergate scandals. Some found the springs of Watergate within the personality and approach to politics of Richard M. Nixon. Relentlessly ambitious, intensely partisan, insecure, perhaps even paranoid, Nixon was willing to use or countenance ruthless, even illegal, means to advance his career or achieve his policy goals. Some analysts located Watergate in the institution of the presidency itself, in the rise of an "imperial presidency" since the 1940s. The presidency dominated the federal government, particularly in the realms of national security and foreign policy. All modern presidents wielded awesome powers and came to be regarded as special people, as a kind of royalty, above the restraints of the Constitution and the claims of morality. Other analysts saw the rise of a Cold War mentality as contributing to the Watergate syndrome. In a struggle for survival against ruthless and powerful adversaries, it is sometimes necessary to employ the same ruthless methods that the Communists used, and to employ them more extensively than they. It was necessary to enter an Orwellian world in which undemocratic methods were required to preserve democracy. Still others saw the Watergate scandals deriving from an ethic that held that winning was so important that there were no limits on what could be done to achieve victory. This do-whatever-it-takes-to-win attitude also reflected the political ethics of the many nouveau-riche Sunbelt politicians who rode to power on Nixon's coattails. Nixon was the leader of this new class of "cowboy" politicians who did not play the game of politics by the traditional establishmentarian rules. They had, therefore, to be destroyed.

George McGovern was right when he labeled Nixon's administration the most corrupt in history. But the corruption of the Nixon White House, Agnew excepted, was not the commonplace corruption of crooks, thieves, bribers, grafters, chiselers, and influence peddlers who have infested past presidencies. It was a more dangerous kind of corruption that threatened the integrity of the American system of government. It threatened to replace a government based on constitutional law with the rule of a powerful leader heading a staff of fanatical loyalists, whose highest calling was to do his bidding and vanquish his enemies. His enemies list included Democratic Party leaders, prominent journalists, bureaucrats, antiwar protesters, black militants, and hippies. They posed threats to the leader's personal authority, which he equated with national security. Their threat would be contained by any means necessary, including wiretapping, surveillance, burglary, blackmail, political sabotage, and intimidation. President Nixon and his men for a time posed the most serious threat to constitutional governance, democratic political processes, and civil liberties in American history.

But they failed. Arbitrary power was thwarted. Eventually, due process ran its course. Three hundred seventy-eight officials, including three former cabinet members and several top-level White House aides, either pleaded guilty or were convicted of Watergate-related offenses. Thirty-one went to prison. Only President Ford's pardon probably kept Nixon from prison. The system met the challenge. A free press sounded alarm bells. Various investigations exposed the culprits. The Supreme Court firmly established the principle that no one, including the president, is above the law. Congress, spearheaded by the Senate Watergate Committee and the House Judiciary Committee, overrode efforts at executive usurpation.

Watergate left a mixed legacy. Paradoxically, it revealed both the terrible vulnerability and the underlying strength and resiliency of American political democracy. The abuses of power by the president and the president's men were finally checked. But it took an agonizingly long time for the mainstream media to get involved, for the public to become aroused, and for the Congress to take action. Suppose the tapes had not been discovered? Or suppose that Nixon had ordered them destroyed? Watergate's outcome provides no guarantee that the system would be able to contain a subsequent president's abuses of power. Watergate, along with the

Vietnam War, made Americans skeptical, even cynical, about politics and politicians. It reminded Americans of what the Founding Fathers knew to be the chief threat to republican government, that power can corrupt fallible leaders. Within the psyches of political leaders, the grubby demons of greed and a lust for power compete with desires to serve and to do good. And, sometimes, the demons prevail. Above all, Watergate reaffirmed the oldest lesson of our political heritage: eternal vigilance is the price of liberty. American democracy could be lost someday simply because, the people, in their innocent carelessness, took it for granted.

POSTMORTEM

Henry Kissinger has written that Richard Nixon's biographer will require the skills of a historian and the literary talents of a dramatist. It is exceedingly difficult to render a balanced judgment of Richard Nixon's presidency. This complex and divided man rendered both great service and great harm to his nation. His was a long and distinguished public career. His presidency was perhaps the most significant since the great Franklin Roosevelt's. He was a bold and innovative diplomatist with major achievements: the historic opening to China, stabilizing relations with the Soviet Union and reducing the threat of nuclear war, eventually ending the disastrous war in Southeast Asia, and placing U.S. foreign policy worldwide on a sound, realistic basis. He ensured that the United States would continue to occupy the central role in world affairs. In the process of bringing about these historic accomplishments, Nixon achieved the stature of world statesman. His accomplishments in domestic policy are less impressive, but he restored a measure of social peace, wrestled energetically with economic problems, and supported some ecological causes. He proposed innovative solutions to welfare problems and arrested the decline of local government.

But, in the ultimate crisis of his political career, he strained the American system of constitutional government that he had sworn to defend, damaged the presidency, harmed the Republican Party, destroyed his public career, and tarnished his historical reputation. He was forced to resign in disgrace and fled into "exile" within his own country.

In the 1980s and 1990s, the American people's anger at Nixon had diminished. He achieved a partial rehabilitation. He acquired the stature of an elder statesman; presidents occasionally sought his advice on matters of foreign policy. He achieved respect as the author of several substantial books about politics and foreign policy. His memoir is the best and most revealing of any president in American history. At his death in April 1994, he was honored with a splendid state funeral in front of the magnificent Nixon presidential library located in his home town of Yorba Linda, California. Thousands of citizens braved driving rains to pay their final respects. Three presidents who spoke at his funeral praised his patriotic service to his nation, especially his foreign policy achievements. No one mentioned Watergate or the fact that his presidency had ended in humiliation and disgrace.

IMPORTANT EVENTS

1968	Nixon is elected president
1969	Secret bombing of Cambodia begins
1969	Warren Burger is appointed Chief Justice of the Supreme Court
1969	Vietnamization is announced
1970	Cambodia is invaded
1971	Lieutenant William Calley is convicted of war crimes
1971	The Pentagon Papers are published
1972	Nixon visits China
1972	Nixon visits the Soviet Union, signs SALT 1
1972	The Watergate break-in occurs
1972	Nixon is reelected by a landslide
1973	American involvement in the Indochina war ends
1973	Existence of Nixon's secret White House taping system is discovered
1973	The Supreme Court decides *Roe v. Wade*
1973	The Yom Kippur war takes place
1973	The first energy crisis occurs
1973	Agnew resigns the vice presidency
1974	Nixon resigns the presidency
1974	Gerald Ford assumes the presidency
1975	South Vietnam falls
1975	The Khmer Rouge seize power in Cambodia

BIBLIOGRAPHY

There have been several major studies of Richard Nixon undertaken in recent years. The best of these is Stephen E. Ambrose's masterful three-volume political biography. Roger Morris, a scholar who also worked for the National Security Council staff under both Johnson and Nixon, has written a major study of Nixon covering the years of his life and political career up to 1952 entitled *Richard Milhous Nixon: The Rise of an American Politician*. Another fine study is by Garry Wills, entitled *Nixon Agonistes*. The former president is himself the author of several books, the best of which is his autobiography, *RN: The Memoirs of Richard Nixon*, the finest presidential memoir ever done. The Nixon administration's foreign policy is analyzed by Henry Brandon in *The Retreat of American Power*. A critical view can be found in Tad Szulc's *The Illusion of Peace: Foreign Policy in the Nixon Years*. Henry Kissinger, Nixon's brilliant foreign policy adviser, has analyzed their policies in *Years of Upheaval*. For Nixon's Vietnam policies, see the relevant chapters of George Donelson Moss's *Vietnam: An American Ordeal*. The best historical study of Watergate is Stanley I. Kutler's *The Wars of Watergate*. Kutler sees Watergate as a reflection of the essence of Nixon's political career and presidency. See also the two books by *Washington Post* reporters Carl Berstein and Bob Woodward, *All the President's Men* and *The Final Days*. The best of many books written by men involved in the scandal is Harry R. Haldeman's *The Ends of Power*. Theodore H. White's *Breach of Faith: The Fall of Richard Nixon* attempts to explain the causes of the Watergate scandal.

CHAPTER 14

An Era of Limits

Vietnam and Watergate ushered in a time of troubles for Americans. They experienced ineffective presidential leadership, partisan squabbling, continuing social divisions, severe economic dislocations, energy crises, and international disorders. All these problems were compounded by a massive loss of faith in politics, especially among young people. They feared that the American system would not be able to maintain affluence at home, and they worried about declining American influence in the world. A social malaise settled over the land. Americans experienced a crisis of confidence, fearful that their leaders and institutions could not find solutions to their many, complex, and often interrelated problems. Many lost faith in themselves and in their institutions.

The decade of the 1970s was also characterized by a series of significant social and cultural transformations that confirmed both the pluralism and the volatility of American life. These changes often paralleled underlying technological, economic, and demographic developments that rapidly altered the contours of American society and changed the ways most Americans lived and worked. New attitudes toward sex, family, and work changed the nature of many important institutions. Many members of two significant groups, African Americans and women, maintaining the momentum generated by the movements of the 1960s, made dramatic gains in the 1970s in education and income. But at the same time, thousands of women and African Americans were taking advantage of new opportunities to achieve middle-class status, many other women and blacks remained locked into low-paying, low-status jobs, or slipped even further into the ranks of welfare dependency and poverty.

The most important development of the 1970s represented a historic shift in the direction of the American economy. The longest boom cycle in American history began during World War II and had continued, with occasional recessions, for thirty years, came to a halt during the early 1970s. The seemingly perpetual prosperity, fueled by a high growth rate, job creation, federal spending, innovative technology, and most of all by consumerism, stalled; to be replaced by the economic double whammy of "stagflation," which eroded purchasing power and lowered living standards for millions of American families. The apparent end of economic progress frustrated and bewildered Americans. Stagflation undermined their morale and robbed them of their sense of control over their destinies. For the first time since the Depression decade of the 1930s, millions of Americans regarded the future with fear and pessimism.

A FORD NOT A LINCOLN

The new president stood in dramatic contrast to his deposed predecessor. Gerald Ford was warm, open, and outgoing. A nation weary of war and political scandal appreciated his personal charm, modesty, and integrity as he reminded his fellow citizens that "I am a Ford, not a Lincoln." He came from the Midwest. He had represented Michigan's fifth district for thirteen consecutive terms until appointed vice president in 1973. He had risen through the ranks of the seniority system to become House Minority Leader in 1965. As president, Ford retained many of Nixon's advisers and tried to continue his policies.

Sensing the malaise of the nation in the wake of war and Watergate, Ford made "binding up the nation's wound" and restoring national confidence his top priorities. But a month after he took office, Ford granted former President Nixon a "full, free, and absolute" pardon for any crimes he may have committed while in office. Ford granted the pardon to spare the nation the divisive spectacle of putting a former president on trial. He insisted that there was no advance understanding between himself and Nixon. Whatever his intent, Ford's decision to pardon Nixon backfired. It ruined his chances for getting bipartisan support for his policies from the Democratic-controlled Congress. Despite his denials, many Americans suspected that Ford and Nixon had made a deal—Nixon had chosen Ford to replace Agnew with the understanding that if Nixon resigned or was removed from office, Ford would pardon him. Further, it was patently unfair to send underlings to jail for their parts in Watergate while the leader whose directives they followed went free. Most Americans believed that if Nixon had broken the law he should have to face trial like any other citizen. Ford appeared to be endorsing the dubious principle that the greater the power, the less the accountability. Ford's pardon of Nixon perpetuated the suspicions and resentments of Watergate that the new leader was trying to dispel, tied his presidency to that of his despised predecessor's, hurt his party in the 1974 elections, and may have cost him the 1976 election.

Ford generated further controversy when he established an amnesty program for the thousands of young men who had violated draft laws or deserted from the military during the Vietnam era. If they agreed to perform public service for one to two years, their prison terms were waived or reduced. Hawks condemned the plan as too lenient; doves denounced it as punitive. Another of Ford's efforts to bind up national wounds had had the opposite effect of reopening them.

The president also provoked another uproar when he selected Nelson Rockefeller as his vice president. During Rockefeller's Senate confirmation hearings, it was learned that he had given some of his vast personal wealth to officials prominent in Ford's administration, including Secretary of State Henry Kissinger, formerly a Rockefeller aide. These gifts and loans gave the appearance that a rich man was trying to buy the vice presidency. Rockefeller's confirmation was delayed and the credibility of the new administration harmed.

The 1974 midterm elections took place amidst an atmosphere of continuing political controversy and public mistrust, much of which had been perpetuated by Ford's own actions. The Democrats gained 43 seats in the House and 4 seats in the Senate, increasing their margins to 291 to 144 in the House and to 61 to 38 in the Senate. The Democrats also won most of the state and gubernatorial elections. More voters than ever before called themselves Independents and split their tickets, and only 38 percent of those eligible to vote went to the polls.

Shortly after the midterm elections, a Senate committee investigating CIA operations discovered that over the years it had been involved in numerous assassinations or attempted murders of foreign leaders including Fidel Castro in Cuba. A commission headed by Vice President Rockefeller found that the CIA had routinely kept citizens under surveillance and had conducted drug experiments on unwitting victims. The CIA had also engaged in illegal domestic espionage and compiled files on dissenters. Other investigations revealed that the FBI had also engaged in a variety of lawless actions including wiretapping, spying, burglary, blackmail, and sabotage. Former FBI director J. Edgar Hoover had conducted a personal vendetta against civil rights leader Dr. Martin Luther King, Jr. FBI agents ha-

President Gerald R. Ford.
Source: National Archives.

rassed King, spied on him and his associates, read his mail, tapped his phones, bugged his hotel rooms, and blackmailed him.

These discoveries of official lawlessness, most occurring during Nixon's presidency, confirmed that the CIA and FBI, in their obsessive pursuit of internal security, had repeatedly violated the constitutional rights of American citizens. In response, President Ford issued new directives providing for greater congressional oversight of CIA activities and restricting its covert operations. The Justice Department issued new guidelines for the FBI. The new FBI director, Clarence Kelly, publicly apologized to the American people for the past sins of the Bureau and pledged they would never recur.

ECONOMIC AND ENERGY WOES

While Americans learned more about official wrongdoing in Washington, their economy deteriorated. The inflation rate soared beyond 10 percent in 1974, spurred by wage hikes, increased consumer demand, budget deficits, and competition from the surging Japanese and Western European economies. The Ford administration, resorting to traditional conservative economic policy, attacked inflation by slowing down the economy with tight money. Tight money brought the worst downturn since the Great Depression of the 1930s. Some traditional U.S. mass production industries with inefficient methods of production, poor quality control, and high payroll costs struggled to compete with manufacturers in Europe and the Pacific Rim. American multinational corporations moved their manufacturing facilities overseas to take advantage of lower costs and cheap labor. The primary manufacturing industry of the U.S. economy, automobiles, lost a sizable portion of its domestic market to Japanese and German imports. Unemployment climbed to 7 percent by year's end and reached 9 percent in 1975, the highest since before World War II. Two years later, the inflation rate had dropped to 5 percent, but at the price of having 8 million workers unemployed.

In October 1973, an alarming new factor disrupted American economic life, the energy crisis, adding to both inflation and recession. It appeared suddenly when the Organization of Petroleum Exporting Countries (OPEC) embargoed oil shipments to the United States. The oil cutoff was initiated by Saudi Arabia and other Arab members of OPEC to protest U.S. support of Israel in its recent war with Egypt and Syria, and to force a settlement of the war favoring the Arabs. Americans experienced shortages of heating oil and power "brownouts." Impatient motorists formed long lines at gas pumps.

The energy crisis had been building for years; the OPEC embargo triggered it. American postwar growth and prosperity had been founded on cheap energy, increasingly derived from petroleum. U.S. domestic oil production began declining in 1969 while demand continued to rise. By 1970, America, with only 6 percent of the world's population, used over one-third of the world's energy. To meet the ever-increasing demand for oil, U.S. oil companies bought more and more imported oil. Daily consumption of imported oil rose from 12 percent in 1968 to

**Energy Crisis USA. . . .
Motorists line up to get
gas at a service station in
Los Angeles.** *Source:* National Archives.

36 percent by 1973. An increasing proportion of imported oil came from OPEC nations, and two-thirds of OPEC oil came from the Middle East. Oil companies became the mechanisms for maintaining the OPEC cartel since they refined the oil for U.S. markets. When OPEC shut off oil in October 1973, these companies reaped huge profits from the accompanying rise in oil prices.

The OPEC embargo was short-lived. Arab countries removed it after a few months and oil supplies returned to normal. But gasoline prices rose from 30¢ to 70¢ a gallon during that period and stayed there. Much higher energy prices became a permanent fact of U.S. economic life. Higher oil prices sent a large inflationary jolt coursing through all facets of the American economy because oil had seeped into the fabric of American life. Oil heated homes; it was synthesized into fibers and plastics; farmers used it for fertilizer, pesticides, and fuel; and it was crucial to all forms of transportation. Rising energy prices struck hardest at the older industrial centers of the Northeast and Great Lakes region, which had to import most of their energy. Factories constructed during the days of cheap energy proved wasteful and inefficient. Cutbacks in federal spending fell hardest on cities in these regions, given their shrinking tax bases, declining industries, and expensive social services. The severity of the fiscal crisis of the "rust belt" cities revealed itself in 1975 when New York City verged on bankruptcy.

Before he was forced to resign, Nixon had battled the energy crisis. He created the Federal Energy Office to formulate a national energy policy and to promote conservation. He proposed a plan called "Project Independence" to make America energy independent by 1980. It called for increasing domestic oil production by tapping Alaskan oil fields and accelerating offshore drilling; producing more natural gas, coal, and nuclear energy, extracting oil from shale deposits; and developing renewable energy sources. Project Independence made little progress.

With the lifting of the OPEC embargo and the return of normal supplies of oil, most people quickly forgot about the energy crisis, although they complained about the high price of gasoline for their cars. As Ford took office, America continued to import one-third of its daily oil requirements.

Ford tried to continue Nixon's energy program, but he encountered much opposition. Environmentalists opposed many features. Antinuclear groups opposed building additional nuclear power plants. Ford tried to deregulate domestic oil and natural gas prices only to be blocked by congressional Democrats who believed that deregulation would hurt low-income families and aggravate inflation. Congress enacted legislation in 1975 giving the president standby authority to ration gasoline, to create a strategic petroleum reserve, and to set mandatory fuel economy standards for new cars. Three years later, the United States still imported 40 percent of its daily oil requirements.

Conflicts between the conservative Republican president and the Democratic-controlled Congress hampered government effectiveness during Ford's tenure. He vetoed sixty-six bills enacted by Congress, including federal aid for education, a health care measure, a housing measure, and a bill to control strip mining. Congress enacted a few important measures, among them extending the Voting Rights Act of 1965 and increasing Social Security benefits. Congress also enacted measures over Ford's vetoes, including a $3 billion public service jobs bill to combat the recession.

FORD, KISSINGER, AND THE WORLD

Henry Kissinger, whom Ford inherited from former President Nixon, doubled as Secretary of State and head of the National Security Council, playing a major part in shaping foreign policy. As a political realist, Kissinger understood that U.S. economic and military power had suffered a relative decline in the world since the late 1960s and that America could no longer expect to dominate its allies in Europe, Latin America, and the Middle East. Kissinger had a major part in implementing U.S. Middle Eastern policy following a fourth Arab-Israeli war that began October 6, 1973. It started when Syria and Egypt both attacked, catching the Israelis off guard because they were observing Yom Kippur, the holiest Jewish holiday. Both sides sustained heavy losses, but America provided Israel with military support, while the Soviets replenished Arab armies.

The United Nations tried to work out a cease-fire formula. Before it became effective, Israeli armies advanced close to the Egyptian capital of Cairo. With Egypt near defeat, its leader, Anwar Sadat, invited both the United States and the Soviet Union to send troops to police a cease-fire. The Soviets accepted Sadat's proposal, but Washington, which did not want Soviet troops in the Middle East, refused it. The Soviets then announced their intention to send troops unilaterally. These actions brought the two superpowers to a point of direct confrontation. As the Soviets prepared to airlift troops to Egypt, the United States placed its armed forces on worldwide alert. These actions provoked the most dangerous U.S.–USSR conflict since the Cuban missile crisis.

The UN, backed by both the United States and the Soviet Union, defused the tense situation by creating a peacekeeping force excluding both American and Soviet forces. Kissinger, shuttling back and forth between Cairo and Jerusalem, persuaded the Egyptians and Israelis to accept a cease-fire. The cease-fire was the first of a series of Middle Eastern agreements facilitated by Kissinger's "shuttle diplomacy." The Suez Canal was reopened. The Arabs lifted their oil embargo. Egypt and Syria resumed diplomatic relations with the United States. Kissinger capped his Middle Eastern efforts in 1975 by arranging an important new Sinai agreement between Egypt and Israel. According to its terms, UN peacekeeping forces would remain and an early warning system would be set up in the Sinai to prevent future surprise attacks by either side. These Sinai Accords made possible the subsequent achievement of the Camp David agreements.

Ford and Kissinger tried to improve relations with China and the Soviet Union, but had little success. Ford visited China in 1975, but American support of Taiwan prevented his forging closer ties. At the time, China's leadership was changing. Rival factions of pragmatists and radicals vied for power as China's aged revolutionary leaders, Jou En-lai and Mao Zedong, passed from the scene. Any new diplomatic initiatives had to wait until a new leadership established control. Efforts to extend détente and forge a second SALT agreement with the Soviets failed. Negotiators got bogged down in technical details as advances in nuclear weapon technologies outstripped efforts to impose political controls. Another effort to extend détente brought Ford and the Soviet leader Leonid Brezhnev together with European leaders at Helsinki in August 1975. Both sides agreed to recognize the political boundaries dividing Eastern and Western Europe since the end of World War II. For the first time, the United States recognized the legitimacy of East Germany. For his part, Brezhnev agreed to ease restrictions of the right of Soviet Jews to emigrate. Kissinger's overtures to the Communists outraged conservatives within the Republican Party like presidential hopeful Ronald Reagan, who denounced both détente and Kissinger for trafficking with the Reds.

The Vietnam War ended in April 1975, when North Vietnamese forces overran the South and captured Saigon, two years after all U.S. forces had been withdrawn. President Ford tried to help the dying South Vietnamese regime, but Congress refused to enact his request for additional aid. About a month later, Cambodian Communists seized an American merchant ship, the *Mayaguez*, cruising near the Cambodian coast. Ford sent in a detachment of 350 Marines to rescue the ship and crew. Most Americans applauded the President's show of force at a time when Americans were feeling pushed around in Southeast Asia. During the final years of the U.S. involvement in Southeast Asia, Congress sought a greater role in the conduct of foreign policy and to reduce the power of the presidency. The War Powers Act, passed over President Nixon's veto in 1973, ordered the president to consult with Congress before sending U.S. forces into war.

An American soldier assisting a family fleeing Vietnam as the Communists take over April 30, 1975. *Source:* U.S. Army Photograph.

THE ELECTION OF 1976

As the 1976 election approached, Ford appeared politically vulnerable. President only by the grace of Nixon's appointment, he had proven to be an ineffective caretaker during his two years of office. He faced a powerful challenge from within Republican ranks from Ronald Reagan, the leader of a resurgent conservative movement. Democrats were confident that they could beat either man. A large field of Democratic contenders sought their party's nomination. Candidates included senators Henry Jackson and Frank Church, governors George Wallace and Jerry Brown, and Morris Udall, an Arizona congressman. The surprise of the 1976 Democratic race proved to be the sudden emergence of James Earl Carter, Jr., who called himself "Jimmy." Carter beat them all to capture the Democratic nomination. Carter was unknown outside his native Georgia, where he had served one term as governor. When he entered the first Democratic primary in New Hampshire, few observers took his candidacy seriously. "Jimmy *who?*" the voters asked. Carter took New Hampshire and was off and running. He waged a skillful primary campaign, capitalizing on the national backlash from Watergate.

He won a series of primary victories both north and south. His political style was earnest and folksy. His major pitch was the need for a leader untainted by the corruptions of Washington, an outsider who could restore integrity to government. People responded to the man and his message. When the Democratic convention opened in New York, Carter had more than enough votes to ensure a first-ballot nomination. He chose a midwestern liberal for his running mate, Senator Walter Mondale of Minnesota, and they ran on a platform attacking Ford's "government by veto" and Kissinger's "manipulative" foreign policy. Carter's capturing of the Democratic Party nomination in 1976 was one of the most remarkable achievements in modern American political history. His victory could only have happened within the context of post-Vietnam, post-Watergate massive disillusionment with politics as usual in this country.

Ford, meanwhile, was locked in a fierce struggle for the Republic nomination with Ronald Reagan, leader of the resurgent Republican Right. Ford adopted a centrist stance, projecting an image of a moderate leader healing the nation's wounds, promoting economic recovery, and keeping the nation at peace. His strategy worked initially. He beat Reagan decisively in the early primaries. But the former California governor kept hammering away. When the Sunbelt primaries came up in the spring, Reagan ran off a string of victories, surging ahead of Ford in the delegate count. Ford rallied with victories in several northern industrial states. Reagan countered with a big win in California. When the Republican convention assembled in Kansas City, the two candidates were so close that the winner would be the one who captured a majority of the few uncommitted delegates. Ford managed to win a close first-ballot nomination, but Reagan forced Ford to move Right in order to survive and influenced the drafting of a conservative platform. Ford chose a sharp-tongued conservative, Kansas Senator Robert Dole, to replace Rockefeller, who chose not to run again. Although Reagan endorsed Ford, many of his supporters did not. Ford led a divided party into battle against a Democratic party united behind Carter.

The presidential campaign turned out to be rather dull and unenlightening. Neither man made much impact on a wary electorate. Neither candidate stood out in a series of three televised debates. Carter appeared especially fuzzy on the issues. Ford ran on his record, which was unimpressive. Carter conducted a vaguely liberal, populistic, and moralistic campaign. A Baptist Sunday school teacher and "born-again" Christian, he promised his audiences, "I'll never lie to you," which inclined many skeptical voters to regard him as either a knave or a fool. He ran against the federal government, promising to tame Washington's "bloated, unmanageable bureaucracy." He pledged a government that is "as good and honest as are the American people."

When the contest started, the polls gave Carter a big early lead. Within six weeks, his waffling and Ford's attacks had eliminated it. On election eve, pollsters termed it too close to call. Carter managed a narrow victory, getting 41 million votes to Ford's 39 million. His winning margin in the electoral vote was 297 to 241. Carter carried the South, several border states, and some northern industrial states. He lost most of the Midwest and carried no state west of the Mississippi River. Black votes provided his margin of victory in the South. He also did well among traditional Democratic voters—labor, urban, Jewish, liberals, and intellectuals. Although the race for the White House was close, the congressional races were not. Carter's party ran much better than he did. Democrats retained their large majorities in both houses of Congress. Voter turnout continued low—only 53 percent of the electorate cast ballots.

Carter's victory suggested that a majority of voters shared his revulsion over abuses of power by Washington-based professional politicians. They were willing to entrust the reins of government to an inexperienced outsider from a southern village. Given a choice between "fear of the known and fear of the unknown," the citizenry opted for someone new who promised to tell the truth.

Carter's winning the Democratic nomination before the convention signaled an important new political reality; most states were now holding presidential primaries. The primary process opened up the nominating process to the mass of voters and reduced the importance of political parties. It also lengthened the campaigns, greatly increased their costs, and enhanced the role of television. Ford and Carter both accepted $22 million of federal funds to finance their fall campaigns and both renounced private fund-raising. They were the first presidential candidates to use new federal spending laws enacted following the Watergate disclosures of fund-raising abuses.

PRESIDENT "JIMMY"

The thirty-ninth President came to the White House via an improbable route. He grew up on a farm in the southwest Georgia village of Plains. His first career choice was the Navy. He graduated from the U.S. Naval Academy in 1946 and spent seven years in the nuclear submarine program. When his father died in 1953, Carter gave up his naval career and returned to Plains to take over the family business. By 1970, he had built up a prosperous enterprise based on raising and processing peanuts. Elected governor of Georgia in 1970, Carter proved an able administrator and moderate reformer. His chief accomplishment was to announce the end of racial discrimination in Georgia. He brought about a marked increase in the number of black state employees. From this modest political base, he forged the political strategies that brought him the presidency in 1976.

Carter possessed a keen intelligence, rigorous self-discipline, a capacity for sustained hard work, deep religious beliefs, and intense patriotism. He was one of the most conscientious, hardest-working chief executives the nation has ever had. He was a reflective, well-read man. There was a steely glint to his soft blue eyes. Behind the ready smile and informal manner lay a grimly serious personality. A private man, aloof, somewhat shy, he was driven by a powerful ambition to succeed, to leave his mark on the national scene.

One of Carter's most valuable political assets proved to be his wife, Rosalyn; she was attractive, strong, and politically shrewd. She made a dynamic First Lady, going well beyond the usual roles of hostess, ornament, and goodwill ambassador. She was her husband's principal adviser on many issues, a member of his inner circle. Not since Eleanor Roosevelt had a First Lady played such important political roles or achieved such power in her own right.

THE OUTSIDER GOES TO WASHINGTON

Carter came to office knowing that millions of Americans were still deeply suspicious of the political system. He strove from the outset to "deimperialize" the White House and to restore popular faith in national politics. He accepted phone calls from ordinary citizens, he hosted radio call-in shows, he appeared at local town meetings, and he even stayed overnight in citizens' homes. He also brought many previously excluded people into government. Of his 1,195 full-time federal appointments, 12 percent were women, 12 percent were black, and 4 percent Hispanic, far more coming from these historically disadvantaged backgrounds than any previous president's appointees. But Carter's populistic campaign style contradicted his managerial and technocratic approach to governing. As Bert Lance, his close friend and first budget director put it, Carter "campaigns liberal, but he governs conservative." Carter was the most conservative Democratic president since Grover Cleveland. His top priorities became slashing the size and cost of government.

Carter's policies also reflected the conservative mood that increasingly gripped the country by the late 1970s. More and more Americans repudiated 1960s-style liberalism, which they associated with foreign policy failures, inflationary domestic policies, oversized government, high taxes, and a generalized permissiveness and moral decline. For many Americans, liberalism no longer worked at home or abroad. The antigovernment, antispending inclinations of voters were expressed dramatically in California's 1978 election. An elderly real estate lobbyist, Howard Jarvis, led a successful taxpayer's revolt that slashed property taxes by two-thirds. National polls showed a large majority of Americans supported cuts in the costs of government. A 1978 poll revealed that conservatives outnumbered liberals by a ratio of more than two to one.

When Carter took office, the inflation rate stood at 6 percent and the unemployment rate at 8 percent. Carter had gotten political mileage during his campaign against Ford by attacking the incumbent's failure to solve these serious economic problems, labeling the combined total of inflation and unemployment rates the "misery index." He called the "misery index" of 14 intolerable and promised to reduce it. He first tried stimulating the economy to reduce unemployment by implementing Keynesian "pump priming" programs. Congress enacted a $6 billion local public works bill, an $8 billion public service jobs bill, tax cuts, and an increase in the minimum wage. Unemployment declined to 6 percent in two years.

But the inflation rate rose, back to 7 percent in 1977 and 10 percent in 1978. It zoomed to 12 percent in 1979 and 13 percent in 1980, the worst two years since World War I. Confronted with runaway inflation, Carter radically shifted his economic focus. He concentrated on attacking inflation, adopting fiscal restraints similar to his conservative predecessor. In 1979, he appointed Paul Volcker chairman of the Federal Reserve Board. Volcker immediately imposed severe monetary restrictions on the economy that drove interest rates to historic highs, pulling the economy into recession without immediately curbing inflation. The ensuing "stagflation" of 1979 and 1980 was far worse than it had been under either Nixon or Ford. In 1980, the "misery

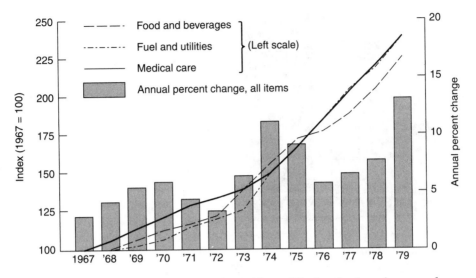

Inflation was the most serious economic problem afflicting the American people during the 1970s. Note that the cost of living, as measured by the consumer price index, nearly doubled between 1967 and 1979. *Source*: Moss, *Moving On*, p. 282.

index" had reached 21, a figure that Carter's Republican opponent in 1980, Ronald Reagan, would use against him with devastating effectiveness.

Declining productivity signaled another kind of economic rot. Productivity had increased an average of 3 percent per year between 1945 and 1965. During the 1970s, productivity only rose at an annual rate of 1 percent. As late as 1968, the American economy had been the most productive in the world; by 1980, it had slipped to the twentieth most productive. Energy problems added to America's economic difficulties. Despite the 1973 energy crisis, Americans continued to use more oil and to import a high proportion of their daily requirements throughout the 1970s. Domestic oil production continued to decline. In April 1977, Carter developed a comprehensive energy plan that he termed "the moral equivalent of war (MEOW)." But Congress did not respond to his leadership and the energy plan failed to pass. In 1979, a second oil crisis hit the deteriorating American economy when Iran cut off its oil exports after the fall of the Shah. Gasoline shortages again forced angry motorists to line up at the pumps. Carter responded to this second crisis with a phased deregulation of domestic oil prices to spur production. Oil deregulation immediately raised gasoline prices 50 percent (from 70¢ to over $1 per gallon) and increased oil company profits, some of which the government siphoned off in excise taxes.

President Carter, baffled by the failures of Americans to solve their serious economic and energy problems, invited 130 leaders from all walks of life to Camp David for ten days of meetings to determine what was wrong with the nation. From these intensive discussions, the president concluded that the nation was facing "a crisis of the spirit." In what proved to be his finest speech, he

Jimmy Carter. *Source:*
National Archives.

told Americans they faced a crisis of confidence that posed a fundamental threat to American democracy—they had lost faith in themselves and their institutions; they had lost faith in the future. Americans faced their mounting economic and energy difficulties with uncharacteristic passivity and pessimism. Where was the old American optimism and "can-do" spirit? Carter pleaded with his fellow countrymen to regain that lost confidence in themselves and their government.

Critics of the Carter administration suggested the nation faced a different problem than loss of national spirit—namely, the failure of presidential leadership. Carter had never been able to outgrow his outsider status. He never firmly grasped the reins of government, never asserted control over executive bureaucracies, and never established effective liaison with Congress. He failed to develop a consistent approach to public policy. He mastered the details of problems, but could never project a broad national vision or a sense of direction. He never learned to communicate effectively with the press or with the American people. His was a perpetually floundering, rudderless government that ultimately lost the trust and respect of most of the citizenry. At the time he made his "malaise" speech, his approval rating in the polls stood at 26 percent. Journalist Tom Wicker called Carter's administration the greatest failure since Herbert Hoover's performance during the Great Depression.

CARTER AND THE WORLD

Carter came to office with almost no background in foreign affairs. His only previous international experience came from having served on the Trilateral Commission, an association of businessmen, bankers, politicians, and intellectuals gathered from the United States, Japan, and European countries committed to strengthening economic ties among major free world nations. Carter recruited his two top foreign policy advisers from the commission, his Secretary of State, Cyrus Vance, a Wall Street lawyer, and his National Security Adviser, Zbigniew Brzezinski, a professor of international relations at Columbia.

Carter announced at the outset of his administration that he would make human rights the distinctive theme of his foreign policy; he said human rights will be "the soul of our foreign policy." The new president's emphasis on human rights expressed both his streak of Jeffersonian-Wilsonian idealism and his desire to move beyond the realm of Nixon-Kissinger realism. He wanted to reclaim the ideological high ground in the ongoing Cold War competition with the Soviet Union. Human rights espoused traditional American ideals and a noble cause, but proved in practice to be a difficult slogan to implement.

Carter's greatest diplomatic triumph occurred in the Middle East where he played a major role in achieving peace between Egypt and Israel. He built upon a foundation laid by Kissinger's shuttle diplomacy and the extraordinary actions taken by the Egyptian leader, Anwar Sadat. Sadat, perceiving that Egyptians could never dislodge the Israelis from the Sinai by force, offered them peace in exchange for the return of Egyptian lands. Sadat electrified the world when he went to Jerusalem in the fall of 1977. He told Israelis that any permanent agreement between Egypt and Israel must include Israeli withdrawal from the West Bank and the Golan Heights, a homeland for Palestinian Arabs, and recognition of the Palestine Liberation Organization (PLO) as their government.

Israeli Prime Minister Menachem Begin was willing to strike a bargain with Egypt on the Sinai, but he balked at the Palestinian issues. Negotiations between the two countries reached an impasse after six months. Carter then invited both leaders to Camp David for conferences. After two weeks of intense negotiations in which Carter was fully engaged, they achieved a framework of peace for the Middle East. Egypt agreed to a separate peace with Israel, and the Israelis agreed to return the Sinai region to Egypt. The Palestine issue was left vague. Both sides agreed to "self-governing" authority for the people inhabiting the West Bank, with their specific political status to be worked out in subsequent negotiations. Sadat and Begin signed the historic peace agreement, which ended more than thirty years of war between their countries on March 26, 1979, in Washington. Egypt and Israel then proceeded to normalize their relations.

President Carter hoped that these Camp David Accords would launch a new era of peace in the Middle East, but insurmountable obstacles persisted. No other Arab nation followed Egypt's lead. Negotiations on the Palestine question went nowhere. Israel refused to recognize the PLO or any other Palestinian political organization, and these groups all refused to recognize the results of any negotiations excluding them. The Palestine issue was further complicated by the outbreak of civil war in Lebanon between Muslim and Christian factions over PLO camps located in southern Lebanon. These camps served both as staging areas for terrorist raids into Israel and as targets of Israeli reprisals.

**The Signing of the Camp David Accords. . . . President Carter looks
on as Israeli Prime Minister Menachem Begin (to Carter's left) and
Egyptian President Anwar Sadat (to Carter's right) sign the historic
pact March 26, 1979, at a formal ceremony held on the North lawn
of the White House.**   *Source*: National Archives.

Carter also had some diplomatic successes in Latin America. In April 1978,
Carter persuaded the Senate to ratify two treaties turning the Panama Canal over
to Panama by the year 2000. These treaties permitted the gradual phasing out of
the last vestiges of U.S. colonialism in Central America. The United States reserved
the right to intervene to keep the canal open and also retained priority of passage
in the event of a foreign crisis. The treaties protected U.S. interests and removed a
source of resentment for Panamanians and other Central American nationalists.

Elsewhere in Latin America, Carter changed U.S. policies, usually in the name
of human rights. He withdrew support for a tyrannical rightist dictatorship in Chile
that Ford and Kissinger had backed. In February 1978, he cut off military and economic aid to the Nicaraguan dictator, Anastasio Somoza. Deprived of aid, Somoza
was soon overthrown by revolutionaries calling themselves Sandinistas. The United
States promptly extended a $75 million aid package to the new left-wing government
containing strong Marxist elements. In El Salvador, Marxist guerrillas, assisted by the
Sandinistas, began a civil war against the government. The rightist government
fought back brutally. The United States suspended aid to the Salvadoran government
following the murder of three American nuns by government troops.

In the Far East, Carter completed the process Nixon had begun with his historic opening to China in 1972. Since that time, both America and China had been
moving toward normalizing relations. Carter wanted to use good relations with

China as a lever to pry cooperation out of the Soviet Union. American business-men eagerly anticipated tapping into China's consumer economy of 1 billion people. The two nations established normal relations with an exchange of ambas-sadors in 1979.

United States relations with black Africa improved during Carter's tenure. He appointed Andrew Young, a black minister and former civil rights activist, to be the U.S. ambassador to the United Nations. President Carter made a successful trip to Liberia and Nigeria in 1978. Good relations with Nigeria were especially im-portant. It was the richest, most populous black African nation and the second-largest foreign supplier of oil to the United States.

THE DECLINE OF DÉTENTE

Détente had already begun to decline under Ford and Kissinger, and it continued to decline during Carter's presidency. Carter's diplomatic efforts toward the So-viet Union were hindered by his inexperience. Influenced initially by Secretary of State Cyrus Vance, Carter sent what he intended to be a friendly signal to the So-viets: He announced his intention to withdraw U.S. troops from Korea. Far from responding in kind, the Soviets took Carter's friendly words and gestures as signs of weakness; the Soviets became more aggressive. Escalating their arms buildup, they extended their influence in Africa using Cuban soldiers as proxies, and in-creased their military forces stationed in Cuba. The president had hoped to achieve quick ratification of SALT II, but he angered the Soviet leaders by proposing addi-tional cuts in the two nations' strategic arsenals. His talk of human rights and granting of full diplomatic recognition to China further annoyed the Soviets. It took years before SALT II negotiators could complete their work. The treaty lim-ited both sides to 2,400 nuclear launchers and 1,320 MIRVs and was intended to further stabilize the arms race.

SALT II also encountered strong opposition within the Senate. The Chief senatorial critic was liberal cold warrior Henry "Scoop" Jackson, who insisted that the proposed agreement allowed the Soviets to retain strategic superiority in several weapons categories. Other critics of SALT II were uncomfortable with the fact that the treaty acknowledged that the Soviets had achieved nuclear parity with the United States, a reality that they interpreted as symbolizing the relative decline of U.S. power. Some liberal senators were unhappy with SALT II because it did not eliminate key weapons systems such as the huge Soviet land-based ICBMs and the new American cruise missiles. Carter himself lost faith in SALT II and did not press the Senate for ratification. Instead, he persuaded NATO allies to agree to install new Pershing II missiles in Western Europe to counter the SS-20 intermediate-range missiles that the Soviets were installing in Eastern Europe. Installing these weapons in Europe represented a major escalation of the nuclear arms race.

While the Senate was debating the merits of SALT II, in December 1979, 85,000 Soviet troops invaded Afghanistan to suppress a Muslim rebellion against a faltering Marxist regime. Alarmed, President Carter called the Soviet invasion "the most serious threat to world peace since the Second World War." Carter canceled grain shipments to the USSR, suspended high-technology sales to the Soviets, and ordered U.S. athletes to boycott the Olympics to be held in Moscow the following summer. He also increased military spending and removed restrictions on CIA covert operations. He withdrew SALT II from Senate consideration and proclaimed the Carter Doctrine for Southwest Asia. Calling the Persian Gulf a vital U.S. interest, he declared that the United States would repel "by any means necessary" an attack in that region by outside forces. Carter's hard line toward Moscow reversed U.S. policies toward the Soviet Union that went back to the Kennedy years. Ironically, the man who began his presidency espousing kind words for the Soviets killed détente and resuscitated the Cold War.

DEBACLE IN IRAN

It was in the Persian Gulf region that America suffered a major foreign policy disaster that humiliated President Carter and contributed to his political downfall. Iran was America's major ally in the Persian Gulf area. It played a key role in containing the Soviet Union. It was a major supplier of top-grade oil, and Iranians annually purchased billions of dollars worth of American arms. The Shah, whom a CIA covert operation had helped restore to power in 1953, permitted the intelli-

National defense outlays. 1945–1980. *Source: Historical Statistics of the United States. Colonial Times to 1970,* and *Statistical Abstract of the United States, 1980.*

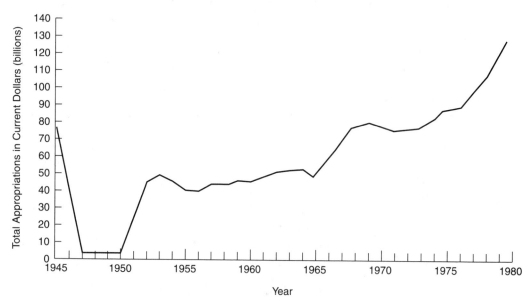

gence agency to station electronic surveillance equipment along Iran's border with the Soviet Union. Tens of thousands of Iranian students attended U.S. colleges and universities. American oil companies supplied the state-owned Iranian oil industry with equipment and technicians and shared in its profits. Iran was a vital U.S. interest, much more important than Korea or Vietnam had ever been. On the surface, Iran and the United States were best friends when Carter took office.

Beneath the surface, Iran in the late 1970s seethed with anti-Shah and anti-American fervor. Only the Shah and a ruling elite were genuinely pro-American. Carter, in contradiction of his human rights policy and unaware of the tensions in Iran, traveled to Iran in late 1977 to pay tribute to the Shah. At a state banquet held in his honor, President Carter toasted the Shah for "the admiration and love your people give to you." He called Iran "an island of stability in one of the most troubled areas of the world." The CIA station chief in Teheran issued a report in 1978 stating that Iran was not even near a revolutionary situation. U.S. intelligence operatives were blind to the faults of the Shah's corrupt, oppressive regime, and equally blind to the existence of revolutionary forces poised to destroy it.

The assault on the Shah was led by fundamentalist Islamic clergy who were intent on replacing Iran's modern, Westernized state with an Islamic republic. Their leader was an aged religious fanatic, Ayatollah Ruholla Khomeini. From exile in France in 1978, Khomeini ordered his legions to demonstrate, to disrupt the economy, to do anything to create chaos in order to force the Shah to abdicate. Carter initially dismissed Khomeini's revolution, assuming the Shah would suppress it. Carter watched in disbelief as Iran's oil production stopped and its economy ground to a halt. The Iranian army, forbidden by the Shah to fire upon the rioters for fear it would ruin the chances of his son succeeding him, was demoralized. On January 16, 1979, the Shah fled his country. Khomeini returned to Iran to a frenzied hero's welcome from revolutionary crowds. One of the most bizarre events of modern times had occurred. A virtually unarmed people led by clergymen had overthrown one of the world's most powerful rulers.

U.S. leaders, thinking in customary Cold War terms, did not know how to deal with a man who denounced both the United States and the Soviet Union with equal vehemence. Fearing Soviet intrusion into Iran and the loss of a crucial source of Western oil, Carter tried to establish normal relations with the new Iranian government. That proved impossible. Khomeini, who called the United States the "Great Satan," refused all American overtures.

Meanwhile, President Carter allowed the Shah, who was suffering from terminal cancer, to enter the United States for medical treatment. In retaliation, on November 4, 1979, Iranian militants overran the U.S. embassy in Teheran and took fifty-three Americans hostage. Khomeini approved the action, which violated the principle of diplomatic immunity observed by all nations. Carter retaliated by ordering the fifty thousand Iranian students within the United States to report to the nearest immigration office. Any found in violation of their visas were deported. He also froze all Iranian assets in the United States, suspended arms sales, and clamped a boycott on all U.S. trade with Iran.

Carter made return of the hostages his number-one priority, which it remained for the rest of his presidency. The hostage crisis dominated U.S. foreign policy for the next fourteen months. The media gave the crisis extensive coverage, keeping it uppermost in the public eye. For months, American officials negotiated futilely for release of the hostages with a series of Iranian governments, but no Iranian leader could acquire the necessary stable authority.

Six months after the hostages were taken, Carter severed diplomatic relations with Iran and authorized a military operation to attempt a rescue. He had previously resisted any suggestions to use force to attempt a rescue because he feared the hostages would be killed. The rescue effort failed because of bad luck, poor leadership, equipment malfunctions, and accidents. The humiliating failure reinforced the popular image in this country of Carter as an irresolute bumbler. The failed rescue attempt also symbolized the impotence of the United States as seen in its inability to protect its citizens against terrorism.

Prospects for resolving the hostage crisis improved in late 1980. The ailing Shah died in July. On September 22, Iraq suddenly invaded Iran and provoked a full-scale war between the two nations. In October, Carter offered to release frozen Iranian assets and to resume normal relations and trade with Iran in exchange for release of the hostages. On November 4, Ronald Reagan was elected president. Khomeini was responsive to the U.S. offer. He needed money for the war with Iraq, and he now had another cause around which to rally support for the revolution. He also feared that the new president might take stronger action. On January 21, 1981, Carter's last day in office, Iran agreed to release the hostages in exchange for the return of $8 billion of Iranian assets. The hostages came home 444 days after their capture.

THE ELECTION OF 1980

As the 1980 election approached, Carter was clearly in deep political trouble. His "misery index," the sum of the rate of inflation plus the unemployment rate, was much higher than when he ran against Ford in 1976. He had failed to fulfill most of his campaign promises. Above all, there was the daily embarrassment of the hostages. Carter had to fight off a primary challenge from Senator Edward "Ted" Kennedy. At the outset of his bid, Kennedy had a big lead over Carter in the polls. But once the battle began, his popularity nose dived. His automobile accident at Chappaquidick on Martha's Vineyard, Massachusetts, in 1969 in which a young woman lost her life continued to dog Kennedy, reviving old doubts about his character and judgment. His old-fashioned liberal philosophy was out of sync with the times. Carter easily deflected Kennedy's challenge. He was renominated on the first ballot.

The Republicans entered the 1980 presidential race brimming with confidence. Many candidates entered the race for the Republican nomination, but from the outset the clear choice of most of the party faithful was the old right-wing war horse, Ronald Reagan. Of the others, only George Bush showed any strength in the primaries. Reaganites controlled the Republican convention and pushed through a conservative platform calling for deep tax cuts, a balanced budget, large increases in defense spending, constitutional amendments banning abortions and restoring prayer in public schools, and opposition to the Equal Rights Amendment. Reagan chose Bush for the vice-presidential slot after failing to get former President Ford for the position.

A third-party candidate joined the race, John Anderson, running as an Independent. He had no organization, no constituency, nor did he have many issues that set him apart from the major candidates. He offered the electorate his self-proclaimed integrity and competence. He qualified for federal election funds, and his campaign received extensive media coverage. Anderson attracted mainly Democratic voters turned off by Carter's performance, although his candidacy had no bearing on the outcome of the election.

Reagan was favored to win when the presidential campaign began in August. But he made several incorrect statements concerning important issues that conveyed the impression of being dangerously out of touch with the times. Within a month, Carter had caught up. Sensing an advantage, Carter attacked Reagan personally. He accused Reagan of racism, war-mongering, and raised the question of his age. At sixty-nine, Reagan was the oldest major party candidate ever to seek the presidency. But Carter's attacks backfired because voters resented them. Polls taken at the end of September showed Reagan back in the lead.

Reagan attacked Carter's handling of the economy at a time of historically high "stagflation." He attacked Carter's handling of foreign policy at a time when the world was especially unstable and when the hostages were in Iranian hands. Carter, hoping to salvage his failing campaign, challenged Reagan to debate him on television. Carter was confident that his detailed knowledge of the issues would expose Reagan as a windy fraud. Reagan agreed to one debate, which took place in Cleveland's Convention Center on October 28.

It was the best of the televised presidential debates. The panelists chose excellent questions about major issues. The candidates were evenly matched through the early rounds of questioning. Then Carter, responding to a question about nuclear arms control, said that he had consulted with his thirteen-year-old daughter, Amy, about the important issues of the campaign. His answer unintentionally suggested to the vast television audience that the president of the United States relied on the advice of a child when considering important policy matters. Reagan scored impressively when he responded to Carter's attacks on his record on Medicare. Using his actor's skills, Reagan shook his head ruefully, saying, "There you go again;" then, in the manner of a parent correcting an erring child, he firmly set the record straight. In terms of content, the debate was a draw. On image and personality, Reagan won decisively. In ninety minutes, he had erased the image of him that Carter had been projecting throughout the campaign, the image of Reagan as a combination scrooge and mad bomber. In the debate, Reagan came across as a firm, genial leader who would never push the nuclear button in panic or anger. He sealed Carter's fate when he closed the debate by asking the huge television audience a series of rhetorical questions: Are you better off than you were four years ago? Is America as respected throughout the world as it was four years ago? Are we as strong as we were four years ago?

A close contest had been turned into a rout for Reagan. He got 44 million votes to Carter's 35 million and Anderson's 5.7 million. Reagan swept the election with 489 electoral votes to Carter's 49, with zero for Anderson. The Republicans gained thirty-three seats in the House. The most surprising outcome of the 1980 election was the Republican reconquest of the Senate for the first time since 1954. Republicans gained 12 senatorial seats, giving them fifty-three, the largest Republican total since 1928. Reagan shattered the Democratic coalition that had elected Carter in 1976. He got nearly half the labor vote. He carried blue-collar voters, middle-income voters, the Catholic vote, the ethnic vote, and the southern vote. He carried all the populous northern industrial states. He split the Jewish vote and got a third of the Hispanic vote. Only African American voters remained faithful to Carter.

The vote revealed two cleavages among voters. African Americans voted 90 percent for Carter; whites voted 56 percent for Reagan. This stark racial division suggested politics during Reagan's presidency could become racially polarized. There was another division among voters. For the first time in the sixty years since women got the vote, a gender gap appeared in the electoral results. Whereas 56 percent of men voted for Reagan and only 36 percent for Carter; only 47 percent of women voted for Reagan and 45 percent for Carter. Reagan's opposition to abortion and the ERA, plus his aggressive foreign policy rhetoric alienated women voters. Many working women, struggling to cope with precarious economic circumstances, perceived that Reagan did not represent their interests and feared that he might call for Congress to eliminate government programs on which they and their families depended.

Some analysts read the 1980 election as a harbinger of a new conservative Republican majority coalition. More saw it as the rejection of an ineffective leader who could not control inflation or retrieve the hostages. The main issue apparently was Reagan himself. Could he be a safe replacement for the discredited incumbent? Many people had their doubts. They thought Reagan too old, too uninformed, too conservative, and too dangerous—until the debate. Reagan's adept performance in that forum turned a close election into a landslide. Reassured, people voted for Reagan by the millions.

A DEMOGRAPHIC PROFILE

The Census Bureau reported that there were 205 million Americans in 1970, 215 million in 1975, and 227 million by 1980. Regionally, southern and western states accounted for 90 percent of that population increase. Many northeastern and midwestern states showed little or no growth, and several lost population. Population trends that had first appeared in this country after World War II continued. The Sunbelt regions, stretching from South Carolina to Southern California, remained

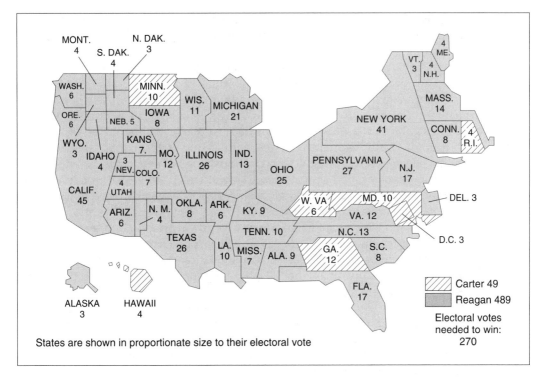

The electoral vote, 1980.   *Source*: Moss, *Moving On,* p. 292.

the dynamic centers of the nation's technological innovation, economic growth, and population increase. The expanding population, productivity, and wealth of the Sunbelt led to increased political clout in Washington. Political leaders including Senator Barry Goldwater, presidents Lyndon Johnson and Richard Nixon were products of Sunbelt politics. Ronald Reagan, the leader of the conservative revival, elected president in 1980, was also a product of Sunbelt politics.

Two additional demographic shifts with profound social implications occurred during the 1970s—the birthrate fell and human longevity increased. Twentieth-century birthrates peaked in 1947 at 26.6 live births per thousand and tumbled to 18.1 per thousand in 1975. Low birthrates meant that adults were not bearing enough children to replace themselves and only expanded immigration prevented long-term U.S. population decline. The steep drop in birthrates reflected several factors at work. The most important of these included the development of the birth control pill, the legalization of abortions, and the changing attitudes and values toward having children among women. Increasing longevity derived from advances in medicine and nutrition. Doctors perfected cures for some forms of degenerative diseases such as heart disease and cancer. But the most important causes of rising longevity were reductions in the infant mortality rate and the childhood death rate.

By 1975, average longevity in America had reached 73.1 years. The fastest-growing age group comprised people age seventy-five and older. Declining birthrates and expanding longevity combined to produce an aging American population. The median age of the U.S. population reached thirty years as of April 1, 1980, making America one of the oldest societies in the world.

Census data also showed that the traditional American household comprising a nuclear family of four declined during the 1970s. Nearly half the households added in the 1970s consisted of persons living alone or with nonrelatives. Declining birthrates, declining marriage rates, high divorce rates, households occupied by unmarried couples, households occupied by single-parent families, and the existence of millions of men and women living alone all suggested that household arrangements in America increasingly reflect the sociological diversity that has become America's most salient characteristic.

By the late 1970s, one of the most rapidly growing population segments comprised the "thirty-somethings," the advance wave of baby boomers. This group received much media attention, particularly the better-educated "Yuppies" among them. Yuppies were upwardly mobile, affluent young Americans earning $40,000 or more per year. Having few or no children, Yuppie couples often held two high-paying jobs. Merchants and advertisers catered to their large disposable incomes and lifestyle preferences based on buying expensive homes, cars, and clothes; dining in expensive restaurants; and taking costly vacations. Yuppies tended to embrace fashionably conservative politics and Social Darwinian ethics. Their lives could be defined in two words: careerism and consumerism.

But Yuppies did not represent the norm. According to census data, of the 78 million baby boomers, only 5 percent had incomes of $40,000 or more in the late 1970s. The median income for baby boomers in 1977 was $16,000, below the national average. The fundamental problem baby boomers faced was one of demographics: too many people chasing too few opportunities. Opportunities for baby boomers were also curtailed by the energy crisis and high inflation of the late 1970s and early 1980s. Further, the annual growth rate of the American economy averaged a sluggish 1.6 percent per annum during the 1970s and long-term unemployment rates were the highest since the 1930s. Baby boomers as a whole were less upwardly mobile than their parents, the first such group in America since the generation that came of age during the Great Depression of the 1930s. Never has a generation of young Americans had to work so hard for so little. Baby boomers could be characterized as victims—victims of advertisers, of their own unrealistic expectations, of demographic trends, of energy crises, and, above all, stagflation.

ECONOMIC STASIS

During the thirty-year boom cycle lasting from the early 1940s to the early 1970s, Americans had enjoyed unprecedented prosperity. Real per capita family income doubled, and the GDP more than doubled during those three decades of strong economic growth. The steadily expanding economy and rising living standards over a long period of time had convinced most Americans that prosperity was perpetual. Americans also believed that economic progress would in time eradicate poverty from the land. But during the early 1970s, stagflation replaced perpetual growth, creating a set of economic circumstances that threatened to erode both prosperity and faith in economic progress.

Signs of decline had first appeared in 1968. President Johnson's failure to raise taxes to pay for the Vietnam War while continuing to fund expensive Great Society reform measures at home increased government deficits and jacked up the inflation rate. During Nixon's presidency, both the deficits and the rate of inflation increased. In 1972, the budget deficit reached $40 billion and the rate of inflation soared to 8 percent.

During the early 1970s, the declining U.S. economy was also showing the effects of strong foreign competition. Rebuilt after having been destroyed during World War II, the industrial economies of West Germany and Japan were more productive than the older U.S. industries. U.S. shares of many world markets declined. Within America, many industries lost large shares of the domestic market to their foreign competitors. In 1970, about 10 percent of new cars sold in America were imported; by 1980, that figure had reached 30 percent.

Inflation, deficits, and loss of both domestic and export markets combined to create a serious balance of payment problem by 1972 that threatened to undermine the value of the dollar. When the Nixon administration devalued the dollar by severing it from gold, this action unleashed an orgy of gold speculation in the world that drove the price of gold from $35 an ounce to over $800 and added to the inflationary burden of American consumers. When the Nixon administration increased wheat sales to the Soviet Union to reduce the American trade deficit, food prices in this country rose sharply.

In geopolitical terms, the U.S. defeat in Vietnam signaled that U.S. hegemony in the world had ended. In economic and financial terms, the declining U.S. position in the world economy likewise signaled that the era of American dominance had ended. The OPEC embargo that kicked in during October 1973 compounded American economic difficulties, added to the inflation rate, and highlighted the dangers of continued dependency on foreign sources of oil. Yet during the 1970s, America became more dependent on foreign sources of oil. The bill for oil imports in 1970 was $5 billion. By 1980, it was in excess of $90 billion! The huge rise in the cost of imported oil was another dramatic sign of American economic decline in the world. It also served as a potent reminder that America no longer controlled its own economic destiny. The American economy had become increasingly connected to the emerging world economic order.

Economic woes continued throughout the 1970s for millions of American families. Industrial productivity stagnated. Living standards declined. During the 1950s, American living standards had been the wonder of the modern world. During the 1970s, American living standards fell below those of several European countries. Stagflation became an integral part of the American way of life, eroding both living standards and American confidence in its economic system.

The struggles of millions of American families for economic survival during the 1970s were exacerbated by structural trends that threatened the economic foundations of American middle-class society. As the economy became based more and more on high-tech service and information-oriented industries, the number of jobs that provided middle-class incomes declined. A service economy employs millions of clerical workers, sales clerks, waiters, bartenders, cashiers, and messengers. Wages for these jobs are comparatively low. While millions of new service-sector jobs were created during the 1970s, the number of higher-paying manufacturing jobs decreased.

During the 1970s, millions of factory jobs disappeared because of declining productivity, cutbacks in capital spending, and because production work became increasingly automated. Trade unions lost hundreds of thousands of members to automation and to declines caused by foreign competition in the steel, rubber, auto, and other manufacturing industries. The manufacturing jobs that disappeared during the 1970s tended to be skilled jobs from middle-income spectra. These displaced workers usually could not find alternative employment that offered comparable pay and fringe benefits. Their options were early retirement, if they could afford it, or to take jobs in the rapidly expanding service sectors of the economy. But most of these service jobs were low-skill, low-paying jobs with minimal opportunities for advancement or for a career. In any case, most of these new service sector jobs went to women, minorities, and youngsters. The fastest-growing sector of the service economy in the 1970s, which carried into the 1980s, was the fast food industry. McDonald's became the nation's largest employer. During the 1970s, the fast food industry added workers faster than manufacturing lost them, at wages that averaged one-third as much.

There were other signs of economic decline during the 1970s. Real income declined 15 percent from 1973 to 1980 in this country. By 1980, working-class-family purchasing power had fallen back to 1960 levels. Meanwhile the inflation engine drove housing and new car prices upward. The median price of new single-family homes doubled during the decade. Stagflation priced the American dream out of reach of young, working-class, and lower-middle-class families. The 1970s appeared to reverse the social and economic trends of the 1950s. There was a wholesale loss of faith in economic progress, in the notion that the next generation of Americans inevitably would be better off than their parents. During the 1970s, millions of families faced what they had been led to believe could never recur—economic retrogression, the first since the 1930s.

For generations, Americans had been sustained by their belief in economic individualism: Talent, initiative, and hard work generated upward mobility and economic security. It enabled men (and women) to provide for their families and ensured that their children would have a better life than they. But during the era of limits, faith in the Protestant ethic was eroded. The question for millions of young people became how many could share in the dream, and for how many would America be more of a nightmare than a dream? Old men evoked the promise of American life, young people had to struggle harder than ever to achieve it. Millions of Americans could not find steady work in the 1970s. Millions who worked found not affluence but subsistence. New technologies consumed more good jobs than they created. The American myth of success asserted that anyone could make it to the top if he or she tried hard enough. Statistical reality suggested something else in postindustrial America. Where abilities were about equal, the chances of a child from an upper-income family making it to the top of his profession was 27 times more likely than a child from a low-income family. For millions of young people, the struggle was not to reach the top, but to not fall any lower. Millions of middle-class youngsters could not realistically expect to earn as much, to own as much, and to be as successful as their parents. American professional mobility appears to have peaked in the mid-1960s and has been declining relatively since. Ironically, at a time when racist and sexist barriers to advancement were shrinking and the American dream was open to all Americans for the first time, there was declining mobility. In an era of limits, declining economic opportunity shrunk the dream.

CARS AND COMPUTERS

Despite stagflation and energy crises, Americans during the 1970s continued their love affair with the automobile. The car culture was alive and well in America during the era of limits. Automobile registrations reached 90 million in 1970 and 118 million in 1980. Millions of Americans purchased automobiles manufactured in Europe and Japan during the 1970s. High-performance small sports cars, pickups, and vans became more popular. Consumers became more value-conscious and safety conscious; manufacturers responded by offering their customers far greater choices of vehicle than had been available previously. The application of new technologies meant that 1970s automobiles were more aerodynamically designed, fuel-efficient, safer, and much easier to handle than the cars of the 1950s and 1960s had been. 1970s automobiles were also much more expensive and, especially the American-made cars, much more prone to break down.

Automobiles continued to be the primary means of intercity travel in the United States during the 1970s, although commercial airlines did increase their share of the travelers' market, from about 5 to 10 percent. Despite sizable increases in their business, most domestic airlines found themselves in serious financial difficulties during the late 1970s. Most of their financial difficulties derived from the deregulation of the airline industry implemented during the Carter presidency. Several well-known airlines went out of business, including Eastern and Braniff.

Deregulation of the airlines probably created more problems than it solved. In the short term, passengers obviously benefited from the far greater variety of flights offered at low prices generated by the new era of cutthroat competition. In the long run, deregulation created conditions reminiscent of the era of cutthroat competition in the railroad industry of a hundred years ago: Weaker competitors were driven to bankruptcy and either forced to shut down or be absorbed by the stronger airlines. Serious questions of reliability and safety have also been raised.

The most dramatic technological innovations of the 1970s were all connected with the computer revolution. America was computerized during the 1970s. There were approximately six thousand computers in use in this country in 1972; by 1980, there were tens of thousands, and the number was expanding exponentially every year. The agent of revolution was the microcomputer. Use of microcomputers enhanced the abilities of individuals working in a wide variety of fields to calculate, sift through, and retrieve information. They could also build statistical models and process words. The key invention that brought forth the microcomputer was Ted Hoff's perfection of the microprocessor, or computer chip, in 1972. Hoff was a young engineer on the staff at Intel Corporation when he designed the world's first microprocessor that started the revolution in electronic technology. The computer revolution made possible the information revolution of the 1970s and 1980s that transformed the way America worked.

The first personal computers were marketed in the mid-1970s. In California's Silicon Valley, a suburban area located about 50 miles south of San Francisco, dozens of small computer companies found themselves on the cutting edge of revolution. In 1976, two young men, Steven Wozniak, a computer genius, and Steve Jobs, who possessed great entrepreneurial talents, opened a small business in a garage they rented for $50 a month. Wozniak designed and Jobs sold small, inexpensive personal computers. They called their fledgling company Apple. Sales were slow at first, nobody appeared much interested in a small personal computer. Sales picked up in the late 1970s; in 1985, Americans bought 6 million PCs. By the mid-1980s, Apple had become a multibillion dollar business; Wozniak and Jobs were rich beyond their wildest dreams.

NEW IMMIGRANTS

Because the Immigration Act of 1965 abolished the discriminatory national origins system dating back to the 1920s, there has been both a large increase in immigration and a significant shift in the sources of immigrants. Most of the millions of immigrants who have come to the United States in the 1970s, 1980s, and 1990s have been Asians and Latin Americans. Mexico furnished the most legal immigrants, and the most illegal ones as well. Along with Mexicans came Cubans, Puerto Ricans, and Central Americans, particularly people from El Salvador and Nicaragua. Some of these new arrivals were fleeing religious and political oppression, but most of them came for the same reasons that have always attracted newcomers to America—opportunities for a good job and a better life for their families that were not available in their homelands.

The United States, true to its ancient heritage, remained one of the few countries in the world freely welcoming millions of newcomers from foreign lands. But many native-born Americans were alarmed by the flood of poor immigrants arriving annually, especially the "illegals" who came mostly from Mexico through a porous membrane called the United States–Mexican border. They feared that these people would take jobs from American workers, lower wages and living standards, overload welfare and school systems, and become an underclass of poor people amidst an affluent society.

Another problem posed by elements in the Hispanic American population, which, fueled by large-scale immigration from Mexico and other Hispanic countries, is growing at more than twice the rate of the general population, is the ancient question of assimilation. By the year 2000, if present growth rates continue, Hispanic Americans will compose the largest minority population group within the United States. This demographic trend worries many native-born Americans who focus on the fact that Hispanics have often formed their own communities, or "barrios," where they can get along quite well without having to speak or write English. Some Hispanics also insist that their children be taught in Spanish-speaking or bilingual schools. The Supreme Court has authorized bilingual instruction in public schools.

Spokesmen for the native-born population have argued that the existence of large, Spanish-speaking populations clustered in southern California, southern Florida, the Southwest, and sections of New York and Chicago pose a threat to national unity and to the political cohesiveness of the American system. Hispanic spokesmen insist on their rights to have their children educated as they see fit. They also insist on retaining their language and identity as a distinct ethnic group within a pluralistic society.

A Mexican American journalist, Richard Rodriquez, has written of the need for Mexican Americans and all other Spanish-speaking citizens of the United States to learn English in order to realize their full opportunities, and he accepts, as a painful necessity, the loss of some parts of the traditional Hispanic culture and the comfort it provided. It is the price exacted for full participation in American life, a price he believes individuals from all immigrant groups must pay.

After Hispanics, Asians have furnished the largest supply of newcomers. They have come mainly from Hong Kong, Taiwan, China, Vietnam, Korea, Japan, and the Philippines. Their numbers boosted by large-scale immigration, the Asian American population has doubled in the past decade, from 2 million to more than 4 million people. Asians are among the most upwardly mobile population groups within American society. Seventy-five percent of Asian Americans have graduated from high school. One-third of Asian American adults have four or more years of college, twice the rate for whites. In the economic sphere, data from the 1980 census show that the Asian American median annual income was more than $2,000 above the white median annual income.

Success has not come easy for Asian Americans. Historically, they have been the victims of exclusion, prejudice, discrimination in various forms, and even of violence. And, not all have achieved success. Many recent Asians immigrants remain mired in poverty, alienated from the mainstream of American life, and tempted by vice and crime. Many struggle to fathom a mysterious language and culture that is neither open nor friendly to them. Incidents of violence against Asian immigrants abound. Many recent arrivals from Vietnam, Cambodia, and Laos, the

**Mr. and Mrs. Van Ngo Vu
stocking shelves in their
family grocery store. Vu's
Market opened in 1987.**
Source: National Archives.

"boat people," refugees from oppression in their homelands, have encountered
only grief and failure in this country. But there is also the saga of Jean Nguyen.
Nguyen, at age eleven, escaped from Vietnam with her family by boat when Saigon
fell to the Communists in 1975. She spoke no English upon her arrival in America
that same year. In 1981, she graduated number one in her high school class and in
May 1985, graduated from West Point, receiving a commission as a second lieutenant in the United States Army. President Reagan paid tribute to Nguyen in his
1985 State of the Union Address, calling her "an American hero."

AFRICAN AMERICANS: A DUAL SOCIETY

For millions of African American families, the 1970s were a decade of significant
progress. Institutionalized racism and other obstacles to black achievement diminished. Affirmative action programs spawned by the civil rights movements of the
1960s paid off for middle-class African Americans in the 1970s and 1980s. The greatest progress for African Americans came in education. By 1980, more than 1 million
black people had enrolled in colleges, and thousands attended the finest universities
and professional schools in the country. Thousands of young African American men
and women became doctors, lawyers, college professors, government bureaucrats,

and business executives. The size of the black middle class had increased rapidly and black per capita income rose appreciably. African American couples married, had children, and bought homes in the suburbs, their lifestyles much like that of their white counterparts in similar circumstances. Many young black professionals, reared and educated in the North, flocked to the Sunbelt cities to live and work. Many blacks found urban life in Atlanta, Houston, and New Orleans more congenial, more nearly integrated, and offering more opportunities for ambitious careerists than the supposedly more liberal northern cities. African American political participation in southern states has also outstripped that of the North.

Despite significant gains for some, millions of African Americans have not made it in white America, and, in fact, they have lost ground. Affirmative action admissions programs were challenged by the *Bakke* case. Allen Bakke, a white applicant to the University of California at Davis Medical School, sued the university when his application was rejected. He showed that his qualifications were superior to several minority candidates who were admitted as "disadvantaged students" under a special quota reserved for them. The state supreme court ruled in his favor as did the Supreme Court, in a 1978 five-to-four decision. The Supreme Court held that Bakke's rights to equal protection under the Fourteenth Amendment had been violated, and it nullified the school's affirmative action program based on racial quotas. But by a similar five-to-four decision, the Court upheld the right of the university to use race as "one element" in their effort to recruit medical students.

But the plight of poor African Americans trapped in urban ghettos worsened in the 1970s and 1980s. Unemployment among African Americans remained high, about twice the national average, averaging 14 percent to 15 percent. Unemployment among African American teenagers skyrocketed to the 40 percent to 50 percent range by 1980. Black median family income was $13,500 in 1985, only half that for whites.

Among poor urban African Americans, recent statistics reveal a frightening pattern of intertwined social pathologies—rising drug usage, delinquency, vice, and crime; rising school dropout rates and unemployment rates; and rising numbers of illegitimate births and households headed by an unmarried female parent. Many social analysts fear a permanent underclass is being forged within black America, without the possibility of integration into the mainstream or of achieving personally fulfilling lives.

Whatever the multiple causes of this decline of black inner-city communities, because African Americans and local governments do not have the resources to solve the overwhelming social problems afflicting the black underclass and because federal officials assign solving these problems a relatively low priority, these conditions will continue to fester. The unattended massive needs of the black underclass represents a ticking time bomb within the vitals of urban America. Within America, African Americans have forged a dual society—on the one hand, a thriving middle class that has achieved a place for itself in recent years that is roughly equal to white America—and on the other hand, a declining underclass rotting on the mean streets of urban ghettos.

WOMEN: CHANGING ATTITUDES AND ROLES

Women in recent years have continued many of the trends established in the late 1960s and early 1970s. Female enrollments in colleges, graduate schools, and professional schools have continued to expand. By 1980, women college enrollment surpassed male enrollment. Middle-class women continued to enter the professional and corporate worlds in ever-increasing numbers. Working-class women continued to join unions, enter the skilled trades, and increase their numbers in previously all-male economic occupations. Both federal and state laws have been enacted that have helped women obtain credit, start their own businesses, and buy homes. Other women made their way in politics.

But despite their many successes, women have continued to encounter barriers in their struggle to overcome historical disadvantages and to achieve genuine equality in contemporary American society. Women antifeminists like Phyllis Schlafly and Anita Bryant have successfully campaigned against the Equal Rights Amendments. They have also fought to repeal the right of women to have an abortion on demand as sanctioned by the Supreme Court. Antifeminists won a partial victory in 1980 when the Supreme Court upheld the constitutionality of a congressional law prohibiting federal funding of abortions for poor women. Antifeminists have charged the women's movement with being responsible for the spiraling divorce rate and the breakdown of family life in America. "No-fault divorces," initially hailed as a great victory for women, have proven to be a two-edged sword because equality before the law has not brought equality in the marketplace. Compounding their economic difficulties, divorced women, who usually have custody of children, have found that former husbands default on child support payments and the courts often do not force them to pay.

Many men have responded negatively to women's liberation and have abandoned their traditional roles as financial provider and authority figure for the family. Sophisticated postfeminist analysts fault the liberal leaders of the women's movement for being too concerned with achieving legal and political equality and, thereby, neglecting fundamental economic pressures that women face in a society in which male economic domination remains a continuing reality. They also criticize feminists who have been obsessed with getting middle-class women into previously all-male professions and occupations, while neglecting the interests of the more numerous working-class women mired in low-paying occupations traditionally reserved for women.

Harsh economic realities continued to limit opportunities for women. For every glittering career success scored by ambitious, capable, upwardly mobile women, many more women work in low-paying jobs, which offer few opportunities for promotion or substantial pay increases. Occupational segregation, in which women remain concentrated in low-paying positions while men earn much higher incomes for their work, remains a persistent problem for women. Most of the new jobs created in the service sectors of the economy have been taken by women, and they invariably pay less than manufacturing or professional jobs.

In 1980, women earned only 60¢ for every dollar earned by men. The 60¢ represented an improvement over previous decades but fell far short of economic parity with men. Women have also been the victims of the "superwoman syndrome." Early feminist leaders proffered an idealized image of the woman who could have it all—career, home, husband, and family—a life of perfect equality and fulfillment. In practice, having it all often meant women worked full-time outside the home then came home to continue working without pay, doing all the cleaning, cooking, and caring for children, while men watched football, drank beer, and played with the dog.

Most women in recent years have worked because they have to support themselves or because they head a single-parent household. Millions of married women have felt it necessary to work to enable their family to enjoy a middle-class lifestyle that, because of inflation, is no longer affordable with a single income. Many women have slipped into the ranks of the working poor in recent years as a result of being divorced and saddled with child-rearing duties. The feminization of poverty and the fact that millions of American children are being reared in poverty are two ominous socioeconomic realities directly affecting the status of women.

EDUCATION

Most American colleges and universities continued to thrive in the 1970s and 1980s. In 1980, an estimated 11 million students were enrolled full- or part-time in the nation's twenty-five hundred institutions of higher learning. Americans continued to spend far more on post-high-school education than any other people, and America possessed a hundred of the world's finest universities. Distinguished university faculty members continued to do important research and publish their findings. American scholars led the world in many disciplines, especially the sciences. American universities are the vital centers of the nation's flourishing intellectual life.

In contrast to the turbulent 1960s, college campuses were mostly tranquil places in the 1970s and early 1980s. Surveys revealed that college students of the 1980s often embraced conservative social and political views. Students were much more interested in preparing for well-paying careers than they were in protesting public issues. Yet, some students could still respond to issues of conscience. Thousands of students joined protests against the nuclear arms race and called for universities to divest themselves of securities issued by companies doing business with the repressive apartheid regime in South Africa.

College students in recent years have been much less interested in the humanities and social sciences than they were a generation earlier. Students of the 1970s and early 1980s flocked to majors in math, economics, finance, business, engineering, and computer science. Many students, including bright ones, demonstrated deficiencies in verbal skills, ignorance of history and literature, and a general decline in cultural literacy.

While colleges flourished, American public schools deteriorated. Scholastic aptitude scores were 50 points lower in 1980 than they were in 1963. The high school dropout rate in 1980 was over 20 percent, the highest since the 1950s. About one in three eighteen-year-olds in this country were declared functionally illiterate in 1980. At a time when competition for jobs and all the accoutrements of the American-style good life is intensifying, when the economic and social life of the nation is becoming more complex and demanding, when employers are demanding brighter and better-educated employees, the public school system increasingly failed to meet individual and national needs.

Many culprits have been blamed for the dismal performance of the public schools. Television has been cited for keeping youngsters from reading books and for fostering boredom in the classroom. Indifferent and incompetent parents, who neither set a good example nor encourage their children to do well in school, have been part of the problem. Popular entertainers and professional athletes whose riches and fame derive from talent rather than study in schools have been indicted for setting bad examples and leading youngsters astray. In addition, the best and brightest college graduates rarely went into teaching. Entry-level salaries were low and teaching commanded little prestige as a profession. Americans once believed that education could solve all social problems; now the schools have become a social problem.

There were signs in the 1980s that educators were trying to turn their public schools in the direction of excellence. Polls showed people willing to pay more taxes to improve their schools. California and other states have implemented legislation lengthening the school day and year, strengthening the curriculum, raising teachers' salaries, and requiring new teachers to pass competency tests. But the jury is still out on whether the nation can improve its most important educational institutions. The fundamental question raised by the public school issue is one of cultural value. How highly does the nation prize learning? How highly do parents prize learning and how much are they willing to pay for good schools? Do students really care about becoming educated or are they only interested in an active social life, careers, and money?

RELIGION IN AMERICA

The United States remained the most religious nation in the Western world. Nearly all Americans espoused a belief in God, and 60 percent of the population claimed membership in a church in 1980. Members of the more liberal Protestant churches and Reformed Jews became more accepting of divorce, homosexuality, birth control, and female members of the clergy. Ministers and rabbis of these groups often urged their congregants to work for a more humane and just social order.

American Catholics in the 1970s and 1980s were concerned with the continuing consequences of Vatican II, the Church Council that had met in the early 1960s to bring the Church more into accord with modern life. The liturgy was given in English and the laity sang hymns during services. Priests were allowed more latitude in their interpretations of the Bible and they sought ecumenical dialogues with ministers and rabbis. Catholics recognized non-Catholic and non-Christian faiths, and condemned anti-Semitism.

Church leaders spoke out on issues. In 1983, American Bishops condemned nuclear war and urged the superpowers to disarm. In 1985, the Bishops criticized the American capitalist economy for not meeting the needs of the millions of disadvantaged Americans. Many educated, liberal middle-class Catholics welcomed the changes induced by Vatican II. But many traditionalists felt betrayed and were disturbed by these changes. They continued to adhere to the Church's traditional teachings on matters of sex, birth control, and abortion.

Among American churches, fundamentalist groups have experienced the greatest growth and social dynamism in recent years. Fundamentalist leaders insisted on literally interpreting Scripture, opposed the teaching of evolution in public schools, and opposed women's liberation. They also condemned homosexuality, premarital sex, and pornography. During the 1970s and 1980s, fundamentalist "televangelists" flourished. Television ministries, viewed weekly by millions, significantly increased the audience for fundamentalist messages. "Televangelists" often blended fundamentalist religious beliefs with Far Right political doctrines. One of the most powerful television preachers, Jerry Falwell, formed a coalition in 1979 of conservative Protestants from various denominations called the Moral Majority to support a right-wing political agenda. Falwell and his followers supported the social agenda of Ronald Reagan in the 1980s—constitutional amendments restoring prayer in public schools and abolishing abortion.

THE "ME DECADE"

While some Americans carried the activist reform spirit of the 1960s into the 1970s and 1980s, many more Americans turned inward. They wanted to change themselves, not the external world of politics and society. They incorporated many of the elements from the hippie countercultural rebellion into their lifestyles—drug use, permissive sexuality, and above all the "consciousness revolution." Participants included mostly young middle-class professionals who prized affluence and professional attainment, but defined success primarily in psychological rather than material terms. It was more important to them to fulfill their "human potential" than to accumulate as much wealth as possible.

The cutting edge of the consciousness revolution could be found in California, home of the new lifestyles based on developing one's inner resources. Facilities like the Esalen Institute at Big Sur offered weekend encounter sessions for seekers wanting to "get in touch with themselves." Another entrepreneur of the human potential movement offered Erhard Seminars Training (est) built around marathon encounter sessions in which participants were encouraged to confront their most powerful feelings. Journalist Tom Wolfe labeled these "psychonauts of inner space" the "Me Generation" and compared their movement to a religious revival.

As millions of Americans joined the consciousness revolution to seek salvation in narcissistic self-absorption, others sought refuge from the stresses of secular society by joining religious cults. Some of these religious orders embraced Eastern mystical religious practices such as transcendental meditation or Zen Buddhism. One cult, led by Indian holy man Bhagwan Shree Rajneesh Mahareshi Yogi, established a flourishing colony near Antelope, Oregon. Thousands of people, attracted by the Bhagwan's message of spiritual rebirth and free sex, lived and worked in apparently joyous harmony for a time. But the cult disintegrated in 1986 because of internal dissension among its leaders. The Rajneesh fled Oregon for India to avoid prosecution on several federal charges.

The most prominent of these cults was the Unification Church, founded by a Korean businessman and preacher, the Reverend Sun Myung Moon, who relocated in the United States. Moon, trained as a Presbyterian minister, developed his own religion. He claimed to be the son of God and to receive divine revelations. His movement was controversial. His disciples were accused of kidnapping and brainwashing some of their teenage recruits. Reverend Moon also ran afoul of the law and was convicted of income tax evasion. Another cult came to a horrible end in November 1978, when its insane leader, Jim Jones, led the cult members from California to Guyana and convinced more than seven hundred members to engage in a ghastly ritual mass suicide by poisoning.

POPULAR CULTURE

America calmed in the early 1970s; the era of limits was also an era of comparative civic and social tranquility. In the words of historian John Wiltz, in America during the 1970s, "the national society became more mellow." No more fiery urban riots or militant campus protests convulsed the nation. Gone was the strident rhetoric of youthful radicals denouncing government policies at home and abroad, and also challenging traditional American values, mores, and institutions. Gone were the calls for a new American revolution.

Several factors accounted for the calming down of America during the 1970s. The end of the Vietnam War removed the single most powerful source of dissidence. The decline of the economy, stagflation, and energy crises shifted attention from political troubles to more fundamental economic and financial dysfunctions. The successes, or at least partial victories, of many of the 1960s movements led some of their participants to cease their activism in the 1970s with a sense of having accomplished their missions. Some radicals, suffering from moral and political exhaustion, abandoned their futile efforts to refashion American politics and society. They retreated into a sullen personalism and quietism. Some joined the "me generation," redirecting their reformist energies away from the world and toward their own personalities. Others, reaching adulthood, prepared to make an accommodation with the system that they had previously rejected. Many a hippie and campus radical abandoned their countercultural ways, shaved their beards and cut their hair, put on three-piece suits, and became Yuppies. Radical rebellion for many, while no doubt sincere and serious, turned out to be evanescent growing pains during a time of troubles and significant transformations.

As the society calmed in the 1970s, Americans, retreating into private realms, embraced an odd assortment of fads and silly activities. One such curious custom was streaking. Naked youths, mostly young men, but also women, streaked across college campuses, along busy streets and highways, and through malls. While a few young people embraced streaking, millions more turned to disco dancing. Disco music appealed mainly because of its strong, rhythmic beat accompanied by simple, repetitive lyrics. Couples danced the night away beneath pulsating lights in one of the hundreds of night clubs that sprang up across America in the mid-1970s. An attractive African American soul singer, Donna Summer, became the Queen of Discoland; her records sold millions of copies during the years of the disco craze. Many, mostly young, people came to discos just to listen to the sound of Summer and other disco artists. Many more learned to dance the "hustle" and the "bus stop" or the myriad of other new disco dances.

During the 1970s, millions of Americans became more diet-conscious than ever before. People reduced their salt intake and their cholesterol intake. Others stopped drinking alcoholic beverages and drinks with caffeine in them. Others rejected processed sugars like the plague. Closely related to dieting and part of the new health consciousness, millions of people embraced the so-called fitness revolution. They became avid weight lifters as well as weight watchers. They swam, they jogged, and they rode bicycles; they joined health clubs, played racquetball, and performed aerobic exercizes. Another indicator of growing health consciousness during the 1907s: millions of people abandoned smoking cigarettes. By the end of the 1970s, approximately 30 percent of the adult population smoked, the lowest percentage since the 1920s.

If Americans were smoking fewer cigarettes during the 1970s, they were drinking more alcoholic beverages, especially beer. Per capita alcoholic consumption increased from 22 gallons in 1970 to 27 gallons in 1980. Two causes of the increased drinking could be found in the growing secularization of American life and the increasing amounts of money the major breweries spent on television advertising. Televised sporting events invariably featured numerous beer commercials associating good times with their products. Directing their ads mainly toward single young men, breweries strove to link beer drinking with male fantasies about sexy young women.

During the late 1970s, alcohol abuse among teenagers and college students became a serious national issue. Studies found that thousands of high school students were teenage alcoholics. In 1975, of the approximately 45,000 Americans killed in traffic accidents, more than half died in accidents in which at least one of the drivers had been drinking. Fatal auto accidents were one of the leading killers of young people between the ages of fifteen to twenty-five. Another survey found that at least 10 million Americans were alcohol abusers.

Americans used other drugs besides ethanol in increasing amounts during the 1970s. The use of marijuana ("pot"), which had become a potent symbol of the youth revolt during the turbulent 1960s, expanded in the 1970s. Pot farming became a major underground industry in many parts of the country. Surveys showed that nearly half of the nation's college students during the 1970s used marijuana. Because most experts believed that the effects of the drug were comparatively mild if used in moderation, the federal government and most states reduced the legal penalties for possession of small amounts of pot from felonies to misdemeanors. A far more serious drug problem arose in the early 1970s when there occurred a surge in heroin addiction. The nation discovered that it had nearly a million heroin addicts on its hands by 1975.

Americans during the 1970s discovered the microwave oven and consumed a record number of TV dinners annually. American families also dined out much more often than ever before, especially at fast food places. Probably the single most important factor accounting for the 1970s' eating-out phenomenon was the fact that more than 50 percent of married women with children now worked full-time outside the home. As the 1970s ended, Americans were spending 40¢ of every $1 they spent for food at restaurants. The new dining-out patterns attested to a major cultural change that had occurred: The great American dinner was being redefined for families with children. Dinner was no longer a private familial activity; it had increasingly become a public activity.

The movie industry flourished during the 1970s. Hollywood turned out many fine films, some of which set box-office records. In 1972, the brilliant young director, Francis Ford Coppola, made the *The Godfather,* starring Al Pacino, Marlon Brando, and Diane Keaton. Based on a novel by Mario Puzo, the film was an epic story of a powerful Mafia family making it in America. In 1973 came an occult classic, *The Exorcist,* starring a talented child actress named Linda Blair. Based on a novel by William Blatty, the film dealt in dramatic fashion with demonic possession and the valiant efforts of a Catholic priest to exorcise the devil from the body of the child. In 1975 came the techno-thriller, *Jaws,* produced by a brilliant young film maker, Stephen Spielberg. It was a terrifying account of a killer great white shark attacking swimmers. The star of the film turned out to be jaws himself, the technological monster that terrorized a New England town: it was shown devouring swimmers in gruesome detail. *Jaws* had the largest box-office gross of any film ever made.

Jaws' record take at the box office was broken in 1977 by *Star Wars*, the first of a brilliant series of original science fiction films by George Lucas, another major film-making talent that burst on the Hollywood scene in the 1970s. Set in the far distant future, *Star Wars* was essentially a child's fantasy, a fairy tale about high-tech adventures in space starring Mark Hamill as Luke Skywalker, Harrison Ford as Han Solo, and Carrie Fisher as Princess Leia. They were supported by a charming cast of bizarre-looking but gentle aliens and human-like machines called androids. The plot is a simple morality tale, of the good guys triumphing over the bad guys who control the evil Galactic Empire. Much of the appeal of *Star Wars* lay in the fact it had no message, no sex, and only the mildest of violence. It could be enjoyed by kids of all ages. It relied on a dazzling array of special effects and technological wizardry to mesmerize its audience. One critic called it a wild west adventure in outer space. Other critics, pondering the deeper meanings of *Star*

Wars, suggested that it pointed the way toward a new mythology in the wake of the disillusionment with the Vietnam War that destroyed the American frontier myth. *Star Wars* represented a creative effort to reclaim lost American innocence.

Studies showed that Americans watched more television shows than ever before during the 1970s. New technologies significantly enhanced the range and capabilities of the electronic medium. Communication satellites in stationary orbits hundreds of miles in space enabled television news to provide live, instantaneous coverage of news events from anywhere on the planet. The 1970s also featured the advent of cable television. Viewers were freed from having to rely on the three major networks that controlled prime-time programming and the few shows worth watching generated by local independent stations. By the late 1970s, thanks to the advent of cable utilizing the VHF channels, viewers who signed on for their services had a choice of twenty to thirty channels to watch. During the 1980s, cable television grew exponentially, and viewers could receive up to eighty channels. The most important new television technology of the 1970s was the introduction in 1975 of the videocassette recorder, or VCR. Early versions of the VCRs were difficult to use and rather expensive; they were slow to catch on. Sales boomed in the 1980s and wrought another revolution in the nation's television and movie-viewing habits.

Because so many sporting events were televised during the 1970s, commercial spectator sports became a more important part of popular culture than ever before. Major professional spectator sports flourished, especially the National Football League (NFL), the National Basketball Association (NBA), and Major League baseball. Thanks in large part to television, professional football became the most popular national sport. Pro football is a fast-paced, complex, highly competitive, violent game played by tough, highly skilled athletes. Some analysts have linked its powerful hold on fans to the fact that pro football was a microcosm of the corporatist economy that America had become in the 1970s.

College sports, particularly football and basketball, grew rapidly in popularity. The growth of these major college sports was tinged with scandals. Some schools recruited athletes who were simply not equipped to succeed academically. Unless they were among the very few elite athletes who went on to successful careers as professional athletes, most of these college athletes left school after their athletic eligibility was expended without degrees and without the prospect of professional careers of any kind.

Other scandals plaguing college football and basketball programs included illegal payments to "amateur" athletes by alumni boosters, and drug use and criminal behavior by some athletes. The National Collegiate Athletic Association (NCAA) exercised a rather ineffectual policing function over intercollegiate athletics. From time to time they would investigate collegiate athletic programs, find illegalities, and impose sanctions. One had a sense that the NCAA sporadically discovered the tip of a scandalous iceberg. Amidst the commercialism and scandals of collegiate sports there was one positive innovation. Women athletes demanded, and eventually achieved, parity with men at the nation's colleges and universities. These breakthroughs for women athletes represented another victory for the powerful women's movement of the 1970s.

A DISMAL DECADE

The 1970s appear to have been a dismal decade for many Americans. The economic growth cycle that had sustained the affluent society for thirty years stalled. American power and prestige in the world declined. Politicians failed to provide effective leadership at home or abroad. The failure of the American war in Vietnam filled most Americans with shame. The revelations of the Watergate scandals filled most Americans with disgust. Revelations of wrongdoing by the CIA and the FBI angered most Americans. The Iranian hostage crisis humiliated most Americans.

For many citizens, 1970s' America no longer worked in accordance with traditional ideals and expectations. Young people coming of age during the 1970s enjoyed fewer opportunities and less mobility than their parents. Double-digit inflation undermined real per capita income. For the first time in over one hundred years, the average workweek lengthened, reversing a long-running historic trend. Millions of Americans had to work harder for less during the 1970s. With more and more married women with children having to work or choosing to work, family life often deteriorated. People had less leisure time and fewer satisfying or fulfilling ways of using it. Those with disposable incomes threw themselves into a mindless and frantic consumerism. They often bought trendy new technologies, only to discard them after a short period of involvement. Many a personal computer sat idle, or perhaps found use as an expensive planter.

Americans of the 1970s had to face a plethora of troubling, divisive problems, many of which proved to be interrelated and intractable. Abortion, legalized by the Supreme Court in 1973, generated enormous strife and anguish. The country's growing dependence on expensive foreign oil remained a worrisome issue. The decline of America's manufacturing industries in the face of fierce foreign competition and the decisions of American-based multinational corporations to export manufacturing operations presaged a bleak economic future for millions of American workers. Rising deficits in international trade balances and the federal budget made America the world's leading debtor nation. The failing public school system suggested that young people would be poorly prepared for good jobs that were becoming scarce. Social problems abounded: Medical care was too expensive for millions of working-class families who did not have health coverage. There were serious shortcomings in the care available for the handicapped, the very elderly, and the terminally ill. An epidemic of drug use swept the nation in the 1970s. There was a rising tide of crime, especially serious and violent crimes. Massive poverty continued, as did discrimination against racial minorities, women, and gay and lesbian people, despite the gains these groups had made during the 1960s. Continuing serious ecological problems fouled the air and poisoned the environment.

Little wonder that the American people turned to an aging former film actor in 1980 who promised to restore American primacy in world affairs and revitalize the American economy. Even more important, Ronald Reagan promised to restore the American dream and to make Americans feel good about themselves again.

IMPORTANT DATES

1974	Gerald Ford assumes the presidency
1974	President Ford pardons Nixon
1975	Saigon falls to the Communists
1976	Jimmy Carter is elected president
1977	Panama Canal treaties are signed
1978	The Supreme Court delivers the *Bakke* decision
1978	Revolution takes place in Iran
1979	Camp David Accords take place
1979	U.S. hostages are taken in Iran
1979	The U.S. and China resume normal diplomatic relations
1979	The USSR invades Afghanistan
1979	The Carter Doctrine is announced
1979	The Sandinistas triumph in Nicaragua
1980	Ronald Reagan is elected president

BIBLIOGRAPHY

One of the most important general studies of American history from 1945 to the mid-1970s is Godfrey Hodgson's *America in Our Time*. Peter N. Carroll's *It Seemed Like Nothing Happened* is a general political and social history of the 1970s. Both presidents Ford and Carter have written their memoirs. Ford's is called *A Time to Heal;* Carter's is entitled *Keeping Faith: Memoirs of a President*. John Osborne has the best account of the Ford presidency: *White House Watch: The Ford Years*. A. James Reichley, in *Conservatives in an Age of Change*, offers an interesting account of the rising conservative cause throughout the 1970s. Peter Steinfels's *The Neo-Conservatives* is a critical account of the emergence of a neoconservative intelligentsia in the late 1970s. A lively account of the rise of the Sunbelt region to political prominence is Kirkpatrick Sale's *Power Shift: The Rise of the Southern Rim and Its Challenge to the Eastern Establishment*. Stanley Hoffmann, in *Primacy and World Order*, offers a critical assessment of Ford administration foreign policy. A critical study of the Carter presidency has been done by Clark Mollenkoff, entitled *The President Who Failed: Carter Out of Control*. Barry Rubin's *Paved with Good Intentions: The American Experience in Iran* is the best study of the Iranian fiasco. A good study of the energy crisis of the 1970s is Richard Victor's *Energy Policy in America since 1945*. CIA abuses of power are portrayed in *The CIA and the Cult of Intelligence*, by Victor Marchetti and John D. Marks. David Halberstam, in *The Reckoning*, presents a good account of the decline of the American auto industry during the 1970s. The implications of recent demographic shifts are discussed by Joseph J. Spengler in *Population and America's Future*. Several economists have done important books on the 1970s economic crises. See Robert L. Heilbroner's *An Inquiry into the Human Prospect*; Lester Thurow's *The Zero Sum Game;* and Robert Reich's *The New American Frontier*. U.S. economic decline during the 1970s is charted by Barry Bluestone and Bennett Harrison in *The Deindustrialization of America*. A fine recent study, edited by Michael A. Bernstein and David E. Adler, is *Understanding American Economic Decline;* it is the best analysis of the causes of the economic downturn that began in the early 1970s. A good study of the impact of computer technology on American society and culture is Tracy Kidder's *The Soul of a New Machine*. For African Americans during the 1970s, read Ken Auletta's *The Underclass* and William J. Wilson's *The Declining Significance of Race*. *Today's Immigrants: Their Stories* is a recent study by Thomas Kessner and Betty Caroli. There is an extensive and generally excellent literature on women during the 1970s and 1980s. See Winifred D. Wandersee's *On the Move: American Women in the 1970s*. Mary Ann Mason, in *The Equality Trap*, gives us a perceptive study of the limitations of liberal feminism and its failure to cope with the economic plight of divorced working women. Christopher Lasch's *The Culture of Narcissism: American Life in the Age of Diminishing Expectations* catches many of the anxieties and discontents of the American people during the era of limits. Gillian Peele's *Revival and Reaction: The Right in Contemporary America* is a study of current religious and political conservatism. Current education trends are analyzed by Sanford W. Reitman in *Education, Society, and Change*.

CHAPTER 15

America in the Eighties

When President Ronald Wilson Reagan addressed the nation on inauguration day January 20, 1981, it marked the coming to power of resurgent conservatism. Left for dead in the wake of the Goldwater debacle of 1964, conservatism had revived, gathered momentum during the 1970s, and captured the White House in 1980 when Reagan easily defeated the discredited Democratic incumbent, Jimmy Carter. In the early 1970s, conservatives began to speak out forcibly on many issues. Espousing a philosophy based on a strong sense of tradition and social order and stressing the cruciality of religion, private property, and family values, these resurgent conservatives voiced their vehement opposition to many public policies that they believed were bringing about too much social change too quickly. They attacked what they called "forced busing" to integrate the public schools. They also denounced affirmative action programs that guaranteed minorities, particularly African Americans, equal opportunity in their quest for schooling and employment. Conservatives opposed the Equal Rights Amendment and helped defeat it. They also opposed efforts to protect the rights of gays and lesbians. They opposed all gun control measures and they favored the restoration of capital punishment. Most conservatives were outraged when the Supreme Court issued its controversial *Roe* v. *Wade* decision (1973), which granted women the right to an abortion on demand during the first trimester of a pregnancy. Conservatives also attacked other Supreme Court rulings made during the 1970s that outlawed prayer in the public schools and appeared to strengthen the rights of criminals at the expense of law enforcement personnel. They attacked welfare programs, high taxes, and many federal bureaucracies. Conservatives deplored the erosion of wave-the-flag patriotism. They championed free enterprise capitalism, criticized government regulation of economic activity, and attacked trade unions.

Resurgent conservatives also believed that Soviet leaders were the personification of evil and responsible for all that had gone wrong in the world since 1945. They insisted that America must maintain an arsenal of thermonuclear and conventional weapons to contain the aggressive tendencies of the Kremlin and its clients. Conservatives lamented the decline of U.S. power and influence in the world symbolized by the Vietnam debacle and the Iranian hostage crisis.

THE MEDIA MAN

Ronald Reagan emerged in the late 1960s as the most articulate champion of conservative causes. His career followed the Horatio Alger pattern of a poor boy who grew up to became rich and famous. He spent his boyhood living in rented apartments and houses in small midwestern towns where his alcoholic father made an inconstant living as a shoe salesman. Reagan worked his way through college, graduating in 1932 during the depths of the Great Depression. Despite the hard times, Reagan managed to find work in radio and within a few years had become a popular midwestern sportscaster. In 1937, he came to Hollywood. He took a screen test at Warner Brothers and won a film contract. By 1941, Reagan had become a movie star, earning $5,000 a picture. Although he made a few serious pictures, Warner's generally cast Reagan as the lead in "B" movies, usually as an All-American action hero. He spent World War II in Hollywood as an Army Air Corps officer making training films and documentaries for the Armed Forces.

After the war, Reagan's film career faded and he became more active politically. His first marriage, to screen actress Jane Wyman, failed. He had embraced New Deal liberalism during the 1930s and early 1940s. Active in Hollywood politics, he served two terms as president of the Screen Actors Guild. As his Hollywood film career declined, he moved into television. As he was changing media, he married another screen actress, Nancy Davis.

Reagan also began drifting to the right politically during the 1950s. He became a devout anti-Communist and cooperated with studio heads and the FBI to ferret out and blacklist writers, directors, and actors suspected of Communist affiliations. General Electric hired Reagan to host its popular television program, "General Electric Theater." He made speeches for GE, becoming comfortable espousing the company's conservative philosophy at business lunches and employee meetings. While making these speeches, Reagan refined the rhetoric that would propel him to leadership of the conservative cause and one day make him president of the United States. He left GE in 1962 and became active in right-wing Republican politics in Southern California. He continued to make speeches and develop his conservative political philosophy.

Reagan emerged nationally in 1964 when he made a television fund-raising speech on behalf of Barry Goldwater's conservative crusade. "The Speech," as it came to be called, had a powerful impact on his audience and launched Reagan's political career. In his first try for public office in 1966, the voters elected Reagan governor of California. Quickly, the former television host, screen actor, and radio sportscaster assumed national leadership of the rising conservative cause. He made his first bid for the presidency in 1968, but was stymied by Nixon's southern strategy at Miami. He tried again in 1976, narrowly losing to Ford, and at age sixty-nine he won the office in 1980 on his third try.

A handsome man of sunny disposition, Reagan's essential traits included a kind of "aw shucks" modesty that voters found irresistible. He also had a sense of himself as destiny's child, a blessed man fated for distinction. Reagan possessed a lively sense of humor and a limitless fund of stories and anecdotes, which he used with great political skill. Reagan believed in the frontier myth of heroic individualism. America was for Reagan a land of innocence and unlimited possibilities.

He mastered the art of media politics. Reagan's ability to deliver prepared remarks rivaled that of Franklin Roosevelt's, the new president's idol and role model. Nicknamed the "Great Communicator," he showed great political skill by appealing to all varieties of conservatives and by keeping these disparate constituencies united as well as attracting a broad spectrum of Democratic voters. The outcome of the 1980 election and the subsequent popularity that he sustained for most his presidency convinced Reagan that most Americans shared his conservative vision and that they rejected what he termed the "liberal special interest groups."

THE ADVENT OF REAGANOMICS

When Reagan took office in January 1981, runaway inflation had ravaged the American economy for years. The average family's annual purchasing power was about $1,000 less than it had been a decade earlier. The new President called upon his fellow Americans to join him "in a new beginning" to clean up "the worst economic mess since the Great Depression." He blamed "the mess" on high levels of government spending and taxation. He said, "Government is not the solution to our problems; government is the problem."

Influenced by an economist on the faculty of the University of Southern California, Arthur Laffer, Reagan grounded his program for economic recovery in "supply-side" economic theory. Contradicting the long-prevailing Keynesian theory, which relied on government spending and tax cuts to boost consumer demand, supply-siders favored cutting both federal spending and taxes at the same time. They believed that the private sector, freed from shackles imposed by government regulation, public spending, and high taxes, would increase its investment in productive enterprises and generate economic growth and create millions of new jobs. Such expansion would also cut inflation and generate tax revenues that would more than offset losses from the reduced tax rates. The expansion would also balance the budget. To many skeptics, "Reaganomics" sounded almost too good to be true. When George Bush had campaigned for the presidential nomination, he had called Reagan's economic notions "voodoo economics."

The president brought a mixed group of advisers to Washington. He appointed James A. Baker his chief of staff. Baker urged Reagan to move quickly on his key issues—tax cuts and the military buildup. At the Treasury Department, he

President Ronald Reagan taking the oath of office from Supreme Court Chief Justice Warren Earl Burger. At the new president's side stands the new First Lady, Nancy Davis Reagan. *Source:* The White House Collection, Bill Fitz-Patrick, photographer.

installed Donald Regan, a securities broker and conservative Republican. David Stockman became Director of the Office of Management and Budget. Stockman, a supply-side zealot, carried Reagan's program of cutting spending and reducing taxes to Congress. A brilliant workaholic and a missionary for cost and tax cuts, Stockman mastered the intricacies of the congressional budgetary process. He was the point-man for Reaganomics. While Stockman overhauled the federal budgetary process, Paul Volcker, a Carter holdover and chairman of the Federal Reserve Board, kept tight reins on the money supply with high interest rates.

Stockman made cutting federal spending the Reagan administration's top priority. He slashed $41 billion in social spending for food stamps, public service jobs, student loans, school lunches, urban mass transit, and welfare payments. Middle-class entitlements, such as Social Security, were exempted and

Reagan also left what he called a "safety net for the truly needy." At the same time, he was cutting back social spending, Reagan increased military spending. He exhibited great political skill by persuading many Sunbelt Democratic congressmen to support his programs. These "boll weevils," led by Representative Phil Gramm of Texas, were crucial to getting his program through the Democratic-controlled House. Reagan made a dramatic personal appearance before a joint session of Congress to plead for his budget only a few weeks after being seriously wounded during an attempt on his life. He built up a strong bipartisan coalition in the House and won a commanding 253-to-176 victory. His winning margin in the Senate was even more impressive, 78 to 20. Many liberal Democrats were skeptical that supply-side economics could work as its disciples insisted it must, but they lacked an alternative program that commanded public support.

The president also succeeded in getting his proposed income tax cuts through. He originally called for cuts of 10 percent per year for three years, but accepted a compromise that cut taxes 5 percent the first year and then 10 percent for the next two years. Both houses of Congress approved them overwhelmingly. Several other tax concessions were written into an omnibus bill. Capital gains, inheritance tax, and gift taxes were also reduced. Business tax write-offs were also enhanced. The Reagan tax cuts, with congressional sanction, amounted to the largest tax reductions in the nation's history.

Reagan also sought to achieve his goal of reducing federal regulation of the economy. He appointed men and women to federal regulatory agencies who shared his views that markets, not government agencies, ought to direct the national economy. He appointed Anne Gorsuch Burford, who opposed air quality and toxic waste regulations, to head the Environmental Protection Agency (EPA). During her tenure, the EPA budget was slashed and all its enforcement efforts were weakened. Reagan's most controversial appointment was James Watt to head the Department of Interior. Watt had directed an antienvironmentalist legal action group before his appointment to the Interior Department. He supported stripmining and opening up public lands to private developers, including offshore oil-drilling sites. Reagan tried to eliminate the Department of Energy; failing that, he settled for severe cuts in its budget and operations. He persuaded Congress to cut spending for elementary and secondary education.

Drew Lewis, Reagan's Secretary of Transportation, removed many of the regulations to reduce pollution and to increase driver safety that had been imposed on the U.S. auto industry during the 1970s. He also persuaded the Japanese to voluntarily restrict automobile imports to the United States. Lewis opposed an illegal strike by an air traffic controller's union (PATCO) in the summer of 1981. President Reagan fired the 11,500 striking workers, decertified the union, and ordered Lewis to train and hire thousands of new air controllers to replace them. The destruction of the air traffic controller's union was the most devastating defeat for organized labor of modern times. It demoralized a labor movement already reeling from the decline of American manufacturing.

By the end of the summer of 1981, "Reaganomics" was in place. The new leader had moved most of his legislative program through Congress. He wielded executive power with great skill and effectiveness. His efforts represented the greatest feat of presidential legislative leadership since the heyday of Lyndon Johnson's Great Society programs of 1964 and 1965. Reagan had asserted a popular mandate, seized the political initiative, redefined the public agenda, and got most of his program implemented. *Time* magazine observed that "No President since FDR had done so much of such magnitude so quickly to change the economic direction of the country." Reaganomics amounted to a radical assault on the liberal welfare state erected during the previous fifty years.

Aware that few African Americans had voted Republican, the Reagan administration was unresponsive to black concerns. Federal support for civil rights weakened. Reagan opposed affirmative action hiring programs, which he believed amounted to reverse discrimination. His attorney general opposed busing to achieve school desegregation. The number of African American officials appointed to major government positions declined. The budgets for federal agencies responsible for enforcing civil rights programs were curtailed. Both the staff and budget of the Civil Rights Division of the Justice Department were cut. The Justice Department filed few school desegregation and fair housing suits during Reagan's first term as president.

Reagan's record on appointments of women was better than his record for African Americans. He appointed a few highly visible women to top government positions. He fulfilled a campaign pledge and made a major symbolic gesture to women when he appointed Sandra Day O'Connor to the Supreme Court, the first women jurist ever chosen. He appointed Jeane Kirkpatrick to be the U.S. Ambassador to the United Nations. Several women served in his cabinet. Feminists, however, pointed out that Reagan appointed far fewer women to federal offices and judgeships than had his Democratic predecessor. Reagan also opposed the Equal Rights Amendment, and he denounced *Roe* v. *Wade*.

RECESSION AND RECOVERY

After a year, it was evident that Reaganomics had not brought an economic revival. Unemployment exceeded 9 percent, the highest since 1941. Business bankruptcies rose to depression levels. Steep interest rates priced homes and cars beyond the reach of millions of families and plunged those two major industries into depression. One year after Reagan's promised new beginning, the nation was mired in its worst slump since the Great Depression. Manufacturing output declined and the construction industry slumped. Big cities fared the worst. In Detroit, unemployment reached 20 percent. A class of "new poor," not seen since the 1930s, appeared on the streets: homeless, unemployed workers and their families.

Sandra Day O'Connor, the first woman to be appointed to the U.S. Supreme Court. *Source:* Supreme Court.

A combination of deep tax cuts, steep hikes in military spending, and drastic economic shrinkage drove the federal budget deficit over $100 billion, the highest ever. The one bright spot in a dark economic picture was declining inflation. It dropped from 13 percent in 1980 to 9 percent in 1981 and fell to 5 percent in 1982. The short-term failure of Reaganomics derived from two fiscal realities: the failure of the tax cuts to stimulate increased business investment and continuing high interest rates that put a crimp in both business spending and consumer purchases. Reagan, confronting a declining economy and rising criticism, pleaded for time. He insisted that Reaganomics did not cause the downturn, that it came from the accumulated mismanagement and mistaken policies of his Democratic predecessors. Reagan promised that prosperity would come, but it would have protracted birthing pains. The recession worsened all through 1982. Toward the end of the year, unemployment reached 10 percent; over 11 million Americans were out of work.

The 1982 midterm elections took place amidst the worst economic conditions this country had seen in over forty years. Undaunted, Reagan campaigned hard for his program and for Republican candidates. The election amounted to a referendum on Reaganomics. The Democrats picked up twenty-five House seats, but the Republicans held on to the Senate. When the new Congress convened in January 1983, Reagan lost his bipartisan majority coalition that had pushed through Reaganomics. House Speaker Thomas "Tip" O'Neill, the leader of the opposition to Reaganomics, forced the president to accept budget compromises in 1983. Cuts in social spending were lessened and increases in military spending were reduced.

The economy recovered strongly in 1983 and the surge continued in 1984. The gross domestic product rose 6.8 percent in 1984, the largest one-year gain since the Korean War. Unemployment and interest rates declined. Housing starts and new car sales picked up; domestic auto makers reported strong sales and record profits in mid-1984. The rate of inflation dropped to 4 percent for both years, the lowest since the early 1970s. Personal income rose, and consumer and business confidence soared. Abundant world oil supplies were an important cause of the drop in the rate of inflation. By the end of 1984, the OPEC cartel was in disarray and world oil prices were falling. The economic expansion that began in 1983 lasted through the 1980s. It was the longest sustained period of prosperity in modern American history. Prosperity generated 18 million new jobs, significantly enhanced productivity, and tripled the price of common stocks by 1990.

Despite the strong rebound, serious problems continued to plague the economy. Tax cuts combined with large increases in military spending to generate record federal deficits. The nation's international trade deficit reached a record $108 billion in 1984. The main causes of the soaring international debt was the nation's continuing thirst for foreign oil along with imported manufactures such as autos and stereos. By the end of his first term Reagan had managed to double the national debt. All talk of balanced budgets had been replaced by a frenzied concern to staunch the flow of red ink. Amidst the economic boom, over 7.5 million Americans remained out of work. The Census Bureau reported the nation's poverty rate reached 15.2 percent in 1983, the highest since 1965. A 15.2 percent poverty rate meant that there were 35 million poor people in America, 6 million more than when Reagan assumed office.

THE COLD WAR REVIVED

Because of his lack of experience and because he made reviving the economy his top priority, Reagan relied heavily on advisers both for forging and implementing U.S. foreign policy. For the new president, the traditional verities of the Cold War still prevailed: America and its allies were locked in a life-or-death struggle for survival with a ruthless, expansionist Soviet empire. Reagan repudiated previous efforts at détente and announced his intention to challenge Soviet interests around the globe. He launched a rapid buildup of military power to give the United States the muscle and confidence that it needed to prevail in the long twilight struggle with its global rival. He announced what came to be known as the Reagan Doctrine—that the United States would help anti-Communist resistance movements anywhere in the world.

He also made clear that he intended to make major use of the CIA as an instrument of American foreign policy, especially its covert paramilitary operations. He freed U.S. arms sales from the restrictions imposed by the Carter administration and scrapped Carter's human rights policies. Reagan appointed his campaign manager and good friend William Casey to head the restored CIA. He denounced the Soviet Union in a speech before the United Nations in 1982, charging that Soviet agents were working everywhere in the world, "violating human rights and unnerving the world with violence." Addressing a convention of Christian evangels in Orlando, Florida, in May 1983, he called the Soviet Union "an evil empire" and declared that the Soviet leaders were "the focus of evil in the modern world."

Ironically, Reagan was only continuing a trend begun under Carter in 1979. After the Iranian revolution and the Soviet invasion of Afghanistan, Carter had abandoned détente and taken a hard line toward the Soviets that had reignited the Cold War. Influenced by his hard-liner foreign policy adviser, Zbigniew Brzezinski, Carter dropped the proposed SALT II treaty, canceled trade with the Soviets, increased American military spending, and sought to put intermediate range missiles in Europe. Whether he acknowledged it or was even aware of it, Reagan's hard-line anti-Soviet policies often built upon Carter's initiatives.

Under Reagan, the U.S. military flourished. Secretary of Defense Caspar Weinberger proposed plans that would double U.S. military spending over five years, from $171 billion in 1981 to over $360 billion in 1986. Weinberger insisted that during Carter's presidency the Soviets had achieved strategic superiority over the United States. A "window of vulnerability" existed for American land-based missiles that could tempt the Soviets to try a "first strike" nuclear attack. Weinberger ordered building a new strategic bomber, a new strategic missile, and an expanded Navy with 450 to 600 ships. Reagan, determined to challenge the Soviet Union, strongly supported all of Weinberger's proposals for the military buildup. When Stockman attempted to cut military outlays, Reagan backed Weinberger and blocked Stockman's efforts. During Reagan's presidency defense budgets were the largest in peacetime history. Reagan and other top officials spoke of being able "to prevail" in the event of a nuclear war with the Soviets. Such rhetoric, yoked to the gigantic increases in military spending, frightened millions of Americans who feared the Reagan was preparing for a nuclear war with the Soviets.

The Reagan administration had difficulty in achieving a unified approach to foreign policy because of internal feuding among key personnel. There were hazards entailed in Reagan's habit of deferring to his foreign policy advisers because they often disagreed among themselves. His first Secretary of State, General Alexander Haig, expected to be the strong man in orchestrating Reagan's foreign policy, turned out to be too aggressive as a turf fighter and ran afoul of Reagan's inner circle of Californians. He was replaced by George Schultz, an economist with extensive experience in government service; but Schultz frequently worked at cross-purposes with Weinberger and Reagan's ambassador to the United Nations, Jeane Kirkpatrick.

Despite his tough anti-Communist rhetoric and expensive military buildup, Reagan found it difficult to assert pressure on Communist states. In late 1981, the Soviet Union forced Poland to impose martial law in order to crush a trade union movement that was pushing Poland toward democratic socialism and away from Soviet Communism. Reagan, outraged, found his options limited. He could not risk nuclear war with the Soviet Union. He could not persuade NATO allies to impose economic blockades on the USSR or Poland. He imposed an American boycott on the nearly bankrupt Polish economy that only caused additional hardship on the Polish people without saving the trade union movement. The Polish crisis demonstrated once again the determination of the Soviets to hold on to their Eastern European empire no matter what U.S. presidents said or did. Reagan also discovered that sovereign and prosperous NATO countries also felt no compunction about resisting some U.S. anti-Communist initiatives.

Reagan met frustration again in Europe in 1982 when he tried to block a major economic arrangement between the Soviet Union and Western European nations. The Soviets agreed to sell natural gas to the West Europeans if they would build a pipeline to transport the gas. The West Europeans had agreed to purchase the natural gas from Siberia and to build the pipeline to transport it. The pipeline required American technology supplied by European corporations. Reagan tried and failed to stop the deal by imposing sanctions against these companies, some of which were partly government-owned.

The Reaganauts had more success in stymieing Soviet efforts to crush Afghanistan's *mujahidin* rebels during the earl 1980s. The CIA set up a clandestine arms supply operation. Arms were shipped to Pakistan and then smuggled into Afghanistan. The Soviets soon found themselves bogged down in a Vietnam-like quagmire. They unleashed a fearsome arsenal of modern high-tech weaponry against the rebels. Soviet aircraft carpet-bombed Afghan villages in an effort to destroy the guerrillas' popular base of support. Soviet infantry battalions, supported by armor, artillery, and helicopter gunships, tried to sweep the rebels from strategic valleys. The Soviets also tried to interdict the movement of arms and supplies from Pakistan and threatened the Pakistanis if they did not desist. All to no avail. The *mujahidin*, despite absorbing heavy casualties, maintained a determined resistance to Soviet efforts to pacify them. The application of the Reagan Doctrine in Afghanistan succeeded.

Reagan succeeded in implementing Carter's 1979 initiative to place 572 intermediate range Cruise and Pershing II missiles in Western Europe that could strike targets in the western regions of the Soviet Union. These missiles would counter Soviet SS-20 missiles already deployed and aimed at NATO countries. This initiative provoked an angry response from the Soviets who tried to stop it. It also aroused opposition from leftist political leaders and peace groups in Europe and from a "nuclear freeze" movement in the United States.

To offset European and domestic opposition to his plan, Reagan offered two new arms control initiatives. The first, called the "zero option," offered to cancel the proposed deployment of Cruise and Pershing missiles in exchange for Soviet removal of their SS-20 missiles. Secondly, at a new series of arms talks between American and Soviet negotiators in Geneva, called START, the United States proposed that both sides scrap one-third of their nuclear warheads and to permit land-based missiles to have no more than half the remaining warheads. The Soviets quickly rejected both proposals. They had no incentive to remove missiles already in place in exchange for cancellation of weapons not yet deployed. They rejected the second offer because 70 percent of their warheads were on land-based missiles compared to about one-third for the United States. However, these U.S. arms control proposals reassured nervous Europeans and slowed the nuclear freeze movement. When the new missiles began arriving in Great Britain and West Germany in 1983, the Soviets broke off the START talks.

The United States escalated the arms race in 1983 when Reagan ordered the Pentagon to develop a Strategic Defense Initiative (SDI). SDI was an immensely complex antimissile defense system that used high-powered lasers to destroy enemy missiles in space. SDI was quickly dubbed "Star Wars" by the media. Many scientists expressed skepticism that SDI could work. If it could be built, they estimated that it would take years and cost $1 trillion. It also posed the danger of destabilizing the arms race, forcing the Soviets to build more missiles and to develop an SDI of their own. President Reagan strongly backed the SDI, assuming that it could be built and would free the world from the deadly trap of deterrence based on mutually assured destruction. He clung to his vision of a world free from the threat posed by the nuclear arms race.

So the costly and dangerous nuclear arms race between the two superpowers roared on. Both sides continued to develop new weapons systems and to refine existing ones. Although both sides observed the unratified SALT II agreement, it placed few curbs on their activities. Arms control negotiations were suspended. The death of the Russian leader, Leonid Brezhnev, followed by two short tenures of old and sick successors, created a succession crisis for the Soviets. It also made any efforts at negotiations between the Soviets and the Americans difficult. In March 1985, a dynamic new leader emerged in the Soviet Union, Mikhail Gorbachev. He quickly established himself as a strong leader. Future negotiations on arms control between the two superpowers again became possible. Although he had only a few diplomatic successes against the Soviets, had escalated the arms race, and deepened the Cold War, Reagan's efforts against the Soviets did restore a measure of American pride and self-confidence. Americans felt good again about themselves and their place in the family of nations.

THE PACIFIC RIM

The Reagan administration also gave much attention to U.S. foreign policy interests in the Far East. Asia comprised a vast region of diverse nation states which, many experts believed, was destined to become the center of American diplomatic concerns by the dawn of the twenty-first century. The most important nations were China, home to a quarter of the planet's 5 billion inhabitants, and Japan, a nation risen from the ashes of total defeat at the end of World War II to become an economic powerhouse by the 1970s. The economies of South Korea, Taiwan, Hong Kong, Maylasia, and Singapore were also thriving in the early 1980s, their prosperity in large measure fueled, like Japan's, on the sale of manufactures to the United States and Western Europe.

The administration did not have good relations with China initially, mainly because of Reagan's efforts to bolster the military forces of Taiwan, which the Chinese considered to be an integral part of their country. In 1984, Sino-American relations improved when Premier Zhao Zivang of the PRC visited the United States and signed agreements pledging cooperation between China and the United States in the crucial areas of industry, science, and technology. Reagan later visited China and signed pacts pledging renewed cultural exchanges between the two countries. Relations between China and America were cordial by the end of Reagan's first term.

Diplomacy with Japan was the Reagan administration's prime Asian concern. Two major problems strained Japanese–American relations in 1981. The first concerned efforts by the Reagan administration to get Japan to pay a far larger share of its defense costs rather than continue to sit comfortably behind the nuclear shield provided by U.S. taxpayers. The Japanese subsequently increased their defense outlays, to about 0.75 of 1 percent of GDP, less than what the Americans wanted, and far lower than the 6 percent of their own GDP that Americans spent annually for defense.

The second, more serious, problem concerned the growing imbalance in U.S.–Japanese trade that increasingly favored the Japanese. The imbalance had reached $10 billion in 1980 and $16 billion in 1981. The largest part of the imbalance derived from the sale of Japanese cars to U.S. consumers. In 1981, Japanese automakers sold almost 2 million cars to American buyers, hurting domestic automakers, who had lost 25 percent of their market to the Japanese in a decade. U.S. negotiators persuaded the Japanese to reduce voluntarily auto shipments to America for 1982, and they also convinced the Japanese to reduce barriers to the importation of U.S. agricultural commodities. Despite these concessions, the trade imbalance continued to grow in favor of Japan. It reached $20 billion in 1983 and shot up to $35 billion in 1984. The fundamental cause of the trade imbalance was rooted in a reality of modern international economic life: Japanese manufacturers were far more adept at producing quality goods that American consumers strongly desired than Americans were at producing goods that Japanese consumers wanted to buy.

In Southeast Asia, the Vietnamese people endured a life of poverty and oppression. Their Communist leaders discovered that they were far better equipped to fight American imperialism than they were to provide good government and a prosperous economy for their people. Soviet subsidies kept the backward Vietnamese economy going. Each year, thousands of Vietnamese fled the country to seek a better life for themselves and their families in Taiwan, Hong Kong, France, and the United States. Vietnam also maintained 200,000 troops in Kampuchea to support a puppet regime that the Vietnamese had installed in 1979. The Reagan administration indicated its displeasure with Vietnamese imperialism and also sought an accounting from the Hanoi government of the fate of thousands of American servicemen still missing in action from the war. Washington made it clear to the Vietnamese leaders that there could be no improvement in official American-Vietnamese relations until Vietnam pulled its troops out of Kampuchea and settled the MIA issue to the satisfaction of the concerned families.

DISASTER IN LEBANON

In the Middle East, the Reagan administration tried to continue the peace process established by Carter of providing Israel with strategic security and giving the Palestinians a homeland on the West Bank. The larger goal of U.S. Middle Eastern policy continued to be containing Soviet influence in that strategic region. While trying to implement its policies, the United States became embroiled in a civil war going on in Lebanon. Israel continued its policy of gradual annexation of the West Bank, ignoring the national aspirations of the Palestinians. In June 1982, in an effort to destroy the PLO, Israeli forces invaded Lebanon and besieged West Beirut, where refugee camps contained thousands of Palestinians and provided a base for PLO fighters. The PLO and other Muslim factions in Lebanon turned to Syria to contain the Israeli forces.

U.S. policy in Lebanon was contradictory. Even as it supported the Israeli invasion, the Reagan administration employed an envoy of Lebanese descent, Philip Habib, who arranged for the Israelis to lift their siege while a UN force supervised the removal of PLO forces. Following the removal of the PLO, the Israelis reoccupied West Beirut. On September 17, 1982, Lebanese Christian militia, working closely with Israeli forces, entered two Palestinian refugee camps and slaughtered hundreds of people in reprisal for the murder three days earlier of a Christian leader. Following the massacre, the United States sent in troops to try to restore peace in Beirut.

But the U.S. forces came under siege themselves as civil war raged in the streets of Beirut between Christian and Muslim militias. Syrian forces, aided by the Soviets, occupied eastern Lebanon and controlled most of the Muslim factions. Israeli troops remained in southern Lebanon. The 1,500 U.S. Marines, isolated at the Beirut airport, without a clear-cut mission nor sufficient force to maintain order, were perceived by the Muslims and their Syrian supporters to be aligned with the Christian forces.

The Middle East, 1947–1981.   *Source:* U.S. State Department.

The United States tried unsuccessfully to restore order to Lebanon and to arrange for Syrian and Israeli withdrawal. Early on the morning of October 23, 1983, a yellow Mercedes truck loaded with explosives and driven by a Muslim terrorist, slammed into the U.S. Marine compound near the Beirut airport and killed 241 Marines sleeping inside. Reagan was forced to withdraw the remaining American forces in February 1984, ending the U.S. presence in Lebanon. The civil war went on. Syria remained the major force in Lebanese affairs. Lebanon became a fertile source of kidnappings and terrorist attacks on American citizens. Moderate

Arab states refused to support U.S. Middle East policy and the peace process appeared hopelessly stalled. Lebanon was a humiliating defeat for the Reagan administration and the slaughter of the Marines constituted the worst U.S. military disaster since Vietnam. Lebanon's agony continued.

POLICING THE WESTERN HEMISPHERE

Reagan administration officials also gave a high priority to Western Hemispheric affairs where the United States had long been the hegemonic power. Canada and America had long been each other's principal trading partner and the two democratic nations shared the longest unfortified international boundary in the world. Canada also was the chief supplier of foreign oil to the United States. Even so, relations between the two countries had not been warm in recent years. Canadian nationalists had long resented U.S. domination of many sectors of their economic life. And, the two countries often were at odds over trade policies, NATO affairs, fishing rights, disarmament policies, and pollution. Relations between the two nations improved after a new conservative government headed by Brian Mulroney came to power in 1984. Mulroney and Reagan soon established a warm personal relationship. Together they brought about a historic agreement: a treaty removing all barriers to trade between their two countries. The agreement went into effect in December 1988, making the Canadian–U.S. market the largest international free trade zone in the world. Achievement of free trade with the Canadians was one of the major diplomatic achievements of the Reagan presidency.

In addition to Canada, the Reagan administration involved itself in the internal affairs of Central American countries. In Nicaragua, Reagan accused the new Sandinista government of suppressing democratic elements within Nicaragua and aiding Marxist rebels in nearby El Salvador. Reagan viewed the Sandinista regime as a serious threat in Central American that must be contained. Otherwise it could become another Cuba, exporting Marxist-Leninist revolution to neighboring countries, using Nicaraguan military bases as staging areas.

At the time Reagan assumed the presidency, the CIA estimated there were about five hundred Cuban, Soviet, and East European military advisers, technicians, and intelligence operatives in Nicaragua. In the spring of 1982, Reagan approved the use of CIA paramilitary operations to interdict arms shipments from Nicaragua to El Salvador and to overthrow the Sandinista regime. Washington's chosen instrument for deposing the Sandinistas was to be a "Contra" military force recruited from various groups of anti-Sandinista Nicaraguans, including former supporters of the deposed dictator, Anastasio Somoza Debayle.

Congress, skeptical of Reagan's Central American policy, enacted the Boland Amendment in December 1982 which forbade the CIA or the Pentagon to provide any funds or training to anyone for the purpose "of overthrowing the government of Nicaragua." Reagan appealed to Congress in 1983 for funds to "hold the line against externally supported aggression" in Central America. Congressional Democrats accused him of exaggerating the Cuban and Soviet threats, of relying too heavily upon military solutions, and of ignoring serious social and economic problems within Central American countries which bred rebellion. Public opinion polls revealed much popular opposition to U.S. military involvement in Central America, and fears of being drawn into another Vietnam. After noisy debates, Congress first rejected the Reagan administration's request for $80 million to support CIA covert operations against Nicaragua. But in December 1983, Congress did approve $24 million for covert operations.

Meanwhile, the CIA continued its war on the Sandinistas. Contra forces, trained by the CIA at bases in neighboring Honduras, began operations inside Nicaragua. Other CIA-trained elements attacked various port installations at several sites. In early 1984, helicopters flown by CIA-trained operatives mined three of Nicaragua's major harbors. When Congress learned that CIA-trained forces had mined Nicaraguan harbors, causing damage to merchant ships, it cut off all American aid for the Contras. The World Court later ruled that the United States had violated international law and Nicaragua could sue America for damages. The Reagan administration ignored the court's ruling. With funding of its secret war in Nicaragua cut off by Congress, Washington made a deal with the Saudi Arabians whereby the United States sold the Saudis four hundred Stinger aircraft missiles in return for which they agreed to provide the Contras with $10 million. The administration also persuaded Israel to aid the Contras and wealthy Americans also chipped in money. The Iran-Contra scandal originated in these efforts at creative financing to keep Washington's proxy war in Nicaragua afloat and circumvent the will of Congress.

In El Salvador, the war between left-wing guerrillas and a right-wing government continued. Carter had cut off U.S. aid to the government, following the murder of three American nuns by government forces. The Reagan administration restored and increased U.S. assistance and sent in forty-five U.S. military advisers to help government forces. The United States backed a government headed by a moderate democrat, José Napoleón Duarte. Duarte defeated the candidate of the extreme Right, Roberto d'Aubisson, in a 1984 election and began a reform program. He also tried to curb the excesses of right-wing "death squads" who had murdered thousands of civilians since the war began. But Duarte's forces could not defeat the rebels. The civil war went on.

While the Reagan administration pursued its proxy war against the Sandinistas in Nicaragua and backed the Duarte government in El Salvador, it also fought a brief miniwar for control of a small island located in the Eastern Caribbean, Grenada. U.S. forces invaded Grenada ostensibly to rescue several hundred American citizens studying medicine there. The main purpose of the invasion was to overthrow a Marxist regime headed by General Hudson Austin who had recently come to power. What most concerned the Reagan administration was the construction of an airport at Point Salines capable of accommodating Fidel Castro's air force. The runway could also serve as a refueling station for Soviet aircraft ferrying weapons to the Sandinistas. American invaders quickly overcame all resistance, deposed the Austin regime, and sent several hundred Cuban militia captured in the fighting back to their island. Most Grenadians welcomed the American armed forces as liberators who had rescued them from a tyrannical regime that had taken control of their island and was turning it into an outpost of Cuban and Soviet power. America installed a friendly interim government and granted it $30 million in military and economic assistance. The United Nations condemned the American incursion into Grenada, but public opinion polls in this country showed Reagan's actions enjoyed broad support.

REAGAN: THE FIRST TERM

Liberal intellectuals savaged Ronald Reagan. They were offended by both the conservative agenda and by his seeming lack of some of the abilities normally associated with occupants of the Oval Office. Historian John Edward Wiltz called him "the least cerebral" of modern presidents. He was portrayed as a kind of ceremonial president: While he looked and acted the part, an inner circle of advisers made policy and ran the country. He tended to disengage himself from the details of his day-to-day administration. On occasion, he dozed off at cabinet meetings while his advisers debated policy options. He was not especially energetic or hardworking; he was America's first nine-to-five president since Calvin Coolidge. He often appeared dependent on his wife Nancy for advice and guidance. He sometimes confused events that had transpired in the celluloid world of Hollywood films with political reality. His knowledge of the world appeared to be impressionistic and anecdotal rather than conceptual and factual. He was often given to misstatements. During his presidency, Reagan's staffers became adept at damage control, at putting the proper "spin" on his more ludicrous and outrageous remarks. At times, Reagan appeared to be an actor playing the role of president rather than functioning as chief executive.

Even though his left-wing detractors attacked his intellectual and administrative shortcomings, Reagan had a clear vision of the direction in which he wanted to move the country and he was determined to succeed. He was determined to reverse the fifty-year trend whereby the federal government assumed increasing responsibility for underwriting the economic security and general welfare of the population. He wanted to slash taxes and eliminate government regulations, which he believed had shackled the entrepreneurial energies of the American people for a half-century. He was also determined to restore American military primacy in the world and to contain Soviet expansionism as Americans had done in the 1940s and 1950s before the Vietnam debacle sapped their will.

Demonstrating great political skill, Reagan largely succeeded in moving the Congress and the American people in accordance with his conservative vision. He retained the trust, admiration, and affection of a majority of his fellow citizens for most of his presidency. He did not destroy the welfare state, if that was his intent, but he trimmed its sails. The social service state was pared down and the social contract was attenuated. The economy, after enduring a bitter recession in 1982, rebounded strongly. Inflation was brought under control, and long-term stable growth for the rest of the decade of the 1980s ensured national prosperity. Reagan strengthened the armed forces and Americans were treated with new respect in the world by both friends and foes. Most Americans became more optimistic about both their present conditions and the future of the nation. Reagan's stirring speeches helped to lift the malaise that had fastened itself on the nation during the era of limits. He proved to be the most popular and successful president since Eisenhower.

But there was a dark side to the Reagan record. Huge deficits in the federal budget and international trade roared out of control. America found itself becoming the world's largest debtor nation. While Yuppies prospered, the number of poor Americans increased. The rich became richer while poor people became poorer. The Reagan administration had scant interest in civil rights or ecological concerns. Drugs poured into the country and crime rates soared. Although popular with a large majority of the population, the Reagan presidency was a controversial one, and it had its legions of detractors. Probably the way in which individuals viewed the Reagan presidency turned mainly on their economic circumstances, their political ideologies, their skin color, and their gender.

THE ELECTION OF 1984

Reagan's landslide reelection victory on November 6, 1984, reaffirmed his personal popularity. His forty-nine-state sweep expressed voter approval of the strong economic recovery and the country's powerful military buildup. Reagan received 525 electoral votes, the largest total in history. Former Vice President Walter Mondale, the Democratic Party candidate, carried only his home state of Minnesota and the District of Columbia. Reagan got 52.7 million votes (59 percent) to 36.5 million (41 percent) for Mondale. The Republicans gained thirteen seats in the House and won seventeen of thirty-three Senatorial elections, retaining a fifty-four to forty-six majority. In state and local races, beyond the reach of Reagan's influence, Democratic candidates fared much better.

Reagan's smashing victory crossed all regional and most demographic lines. The Democrats appeared to have no remaining regional base of support. In the once Solid South, every state went for Reagan by decisive majorities. In the West and Southwest, Reagan won easily. The Northeast, once the stronghold of both moderate Republicans and liberal Democrats, voted for Reagan. He also swept the industrial states of the Great Lakes and the midwestern farm belt, despite continuing economic problems in both of these regions. All age groups voted for him. Baby-boomers, voters in their twenties and thirties, voted two to one for Reagan. Half of union members voted for Reagan even though Mondale's chief backers were the AFL-CIO leadership. Class and ethnic differences were visible in the voting returns. Middle-class and wealthy voters overwhelmingly supported Reagan. Less affluent voters generally supported Mondale. Blacks voted 90 percent for Mondale as did 60 percent of the Hispanics. Election results showed Hispanics to

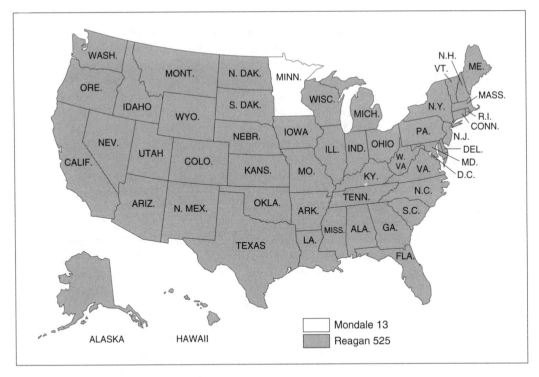

The electoral vote, 1984.   *Source:* Moss, *Moving On,* p. 337.

be an emerging political force, constituting large voting blocs in key states such as California, Texas, and Florida.

At the outset of the election campaign, Reagan had appeared vulnerable to charges that Reaganomics unfairly favored the rich and hurt the poor. His Middle East policy had failed in Lebanon. His Central American policy was controversial, and the Soviets had broken off arms control talks. There had been several scandals involving Administration members. But Reagan mounted a bouyant and energetic campaign. His reelection bid used slick television commercials that emphasized the restoration of the national economy and national pride while avoiding specific issues. His commercials stressed the themes of redemption, family values, and patriotism. His chief speech writer, Peggy Noonan, wrote the best line of his campaign: "America is back: it's morning again." Garry Wills suggested that much of Reagan's remarkable personal popularity derived from nostalgia, from a yearning for a sense of restoration of a lost community.

Reagan was also helped significantly by what Congresswoman Pat Schroeder called the "Teflon president:" the public and most of the established media did not hold Reagan accountable for his policy failures or for wrong-doing by members of his administration. For the duration of the 1984 campaign, it appeared as if the American people were determined to enjoy a successful and popular presidency no matter what, after so many scandals and so many failures. Reagan, during his first term, enjoyed the most favorable press of any modern president. As journalist Bill Moyers observed, Americans voted for Reagan because they wanted "to feel good."

Mondale tried to focus the campaign on issues, but he never found one that enabled him to cut into the president's huge lead. Public opinion polls showed voters disapproved of many of Reagan's specific policies, but they were voting for him because they liked and trusted the man. Given world and national conditions, probably no Democrat could have beaten Reagan in 1984. Mondale also hurt whatever chance he might have had to win by announcing bluntly to American voters at the outset of his campaign that he intended to raise taxes if he won. Polls showed most Americans believed they were better off economically in 1984 than they had been in 1980 and were pleased to find the nation at peace. Compounding Mondale's problems, he came across poorly an television. His droopy-eyed appearance and the nasal twang in his voice projected negativism and pessism. By contrast, Reagan, the Great Communicator, exuded energy, goodwill, and unrelenting optimism.

In defeat, the Democrats made history twice. First, Jesse Jackson, the first serious black candidate for president, conducted a spirited primary campaign, getting 18 percent of the vote and winning 373 delegates to the Democratic convention Second, Mondale's running mate, Representative Geraldine Ferraro, the first woman vice-presidential candidate on a major party ticket, conducted a historic campaign. But Ferraro was on the defensive during much of her campaign because of her violations of campaign spending laws and because of her husband's questionable business practices. She neither strengthened a weak Democratic ticket nor enabled Mondale to exploit the "gender gap." Jackson's campaign proved to be too radical and divisive. His promised "rainbow coalition" of all disadvantaged Americans failed to congeal; his political base never reached much beyond the black community.

THE SECOND TERM

President Reagan began his second term in January 1985, convinced that most Americans endorsed his policies. He was determined to provide more of the same. He reorganized his White House staff with not entirely happy results. His chief of staff, James Baker, switched jobs with Secretary of the Treasury Donald Regan. Regan never developed the rapport with the president that Baker had enjoyed, nor did he have the ability to compensate for or protect Reagan from his shortcoming as had Baker. Two other personal advisers also departed: Michael Deaver and Edwin Meese, who, along with Baker, had formed a "Troika" that was responsible for much of the Reagan's presidency's legislative successes during the first term. Deaver formed a public relations firm to cash in on his White House connections; he promptly ran afoul of laws forbidding influence peddling. Edwin Meese became Attorney General and managed to established the lowest ethical and legal standards for the nation's top law enforcement office since the days of Warren G. Harding. Meese was in continual difficulty with congressional investigators because of some of his unsavory associations and because of the slipshod manner in which he handled his personal finances.

Reagan made tax reform his top legislative priority. The federal tax system had become exceedingly complex over the years as Congress had factored in a great many exemptions and loopholes favoring corporations and wealthy individual taxpayers. Polls showed strong popular support for revising a tax structure that former President Carter had called a "disgrace to the human race" and Reagan himself had termed "un-American."

Bipartisan support for tax revision gradually emerged in Congress, led by Democratic Congressman Daniel Rostenkowski and Republican Senator Robert Packwood. In the summer of 1986, Congress passed the Tax Reform Act that brought the first fundamental overhaul of the modern federal income tax system since its inception during World War II. The act simplified the tax code by eliminating many tax shelters and deductions. It reduced multiple tax brackets on individuals to just three, at rates of 15, 28, and 33 percent. It also restored a measure of fairness to a tax system that had long been skewed in favor of the wealthy. It removed 6 million poor Americans from the federal income tax rolls and lowered the tax burden for a majority of taxpayers. The new law shifted some of the tax burden to the business community by closing loopholes and eliminating write-offs and exemptions. Many corporations that had paid little or no federal income tax would pay more under the new law. The Tax Reform Act represented a triumph for supply-side economics. President Reagan predicted that lower taxes would translate into greater consumer spending, expanded productivity, and greater prosperity. Critics predicted the tax law would hurt business enterprise and slow economic growth.

Reagan shared another major achievement when his administration supported a landmark immigration bill passed by Congress in October 1986. The bill revamped the 1965 act, offering legal status to millions of aliens living illegally in the United States. It also required employers to ask for identification verifying the citizenship of job applicants and levied fines on employers who hired illegal aliens. This legislation solved some of the most pressing problems posed by the inability of the nation to police its borders effectively and to control the immigration process.

Another pressing problem to which Reagan was slow to respond was the AIDS epidemic which swept the country during the mid-1980s. This hideous illness, for which there is yet no cure nor even an immunizing agent, believed by many experts to be inevitably fatal to all who contract the virus, each year killed thousands of mostly gay men. For years, the administration refused to publicly acknowledge the disease, and was, at least in the eyes of those most concerned about fighting AIDS, painfully slow to support increased research and study of the dread disease. Administration officials mainly called for mandatory testing of categories of people thought to be at risk or who held positions of public responsibility. Meanwhile, the disease continued to wreak devastation and to blight the lives of the vulnerable. AIDS threatened to become a worldwide epidemic and struck with special fury among the people of several Central and East African nations.

Another serious health problem that Reagan showed more interest in was the growing epidemic of drug use in America. Reagan came to Washington in 1981 committed to waging a war on drugs and bringing the international drug trade under control. Drug traffic in marijuana, cocaine, and heroin flourished in the mid-1980s. America was the world's major consumer of illicit drugs. The immense costs of America's gargantuan drug habit included thousands of deaths annually, health problems for millions, huge increases in urban crime, corruption in the criminal justice system, and loss of productivity. Efforts to enforce drug laws and American-financed efforts to eradicate drug crops at their source in Asia and Latin America continued to be ineffective. One of the major reasons for the failure of the Reagan administration's war against drugs, popularized by First Lady Nancy Reagan, was its inability to slow the great American appetite for drugs. All efforts to curtail the supply side of the drug problem were doomed to fail until a measure of control could be imposed on the demand side.

After years of activity and having spent $3 billion, Reagan announced early in 1988 that the war against drugs had been won. His claim was preposterous. According to contemporary surveys, 25 million Americans regularly used marijuana, 6 million regularly used cocaine, particularly "crack," and another million were heroin addicts. Public opinion polls showed that Americans considered the drug epidemic to be the nation's number-one domestic problem. Washington's policy of criminalizing drug use and interdicting the supply either at the source or at the point of entry into this country was failing as Reagan's presidency ended. Some experts suggested that an alternative policy that focused on educating people, especially young people, about the hazards of drug use, and that relied on therapies, counseling, and community support groups to wean people from drug dependencies promised better results over the long term.

THE "GO-GO" ECONOMY

The economy continued to perform strongly through the second term of Reagan's presidency. Inflation remained under control and oil supplies were plentiful. When inflation and higher taxes were taken into account, motorists were filling their tanks with cheap and plentiful gasoline. Growth rates averaged 3 to 4 percent per annum; many corporations enjoyed record sales and profits and continually expanded production. The stock market continued to push through record highs as the great bull market of the 1980s roared on. Consumer spending and consumer confidence remained high.

Despite the economy's strong performance, serious problems plagued the American economy. Individual and corporate indebtedness increased rapidly. The takeover mania that gripped Wall Street during the 1980s continued. Most of these corporate buyouts were severely "leveraged;" that is, they were financed by consortia of bankers and brokerage houses who often sold huge portfolios of "junk bonds" (high-yield, high-risk securities issued by companies with low credit ratings) to raise the vast sums of capital needed to buy out shareholders at above-market prices. Once the corporate raiders acquired operating control of the company, they often had to sell off its profitable assets to raise the sums required to meet the huge interest payments on the indebtedness they had contracted to buy out the former stockholders.

LBOs (leveraged buyouts) usually did not make the economy more productive or competitive; in fact, they often left companies weaker and in serious debt with no funds for research or the development of new products. Aggregate net capital investment also was not enhanced by these takeovers and mergers. Toward the end of Reagan's presidency, investigations exposed some of the financial wizards who had brokered corporate takeover deals as criminals who had violated laws against insider trading. The two biggest names were high-fliers Ivan Boesky and Michael Milken, both of whom served years in jail, paid millions of dollars in fines, and saw their business careers and personal reputations ruined.

Budget deficits continued to grow, exceeding $200 billion in 1986. During Reagan's presidency, the national debt tripled—from $1 trillion to $3 trillion! By 1989, each American's share of the national debt exceeded $12,000. Paying the annual interest due on the national debt became the third-largest item in the federal budget, after social security and defense. The massive indebtedness came about as a result of a tacit agreement between the Reagan White House and many Democrats in Congress. They agreed to support large increases in military spending, modest cuts in social spending, and deep tax cuts.

The national debt became so large during Reagan's presidency that servicing it absorbed most of the net savings accrued by individuals and businesses each year. Pressures on interest rates were eased because foreign investors, particularly Germans, Japanese, and Saudi Arabs, bought up about 20 percent of the U.S. debt each year. Even so, the federal government had to take so much money from the private capital markets to fund the debt each year that money available for investment in research, product development, new technologies, and increased productive capacity were significantly curtailed. There was a link between the huge federal indebtedness and declining American competitiveness in the world's marketplaces. Both the federal government and the private sector became dependent on large annual infusions of foreign capital.

In December 1985, Congress enacted the Gramm-Rudman Act, a measure that required automatic annual reductions in the budget deficit if the president and Congress failed to agree on cuts. The following year, the Supreme Court nullified the law and the deficit for 1986 came in at a record $226 billion. Congress then enacted a modified version of Gram-Rudman, but then the White House and congressional legislators agreed to accounting procedures that effectively gutted the law. Several large spending programs were declared "off-budget" and not included when figuring the deficit in order to evade Gramm-Rudman limits. The 1987 deficit was smaller, but it took a record crash of the stock market on October 19, 1987, and fears of impending recession to force Reagan and the Congress to reduce the budget deficit.

Trade deficits also had expanded rapidly between 1980 and 1985 as imports increased 41 percent while exports decreased slightly. Every week during the Reagan presidency, American consumers spent about $1 billion more buying imported goods than foreigners spent buying American-made products. To offset that imbalance in international trading, huge amounts of American securities, real estate, and factories were purchased by foreign investors who had to recycle their surplus dollars. By the end of Reagan's presidency, U.S. assets in foreign lands totaled less than the U.S. assets owned by foreigners. Until the early 1970s, America had been the world's leading creditor nation. By the end of the Reagan presidency, America had become the world's leading debtor.

Other economic trends alarmed Americans. Increasing numbers of American manufacturing concerns moved their operations overseas to get away from unionized workers and high taxes, and they took thousands of good jobs with them. At the same time, foreign investors from the Middle East, Japan, Hong Kong, and various European countries continued buying up American assets. By the end of Reagan's presidency, foreign corporations owned American banks, investment houses, fast food restaurants, motion picture studios, landmark skyscrapers, thousands of acres of farm land, publishing firms, and supermarket chains.

While foreigners continued to buy up U.S. properties, other foreign competitors steadily increased their share of American domestic markets for autos, electronic products, cameras, textiles, and shoes. Many of these developments reflected a new reality—that the economic lives of nations were increasingly intertwined. By the mid-1980s, the American economy was intricately plugged into a world economic system. Henceforth, more and more of the economic and financial activities of Americans would be influenced by decisions made in corporate boardrooms in Tokyo, Riyadh, and Bonn. But many Americans, who tended to intermingle nationalistic feelings with economic activity, felt threatened by what appeared to them to be losses of autonomy and signs of relative decline.

Another sign of trouble in America that surfaced in the late 1980s—disasters in the savings and loans industry—was entirely homegrown. The savings and loan debacle was an unintended consequence of bipartisan good intentions. Deregulation was a policy idea first implemented during the Carter years, in the airline and trucking industries. The Reaganauts embraced and expanded upon deregulation in the name of greater productivity plus economy in government. Under the influence of supply-side economic theory, federal agencies relaxed or abolished rules and regulations affecting the operations of a wide range of American industries. One of these was savings and loans banks. Historically, S&Ls loaned money to individuals to buy homes in local areas where the banks were located. Home mortgages tended to be low-risk, low-profit investments. Savings and loans banks were noted for being safe, sound, and a little dull.

At the urging of the Reagan administration, Congress deregulated the savings and loan industry in 1982. Consequently, S&Ls could offer a much wider range of loans; they could invest depositors's funds in commercial real estate, undeveloped land, and, in fact, just about any kinds of high-risk projects imaginable. They could also loan funds for projects nationally and even internationally. Even if these high-risk operations went bust and the banks collapsed, the existence of the Federal Savings and Loan Insurance Corporation (FSLIC) meant that the bankers would not incur personal liabilities and depositors would get their money back from the government.

In many parts of the nation, especially in the Southwest and West, the new era of deregulation in the S&Ls attracted a generation of incompetent and crooked buccaneers into the banking industry. They proceeded to invest billions of dollars of depositors' funds in a bewildering variety of dubious projects, knowing that they might reap huge profits from their high-risk undertakings but also running no risk of incurring personal responsibility for any losses because of the existence of FSLIC. Deregulation of the savings and loans industry eventually reaped a financial disaster that left the taxpayers saddled with a tab that ran into hundreds of billions of dollars.

Although the economic expansion of the "go-go" years of the 1980s was real and impressive, it was also selective and spotty. It excluded vast numbers of Americans. The chief regional beneficiaries of the Reagan boom years were the Northeast and California. Both regions were on the cutting edge of the computer revolution and both had extensive military and aerospace industries. In these areas, good jobs at good salaries abounded; real estate prices for both residential and commercial properties shot upwards.

But in the states of the upper Midwest, site of the traditional smokestack industries, economic conditions deteriorated. Agricultural states and energy-producing states also slumped during the 1980s. While the Northeast and West Coast boomed, much of the rest of the country was mired in a decade-long stagnation and recession. Real wages, adjusted for inflation, continued to stagnate in many parts of the country during the 1980s. Real take-home pay for factory workers declined slightly from 1975 to 1987.

There were other victims of Reaganomics during the 1980s. Revenue-sharing with state and local governments, enacted by Richard Nixon in 1972, was cut during the Reagan presidency. Infrastructure repairs to roads and bridges were neglected. Cities, strapped for funds by shrinking tax bases and increasingly needy populations, were especially hard hit by these losses of federal funds. Social services deteriorated.

During the 1980s, income differentials between upper-income and lower-income families widened. The number of poor women and children increased. One of the main reasons poverty was increasingly feminized was because of a sharp increase in the number of unwed mothers; the rate of children living with a never-married mother increased threefold during the 1980s. By the end of the 1980s, one-fourth of the children born in the United States was born to an unwed mother. The Reagan administration, although not responsible for the rapid rise of poor unmarried women with children, made matters worse for them by cutting funds for the Women-Infants-Children program (WIC) that provided both pre- and postnatal care and food monies to low-income women.

During the 1980s, the poverty rate in America regressed to about where it had been in the mid-1960s, to about 13 percent. But poverty in America had changed by the mid-1980s. Whereas the elderly had comprised a majority of the poor people in America in the mid-1960s, by the mid-1980s, most of the poor consisted of single mothers, children, and young men with low educational and job skills. A sizable proportion of the 1980s poor worked full- or part-time at minimum-wage levels. Millions of the new jobs created during the 1980s were full or part-time service-sector jobs that paid only minimum wages.

Homeless people constituted a growing proportion of the 1980s poor population. The homeless, the poorest of the poor, came from many backgrounds: the unemployed, the mentally ill, drug and alcohol abusers, people with serious medical problems, including AIDS victims; racial minorities, runaways, dysfunctional Vietnam veterans, and women fleeing abusive husbands. Many of the homeless struggled to survive, living on the streets of large cities and begging for food and money. Sometimes aggressive panhandlers frightened or angered prosperous shoppers as they walked along sidewalks or entered stores. If prospering Yuppies represented the glittering successes of the Reagan era, the homeless represented the abject failures. In the new Gilded Age, the homeless were the prime victims of recrudescent Social Darwinism. Nobody knew exactly how many homeless there were in America in the 1980s. Estimates ranged from a low of 200,000 up to more than a million. President Reagan, while expressing his personal sympathy for the plight of the homeless, proposed no new federal programs to alleviate their suffering or to get them off the streets. What assistance there was for the pathetic armies of the homeless mostly came from local governments, private charities, churches, and compassionate individuals.

THE REAGAN COURT

President Reagan had long opposed most civil rights laws and supported a constitutional amendment outlawing busing to achieve school integration. The Supreme Court in 1983 blocked attempts by the Justice Department to restore tax benefits to segregated private schools and colleges. When the 1965 Voting Rights Act was up for renewal, Reagan advised Congress to kill it. Congress renewed it by large majorities.

In the field of civil liberties, Reagan, like most conservatives, believed that the court system favored the rights of accused criminals over those of law-abiding citizens, who were often victims of violent crimes. During the 1980s, both the Congress and the states, responding to widespread popular concerns, took a stronger law-and-order line. Longer, mandatory sentences were imposed for many crimes. Many states reinstituted the death penalty for heinous crimes. Jail populations rapidly increased and construction of new prison facilities lagged behind demand. By the end of the 1980s, over a million Americans were incarcerated, the highest rate of incarceration for any country in the world.

Over the course of his presidency, Reagan appointed over four hundred federal judges; these jurists constituted about 60 percent of all sitting federal judges in 1989. The president also appointed a chief justice and three associate justices to the Supreme Court. The administration searched for strict constructionists whose constitutional views could also incorporate right-wing social agendas, including opposition to affirmative action programs, abortion, and pornography, and favoring harsher justice for accused criminals. Reaganite judges were also expected to support efforts to restore prayer in the public schools and to favor the death penalty. Most of the four hundred Reaganite judges were youngish white males with conservative judicial philosophies.

The president's appointments to the Supreme Court allowed him to reshape that venerable institution. In 1981, he had appointed Sandra Day O'Connor and in 1986 he had selected Antonin Scalia to be associate justices. Both O'Connor and Scalia were conservatives. Reagan had also replaced retiring Chief Justice Warren Burger with Associate Justice William Rehnquist, the most conservative member of the Court. Reagan's efforts to add a third justice to the High Court in July 1987 proved embarrassing to the elderly chief executive. His first nominee, Appellate Judge Robert Bork, was rejected by the Senate because of his extreme views concerning First Amendment rights. Reagan's second choice, Douglas Ginsburg, had to withdraw his name from consideration after revealing to the press that he had smoked marijuana when a student. Reagan's third choice, also a judicial conservative, Anthony Kennedy, was unanimously confirmed by the Senate in February 1988.

Gradually, the Reagan appointees on the Supreme Court shifted the tenor of its decisions in a conservative direction. It chipped away at some of rights of the accused established in previous decisions. For example, the court now permitted the use of illegally seized evidence in court in some instances. The Reagan court also undermined affirmative action. In *City of Richmond* v. *J. A. Croson Company* (1989), the Court nullified a government set-aside program that reserved a proportion of government contracts for minority groups.

FOREIGN POLICY

During his second term, President Reagan had to face many international problems. Global financial crises threatened as Third World nations sank ever deeper into debt. The collective debt of Argentina, Brazil, and Mexico approached $250 billion, most of it owed to American and European banks. The possibility of these countries ever repaying their debts appeared nil, and default, which could derange international financial transactions and trade and do serious harm to major U.S. banks, remained a constant danger.

International terrorism was another mounting problem. Between 1981 and 1986, thousands of people were kidnapped, injured, or killed by terrorist attackers. The State Department estimated that about seven hundred major terrorist assaults occurred in the world in 1985. Many terrorists had their roots in the bitter conflicts in Lebanon between Christian and Arab factions, and in the continuing battle to the death between Israelis forces and Palestinian fighters. Arab terrorist organizations, dedicated to the destruction of Israel and to attacking its Western supporters, frequently targeted Americans. The slaughter of the American Marines in Beirut in 1983 was the worst of many Muslim terrorist attacks against Americans. In June 1985, Lebanese Muslim terrorists hijacked an American jetliner and held thirty-nine Americans hostage for seventeen days. In October 1985, four members of the Palestinian Liberation Army seized an Italian cruise ship, the *Achille Lauro,* killing an elderly American in a wheelchair. In April, U.S. military installations in West Germany were bombed by Palestinian terrorists supported by Libya. In retaliation, American bombers attacked targets in and near the Libyan capital of Tripoli. Public opinion within the United States supported the air attack, but most of America's European allies, their citizens often the victims of terrorist assaults and kidnappings, called the bombing counterproductive and likely to provoke further terrorist attacks.

In South Africa, a racist, white minority continued its rule over black, Asian, and mixed-race groups that composed 86 percent of the population. The Reagan Administration, following a policy it called "constructive engagement" toward the South African apartheid regime, refrained from public criticism and tried to nudge it toward democracy. The policy produced few results and South Africa was racked by violence in the mid-1980s as government security forces violently repressed black demonstrators. Angry and frustrated blacks at times retaliated with terrorist attacks of their own.

Critics of "constructive engagement" believed that only economic pressure could force the South African government to dismantle apartheid. Fourteen states and forty-one cities passed divestiture laws restricting or prohibiting the investment in South Africa of pension funds and requiring the selling off of current holdings in South African securities. The divestiture issue activated protests on college campuses. Some universities, responding to protests, ordered partial or full divestment. In October 1986, Congress, overriding a presidential veto, imposed economic sanctions on South Africa, including a boycott of South African products and a ban on new U.S. loans and investment in that country. Some U.S. corporations voluntarily sold off their South African operations.

The Reagan administration also had to confront a crisis in the Philippines, the former territory and longtime ally of the United States. For several years, a corrupt military dictator, whom Washington had supported, Ferdinand Marcos, had been losing power. Communist rebels were gaining strength in several regions of the country. Pressure from U.S. officials forced Marcos to permit elections which had been suspended since he took office. In February 1986, he was challenged by Corazon Aquino, the widow of an assassinated political opponent of Marcos. Both sides claimed victory in an election marked by violence and fraud. U.S. officials, worried about the declining Philippine economy and the rising Communist insurgency in a strategically important country, pressured Marcos to resign. He fled Manila in March 1986, and Aquino assumed office. She worked to restore political democracy, to revamp the economy, to maintain friendly relations with America, and to remove the Communist threat. During her first two years of power, Aquino had succeeded in restoring political democracy and the economy was growing after years of stagnation. But she had to survive two coup attempts led by army officers who wanted to restore Marcos to power.

THE IRAQI-IRANIAN WAR

The continuing Iraqi-Iranian war reached menacing proportions in 1987. After six years of fighting that claimed nearly 2 million lives, the stalemated war spilled into the Persian Gulf and threatened vital oil shipments that flowed daily from Gulf oil fields to Europe, Japan, and the United States. Iraq attacked Iran's oil-export terminals and also struck at Iranian tankers carrying oil from the gulf. Iran could not strike at Iraqi oil shipments directly because Iraq's oil traveled via pipelines to terminals on the Mediterranean and Black Seas, but the Iranians undertook reprisals by attacking ships hauling oil from Kuwait, an oil-rich Arab Emirate that was bankrolling Iraq's war against Iran.

Soviet entry into the Gulf, along with both Iraqi and Iranian threats to Gulf oil shipping, caused President Reagan to send a large fleet of U.S. Navy vessels to the region and to provide naval escorts for oil convoys. In what amounted to armed intervention into the shipping war, Washington agreed to reflag and escort tankers carrying oil produced by Kuwait. In the summer of 1987, an American guided-missile frigate on station in the Gulf, was attacked, apparently by accident, by an Iraqi plane, with the loss of thirty-eight lives. Then on July 3, 1988, there occurred an even more ghastly accident when a U.S. destroyer, the USS *Vincennes*, fired a missile that brought down an Iranian airliner, killing all 290 people aboard. Crewmen aboard the American destroyer apparently thought that it was an Iranian fighter closing on their ship for an attack.

The United States feared that a victory by either Saddam Hussein's secular Iraqi regime or Khomeini's Islamic fundamentalist Iranian government would make the winner the dominant power in the Persian Gulf. To prevent either side from winning the war—a victory that could threaten the political stability of Saudi Arabia, Kuwait, and other moderate Arab regimes, and disrupt the flow of oil to the United States and its allies—America, behind an official facade of neutrality, secretly aided whichever side appeared to be losing. In the early years of the war, Washington helped Iran, but after 1986, America aided Saddam. There had been several incidents involving attacks on merchant shipping by Iranian speedboats and several ships had been damaged by mines lain by Iranians. U.S. ships and helicopter gunships had retaliated for some of the Iranian attacks, sinking speedboats and damaging an Iranian oil platform in the Gulf. In April 1988, there occurred a series of clashes between American and Iranian naval units. As a consequence of American intervention in the Persian Gulf, Iran and the United States were engaged in an undeclared naval war.

The Iraq-Iran war ended suddenly in August 1988 when Ayatollah Khomeine accepted a UN-proposed cease-fire. At the time Iraq had gained the upper hand and the Iranian enthusiasm for war had subsided after six years of slaughter. Although he had seized the initiative, Saddam, weary of the long war, readily consented to the cease-fire. Mutual exhaustion had brought an end to war. During the war, the Iraqis had used poison gas against the Iranians and were feverishly at work developing nuclear weapons. Despite the ominous indicators, the Reagan administration continued to back Iraq, considering it to be a necessary counterforce to the Iranians. Washington's support of Saddam in the late 1980s is one of the background causes of the 1991 Persian Gulf War.

As the war between Iraq and Iran ended, the Arab-Israeli conflict took a violent turn. Palestinians living in the West Bank and Gaza took to the streets to protest continuing Israeli occupation of the two territories. Roving bands of Palestinian youths, armed with rocks and Molotov cocktails, clashed with Israeli army squads. This Palestinian *intifidah* (uprising) continued intermittently through 1988 and 1989, resulting in the deaths of hundreds of Palestinians and a dozen Israeli soldiers. The Israeli government headed by Prime Minister Yitzhak Shamir refused to consider any resolution of the conflict that established a Palestinian state in the territories. He also refused to meet with Yasir Arafat and the PLO, the only organization that represented a majority of the Palestinians. The Reagan administration backed the Shamir government's refusal to meet with PLO leaders, but did favor some kind of political arrangement in the occupied territories that would give the Palestinians autonomy.

CENTRAL AMERICA

The Reagan administration continued its support of the Contra rebels fighting to overthrow Nicaragua's Sandinista regime. In the summer of 1985, Congress narrowly approved $100 million in support of the Contras. The policy continued to draw criticism from the media and liberal Democrats. Public opinion polls showed a majority of Americans opposed to Contra aid and fearful that American troops would be sent to fight the Sandinistas if the rebels failed. The intermittent civil war went on.

A peaceful alternative to war in Nicaragua surfaced late in 1987 when President Oscar Arias Sanchez of Costa Rica, speaking for the leaders of four Central American republics meeting in Guatemala City, proposed a plan calling for an end to U.S. military backing of the Contras, the restoration of democracy in Nicaragua, and negotiations between the Sandinista government and Contra leaders leading to a cease-fire. Reagan administration officials expressed a willingness to let Arias try to implement his plan, and Nicaraguan leader Daniel Ortega Saavedra appeared willing to accept some of the proposals. In April 1988, both sides agreed to a temporary cease-fire and Congress voted $48 million in nonlethal humanitarian aid for the Contras. In nearby El Salvador, efforts to get negotiations going between the Duarte government and the Marxist rebels continued to fall, and the civil war in that tormented country went on.

THE IRAN-CONTRA SCANDAL

President Reagan's personal popularity remained high through the first half of his second term. Most Americans remained optimistic about their own and their nation's prospects, and they strongly endorsed Reagan's style of presidential leadership. But two weeks after the midterm elections in November 1986, the worst political scandal since Watergate erupted in Washington. Americans were shocked to learn that the Reagan administration had entered into secret negotiations with Iranian officials that involved selling them arms in exchange for the release of American hostages held captive in Lebanon by Muslim terrorists. Two weeks after Americans had learned of the arms-for-hostages deals with Iran, Attorney General Edwin Meese told a stunned press conference audience that his investigators had discovered that profits from the Iranian arms sales had been sent to Contra rebels fighting in Nicaragua even though Congress had enacted legislation forbidding American military aid to the rebel fighters.

At a hastily called press conference, President Reagan denied that arms had been traded for hostages. He insisted that a relatively low-level operative with the National Security Council, Marine Lieutenant Colonel Oliver North, was mainly responsible for both the dealings with Iran and the Contra arms sales, and that only North's immediate superior, National Security Adviser, Vice Admiral John Poindexter, knew of his activities. Reagan's statements were simply not credible. For the first time in his presidency, Reagan's integrity and competence were seriously questioned by the citizenry. His public approval rating dropped precipitously, from 67 percent to 46 percent.

The origins of the Iran Contra scandals went back to 1981 when President Reagan ordered CIA director William Casey to organize an anti-Sandinista force among Nicaraguan exiles living in Honduras. Over the next several years, these Contra forces waged a guerrilla war against the Sandinista forces. Congress, concerned about reports that the Contras had killed many civilians and had also sown mines in Nicaraguan harbors that had damaged merchant ships belonging to other countries, enacted the Boland Amendment. The Boland Amendment limited American aid to the Contras to $24 million and forbade the use of any U.S. funds for the purpose of trying to overthrow the Sandinista government, a government that the United States recognized.

Reagan, committed to the goal of overthrowing the Sandinistas and, in his view, eliminating a Communist threat to Central America, and contemptuous of the democratically-controlled Congress, instructed the CIA, the National Security Council, and the Pentagon to circumvent congressional restrictions on aiding the Contra forces. In the summer of 1984, Congress, responding to Reagan administration efforts to continue its clandestine proxy war in Nicaragua, tightened the

Boland Amendment. It forbade the CIA and any other U.S. government agency from aiding the Contras.

The tighter version of the Boland Amendment failed to deter the president and his men. Casey, National Security Adviser Robert McFarlane, and one of McFarlane's aides, Marine Lieutenant Colonel Oliver North, persuaded a handful of U.S. allies to proved funds for the Contras. Nations contributing monetary support for the rebels included Israel, South Africa, Saudi Arabia, South Korea, and Taiwan. At the same time they raised funds from allies for the Contra cause, Casey, North, and others also solicited additional funds from wealthy American individuals to support the rebels.

While President Reagan and his subordinates were circumventing the will of Congress and violating the Boland Amendment by continuing the war in Nicaragua that Congress was trying to stop, the administration also began an involvement with Iran aimed at freeing U.S. hostages being held in Lebanon by pro-Iranian Muslim terrorists. President Reagan had been deeply moved when the families of seven American citizens held hostage in Lebanon had pleaded with him to arrange for the release of their loved ones. Reagan was also aware of the major political dividends that would accrue to him and the Republican party in the upcoming elections if he could bring the hostages home.

In July 1985, an Iranian arms dealer, Manucher Ghobanifar, met with McFarlane. Ghobanifar claimed to represent a moderate faction within the Iranian government that wanted to improve relations with America. He proposed to McFarlane that the United States, working through Israeli middlemen, arrange for the delivery to Iran of TOW antitank missiles that the Iranians desperately needed for their ongoing war with Iraq. In return, the moderates would work to arrange the release of some of the American hostages. A few months later, Reagan authorized the sale of 100 TOW missiles to Iran. At the time that he authorized the sale of the weapons, Reagan understood that the United States was trading arms for hostages. He also knew that it was against the law and contrary to American policy, which he had publicly affirmed, to sell weapons to Iran because of its support of international terrorism.

But no hostages were freed after this transaction. Ghobanifar told McFarlane that the Iranians wanted an additional 400 missiles in exchange for the release of a single hostage. McFarlane arranged for the missiles to be sent, and on September 15, 1986, one of the American hostages, Benjamin Weir, was set free. In November Ghobanifar was back with another deal: send Iran 100 HAWK surface-to-air missiles and five American hostages would be freed. In December, President Reagan signed a secret document, called a finding, which approved the proposed sale. The finding described the transaction as an arms-for-hostages deal. At the time that the deal was made, Oliver North wrote a memorandum equating the 100 HAWK missiles with five American hostages that were supposed to be released. No hostages were released.

Even though the several arms sales to Iran had only yielded one released hostage, Reagan's enthusiasm for the project remained undiminished. Poindexter, who replaced McFarlane as National Security Adviser in December 1985, working through North, arranged for another shipment of arms to Iran. This time, 3,000 TOW missiles and another 100 HAWKs would be sent in exchange for the remaining six Americans still held captive by terrorists in Lebanon. Both Secretary of State George Schultz and Secretary of Defense Caspar Weinberger opposed the arms-for-hostages transactions because they were illegal, because they were contrary to stated American foreign policy, and because they did not serve the national interest. Vice President George Bush, although not a major player in the transactions, attended several meetings at which the arms-for-hostages deals were discussed. Bush never gave any indication that he was opposed to them.

Oliver North came up with the plan to divert the profits from the sale of arms to the Iranians to the Contras. Did President Reagan direct North to send the money to the Contras? Reagan later could not remember if he approved the funds; Poindexter testified that the president did. In February 1986, a sale of 1,000 TOW missiles to the Iranians netted a profit of about $8 million. North gave the money to a retired Air Force Major General, Richard Secord, to buy arms for the Contras. No hostages were released; in fact, two more Americans in Lebanon were taken hostage.

After at least four arms shipments to the Iranians, more Americans than ever were held hostage. But Reagan's zeal for the cause remained undiminished. On July 26, Iran arranged for the release of another American hostage, Lawrence Jenco, a Catholic priest. Another shipment of missiles was sent to Iran, but it resulted in no further prisoners being freed. On November 2, just before the midterm elections, a final arms shipment was sent to Iran via Israeli middlemen. It produced the release of another hostage, David Jacobsen. But all the frantic deals with the Iranians did not net the Reagan administration its hoped-for political boost. Instead, they had generated a serious election-eve political crisis for the president and his men.

The cover on the bizarre secret schemes was blown in late October and early November. On October 5, 1986, a plane hauling weapons to the Contras was shot down and the Sandinistas captured an aircrewman, an American named Eugene Hasenfus. Hasenfus confessed to his captors that he was part of a secret American program to aid the Contras. On November 1, a Lebanese magazine, *Al Shiraa*, ran a story about the U.S. arms-for-hostages deals with Iran. Iranian officials quickly confirmed the story and told the world that the so-called moderates were agents of the Khomeini government. They bragged that they had tricked the Americans into selling them modern weapons that were urgently needed for their war with the Iraqis. Three weeks later, Edwin Meese made his stunning announcement that money from the sale of arms to Iran had been diverted to the Contra war effort against the Sandinistas.

In some ways, the fallout from the Iran-Contra scandal was worse than Watergate. It severely damaged U.S. foreign policy. The American policy of taking a hard-line against terrorism had been exposed as hypocritical. The Saudis and other moderate Arab states felt an acute sense of betrayal at the news that U.S. officials had sold antitank and antiaircraft missiles to Khomeini's government in the hopes of securing the release of seven Americans being held hostage in Lebanon by groups of Islamic fundamentalists controlled by Teheran. At home, conducting a clandestine foreign policy in Central America against the expressed wishes of Congress and contrary to public opinion and perhaps the law, weakened Reagan's ability to govern effectively. His chances of getting his legislative program through the Democratically controlled Congress were sharply reduced. Iran-Contra badly wounded the Reagan presidency, eroding both its power and popularity.

In the aftermath of the scandalous revelations, there were several official investigations of its details. A federal court appointed an independent counsel to investigate the scandal. President Reagan appointed a commission headed by former Senator John Tower to investigate the affair. Congress also appointed committees to investigate the scandals. The Tower Commission's report was made public in March 1987. It portrayed Reagan as an out-of-touch president who had surrounded himself with irresponsible advisers pursuing ideologically driven policies that hurt the national interest.

Reagan responded with a speech to the American people on March 4 in which he tried to restore his faltering hold on events. He acknowledged responsibility for Iran-Contra, but he insisted that it was not his intent to trade arms for hostages and that he knew nothing about using some of the money obtained from Iran to buy arms for the Contras. In effect, he denied all responsibility for any wrongdoing. He was forced to plead a fool's defense to avoid being branded a knave. Reagan's speech neither improved his image nor enabled him to regain the political initiative.

Following the Tower report, the combined congressional committees began holding televised hearings that ran through the summer of 1987. At times, the hearings evoked memories of Watergate as congressmen tried to follow the money trail, to find out how the profits from arms sales to Iran were channeled to the Contras, and to find who profited from all these weird transactions.

Two of the witnesses appearing before the committees, retired Air Force Major General Richard Secord, who was recruited by Colonel North to run the Contra weapons supply system, and former National Security Adviser Robert McFarlane, who had arranged the Iranian arms sales, both implicated the President in their testimony. They insisted that Reagan was repeatedly briefed about the arms sales to Iran and approved of the efforts to get the hostages released. They also implicated the late CIA Director William Casey, who may have been the mastermind behind the Iran-Contra operations, and who may have worked through Colonel North and former national security adviser Admiral John Poindexter, to avoid congressional oversight and public disclosure as required by law. The two key witnesses to appear before the Committee, Colonel North and Admiral Poindexter, both insisted that they had kept President Reagan uninformed about the details of the Iranian negotiations and that they never told him of the government's involvement in shipping arms to the Contras. They also admitted that they had deliberately misinformed Congress and the press about their actions—actions which they believed were serving the national interest and accorded with the president's wishes. The flamboyant and unrepentant North was clearly the star of the televised hearings. He passionately defended his actions as moral and patriotic even if they did defy Congress and break the law.

The committee hearings were seriously flawed. They were hastily conducted and investigators lacked crucial documents that would have enabled them to get at more of the truth about the Iran-Contra scandals. Key witnesses lied or gave evasive answers. The investigating committees clearly did not have the stomach to press their investigation too close to Reagan nor to consider the possibility of impeaching him, even though they possessed evidence suggesting that he had knowingly and deliberately broken laws. Committee members knew that most Americans could not care less whether funds from arms sales were diverted to the Contras. While resenting the arms sales to Iran, many Americans could also see Reagan's good intentions: he was trying to free the hostages even if the means chosen were dubious. Lawmakers also feared political reprisals at the hands of the people if they stood guilty once again of regicide. Besides, there was no "smoking gun" in the Iran-Contra scandals that irrefutably implicated the president. Liberal Democrats, who were most outraged by Iran-Contra, given their low estimations of Reagan, found his fool's defense plausible. They really could believe that he was an out-of-touch leader who did not know what was happening inside his own administration.

The committees issued a joint 450-page report on November 18, 1987, that was scathingly critical of the president. It bluntly accused Reagan of not obeying his oath to uphold the Constitution and the laws of the land and said he bore "the ultimate responsibility" for the wrongdoing of his aides. The congressional report also provided the most accurate accounting to date of how nearly $48 million raised from the arms sales had been distributed. In a sweeping criticism of the officials involved, the report stated that the Iran-Contra affair was "characterized by pervasive dishonesty and inordinate secrecy." It also voiced the suspicion that the president knew more about the arms sales and Contra funding efforts than he acknowledged. It also challenged the credibility of Colonel North's and Admiral Poindexter's testimony. Without citing specific individual actions or naming specific laws, the report asserted that "laws were broken" in the Iran-Contra affair. The report concluded that the president's protestations of ignorance could not absolve him from responsibility because the scandal occurred on his watch.

Coming a year after the original revelations, the report failed to elicit much public interest, and White House spokesmen dismissed the report as containing nothing that was new. But the Iran-Contra revelations had severely damaged Reagan's presidency. They also seriously crippled his crusade to overthrow the Sandinistas. Public opinion polls revealed that a majority of Americans believed that the president knew about the government's involvement in the Contra arms shipments, and President Reagan's popularity ratings remained far lower than they had been before the news of the scandal had broken.

In March 1988, the independent counsel, Lawrence Walsh, issued grand jury indictments to four of the most prominent participants in Iran-Contra scandal, including Colonel North and Admiral Poindexter. All were charged with multiple offenses, including conspiracy, fraud, theft, perjury, and covering up illegal operations. At his trial in 1990, Poindexter repudiated his testimony previously given before the congressional committees. He stated that Reagan was in charge of the Iran-Contra operations from the beginning and had ordered him, North, and others to break the law.

The former president was called to testify at Poindexter's trial. In answers to 127 questions put to him by prosecutors, Reagan frequently gave confused and vague answers, and often could not recall the names of subordinates or their activities. He reiterated that he was not involved in any wrongdoing and that he did not know what his subordinates were doing, or that they traded arms for hostages or diverted the profits to the Contras. Poindexter was convicted of five felonies, including perjury. North was convicted of obstructing congress and destroying confidential documents. The trials of the Iran-Contra conspirators concluded this shabby episode that marred the reputation and undermined the popularity and power of President Reagan.

THAWING THE COLD WAR

During Reagan's second term, both the United States and the Soviet Union urgently needed to stabilize the nuclear arms race in order to free their people and the planet from its spiraling cost and danger. For reasons about which we can only speculate, Ronald Reagan, the quintessential Cold Warrior, to the amazement of most his leading advisers, began to soften his hard-line anti-Soviet thinking. He authorized the resumption of arms negotiations with the Soviets which began in March 1985. A dramatic moment in world history occurred when the Soviet leader, Mikhail Gorbachev, and President Reagan met in Geneva from November 24 to 27, 1985, the first summit conference since Carter had journeyed to Moscow in 1979. But their six hours of private talks were inconclusive. They achieved no major agreements on arms control. The major block was Reagan's insistence that America would continue development of the Strategic Defense Initiative (SDI). Gorbachev demanded that the United States abandon the SDI before he would agree to any cuts in nuclear weaponry or sign any arms control agreements. At the summit's conclusion, Reagan and Gorbachev produced a four-and-one-half page communiqué pledging to accelerate arms control negotiations.

The summit was an exercise in global public relations by both sides. But it was also an important historic event, giving further diplomacy a needed impetus. A budding friendship between the two world leaders was the main consequence of the meetings. President Reagan toned down his anti-Communist rhetoric, saying Gorbachev was a man with whom he could do business. In the Soviet press, a new image of Reagan as a man who could be reasoned with had replaced a hostile version in which he had often been compared to Hitler. But the great expectations generated by the Geneva summit failed to materialize.

At a hastily called summit meeting at Reykjavik, Iceland, in October 1986, Gorbachev and Reagan came close to reaching major agreements on nuclear arms controls. But the opportunity for a comprehensive arms control treaty was missed when Gorbachev demanded a limitation on development of the U.S. Strategic Defense Initiative that President Reagan refused to consider.

During the next year, Reagan replaced many of his hard-line anti-Communist advisers with a new breed of more flexible and pragmatic bureaucrats. Frank Carlucci replaced Weinberger at Defense. Army General Colin Powell became the new head of the National Security Council. Senator Howard Baker replaced Donald Regan as the president's chief of staff. These men favored reaching arms control agreements with the Soviets. First Lady Nancy Reagan, concerned about her husband's place in history in the aftermath of Iran-Contra, urged him to seek a major arms control agreement with Gorbachev. She wanted an accommodation with the Soviet Union to be the chief legacy of a Reagan presidency.

A year after Reykjavik, joint arms control efforts finally resulted in a major agreement between the two superpowers. Gorbachev journeyed to the United States, and he and Reagan signed a historic treaty in December 1987 that eliminated an entire class of weapons—intermediate range thermonuclear missiles—which had been located mostly in Europe. Both sides had, in effect, accepted the "zero option" originally proposed by Reagan in 1983. The agreement, known officially as the Intermediate Nuclear Forces (INF) Treaty, was the first nuclear arms control agreement ever reached that required the destruction of deployed nuclear weapons systems. It also provided for inspectors of both powers to observe the dismantling and destruction of the intermediate-range missiles. The INF Treaty and the return of cordial relations with the Soviet Union represented President Reagan's most important diplomatic achievements.

The signing of the INF Treaty and return of détente with the Soviets also held out the promise of future agreements cutting strategic weaponry on both sides. Negotiators from both countries continued to work on a Strategic Arms Reduction Treaty (START). The Soviets also announced that they were ending their costly and futile war in Afghanistan. In addition to phasing out the Afghan adventure, Gorbachev undertook a worldwide scaling back of Soviet diplomatic activity. He indicated that the Soviets might end their economic and military support of the Sandinistas. He urged the PLO to recognized Israel's right to exist. He pressured Hanoi to pull its troops out of Kampuchea. He pulled Soviet forces back from the Sino-Soviet border regions, and he urged the Soviet satellites in Eastern Europe to reform their economies and become more involved with the nations of Western Europe.

The sudden and quite remarkable turnabout in U.S.–Soviet relations culminated in Reagan's triumphant visit to Moscow in June 1988. To anyone familiar with Reagan's long record of ferocious anti-Communism, his appearance in the heart of the "evil empire" was astonishing. When asked if he still believed the Soviet Union was the "focus of evil in the modern world," he responded, "They've changed." He spoke to the Soviet people on television and embraced his friend

Mikhail Gorbachev at the site of Lenin's tomb. After such acts of reconciliation, no one appeared to care that both nations still had thirty-thousand nuclear warheads aimed at each other. Gorbachev made another visit to America in December 1990. Good pals "Ron" and "Gorby" staged a photo opportunity in front of the Statue of Liberty. Even the First Ladies, Nancy Reagan and Raisa Gorbachev, who had taken a chilly dislike to each other since their first meeting, exchanged warm smiles. The Cold War appeared to be melting.

THE SLEAZE FACTOR

While Iran-Contra investigations raised troubling questions about the integrity and competence of high government figures, other scandals rocked the Reagan administration. In December 1987, former White House adviser Michael Deaver, who operated a political consulting service, was convicted on three counts of perjury for denying that he improperly used his White House connections to help clients. In February 1988, Attorney General Edwin Meese became the latest in a long line of Reagan administration officials to be accused of conflict-of-interest and improper conduct. The charges against Meese stemmed from his alleged financial relations with a small company that received a defense contract. He came under further attack for his alleged awareness of a proposal to bribe Israeli officials to guarantee that they would not attack a planned oil pipeline construction project in the Middle East. Further problems for Meese developed at the Justice Department when several top officials resigned in April 1988 because they feared Meese's mounting problems prevented him from exerting strong leadership of the Department and also hindered several ongoing Justice Department operations. Despite his troubles and declining credibility, Meese continued to enjoy the support of President Reagan, who gave his long-time friend and adviser a strong vote of confidence.

On top of these revelations of wrongdoing and improprieties at high levels in the White House came the incredible disclosure in 1988 via the memoirs of Donald Regan, Reagan's former chief of staff, that the president had permitted his wife Nancy, after she had consulted with an astrologer, to influence his scheduling. By the end of Reagan's presidency, allegations of illegal and unethical activities tarnished the reputations of more than one hundred White House officials.

Reagan administration officials were by no means the only politicians to be plagued by scandal in 1987 and 1988. The leading contender for the Democratic presidential nomination, Gary Hart, had to abandon his campaign for seven months when a newspaper reporter disclosed that Hart had spent a weekend with an attractive model. When Hart belatedly reentered the race in 1988, he found that he had lost all his organization and most of his popular support. He soon gave up his now hopeless candidacy. Another Democratic presidential hopeful, Senator Joseph Biden of Delaware, had to withdraw when reporters learned that he had frequently plagiarized from the speeches of other politicians and had falsified his academic record.

IMPORTANT EVENTS

1981	Ronald Reagan is inaugurated as the fortieth president of the United States
1981	Reaganomics is implemented
1981	The U.S. military buildup begins
1982	Covert aid to Contras in Nicaragua begins
1982	Congress enacts the Boland Amendment
1983	The U.S. deploys intermediate range Pershing missiles in Western Europe
1983	Reagan proposes SDI (Star Wars)
1983	Muslim terrorist kills 241 U.S. Marines in Beirut
1983	The U.S. invades Grenada
1984	Reagan is reelected by landslide margin
1985	The Geneva Summit takes place
1985	The Gramm-Rudman Act is passed
1985	The U.S. becomes a debtor nation for the first time since 1915
1986	The Tax Reform Act is passed
1986	The U.S. adopts economic sanctions against South Africa
1986	The Reykjavik Summit takes place
1986	The Immigration Reform Act is passed
1986	The Democrats regain control of the Senate
1987	The U.S. intervenes in the Persian Gulf shipping war
1987	The Iran-Contra scandal erupts
1987	The stock market crashes
1987	The U.S. and Soviet Union sign the INF Treaty
1987	The Soviet Union begins scaling back its international commitments
1988	George Bush is elected president

BIBLIOGRAPHY

A sizable historical and journalist literature has already accumulated for the 1980s. F. Clifton White, in *Why Reagan Won: A Narrative History of the Conservative Movement, 1964–1981*, tells the story of the conservative movement from the Goldwater debacle to Reagan's successful bid for the presidency in 1980. Haynes Johnson, in *Sleepwalking Through History: America in the Reagan Years*, offers a critical journalistic account of the Reagan era. The most informed account of the Reagan presidency is Lou Cannon's *President Reagan: The Role of a Lifetime*. President Reagan has written a memoir, *An American Life*. A fine recent study by Stephen Vaughn, *Ronald Reagan in Hollywood: Movies and Politics*, explores the important relationships among Reagan's film and political careers. Two important books that interpret the public career of Ronald Reagan are by Garry Wills (*Reagan's America: Innocents at Home*) and Michael P. Rogin (*Ronald Reagan: The Movie*). A good account of the early years of the Reagan presidency is Laurence I. Barrett's *Gambling with History: Reagan in the White House*. P. C. Roberts, in *The Supply-Side Revolution*, defends Reaganomics. T. B. Edsall, in *The New Politics of Inequality*, challenges the president's economic policies. Strobe Talbott's *Deadly Gambit* is a lucid and fascinating analysis of the arcane complexities of arms control. Edward N. Luttwack, in *Making the Military Work*, presents a critical study of 1980s military policies. See *Central America: Anatomy of Conflict*, edited by R. S. Leiken, which contains useful studies of that important region. *Visions of America* is a lively account of the 1984 election. The most thorough account of the Iran-Contra scandal that rocked the Reagan administration in 1986 and 1987 is Theodore Draper's *A Very Thin Line: The Iran-Contra Affairs*. Bob Woodward, in *Veil*, has written an account of the Iran-Contra affair in which he contends that it was master-minded by William Casey. Seth P. Tillman's *The United States and the Middle East: Interests and Obstacles* is a balanced treatment of American policy in that troubled region. Stansfield Turner's *Terrorism and Democracy* is a thoughtful study of one of the most serious and ago-nizing problems that U.S. presidents have to deal with. Michael Mandebaum's *Reagan and Gorbachev* is a good account of their personal diplomacy. Roy Gutman, in *Banana Diplomacy*, gives us a critical study of U.S. foreign policy in Nicaragua and El Salvador in the 1980s. Michael Schaller is the first historian to write an account of the Reagan years. His *Reckoning with Reagan: America and Its President in the 1980s* is a fine, brief study of what happened and why during the Reagan presidency.

CHAPTER **16**

Epilogue:
The 1990s

As Americans entered the final decade of the twentieth century, they faced a rapidly changing international world and a myriad of perplexing internal economic, social, political, and cultural problems. Americans struggled to find new solutions and to chart new directions both at home and abroad. The opening of the Berlin Wall on November 9, 1989, was the first in a series of stunning events that culminated in the collapse of the Soviet Union and the end of the Cold War that had dominated world affairs for nearly a half-century. As Americans confronted a transformed global situation, they had to deal with changing demographics, economic decline, a fragmented social order, ethnic conflict, cultural warfare, and ideologized politics. Many Americans expressed dismay over environmental degradation and decaying public schools. They worried about their personal and the nation's long-term economic prospects. In 1992, after twelve years of Republican rule, voters sent Democrat Bill Clinton to the White House. His administration sought to craft a new moderate reform agenda for the conservative political climate of the 1990s.

A DEMOGRAPHIC PROFILE FOR THE NINETIES

Census takers, combing the country during 1990, discovered that dramatic changes had occurred in the nation's demographic profile during the go-go years of the 1980s. In 1990, the national population totaled 247 million, nearly a 10 percent increase over 1980. By 1996, the population exceeded 261 million and the median age had reached thirty-four, making Americans one of the oldest national populations on the planet. One of the most important findings of the 1990 census: the advance wave of baby-boomers had entered middle age.

The fastest-growing age groups continued to be older Americans. This "graying of America" raised serious issues. How well would society be able to maintain its oldest citizens and at what cost? Corporations found their pension costs inflating out of control. The social security system, although fiscally solvent for the foreseeable future barring catastrophe, was increasingly strained. Young workers had to pay higher social security taxes to fund pensions paid to an ever-higher proportion of retirees. Many of the retirees were far more affluent than the workers paying their social security pensions. In the early 1990s, many retirees were also drawing generous pensions relative to the amounts they had contributed to the social security system during their working years. Social security taxes increased 25 percent during the 1980s. Many young working people in the early 1990s remained openly skeptical that social security benefits would be there for them when they reached retirement age. There were also special problems with Medicare and Medicaid, both funded through the social security system. By 1996, it was clear that Medicare costs had to be trimmed sharply or the system would be bankrupt before the end of the century.

The 1990 census confirmed that Americans remained a people on the move. Migration patterns that originated during World War II continued. The Sunbelt states retained their magnetic abilities to attract new residents from the Northeast and Midwest. Population increases in sunbelt states stretching from South Carolina to Southern California continued to account for most of the nation's population growth in the 1980s. California, fueled by immigration from Mexico, Asia, and the Pacific Islands, added 5 million people and accounted for 25 percent of the total population growth during the decade.

Continuing population shifts from the Northeast and Midwest to the South and Southwest also meant that the locus of political power continued to shift in the same direction. In the new House of Representatives elected in 1992, California gained seven seats, Florida gained three, and Texas gained two. Several of the older states of the Northeast and Midwest lost representation. The 1990 census also revealed that the national population continued to gravitate toward the nation's urban centers. Most of the decade's population growth occurred in cities containing more than 100,000 people.

The 1990 census also reflected the growing variety of household living arrangements in America. The number of traditional families, of married parents with children, continued to decline. Nuclear families made up only about one-fourth of the nation's households in 1990. As many households were made up of a person living alone. The number of single mothers heading a household increased rapidly during the decade, especially among minority populations. In 1996, there were nearly 12 million single-parent families, most of them headed by a woman who had never married. During the 1990s, the number of people choosing not to marry increased rapidly. In 1996, approximately 14 percent of American households were poor, about the same proportion as could be found in this country in 1965.

The large increase in poor, single-parent families during the 1990s had ominous implications for millions of America's children. Observers noted that in addition to the usual adolescent disaffection, some of which adults suspected was designed simply to annoy them—peculiar dress, weird hair styles, and a taste for bad music—many young people exhibited genuine confusion, anguish, and despair. In 1996, rates of teenage eating disorders, drug use, depression, and suicide were all rising. Adolescents were one of the highest-risk groups for contracting AIDS. At the same time that teenage pathologies were rising at an alarming rate, SAT scores were dropping. Young people also had to deal with a collapsing public school system and diminishing opportunities for higher education. Economy-minded congresses reduced the amounts of money available for student grants, loans, and work-study programs. There were fewer good jobs available and competition for them was intensifying.

THE DECLINE OF THE MIDDLE CLASSES

Many serious, intertwined economic problems, exacerbated by the recession that struck during the early 1990s, vexed the American people. The annual trade deficit ranged between $40 and $60 billion. Annual federal deficits continued to run up huge amounts of red ink. The national debt reached $4 trillion in 1992 and was approaching $5 trillion in 1996. That year, annual interest payments on the national debt reached $250 billion, consuming 16 percent of all federal spending.

During the recession, unemployment rose; it reached 7.8 percent during the summer of 1992, meaning that about 9 million workers were without jobs. Housing starts, new car sales, and business investment plummeted. The Federal Reserve Board slashed interest rates to thirty-year lows, but the economy did not pick up. The first recession to afflict the American people in a decade had two major causes: cuts in military spending in the aftermath of the Cold War and the collapse of commercial real estate markets in the wake of the overexpansion of the 1980s. A further cause derived from the spending binge that Americans had gone on during the go-go decade of the 1980s. Then their bills came due in the early 1990s and the economy contracted.

More importantly, the long-term structural weaknesses of the U.S. economy that had first appeared during the early 1970s, persisted into the 1990s. The employment shift from industrial to service sector jobs continued, with many of the latter positions low-paying and unskilled. Large corporate employers, facing increasingly stiffer world-wide competition, continued to streamline their operations. As they computerized and downsized, they laid off thousands of workers, not only production workers, but also managerial personnel, especially middle-management types whose work could be done more efficiently by computers.

The most serious long-term structural weakness that has eroded the economic underpinnings of millions of American middle-class families since 1973 has been the slow rate of economic growth. From 1890 through 1970, the U.S. economy grew at an annual rate of 3.5 percent, adjusted for inflation. More than any other single factor, that high rate of economic growth sustained over much of the twentieth century, creating a large and prosperous middle-class society. Since 1970, including the boom years of the 1980s, the annual rate of growth has averaged 2.2 percent. This sharp decline (37 percent) in long-term annual growth rates has had devastating impacts on many middle-class families. Real income for the middle classes has been declining since 1973. During those years, the annual share of national income earned by the middle classes has also been declining. Slower rates of growth mean declining economic opportunity and lowered social mobility.

During the 1990s, despite recession and continuing structural weaknesses, the U.S. economic performance included some bright spots. In the mid-1990s, the U.S. economy remained the largest and strongest national economy in the world. In 1996, American industry once again led the world in productive efficiency. Aided by a weak dollar and quotas imposed on Japanese imports, American automakers improved their domestic market share. It reached 75 percent in 1996, up from 68 percent in the late 1980s. By the mid-1990s, U.S. automakers were turning out fuel-efficient and reliable vehicles that were as good as the foreign competition and often cost thousands of dollars less. American automakers dominated the markets for the popular minivans, light trucks, and off-road vehicles. In 1995 and 1996, American high-tech industries flourished. U.S. electronics companies continued to lead the world in such diverse fields as desktop computers, software applications, and telecommunications. Even though American companies overall ran a large annual trade deficit, U.S. high-tech industries enjoyed a growing annual trade surplus that exceeded $50 billion in 1995.

A NATION OF IMMIGRANTS

During the decade of the 1980s, 6 million legal immigrants entered the country. No one knows how many illegal immigrants entered the country during the same period, but conservative estimates put the figure at hundreds of thousands per annum. If the estimated illegal immigrants are added to the legal immigrants, between 9 and 10 million people emigrated to America during the 1980s, the largest number for any decade in American history. Europeans represented only 12 percent of the 1980s immigration. Experts estimate that the rate of immigration established during the 1980s has continued into the 1990s. Most of the immigrants emigrated from a Hispanic country within the Western Hemisphere or from a Pacific Island or Asian nation.

Most of the 1980s immigrants clustered in a few states and cities. According to the 1990 census, California was the home of two-thirds of the Asian American population and over one-third of the Hispanic American population. In New York, Los Angeles, San Francisco, Chicago, and other great cities, the new Hispanic and Asian populations settled into ethnic neighborhoods. They brought their distinctive manners, cultural mores and styles; they brought their distinctive languages, cuisine, dress, and music. America's big cities became home to the most culturally diverse populations in world history.

While cultural diversity brought energy and vitality and made America's big cities the most vibrant urban centers in the world, it also brought tensions, dislocations, and serious problems and pressures. African Americans were most vulnerable to the economic competition posed by striving newcomers. The huge influx of new people during the 1980s and 1990s triggered an upsurge of nativism. Drives to repeal bilingual education and to make English the official national language reflected this resurgent nativism. Governor Pete Wilson of California tried unsuccessfully to parlay nativist attacks on immigrants and affirmative action programs into a drive to win the Republican nomination for president in 1996.

BLACK AND WHITE, BUT NOT TOGETHER

Festering ethnic tensions exploded in May 1992 when a California jury acquitted four white police officers charged with savagely beating an African American suspect, Rodney King. A bystander had recorded the incident on a video camera and portions of the tape were repeatedly broadcast to the nation. To nearly all who observed the gruesome sequences, the television camera presented compelling images of police brutality. The verdict to acquit the four policemen, rendered by a politically conservative suburban jury containing no African American members, astonished and angered the nation.

The verdict also ignited the most violent race riot in the nation's history in south-central Los Angeles. Thousands of businesses were looted and destroyed, many of them burned. Fifty-four people were killed, thousands were injured, and over seventeen thousand people were arrested. The costs of the riot exceeded $1 billion. The Los Angeles police, poorly led and confused, initially were slow to respond to the riot and allowed events to get out of control. National Guard troops rushed to Los Angeles to quell the rioters. Within a few days order was restored, but only after enormous property damage and loss of life had occurred.

The riot was reminiscent of the 1965 Watts upheaval: mobs of angry black rioters burning and looting their neighbor businesses. But there were also significant differences. The 1965 riot had pitted black against white. The 1992 riot had much more complex ethnic dynamics. In May 1992, blacks attacked other blacks as well as whites. Hispanics attacked whites. Blacks and Hispanics both attacked Asians, mostly Koreans. Gangs of African American and Hispanic thugs also engaged in violence and looting. No simple analysis sufficed to account for the ominous upheaval. The King verdict obviously triggered the riot, but the underlying causes appeared to be a potent mix of ethnic antagonisms, poverty, and government neglect, all exacerbated by a severe economic recession that hit poor people, working-class people, and small businessmen especially hard.

In 1995, an ironic sequel to the Rodney King case occurred in the tormented city of Los Angeles. From January to October, a former star athlete turned television sportscaster and film actor, O. J. Simpson, stood trial for the murder of his former wife, Nicole Brown Simpson, and her friend, Ronald Goldman. After a lengthy trial, a jury acquitted Simpson of all charges.

Because of the political and cultural contexts in which the trial occurred, it acquired a significance that far transcended the guilt or innocence of one prominent individual. The O. J. Simpson murder trial became the most famous media event in American history. Virtually all the major media provided constant coverage of the trial for months. Due process became judicial theater, a media circus, and Hollywood showbiz. A terrible tragedy became a mass spectacle. A brutal double murder became prime time entertainment, a real-life who-dunnit?

In the eyes of a substantial majority of viewers and expert commentators, the state presented a strong case based on physical evidence that implicated Simpson beyond a reasonable doubt in the two murders. The fact that Simpson, a rich and famous man, whose resources matched those that Los Angeles county could allocate for the trial, hired a battery of high-priced attorneys to mount a successful defense, proved to many Americans the dubious proposition that he was immune to the justice system. Simpson's acquittal also reinforced the widely held cynical notion that in America there was one standard of justice for the rich and another, harsher standard for the poor. The outcome of the trial suggested to many observers that the American system of criminal justice had been tried and found wanting. The jury system appeared to sacrifice impartial justice to political goals and ethnic agenda.

The trial also raised the spectre of domestic violence. The prosecution, although failing to convince the jury that he was a murderer, did show that Simpson had frequently battered his wife prior to their divorce. Statistics showed that domestic violence was the leading cause of injury to women each year. During 1994, over fourteen hundred women died as a result of domestic violence.

Looming over all aspects of the trial was the ugly reality of racism. Because the murder victims, Nicole Brown Simpson and Ronald Goldman, were white, and Simpson was a black celebrity, racial attitudes in this country became central to the outcome of the trial and how people viewed that outcome. The jury, consisting of nine African Americans, eight of them women; an Hispanic male; and two white women, reached a verdict of acquittal within four hours! The jurors all rushed to judgment without seriously considering the mountain of evidence, much of it quite complex and technical, presented by 133 witnesses who testified during the long trial. Polls showed that 87 percent of black Americans agreed with the jury's verdict and 65 percent of whites believed Simpson to be guilty as charged. The black-white racial chasm that existed in this country was highlighted on October 3, 1995, when the clerk of court read the jury's verdict. Around the country, wherever crowds of black Americans had gathered to hear the verdict, they broke into cheers and hugged each other at what appeared to them to be a triumphal deliverance. Wherever crowds of whites had gathered to hear the verdict, they stood in stunned silence or stared in disbelief at what appeared to them to be a brutal miscarriage of justice. These differential responses showed that white and black Americans stared uncomprehendingly at each other from across a vast cultural divide. Seemingly lost in all the furor over the verdict of acquittal was the fact that Simpson still faced civil suits brought by the families of the murder victims accusing him of the "wrongful deaths" of Nicole Brown Simpson and Ronald Goldman.

Two weeks after the conclusion of the Simpson trial, another dramatic event accentuated the black-white racial divide rending the American social fabric. The controversial leader of the Nation of Islam, Louis Farrakhan, led a "Million Man March" on Washington. About 500,000 black men gathered on the Mall in front of the Washington monument. For the huge gathering it was a day of atonement, of renewal, and an affirmation of their black manhood. For most of the participants, it was a deeply moving experience. Strangers listened to speeches, chatted, sang, cried, and hugged one another. Time will tell whether the march was a vivid but perishable event, a Woodstock for African American men, or a turning point in black history—a moment when black men took responsibility for their lives and returned to their homes and communities determined to build a better society. The march also demonstrated how far America had yet to travel to achieve Martin Luther King's vision of an individualistic, integrated, color-blind society, a society in which people were judged not by the color of their skin but by the content of their character.

A more significant indicator of the growing separation of blacks and whites occurred in the cities and suburbs of the nation during the mid-1990s. The pace at which school districts were undoing mandatory school desegregation accelerated. A conservative federal judiciary, which had staked its authority on vigorous enforcement of desegregation orders, often in the teeth of massive resistance, appeared eager to depart the field. After decades of progress toward integration of public schools, the separation of black children was fast approaching early 1970s levels, before busing was implemented.

In 1996 over one-third of black youngsters attended schools that were 90–100% minority, that is African American, Hispanic, Asian, and Native American. Ironically, the Northeast was the most segregated region, and many states of the Old South were among the least segregated. A combination of legal revisionism and continuing residential segregation effectively undermined the nation's effort to integrate its public schools. The relentless tides of demographic change were resegregating the nation's public schools. White flight from the cities to the suburbs left many of the nation's largest public school systems with too few white students to have a meaningful integration. Boston, scene of some of the ugliest resistance to school integration in the early 1970s, illustrated the problem. In 1972, the year desegregation began, about 60 percent of Boston's 90,000 students were white. In 1996, there were 63,000 students in Boston public schools, and only 18 percent were white.

A FRAGMENTED SOCIETY

During the 1980s and 1990s, there occurred a dramatic transformation in the ethnic and racial composition of the American population, the greatest since immigrants from southern and eastern Europe flooded into America during the first fifteen years of the twentieth century. According to the 1990 census, one in four Americans claimed African, Hispanic, Asian, or Native American ancestry. African Americans represented 12 percent of the total; Hispanic Americans represented 9 percent of the total; Asian Americans represented 3 percent of the total; and Native Americans 1 percent of the total population of 247 million. By 1996, the nation's population had grown to some 261 million people; it constituted a mosaic of Native Americans, African Americans, Hispanic Americans, Asian Americans, and European Americans. Each of these large groups comprised, in turn, an array of subgroups differentiated by region, national origin, ethnicity, religion, education, gender, age, and class. Because of the continuing high rate of immigration, both legal and illegal, to America, the percentage of foreign born had reached 10 percent by the mid-1990s, the highest since the 1920s, and up from 5 percent in 1970.

In 1996, more than 2 million people identified themselves as Native Americans, more than twice the 1970 total. This figure reflected not only a rapid natural increase in the AmerIndian population but also the growing number of people of mixed-race ancestry eager to affirm their ethnic roots. A network of tribal-controlled colleges and universities provided Native Americans with relevant educations and cultural sustenance. Many tribes energetically pursued various business ventures from growing wild rice to operating profitable gambling casinos. Despite much economic progress during the 1990s, Native Americans remained the nation's poorest and most oppressed major ethnic group. Both on reservations and in the nation's cities and suburbs, unemployment, alcoholism, accidents, and suicide continued to take their toll on the nation's most vulnerable people.

Fed by continuing high rates of immigration, the Asian American population continued to grow rapidly during the decade of the 1990s. People from Korea, the Philippines, Vietnam, and China continued to come to the United States in large numbers. In 1996, more than 10 percent of Los Angeles's 3.5 million residents were Asians, more than double the proportion a decade earlier. Strengthened by family cultures and prizing academic success, Asian Americans showed high rates of college attendance and upward mobility. However, Asian American communities experienced generational tensions as young people got caught between the tug of traditional ways and the lure of American popular culture.

In the mid-1990s, the African American community remained divided along class lines. At one end of the social spectrum, a large and growing class of educated black professional and business men and women enjoyed successful careers and affluent life styles. A 1996 survey showed that 13 percent of adult blacks had obtained their bachelor's degrees and nearly 75 percent had received their high school diplomas. Yet, despite the tremendous increase in the number of highly educated African Americans in recent years, significant disparities in annual earnings persisted. Median annual income for African American families in 1996 was only about 60 percent of whites: ($25,000 per year for black families compared to $42,000 per year for whites).

At the other end of the spectrum could be found the impoverished inner city blacks. These poorest of the poor constituted an "underclass" trapped within the inner cities. Although intact families, thriving churches, and other strong institutions could be found in the inner cities, this culture of decency was often overwhelmed by social pathologies. As factory jobs once open to urban workers disappeared, young people faced life on the mean streets or held marginal service-sector jobs in car washes and fast-food restaurants. Inner-city pathologies such as high crime rates, drug abuse, welfare dependency, and teenage pregnancies could not be separated from the fundamental problems: lack of good educational and job opportunities.

In 1996, the nation's 22 million Hispanics, more than double the total in 1975, represented America's fastest-growing minority. Hispanic Americans are themselves a diverse group; they include 16 million Mexican Americans concentrated in California and the American Southwest; 1 million Cuban Americans mostly living in south Florida; and between 1 and 2 million immigrants from the Caribbean region and Central America living mostly on the East Coast or in California. The Hispanic American population also included 2 million Puerto Ricans, who are American citizens by birth.

Most Hispanics, regardless of national origins, emigrated to America in search of a better life for themselves and their families. Millions have found success. Hispanic family, church, and cultural institutions have sustained hardworking people struggling to make it in America. But life remained harsh for millions of Hispanic families. In 1996, 20 percent of Mexican Americans and one-third of Puerto Ricans lived in poverty. Hispanic communities were often devastated by alcohol and drug abuse, soaring crime rates, gang violence, and high rates of school dropouts and teenage pregnancies.

As American society grew more fragmented in the 1980s and 1990s, the sense of a common national community proved ever more elusive. The American people appeared to share only consumerist cultural experiences such as shopping at malls and watching prime-time television programs. Debate erupted, as groups hitherto marginalized or excluded from the mainstream of American life demanded cultural as well as political equality.

The multiculturalism controversy took many forms. High school and college course offerings became contested arenas in the "culture wars." Newly empowered advocates for women, African Americans, Hispanic Americans, Asian Americans, Native Americans, gays and lesbians, and fundamentalist religious groups demanded that high schools and colleges revise their curricula. Professors of literature revised reading lists to include works by women, persons of color, and Third World writers. Multiculturalists challenged course reading lists that continued to privilege "DWEMs" (dead white European males). History professors hastened to rewrite textbooks to give more space to previously neglected or excluded nonelite groups.

The multiculturalist reforms provoked a backlash. Traditionalists insisted that these efforts at more inclusive scholarship eroded any sense of a shared national identity. They worried lest a heedless rush to multiculturalism undermine the basic unity of the most successful pluralistic society in world history. Some teachers expressed dismay at working in repressive environments in which newly empowered champions of multiculturalism and "politically correct" speech imposed a new bureaucratic orthodoxy that stifled academic freedom and encouraged an aggressively litigious culture of victimization.

Yet a number of voices resisted all efforts to polarize Americans into warring factions and insisted that multiculturalism's many positive contributions could be retained, while rejecting its extremist claims. In this view, the cultures carried by ethnically and racially defined communities could be appreciated without expecting every individual to define themselves narrowly as members of the descent-based community into which they were born. David Hollinger, perhaps America's most eminent intellectual historian, distinguished sharply between biology and culture, complaining that multiculturalism too often assumed that a person's values and tastes followed from skin color or the shape of the face. In a brilliant and timely book, *Postethnic America: Beyond Multiculturalism*, Hollinger offered his cosmopolitan and inclusive vision of a dynamic, pluralistic society embracing all people of whatever descent:

> Postethnicity prefers voluntary to prescribed affiliations, appreciates multiple identities, pushes for communities of wide scope, recognizes the constructed character of ethno-racial groups, and accepts the formation of new groups as part of the normal life of a democratic community.[1]

WOMEN AND WORK

By the mid-1990s, women had smashed through many sexist barriers to higher education and the workplace. In many fields, long virtually closed to women, such as medicine, law, engineering, and business management, many women energetically pursued productive careers. In 1996, one-fourth of all doctors and lawyers were women. There were also huge increases in the number of women holding public office in the 1980s and 1990s. President Reagan had appointed Sandra Day O'Connor to the Supreme Court in 1991. President Clinton added Ruth Bader Ginsburg to the Court in 1993. In 1996, the number of working mothers with children exceeded the number of mothers with children not working outside the home. By 1996, women constituted 48 percent of the total workforce.

But even as increasing numbers of women moved into formerly male-dominated occupations and professions, disparities continued in the pay they received for performing comparable work. Women who worked full-time in 1996 earned about 73¢ for every $1 a man earned. Experts offered several explanations to account for continuing pay inequities for women: Women constituted most of the newer entrants into the job market; they had more interruptions in their work careers; they more likely worked in occupations that were not unionized; they sometimes traded higher pay for more convenient or flexible hours; and, of course, they were victims of continuing discrimination. Many women still confronted a segregated job market in the mid-1990s. Over 60 percent of working women held "pink collar" jobs.

---

[1]David A. Hollinger, *Postethnic America: Beyond Multiculturalism* (New York: Basic Books, Copyright 1995, p. 116.

Many women who had reached managerial positions in business in the mid-1990s felt that they were paying too high a personal price for their professional successes. Others complained that they could not fulfill family obligations at home and perform their jobs at the highest levels. Felice Schwartz, the head of a research institute that studied women in business, suggested that these women might pursue a slower career track in business to have more time for family responsibilities. But feminists denounced Schwartz's so-called "mommy track." They claim that it perpetuated the very second-class status of women in business that they were trying to surmount.

Long-term structural changes in the economy have adversely affected working women. The rise of service industries and the implementation of new technologies created millions of new jobs for women, but they have also created new limits and liabilities. For example, computers have degraded the labor and status of clerical employees. Automated offices have become the sweatshops of the 1990s. In addition, many businesses, to cut costs, have increasingly hired part-time and temporary clerical workers. These contingent workers typically received less pay and fewer benefits than full-timers.

Long-term structural changes in family relations affected working women more adversely than economic changes. In the 1990s, the divorce rate continued to rise, as did the numbers of women living alone and the numbers of single-parent households headed by women. In 1996, about half of female workers had never been married or had been divorced and not remarried. Much of the increase in the poverty rate in the United States in the 1990s has been attributed to the rapid increase in the number of single-parent households headed by a woman.

Cultural changes have also accompanied the advent of women into the workplaces of America. Most notably, there have been changes in women's consciousness. Many women in the mid-1990s feel that they are the equal of men in the market place and they have greater ambitions and expectations than previous generations of women. But traditional values and stereotypes have also exhibited strong staying powers. Advertisers no longer celebrated domesticity as women's only appropriate realm, but they still insisted that the busy career woman had to keep her weight down and look pretty. Women spent far more of their incomes on clothes, beauty aids, and diet and exercise programs than men.

THE ELECTION OF 1988

As 1988 began, the economy continued to perform strongly. One hundred and fourteen million Americans, the most ever, were working and the economy continued to generate thousands of new jobs each month. Inflation remained in check. The expansionist trend that had begun in 1983 continued.

As candidates in both parties geared up for the 1988 elections, the race for the presidency appeared to be wide open. For the Republicans the major contenders included Vice President George Bush, Senate Republican leader Robert Dole, and former "televangelist" Pat Robertson. For the Democrats, a large field of candidates sought their party's nomination. They included the ill-starred Gary Hart and Senator Joseph Biden, also Congressman Richard Gephardt of Missouri, Senators Paul Simon of Illinois and Albert Gore of Tennessee, Governor Michael Dukakis of Massachusetts, former governor Bruce Babbit from Arizona, and the charismatic black leader, the Reverend Jesse Jackson. The primaries, beginning with the Iowa caucuses in January 1988, served to winnow out the candidates. When the lengthy, costly, and exhausting primary process finally ran its course in June, the survivors were Reagan's sixty-four-year-old vice president, George Bush, and the governor of Massachusetts, Michael Dukakis.

The Democrats held their convention in July in Atlanta where the flamboyant Jesse Jackson, who had finished a strong second in the primary balloting to Dukakis, sought the vice presidency. However, Dukakis chose instead an elderly conservative Senator from Texas, Lloyd Bentsen. The Dukakis camp expected the more conservative Bentsen to strengthen the Democratic ticket's appeal in Texas and other southern states by offsetting the Massachusetts technocrat's more liberal image. At the time the Democrats chose their ticket, public opinion polls favored Dukakis over Bush. Dukakis was perceived as a competent administrator who had presided over the economic revitalization of Massachusetts.

But by the time the Republicans had held their convention in New Orleans in mid-August, Bush had staged a remarkable political comeback. Polls gave Bush a lead that he never lost. He easily survived a mini-controversy over his selection of youthful Senator J. Danforth Quayle of Indiana to be his vice-presidential running mate. Quayle was thought to be too young and inexperienced to be "a heartbeat away from the presidency." Media investigations also revealed that Quayle had allegedly used family political influence to gain entry to an Indiana National Guard unit in 1969 and thereby avoid a possible tour of duty in Vietnam. All such misgivings about Quayle did not cost Bush many votes.

The Reverend Jesse Jackson campaigning for the presidency in 1988.
Source: Mercantile Library, St. Louis. Used with permission.

After Bush's victory in November, disappointed Democrats would charge Dukakis with losing an election that he could have won. They said his campaign had been poorly organized, his television commercials had been ineffective, he had failed to respond effectively to Republican attacks, and that he had lacked the passion required to excite voters. While Dukakis's uninspired campaign may have contributed to his downfall, there were other, more important, reasons for George Bush's impressive victory in November. The Republicans conducted a richly financed, efficient, and professional campaign. The Bush campaign easily won what media analysts have called the "battle of the sound bites," that is, the vivid ten-to-twenty-second pronouncements uttered daily by the candidates as they campaigned across the nation that would be picked up on the evening television news programs and beamed into millions of living rooms nightly until election day. Bush also found most of the "hot" electoral buttons to push during the contest with Dukakis. He projected a vision of a "kinder, gentler nation," and encouraged Americans to be more compassionate, to help one another and shine forth from "a thousand points of light." He pledged "no new taxes," and when questioned about his commitment, responded á la popular Clint Eastwood movie character, with "read my lips." Bush stated that he wanted to be known as the "education president" and the "environmental president."

Bush also waged a long and relentless assault on Dukakis as an example of all that was wrong with contemporary liberalism. He charged that Dukakis was weak on foreign policy and national security matters. Republican campaign ads implied that Dukakis was unpatriotic for not supporting legislation that required Massachusetts teachers to lead children in the daily recitation of the Pledge of Allegiance. The most notorious (and effective) Bush television attack commercial suggested that Dukakis was soft on crime because while he was governor a convicted rapist and a murderer was allowed a weekend furlough from prison during which he committed more outrageous crimes.

Dukakis disdained negative campaigning and he refused even to respond to the Bush attacks. Instead, Dukakis tried to direct the campaign to the issues. Unfortunately for his electoral chances, his approach failed. His campaign never caught fire and eventually floundered. He never found a focus, a telling issue, or a coherent theme that resonated among the voters. During two televised debates between the candidates, Dukakis failed to cut into Bush's lead or even slow his momentum.

On election day, the Bush-Quayle ticket buried Dukakis and Bentsen, winning 54 percent of the popular vote to 46 percent, 48 million votes for the Republicans to 41 million for the Democrats. Bush carried forty of the fifty states and had a 426-to-112 advantage in the electorate vote. Dukakis's defeat could be attributed in part to the continued flight of white voters who made up over 80 percent of the electorate. Since 1948, the only Democratic presidential candidate to get a majority of the white vote was Lyndon Johnson. Dukakis got about 38 percent of the white vote in 1988 while carrying 88 percent of the African American vote. The once solidly Democratic South was now solidly Republican, as was most of the Midwest and West. Blue-collar workers, once a Democratic mainstay, who had defected to the Republicans during the 1970s, voted for Bush. The Democratic coalition had vanished at the top of the ticket.

Despite being beaten in the presidential vote, the Democrats retained control of both houses of congress, two-thirds of state governorships, and control of thirty-six state legislatures. Although they had lost five of the last six presidential elections, the Democrats in 1988 retained considerable political power at the local, state, and congressional levels. Voter turnout in 1988 was the lowest since 1924. Potential voters were also turned off by the excessive negative campaigning, which focused on character assassination rather than on the issues. Of the estimated 183 million Americans eligible to vote, only 91.6 million (50.1 percent) bothered to vote, the lowest percentage for any of the world's developed democratic nations.

The factor that had ensured Bush's victory: he was Reagan's heir apparent. True, the old leader had lost some of his luster as a consequence of the Iran-Contra scandal and the "sleaze factor." Towards the end of his presidency, Reagan clearly showed the effects of age, failing health, and fatigue. Dukakis and the Democrats also called attention to a long list of national problems that eight years of conservative Republicanism had either created or slighted: the huge federal deficits, the neglect of the poor, indifference to civil rights, the deterioration of the environment, scant interest in consumer protection or safety in the workplaces of America, the decline of unions, the erosion of public education, and the fact that a third of Americans could not afford adequate medical care. Further, Democrats raised a basic question of fairness. They charged that Reaganomics had always favored the rich and the affluent at the expense of the middle classes, the working classes, and the poor. In addition, Democrats pointed to a series of Reagan foreign policy failures in Central America and the Middle East.

But the majority of Americans voting in 1988 no longer held liberal values and no longer looked to the Democratic Party for presidential leadership on either domestic or foreign policy. For most American voters, talk of national debts involved incomprehensible abstractions that did not seem to have any relevance to their daily lives. Most voters in 1988 were not poor, were not minorities, and did not appear much concerned about the folks who were. Eight years of Reagan's rule had coincided with the longest sustained period of economic growth in U.S. history. Since 1983, the economy had grown at an annual rate of over 4 percent. During the decade, 20 million new jobs were created.

Even though he had numerous failures and shortcomings, Ronald Reagan remained the most popular and admired political leader in America in 1988. Reagan presided over a peaceful and prosperous America, and relations with the Soviets were better than they had been since World War II. The 1988 election was essentially a referendum on Reaganism. A large majority of the electorate concluded that George Bush was more likely than Michael Dukakis to keep the nation at peace and to keep the good times rolling.

THE PATRICIAN AS PRESIDENT

Born June 12, 1924, in Milton, Connecticut, George Herbert Walker Bush grew up in Greenwich, Connecticut, a posh suburb of New York City. His father, Prescott Bush, a wealthy Wall Street investment banker, served two terms in the Senate representing the state of Connecticut. Soon after graduating from Philips Academy, an exclusive preparatory school, in 1942, a seventeen-year-old George Bush joined the Navy. He went through flight training and served in the South Pacific with a carrier-based torpedo squadron. He was the youngest ensign flying combat missions in the Pacific war. While flying a mission on September 2, 1944, Bush had to bail out of his flak-damaged plane. He spent four hours in the water before being picked up by a submarine. An authentic war hero, Bush was awarded the Distinguished Flying Cross for bravery in combat.

Rotated back to the United States in 1945, he soon married Barbara Pierce, the daughter of a publishing magnate. After the war, Bush attended Yale University where he majored in economics and captained the baseball team. After graduating from Yale, Bush headed west to seek his fortune. He settled in west Texas and went into the oil-drilling business. Within ten years he had become president of his own company, the Zapata Offshore Company, headquartered in Houston where he lived with his wife and five children.

As he pursued his business interests, George Bush also got involved in Texas Republican politics. From 1966 to 1970, he served two terms in the House representing the seventh congressional district. He tried to move up to the Senate in 1970, only to be defeated by Lloyd Bentsen. Following Bush's defeat in the senatorial race, President Nixon appointed him to be U.S. Ambassador to the United Nations. There followed a series of high-level appointive jobs in both the Nixon and Ford administrations: national chairman of the Republican Party, chief U.S. emissary to China, and director of the CIA.

In 1979, Bush announced that he would seek the presidency. He started strongly in the 1980 primaries, but his candidacy was soon overwhelmed by the Reagan juggernaut. After Reagan failed to get his first choice for vice president, former president Ford, he turned to Bush. As Reagan's vice president for eight years, Bush proved to be one of his ablest and most loyal advisers. Reagan in turn gave his vice president important assignments and made it clear in 1988 that George H. W. Bush was his personal choice to be his successor in the Oval Office. He got the Republican nomination and went on to a sweeping victory over Michael Dukakis in November 1988.

ECONOMIC AND SOCIAL POLICY

The Bush presidency was noteworthy mainly for the absence of many new initiatives emanating from the White House. Bush clearly lacked Reagan's sense of ideological mission nor did he appear capable of articulating a compelling vision that would inspire his fellow citizens or provide them with a sense of direction. He did

George Bush, forty-first president.   *Source:* The White House.

not appear to have much interest in domestic affairs, nor did he have the political skill to work effectively with an oppositionist Congress.

Bush's presidency began with a series of political gestures. He met with the leaders of the Democratic opposition to tell them that he wanted a cooperative relationship with Congress rather than to continue the partisan confrontational style of his predecessor. He also met with African American leaders to assure them of his sympathetic understanding of their problems. By these actions, Bush signaled that his administration would be more moderate and more conciliatory than Reagan's had been. The new president and his unpretentious wife, Barbara, also showed their fellow Americans that life in the Bush White House would be comfortable, low-key, and family oriented. Patrician informality and concern for the sensibilities of ordinary Americans would be in; Hollywood-style nouveau riche glitz and glamor was out.

Bush's first budgetary proposals sent to Congress in February 1989 offered a few programs to combat drug abuse and to improve the nation's public schools. He also sought additional funding for child care, clean air, AIDS research, and to assist the homeless. In keeping with his campaign promises, he sought no new taxes to pay for these programs; indeed he proposed a tax cut—he wanted Congress to reduce the capital gains tax by 15 percent. He insisted that, even with his tax cut, his new funding proposals could be paid for, the deficit reduced, and the bankrupt savings and loans banks resuscitated by the increased revenues flowing into the federal treasury from accelerated economic growth. Few economists out-side his administration shared Bush's faith in the miraculous powers of supply-side economics. They feared that the new president might be practicing his own brand of "voodoo economics."

The new administration was dominated by two overriding concerns: the sav-ings and loan crisis and reducing the huge federal deficits. Bush proposed a rescue plan to either close or sell the bankrupt S&Ls and to repay depositors. Congress created a new agency, the Resolution Trust Corporation (RTC), to sell off the assets of the failed thrifts to solvent banks, often on very favorable terms. At the same time, the FSLIC was folded into the Federal Deposit Insurance Corporation (FDIC) to provide the billions needed to bail out depositors.

The new president acknowledged that "our will is strong, but our wallet is weak," that is, Bush insisted that straitened circumstances precluded new federal initiatives, however desirable, that cost much money. The Reagan legacy included a prosperous economy, but its prosperity could only be sustained by huge deficit spending—deficit spending by the federal government, by business, and by indi-vidual consumers. Reagan's tax cuts had compounded the federal government's enormous debt problems. The budget deficits would have been even larger if it were not for the fact that huge surpluses from the Social Security trust fund went into general revenues and the enormous sums being spent on bailing out bankrupt savings and loans banks and paying off their depositors were excluded from bud-getary calculations.

Bush's own innate sense of caution, reinforced by his sense of financial strin-gency, ensured that his administration could not solve the myriad social problems plaguing Americans in the early 1990s. In the spring of 1991, Bush, under heavy pressure from Congress to reduce the federal debt, conceded the need to accept some new taxes. His concession promptly outraged his conservative supporters and many citizens who had voted in good faith for Bush and his no-new-taxes promise. In October, the Bush administration and the Democratically controlled Congress finally agreed on a combination of tax hikes and budget cuts that promised modest reductions in the budget deficits over the next four years.

About the time the President and Congress worked out their budget deal, the economy slipped into a recession, the first in nearly a decade. Despite complaints emanating from many workers who had lost their jobs, congressional Democrats, and even some Republicans, Bush denied for months that the economy had lapsed into recession, and then appeared unable to devise a program of economic restora-tives. The recession, combined with Bush's denials, seriously undermined his popularity with American voters.

Bush also inherited a host of serious social problems from the Reagan years. The most feared pathology was the ongoing AIDS epidemic. By 1990, the disease had claimed over 110,000 lives and an estimated 1.5 million people tested HIV-positive. Most of the AIDS-infected cases involved gay men, but in the early 1990s, the proportion of AIDS cases among African American and Hispanic American in-travenous drug-users was growing rapidly. The number of women infected with the AIDS virus was also growing rapidly. Despite huge sums spent on research, there was no prospect for an early cure or even the development of an effective vaccine. Some progress occurred in the development of drugs and therapies that suppressed or delayed AIDS symptoms, but these treatments proved to be expensive and often produced unpleasant side effects.

Bush continued the war on drugs begun during Reagan's years. He pushed for more stringent drug-testing in the workplaces of America, better enforcement of existing drug laws, and additional measures taken to interdict the flood of illicit drugs pouring into the country from Mexico, Peru, and Colombia. Despite stepped-up efforts on all three fronts, drugs, especially "crack" cocaine, remained widely available within the United States.

There was also a connection between widespread crack use and the rising level of violence amidst the inner cities of America. Even though the Bush presidency spent billions of dollars on its war on drugs, it failed to curb the great American appetite for drugs. No one in the Bush administration appeared willing to address the key questions: Why were so many Americans, especially young Americans of minority backgrounds, attracted to illegal drugs? How might the great American drug thirst be curtailed?

THE SUPREME COURT IN THE NINETIES

By the late 1980s the Supreme Court, because of the presence of three Reagan appointees, Sandra Day O'Connor, Antonin Scalia, and Anthony Kennedy, had taken a conservative turn. In *Webster* v. *Reproductive Health Care Services* (July 1989), the Court, by a five-to-four majority decision, sustained a Missouri statute that made it more difficult for women to obtain an abortion.

But in other important constitutional areas, the Court adhered to liberal precedents. In *Texas* v. *Johnson,* a five-to-four majority ruled that burning an American flag as a form of protest was protected as free speech under the First Amendment. President Bush denounced the Court's ruling. Public opinion polls showed the overwhelming majority of Americans favored punishing flag burners. Congress, seeking to get around the Supreme Court, overwhelmingly passed a law making flag burning a crime. The Supreme Court then promptly nullified the new law. Efforts by President Bush and the Congress to propose a new constitutional amendment that would have outlawed flag burning failed.

With the retirement from the Court in 1990 and 1991 of William Brennan and Thurgood Marshall, two aged liberal associate justices, Bush got opportunities to add additional conservative jurists to the Supreme Court. His first appointment, David Souter, an obscure federal judge from New Hampshire, was quickly confirmed by the Senate with little opposition. Bush's second appointee, Clarence Thomas, a conservative African American jurist, was narrowly confirmed by the Senate in October 1991 by a vote of fifty-two to forty-eight.

Judge Thomas had to survive challenges from many Senators dissatisfied with his evasive answers to their questions concerning his views on abortion and other issues. In dramatic televised hearings before the Senate Judiciary Committee, Thomas also had to refute charges brought by an Oklahoma University law professor, Anita Hill, that he had sexually harassed her when she had worked for him at two federal agencies in 1982 and 1983. The nation was treated to three days of often sexually explicit testimony. Public opinion polls showed that about 75 percent of all Americans and two-thirds of U.S. women believed Thomas when he denied all of Hill's allegations. The close Senate vote to confirm Thomas was not appreciably affected by the hearings; nearly all the negative votes were cast by senators who would have voted against Thomas had Hill never made her charges.

The controversy attending Thomas's confirmation hearings brought three significant realities to the fore: the confirmation process for Supreme Court Justices had been thoroughly politicized, intimate details of the private lives of appointees to high office had become legitimate areas of public inquiry, and, most important, the troubling matter of sexual harassment of women in the workforce and political system, both of which remained male-dominated at the higher levels. The hearings also heightened public disgust with the performance of Washington politicians and made people more aware of the seriousness of the problems women face in the work places of America.

With the addition of George Bush's nominees, David Souter and Clarence Thomas, the court took on a strong conservative tone.   *Source:* National Geographic Society. Photo by Joseph H. Bailey.

The insensitive treatment accorded Hill by some male senators bent on discrediting her testimony revived the moribund feminist political movement. Patricia Ireland, a spokeswoman for the National Organization for Women (NOW), vowed that women would no longer depend on men for their rights, but would seek to replace male office holders with qualified women. Using as their rallying cry, "they still don't get it," woman entered mainstream politics in unprecedented numbers during the 1992 elections.

THE END OF THE COLD WAR

The advent of the Bush presidency coincided with dramatic changes occurring in the international realm that brought about the most fundamental changes in American foreign policies since World War II. The most important of these changes was the decline of Communism as evidenced by the disintegration of the Soviet empire in eastern Europe and then the disintegration of the Soviet Union itself. The Soviet revolution, which had convulsed the world in 1917, and had been one of the most potent shapers of twentieth-century history, disintegrated. The Cold War, which had been the dominant reality of international life for nearly half a century, suddenly ended. It ended when the Soviet Union had to withdraw from international competition because of severe internal economic weaknesses. In all these extraordinary developments, occurring unexpectedly and with bewildering rapidity from 1989 to 1991, Americans, although the prime beneficiaries, could only stand on the sidelines and watch in amazement.

Although many neoconservatives were quick to say that the rapid American military buildup in the 1980s coupled to the aggressive anti-Communist foreign policy initiatives embodied in the Reagan Doctrine brought about the demise of Communism and the Soviet Union, and thus gave America victory in the Cold War; it appeared more likely that Communism had simply imploded. Communism collapsed from within, the victim of its own unresolvable contradictions. Perhaps America's aggressive anti-Communist strategies and the pressures of trying to compete with the Americans hastened the Soviet collapse. While the Soviet Union clearly was a loser in a long struggle, America lost as well. The United States ultimately paid heavily for perpetuating the conflict: a weakened economy, strained international relations, and impaired moral stature at home and abroad.

The sudden demise of Communism caught official Washington and all American Sovietologists by complete surprise. Neither the CIA nor any of the other American intelligence agencies, nor any of the myriad of experts inhabiting prestigious U.S. institutes and think tanks had the slightest inkling that the Soviet system was on the verge of collapse until it disintegrated. Communism failed primarily because it did not work; it was an inherently dysfunctional system of political economy. It failed to deliver on its promises of material abundance and social equality. It also failed to transform humanity and reshape society and history. The workers' paradise failed to materialize. The basic failure was economic. Communism's political and ideological failures derived from its economic failure. Communism never achieved legitimacy and it finally had to be scrapped, consigned to the dustbin of history.

Mikhail Gorbachev presided over the death of the Soviet Union. He understood that the Achilles heel of the Soviet empire was its stagnating economy and lagging technology, especially in the areas of computer technology and information processing. By the mid-1980s, Gorbachev perceived that the Soviet Union could no longer maintain the arms race with the United States and feed its own people. In an effort to revive a failing system, Gorbachev proclaimed an era of *perestroika* (economic restructuring) and *glastnost* (openness). Economic controls were loosened and censorship was lifted. A civic awakening occurred, characterized by a new freedom and energy. Government was recreated and revitalized. An elected parliament supplanted party aparatchiks.

Although Soviet politics were reformed, the economy continued to deteriorate. Economic rot forced Gorbachev to curtail Soviet imperialism. He pulled Soviet troops out of Afghanistan ending a nine years' war in that country. In July 1989, Gorbachev repudiated the Brezhnev doctrine that gave Soviet troops the right to intervene in Eastern European countries. He cut loose from client governments in Poland, Czechoslovakia, East Germany, Hungary, Bulgaria, and Romania. Once the people of these countries understood that Soviet tanks no longer protected their rulers, they promptly toppled all those hated regimes like a row of dominoes. Communist rule ended first in Poland and Hungary. Then Reds were ousted in Czechoslovakia and Bulgaria. In December 1989, Romanian troops joined the people to bring down the hated tyrant Nicolae Ceausescu. He and his wife were executed on Christmas Day. In each of these nations, a different form of government evolved, from parliamentary democracy in Poland to a government in Romania that included many Communist elements. All experienced significant economic dislocation as they began the difficult task of privatizing their economies after enduring nearly a half-century of Communism.

The most dramatic event during the collapse of the Soviet empire in Eastern Europe occurred November 9, 1989 when the Berlin Wall that had so long served as a hated symbol of the impasse between East and West was breached. Young Germans defiantly spat on the wall and wrote obscene graffiti on it. Thousands of East and West Germans crossed the former barrier as the long-standing division of their country began to end. With the borders between East and West Germany fully open, the Communist government of East Germany simply collapsed. A democratic government quickly replaced it and on October 3, 1990, East Germany reunited with West Germany. The reunited Germany remained in NATO and the Warsaw Pact disintegrated. Since disputes between the Soviets and Americans over Germany were the major cause of the Cold War during the mid-1940s, it was historically appropriate that the reunion of Germany signalled the end of the Cold War era.

The American leaders, Reagan and his successor, George Bush, supported the Gorbachev revolution, understanding that it obviously served U.S. interests to end the Cold War, dismantle the Soviet empire, end the arms race, and reform the

Soviet Union. Many U.S. corporations quickly penetrated the Soviet Union. Mc-Donald's opened a large restaurant just off Red Square. But it was the Germans who led the drive to dominate East European and Soviet markets in the immediate aftermath of the Cold War. Gorbachev and the West Germans cut a deal: The Germans would provide about $30 billion to prop up the Soviet economy and in return Gorbachev accepted speedy German reunion and the end of the Warsaw Pact.

U.S. foreign policy in Latin America also benefited from the end of the Cold War. Gorbachev announced that Soviet aid to prop up the Cuban economy, which had been running at $5 billion per annum, would be drastically curtailed. In the post-Cold War era, Castro appeared to be only an aging caudillo clinging to power in an impoverished insular backwater within a hemisphere that had abandoned dictatorship of either the leftist and rightist variety and had turned to U.S.–style liberal democracy. In Nicaragua, the Sandinistas also felt the impact of the end of the Cold War. The Soviet Union, which had subsidized the Marxist-oriented Sandinistas to the tune of $500 million a year, turned off the spigot. In early 1990, the Sandinistas permitted free elections to take place in Nicaragua. To their great surprise, a coalition of anti-Sandinista forces led by Violetta Chamorro won. Isolated from their Soviet patron and repudiated by the people of Nicaragua, the Sandinistas surrendered their power. Chamorro became Nicaragua's first freely elected president in more than sixty years.

While supporting the spread of Democracy in Nicaragua, the United States also settled some scores in Panama. In December 1989, the U.S. sent military forces into Panama to overthrow dictator Manuel Noriega and to install a pro-American government. Noriega had previously worked with the CIA. He later broke with the Americans, supported the Sandinistas, and got rich as a drug trafficker for the Medellin cartel. Previously, U.S. federal grand juries had indicted Noriega for drug smuggling, gun running, and money laundering. One of the purposes of the invasion was to capture Noriega and bring him to the United States to stand trial.

Most Panamanians welcomed the twenty-five thousand U.S. troops sent to Panama as liberators. Noriega was captured, and brought to the United States for trial. Only twenty-three American soldiers were killed in the military operation but thousands of Panamanians were killed and wounded, many of them civilians. Public opinion polls showed the Panamanian intervention, which was of dubious legality, to be overwhelmingly popular with Americans. President Bush's popularity soared. In April 1992, Noriega was convicted on many counts of racketeering and drug smuggling and sent to a U.S. federal prison.

China also felt the impact of rising anti-Communism. During the early 1980s, China's Communist leader, Deng Xiaoping began modernizing China's unproductive economy by introducing market incentives. But at the same time Deng was freeing up the Chinese economy, he insisted on maintaining the Communist party's monopoly of political power. In early 1989, Deng sent army units into Tibet to crush a Tibetan bid for greater autonomy. In April 1989, thousands of Chinese students and intellectuals gathered in Beijing's Tiananmen Square to demand democracy for China. The prodemocracy movement spread rapidly and soon demonstrations sprouted in Nanjing, Shanghai, and other Chinese cities. Americans strongly supported the prodemocracy forces. For a time Chinese authorities appeared uncertain how to respond to the challenge because of the extensive media coverage the prodemocracy movement received in the world's press. But on the morning of June 4, 1989, Deng ordered the Chinese army to crush the drive for democracy. A brutal massacre ensued that claimed the lives of at least a thousand people. Dissident democrats were hunted down and jailed en masse. The nascent prodemocracy movement was violently suppressed.

President Bush publicly condemned the Chinese regime's slaughter of its own people and ordered the U.S. Immigration service to extend the visas of Chinese students in the United States. But Bush would take no actions that might weaken the friendly relations carefully cultivated between the Chinese and American governments since Richard Nixon's historic journey to Beijing in 1972. Bush refused to consider adopting any reprisals that might discomfit China's Communist gerontocracy, which he insisted would do nothing to salvage democracy in China and might harm U.S. interests.

Outside of China, Communism survived in the early 1990s as a pathetic remnant of a once-mighty world movement. It persisted only in a few small and poor Third World countries where it served mainly as an ideological prop for the absolutist power of bureaucratic elites. When these elites lose power Communism will probably wither away in these few remaining countries.

While Communist regimes were collapsing in Eastern Europe, rightist authoritarian regimes were also succumbing to the world democratic revival. In Chile in 1989, General Pinochet's stern regime gave way to a democratically elected government. In South Africa, Frederick DeKlerk became prime minister in August 1989. Within a few months, he released African National Conference leader Nelson Mendela from prison, where he had languished for more than twenty-five years. In 1991, as DeKlerk began dismantling apartheid, President Bush lifted American sanctions. In April 1994, occurred one of the most thrilling moments in modern world history: South Africa held its first elections in which all South Africans could vote. Mendela was elected president; a multiracial parliament was chosen. Democracy had trumped apartheid. In 1995 and 1996, South Africans of all races, under the inspired leadership of Mendela, worked to achieve a genuine multiracial society.

Elsewhere in Africa, drought and famine threatened millions of people, especially in Somalia, where years of civil war had destroyed any semblance of government. In December 1992, when warring Somali factions diverted UN-sanctioned food relief shipments to black markets, Washington sent in thirty thousand American troops to protect food deliveries. In the post–Cold War era, President Bush responded less to any economic or strategic interests the United States might have in that region, and more to a desire to alleviate human misery. He and millions of his fellow Americans were sickened by nightly television images of starving and dying children lying in filthy, fly-infested streets—and they sought to help. In time, the American intervention in Somalia became controversial. Tensions arose between UN and U.S. officials there. Under President Clinton, the American mission expanded to include restoring order and state building. Eighteen U.S. Marines were killed in fighting the forces of Somali warlord, Mohammed Farah Aidid. Yielding to public pressure to bring the troops home, Clinton withdrew all American forces from Somalia in 1994.

WAR IN THE PERSIAN GULF

During January and February 1991, in the first major military action of the new post–Cold War era, America and its allies fought a war in the Persian Gulf against Iraq. The war had a long preparation time and derived in part from some questionable U.S.–Middle Eastern diplomatic policies. During the Iraq-Iranian War, America often aided Iraq to prevent an Iranian victory that Washington feared could threaten the oil-rich Saudis. During the late 1980s, America sent the Iraqis nearly $1 billion worth of agricultural, economic, and technical aid. These aid packages included high-tech equipment such as advanced computers and lasers that could be used to produce weapons of mass destruction.

Soon after Iraq's war with Iran ended in a draw under the terms of an agreement negotiated by UN representatives, Kuwait, which, along with Saudi Arabia, had bankrolled Iraq's war with the Iranians, increased its production of oil in violation of OPEC rules. World oil prices dropped, hurting Saddam's government, deeply in debt and dependent on oil revenues for sustaining the Iraqi economy. Saddam was also annoyed by the Kuwaitis and the Saudis for their refusal to forgive Iraq's huge indebtedness to them. He also asserted claims to Kuwaiti territory based on maps predating the 1919 political settlement that had created the modern nation state of Iraq. Saddam appeared to harbor grandiose ambitions of becoming the dominant power in the Gulf area.

Even as Iraq prepared for war, U.S. leaders did not anticipate military action in the region. Washington was preoccupied with the historic events that ended the Cold War and collapsed the Soviet empire in Eastern Europe. Washington's policies in the Gulf region still turned on the notion that Iraq was the major counterweight to Iranian revolutionary aggression. On the eve of Iraq's invasion of Kuwait, the American ambassador to Baghdad, April Gillespie, told Saddam that the United States would not become involved in regional disputes, although America would defend its vital interests. Saddam apparently interpreted Gillespie's remark as a green light for aggression.

On August 2, 1990, Iraqi forces occupied Kuwait and appeared to threaten neighboring Saudi Arabia, possessor of more than a fifth of the world's proven oil reserves. Bush, determined to force Saddam Hussein to withdraw his forces from Kuwait, forged an international coalition under United Nations auspices to thwart Iraqi aggression. As a result of Bush's skilled leadership, Iraq was soon isolated and condemned by world opinion. Bush also persuaded the Soviet leader, Mikhail

Gorbachev, to abandon his former Iraqi client and support the UN initiative. Saddam had not anticipated the strong reaction by the United States, the nearly universal indignation of the international community, nor that his erstwhile Communist patron would support American foreign policy initiatives.

The United Nations quickly enacted Resolution 661 authorizing a trade embargo against Iraq. The international community clamped a tight economic boycott on Iraq and deployed a military force of some 250,000 troops to defend Saudi Arabia from possible attack. Most of these forces, dubbed Operation Desert Shield, were American under the command of American Army General Norman Schwarzkopf. But Schwarzkopf's forces also included a sizable representation from Great Britain, France, and several Arab countries including Saudi Arabia, Egypt, Syria, Morocco, Oman, and the United Emirates.

Initially, Bush appeared willing to use military force defensively, to protect Saudi Arabia and other possible Iraqi targets from attack and to let economic pressures force Saddam out of Kuwait. But almost from the beginning of Gulf military operations, Pentagon planners were preparing for offensive military action. Bush soon became convinced that the boycott would not work, or else would take too long. During November the military forces in and near Saudi Arabia more than doubled. Five hundred fifty thousand forces representing some twenty countries prepared for offensive military operations to liberate Kuwait.

Congress, apprehensive about the rapid military buildup and the preparations for offensive military operations, erupted in debate. Many liberal Democrats opposed military action against Iraq. They believed that the economic boycott ought to be given a chance to work and they also did not want America to go to war without congressional approval. The United Nations enacted Resolution 629 on November 29 which set January 15, 1991, as a deadline for Iraqi withdrawal from Kuwait and authorized the use of force to drive the Iraqis from Kuwait if they did not leave by that date. On January 12, both the House and Senate, after passionate debates and by narrow majorities, enacted resolutions formally approving the use of American military force in the Gulf. Last-minute negotiations between U.S. Secretary of State James Baker and Iraqi Foreign Minister Tariq Aziz failed to achieve an Iraqi withdrawal from Kuwait.

On January 16, 1991, the war in the Persian Gulf, Operation Desert Storm, commenced when President Bush ordered an Allied air assault on Iraqi targets. Deploying an impressive arsenal of high-tech weaponry, America and its allies waged a destructive five-week air war against the Iraqis. Priority targets included Iraqi chemical, biological, and nuclear production, command and control facilities, airfields, roads, and elite military forces.

Meanwhile, Allied ground forces stood poised to strike at Saddam's forces dug into the Kuwaiti and southern Iraqi deserts. On February 23, 1991, General Schwarzkopf ordered his forces, now 700,000 strong, to attack Iraqi positions in Kuwait and southern Iraq. The key military operation involved sending 200,000 American, British, and French armored forces across the undefended Iraqi border with Saudi Arabia 200 miles to the west of Kuwait. They smashed into the elite

Republican Guard forces and quickly demolished them. Iraqi soldiers surrendered in droves. Within four days, Allied forces had overwhelmed the Iraqis, whose fighting capabilities had been seriously eroded by the weeks of the air attacks that preceded the invasion. One hundred hours after the ground war began, President Bush offered a cease-fire and the Iraqis quickly accepted it. At war's end, the allied forces occupied Kuwait and held southern Iraq.

Only 148 Americans were killed and 467 wounded during the short war, to the immense relief of Americans who had feared that thousands might perish in the desert fighting. Saddam Hussein had vowed that, in the mother of all battles, his soldiers would kill thousands of American troops if they invaded Kuwait. But it was mostly Iraqis who died in the Persian Gulf war, an estimated 100,000 Iraqi soldiers and civilians. In addition to light casualties, the dollar costs of the war to Americans also proved light because the $30 billion tab for the war was picked up by wealthy U.S. allies who did not send combat forces.

Americans erupted in frenetic celebration of the glorious victory that had been achieved so quickly and at such low cost. Tumultuous parades and celebrations, the likes of which had not been since 1945, welcomed home the conquering heroes. Flags cropped up in many a front yard and yellow ribbons festooned homes across the land. Polls gave President Bush approval ratings of 90 percent. The Gulf War made a national hero of General Schwarzkopf, the commander who had led Allied forces to a quick victory at a relatively light cost. Schwarzkopf, affectionately called "Stormin Norman" by his troops, made an appealing hero; he appeared to be an old-fashioned patriot who was personally concerned about the welfare of soldiers entrusted to his command.

Even though the Persian Gulf War scarcely resembled the Vietnam War in any way, President Bush announced that Americans had finally kicked the "Vietnam syndrome," that is, they were no longer afraid to commit their military forces to a major foreign operation. The Gulf War was the most popular war since the Spanish-American War. Americans also reveled in the thought that, in the first major crisis of the post–Cold War era, America had asserted its leadership of the world community and the Soviets had followed the U.S. lead. They echoed Bush's talk of forging a "new world order" under American stewardship.

The war also received saturation media coverage. American home audiences followed the war around the clock on the Cable News Network (CNN). CNN continually provided live, on-the-spot coverage of the conflict. But the U.S. military tightly controlled television reportage and American TV viewers were allowed to watch only a heavily censored version of the war. Pentagon officials believed, mistakenly, that biased media coverage of the Vietnam War had contributed to the American defeat in Indochina.

Television journalists, with few exceptions, willingly allowed themselves to be manipulated by the military in exchange for access to war stories. Reporters were formed into pools and learned about Gulf military operations during official briefings. Reporters were allowed in the field only with military escorts who controlled what they saw and whom they interviewed. The televised version of the

Gulf War presented to American audiences was a sanitized affair that featured stories about high-tech weaponry and interviews with American soldiers preparing for battle. Americans saw little of the gory realities of a war that included civilian casualties and the slaughter of tens of thousands of Iraqi soldiers.

American foreign policy goals in the Persian Gulf War included liberating Kuwait. Larger American strategic goals included keeping the vast Middle Eastern oil reserves in friendly hands and destroying Saddam Hussein's capacity to wage offensive war or to achieve paramountcy in the Persian Gulf region.

Even though the Persian Gulf War was a great success, thoughtful critics of American foreign policy raised several important issues. They pointed out that short-sighted U.S. policy had helped create the Iraqi threat by selling them technology that had military applications during the 1980s when they were fighting the Iranians. Further, the Bush administration failed to inform Saddam Hussein that the United States would strongly oppose aggression against Kuwait. The American failure to send the proper message to the Iraqi leader encouraged him to think that he could get away with plundering the Kuwaitis.

In addition, critics observed that even though the allied coalition succeeded in driving the Iraqis out of Kuwait, it failed to bring down Saddam Hussein. Bush encouraged ethnic Kurds and Shiite Muslims within Iraq to rebel, but when they did Washington allowed Saddam to crush them. Thousands of Kurds and Shiites died because of America's unwillingness to continue the war against Iraq until Saddam was deposed. Bush's reluctance to continue the war derived from Saudi fears that if Saddam were deposed, Iraq would disintegrate. The Saudis preferred a defanged Saddam presiding over a stable Iraq than chaos and civil war on their border. The Saudis also feared Iranian hegemony in the region in the wake of an Iraqi collapse, a fear that Washington also held.

The fact that Saddam remained in power and had crushed the two rebellions quickly took much of the luster off of the allies' shining victory in the Gulf war. Ironically, both Syria and Iran, two sponsors of international terrorism, emerged as the dominant powers in the Persian Gulf region in the aftermath of Iraq's shattering defeat. The use of force in the Middle East did not significantly increase American diplomatic options in that violent region nor did it promise long-term solutions to its seemingly intractable problems.

The short war had a negligible impact on the American economy. Domestic oil prices dropped, but the economy remained mired in recession. President Bush's high approval ratings at the time of the war dissipated during the next six months as the U.S. economy remained in the doldrums. Because of the Soviet collapse and the smashing Iraqi defeat, Israel felt more secure than any time since the Jewish state was founded. Responding to American pressures, Israeli leaders agreed to participate in an international conference convened in Madrid in December 1991 to resolve the Palestinian issue and to achieve a comprehensive Middle East peace treaty. Delegates from several Arab nations and representatives of the Palestinians engaged in dialogues with Israeli envoys. In the spring of 1993, the talks were placed on hold as Israeli security forces fought with the Palestinian militants in the occupied territories.

THE DEMISE OF COMMUNISM

The collapse of Communism did not usher in a safe new world. The Cold War had been a managed superpower rivalry, and since that terrifying moment during the Cuban Missile Crisis of October 1962 when a nuclear catastrophe became possible, both American and Soviet leaders were exceedingly careful and took extreme precautions to avoid any replication of that event for the duration of the Cold War. In the wake of the economic decline and political disintegration of the Soviet Union, Soviet ethnic nationals fell to warring among themselves. The Baltic states made good on their bid for independence; and others declared their determination to achieve independence.

On August 19, 1991, Stalinist reactionaries among the Red Army, the KGB, and the bureaucrats who controlled the Soviet economy attempted a military coup. It failed because of their own ineptitude and indecisiveness. It also failed because forty thousand citizens of Moscow defied the putschists and rallied around the courageous leadership of the radical populist, Boris Yeltsin.

For a few months Gorbachev clung to power, but he presided over a center that was rapidly disintegrating. The death of the Soviet Union was officially proclaimed on December 21, 1991 by Boris Yeltsin and several other leaders who announced the formation of a new federation of sovereign states. The former USSR had mutated into an eleven-republic Commonwealth of Independent States, three independent Baltic nations, and an independent Georgia. On December 26, major European powers and the United States officially recognized the Russian republic under Yeltsin's leadership as the de facto successor to the defunct Soviet Union. Powerless and presiding over nothing, Gorbachev resigned on December 27. Ironically, it was the actions of Gorbachev more than those of any other individual that were responsible for the demise of the Soviet Union. The process that he had set in motion five years earlier to reform the Communist system had resulted in its destruction and his fall from power. It turned out that the Soviet Union could not be reformed, it could only be destroyed. Reform had foundered on economic failure. As one Muscovite put it, "Gorbachev knew how to bring us freedom but he did not know how to make sausage."

During the first two years following the collapse of the Soviet Union, severe economic shrinkage halved the Russian GDP and impoverished 80 percent of its 145 million people. Inflation, especially for basic food commodities, raced along at a rate of 25 to 50 percent per month. While falling production and hyperinflation battered the Russian economy and while Russians starved in the streets, right-wing nationalists and former Communist apparatchiks tried to bring Yeltsin down. Yeltsin eventually crushed his opponents. In elections held two months later, disgruntled voters gave strong support to a political party led by Vladimir Zhirinovsky, a rabidly nationalistic, antisemitic, and neofascistic boor who openly admired Adolph Hitler.

Russia found itself in the throes of three simultaneous, painful, and interlinked transitions: from multinational empire to nation-state, from totalitarian to democratic government, and from a command economy to a free market capitalist system. The United States had a stake in the outcome of these transitions. Could Russia make these transitions and emerge as a peaceful democratic capitalist nation under the rule of law? President Clinton held a summit with the embattled Russian leader at Vancouver on April 3 and 4, 1993. He made a strong show of support and pledged $1.6 billion in aid.

As the Soviet Union receded from the world stage, Europe, led by a reunified Germany, moved to form a European community free of tariffs, travel restrictions, and monetary impediments. Although that drive was stalled by recession, disputes over national currencies, and fear of German domination, it will probably go forward. Twelve nations with a population of about 350 million would constitute the world's richest market. America's relationship to this emergent Europe has not yet been defined, but it suggests that the United States will face formidable economic and financial competition from its erstwhile dependents.

Along the Pacific Rim, Japan suffered a series of financial and economic setbacks in the 1990s. Even so, America's Asian and Pacific trade in 1995, over half of it with the Japanese, was much larger than its trade with Europe. China, its economy freed from Communist shackles, had the world's fastest-growing major economy. China, with its rich resources, vast population, and dynamic economy, appeared on track to become the next world superpower sometime during the 21st century.

The former Soviet Union.   *Source:* U.S. State Department.

THE 1992 ELECTION

In the summer of 1990, the economy slid into a recession, the first downturn in eight years, ending the longest period of growth and prosperity in modern American history. Its major causes included a combination of private and public indebtedness, excess productive capacity, and declining consumer confidence. Other causes included low rates of savings and investment, a slump in the world economy that hurt American export sales, and cuts in military and aerospace spending in the post–Cold War era.

Although the recession was not a severe one, the American people reacted very negatively to it. The economic downturn undermined Bush's popularity; the president compounded his political troubles by refusing to acknowledge that the economy had been hit by recession until six months after its onset. Following his belated admission that a recession had struck the nation, Bush appeared to be more concerned about foreign policy than with the struggles of ordinary Americans trying to cope amidst a stagnant economy. Although the depression was not deep in most parts of the nation, it lingered on. It was the slow recovery from the recession coupled to Bush's political failures that put the long-term Republican hold on the White House in jeopardy. The state of the economy and jobs for the people became the dominant issues in the 1992 elections.

In the fall of 1991, when Democratic leaders declared their candidacies for their party's 1992 presidential nomination, the most prominent names opted out. House leader Richard Gebhardt, Senators Albert Gore and Bill Bradley, and the best-known Democrats, Governor Mario Cuomo of New York and the Reverend Jesse Jackson, all decided not to run, fearful that George Bush was unbeatable. Their withdrawals opened the door for a young, energetic governor, William Jefferson "Bill" Clinton of Arkansas. Clinton was a relatively obscure political figure in the fall of 1991, and, like the most recent Democratic president, Jimmy Carter, he was a southerner who took moderate positions on most issues.

Bill Clinton brought some impressive credentials to the presidential fray. He had been a Rhodes Scholar and had received a law degree from Yale. As governor of Arkansas he had been a popular and effective leader. During his eleven-year tenure of office, Arkansas's public schools had improved and the state economy had grown steadily. Clinton, during the 1980s, had been critical of both conservative Republican economic policies and of what he called liberal Democratic "tax-and-spend" alternatives. He had served as chairman of the Democratic Leadership Council, a group of moderates intent on winning control of the national party to steer it away from left-wing interest groups and back to the center of the political spectrum inhabited by most voters.

Clinton also brought some liabilities and questions about his character and performance to the race. Early in the campaign, he had to respond to allegations that he had had an affair with a woman who had worked in the governor's office in Little Rock. He also acknowledged smoking marijuana while a college student.

Post–Cold War Europe, 1992. *Source:* U.S. State Department.

More seriously, he appeared to have manipulated the selective service system to avoid military service during the Vietnam War era. Another disturbing quality emerged as Clinton campaigned in the early Democratic primaries. His answers and explanations to the myriad of accusations that came his way seemed designed more to evade or appease than to clarify. Nevertheless, Clinton moved ahead quickly in the Democratic primaries. He rather easily defeated two weak rivals, former Massachusetts senator Paul Tsongas and former California governor Jerry

Brown. Clinton demonstrated resiliency, an ability to hit back at detractors, and, most of all, an impressive grasp of the important issues facing the American people in 1992.

The Democratic convention held in Madison Square Garden in New York in July was an impressive show of unity by a party that had long been riven by clashing interest groups and ideological wars. The delegates proceeded to nominate the first baby-boomer ticket in American political history: forty-five-year-old Bill Clinton for president and forty-two-year-old Albert Gore as vice president. In his crisp acceptance speech, Clinton pronounced an end to spendthrift liberalism and special interest politics. He called for a "new covenant" between the federal government and the American people that included welfare reform, affordable health care for all Americans, a tax cut for the middle class, higher taxes for rich people, tax breaks for small businesses, and sharp reductions in military spending. Clinton emerged from the convention as the candidate of a unified party prepared to wage a well-financed, sophisticated, and moderate campaign against a vulnerable incumbent. Polls taken shortly after the Democratic convention gave the Clinton-Gore ticket substantial leads over Bush and Quayle.

To make matters worse for President Bush, he was challenged in the Republican primaries by Patrick Buchanan, a conservative former aide to both presidents Nixon and Reagan. Buchanan assailed Bush for breaking his no-new-taxes pledge and for betraying conservative principles. He had opposed the Gulf War and wanted all American forces stationed overseas brought home. Although he had no chance of winning, Buchanan stayed in the race long enough to demonstrate George Bush's fragile hold on conservative Republican voters and to weaken seriously the President's drive for reelection.

The Republican convention further weakened Bush's prospects for victory in November. Although on the surface, the party faithful rallied around the candidacy of the incumbent leader, the convention was co-opted by the Religious Right. The party platform took extreme positions on a whole range of controversial social issues such as abortion, positions at variance with those held by mainstream Americans. Buchanan strongly supported traditional family values, but while doing so he appeared to be saying that anyone who did not belong to a white Christian middle-class nuclear family was less wholesome, and less American than he and his fellow conservatives. Such atavistic displays of nativism were politically counterproductive in 1992 because they offended so many gays, lesbians, female heads of households, people of all ages living alone, co-habitors, secular people, Jews, and other minorities.

The development that made the 1992 election one of the most significant and unpredictable of modern times was the entry of a strong third-party candidate, a maverick Texas billionaire populist, H. Ross Perot. While Bush and Clinton battled their way through the primaries, Perot's electronic grass-roots campaign was fueled by voter outrage, outrage at a political system that suffered from corruption and gridlock, a system that could not even address the real problems facing ordinary Americans much less solve them. The feisty Texan with a quick wit and a keen sense of what many Americans were thinking enlivened the political landscape with his presence during the election of 1992.

By May, Perot was outpolling both Clinton and Bush in some national surveys. Suddenly, in mid-July, Perot announced that he was withdrawing from the presidential race and threw his support to Bill Clinton, whom, Perot claimed, had taken up his issues. He also indicated that he got out of the race because he wasn't enjoying it. Some observers speculated that Perot withdrew because he did not want to subject himself and his family to intense media scrutiny.

During the fall campaign Clinton consistently attacked what he called the "trickle-down" economic policies of the Reagan and Bush administrations while carefully avoiding the label of liberal big spender. He portrayed himself as "an agent of change" to appeal to Perotistas. Clinton called for welfare reform to get the votes of Reagan Democrats. He repeated his proposals made at the Democratic convention for affordable health care for all Americans, taxing the rich, and tax breaks for the middle class. He also proposed moderate reductions in the budget deficits at the same time proposing a stimulus package to jump-start the economy and provide up to 500,000 new jobs. In an effort to reach young voters he proposed college scholarships linked to voluntary national service for two years following graduation.

Bush, comparing himself to Harry Truman in 1948 who overcame seemingly insurmountable obstacles to score a historic upset victory, made a strenuous bid for reelection. He tried to run on his foreign policy record, but in 1992, in the post–Cold War era, the American people considered foreign policy issues secondary or peripheral. Bush blamed the Democratically controlled Congress for political gridlock, the lingering recession, and the runaway deficits. Mostly he concentrated his fire on Bill Clinton. He charged Clinton with being an old-fashioned tax-and-spend liberal disguised as a moderate. He questioned Clinton's character and his judgment. He challenged Clinton's patriotism for being a draft-avoider and even questioned his loyalty for having visiting the Soviet Union. "Who do you trust?" became the focal point of Bush's campaign in its frantic final weeks. Polling evidence suggested that Bush's shrill attacks on Clinton had little impact on voter behavior. Clinton began the campaign with a sizable lead over Bush and held it to election day.

The Republican media blitz that had been so brilliantly successful against Dukakis in 1988 failed to work its magic in 1992. Bush did not win the "battle of the sound bites" this time around. The major television networks did not carry Bush's one-liners and accusations as unmediated news in 1992. The Clinton campaign, unlike the passive and proud Dukakis, quickly responded to all the Bush charges and often countered with accusations of their own. Most importantly, this time around Bush was not running as Reagan's heir-apparent promising four more years of prosperity; he was running on his own lackluster record of poor leadership on domestic issues.

In the final month of the campaign, the unpredictable Ross Perot leaped back into the ring. Once again, the election became a three-way contest. Perot joined

Clinton and Bush to participate in three televised presidential debates. The debates did not affect the electoral outcome appreciably but they did offer the three candidates forums before massive audiences of prospective voters. Clinton probably showed to best advantage in the debates because he consistently demonstrated his mastery of the details of public policy.

The election results confirmed the lead that Clinton had long maintained in the polls. He received 43.7 million votes to 38.1 million for Bush and 19.2 million for Perot. Clinton's victory was much more decisive in the electoral vote column. He carried thirty-two states and the District of Columbia with a total of 370 electoral votes to 168 for Bush and 0 for Perot. For the first time since 1977, the Democrats won control of both the White House and the Congress.

With three popular candidates in the field, some traditional voting patterns were blurred. Nevertheless, Clinton's clever campaign partially restored the old Democratic coalition that had been ripped to shreds by Nixon and Reagan. Clinton retained the African American vote although the Arkansas governor made fewer gestures in the direction of blacks than any Democratic candidate since the 1950s. Hard times and Bush's failed policies brought a lot of Reagan Democrats home to Clinton's party, especially in the midwestern industrial states. Clinton probably won the election by carrying Ohio, Illinois, Michigan, and Pennsylvania—all of which had voted for Bush in 1988. In these states, the Reagan Democrats turned away from Bush and voted either for Clinton or Perot. Clinton also got a majority of the women's vote and the youth vote. Clinton and Gore, both moderate southerners, also chipped away at the Solid South, which had been solid for Republicans in recent elections. They carried their home states of Arkansas and Tennessee, and also picked up Louisiana and Georgia. They also carried normally Republican California with its huge bloc of 54 electoral votes.

Perot also scored well in California, getting over 2 million votes, 20 percent of the total. Perot got more votes than any third-party candidate in American political history. Perot scored best in states hardest hit by recession such as Maine, Alaska, and California. His presence in the race also accounted for the higher voter turnouts in 1992. Almost 55 percent of eligible voters went to the polls in 1992, compared to 50 percent in 1988. The higher levels of voter involvement in 1992 reversed a trend that had begun in the 1960s.

Analysts probing for the deeper meanings inherent in the outcomes of the 1992 election suggested that it might represent another turning point in modern American electoral politics. There was a decline in the saliency of social issues and the black-white race issues. Clinton did better among white voters than any of his Democratic predecessors since Lyndon Johnson in 1964—barely losing their vote, 39 percent to 40 percent. Polls consistently showed throughout the 1992 campaign that the issues that mattered most to most voters were the state of the economy, jobs, education, and health care.

Perhaps the biggest political news of 1992 was not the presidential race but the congressional races for the House and Senate. The Democrats picked up one senate seat giving them a fifty-eight to forty-two edge. The large Democratic majority in the House of Representatives shrank a little, from 266 to 166 to 260 to 174. Although the shift in relative strength of the major parties was slight, 1992 represented a year of upheaval in congressional voting. Elections for the House were held for the first time under the reapportionment brought about by the 1990 census. Demographic trends underway since World War II continued to prevail. Sunbelt states like California, Arizona, Texas, and Florida were the big winners, gaining many additional seats. The Northeastern states and the old industrial states of the Upper Midwest continued to be the big losers, losing the seats that the southern rim states gained.

Voters vented their anger on congressional incumbents for voting themselves a pay raise during a recession and for writing overdrafts on their special House bank accounts. Many voters perceived legislators as being more concerned about office perks than serving the public. In the wake of the House scandals, more incumbents resigned or were defeated in primary elections than for any election since 1946. Women, African Americans, Asian Americans, and Hispanics were elected to the House in record numbers. In the Senate, women scored a major breakthrough. Eleven women won major party nominations and five of them, all Democrats, won in November. Carol Moseley Braun, from Illinois, became the first African American woman to serve in the Senate. California sent two women to the Senate and Colorado sent a Native American, Ben Nighthorse Campbell.

THE DEMOCRATS RETURN

As in 1960, the 1992 election wrought both a change of party in the White House and a generational shift along the corridors of power. With Clinton and Gore in office, and over a hundred new members of Congress in place, the baby boomers assumed national leadership. Because the Democrats had majorities in both houses of Congress, it appeared possible to bring an end to the gridlock that had rendered the federal government ineffective for years. Clinton made good on his pledge to diversify the upper echelons of the executive branch by selecting many women and minority candidates. Women headed the Environmental Protection Agency and the Council of Economic Advisers. Janet Reno was picked to be the first woman Attorney General. Clinton's determination to select women for important offices also reflected the influence of the new president's wife, Hillary Rodham Clinton, who promised to be the most influential First Lady since the great Eleanor Roosevelt. Hillary had been a corporate lawyer prior to coming to Washington and clearly intended to involve herself in most of the new administration's important issues. The president named his wife to chair the Task Force on National Health Care Reform.

The new president quickly got embroiled in a controversy with the Pentagon over his proposal to allow openly gay and lesbian people to serve in the armed forces. Because of the deeply ingrained hostility within the military services toward openly gay and lesbian people serving on active duty, Clinton was forced to delay implementation of this reform. In July 1993, Clinton announced a compromise policy that had the support of the Joint Chiefs of Staff: The military would no longer ask prospective recruits questions about their sexual orientation and would no longer employ security forces to hound suspected gays and lesbians out of the armed forces. But gays and lesbians serving in the military could not engage in overt homosexual behavior on or off military duty stations; also, open acknowledgment of gay or lesbian preferences would be grounds for dismissal from military service. This "don't ask, don't tell, don't pursue" compromise failed to satisfy gay and lesbian activists who vowed to continue their campaign to achieve equality within the armed forces in the courts, and it angered those who opposed any change in the anti-gay/lesbian policies of the military services. In 1995 and 1996, gay and lesbian individuals serving in the armed forces continued their struggle to achieve full acceptance.

The new president reversed the Bush administration's efforts to restrict the right of women to an abortion. But he also displayed a tendency to abandon or delay many of his campaign commitments, giving rise to the fear that he was less an "agent of change" than a canny politician who exploited popular resentment against the performance of a lackluster incumbent to get elected. His proposals to stimulate the economy and generate new jobs ran into serious political trouble. Republicans in the Senate and opposition from his own party leaders in both houses forced him to abandon his proposal to give tax breaks to small businesses and reduce the size of his stimulus package.

Although the recession was clearly over in the spring of 1993 and the economic growth rate exceeded 4 percent per annum, the high rate of unemployment refused to decline. It remained fixed at 7 percent. Thirty-six million Americans

Baby boomers in the White House . . . President Bill Clinton and First Lady Hillary Rodham Clinton. *Source:* Official White House Photograph.

lived in poverty. More Americans than ever before were receiving food stamps. In the post–Cold War era, cuts in military and aerospace spending brought massive layoffs at prime defense contractors such as Boeing, McDonnell-Douglas, and Lockheed. American businesses both large and small were forced to become more efficient to meet the rigors of world economic competition in the 1990s. They laid off workers and mid-level managers to become more cost-effective operations. Companies replaced human workers with computers and computer-driven machines. Computers worked efficiently around the clock; they did not make mistakes, they did not get drunk, use drugs, have personal problems, or show up for work with an attitude. And, they put people who needed jobs out of work.

Millions who continued to work had to work harder and longer than ever before. Pressures on workers to be more productive were unrelenting and intensifying. Workers complained of anxiety and job burnout in ever increasing numbers. Record numbers of workers have filed disability claims in recent years, their disabilities linked to stress or to disabling injuries caused by spending too many hours on computer terminals. All of these matters involving structural unemployment, longer hours of work, and work-related stresses and disabilities had ominous implications. Millions of workers and their families in the cutthroat 1990s suffered serious declines in the quality of their lives. They had to work longer and harder than their parents, endure more stress, and were less well compensated. They worried about retirement and pensions, and whether social security will be there when they are elderly.

The continuing decline of trade unions also contributed to the deteriorating status of working people. In 1995, scarcely 15 percent of American workers belonged to unions. Beset by corporate downsizing, the wholesale transfer of jobs overseas, harsh union-busting tactics, and increasingly conservative Congresses that were indifferent or hostile to trade union interests, unions have been powerless to lift the wages of most workers or even protect their jobs. Adjusted for inflation, wage levels in unionized industries have been stagnant for over twenty years, even as productivity and corporate profits have soared.

In August 1993, Congress enacted a five-year economic renewal program that incorporated some of Clinton's proposals. It raised the top marginal income tax rates from 31 to 36 percent, eased taxes on low-income families, and provided funding for education, retraining, and apprenticeship programs aimed at upgrading workers' skills. The program also brought about modest reductions in the budget deficit, which continued to exceed $200 billion annually in 1994 and 1995.

Clinton also expected the North American Free Trade Agreement (NAFTA) to boost efforts at economic renewal. Negotiated by the Bush administration, NAFTA incorporated Mexico into a free trade zone already created by Canada and the United States during Reagan's presidency. NAFTA aroused both strong support and fierce oppostion. Liberal Democrats and trade union leaders led the opposition, insisting NAFTA would send thousands of U.S. jobs south of the border. NAFTA supporters argued that NAFTA would create jobs by opening Mexican markets to a greater array of U.S. products. With strong support from Republicans,

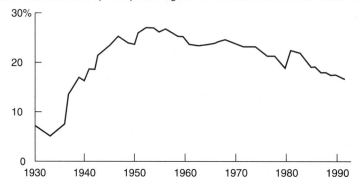

Labor union membership, 1930–1990.   *Source:* Bureau of Labor Statistics, Department of Labor.

NAFTA carried Congress, giving Clinton a political victory over the liberal wing of his own party. In 1994, Clinton followed his NAFTA victory by reducing trade barriers with major Pacific Rim nations. In 1995, he became embroiled in a nasty trade dispute with Tokyo over their refusal to allow American companies to sell automotive spare parts to the Japanese. Only after Clinton threatened to impose sanctions that would have severely hurt sales of Japanese luxury automobiles to the United States did the Japanese make concessions.

In October 1993, following the lead of Hillary Rodham Clinton, the Clinton administration moved to implement health care reform. The Task Force unveiled a complex plan that had three main goals: provide coverage for the 37 million Americans who had no health insurance, hold down costs, and preserve the high quality of available health care for all Americans. The plan would have drastically restructured the existing health care system. All Americans would be enrolled into large regional health alliances. Individuals could enroll in either a fee-for-service plan, enabling them to choose their own physicians, or in less expensive health maintenance organizations (HMOs) where they would see doctors on the HMO staffs. Employers would pay 80 percent of workers' insurance costs. Self-employed workers would buy their own insurance and Medicaid would continue to cover the poor. To cover the plan's estimated $100 billion in added costs, Congress would enact large tax increases on tobacco products.

The administration's health care reform proposal instantly attracted legions of critics. Health care providers furnished much of the opposition. Conservatives worried about its costs, government intrusion, decline in the quality of health care, and the loss of privacy. Liberals in Congress complained that setting up the regional health alliances that would compete with one another for customers merely substituted one costly and confusing system of medical care for another. They proposed a single-payer system, modeled after Medicare, to be administered uniformly through direct government reimbursements. Lobbyists for small businesses insisted that many small businessmen would be driven to bankruptcy if they were forced to buy health insurance for all their employees.

After six grueling months of hearings, the administration conceded defeat on health care reform and settled for some token reforms to contain costs. One of the principal reasons for the defeat of health care reform was the failure of traditional liberal constituencies to provide strong support. The big losers were the 37 million Americans who remained without health insurance.

The 1994 midterm elections amounted to a popular referendum on Clinton's performance during his first two years in office. A sizable majority of voters used the occasion to voice their dissatisfaction with the first "Yuppie" president. Elected by only 43 percent of the voters, Clinton's approval ratings in the polls had rarely exceeded that figure during the first two years of his presidency. Clinton also received the most critical media coverage of any modern president. He brought energy, enthusiasm, and good intentions to the job. He possessed an affable personality and considerable political skills. But he made mistakes and his image was tarnished by scandals. Most of all, he failed to provide strong leadership or project a coherent vision for the nation. He failed to get most of his important programs through a Democratic Congress. There appeared to be two President Clintons—the moderate New Democrat and the paleoliberal committed to discredited tax-and-spend policies. Clinton was also hurt by popular anger at government and politicians generally, fears about rising crime rates, unresolved social issues, cultural conflicts, and by continuing economic insecurities and discontents.

The results brought a resurgent conservative Republican Congress to power, the first since 1952. The new Senate contained a fifty-six to forty-four Republican majority and the new House had 227 Republicans to 199 Democrats. Clinton was the first Democratic president to face a Republican-controlled Congress in a half-century. Congress's Democratic minority was in complete disarray, with many of its leaders retired or defeated. The shock troops leading this Republican political "earthquake" were a group of seventy-three mostly young conservative reformers, many of them with strong ties to the Religious Right. The new Speaker of the House of Representatives, Newt Gingrich, was the leader of the Republican revolt. A controversial politician, Gingrich had for years been the House minority leader. He was best known for his ideological assaults on the liberal leadership of the House. The New Right oppositionist made a quick transition from gadfly to power broker; Gingrich was now the second most powerful politician in Washington.

Gingrich read the election results as a mandate for implementing his "Contract with America," a conservative economic, social, and cultural agenda for the 1990s. In 1995, with Gingrich and his shock troops leading the way, the most activist Congress in decades enacted legislation that reformed the way the House worked, weakened affirmative action programs, cut foreign aid, cut taxes, reduced budget deficits, and moved to reform the welfare system. Following Gingrich's lead, the 104th Congress set out to downsize the federal government and dismantle the welfare state. It was intent on reversing fifty years of liberal social policy. A chastened Clinton, his power significantly reduced by the election outcome, could only watch passively as the Republicans seized the legislative initiative. The election also forced Clinton to move Right and to rediscover that he was a moderate New Democrat. Clinton was forced to adopt a defensive political strategy—of trying to fend off Republican efforts to cut deeply or destroy liberal programs whenever he sensed that he had public opinion on his side, and of trying to position himself to win reelection within an increasingly conservative political environment.

As the 1996 presidential campaign unfolded, President Clinton's reelection prospects appeared to improve. He outmaneuvered the Republican congressional leadership in bruising battles with them over balancing the federal budget and cutting Medicare benefits. Public opinion polls showed that the American public viewed Clinton as a responsible leader concerned with fending off congressional extremism. Newt Gingrich's power and popularity diminished. The 72-year-old Senate majority leader Robert Dole, achieved his long-sought goal of winning the Republican presidential nomination with a sweeping series of primary victories in February and March. However, his candidacy continued to be challenged by conservative Pat Buchanan who was determined to drive Dole to the Right and influence the drafting of the Republican Party platform. Dole supporters also fretted about the possibility of Buchanan running as a third party independent and perhaps the return of Ross Perot. Either a Buchanan or Perot third-party entry could ensure Clinton's reelection. Both Dole and Clinton were relieved when Colin Powell, the popular African American military hero, declined to seek the Republican presidential nomination. Powell probably would have gotten the nomination and beaten Clinton in November.

Newt Gingrich, the first Republican Speaker of the House of Representatives in more than 40 years. *Source:* Official House of Representatives Photo.

TOWARD THE TWENTY-FIRST CENTURY

Upon taking office in January, 1993, Clinton reversed Bush's priorities. For Clinton, an unreconstructed domestic policy wonk, internal affairs took priority over foreign policy issues. In the conduct of foreign affairs, Clinton was handicapped by his lack of experience plus his failure to appoint strong leaders to key positions. The Clinton administration also faced the daunting task of developing and implementing effective foreign policies in the post-Cold War era, of redefining America's global role in a new environment. The most serious problems with the Clinton administration's conduct of foreign policy appeared to be its lack of focus and its inability to set priorities. Because Clinton and his foreign policy advisers lacked clear objectives and did not have a consistent set of criteria to apply, Washington could never decide when or how much U.S. power and prestige to commit in situations that did not involve vital national interests. A pattern of ad hoc responses to crises as they arose characterized the Clinton administration's approach to foreign policy. Clinton tried to downplay international politics and the use of military force. He focused American foreign policy on economic issues—on promoting world recovery from recession and stimulating economic growth. In the area of foreign economic policy, he had major achievements. He supported NAFTA, normalized relations with Vietnam, and negotiated trade agreements with Pacific Rim nations.

The shortcomings of the Clinton approach to foreign policy were glaringly evident in Bosnia and Herzegovina where the largest war in Europe since World War II had been raging since 1991. By the time of the Clinton administration's accession to power in January 1993, vicious ethnic fighting among Serbs, Bosnian Muslims, and Croats had killed over 100,000 people and generated over 3.5 million refugees. Even though the Bosnian Muslims were clearly the victims of aggression and atrocities, and were hindered in their efforts at self-defense by an arms embargo, Washington appeared more concerned about avoiding significant military involvement and confining the conflict to the petty successor states of the now defunct Yugoslav federation than aiding the outgunned Bosnians. Murderous warfare raged on in 1993, 1994, and 1995 despite feckless UN efforts to broker a cease-fire and negotiate a settlement that would have divided Bosnia and Herzegovina into a patchwork of ethnic regions.

Finally, in the fall of 1995, Washington took action. Clinton perceived that the UN and Europeans were incapable of effective action in Bosnia. Bringing the leaders of the three warring factions to Dayton, Ohio, in December, Washington brokered a cease-fire, and complex political settlement to be implemented gradually over the next year. The settlement involved sending a NATO force of 60,000 troops, of which 20,000 would be U.S. combat soldiers, to police the cease-fire and allow the political settlement to gradually take hold. A vocal majority in Congress and among the American public opposed sending American forces to Bosnia because no vital U.S. interests appeared to be at issue and because prospects for success appeared problematic. There was also a reluctance to place American troops in a dangerous and violent region where they could incur casualties. The Bosnian intervention reflected Washington's concern about maintaining the NATO alliance and America's leadership role in European affairs.

On another front, the hijackings and other terrorist acts that had tormented the presidencies of Carter and Reagan declined during the early 1990s. Suddenly, in February 1993, terrorism struck the United States when a powerful explosion ripped through the World Trade Center located in New York, killing five people and injuring scores of others. In 1995, following a dramatic trial, a militant sheik and four of his Shiite followers were convicted of the bombing. In April 1995, Americans discovered to their horror that they did not have to import terrorists when a car bomb of tremendous explosive power demolished a nine-story federal building in Oklahoma City, killing 168 people, many of them children enrolled in a preschool nursery housed on the second story, and injuring hundreds. The FBI soon arrested Timothy McVeigh and Terry Nichols who were charged with the crime. Both men had ties with the militia movement, a Rightwing fringe group who viewed governmental efforts to impose a measure of gun control as part of a larger conspiracy by the federal government to extinguish freedom in America. In March 1996, FBI agents arrested 53-year-old Theodore Kaczynski, as the suspected Unabomber, a serial killer who had waged a campaign of terror-bombing since 1979 that had killed 3 people and injured 23 others in 16 separate attacks.

While terrorists recruited from various Middle Eastern countries bombed the Trade Center, Washington's efforts to bring peace to the Middle East at last bore fruit. Building on the previous efforts of Presidents Reagan and Bush, Clinton's Secretary of State, Warren Christopher, urged Israeli and Palestinian leaders to continue the dialogue begun at Madrid following the smashing Allied victory in the Persian Gulf War. In September 1993, following secret talks, there occurred a startling breakthrough. Israel and the Palestine Liberation Organization (PLO) announced an accord granting the Palestinians limited autonomy in the Gaza Strip and areas of the West Bank. In return, Yassir Arafat, the PLO leader, renounced terrorism and recognized Israel. On September 13, 1993, in Washington, as a beaming Bill Clinton looked on, Israeli Prime Minister Yitzhak Rabin and Yassir Arafat signed the accord and shook hands. It was as if decades of discord and heartache had suddenly dropped away. In 1995 and 1996, despite sporadic efforts by Palestinian militants to disrupt the peace process, the Israeli-PLO Accord remained in place.

Experts concerned about the future of the small planet we inhabit fear that rapid world population increases and severe environmental problems pose far more serious long-term threats to our living standards and general sense of well-being than do political and economic problems. In 1996, the world's estimated population exceeded 5.7 billion people. Demographers predict that by the year 2020, the world's population will reach 8 billion. The consequences of such population growth will all be dire. Mass immiseration, especially in Third World countries, will breed extremist political and religious movements that ensure a turbulent future. Surging populations will also use up huge quantities of the earth's finite resources, wipe out millions of acres of rain forests necessary to cool and purify the planet, and extinguish thousands of species of plants and animals. As the twenty-first century approaches, Americans face many challenges at home and abroad. And they must cope with that daunting future that will soon explode among us at a time when America's basic economic, social, and political institutions are increasingly strained.

IMPORTANT EVENTS

1988	George H. W. Bush is elected president
1989	Tiananmen Square massacre takes place
1989	The Cold War ends
1989	The United States invades Panama to overthrow and capture Manuel Noriega
1990	Violetta Chamorro is elected president of Nicaragua
1990	Germany is reunited
1990	Iraq invades Kuwait
1991	The Persian Gulf War occurs; Kuwait is liberated
1991	Clarence Thomas becomes an associate justice of the Supreme Court
1991	The Middle East peace conference occurs
1991	The Soviet Union disintegrates
1992	South Africa votes to end apartheid
1992	Bill Clinton is elected president
1993	Ruth Bader Ginsberg is appointed to Supreme Court
1993	Israeli-PLO agreement takes place
1994	Republicans win control of Congress
1995	The O. J. Simpson murder trial becomes the "trial of the century"
1995	Terrorists bomb the federal building in Oklahoma City
1996	U.S. troops are sent to Bosnia-Herzegovina

BIBLIOGRAPHY

Recent military, political, and diplomatic history is covered best in the *New York Times*, and other fine newspapers and weekly newsmagazines such as *Time* and *Newsweek*. The *National Review* covers recent history from a conservative perspective and the *New Republic* covers the same events from a moderate liberal perspective. We also have several book-length accounts of recent historical developments. Those interested in the troubling world environmental problems of the 1990s will want to read *Crossroads: Environmental Priorities for the Future*, edited by Peter Borrelli. Kevin Philips, a conservative political analyst, has written *The Politics of Rich and Poor*, which is concerned about the social inequities deriving from contemporary economic policies. On the matter of women's pay issues, see *Wage Justice: Comparable Worth and the Paradox of Technocratic Reform* by Sara M. Evans and Barbara J. Nelson. There is an extensive literature on the AIDS epidemic. One of the best books is Randy Shilts's *And the Band Played On*. On contemporary drug problems plaguing Americans, see Erich Goode's

Drugs in American Society. Ellis Cose's *The Rage of a Privileged Class: Why Are Middle-Class Blacks Angry?* is an important and disturbing book. See William Wei's *The Asian American Movement* for a study of an important group of Americans who lack an extensive historical literature. There is a growing literature on all the historic changes occurring in eastern Europe and the Soviet Union. See *Reform in Russia and the USSR* (edited by Robert O. Crummey) and *Central and Eastern Europe: The Opening Curtain* (edited by William E. Griffith). Two American Sovietologists, Robert Jervis and Seweryn Bailer (eds.), present diverse looks at the post–Cold War world in *Soviet-American Relations After the Cold War.* For American-Japanese relations, a book edited by Akira Iriye and Warren I. Cohen, *The United States and Japan in the Postwar World,* is very good. For recent developments in Central America, consult *Understanding Central America,* by John A. Booth and Thomas W. Walker. *Saddam Hussein,* by Judith Miller and Laurie Mylorie, is an informative study that sheds light on the motivations of the Iraqi leader and the genesis of the Persian Gulf crisis. A recent study looking to the future of international relations is Paul Kennedy's *Preparing for the Twenty-First Century.* David A. Hollinger, *Postethnic America: Beyond Multiculturalism,* is a brilliant and timely effort to reconcile the reasonable claims of multiculturalists with the need to maintain a coherent national culture that includes all Americans.

Appendixes

APPENDIX A:

*AMENDMENTS TO THE CONSTITUTION ADDED
DURING THE TWENTIETH CENTURY*[1]

The Fifteenth Amendment. For nearly a century after it was drafted, the Fifteenth Amendment was evaded by various devices that hindered blacks from registering and voting. The Voting Rights Act of 1965 is the most recent attempt to enforce the amendment by providing federal supervision of voter registration in localities with a history of discrimination.

The Progressive amendments. The Sixteenth through Nineteenth amendments were the product of the Progressive movement. The Sixteenth was necessitated by a Supreme Court decision in the 1890s that a federal income tax violated the constitutional requirements that direct taxes (as opposed to excises) had to be apportioned among the states, which in turn would collect from the people. The Seventeenth Amendment was intended to democratize the "millionaires' club," the U.S. Senate, by requiring that its members be

Amendment XVI [1913]

The Congress shall have power to lay and collect taxes on incomes, from whatever source derived, without apportionment among the several States, and without regard to any census or enumeration.

Amendment XVII [1916]

The Senate of the United States shall be composed of two Senators from each State, elected by the people thereof, for six years; and each Senator shall have one vote. The electors in each State shall have the qualifications requisite for electors of the most numerous branch of the State legislators.

When vacancies happen in the representation of any State in the Senate, the elected directly by the people. The Eighteenth Amendment authorized prohibition, and the Nineteenth women's suffrage.

executive authority of such State shall issue writs of election to fill such vacancies: *Provided*, That the legislature of any State may empower the executive thereof to make temporary appointments until the people fill the vacancies by election as the legislature may direct.

This amendment shall not be so construed as to affect the election or term of any Senator chosen before it becomes valid as part of the Constitution.

Amendment XVIII [1919]

Section 1. After one year from the ratification of this article the manufacture, sale, or transportation of intoxicating liquors within, the importation thereof into, or the exportation thereof from the United States and all territory subject to the jurisdiction thereof for beverage purposes is hereby prohibited.

Section 2. The Congress and the several States shall have concurrent power to enforce this article by appropriate legislation.

Section 3. This article shall be inoperative unless it shall have been ratified as an amendment to the Constitution by the legislatures of the several States, as provided in the Constitution, within seven years from the date of the submission hereof to the States by the Congress.

Amendment XIX [1920]

The right of citizens of the United States to vote shall not be denied or abridged by the United States or by any State on account of sex.

Congress shall have power to enforce this article by appropriate legislation.

The lame duck amendment. The Twentieth Amendment did away with an anomaly created by Article I of the Constitution , the requirement that elections would be held in November but inaugurations delayed until March. This resulted in a "lame duck" session of Congress, lasting from December until March in even-numbered years, when members, many of whom had failed to be reelected and were on their way to private life, were voting on matters of national importance. By moving inauguration day back from March 4 to January 20, the amendment shortens the interval between popular selection and the exercise of presidential and legislative power.

Amendment XX [1933]

Section 1. The terms of the President and Vice President shall end at noon on the 20th day of January, and the terms of Senators and Representatives at noon on the 3rd day of January, of the years in which such terms would have ended if this article had not been ratified; and the terms of their successors shall then begin.

Section 2. The Congress shall assemble at least once in every year, and such meeting shall begin at noon on the 3d day of January, unless they shall by law appoint a different day.

Section 3. If, at the time fixed for the beginning of the term of the President, the President elect shall have died, the Vice President elect shall become President. If a President shall not have been chosen before the time fixed for the beginning of his term, or if the President elect shall have failed to qualify, then the Vice President elect shall act as President until a President shall have qualified; and the Congress may by law provide for the case wherein neither a President elect nor a Vice President elect shall have qualified, declaring who shall then act as President, or the manner in which one who is to act shall be selected, and such person shall act accordingly until a President or Vice President shall have qualified.

Section 4. The Congress may by law provide for the case of the death of any of the persons from whom the House of Representatives may choose a President whenever the right of choice shall have devolved upon them, and for the case of the death of any of the persons from whom the Senate may choose a Vice President whenever the right of choice shall have devolved upon them.

Section 5.   Sections 1 and 2 shall take effect on the 15th day of October following the ratification of this article.

Section 6.   The article shall be inoperative unless it shall have been ratified as an amendment to the Constitution by the legislatures of three-fourths of the several States within seven years from the date of its submission.

Amendment XXI [1933]

Section 1.   The eighteenth article of amendment to the Constitution of the United States is hereby repealed.

Section 2.   The transportation or importation into any State, Territory, or possession of the United States for delivery or use therein of intoxicating liquors, in violation of the laws thereof, is hereby prohibited.

Section 3.   This article shall be inoperative unless it shall have been ratified as an amendment to the Constitution by conventions in the several States, as provided in the Constitution, within seven years from the date of the submission hereof to the States by the Congress.

The Twenty-first Amendment.   The Twenty-first Amendment repealed the Eighteenth, and thereby repealed prohibition. It is the only amendment that provides for its ratification by specially selected conventions, and it is the only one that has been approved in this way.

Amendment XXII [1951]

No person shall be elected to the office of the President more than twice, and no person who has held the office of President, or acted as President, for more than two years of a term to which some other person was elected President shall be elected to the office of the President more than once.

But this Article shall not apply to any person holding the office of President when this Article was proposed by the Congress, and shall not prevent any person who may be holding the office of President, or acting as President, during the term within which this Article becomes operative from holding the office of President or acting as President during the remainder of such term.

The Twenty-second Amendment.   The Twenty-second Amendment, a belated slap at Roosevelt by a Republican-dominated Congress, limits the president to two terms in office. Ironically, the two presidents to which it has applied were Republicans, Dwight D. Eisenhower and Ronald Reagan.

The Twenty-third Amendment. The Twenty-third Amendment allows residents of the District of Columbia to vote in presidential elections.

Amendment XXIII [1961]

Section 1. The District constituting the seat of Governor of the United States shall appoint in such manner as the Congress may direct:

A number of electors of President and Vice President equal to the whole number of Senators and Representatives in Congress to which the District would be entitled if it were a State, but in no event more than the least populous State; they shall be in addition to those appointed by the States, but they shall be considered, for the purposes of the election of President and Vice President, to be electors appointed by a State; and they shall meet in the District and perform such duties as provided by the twelfth article of amendment.

Section 2. The Congress shall have the power to enforce this article by appropriate legislation.

The poll tax amendment. The Twenty-fourth Amendment prevents the states from making payment of a poll tax a condition for voting. Common at the time among southern states, the poll tax was a capitation (poll, or head) tax on individuals. A poll tax receipt was often required in order to vote. It was designed to prevent uneducated people, especially blacks, who were unaccustomed to saving receipts, from voting.

Amendment XXIV [1964]

Section 1. The right of citizens of the United States to vote in any primary or other election for President or Vice President, for electors for President or Vice President, or for Senator or Representative in Congress, shall not be denied or abridged by the United States or any State by reason of failure to pay any poll tax or other tax.

Section 2. The Congress shall have the power to enforce this article by appropriate legislation.

The Twenty-fifth Amendment. The Twenty-fifth Amendment, inspired by President Eisenhower's heart attack and President Johnson's abdominal surgery, provides for the temporary replacement of a president who is unable to discharge the duties of the office.

Amendment XXV [1967]

Section 1. In case of the removal of the President from office or his death or resignation, the Vice President shall become President.

Section 2. Whenever there is a vacancy in the office of the Vice President, the President shall nominate a Vice President who shall take the office upon confirmation by a majority vote of both houses of Congress.

Section 3. Whenever the President transmits to the President pro tempore of the Senate and the Speaker of the House of Representatives his written declaration that he is unable to discharge the powers and duties of his office, and until he transmits to them a written declaration to the contrary, such powers and duties shall be discharged by the Vice President as Acting President.

Section 4. Whenever the Vice President and a majority of either the principal officers of the executive departments, or of such other body as Congress may be law provide, transmit to the President pro tempore of the Senate and the Speaker of the House of Representatives their written declaration that the President is unable to discharge the powers and duties of his office, the Vice President shall immediately assume the powers and duties of the office of Acting President.

Thereafter, when the President transmits to the President pro tempore of the Senate and the Speaker of the House of Representatives his written declaration that no inability exists, he shall resume the powers and duties of his office unless the Vice President and a majority of either the principal officers of the executive departments, or of such other body as Congress may by law provide, transmit within four days to the President pro tempore of the Senate and the speaker of the House of Representatives their written declaration that the President is unable to discharge the powers and duties of his office. Thereupon Congress shall decide the issue, assembling within 48 hours for that purpose if not in session. If the Congress, within 21 days after receipt of the latter written declaration, or, if Congress is not in session, within 21 days after Congress is required to assemble, determines by two-thirds vote of both houses that the President is unable to discharge the powers and duties of his office, the Vice President shall continue to discharge the same as Acting President; otherwise, the President shall resume the powers and duties of his office.

The Twenty-sixth Amendment. The Twenty-sixth Amendment corrected a historic injustice: young men could be drafted and sent to war at the age of eighteen, but not allowed to participate in the nation's democratic processes until they were twenty-one. It extended the vote to eighteen-year-olds.

Amendment XXVI [1971]

Section 1. The rights of citizens of the United States, who are 18 years of age or older, to vote shall not be denied or abridged by the United States or any state on account of age.

Section 2. The Congress shall have the power to enforce this article by appropriate legislation.

The Twenty-seventh Amendment. Originally proposed by Congress in 1789, it was not ratified by the states until 1992. It was rapidly enacted in the wake of public outrage aimed at Congresspersons who had voted themselves a substantial pay raise.

Amendment XXVII [1992]

No law, varying the compensation for the services of the Senators and Representatives shall take effect, until an election of Representatives shall have intervened.

APPENDIX B:
PRESIDENTIAL ELECTIONS, SINCE 1896

YEAR	CANDIDATES RECEIVING MORE THAN ONE PERCENT OF THE VOTE (PARTIES)	POPULAR VOTE	ELECTORAL VOTE
1896	WILLIAM McKINLEY (Republican)	7,102,246	271
	William J. Bryan (Democratic)	6,492,559	176
1900	WILLIAM McKINLEY (Republican)	7,218,491	292
	William J. Bryan (Democratic; Populist)	6,356,734	155
	John C. Wooley (Prohibition)	208,914	0
1904	THEODORE ROOSEVELT (Republican)	7,628,461	336
	Alton B. Parker (Democratic)	5,084,223	140
	Eugene V. Debs (Socialist)	402,283	0
	Silas C. Swallow (Prohibition)	258,536	0
1908	WILLIAM H. TAFT (Republican)	7,675,320	321
	William J. Bryan (Democratic)	6,412,294	162
	Eugene V. Debs (Socialist)	420,793	0
	Eugene W. Chafin (Prohibition)	253,840	0
1912	WOODROW WILSON (Democratic)	6,296,547	435
	Theodore Roosevelt (Progressive)	4,118,571	88
	William H. Taft (Republican)	3,486,720	8
	Eugene V. Debs (Socialists)	900,672	0
	Eugene W. Chafin (Prohibition)	206,275	0
1916	WOODROW WILSON (Democratic)	9,127,695	277
	Charles E. Hughes (Republican)	8,533,507	254
	A. L. Benson (Socialist)	585,113	0
	J. Frank Hanly (Prohibition)	220,506	0
1920	WARREN G. HARDING (Republican)	16,143,407	404
	James M. Cox (Democratic)	9,130,328	127
	Eugene V. Debs (Socialist)	919,799	0
	P. P. Christensen (Farmer-Labor)	265,411	0
1924	CALVIN COOLIDGE (Republican)	15,718,211	382
	John W. Davis (Democratic)	8,385,283	136
	Robert M. LaFollette (Progressive)	4,831,289	13
1928	HERBERT C. HOOVER (Republican)	21,391,993	444
	Albert E. Smith (Democratic)	15,016,169	87
1932	FRANKLIN D. ROOSEVELT (Democratic)	22,809,638	472
	Herbert C. Hoover (Republican)	15,758,901	59
	Norman Thomas (Socialist)	881,951	0
1936	FRANKLIN D. ROOSEVELT (Democratic)	27,752,869	523
	Alfred M. Landon (Republican)	16,674,665	8
	William Lemke (Union)	882,479	0
1940	FRANKLIN D. ROOSEVELT (Democratic)	27,307,819	449
	Wendell L. Willkie (Republican)	22,321,018	82
1944	FRANKLIN D. ROOSEVELT (Democratic)	25,606,585	432
	Thomas E. Dewey (Republican)	22,014,745	99
1948	HARRY S. TRUMAN (Democratic)	24,179,345	303
	Thomas E. Dewey (Republican)	21,991,291	189
	J. Strom Thurmond (States' Rights)	1,176,125	39
	Henry Wallace (Progressive)	1,157,326	0
1952	DWIGHT D. EISENHOWER (Republican)	33,936,234	442
	Adlai E. Stevenson (Democratic)	27,314,992	89

1956	DWIGHT D. EISENHOWER (Republican)	35,590,472	457
	Adlai E. Stevenson (Democratic)	26,022,752	73
1960	JOHN F. KENNEDY (Democratic)	34,226,731	303
	Richard M. Nixon (Republican)	34,108,157	219
1964	LYNDON B. JOHNSON (Democratic)	43,129,566	486
	Barry M. Goldwater (Republican)	27,178,188	52
1968	RICHARD M. NIXON (Republican)	31,785,480	301
	Hubert H. Humphrey (Democratic)	31,275,166	191
	George C. Wallace (American Independent)	9,906,473	46
1972	RICHARD M. NIXON (Republican)	45,631,189	521
	George S. McGovern (Democratic)	28,422,015	17
	John Schmitz (American Independent)	1,080,670	0
1976	JAMES E. CARTER, JR. (Democratic)	40,274,975	297
	Gerald R. Ford (Republican)	38,530,614	241
1980	RONALD W. REAGAN (Republican)	42,968,326	489
	James E. Carter, Jr. (Democratic)	34,731,139	49
	John B. Anderson (Independent)	5,552,349	0
1984	RONALD W. REAGAN (Republican)	53,428,357	525
	Walter F. Mondale (Democratic)	36,930,923	13
1988	GEORGE H. W. BUSH (Republican)	47,917,341	426
	Michael Dukakis (Democrat)	41,013,030	112
1992	WILLIAM J. CLINTON (Democrat)	44,908,254	370
	GEORGE H. W. BUSH (Republican)	39,102,343	168
	ROSS PEROT (Independent)	19,741,065	0

From Irwin Unger, *These United States: The Questions of Our Past, Volume II: Since 1865,* 3rd ed., pp. 821–822. Reprinted with permission of Prentice Hall.

APPENDIX C:
PRESIDENT, VICE PRESIDENT, AND CABINET OFFICERS, FROM 1897.

PRESIDENT AND VICE PRESIDENT	SECRETARY OF STATE	SECRETARY OF TREASURY	SECRETARY OF WAR	SECRETARY OF NAVY	POSTMASTER GENERAL	ATTORNEY GENERAL	SECRETARY OF INTERIOR
25. **William McKinley** (1897) Garret A. Hobart (1897) Theodore Roosevelt (1901)	John Sherman (1897) William R. Day (1897) John Hay (1898)	Lyman J. Gage (1897)	Russell A. Alger (1897) Elihu Root (1899)	John D. Long (1897)	James A. Gary (1897) Charles E. Smith (1898)	Joseph McKenna (1897) John W. Griggs (1897) Philander C. Knox (1901)	Cornelius N. Bliss (1897) E. A. Hitchcock (1899)
26. **Theodore Roosevelt** (1901) Charles Fairbanks (1905)	John Hay (1901) Elihu Root (1905) Robert Bacon (1909)	Lyman J. Gage (1901) Leslie M. Shaw (1902) George B. Cortelyou (1907)	Elihu Root (1901) William H. Taft (1904) Luke E. Wright (1908)	John D. Long (1901) William H. Moody (1902) Paul Morton (1904) Charles J. Bonaparte (1905) V. H. Metcalf (1906) T. H. Newberry (1908)	Charles E. Smith (1901) Henry Payne (1902) Robert J. Wynne (1904) George B. Cortelyou (1905) George von L. Meyer (1907)	Philander C. Knox (1901) William H. Moody (1904) Charles J. Bonaparte (1907)	E. A. Hitchcock (1901) James R. Garfield (1907)
27. **William H. Taft** (1909) James S. Sherman (1909)	Philander C. Knox (1909)	Franklin MacVeagh (1909)	Jacob M. Dickinson (1909) Henry L. Stimson (1911)	George von L. Meyer (1909)	Frank H. Hitchcock (1909)	G. W. Wickersham (1909)	R. A. Ballinger (1909) Walter L. Fisher (1911)
28. **Woodrow Wilson** (1913) Thomas R. Marshall (1913)	William J. Bryan (1913) Robert Lansing (1915) Bainbridge Colby (1920)	William G. McAdoo (1913) Carter Glass (1918) David F. Houston (1920)	Lindley M. Garrison (1913) Newton D. Baker (1916)	Josephus Daniels (1913)	Albert S. Burleson (1913)	J. C. McReynolds (1913) T. W. Gregory (1914) A. Mitchell Palmer (1919)	Franklin K. Lane (1913) John B. Payne (1920)
29. **Warren G. Harding** (1921) Calvin Coolidge (1921)	Charles E. Hughes (1921)	Andrew W. Mellon (1921)	John W. Weeks (1921)	Edwin Denby (1921)	Will H. Hays (1921) Hubert Work (1922) Harry S. New (1923)	H. M. Daugherty (1921)	Albert B. Fall (1921) Hubert Work (1923)
30. **Calvin Coolidge** (1923) Charles G. Dawes (1925)	Charles E. Hughes (1923) Frank B. Kellogg (1925)	Andrew W. Mellon (1923)	John W. Weeks (1923) Dwight F. Davis (1925)	Edwin Denby (1923) Curtis D. Wilbur (1924)	Harry S. New (1923)	H. M. Daugherty (1923) Harlan F. Stone (1924) John G. Sargent (1925)	Hubert Work (1923) Roy O. West (1928)
31. **Herbert C. Hoover** (1929) Charles Curtis (1929)	Henry L. Stimson (1929)	Andrew W. Mellon (1929) Ogden L. Mills (1932)	James W. Good (1929) Patrick J. Hurley (1929)	Charles F. Adams (1929)	Walter F. Brown (1929)	W. D. Mitchell (1929)	Ray L. Wilbur (1929)
32. **Franklin D. Roosevelt** (1933)	Cordell Hull (1933) E. R. Stettinius, Jr.	William H. Woodin (1933)	George H. Dern (1933)	Claude A. Swanson (1933)	James A. Farley (1933)	H. S. Cummings (1933)	Harold L. Ickes (1933)

President / Vice President	Secretary of State	Secretary of the Treasury	Secretary of War / Defense	Secretary of the Navy	Postmaster General	Attorney General	Secretary of the Interior
John Nance Garner (1933) Henry A. Wallace (1941) Harry S. Truman (1945)	(1944)	Henry Morgenthau, Jr. (1934)	Harry H. Woodring (1936) Henry L. Stimson (1940)	Charles Edison (1940) Frank Knox (1940) James V. Forrestal (1944)	Frank C. Walker (1940)	Frank Murphy (1939) Robert Jackson (1940) Francis Biddle (1941)	
33. **Harry S. Truman** (1945) Alben W. Barkley (1949)	James F. Byrnes (1945) George C. Marshall (1947) Dean G. Acheson (1949)	Fred M. Vinson (1945) John W. Snyder (1946)	Robert P. Patterson (1945) Kenneth C. Royall (1947) SECRETARY OF DEFENSE James V. Forrestal (1947) Louis A. Johnson (1949) George C. Marshall (1950) Robert A. Lovett (1951)	James V. Forrestal (1945)	R. E. Hannegan (1945) Jesse M. Donaldson (1947)	Tom C. Clark (1945) J. H. McGrath (1949) James P. McGranery (1952)	Harold L. Ickes (1945) Julius A. Krug (1946) Oscar L. Chapman (1949)
34. **Dwight D. Eisenhower** (1953) Richard M. Nixon (1953)	John Foster Dulles (1953) Christian A. Herter (1959)	George M. Humphrey (1953) Robert B. Anderson (1957)	Charles E. Wilson (1953) Neil H. McElroy (1957) Thomas S. Gates (1959)		A. E. Summerfield (1953)	H. Brownell, Jr. (1953) William P. Rogers (1957)	Douglas McKay (1953) Fred Seaton (1956)
35. **John F. Kennedy** (1961) Lyndon B. Johnson (1961)	Dean Rusk (1961)	C. Douglas Dillon (1961)	Robert S. McNamara (1961)		J. Edward Day (1961) John A. Gronouski (1963)	Robert F. Kennedy (1961)	Stewart L. Udall (1961)
36. **Lyndon B. Johnson** (1963) Hubert H. Humphrey (1965)	Dean Rusk (1963)	C. Douglas Dillon (1963) Henry H. Fowler (1965) Joseph W. Barr (1968)	Robert S. McNamara (1963) Clark M. Clifford (1968)		John A. Gronouski (1963) Lawrence F. O'Brien (1965) W. Marvin Watson (1968)	Robert F. Kennedy (1963) N. deB. Katzenbach (1965) Ramsey Clark (1967)	Stewart L. Udall (1963)
37. **Richard M. Nixon** (1969) Spiro T. Agnew (1969) Gerald R. Ford (1973)	William P. Rogers (1969) Henry A. Kissinger (1973)	David M. Kennedy (1969) John B. Connally (1970) George P. Shultz (1972) William E. Simon (1974)	Melvin R. Laird (1969) Elliot L. Richardson (1973) James R. Schlesinger (1973)		Winton M. Blount (1969)	John M. Mitchell (1969) Richard G. Kleindienst (1972) Elliot L. Richardson (1973) William B. Saxbe (1974)	Walter J. Hickel (1969) Rogers C. B. Morton (1971)

PRESIDENT, VICE PRESIDENT, AND CABINET OFFICERS, FROM 1897 *(continued)*

PRESIDENT AND VICE PRESIDENT	SECRETARY OF STATE	SECRETARY OF TREASURY	SECRETARY OF DEFENSE	ATTORNEY GENERAL	SECRETARY OF INTERIOR
38. Gerald R. Ford (1974) Nelson A. Rockefeller (1974)	Henry A. Kissinger (1974)	William E. Simon (1974)	James R. Schlesinger (1974) Donald H. Rumsfeld (1975)	William B. Saxbe (1974) Edward H. Levi (1975)	Rogers C. B. Morton (1974) Stanley K. Hathaway (1975) Thomas D. Kleppe (1975) Cecil D. Andrus (1977)
39. James E. Carter, Jr. (1977) Walter F. Mondale (1977)	Cyrus R. Vance (1977) Edmund S. Muskie (1980)	W. Michael Blumenthal (1977) G. William Miller (1979)	Harold Brown (1977)	Griffin B. Bell (1977) Benjamin R. Civiletti (1979)	
40. Ronald W. Reagan (1981) George H. W. Bush (1981)	Alexander M. Haig, Jr. (1981) George P. Shultz (1982)	Donald T. Reagan (1981)	Caspar W. Weinberger (1981)	William French Smith (1981)	James G. Watt (1981) William Clark (1983) Donald P. Hodel (1985)
41. Ronald W. Reagan (1985) George H. W. Bush (1985)	George P. Shultz (1985)	James B. Baker III (1985)	Caspar W. Weinberger (1985)	Edwin Meese III (1985)	
42. George H. W. Bush (1989) J. Danforth Quayle (1989)	James B. Baker III (1989)	Nicholas Brady (1989)	Richard Cheney (1989)	Richard Thornburgh (1989)	Manuel Lujan (1989)
43. William Jefferson Clinton (1993) Albert Gore (1993)	Warren Christopher (1993)	Lloyd Bentsen (1993)	Les Aspin (1993)	Janet Reno (1993)	Bruce Babbitt (1993)

SECRETARY OF AGRICULTURE	SECRETARY OF VETERAN AFFAIRS	SECRETARY OF COMMERCE	SECRETARY OF LABOR	SECRETARY OF HEALTH AND HUMAN SERVICE	SECRETARY OF HUD	SECRETARY OF EDUCATION
Clayton Yeutter (1989) Mike Espey (1993)	Edwin Derwinski (1989) Jesse Brown (1993)	Robert Mosbacher (1989) Ron Brown (1993)	Elizabeth Dole (1989) Robert Reich (1993)	Louis W. Sullivan (1989) Donna Shalala (1993)	Jack Kemp (1989) Henry Cisneros (1993)	Richard Riley (1993)

SECRETARY OF ENERGY						SECRETARY OF TRANSPORTATION
James Walters (1989) Hazel O'Leary (1993)						Samuel K. Skinner (1989) Frederico Peña (1993)

Source: From Unger, pp. 826–828. Reprinted by permission of Prentice Hall.

APPENDIX D:
POPULATION OF THE UNITED STATES, 1890–PRESENT (EST.)

1890	63,000,000
1900	76,000,000
1910	92,000,000
1920	106,000,000
1930	122,000,000
1940	132,000,000
1950	151,000,000
1960	179,000,000
1970	205,000,000
1980	227,000,000
1990	247,000,000
1996 (est.)	261,000,000

APPENDIX E:
U.S. TERRITORIAL EXPANSION SINCE 1898

Hawaii	1898
The Philippines	1898–1946
Puerto Rico	1899
Guam	1899
American Samoa	1899
Canal Zone	1904
U.S. Virgin Islands	1917
Pacific Island Trust Territories	1947

Index